Marketing Research

Ninth Edition

Marketing Research

Ninth Edition

Carl McDaniel, Jr.
University of Texas
at Arlington

Roger Gates
DSS Research

John Wiley & Sons, Inc

VICE PRESIDENT & PUBLISHER   George Hoffman
SENIOR ACQUISITIONS EDITOR   Franny Kelly
ASSISTANT EDITOR   Emily McGee
PRODUCTION MANAGER   Dorothy Sinclair
SENIOR PRODUCTION EDITOR   Janet Foxman
PRODUCTION EDITOR   Erin Bascom
MARKETING MANAGER   Kelly Simmons
CREATIVE DIRECTOR   Harry Nolan
SENIOR DESIGNER   Wendy Lai
PRODUCTION MANAGEMENT SERVICES   Furino Production
SENIOR ILLUSTRATION EDITOR   Anna Melhorn
PHOTO EDITOR   Sheena Goldstein
EDITORIAL ASSISTANT   Melissa Solarz
EXECUTIVE MEDIA EDITOR   Allison Morris
MEDIA SPECIALISTS   Elena Santa Maria and Tom Caruso
COVER PHOTO   © Stephen Hobson/iStockphoto
            © Angela Waye/iStockphoto

This book was set in Adobe Garamond by MPS Limited, and printed and bound by Quad Graphics/Versailles. The cover was printed by Lehigh Phoenix.

This book is printed on acid free paper. ∞

Founded in 1807, John Wiley & Sons, Inc. has been a valued source of knowledge and understanding for more than 200 years, helping people around the world meet their needs and fulfill their aspirations. Our company is built on a foundation of principles that include reposnibility to the communities we serve and where we live and work. In 2008, we launched a Corporate Citizenship Initiative, a global effort to address the environment, social, economic, and ethical challenges we face in our business. Among the issues we are addressing are carbon impact, papter specifications and procurement, ethical conduct within our business and among our vendors, and community and charitable support. For more information, please visit our website: www.wiley.com/go/citizenship.

Evaluation copies are provided to qualified academics and professionals for review purposes only, for use in their courses during the next academic year. These copies are licensed and may not be sold or transferred to a third party. Upon completion of the review period, please return the evaluation copy to Wiley. Return instructions and a free of charge return shipping label are available at www.wiley.com/go/returnlabel. Outside of the United States, please contact your local representative.

ISBN-13 978-0470-08702-2

Printed in the United States of America

10 9 8 7 6 5 4 3 2 1

Dedicated to
Mimi Olsen
Abby, Will, Connor, Will, Cole, Jake, Knox

PREFACE

Welcome To Our World Of Marketing Research

Our world-view is that of marketing research. We are here every day, not as observers, but participants. Roger Gates, one of your co-authors is President of DSS Research, one of America's largest health-care marketing research firms. You can learn more at www .dssresearch.com. Carl McDaniel was a co-founder of a marketing research company that is vibrant today. He also was a co-founder of the Master of Science in Marketing Research program at the University of Texas at Arlington. Along with Roger Gates and several others, Carl created the MSMR Advisory Board. The Advisory Board consists of leaders and shakers in the marketing research industry (go to www.uta.edu/msmr/advisory-board/advisory-board-members.com). You are holding the only text written by marketing research insiders. It is like writing about football as you witness the game from the stands or writing about the sport as a player on the field. We are not spectators viewing marketing research from afar. Unlike authors of other research texts, we are on the field and continue to offer you Real Data, Real People, and Real Research. **Welcome to the real world of marketing research**.

As A Global Leading Marketing Research Text-We Practice What We Preach

Marketing research is a managerial tool used to better understand the customer, potential customers, and the marketplace. To stay on top, we must deliver a text that meets ever-changing needs. Recently, John Wiley and Sons commissioned a virtual focus group that helped us more efficiently plan this 9th edition. We are grateful to The Grandview Group for conducting the research and to the following participants for their excellent feedback: –Joseph Ballenger (Stephen F. Austin State University), Joseph Cangelosi (University of Central Arkansas), Curt Dommeyer (California State University, Northridge), Maxwell Hsu (University of Wisconsin), William Johnson (Nova Southeastern University), Ben Ong (California State University, Fresno), Carolyn Predmore (Manhattan College), Kabir Sen (Lamar University). Their suggestions have made a market-leading textbook even better.

Make Marketing Research Come Alive with the Global Leader in Marketing Research Texts

We Offer Real Data/Real People/Real Research

Real Data

We have retained our three popular data cases, which are based on a nationwide sample of 2,000 college-aged students. The sample was drawn by the world leader in sampling solutions, Survey Sampling International. You can find out more about them at *www.surveysampling.com*. Each of the three cases focuses on topics of interest to college students. They include an Online Dating Service, an Online Student Travel Service, and a new chain of combination fast-food and convenience store located near college campuses. Not only do we have demographic and attitudinal data for each respondent, but working with Claritas, a leading provider of marketing databases (*www.claritas.com*), we offer students a chance to work with PRIZM NE appended to our data sets. This latest version of the original PRIZM is the most widely used target marketing system in the United States! The new PRIZM NE is a 66-segment model. These segments are arranged to make up two standard sets of groups: Social Group and Lifestage Group.

In addition to the three new data cases, we have retained the data case, Rockingham National Bank Visa Card Survey, for the ninth edition. This was done in response to many requests from our users. We know that you will enjoy working with this student favorite!

Real People

Roger Gates, president of DSS Research, is one of the authors of this text. His firm is privately held and therefore does not publicly disclose revenue. However, if it did, it would be one of the 35 largest research firms in America! DSS specializes in healthcare products and services. We have retained the **From the Front Line** feature, which highlight a wide range of DSS professionals from new MBAs to Roger himself. Each person was asked to discuss a provocative question that we thought would be of interest to students. Some of the topics discussed in the From the Front Line features include:

- Secrets of conducting good focus groups
- Secrets of good questionnaire design
- How to develop a good set of tables
- Courses I wish that I had taken before becoming a marketing researcher, and why

Feedback from both professors and students tells us that our readers found these stories interesting and helpful in understanding marketing research.

Real Research

What could be more real than a nationwide survey drawn by Survey Sampling International? Not only was the sample professionally drawn, but the questionnaires were created by research professionals at DSS Research. The Rockingham National Bank Visa Card Survey is also based on actual data from one of America's largest research firms. All end-of-chapter cases and data cases are real. It is part of our commitment to bring the student the most authentic, real-world marketing research text on the market.

What's New? Cutting–Edge Trends And Methodology In Every Chapter

We learned through our research that opening vignettes were not necessary. They have been dropped from this edition. You find our real end-of-chapter cases useful and interesting to read, so we update them and added a new, real-world case in each chapter. Students have told us that they thoroughly enjoy our **From the Front Line** feature which highlights a wide range of DSS Research professionals from new MSMR graduates to Roger himself. Each person discusses a provocative question, related to the chapter material, that we have found to be interesting to the students. We have added five new From the Front Line interviews in this edition.

New Content by Chapter:

Chapter 1—The Role of Marketing Research in Management Decision Making

New section on social media and user-generated content. New discussion of basic research. Updated and added new material on the role of the Internet in marketing research. New examples throughout.

Chapter 2—The Marketing Research Industry and Research Ethics

Updated list and discussion of the United States' largest marketing research firms. New material on online tracking firms. Revised discussion on research outsourcing. New material on the state of the marketing research industry. Expanded section on privacy.

Chapter 3—Problem Definition, Exploratory Research, and the Research Process

New box on "What Do You Need to Know." New box entitled, "Where Do I Send the RFP?" New examples throughout.

Chapter 4—Secondary Data and Databases

Major new sections on behavioral targeting and the privacy battle.

Chapter 5—Qualitative Research

New box entitled, "Building a Strong Bond with Focus Group Participants." New discussion of the client's role in focus group research. New section on focus group trends. New material on focus group participants. New box entitled, "Getting Consumers to Tell Their Stories."

Chapter 6—Traditional Survey Research

New discussion on predictive dialing. New material on cell phone interviewing.

Chapter 7—Online Marketing Research

Updated online statistics. Updated and added sources of secondary data online. New material on researchers' use of blogs. New box entitled, "Advantages of Online Focus Groups in B2B Research." New material on online individual depth interviewing. New box entitled, "The Primacy of Online Research." New material on mobile Internet research.

Chapter 8—Primary Data Collection: Observation

Greatly expanded material on ethnographic research. Discussion on ethnography and focus groups. New material on mystery shopping. New discussion on observation using an MRI. New material on eye tracking. New section on gender and age recognition systems. Update on people meters. New section on the

Symphony IRI Consumer Network. Major new discussion on Internet tracking. New discussion on Internet scraping. New section on comScore.

Chapter 9—Primary Data Collection: Experimentation and Test Markets

New box entitled, "Data Use: The Insidious Top Box and Its Effect on Measurement," New discussion of test marketing. New box entitled, "What Makes a Good Test Market?"

Chapter 10—The Concept of Measurement

New examples.

Chapter 11—Using Measurement Scales to Build Marketing Effectiveness

New box entitled, "Comparing the Traditional Likert Scale and Alternative Slider Scales." New box entitled, "Cross-Cultural Segmentation: Accounting for Cross-Cultural Response Differences When Using Survey Rating Scales." New box entitled, "To Choose or Not to Choose? Are Choice Techniques the Right Choice?" New box entitled, "The 10 Point Scale versus the 7 Point Scale."

Chapter 12—Questionnaire Design

New box entitled, "It's All About the Objectives." New section on laddering. New material on probing. New material on interview instructions. New section on using Facebook as a survey research platform.

Chapter 13—Basic Sampling Issues

New material on address-based sampling. New examples throughout.

Chapter 14—Sample Size Determination

New material on sample size and sample size tables. New discussion on sample size in qualitative research.

Chapter 15—Data Processing and Fundamental Data Analysis

New material on interview validation. New discussion on data analysis software.

Chapter 16—Statistical Testing of Differences and Relationships

New box entitled, "Choosing the Right Test for the Right Situation." New box entitled, "Does Statistical Precision Validate Results?" New examples throughout.

Chapter 17—Bivariate Correlation and Regression

New material on explaining correction results.

Chapter 18—Multivariate Data Analysis

New material on the trade-off matrix.

Chapter 19—Communicating the Research Results

New box entitled, "The Relationship Between Clarity and Project Success." New box entitled, "Getting to the Heart of Writing Quantitative Research Reports." New material on challenges researchers face in communicating their results to clients. New material on presentations on the Internet.

Chapter 20—Managing Marketing Research

New material on the state of the marketing research industry. New section on the key role of the project manager. New material on the movement toward insourcing. New section on researcher pay. New box entitled, "Soft Skills of an Ideal Marketing Researcher." New section on client-supplier partnerships. New box on "Picking a Russian Research Supplier." New section on how internal marketing research departments can achieve strategic consultative relevance. New material on creative problem solving. New material quantifying the economic value of research. New material on project control.

Outstanding Resources For All Teaching Needs

Classroom-Tested Instructor's Manual

We have done everything possible to facilitate your teaching marketing research with a comprehensive instructor's manual. Each chapter contains the following:

- ■ *Suggested Lesson Plans.* Suggestions are given on how to decide the chapter material, based on the frequency and duration of your class period.

- ■ *Chapter Scan.* A quick synopsis highlights the core material in each chapter.

- ■ *Learning Objectives.* The list of learning objectives found in the test is repeated here.

- ■ *General Chapter Outline.* The main headers provide a quick snapshot of all the content areas within the chapter.

- ■ *List of Key Terms.* The key terms introduced to the students in the text are repeated here.

- ■ *Detailed Chapter Outline.* This outline fleshes out the general outline given previously. It also indicates where ancillary materials fit into the discussion: PowerPoint slides, exhibits from the text, learning objectives, and review questions. Boxed features are also included in this outline.

- ■ *Summary Explaining Learning Objectives.* An explanation of how the learning objectives are satisfied by chapter material is the basis of the Instructor's Manual summary.

- ■ *Answers to Pedagogy.* Suggested answers and approaches to the critical thinking questions, the Internet activities, the cases, the cross-functional questions, and the ethical dilemmas are offered at the end of each chapter or part.

  Instructors can access the electronic files on the Instructor Companion Site at *www.wiley.com/college/mcdaniel.*

Comprehensive PowerPoint Package

We have created a comprehensive, fully interactive PowerPoint presentation with roughly 400 slides in the package. You can tailor your visual presentation to include the material you choose to cover in class. This PowerPoint presentation gives you the ability to completely integrate your classroom lecture with a powerful visual statement of chapter material. Keep students engaged and stimulate classroom discussion! The entire collection of slides will be available for download from our Web site at *www.wiley.com/college/mcdaniel.*

Classroom-Tested Comprehensive Test Bank

Our test bank is comprehensive and thoroughly classroom-tested. The questions range from definitions of key terms to basic problem-solving questions to creative-thinking problems. This new and improved test bank includes approximately 60 questions per chapter consisting of multiple-choice, true/false, and essay questions. Regardless of the type and level of knowledge you wish to test, we have the right questions for your students. A computerized version of this newly created test bank is also available on the book's companion Web site so that you can customize your quizzes and exams. Instructions can access the electronic files on the Instructor's Companion Site at *www.wiley.com/college/mcdaniel.*

Focus Group Video and Lecture Launches

Additional *Real Research* is offered through a focus group video conducted by another one of our research partners. Jerry Thomas, president of Decision Analyst (*www.decisionanalysis.com*). Decision Analyst, Incorporated is a large international marketing research firm. The focus group subject is online dating data case. We also offer several interviews featuring Jerry Thomas and your author, Carl McDaniel, discussing key topics in marketing research. For more information on this 45-minute video, available on DVD, please contact your local Wiley representative.

New Wiley Marketing Research Video Series

Brand new interview-style video clips of top marketing research companies. Each video, six to eight minutes in length, presents interviews with key personnel to discuss how they apply the major concepts of marketing research to their business. The Marketing Wiley Research Video Series can be accessed on the student and Instructor's Companion site at www.wiley.com/college/mcdaniel.

Acknowledgments

This book could not have been written and published without the generous expert assistance of many people. A big thanks goes to Pam Rimer for typing Carl McDaniel's portion of the manuscript and to Jan Schneider for all the assistance she provided to Roger Gates on this edition.

Our deepest gratitude goes to the team at John Wiley and Sons for continuing the trend of excellence established by this text. Thank you to Fanny Kelly (Senior Acquisition Editor), Emily McGee (Assistant Editor) and Melissa Solarz (Editorial Assistant).

CONTENTS IN BRIEF

CONTENTS

The Role of Marketing Research in Management Decision Making

CHAPTER 1

LEARNING OBJECTIVES

1. To review the marketing concept and the marketing mix.

2. To comprehend the marketing environment within which managers must make decisions.

3. To define marketing research.

4. To understand the importance of marketing research in shaping marketing decisions.

5. To learn when marketing research should and should not be conducted.

6. To learn how the Internet is changing marketing research.

7. To understand the history of marketing research.

Welcome to the fascinating world of marketing research! How does marketing research help managers reach their goals? How did the field of marketing research evolve? We will explore this topic in chapter one.

Nature of Marketing

> **marketing**
> The process of planning and executing the conception, pricing, promotion, and distribution of ideas, goods, and services to create exchanges that satisfy individual and organizational objectives.

Marketing is the activity, set of institutions, and processes for creating, communicating, delivering, and exchanging offerings that have value for customers, clients, partners, and society at large.[1] Good customer relationships often result in exchanges; that is, a good or service is exchanged for money. The potential for exchange exists when there are at least two parties and each has something of potential value to the other. When the two parties can communicate and deliver the desired goods or services, exchange can take place. How do marketing managers attempt to stimulate exchange? They follow the "right" principle. They attempt to get the right goods or services to the right people at the right place at the right time at the right price, using the right promotion techniques. The "right" principle describes how marketing managers control the many factors that ultimately determine marketing success. To make the "right" decisions, management must have timely decision-making information. Marketing research is a primary channel for providing that information.

The Marketing Concept

> **marketing concept**
> A business philosophy based on consumer orientation, goal orientation, and systems orientation.

To efficiently accomplish their goals, firms today have adopted the **marketing concept**, which requires (1) a consumer orientation, (2) a goal orientation, and (3) a systems orientation. A **consumer orientation** means that firms strive to identify the people (or firms) most likely to buy their product (the target market) and to produce a good or offer a service that will meet the needs of target customers most effectively in the face of competition. The second tenet of the marketing concept is **goal orientation**; that is, a firm must be consumer-oriented only to the extent that it also accomplishes corporate goals. The goals of profit-making firms usually center on financial criteria, such as a 15 percent return on investment.

> **consumer orientation**
> The identification of and focus on the people or firms most likely to buy a product and the production of a good or service that will meet their needs most effectively.

The third component of the marketing concept is a **systems orientation**. A system is an organized whole—or a group of diverse units that form an integrated whole—functioning or operating in unison. It is one thing for a firm to say it is consumer-oriented and another actually to *be* consumer-oriented. First, systems must be established to find out what consumers want and to identify market opportunities. As you will see later, identifying target market needs and finding market opportunities are the tasks of marketing research. Next, this information must be fed back to the firm. Without feedback from the marketplace, a firm is not truly consumer-oriented.

> **goal orientation**
> A focus on the accomplishment of corporate goals; a limit set on consumer orientation.

Opportunistic Nature of Marketing Research

> **systems orientation**
> The creation of systems to monitor the external environment and deliver the desired marketing mix to the target market.

Marketing research is an excellent tool for discovering opportunities in the marketplace. Marketing research recently discovered that when it comes to selecting cosmetics, consumers look for brands they trust and brands that make makeup—both buying it and applying it—natural and easy. Seventy percent of the respondents claim that they use makeup. They favor Cover Girl over any other brand. Out of 60 cosmetic brands, Cover Girl was cited by 14 percent as their favorite, placing it on top. Clinique was second on the list with 10 percent of the mentions, and Maybelline (L'Oreal) and Mary Kay tied for third with 8 percent each.

When the consumers were asked what they loved most about their favorite makeup line, they chose brand trust over all the other factors; the actual product attributes mattered much less. More than two-thirds said they love their makeup because they trust the brand, while only one-third cited loving it "because it feels wonderful." Factors like "uses humane testing/is environmentally safe" were not weighted strongly and emerged toward the bottom of the list.

Cover Girl led the other brands in most of the attributes consumers care about most, scoring highest in categories such as great value, brand trust, wears well throughout the day, and easy, no-mess application.

A common sentiment that emerged in the survey is that makeup wearers want a natural and authentic look rather than something ultramodern.

Among those still buying new products, tween girls (ages 8–12) have upped their product usage, while teens (ages 13–17) and young women (18–24) reported declines in their usage of beauty products.

Significantly more influential to tweens than TV and even their friends, these girls say that they "look to their parents and siblings to see what they are using to help decide what to buy and use."[2]

So marketing research has identified the market leaders, determined why specific brands are popular, learned the "look" that makeup wearers are seeking, ascertained which market segments for new products are growing and which are in decline, and, for the growth segment (tweens), who influences their purchase decisions. Insights such as these will help a cosmetic marketing manager create a more powerful and effective marketing mix.

External Marketing Environment

Over time, the **marketing mix** must be altered because of changes in the environment in which consumers and businesses exist, work, compete, and make purchasing decisions. Some new consumers and businesses will become part of the target market, while others will drop out of the market; those who remain may have different tastes, needs, incomes, lifestyles, and purchase habits than the original target consumers.

Although managers can control the marketing mix, they cannot control elements in the external environment that continually mold and reshape the target market. Unless management understands the external environment, the firm cannot intelligently plan its future, and organizations are often unaware of the forces that influence their future.

Marketing research is a key means for understanding the environment. Knowledge of the environment helps a firm not only to alter its present marketing mix, but also to identify new opportunities. For example, when Ann Arbor, Michigan-based Domino's Pizza introduced its pizza delivery in Japan, a major change in Japanese consumers' behavior was needed as well. Yet Domino's managed to rise to the challenge successfully. If Domino's had merely tested the acceptability of the service it delivered in other parts of the world, it never would have entered Japan. Japanese consumers typically don't eat tomato-based food, and Asians tend to have allergies to milk products. Home delivery was not widely accepted, housewives were reluctant to give up cooking, houses were small, and finding customers in the labyrinthine streets of Tokyo seemed impossible. A market for pizza didn't exist, nor was there any sign of hope for creating one.

Instead of trying to sell its existing product and service to the market, Domino's used its marketing research about customers to design a new product and service offering for Japan. It introduced toppings such as fish and sushi. To sustain its 30-minute delivery, Domino's developed a complex address database and small scooters to navigate the narrow streets in Tokyo. Through this research process this pizza-delivery service that no one asked for became a big hit in Japan.[3]

> **marketing mix**
> The unique blend of product/service, pricing, promotion, and distribution strategies designed to meet the needs of a specific target market.

Marketing Research and Decision Making

Marketing research plays two key roles in the marketing system. First, as part of the marketing intelligence feedback process, marketing research provides decision makers with data on the effectiveness of the current marketing mix and offers insights into necessary changes. Second, marketing research is the primary tool for exploring new opportunities in the marketplace. Segmentation research and new product research help identify the most lucrative opportunities for a firm.

Marketing Research Defined

Now that you have an understanding of how marketing research fits into the overall marketing system, we can proceed with a formal definition of the term, as stated by the American Marketing Association:

Marketing research is the function that links the consumer, customer, and public to the marketer through information—information used to identify and define marketing opportunities and problems; generate, refine, and evaluate marketing actions; monitor marketing performance; and improve understanding of marketing as a process. Marketing research specifies the information required to address these issues, designs the method for collecting information, manages and implements the data collection process, analyzes the results, and communicates the findings and their implications.

> **marketing research**
> The planning, collection, and analysis of data relevant to marketing decision making and the communication of the results of this analysis to management.

We prefer another definition: **Marketing research** is the planning, collection, and analysis of data relevant to marketing decision making and the communication of the results of this analysis to management.

Importance of Marketing Research to Management

Marketing research can be viewed as playing three functional roles: descriptive, diagnostic, and predictive. Its **descriptive function** includes gathering and presenting statements of fact. What is the historic sales trend in the industry? What are consumers' attitudes and beliefs toward a product? Opening a pack of bacon is a messy job. Bacon lovers have to reach into the package, and if they only pull out a few slices, there's no easy way to store the remainder. Oscar Mayer marketing researchers hear plenty from consumers about what they disliked about its former bacon packaging. So marketers figured the best solution would be a packaging innovation that eliminated the chore of placing the opened pack in a resealable plastic bag or wrapping it in plastic or foil. This unwanted task was done so that the last piece of bacon would be as fresh as the first.

> **descriptive function**
> The gathering and presentation of statements of fact.

Oscar Mayer Center Cut Bacon was introduced in a new "Stay-Fresh Reclosable Tray." The flip top lid allows easy access to the bacon inside. The top snaps closed, making it readily resealable. The flat tray makes for simplified storage in the refrigerator.

The second role of research is the **diagnostic function**, wherein data and/or actions are explained. For example, what was the impact on sales when the Oscar Mayer package design was changed? How can product/service offerings be altered to better serve customers and potential customers? Since kids eat over 5 billion ounces of ketchup each year, Heinz decided that the heavy users (kids) should have a lot to say (via marketing research) about how to make ketchup fun. Heinz listened and watched children using ketchup, which resulted in a new bottle design and name selection. The true ketchup connoisseurs helped create Heinz EZ Squirt ketchup!

> **diagnostic function**
> The explanation of data or actions.

The final role of research is the **predictive function**. How can the firm best take advantage of opportunities as they arise in the ever-changing marketplace? Kraft Foods

> **predictive function**
> Specification of how to use descriptive and diagnostic research to predict the results of a planned marketing decision.

noticed that consumers were flocking to "low-carb" diets. The company used marketing research to determine whether this was a fad or a long-term trend. Determining that "low carb" was more than a fad, it entered into an alliance with Arthur Agatston, the creator of the South Beach Diet. The result was certain Kraft products being labeled "South Beach Diet Recommended." Further marketing research led to a broad line of products entitled "The South Beach Diet" brand. Products include cereal, meal replacement and cereal bars, refrigerated sandwich wraps, frozen entrees, and frozen pizza.

The Unrelenting Drive for Quality and Customer Satisfaction   Quality and customer satisfaction have become the key competitive weapons as America emerges from the worst recession since the 1930s. American automobile manufacturers have been among the most battered in recent years. Now, the watchwords are quality and customer service. As one auto executive puts it:

If you go back to even a very short time ago, our whole idea of a customer was that we would wholesale a car to a dealer, the dealer would then sell the car to the customers, and we hoped we never heard from the customer—because if we did, it meant something was wrong. Today, we want to establish a dialogue with the customer throughout the entire ownership experience. We want to talk to and toumers are every step of the way. We want to be a consumer-products and services company that just happens to be in the automotive business.[4]

Where does marketing research come into play? The J. D. Power Awards rank cars based on the level of customer satisfaction. This, in turn, drives sales of specific companies and models. Lexus has always done well in a number of quality and customer satisfaction studies. This has helped increase sales of the IS, LS, and RX models. At some Lexus dealers, you can get a manicure and a massage while having your oil changed. Automobile manufacturers use marketing research to aid designers, determine what new features to add to specific models, and learn how their cars stack up with those of the competition.

Quality that means little to customers usually doesn't produce a payoff in improved sales, profits, or market share; it represents wasted effort and expense. Today, the new mantra is **return on quality**, which means that (1) the quality being delivered is the quality desired by the target market and (2) the added quality must have a positive impact on profitability. For example, banking giant Bank of America measures every improvement in service quality, from adding more tellers to offering new products, in terms of added profitability.

The passion to drive down costs can destroy the delicate balance between efficiency and service. For example, the University of Michigan annual marketing research survey entitled the American Customer Satisfaction index revealed that Home Depot slipped to dead last among major U.S. retailers.[5] Cost cutting, including replacing many full-time workers with part-timers and reducing the profit-sharing pool for all workers, created a customer service disaster. As a result, same-store sales at Home Depot lagged far behind the much better liked Lowe's. New management has now placed a priority on customer service, and sales are improving.

Paramount Importance of Keeping Existing Customers   An inextricable link exists between customer satisfaction and customer loyalty. Long-term relationships don't just happen; they are grounded in the delivery of service and value. Customer retention pays big dividends for firms. Powered by repeat sales and referrals, revenues and market share grow. Costs fall because firms spend less funds and energy attempting to replace defectors. Steady customers are easy to serve because they understand the modus operandi and make fewer demands on employees' time. A firm's ability to retain customers

> **return on quality**
> Management objective based on the principles that (1) the quality being delivered is at a level desired by the target market and (2) the level of quality must have a positive impact on profitability.

also drives job satisfaction and pride, which leads to higher employee retention. In turn, long-term employees acquire additional knowledge that increases productivity.

A Bain & Company study estimates that a 5 percent decrease in the customer defection rate can boost profits by 25 to 95 percent.[6] Another study found that the customer retention rate has a major impact on the value of the firm.[7]

The ability to retain customers is based on an intimate understanding of their needs. This knowledge comes primarily from marketing research. For example, British Airways recast its first-class transatlantic service based on detailed marketing research. Most airlines stress top-of-the-line service in their transatlantic first-class cabins. However, British Air research found that most first-class passengers simply want to sleep. British Air now gives premium flyers the option of dinner on the ground, before takeoff, in the first-class lounge. Then, once on board, they can slip into British Air pajamas, put their heads on real pillows, slip under blankets, and enjoy an interruption-free flight. On arrival at their destination, first-class passengers can have breakfast, use comfortable dressing rooms and showers, and even have their clothes pressed before they set off. These changes in British Air's first-class service were driven strictly by marketing research.

Understanding the Ever-Changing Marketplace

Marketing research also helps managers to understand trends in the marketplace and to take advantage of opportunities. Marketing research has been practiced for as long as marketing has existed. The early Phoenicians carried out market demand studies as they traded in the various ports on the Mediterranean Sea. Marco Polo's diary indicates he was performing a marketing research function as he traveled to China. There is evidence that the Spanish systematically conducted marketing surveys as they explored the New World, and examples exist of marketing research conducted during the Renaissance.

Social Media and User-Generated Content

In the past few years, the world of promotion has been turned upside down. Previously, marketers created a message and then one, or a series, of traditional media, TV, print, radio, billboards to deliver that message to a target market. Now, we have more people than ever participating in blogs, forums, online communities, product/service reviews—think Trip Advisor—and social media sites that created user-generated content (UGC). The opinions expressed in the venues are unsolicited, typically honest, candid, and passionate and can be extremely thoughtful. Social media such as Twitter, Facebook, and Linked-In generate millions of comments a day about products and services. About 20 percent of all Tweets are about brands.[8]

Asking the right questions in marketing research can be as important as getting good answers. UPS found that customers wanted more interaction with their UPS driver. Go to http://www.ups.com to find out how UPS uses marketing research to better serve its customers.

Marketing researchers are tapping into these huge streams of data to determine what people think about their products and services as well as those of the competition. Researchers are building profiles of persons online and using this data to target their promotional efforts. Other researchers tap online communities to build new products and services.

Indications are that the stream of UGC and social media users will do nothing but continue to grow. For example, 56 percent of social media users need to check Facebook at least once day and 12 percent check in every couple of hours. Forty-eight percent said that they check their Facebook or Twitter pages before bed, during the night, or as soon as they wake up. After going to bed, persons under 25 were much more likely to check their social media during the night.[9]

The skyrocketing growth of UGC and social media has already brought numerous changes to the marketplace and to the field of marketing research. We will be touching on these changes throughout the book, including the emotionally charged issue of Internet privacy.

Proactive Role of Marketing Research

Understanding the nature of the marketing system is a necessity for a successful marketing orientation. By having a thorough knowledge of factors that have an impact on the target market and the marketing mix, management can be proactive rather than reactive. Proactive management alters the marketing mix to fit newly emerging patterns in economic, social, and competitive environments, whereas reactive management waits for change to have a major impact on the firm before deciding to take action. It is the difference between viewing the turbulent marketing environment as a threat (a reactive stance) and as an opportunity (a proactive stance). Apple, for example, has been very proactive about bringing cutting-edge technology products to the marketplace. This, in turn, has generated huge profits for the company.

A proactive manager not only examines emerging markets but also seeks, through strategic planning, to develop a long-run **marketing strategy** for the firm. A marketing strategy guides the long-term use of the firm's resources based on the firm's existing and projected internal capabilities and on projected changes in the external environment. A good strategic plan is based on good marketing research. It helps the firm meet long-term profit and market share goals.

> **marketing strategy**
> A plan to guide the long-term use of a firm's resources based on its existing and projected internal capabilities and on projected changes in the external environment.

Applied Research versus Basic Research

Virtually all marketing research is conducted to better understand the market, to find out why a strategy failed, or to reduce uncertainty in management decision making. All research conducted for these purposes is called **applied research**. For example, should the price of DiGiorno frozen pizza be raised 40 cents? What name should Toyota select for a new sedan? Which commercial has a higher level of recall: A or B? On the other hand, **basic**, or **pure**, **research** attempts to expand the frontiers of knowledge; it is not aimed at a specific pragmatic problem. Basic research is conducted to validate an existing theory or learn more about a concept or phenomenon. For example, basic marketing research might test a hypothesis about high-involvement decision making or consumer information processing. In the long run, basic research helps us understand more about the world in which we live. The findings of basic research usually cannot be implemented by managers in the short run. Most basic marketing research is now conducted in universities; the findings are reported in such publications as *The Journal of Marketing Research* and *The Journal of Marketing*. In contrast, most research undertaken by businesses is applied research because it must be cost-effective and of demonstrable value to the decision maker.

> **applied research**
> Research aimed at solving a specific, pragmatic problem—better understanding of the marketplace, determination of why a strategy or tactic failed, or reduction of uncertainty in management decision making.

> **basic, or pure, research**
> Research aimed at expanding the frontiers of knowledge rather than solving a specific, pragmatic problem.

Although basic research is still important at some firms, particularly high tech, the notion of time-to-market has changed. That is, the basic research can be fairly long term but must have a focus on ultimately solving real-world problems. Companies conducting basic research include Microsoft, IBM, Xerox, and Hewlett-Packard. H-P's research arm, for example, has been doing work in areas such as nanotechnology and computer algorithms that could more efficiently sift the Internet for huge amounts of public data to predict business trends.

Prith Banerjee, director of HPLabs, said that about two-thirds of the labs' projects are relatively short-term initiatives that are intended to produce results within about five years. The remaining third is basic research that may not pan out for a decade or more.[10]

Nature of Applied Research

programmatic research
Research conducted to develop marketing options through market segmentation, market opportunity analyses, or consumer attitude and product usage studies.

selective research
Research used to test decision alternatives.

evaluative research
Research done to assess program performance.

Marketing research studies can be classified into three broad categories: programmatic, selective, and evaluative. **Programmatic research** is conducted to develop marketing options through market segmentation, market opportunity analysis, or consumer attitude and product usage studies. **Selective research** is used to test decision alternatives. Some examples are testing concepts for new products, advertising copy testing, and test marketing. **Evaluative research** is done to assess program performance; it includes tracking advertising recall, doing organizational image studies, and examining customer attitudes on a firm's quality of service.

Programmatic research arises from management's need to obtain a market overview periodically. For example, product management may be concerned that the existing market information base is inadequate or outdated for present decision making, or marketing plans may call for the introduction of new products, ad campaigns, or packaging. Whatever the specific situation, current information is needed to develop viable marketing options. Typical programmatic research questions include the following:

- Has its target market changed? How?
- Does the market exhibit any new segmentation opportunities?
- Do some segments appear to be more likely candidates than others for the firm's marketing efforts?
- What new product or service opportunities lie in the various segments?

Equidistant between Los Angeles and San Francisco in the Eastern Sierra Nevada Mountains, Mammoth Mountain has been serving the skiers and snowboarders of central California for 50 years. With the summit reaching above 11,000 feet and average annual snowfall hitting 400 inches, thousands of customers flock to the slopes and the lodges annually.

Yet, the resort's longstanding direct-mail program just wasn't driving the traffic. While the resort wasn't losing visitors (most resort traffic industrywide comes from existing skiers and snowboarders rather than those new to the sports), executives hoped to gain some ground in an overall stable market by injecting some life into what had become an out-of-date marketing campaign—and to increase the frequency of visits by the 900,000 customers in its database.

Resort executives used programmatic research collected from an annual survey, the National Skier and Snowboarder Opinion Survey conducted on behalf of resorts across the country, and found that 94 percent of Mammoth's users in particular acknowledge using the Internet to find information about everything from weather advisories to checking room rates at one of Mammoth's lodges.

This information led to the creation of an e-mail marketing system that reaches 18,000 subscribers. The format is chatty and informing. For example, "The weather has been beautiful here lately, and with a 12- to 14-foot base you can't go wrong anywhere on the mountain. At 1:15 P.M. the temperature is 34 degrees at Main Lodge with clear skies and moderate to gusty winds. It's extremely windy and cold on top at 17 degrees, so be sure to bundle up." Skier visit numbers have been increasing 5 percent or more annually as a result of the programmatic research![11]

"I don't *know* what I'm doing—this is pure research!"

Selective research typically is conducted after several viable options have been identified by programmatic research. If no one alternative is clearly superior, product management usually will wish to test several alternatives. However, selective research may be required at any stage of the marketing process, such as when advertising copy is being developed, various product formulations are being evaluated, or an entire marketing program is being assessed, as in test marketing.

The need for evaluative research arises when the effectiveness and efficiency of marketing programs must be evaluated. Evaluative research may be integrated into programmatic research when program changes or entirely new options are demanded because of present performance such as at Mammoth Mountain.

Decision to Conduct Marketing Research

A manager who is faced with several alternative solutions to a particular problem should not instinctively call for applied marketing research. In fact, the first decision to be made is whether to conduct marketing research at all. In a number of situations, it is best not to conduct research.

■ *Resources are lacking.* There are two situations in which a lack of resources should preclude marketing research. First, an organization may lack the funds to do the research properly. If a project calls for a sample of 800 respondents but the budget allows for only 50 interviews, the quality of the information would be highly suspect. Second, funds may be available to do the research properly but insufficient to implement any decisions resulting from the research. Small organizations in particular sometimes lack the resources to create an effective marketing mix. In one case, for example, the director of a performing arts guild was in complete agreement with the recommendations that resulted from a marketing research project. However, 2 years after the project was completed, nothing had been done because the money was not available.

■ *Research results would not be useful.* Some types of marketing research studies measure lifestyle and personality factors of steady and potential customers. Assume that a study finds that introverted men with a poor self-concept, yet a high need for achievement, are most likely to patronize a discount brokerage service. The management of Charles Schwab's discount brokerage service might be hard-pressed to use this information.

■ *The opportunity has passed.* Marketing research should not be undertaken if the opportunity for successful entry into a market has already passed. If the product is in the late maturity or decline stage of the product life cycle (such as cassette recorders or black-and-white television sets), it would be foolish to do research on new product entry. The same may be true for markets rapidly approaching saturation, such as super-premium ice cream (Häagen-Dazs, Ben and Jerry's). For products already

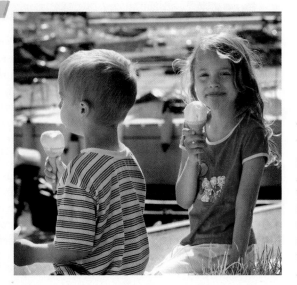

The super-premium ice cream market is reaching saturation. At this point, it might not be wise to enter this market. However, marketing research is necessary to keep products already in the market ahead of the competition.

in the market, however, research is needed to modify the products as consumer tastes, competition, and other factors change.

■ *The decision already has been made.* In the real world of management decision making and company politics, marketing research has sometimes been used improperly. Several years ago, a large marketing research study was conducted for a bank with over $800 million in deposits. The purpose of the research project was to guide top management in mapping a strategic direction for the bank during the next 5 years. After reading the research report, the president said, "I fully agree with your recommendations because that was what I was going to do anyway! I'm going to use your study tomorrow when I present my strategic plan to the board of directors." The researcher then asked, "What if my recommendations had been counter to your decision?" The bank president laughed and said, "They would have never known that I had conducted a marketing research study!" Not only was the project a waste of money, but it also raised a number of ethical questions in the researcher's mind.

■ *Managers cannot agree on what they need to know to make a decision.* Although it may seem obvious that research should not be undertaken until objectives are specified, it sometimes happens. Preliminary or exploratory studies are commonly done to better understand the nature of the problem, but a large, major research project should not be. It is faulty logic to say "Well, let's just go ahead and do the study and then we will better understand the problem and know what steps to take." The wrong phenomena might be studied, or key elements needed for management decision making may not be included.

■ *Decision-making information already exists.* Some companies have been conducting research in certain markets for many years. They understand the characteristics of their target customers and what they like and dislike about existing products. Under these circumstances, further research would be redundant and a waste of money. Procter & Gamble, for example, has extensive knowledge of the coffee market. After it conducted initial taste tests, P&G went into national distribution with Folger's Instant Coffee without further research. The Sara Lee Corporation did the same thing with its frozen croissants, as did Quaker Oats with Chewy Granola Bars. This tactic, however, does not always work. P&G thought it understood the pain reliever market thoroughly, so it bypassed marketing research for Encaprin, encapsulated aspirin. The product failed because it lacked a distinct competitive advantage over existing products and was withdrawn from the market.

■ *The costs of conducting research outweigh the benefits.* Rarely does a manager have such tremendous confidence in her or his judgment that additional information relative to a pending decision would not be accepted if it were available and free. However, the manager might have sufficient confidence to be unwilling to pay very much for it or wait long to receive it. Willingness to acquire additional decision-making information depends on a manager's perception of its quality, price, and timing. The manager would be willing to pay more for perfect information (that is, data that leave no doubt as to which alternative to follow) than for information that leaves uncertainty as to what to do. Therefore, research should be undertaken only when the expected value of the information is greater than the cost of obtaining it.

Two important determinants of potential benefits are profit margins and market size. Generally speaking, new products with large profit margins are going to have greater potential benefit than products with smaller profit margins, assuming that both items have the same sales potential. Also, new product opportunities in large markets are going to offer greater potential benefits than those in smaller markets if competitive intensity is the same in both markets (see Exhibit 1.1).

EXHIBIT 1.1	Deciding Whether to Conduct Marketing Research	
Market Size	**Small Profit Margin**	**Large Profit Margin**
Small	Costs likely to be greater than benefits (e.g., eyeglass replacement screw, tire valve extension). DON'T CONDUCT MARKETING RESEARCH.	Benefits possibly greater than cost (e.g., ultra-expensive Lamborghini-type sportswear, larger specialized industrial equipment like computer-aided metal stamping machines). PERHAPS CONDUCT MARKETING RESEARCH. LEARN ALL YOU CAN FROM EXISTING INFORMATION PRIOR TO MAKING DECISION TO CONDUCT RESEARCH.
Large	Benefits likely to be greater than costs (e.g., Stouffers frozen entrees, Crest's teeth whitener strips). PERHAPS CONDUCT MARKETING RESEARCH. LEARN ALL YOU CAN FROM EXISTING INFORMATION PRIOR TO MAKING DECISION TO CONDUCT RESEARCH.	Benefits most likely to be greater than costs (e.g., medical equipment like CAT scanners, Toshiba's 3D television). CONDUCT MARKETING RESEARCH.

Development of Marketing Research

The many benefits that accrue to management from using marketing research served as the initial impetus to begin conducting marketing research in the United States. In light of the competitive advantage a company can gain from engaging in marketing research, it is surprising that the industry did not move out of its embryonic stage until 1900.

Inception: Pre-1900

The first recorded marketing research survey was taken in July 1824 by the *Harrisburg Pennsylvanian*. It was an election poll in which Andrew Jackson received 335 votes; John Quincy Adams, 169; Henry Clay, 29; and William H. Crawford, 9. Later the same year, another newspaper, the *Raleigh Star*, canvassed political meetings held in North Carolina, "at which the sense of the people was taken." Perhaps the first marketing researcher was John Jacob Astor, who in the 1790s employed an artist to sketch the hats worn by fashionable New York women so that he could keep abreast of fashion trends.[12]

The first documented use of research to make informed marketing decisions was carried out by the advertising agency N. W. Ayer in 1879. That systematic effort was a simple survey of state and local officials to determine expected levels of grain production. The purpose of the research was to develop the scheduling of advertising for a producer of farm equipment. The second documented instance of marketing research appears to have been at E. I. duPont de Nemours & Company toward the end of the 19th century. It involved the systematic compilation of salespersons' reports on a variety of customer characteristics. The response to this second research effort was a harbinger of things to come. The salespersons who were responsible for obtaining and reporting the data were outraged because they didn't like the extra paperwork.

Academic researchers entered into marketing research about 1895, when Harlow Gale, a professor of psychology at the University of Minnesota, introduced the use of mail surveys to study advertising. He mailed 200 questionnaires and received 20 completed questionnaires, a 10 percent response rate. Gale's work was quickly followed by the pioneering work of Walter Dill Scott at Northwestern University. Scott introduced the use of experimentation and psychological measurement to the fledgling practice of advertising.

Early Growth: 1900–1920

It was not until after the turn of the century that consumer demand surged; the growth of mass production meant larger and more distant markets. No longer was America characterized by cottage industries where the craftsman–seller was in daily contact with the marketplace. The need arose to understand consumers' buying habits and attitudes toward manufacturers' wares. In response to this need, the first formal marketing research department was established by the Curtis Publishing Company in 1911. The research focused primarily on the automobile industry, as manufacturers had decided that everyone who had the money and inclination to buy a car had done so. The manufacturers were seeking a new group of consumers to which to target their promotions. A few years later, Daniel Starch pioneered recognition measures of advertising response, and E. K. Strong introduced recall measures and scaling to marketing research.

Adolescent Years: 1920–1950

Percival White developed the first application of scientific research to commercial problems. White's words express his realization of the need for systematic and continual marketing research:

Perhaps the greatest advantage of the company's having its own market analysis department is that the work then becomes a continuous process, or at least a process which is carried forward at periodic intervals, so that altered conditions in the market and in the industry at large are always kept in view. The necessity for regarding markets as constantly changing and not as fixed phenomena should not be lost sight of.[13]

White's book bore scant resemblance to this text. For example, the book avoided the use of statistics and mathematics, only briefly mentioning the U.S. Census.

The 1930s saw widespread use of survey research. A. C. Nielsen entered the research business in 1922. He expanded on White's earlier work by developing the "share of market" concept and many other services that became the foundation for one of America's largest marketing research organizations. It was not until the late 1930s that formal courses in marketing research became common on college campuses; a substantial body of knowledge developed within both the practice and academic communities. Two events—the spread of broadcast media and World War II—helped the fledgling discipline coalesce into a well-defined profession. Social scientists found that broadcast media created interesting new phenomena and increased the variability of human behavior.

By the end of the 1930s, simple examinations of respondents' replies were becoming categorized and compared across groups classified by differences in income, gender, or family status. Simple correlation analysis came into use but was not widespread; those who would use it had to be able to go directly to the statistical sources for such techniques, using texts by some of the pioneers in the field at this time, including G. Udney Yule, Mordecai Ezekiel, and Horace Sechrist.

The requirements of World War II pressed social scientists into service on a number of fronts. Tools and methods that had been novelties before the war were adopted and adapted to study the consumer behavior of soldiers and of their families on the home front. Among those tools were experimental design, opinion polling, human factors research, and operations research techniques.

In the 1940s, focus groups developed under the leadership of Robert Merton. During the late 1940s, the importance of random selection in sampling became widely recognized, and major advances were made in sampling techniques and polling procedures. A small number of psychologists who had been assigned to work in the Army Quartermaster Corps found their way into industry, where they introduced techniques for consumer tests of products.[14]

Mature Years: 1950–2000

The change from a seller's market to a buyer's market (resulting from post–World War II pent-up demand) necessitated better marketing intelligence. No longer could producers sell all of anything they made. The rising costs of production "tooling up," advertising, inventories, and other factors made the price of failure much higher than it had been in the past. Now, marketing research first determines what the market wants and then goods are crafted to meet those needs.

The mid-1950s brought the concept of market segmentation, based largely on easily identifiable demographic characteristics of customers. The same period gave rise to motivation research, with its emphasis on why consumers behave as they do. The underlying concepts of segmentation and motivation analysis, combined with the power of survey techniques, led to such innovations as psychographics and benefit segmentation. In the 1960s, mathematical models were developed for description and prediction—stochastic models, Markovian models, linear learning models. Even more significant was the development of the computer during the early 1960s, greatly enhancing the researcher's ability to quickly analyze, store, and retrieve large amounts of data.

Bill Neal, founder of SDR Consulting, discusses what's good about marketing research in the "Practicing Marketing Research" box that follows.

PRACTICING MARKETING RESEARCH

What Is Good about Marketing Research Today

William D. Neal is founder and senior executive officer of SDR Consulting in Atlanta. Bill talks about what he believes is good about marketing research today.

Looking back over the last 40 years, marketing research on the whole has contributed significantly to business success. Investments in marketing research have continued to increase far above the rate of inflation, and operational marketing managers depend more on marketing research to reduce the risks in undertaking new marketing initiatives.

Voice of the customer. More than ever, businesses and other institutions are measuring and monitoring customer satisfaction and loyalty on a continuous basis, using that information to improve processes and stem defections. Fifteen years ago, very little customer satisfaction and loyalty tracking research was supported or funded at all. Now, most major firms and many smaller firms track their customers' levels of satisfaction. And a smaller number are tracking customers' attitudinal and/or behavioral loyalty. Clearly, both the organization and the customer benefit from this revived focus on customer care.

Management metrics. Slowly, but surely, marketing research is beginning to provide some of the key metrics to senior management. Long the exclusive territory of the purveyors of financial numbers, management metrics are beginning to include marketing components— brand health measures, changes in brand equity, advertising and promotional effectiveness measures, indices of customer satisfaction, and several other measures of marketing impact.

New products. Research has often been blamed for the historically abysmal rate of new product failures. However, some of the more recent investigations into new product failures tend to exonerate at least some of the research. More often, the failures occur because (1) there were inadequate investments in research, (2) the research was ignored, (3) what was researched was not what was launched, (4) there was inadequate marketing and promotional support, or (5) there was inadequate sales or fulfillment support. We have several new tools for testing new products, from concept to prelaunch. When used properly, these newer tools greatly reduce the risks inherent in a new product launch and accurately predict trial and repurchase rates under different levels of marketing support.

Branding. After the branding debacles of the 1990s, many firms began to recognize that their greatest asset is their brands. Unlike any other aspect of the marketing mix, brands represent a component of value that can't be replicated by a competitor. Thus it represents a unique, defensible asset for the owner and a launch pad for new product development and deployment. Unfortunately, branding has long been resistant to the imposition of scientific investigation, relying too much on the creative arts of advertising and promotion. But that is changing. There are now several research-based models for measuring brand value and brand equity and uncovering their key drivers. Quantifiable changes in brand equity represent the ultimate measure of return on marketing investment.[15]

The Connected World: 2000–Present

The Internet has brought profound changes to marketing research. In a global survey, 94 percent of the research firms stated that they were conducting online research.[16] Some firms are beginning to focus on mobile interviewing—mobile self-completion on a smartphone, iPhone, Blackberry, Droid, and the like. Today, 47 percent of Americans go online wirelessly via a laptop; 40 percent do so using a smartphone.[17] And, over 85 percent of the U.S. population has Internet access.[18]

The Internet has produced many benefits for marketing researchers:

■ Provides more rapid access to business intelligence, which allows for better and faster decision making.

■ Improves a firm's ability to respond quickly to customer needs and market shifts.

■ Facilitates conducting follow-up studies and longitudinal research.

■ Slashes labor- and time-intensive research activities (and associated costs), including mailing, telephone solicitation, data entry, data tabulation, and reporting.

Conducting surveys and analyzing mountains of user data are not the sum total of the Internet revolution in marketing research. The Internet has also greatly enhanced management of the research process and dissemination of information. Specifically, the Internet has greatly affected several key areas.

■ *Libraries and various printed materials, which may be virtually replaced as sources of information.* On its Web site, the Bureau of Census (*http://www.census.gov*) indicates that it plans to gradually make the Internet the major means of distributing census data. The same is true for a number of other government agencies. Information from countless databases (both governmental and nongovernmental) can be called up almost instantaneously on the user's desktop, notebook, Blackberry, Kindle, iPad, or other E-reader.

- *The distribution of requests for proposals (RFPs) and the proposals themselves.* Companies can now quickly and efficiently send RFPs to a select e-mail list of research suppliers. In turn, the suppliers can develop proposals and e-mail them back to clients. A process that used to take days now occurs in a matter of hours.

- *Collaboration between the client and the research supplier in the management of a research project.* Both the researcher and the client might look at a proposal, RFP, report, or some type of statistical analysis at the same time on their computer screens while discussing it over the telephone. This is very effective and efficient, as changes in sample size, quotas, and other aspects of the research plan can be discussed and changes made immediately.

- *Data management and online analysis.* Clients can access their survey via the research supplier's secure Web site and monitor the data gathering in real time. The client can use sophisticated tools to actually carry out data analysis as the survey develops. This real-time analysis may result in changes in the questionnaire, sample size, or types of respondents interviewed. The research supplier and the client become partners in "just-in-time" marketing research.

- *Publishing and distribution of reports.* Reports can be published directly to the Web from such programs as PowerPoint and all the latest versions of leading word processing, spreadsheet, and presentation software packages. This means that results are available to appropriate managers worldwide on an almost instantaneous basis. Reports can be searched for content of specific interest, with the same Web browser used to view the report.

- *Oral presentations of marketing research surveys,* which now can be viewed by widely scattered audiences. Managers throughout the world can see and hear the actual client presentation on password-protected Web sites. This saves firms both time and money, as managers no longer need to travel to a central meeting site.

As we pointed out earlier, the Internet represents the present and the future of a significant portion of the world of marketing research. Its impact is limited only by the researcher's imagination. Chapter 7 is devoted to Internet research as are parts of Chapter 8.

SUMMARY

Marketing is an organizational function and a set of processes for creating, communicating, and delivering value to customers and for managing customer relationships in ways that benefit the organization and its stockholders. Marketing managers attempt to get the right goods or services to the right people at the right place at the right time at the right price, using the right promotion technique. This may be accomplished by following the marketing concept, which is based on consumer orientation, goal orientation, and systems orientation.

The marketing manager must work within an internal environment of the organization and understand the external environment over which he or she has little, if any, control. The primary variables over which the marketing manager has control are distribution, price, promotion, and product/service decisions. The unique combination of these four variables is called the *marketing mix.*

Marketing research plays a key part in providing the information for managers to shape the marketing mix. Marketing research has grown in importance because of management's focus on customer satisfaction and retention. It also is a key tool in proactive management. Marketing research should be undertaken only when the perceived benefits are greater than the costs.

A marketing research study can be described as programmatic, selective, or evaluative. Programmatic research is done to develop marketing options through market segmentation, market opportunity analysis, or consumer attitude and product usage studies. Selective research is used to test decisional alternatives. Evaluative research is done to assess program performance.

Marketing research in the United States traces its roots back to 1824, when the first public poll was taken. Its early growth period, from 1900 to 1920, was characterized by the establishment of the first formal marketing research department. Its adolescent years, from 1920 until 1950, saw the widespread use of marketing research. The maturing of marketing research began in 1950 and continues through 2012.

The Internet has had a major impact on the marketing research industry. The use of Internet surveys has increased dramatically because they can be quickly deployed, cost significantly less, are readily personalized, have high response rates, and provide the ability to contact the hard-to-reach respondent. Most importantly, as Internet participation by households has increased, identical online and offline surveys have been shown to produce the same business decisions.

Marketing research has also found other uses for the Internet. It serves as a major information source, aids in the distribution of request for proposals and proposals, facilitates collaboration between the client and the research supplier in the management of a research project, provides data management and online analysis, and allows for the publication and distribution of reports and the viewing of oral presentations by a widely scattered audience. The Internet represents the present and the future of marketing research.

KEY TERMS & DEFINITIONS

marketing An organizational function and a set of processes for creating, communicating, and delivering value to customers and for managing customer relationships in ways that benefit the organization and its shareholders.

marketing concept A business philosophy based on consumer orientation, goal orientation, and systems orientation.

consumer orientation The identification of and focus on the people or firms most likely to buy a product and the production of a good or service that will meet their needs most effectively.

goal orientation A focus on the accomplishment of corporate goals; a limit set on consumer orientation.

systems orientation The creation of systems to monitor the external environment and deliver the desired marketing mix to the target market.

marketing mix The unique blend of product/service, pricing, promotion, and distribution strategies designed to meet the needs of a specific target market.

marketing research The planning, collection, and analysis of data relevant to marketing decision making and the communication of the results of this analysis to management.

descriptive function The gathering and presentation of statements of fact.

diagnostic function The explanation of data or actions.

predictive function Specification of how to use descriptive and diagnostic research to predict the results of a planned marketing decision.

return on quality Management objective based on the principles that (1) the quality being delivered is at a level desired by the target market and (2) that level of quality must have a positive impact on profitability.

marketing strategy A plan to guide the long-term use of a firm's resources based on its existing and projected internal capabilities and on projected changes in the external environment.

applied research Research aimed at solving a specific, pragmatic problem—better understanding of the marketplace, determination of why a strategy or tactic failed, or reduction of uncertainty in management decision making.

basic, or pure, research Research aimed at expanding the frontiers of knowledge rather than solving a specific, pragmatic problem.

programmatic research Research conducted to develop marketing options through market segmentation, market opportunity analyses, or consumer attitude and product usage studies.

selective research Research used to test decision alternatives.

evaluative research Research done to assess program performance.

QUESTIONS FOR REVIEW & CRITICAL THINKING

1. The role of marketing is to create exchanges. What role might marketing research play in facilitating the exchange process?
2. Marketing research traditionally has been associated with manufacturers of consumer goods. Today, an increasing number of organizations, both profit and nonprofit, are using marketing research. Why do you think this trend exists? Give some examples.
3. Explain the relationship between marketing research and the marketing concept.
4. Comment on the following statement by the owner of a restaurant in a downtown area: "I see customers every day whom I know on a first-name basis. I understand their likes and dislikes. If I put something on the menu and it doesn't sell, I know that they didn't like it. I also read the magazine *Modern Restaurants* to keep up with industry trends. This is all the marketing research I need to do."
5. Why is marketing research important to marketing executives? Give several reasons.

6. What differences might you note among marketing research conducted for (a) a retailer, (b) a consumer goods manufacturer, (c) an industrial goods manufacturer, and (d) a charitable organization?

7. Comment on the following: Ralph Moran is planning to invest $1.5 million in a new restaurant in Saint Louis. When he applied for a construction financing loan, the bank officer asked whether he had conducted any research. Ralph replied, "I checked on research, and a marketing research company wanted $20,000 to do the work. I decided that with all the other expenses of opening a new business, research was a luxury that I could do without."

8. What is meant by "return on quality"? Why do you think that the concept evolved? Give an example.

9. Describe three situations in which marketing research should not be undertaken. Explain why this is true.

10. Give an example of (a) the descriptive role of marketing research, (b) the diagnostic role of marketing research, and (c) the predictive function of marketing research.

11. Using the Internet and a Web browser, visit a search engine such as Google or Yahoo! and type, "marketing research." From the thousands of options you are offered, pick a Web site that you find interesting and report on its content to the class.

12. Divide the class into groups of four. Each team should visit a large organization (profit or nonprofit) and conduct an interview with a top marketing executive to discover how this firm is using marketing research. Each team then should report its findings in class.

13. How is the Internet changing the field of marketing research?

(Team Exercise)

REAL-LIFE RESEARCH • 1.1

Give Me a Coupon That I Can Use Online!

While consumers certainly enjoy coupons, what do retailers stand to gain? Turns out, plenty. The study suggests that coupons have a significant impact on retailers' bottom lines in addition to the obvious consumer benefit as couponers are likely to spend more, have higher satisfaction, and return to the retailer where the coupon was used, according to Online Shopper Intelligence, a study from Boston research company Compete.

More than half of the consumers who used a coupon code during their last online purchase said that if they had not received the discount, they would not have bought the item(s)—57 percent said no, 43 percent yes—and more online shoppers are using coupons now than ever. One-third of online shoppers reported that they generally use coupon sites while shopping online, and 35 million consumers visited coupon sites monthly. Coupons have a high return on investment, as the small discount consumers receive encourages them to spend money. When asked how much they spent on their most recent online purchase, consumers who use a coupon spent almost twice as much as consumers who did not use a coupon ($216 with a coupon versus $122 without).

Coupons can be an effective way for retailers to build good-will with consumers and increase customer satisfaction. When asked about their overall shopping experience, satisfaction was higher for consumers who used a coupon than for those who did not. Ninety-two percent of coupon shoppers were extremely or very satisfied versus 88 percent of noncouponers. Consumers who used a coupon also said they are more likely to buy from the retailer again when compared to those who did not use a coupon. Ninety-one percent of consumers with coupons reported being extremely or very likely to shop again at the retailer where the coupon was redeemed versus 86 percent of consumers without coupons.[19]

Questions

1. How might a firm like Home Depot use this information? Would Amazon.com use the same couponing strategy as Home Depot?

2. Do you think that Home Depot might need more research before it develops a couponing strategy? If so, what does it need to know?

3. Do you think it is necessary for online retailers to conduct marketing research? Why?

REAL-LIFE RESEARCH • 1.2

Young Consumers Searching for a Bank Still Want the Personal Touch

Raised in an age of evolving technology, many young consumers are still banking the way their parents historically have done, according to a report by Chicago research firm Mintel. The firm found that only 33 percent of consumers 18–34 are using online banking services. In addition, 37 percent of those ages 18–34 say that "better customer service" would cause them to switch banking providers.

With numerous financial service options available, Mintel's research also shows that younger consumers still have concerns about the security of online banking. Some 40 percent of those who do not use online banking state it is because they "don't trust transactions on the Internet."

"Financial services companies continue to elevate their level of safety and security messaging to their consumers, but it is interesting that the Echo Boom and Gen X groups have not necessarily had their fears laid to rest," says Susan Menkie, senior financial services analyst for Mintel. "The fact that many of them still rely upon human interaction for their banking is actually surprising, given the fact that these generations have grown up with the Internet already being a staple in American culture."

In addition, with 80 percent of respondents in the 18–24-year-old range and 83 percent of 25–34-year-olds owning debit cards, credit card ownership has been dropping in recent years for these age groups. However, contactless credit cards provide a new outlet for attracting new consumers, with over 60 percent of consumers in this age range showing interest in the newer option.

"Young consumers understand that many of their parents have dealt with credit card debt, specifically during the boom of these types of products and services," says Menke. "Because they have been able to see older consumers dealing with potential debt challenges, it has made some younger consumers more cautious when it comes to using credit cards. Over 70 percent of respondents in the 22–24 age range stated that they do not like the idea of being in debt, and that can significantly impact their relationship with credit card companies."[19]

Questions

1. How might a bank use this information?
2. Could this research have been conducted over the Internet? What other means might have been used to gather the data?
3. Is this basic or applied research? Why?
4. What other type of marketing research information might a bank need to effectively market to young consumers?

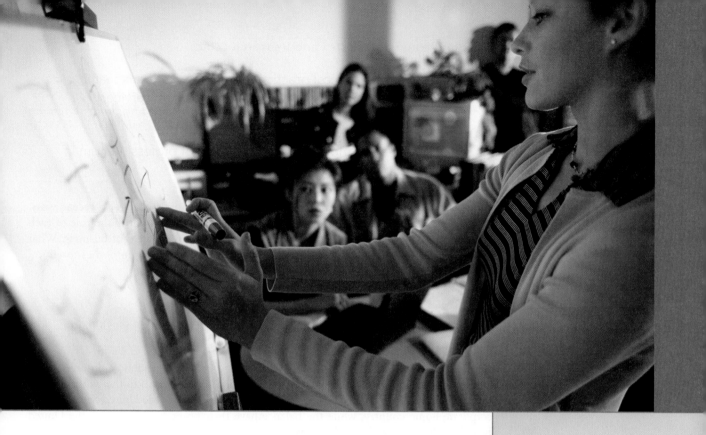

The Marketing Research Industry and Research Ethics

LEARNING OBJECTIVES

1. To appreciate the structure of the marketing research industry.

2. To comprehend the nature of corporate marketing research departments.

3. To learn about the various types of firms and their functions in the marketing research industry.

4. To understand the impact of the Internet on the marketing research industry.

5. To learn who uses marketing research.

6. To understand the growing importance of strategic partnering.

7. To appreciate trends in global marketing research.

→ **8.** To examine unethical practices among marketing research suppliers, clients, and marketing research field services.

→ **9.** To become familiar with respondents' rights.

→ **10.** To discover methods by which the level of professionalism in marketing research can be raised.

The marketing research industry has undergone tremendous change in recent years. Where is the industry going and who are the key players? What is the role of each player? Ethics is one of the most important topics taught in the field of business. What are the ethical issues in marketing research? What are several key approaches to ethical decision making? We discuss each of these issues in chapter two.

Evolving Structure of the Marketing Research Industry

Today, over $31 billion a year is spent on marketing/advertising/public opinion research services around the world.[1] The 25 largest marketing research firms in the world account for 56 percent of this total. Of the top global 25 firms, 14 have the United States as their corporate home country, while the balance have their home base in Japan, the United Kingdom, France, Brazil, or Germany.[2]

Within the United States, marketing research revenues of the 50 largest firms slightly exceed $17 billion. This number is expected to grow significantly as the economy continues to expand after the worst recession since the 1930s. A number of the top 50 firms are basically large database companies that have long-term contracts with their clients (package goods manufacturers, retailers, durable goods manufacturers, and high-tech firms). Firms with long-term contracts fared well during the recent recession, whereas many who specialize in custom, one-of-a-kind research projects saw sales decline.

The various types of organizations encountered in the marketing research industry are summarized in Exhibit 2.1. Exhibit 2.2 depicts the structure of the marketing research industry.

Primary Information Users (Client Organizations) Consumer and Industrial Goods and Services Producers

Producers of goods and services, such as Procter & Gamble and American Airlines, are the ultimate users of the research data. Their primary business is the sale of products and services. They use marketing research data on an ongoing basis in a variety of ways to support the marketing decision-making process such as:

1. To determine how various target groups will react to alternative marketing mixes.
2. To evaluate the ongoing success of operational marketing strategies.
3. To understand what customers and noncustomers are saying about their brands and competing brands.
4. To assess changes in the external, or uncontrollable, environment and the implications of those changes for their product or service strategy.
5. To identify new target markets.
6. To measure the quality of customer service and level of satisfaction.
7. To more effectively target their promotion.

We will discuss users of marketing research in greater detail later in the chapter.

EXHIBIT 2.1	General Categories of Organizations Involved in Marketing Research
Organization	**Activities, Functions, and Services**
Consumer and industrial goods and services producers	Firms such as Kraft General Foods, Procter & Gamble, Ford Motor, and Caterpillar
Media companies	Advertising agencies such as J. Walter Thompson, Young & Rubicam, and Draftfcb. Public relations companies such as Hill and Knowlton. Sales promotion firms such as Acosta
Syndicated service firms	Marketing research data gathering and reporting firms such as The Nielsen Company, Arbitron, and Symphony IRI, which collect data of general interest to many firms but for no one firm in particular (i.e., anyone can buy the data they collect); prominent in the media audience field and retail sales data
Online tracking firms	Companies like Nielsen, Buzz Metrics, and TNS Cymfony on social media sites such as Twitter, along with blogs and discussion boards. Buzz Metrics collects information from 130 million blogs and 8,000 message boards. Firms like Clearspring and Rap Leaf, and Google's Double Click gather information about a person's online activities. This data is sold to firms to be used for targeted advertising.
Custom research firms	Marketing research consulting firms such as Ipsos, DSS Research, and Burke, Inc., which do customized marketing research projects that address specific problems for individual clients
Field service firms	Firms that collect data only, on a subcontract basis, for corporate marketing research departments, ad agency research departments, custom research firms, or syndicated research firms
Specialized service firms	Firms that provide specialized support services to the marketing research industry, such as SDR in Atlanta, which provides sophisticated quantitative analysis or SSI, which provides samples for marketing research suppliers
Others	Government agencies, university research bureaus, individual university professors, and database providers

Exhibit 2.2

Structure of the Marketing Research Industry

Federal, State, and Local Governments

The various branches of government are large buyers of marketing research information. This information includes everything from where a new city park should be located to Americans' attitudes toward nutritional labeling. Although no estimates are available for marketing research expenditures at the state and local levels, federal marketing research expenditures are estimated at $5 billion annually.[3] Except for Westat, America's fourth largest market research firm, little of this money goes to traditional marketing researchers. Instead, the bulk of the work is either done in-house or conducted through academic nonprofits, such as the National Opinion Research Center (University of Chicago), Institute for Social Research (University of Michigan), or Research Triangle

Institute—as well as think-tank for-profits such as Rand Corporation and Mathematica Policy Research.

Media Companies

Media companies include advertising agencies, sales promotion companies, public relations agencies, and direct marketing firms. All are concerned with getting the right message to the right target market. Marketing research information is often required to accomplish this goal. Media companies may obtain the data from custom or syndicated research firms and in some cases may conduct the research themselves.

Retailers and Wholesalers

In the highly competitive retail market, understanding the customer is paramount. Wal-Mart, Home Depot, Saks Fifth Avenue and Bass Pro Shop, as well as many others want to understand their customers' level of satisfaction, the reasons for the satisfaction or dissatisfaction, and what they can do to improve. Those firms that do not understand the customer are destined to failure.

Manufacturers

A key to turning the American automobile industry around is producing cars that people want to buy. Ford, General Motors, and Chrysler are all moving more to marketing research to guide them in producing the right vehicles at the right price points. Even industrial goods manufacturers like Caterpillar use marketing research to measure both dealer and customer satisfaction.

Marketing Research Suppliers

Custom, syndicated, and limited function marketing research firms represent the front line of the research industry. They sell research services, design research studies, analyze the results, and make recommendations to their clients. They will be discussed in detail below. Online tracking firms will be discussed in Chapters 7 and 8.

Marketing Research Supplier Service Firms

As the heading above implies, these firms service the research industry. Services range from software providers, such as Sawtooth Software, to providers of samples, such as SSI. There are several large online panel (groups of persons willing to answer marketing surveys) providers to the marketing research industry. Harris Interactive claims to have the largest panel in the world with members from over 200 countries. Service firms will be described in more detail below.

Consumer and Industrial Corporate Marketing Research Departments

Because corporations are the final consumers and the initiators of most marketing research, they are the logical starting point in developing an understanding of how the industry operates. Most large corporations (and virtually all consumer package goods manufacturers of any size) have marketing research departments. Currently, some are melding marketing research and strategic planning, whereas others are combining marketing research and customer satisfaction departments.

The average size of marketing research departments is quite small. One study found that only 15 percent of service companies such as Federal Express and American Airlines had marketing research departments with more than 10 employees. Only 23 percent of manufacturers' research departments had more than 10 employees. The size of marketing research departments has been experiencing a downward trend because of mergers and reengineering. The recent recession has reversed a long-running trend of more outsourcing to marketing research suppliers. Today, insourcing is the watchword. Corporations are trying to find ways to do more with less.[3] This will mean more work for supplier service firms such as Confirmit, Marketingsight, and Vovici, who provide online survey software, and tools for analyzing and reporting survey data.

Because we cannot cover all types of marketing research departments in this text, we will focus our attention on those found in larger, more sophisticated companies, where marketing research is a staff department and the director of the department generally reports to the top marketing executive. Most of the work of the department is with product or brand managers, new product development managers, and other front-line managers. With the possible exception of various recurring studies that may be programmed into a firm's marketing information system, the marketing research department typically does not initiate studies. In fact, the research manager may control little or no actual budget. Instead, line managers have funds in their budgets earmarked for research.

When brand managers perceive that they have a problem that requires research, they go to the marketing research department for help. Working with the marketing research manager or a senior analyst, they go through a series of steps that may lead to the design and execution of a marketing research project.

Research Suppliers

Although the marketing research industry is characterized by hundreds of small firms, there are some giants in the industry. Exhibit 2.3 shows total revenues for the 40 largest marketing research firms. The largest firm in the industry—The Nielsen Company is largely a syndicated service firm.

The Nielsen Company was founded in 1923. It has been America's largest research firm for over 40 years.[4] Nielsen has offices in more than 100 countries and employs more than 33,000 people. The firm is a global information and media firm offering services in marketing and consumer information, TV and other media measurements, online intelligence, mobile measurement, trade shows, and business publications. Nielsen is divided into two divisions: Watch, which does media research, and Buy, which focuses on consumer research.

Consumer Watch

Nielsen's Watch segment includes measurement and analytical services related to TV, online, and mobile devices, and provides viewership data and analytics primarily to the media and advertising industries. Its media clients use the data to price their advertising inventory and maximize the value of their content, and its advertising clients use the data to plan and optimize their advertising spending and to better ensure that their advertisements reach the intended audiences. Nielsen provides measurement services across three screens: TV, online, and mobile.

Nielsen provides two principal TV ratings services in the United States: measurement of national TV audiences and measurement of local TV audiences in all

EXHIBIT 2.3 | The 40 Largest U.S. Marketing Research Firms*

U.S. Rank	Organization	Headquarters	Web Site www.	U.S. Research Revenue ($, in millions)
1	The Nielsen Co.	New York	nielsen.com	$2,298.0
2	Kantar*	London & Fairfield, CT.	kantar.com	850.9
3	IMS Health Inc.	Norwalk, CT	imshealth.com	801.1
4	Westat Inc.	Rockville, Md.	westat.com	502.4
5	Symphony IRI Group	Chicago	symphonyiri.com	441.7
6	Arbitron Inc.	Columbia, MD	Arbitron.com	379.1
7	Ipsos	New York	ipsos-na.com	288.8
8	GfK AG USA	Nuremberg, Germany	gfk.com	288.5
9	Synovate	London	synovate.com	214.5
10	J.D. Power and Associates	Westlake Village, Calif	jdpower.com	164.4
11	The NPD Group Inc.	Port Washington, NY	npd.com	164.1
12	Maritz Research	Fenton, Mo.	maritzresearch.com	132.1
13	comScore Inc.	Reston, VA	comscore.com	108.0
14	Harris Interactive Inc.	New York	harrisinteractive.com	100.1
15	dunnhumbyUSA	Cincinnati	dunnhumby.com/us/	87.4
16	Lieberman Research Worldwide	Log Angeles	lrwonline.com	73.4
17	Market Strategies International	Livonia, Mich.	marketstrategies.com	66.8
18	Opinion Research Corp.	Princeton, NJ	opinionresearch.com	63.3
19	Abt SRBI Inc.	Cambridge, MA	abtassociates.com	57.5
20	OTX	Los Angeles	otxresearch.com	56.2
21	National Research Corp.	Lincoln, NEB	nationalresearch.com	43.8
22	MVL Group Inc.	Jupiter, FL	mvlgroup.com	39.9
23	Burke Inc.	Cincinnati	burke.com	38.9
24	International Communications	Media, PA	icrsurvey.com	36.3
25	Knowledge Networks Inc.	Menlo Park, CA	knowledgenetworks.com	35.4
26	Communispace Corp.	Watertown, MA	communispace.com	34.7
27	Directions Research Inc.	Cincinnati	Directionsresearch.com	33.7
28	Phoenix Marketing International	Rhinebeck, NY	phoenixmi.com	31.4
29	MarketCast	Los Angeles	marketcastonline.com	28.5
30	Service Management Group Inc.	Kansas City, MO	servicemanagement.com	28.4
31	Radium Global Market Research	New York	radius-global.com	27.6
32	Lieberman Research Group	Great Neck, NY	liebermanresearch.com	25.1
33	Informa Research Services Inc.	Calabasas, CA	informars.com	23.4
34	National Analysts Worldwide	Philadelphia	nationalanalysts.com	23.2
35	C&R Research Services Inc.	Chicago	crresearch.com	22.8
36	Morpace Inc.	Farmington Hills, MI	morpace.com	22.2
37	MarketVision Research Inc.	Cincinnati	mv-research.com	21.7
38	KS&R Inc.	Syracuse, NY	ksrinc.com	19.7
39	Market Probe Inc.	Milwaukee	Marketprobe.com	18.5
40	Q Research Solutions Inc.	Old Bridge, NJ	qresearchsolutions.com	15.8

Source: "Honomichl Top 50", *Marketing News* (July 20, 2010), pp. 25–26.
*Some large privately held firms, such as DSS Research and Decision Analyst, would be included in the list, but they do not disclose financial data.

FROM THE FRONT LINE

Discovering Marketing Research and Why You Should Too

Kristin Chatila, Project Manager, DSS Research

I first discovered marketing research in graduate school, almost by accident, thanks to a dear friend. I had an undergraduate degree in marketing and was pursuing an MBA. Though I thoroughly enjoyed marketing, I was looking for something more than your typical four marketing P's—product, price, place and promotion. After assessing the Master of Marketing Research program, I decided to try one class: Research for Marketing Decisions. Needless to say, I was hooked from day one.

As the marketing research coursework delved deeper and deeper, I sensed I was beginning to uncover the means to what permits the product, price, place and promotion strategies to be successful. Most strategies begin with intuition, navigating through an undefined path. Marketing research, however, allows marketing strategies to have a clear and defined course of action clarifying who, what, where, when, how and (most importantly) why, from conception.

I remember sitting in the Multivariate Analysis class learning a new topic—factor analysis. The mere aspect of mathematically grouping like things (observed variables) was astonishing. That night I dreamt about factor analysis. I was beginning to understand the pieces as to *why* a certain group of people is targeted with a certain type of product and with a certain marketing campaign.

After my graduate studies ended, a new revelation occurred. The basic principals of marketing research can be applied in any industry—supplier or client side. With that being said, there are different types of marketing research positions for different types of people. For example, if you enjoy statistics you may want to pursue a statistician role; if you enjoy uncovering the story the data reveals you may want to pursue an analyst position; if you enjoy sales you may want to pursue an account executive position; if you enjoy multiple aspects of the research process (questionnaire design, sampling, data collection and client relations) you may want to pursue a project management position.

My role as a project manager for a research supplier enables me to utilize my core skills and abilities and what I like to do. Now, the question is "What are your core skills and abilities and how can marketing research add value to your career and life?"

210 designated local TV markets. It uses various methods to collect the data from households including electronic meters and written diaries. The methods collect not only TV viewing data, but also the demographics of the audience from which it calculates estimates of total TV viewership.

Online Audience Measurement Services: Nielsen is a global provider of Internet media and market research, audience analytics, and social media measurement on the behavior of online audiences for online publishers, Internet and media companies, marketers, and retailers. The firm measures Internet surfing, online buying, and video viewing (including TV content) of online audiences, providing advertising metrics such as audience demographics, page and ad views, and time spent and quantifying the effectiveness of advertising by reporting online behavioral observations, attitudinal changes and actual offline purchase activity. Nielsen analyzes consumer-generated media including opinions, advice, peer-to-peer discussions, and shared personal experiences on more than 100 million blogs, social networks, user groups, and chat boards.

Consumer Buy

Nielsen's Buy segment provides market research and analysis primarily to businesses in the consumer packaged goods industry. This segment is organized into two areas: Information, which provides retail scanner and consumer panel-based measurement, and Insights, which provides a broad range of analytics. Buy clients use the data in an effort to better manage their brands, uncover new sources of demand, launch and grow new products, improve their marketing mix, and establish more effective consumer relationships. The measurement data is used as the method for measuring sales and market share in the CPG industry by tracking sales transactions in retail outlets around the world. Its database of retail and consumer information, combined with its advanced analytical capabilities, helps generate strategic insights for clients' key business dscisions.

Custom Research Firms

> **custom research firms**
> Companies that carry out customized marketing research to address specific projects for corporate clients.

Custom research firms, as noted earlier, are primarily in the business of executing custom, one-of-a-kind marketing research projects for corporate clients. If a corporation has a new product or service idea, a packaging idea, an ad concept, a new pricing strategy, a product reformulation, or a related marketing problem or opportunity, it typically will go to a custom research firm for research help.

There are thousands of custom marketing research firms in the United States. Examples of large custom research firms include Market Facts, Inc., the MARC Group, Opinion Research Corp. International, Elrick and Lavidge Marketing Research, Burke, Inc., DSS Research, and Decision Analyst. However, the overwhelming majority of custom marketing research firms are small, with billings of less than $1 million and fewer than 10 employees. They may limit their client base to their local area and may or may not specialize by type of industry or type of research.

Syndicated Service Firms

> **syndicated service research firms**
> Companies that collect, package, and sell market research data to many firms.

In sharp contrast to custom research firms, **syndicated service research firms** collect and sell marketing research data to many firms. Anyone willing to pay the price can buy the data these firms collect, package, and sell. Syndicated service firms are relatively few and, compared to custom research firms, relatively large. They deal primarily with media audience and product movement data and are based on serving information needs common to many companies. For example, companies that advertise on network television want to select shows that reach their target customers most efficiently. They need information on the size and demographic composition of the audiences for various TV programs. It would be extremely inefficient for each company to collect these data itself.

Firms like The Nielsen Company sell standardized TV ratings to a group of clients known as a syndicate—thus, the term *syndicated data*. Some syndicated firms, like Roper Starch Worldwide, sell lifestyle data that is both syndicated and customized. The standardized process is the same to gather the data, but some members of the syndicate may want special information just for their company. This, in fact, is quite common. An additional charge is levied for each custom question added to the syndicated survey.

Exhibit 2.4 shows some syndicated service firms and the specific type of marketing research they offer.

Limited-Function Research Firms

Some firms specialize in one or a few activities. They may, for example, serve only one industry. Westat, for example, serves various government agencies, whereas IMS Health

EXHIBIT 2.4	Syndicated Service Research Firms
Firm	**Syndicated Services**
The Nielsen Company New York, NY	Television ratings Scanner-based data Wholesale/retail audits Internet research
FIND/SVP New York, NY	Large variety of industry/product studies
Maritz Marketing Research Inc. Fenton, MO	Customer satisfaction studies
GfK NOP New York, NY	Public opinion surveys Lifestyle data Media/advertising effectiveness data
Symphony IRI Chicago	Scanner-based data

and DSS Research focus on healthcare. Other firms use a single research technique or a special type of research technique. Mystery Shopper organizations, such as Shop 'n Check and Speedmark, engage only in mystery shopping (discussed in Chapter 7). The Pretesting Company uses devices such as the People Reader to measure how much time is spent reading an ad in a magazine or newspaper.

Many new marketing research firms conduct research only via the Internet. A pioneer in this area is Greenfield Online, *http://www.greenfieldonline.com*, which conducts both quantitative research and qualitative research (research not subject to quantitative analysis). Greenfield claims to have the world's largest Internet-based marketing research panel. A **research panel** consists of a group of individuals who agree to participate in a series of research studies over time. Often, participants receive cash or gifts.

→ **research panel**
A group of individuals who agree to participate in a series of research studies over time.

Marketing Research Supplier Service Firms

A number of firms service marketing research suppliers. When research departments of corporations, such as Kraft General Foods, are conducting their own research, these service firms also cater to them. The two largest categories of service firms are field service organizations and sampling firms.

A true **field service firm** does nothing but collect survey data—no research design, no analysis. Field service firms are data-collection specialists, collecting data on a subcontract basis for corporate marketing research departments, custom research firms, ad agency research departments, and others.

→ **field service firms**
Companies that only collect survey data for corporate clients or research firms.

The following description of the sequence of activities undertaken by a typical field service company provides a good idea of how these firms operate:

1. *Client contact.* Custom or syndicated research firm or corporate or ad agency research department alerts field service firm, usually by e-mail, that it wants to conduct a particular type of study (telephone interview, mall interview, focus group, taste test, etc.).

2. *Interviewer training.* The day the job is to begin, a briefing or training session is held to acquaint interviewers with the requirements of the particular job or questionnaire.

3. *Interviewing status reports.* Daily progress reports are made via e-mail to the client regarding number of interviews completed and costs incurred. These reports permit the client to determine whether the job is on schedule and within budget and allow the field service to advise the client of any problems.

4. *Quality control.* The interviews are edited; that is, specially designed software is used to verify that they were completed correctly.

5. *Ship to client.* Finally, the completed, edited interviews are shipped (typically electronically) to the client.

Most custom research firms rely on field services because it is not cost-effective for them to handle the work themselves. There are too many geographic areas to cover, and it is hard to know which areas will be needed over time. On the other hand, field service firms in particular areas maintain a steady work flow by having numerous research firms and corporate and ad agency research departments as their clients.

The major field service firm of today has a permanent office. It probably has one or more permanent mall test centers, focus group facilities, a central telephone interviewing facility, as well as other specialized facilities and equipment. A recent trend among field service firms is the establishment of satellite offices in multiple cities.

Sampling Firms   Sampling firms provide samples (persons to interview) to marketing research suppliers and other research creators. The largest sampling firm is Survey Sampling Inc. (SSI); this firm does nothing but generate samples for mail, telephone, or Internet surveys. SSI's Survey Spot Internet panel has over 6 million members. The firm's SSI-Lite eSample is a panel categorized by lifestyles; the panel contains over 3,500 topical lists and 12 million names. Other firms such as Harris Interactive and Decision Analyst have huge Internet panels that they use for their own research and rent to other research suppliers.

Software Firms   A number of companies specialize in providing software for statistical analysis and/or Internet interviewing. The most popular statistical package, used by over two-thirds of all research suppliers, is SPSS. This is the same software that we provide you when you purchase a new text. Other companies, like Perseus and Web Surveyor, sell software for online interviewing. The firms also will host surveys on their own servers.

Other Service Companies   Other service companies provide a variety of services to research firms. For example, SDR Consulting, located in Atlanta, offers sophisticated data analysis to marketing research suppliers. MarketingResearchCareers.com specializes, as the name implies, in careers in the marketing research field. Quirk's publishes a magazine, *Quirk's Marketing Research Review*, and directories such as directories of field service firms, international research companies, focus group facilities, and others. Quirk's also hosts an online forum for marketing researchers.

Using Marketing Research—A Corporate Perspective

Now that you are familiar with the marketing research industry, let's look in more detail at research users. There is a very good possibility that any future encounters that you, as a businessperson, will have with marketing research will be as a research user. Exhibit 2.5 shows some of the various types of marketing research clients. Despite the importance of nonmarketing, *internal* clients, such as finance or manufacturing, to the success of an organization, some firms' research departments have paid little attention to nonmarketing clients' specific marketing information needs. As you might expect, these poorly served clients have demonstrated little interest in marketing research information. It has

Exhibit 2.5

Using Marketing Research—A Corporate Perspective

been our experience that the most successful marketing research departments and firms are those committed to the complete satisfaction of all of their clients. Let's take a closer look at the types of information these various clients need and use.

External Clients

Because marketing research can be a valuable source of information about new or improved competitive advantages and because such information is often very expensive to gather, data gathered by a firm's research department is rarely circulated outside of the firm. Many firms don't provide any information to outsiders, such as suppliers. However, those that do usually find that it is to their mutual benefit.

Vendors Manufacturers are moving into **strategic partnerships** with their vendors in order to implement just-in-time manufacturing. These alliances are based on fully integrated manufacturer–supplier logistics systems that get the component to the assembly line just when it is needed. The result is little or no raw materials inventory and significantly reduced carrying costs. The backbone of this system is shared information. Large retailers, such as Wal-Mart, have such relationships with their major vendors.

    Within the framework of strategic partnering, marketing research information is fed back to a manufacturer's suppliers when consumers voice opinions about a component on the manufacturer's customer satisfaction surveys. For example, if Pioneer was supplying radios for Honda automobiles and customers were complaining about how difficult a certain model was to program, this research information would be shared with Pioneer. In one case, a major retail chain commissioned a study on changes in customer preferences for Christmas-related items such as gift wrap, cards, artificial trees, and ornaments, to help its suppliers of production materials understand the importance of making specific product changes and to provide guidance in making those changes.

Franchisees Most major franchisors of consumer goods and services provide marketing research data to their franchisees. Perhaps the most common way of gathering data is from *mystery shoppers*. A mystery shopper, posing as a customer, observes how long it takes to be waited on and/or make a purchase, the courtesy of the clerks,

strategic partnership
An alliance formed by two or more firms with unique skills and resources to offer a new service for clients, provide strategic support for each firm, or in some other manner create mutual benefits.

A major retail chain commissioned a study on changes in customer preferences for Christmas-related items in order to help suppliers understand the need for product change and what product changes to make.

the cleanliness of the operation, and whether his or her purchase or order was properly prepared. Mystery shopping is discussed in detail in Chapter 7.

Franchisors also share marketing research information with their franchisees to support certain recommendations or actions. When McDonald's suggests to a franchisee that a restaurant be remodeled in a particular style, it will show research data indicating that the building is perceived as out-of-date or old-fashioned. Other data might reveal which theme or style current customers prefer. When Burger King launches a major new promotional campaign, it may share with franchisees research data showing that the selected campaign theme was preferred by customers and noncustomers over alternative themes.

Internal Clients

Marketing Managers   Virtually every manager within an organization will, at some point, be a user of marketing research information. However, marketing managers use research data more than any other group. Recall that the marketing mix consists of decisions regarding products or services, promotion, distribution, and pricing. Marketing research helps decision makers in each of these areas make better decisions. Product managers, for example, begin by using research to define their target market. In some cases, managers use research to determine the heavy users of their product within the target market. Marketing research revealed that heavy users of Miracle Whip consume 550 servings, or 17 pounds, of the product a year. These data were used to target a $30 million promotional campaign to core users, telling them not to "skip the zip." As a result, Miracle Whip's market share went up 2.1 percent, to $305 million in annual sales.[5] The ad campaign also was thoroughly tested for effectiveness by marketing research before it was launched.

New product development managers are among the heaviest users of marketing research. From qualitative research techniques that generate product ideas to concept testing, product prototype testing, and then test marketing, marketing research is the key to creating a new product. For example, Post's research on cereals had always shown that bananas are America's favorite cereal fruit. Therefore, why not a banana-flavored cereal? Post's new product manager concocted cereals with dried banana pieces, but they failed marketing research taste tests. Further research, conducted to explain why this happened, uncovered the fact that consumers saw no reason to buy a cereal with preserved bananas, as the fresh fruit is quite cheap year-round. If consumers wanted a banana-flavored cereal, they'd peel a banana and make one on the spot. One day, the new product manager had an inspiration: Consumers had said that they liked banana nut bread; it conjured up thoughts of something delicious that grandma used to make. The manager had Post's labs create a new cereal for test marketing in consumers' homes, where it received very high consumer test scores. Thus, Post Selects Banana Nut Crunch, one of Post's hottest cereals, was born. It is solely a product of marketing research, created from the initial concept of a new product manager.

Marketing research also plays an important role in the distribution function. It is used to choose locations for new stores and to test consumer reactions to internal store design fixtures and features. Banana Republic, for example, has relied on marketing research to create the right atmosphere in its stores.

Within larger organizations, pricing decisions are usually made by committees composed of representatives from marketing, finance, production, and perhaps other departments. A few years ago, Procter & Gamble examined the electric toothbrush market and noted that most electric toothbrushes cost over $50. The firm conducted pricing marketing research and found the demand for electric toothbrushes to be very elastic. The company brought out the Crest SpinBrush that works on batteries and sells for just $5. It is now the nation's best-selling toothbrush, manual or electric, and has helped the Crest brand of products become P&G's twelfth billion-dollar brand.

Marketing research helped Gatorade position its product toward those who use it most often—men between the ages of 19 and 44. Go to *http://www.gatorade.com* to see if the company positions its Web site for this demographic.

Top Management   Procter & Gamble has brought marketing research to the forefront of the company. This, in turn, has meant rising market share, profits, and shareholder value. The president of Harley Davidson decided to create a second line of motorcycles, called Buell, after consulting marketing research data. This new strategic direction opened a whole new market segment (sport/performance) for Harley. Top executives at DuPont, Wal-Mart, Marriott, Carnival Cruise Lines, and Amazon.com look to marketing research for strategic guidance.

Other Internal Users   From time to time, other individuals besides marketing managers and senior management find a need for marketing research. Toyota's engineers sometimes invent new items for which demand must be assessed. Toyota's marketing research, however, feeds engineering management a steady stream of consumer desires and dislikes. Manufacturing also receives continual feedback, from customer satisfaction surveys, about loose-fitting door panels, balky sunroof openers, sudden acceleration, and the like.

Finance departments use test market data to forecast revenue streams for 1 to 3 years. Similarly, repositioning research helps financial managers forecast revenue spurts from older products. Originally, Gatorade was promoted as a drink for competitive athletes. Marketing research found that its main users were men, aged 19 to 44, who understood the product, had a good perception of what it did, and knew when to drink it. The product was repositioned toward physical activity enthusiasts as a drink that would quench their thirst and replenish the minerals lost during exercise better than other beverages did. The new positioning dramatically increased sales.

Human resource managers may call on marketing research to survey employees about a variety of topics. Quality customer service requires that employees have a positive image of the company, an attitude that they then convey to customers. Firms such as Southwest Airlines and Nations-Bank monitor employee attitudes through survey research.

Companies are increasingly turning to marketing research to win their cases in court. Schering-Plough and Pfizer went to court over physicians' perceptions about various antihistamines and sales messages used by sales reps about the products. Marketing research is also used to prove or disprove consumer perceptions regarding similar brand names.

A San Francisco jury ruled against Kendall-Jackson Winery in its case against E. & J. Gallo Winery. Kendall-Jackson claimed that Gallo copied the design of its Vintner's Reserve label, which features a grape leaf with fall colors, by using a similarly styled logo on the Gallo Turning Leaf line of varietal wines. Marketing research won the case for Gallo.

When law firms, top management, or product managers decide to hire a research supplier, they must find the right company to do the job. Jerry Thomas, president and CEO of Decision Analyst, Inc., discussed what to watch out for when hiring a research supplier in the Practicing Marketing Research box below.

PRACTICING MARKETING RESEARCH

Look for the Danger Signals When Evaluating Research Suppliers

Jerry Thomas, president and CEO of Decision Analyst, says that clients should watch for these danger signs in evaluating research suppliers:

- **Magic techniques.** Exotic approaches. Revolutionary technology. Let them experiment on your competitors. **Rule One:** If you don't understand it, don't buy it.

- **Guaranteed solutions.** They know they can solve your problem. They are absolutely certain they are right. They are in possession of the Holy Grail. Let them bring salvation and ultimate truth to your competitors. **Rule Two:** Don't do business with prophets or other types of management consultants.

- **Price variance.** If the prices quoted for research are extremely high, you should be wary and careful (even if they are management consultants). Make sure you are getting extra value for the extra price. Equally risky are the companies that quote extremely low prices; be especially careful in using these companies. **Never, never** choose a research company just because its prices are the lowest. Typically, research costs are a small part of a project's budget. Don't save $2,000 or $3,000 on a research project and run the risk of making wrong decisions that could cost your company millions of dollars.

So you've chosen a research partner. How do you get the most from the research company you choose?

- **Build a relationship.** Involve the research company in your business. Generally, the more you work with one company, the better the job that company will do for you.

- **Set forth clear objectives.** Tell the research company what decisions you wish to make. Be sure the research firm understands your objectives.

- **Look in on the research while it is in process.** Listen to some of the telephone interviews. Observe the focus groups or depth interviews.

Once a study is completed and you've reviewed a draft of the report and its recommendations, ask the research company to present the results of the study to all of your key people **in one room at one time**. This is an absolutely essential step for two reasons: First, most of your employees don't read research reports; second, even if they do read them, many people don't understand research reports. A real live presentation with all the key decision makers in one room allows the researcher to explain the results, answer all questions, and clear up any confusion or misunderstandings. A great added benefit of a presentation is that it helps your key executives reach a consensus on what the research results mean and what actions need to be taken.

Research is not the answer to every question, but if used wisely, it just might help your business avoid the next speculative meltdown. The future belongs to the informed, to the rational, to those who make decisions based on objective, research-based realities.[6]

The State of the Marketing Research Industry

In 2009, research industry revenue fell for the first time since industrywide data was first gathered in the early 1980s. Employment also fell in the United States from over 34,000 persons to slightly over 32,000.[7] The recession of 2007–2009 took its toll om the industry. Yet, the recession also presented an opportunity for researchers to prove their value to client organizations. Manufacturers and retailers are seeking insights that will enable them to gain a competitive advantage to not only survive difficult times but to thrive.

The recession reinforced the importance of speed and nimbleness to business survival, and this, by effect, has changed the types and amount of research being done. "Tactical (short term) and strategic research initiatives still have roles in improving the way decisions are made; however during the recession the balance has shifted," says Jamie Baker-Prewitt, senior vice president and director of decision sciences at Burke Inc. in Cincinnati. "Research execs unanimously reported [in a Burke survey to clients] that [companies] are making more tactical decisions without research."[8]

Instead, Baker-Prewitt says, businesses are redirecting research toward strategic work—the potentially high-value projects that may be key to their survival. A study of market researchers and corporate line managers conducted by Boston Consulting Group found that, on average, 20 to 35 percent of a company's market research budget is invested in strategic research studies.[9]

The development of online research, such as monitoring for Web chatter relevant to your brand or product and specific online communities developed to glean research for real-time insights, also has been spurred by the need for real-time insights and budget constraints, notes Rose Cameron, Chief Strategy Officer at the marketing agency Euro RSCG in Chicago. "Online overall is, I think, getting a real workout right now. . . . There's the whole need to do things faster and cheaper. [Researchers] can't necessarily go out or have the time or budget. Our focus has gone to funding research based on the Internet because it is cost- and time-effective.[10]

Burke's Baker-Prewitt recommends a balanced approach to online, saying it still has a long way to go to being able to deliver insights that are both quick and accurate. "Social media online communities, online listening approaches, many companies are still determining how to learn to use these. Even [the tracking firms] are still figuring out how to best integrate their findings into [helping make] tactical and strategic decisions," she says.[11]

Ravi Parmeswar at Citi takes a slightly different perspective on tactical versus strategic research as explained in the Practicing Marketing Research box.

Most research clients feel that suppliers are doing the basics well—that is, using the right methodologies, asking questions in the right way, surveying the right people, and analyzing the data in a proper manner.[13] Yet, this is not enough. Research clients want suppliers to be partners rather than simply suppliers of data and insights. Clients want suppliers to fully understand their companies and industries. A supplier partner will anticipate problems, offer unique insights, and help their clients get the attention of executives with the authority to make decisions. The trend toward partnering has meant that clients are reviewing their lists of vendors and cutting it down to a relative few.[14] Long-term strategic partnerships require frequent contact and communication to develop the intimate knowledge necessary for success. This means dealing with a select few suppliers.

A discussion of the state of the art of the marketing research industry would not be complete without mentioning ethics.

PRACTICING
MARKETING RESEARCH

Strategic Research Is Fine But Firms Must be Nimble in Today's Marketplace

Ravi Parmeswar, managing director of global consumer and marketplace insights at Citi, a division of New York-based Citigroup Inc., contends that long-term research is important, but researchers working within business institutions must be ready to deliver on the changes demanded at the business decision-making stage, too:

"There will always be certain studies that are OK that take three to six months; those are strategic rather than tactical. There is space for the research, but when you are running a business and looking at this quarter's numbers, you have to put systems in place that are more real-time, where it is about getting the [essential] information [to help make a decision] faster. It is more about knowing that you are never going to have 100% of the information . . . and that you're not going to mitigate all the risk. The real competency is about taking action and making real-time changes are you experience it."[12]

Marketing Research Ethics

→ **ethics**
Moral principles or values, generally governing the conduct of an individual or group.

The two most important factors for research clients in their relationships with research departments/suppliers are client confidentiality and honesty. Each is a question of ethics. **Ethics** are moral principles or values generally governing the conduct of an individual or group. Ethical behavior is not, however, a one-way relationship. Clients and suppliers, as well as field services, must also act in an ethical manner.

Ethical questions range from practical, narrowly defined issues, such as a researcher's obligation to be honest with its customers, to broader social and philosophical questions, such as a company's responsibility to preserve the environment and protect employee rights. Many ethical conflicts develop from conflicts between the differing interests of company owners and their workers, customers, and surrounding community. Managers must balance the ideal against the practical—the need to produce a reasonable profit for the company's shareholders with honesty in business practices, and larger environmental and social issues.

Ethical Theories

People usually base their individual choice of ethical theory on their life experiences. The following are some of the ethical theories that apply to business and marketing research.[15]

Deontology   The deontological theory states that people should adhere to their obligations and duties when analyzing an ethical dilemma. This means that a person will follow his or her obligations to another individual or society because upholding one's duty is what is considered ethically correct. For instance, a deontologist will always keep his promises to a friend and will follow the law. A person who follows this theory will produce very consistent decisions since they will be based on the individual's set duties.

Note that this theory is not necessarily concerned with the welfare of others. Say, for example, a research supplier has decided that it's his ethical duty (and very practical!) to always be on time to meetings with clients. Today he is running late. How is he supposed to drive? Is the deontologist supposed to speed, breaking his duty to society to uphold the law, or is the deontologist supposed to arrive at his meeting late, breaking his duty to be on time? This scenario of conflicting obligations does not lead us to a clear ethically correct resolution, nor does it protect the welfare of others from the deontologist's decision.

Utilitarianism The utilitarian ethical theory is founded on the ability to predict the consequences of an action. To a utilitarian, the choice that yields the greatest benefit to the most people is the choice that is ethically correct. One benefit of this ethical theory is that the utilitarian can compare similar predicted solutions and use a point system to determine which choice is more beneficial for more people. This point system provides a logical and rational argument for each decision and allows a person to use it on a case-by-case context.

There are two types of utilitarianism: act utilitarianism and rule utilitarianism. *Act utilitarianism* adheres exactly to the definition of utilitarianism as described in the above section. In act utilitarianism, a person performs the acts that benefit the most people, regardless of personal feelings or the societal constraints such as laws. *Rule utilitarianism*, however, takes into account the law and is concerned with fairness. A rule utilitarian seeks to benefit the most people but through the fairest and most just means available. Therefore, added benefits of rule utilitarianism are that it values justice and doing good at the same time.

As is true of all ethical theories, however, both act and rule utilitarianism contain numerous flaws. Inherent in both are the flaws associated with predicting the future. Although people can use their life experiences to attempt to predict outcomes, no human being can be certain that his predictions will be true. This uncertainty can lead to unexpected results, making the utilitarian look unethical as time passes because his choice did not benefit the most people as he predicted.

Another assumption that a utilitarian must make is that he has the ability to compare the various types of consequences against each other on a similar scale. However, comparing material gains such as money against intangible gains such as happiness is impossible since their qualities differ so greatly.

Casuist The casuist ethical theory compares a current ethical dilemma with examples of similar ethical dilemmas and their outcomes. This allows one to determine the severity of the situation and to create the best possible solution according to others' experiences. Usually, one will find examples that represent the extremes of the situation so that a compromise can be reached that will hopefully include the wisdom gained from the previous situations.

One drawback to this ethical theory is that there may not be a set of similar examples for a given ethical dilemma. Perhaps that which is controversial and ethically questionable is new and unexpected. Along the same line of thinking, this theory assumes that the results of the current ethical dilemma will be similar to results in the examples. This may not be necessarily true and would greatly hinder the effectiveness of applying this ethical theory.

Understanding ethical theories will help us better decide how certain unethical practices in marketing research should be resolved. Exhibit 2.6 details some of the unethical practices most common among the various groups involved in marketing research.

Research Supplier Ethics

Unethical research supplier practices range from low-ball pricing to violating client confidentiality.

EXHIBIT 2.6	Unethical Practices in Marketing Research	
Research Suppliers	**Research Clients**	**Field Services**
Low-ball pricing	Issuing bid requests when a supplier has been predetermined	
Allowing subjectivity into the research	Soliciting free advice and methodology via bid requests	Using professional respondents
Abusing respondents	Making false promises	Not validating data
Selling unnecessary research	Issuing unauthorized requests for proposal	
Violating client confidentiality		
Black box branding		

Low-Ball Pricing A research supplier should quote a firm price based on a specific incidence rate (percentage of the respondents in the sample that will qualify to complete the survey) and questionnaire length (time to complete). If either of the latter two items changes, then the client should expect a change in the contract price. Low-ball pricing in any form is unethical. In essence, **low-ball pricing** is quoting an unrealistically low price to secure a firm's business and then using some means to substantially raise the price. For example, quoting a price based on an unrealistically high incidence rate is a form of low-ball pricing. Offering to conduct a focus group at $8,000 a group and, after the client commits, saying, "The respondents' fees for participating in the group discussion are, of course, extra" is a form of low-balling.

> **low-ball pricing**
> Quoting an unrealistically low price to secure a firm's business and then using some means to substantially raise the price.

Allowing Subjectivity into the Research Research suppliers must avoid using biased samples, misusing statistics, ignoring relevant data, and creating a research design with the goal of supporting a predetermined objective. One area of research today is so-called *advocacy studies*. These studies are commissioned by companies or industries for public relations purposes or to advocate or prove a position. For example, Burger King once used positive responses to the following question in an advocacy study in an attempt to justify the claim that its method of cooking hamburgers was preferred over that of McDonald's: "Do you prefer your hamburgers flame-broiled or fried?" When another researcher rephrased the question—"Do you prefer a hamburger that is grilled on a hot stainless-steel grill or cooked by passing the meat through an open gas flame?"—the results were reversed: McDonald's was preferred to Burger King.

When studies are released to the news media, the methodology should be readily available to news reporters. A survey done for a coupon redemption company found that "a broad cross-section of Americans find coupons to be true incentives for purchasing products." The description of the methodology, however, was available only for a price of $2,000.

Kiwi Brands, a shoe polish company, commissioned a study on the correlation between ambition and shiny shoes. The study found that 97 percent of self-described ambitious young men believe polished shoes are important. In many cases, advocacy studies simply use samples that are not representative of the population. For example, a news release for a diet products company trumpeted: "There's good news for the 65 million Americans currently on a diet." A company study had shown that people who lose weight can keep it off—the sample consisted of 20 graduates of the company's program, who also endorsed its products in commercials.

When studies are released to the news media, the methodology should be readily available to news reporters. Typically, this information is withheld, often on the ground that the material is proprietary. A survey done for Carolina Manufacturer's Service, a coupon redemption company, found that "a broad cross-section of Americans find coupons to be true incentives for purchasing products." The description of the methodology was available only at a price: $2,000.

Abusing Respondents   Respondent abuse can take several forms. Perhaps the most common is lengthy interviews. This problem stems in part from the "as long as you're asking questions" mentality of many product managers. It is not uncommon for clients to request additional "nice to know" questions, or even exploratory questions on an entirely separate project. This leads to lengthy questionnaires, 30-minute telephone or Internet interviews, and 40-minute mall-intercept interviews. As a result of long interviews and telephone sales pitches, more and more Americans are refusing to participate in survey research. The refusal rate for telephone surveys now averages 60-plus percent, an increase of 10 percent over 10 years. Forty-nine percent of the people who do participate say the surveys are "too personal." Fortunately, more people are willing to participate in Internet surveys than other types of research.

Interest in a product or service is often discerned during the interviewing process, and the researcher knows the interviewees' potential purchasing power from their answers to income and other pertinent financial questions. Although the introduction phase of the questionnaire usually promises confidentiality, some researchers have sold names and addresses of potential customers to firms seeking sales leads. Individuals willing to participate in the survey research process have a right to have their privacy protected.

The state of New York sued Student Marketing Group for selling information on a broad scale to direct marketers. The survey filled out by students included age, gender, religious affiliation, career interests, and grade point average. The company said that it was gathering the data for universities to help the students gain admission and financial aid. Actually, direct marketers used the information to sell credit cards, magazines, videos, cosmetics, and other products.[16]

Selling Unnecessary Research   A research supplier dealing with a client who has little or no familiarity with marketing research often has the opportunity to "trade the client up." For example, if a project called for four focus groups and an online survey of approximately 350 consumers, the research supplier might sell eight groups and 1,000 Internet interviews, with a 400-interview telephone follow-up in 6 months.

It is perfectly acceptable to offer a prospective client several research designs with several alternative prices when and if the situation warrants alternative designs. The supplier should point out the pros and cons of each method, along with sample confidence intervals. The client, in consultation with the supplier, then can decide objectively which design best suits the company's needs.

Violating Client Confidentiality   Information about a client's general business activities or the results of a client's project should not be disclosed to a third party. The supplier should not even disclose the name of a client unless permission is received in advance.

The thorniest issue in confidentiality is determining where "background knowledge" stops and conflict arises as a result of work with a previous client. One researcher put it this way:

I get involved in a number of proprietary studies. The problem that often arises is that some studies end up covering similar subject matter as previous studies. Our code of ethics states that you cannot use data from one project in a related project for a competitor. However, since I often know some information about an area, I end up compromising my original client. Even though upper management formally states that it should not be done, they also expect it to be done to cut down on expenses. This conflict of interest situation is difficult to deal with. At least in my firm, I don't see a resolution to the issue. It is not a onetime situation, but rather a process that perpetuates itself. To make individuals redo portions of studies which have recently been done is ludicrous, and to forgo potential new business is almost impossible from a financial perspective.[17]

Black Box Branding

Marketing research suppliers have discovered branding. Synovate has over 25 branded product offerings, including Brand Vision and M2M. Maritz Research offers Loyalty Maximizer, and Harris Interactive has TRBC, a scale bias correction algorithm. Go to virtually any large marketing research firm's Web site, and you'll see a vast array of branded research products for everything from market segmentation to customer value analysis—all topped off with a diminutive [SM], [TM], or [®].

A common denominator across some of these products is that they are proprietary, which means the firms won't disclose exactly how they work. That's why they're also known pejoratively as black boxes. A black box method is proprietary—a company is able to protect its product development investment. And if customers perceive added value in the approach, suppliers can charge a premium price to boot. (Black boxes and brand names are not synonymous. Almost all proprietary methods have a clever brand name, but there are also brand names attached to research methods that are not proprietary.)

At least two factors have given rise to this branding frenzy. First, competitive pressures force organizations to seek new ways to differentiate their product offerings from those of their competitors. Second, many large research companies are publicly held, and publicly held companies are under constant pressure to increase sales and profits each quarter. One way to do this is to charge a premium price for services. If a company has a proprietary method for doing a marketing segmentation study, presumably it can charge more for this approach than another firm using publicly available software such as SPSS or SAS.

Clients have no objective way of determining whether the results of a proprietary method would vary significantly from those of more standard approaches, and neither have we. Go to five different companies that have five different black boxes for choice modeling, for example. Each company claims its method is superior, yet it's impossible to assess, from a psychometric perspective, which possesses the highest level of validity.

Of course, no one is forcing clients to purchase a black box method, and they can always contact other organizations that have used a supplier's proprietary method to assess its effectiveness. Often clients will obtain multiple bids on a project so that they can select from a variety of approaches to help them answer their research questions.[18]

Client Ethics

Like research suppliers, clients (or users) also have a number of ethical do's and don'ts. Some of the more common client problems are requesting bids when a supplier has been predetermined, requesting bids to obtain free advice and methodology, making false promises, and issuing unauthorized RFPs.

Requesting Bids When a Supplier Has Been Predetermined   It is not uncommon for a client to prefer one research supplier over another. Such a preference may be due to a good working relationship, cost considerations, ability to make deadlines, friendship, or quality of the research staff. Having a preference per se is not unethical. It is unethical, however, to predetermine which supplier will receive a contract and yet ask for proposals from other suppliers to satisfy corporate requirements. Requiring time, effort, and money from firms that have no opportunity to win the contract is very unfair. Why more than a single RFP? Some corporations require more than one bid.

Requesting Bids to Obtain Free Advice and Methodology   Client companies seeking bargain basement prices have been known to solicit detailed proposals, including complete methodology and a sample questionnaire, from a number of suppliers. After "picking the brains" of the suppliers, the client assembles a questionnaire and then contracts directly with field services to gather the data. A variation of this tactic is to go to the cheapest supplier with the client's own proposal, derived by taking the best ideas from the other proposals. The client then attempts to get the supplier to conduct the more elaborate study at the lower price.

Making False Promises   Another technique used by unethical clients to lower their research costs is to hold out a nonexistent carrot. For example, a client might say, "I don't want to promise anything, but we are planning a major stream of research in this area, and if you will give us a good price on this first study, we will make it up to you on the next one." Unfortunately, the next one never comes—or if it does, the same line is used on another unsuspecting supplier.

Requesting Proposals without Authorization   In each of the following situations, a client representative sought proposals without first receiving the authority to allocate the funds to implement them:

1.   A client representative decided to ask for proposals and *then* go to management to find out whether she could get the funds to carry them out.

2.   A highly regarded employee made a proposal to management on the need for marketing research in a given area. Although managers were not too enthused about the idea, they told the researcher to seek bids so as not to dampen his interest or miss a potentially (but, in their view, highly unlikely) good idea.

3.   A client representative and her management had different ideas on what the problem was and how it should be solved. The research supplier was not informed of the management view, and even though the proposal met the representative's requirements, management rejected it out of hand.

4.   Without consulting with the sales department, a client representative asked for a proposal on analyzing present sales performance. Through fear of negative feedback, corporate politics, or lack of understanding of marketing research, the sales department blocked implementation of the proposal.

Retailer Ethics   Intense competition at the retail level has resulted in a mushrooming of customer satisfaction surveys. Perhaps this is nowhere more evident than in auto dealerships. As many auto manufacturers, particularly American, have drastically cut their number of dealerships, those remaining are under strong pressure to provide exceptional customer service. The level of service is measured by manufacturer-supplied customer relationship surveys. One survey of 1,700 new car buyers found that 45 percent of the respondents believed that the dealership tried to influence their survey responses.[19] Some buyers weren't sure when the dealer asked, "Please let us address any problems rather than reporting them." Is this an attempt to influence the buyer or just good customer service?

Specifically, customers responded in the following ways to the question, "When you purchased your car, what did the salesperson or manager say about the survey?":

- 25 percent—They never mentioned the survey.
- 30 percent—They mentioned that I would receive a survey (but none of the following).
- 36 percent—They asked me to let them address the problems rather than reporting them.
- 28 percent—They asked me to tive them perfect scores but did not beg.
- 8 percent—They begged me for perfect scores.
- 9 percent—They said they would only get a bonus if I gave them perfect scores.
- 2 percent—They asked me to bring the survey in to the dealer and fill it out while they watched.
- 2 percent—They asked me to bring the blank survey to the dealer so they would fill it out.
- 2 percent—They offered me a gift in exchange for one of the above.[20]

As you can see, responses exist on a continuum, but a number are clearly unethical. Manufacturers can help solve the problem by sending the questionnaire to the respondent's home; establishing and enforcing a strong policy against survey manipulation allows the respondents to remain anonymous.

Field Service Ethics

Marketing research field services are the traditional production arm of the research industry requiring telephone or face-to-face interviews. They are the critical link between the respondent and the research supplier. It is imperative that they properly record information and carefully follow sampling plans. Otherwise, even the best research design will produce invalid information (garbage in; garbage out). Maintaining high ethical standards will aid a field service in procuring good raw data for the research firm.

Using Professional Respondents   The problem of professional respondents arises most often in the recruitment of focus group participants. Virtually all field services maintain a database of people willing to participate in qualitative discussion groups, along with a list of their demographic characteristics. Maintaining such a list is good business and quite ethical. When qualifications for group participants are easy (for example, pet owners, persons who drive SUVs), there is little temptation to use professional respondents. However, when a supplier wants, for example, persons who are heavy users of Oxydol detergent or who own a Russian Blue cat, it is not unheard of for a group recruiter to call a professional respondent and say, "I can get you into a group tomorrow with a $75 respondent fee and all you need to say is that you own a Russian Blue cat."

In an attempt to weed out professional respondents, a research supplier may specify that the participant must not have been a member of a qualitative discussion group within the past 6 months. However, dishonest field services will simply tell the professional respondent to deny having participated in a group within the past 6 months.

Respondents' Rights

Respondents in a marketing research project typically give their time and opinions and receive little or nothing in return. These individuals, however, do have certain rights that should be upheld by all marketing researchers. All potential participants in a research project have the right to choose, the right to safety, the right to be informed, and the right to privacy.

Right to Choose Everyone has the right to determine whether or not to participate in a marketing research project. Some people, such as poorly educated individuals or children may not fully appreciate this privilege. A person who would like to terminate an interview or experiment may give short, incomplete answers or even false data.

The fact that a person has consented to be part of an experiment or to answer a questionnaire does not give the researcher carte blanche to do whatever she or he wants. The researcher still has an obligation to the respondent. For example, if a person participating in a taste test involving a test product and several existing products prefers the test product, the researcher does not have the right to use the respondent's name and address in a promotion piece, saying that "Ms. Jones prefers new Sudsies to Brand X."

Right to Safety Research participants have the right to safety from physical or psychological harm. Although it is unusual for a respondent to be exposed to physical harm, there have been cases of persons becoming ill during food taste tests. Also, on a more subtle level, researchers rarely warn respondents that a test product contains, say, a high level of salt. An unwitting respondent with hypertension could be placed in physical danger if the test ran several weeks.

It is much more common for a respondent to be placed in a psychologically damaging situation. Individuals might experience stress when an interviewer presses them to participate in a study. Others might experience stress when they cannot answer questions or are given a time limit to complete a task (for example, "You have 5 minutes to browse through this magazine, and then I will ask you a series of questions").

Right to Be Informed Research participants have the right to be informed of all aspects of a research task. Knowing what is involved, how long it will take, and what will be done with the data, a person can make an intelligent choice as to whether to participate in the project.

Often, it is necessary to disguise the name of the research sponsor to avoid biasing the respondent. For example, it is poor research practice to say, "We are conducting a survey for Pepsi; which brand of soft drink do you consume most often?" In cases in which disguising the sponsor is required, a debriefing should take place following the completion of the interview. The debriefing should cover the study's purpose, the sponsor, what happens next with the data, and any other pertinent information. A debriefing can reduce respondent stress and build goodwill for the research industry. Unfortunately, taking the time to debrief a respondent is a cost that most companies are unwilling to incur.

In some business and academic research, the researcher may offer to provide the respondent with a copy of the research results as an incentive to obtain his or her participation in the project. When a commitment has been made to disseminate the findings to survey respondents, it should be fulfilled. On more than one occasion, we have participated in academic surveys where the carrot of research results was offered but never delivered.

Right to Privacy All consumers have the right to privacy. All major research organizations, including the MRA (discussed above), CASRO, the Internet Marketing Research Association (IMRO), the American Marketing Association (AMA), and the Advertising Research Foundation (ARF), have privacy codes. For example, with online survey research, lists of potential respondents must have one of two characteristics. Potential respondents must have either a prior opt-in for contact or they must have an existing business relationship with the sender through which an e-mail contact would not be considered a random, unsolicited e-mail (spam).

The privacy battle is most heated in the area of what online tracking companies are gathering. Tracking companies know what you do online but either can't or won't keep your name in their databases. The industry often cites this layer of anonymity as a reason online tracking shouldn't be considered intrusive. However, some tracking companies meld a number of online and offline databases so they know your name, e-mail address, and a lot of personal offline information.

RapLeaf recently provided a conservative politician with e-mail addresses to target his election campaign. In one example, RapLeaf knew a woman's name, that she was conservative, had an interest in the Bible, and contributed to environmental and political causes. RapLeaf claims it strips out personal information like names before selling them for online advertising. Data gathered and sold by RapLeaf can be very specific. According to documents reviewed by the Wall Street Journal, RapLeaf's segments recently included a person's household income range, age range, political leaning, and gender and age of children in the household, as well as interests in topics including religion, the Bible, gambling, tobacco, adult entertainment, and "get rich quick" offers. In all, RapLeaf segmented people into more than 400 categories.[21]

We will address privacy issues throughout the text. Technology is evolving so rapidly that federal and state laws are woefully behind. More privacy legislation will be forthcoming, though no one is sure what form it will take.

Repeating icon credits: Books - © Baris Simsek/iStockphoto, Globe - Purestock /Getty Images, Inc., Businesspeople - © franz pfluegl/ iStockphoto

The Global Research feature below explains the Safe Harbor Program, its privacy provisions, and why it is important to global marketing researchers.

GLOBAL RESEARCH

Safe Harbor in a Privacy Storm

The European Commission's Directive on Data Protection went into effect in October 1998 and prohibits the transfer of personal data to non-European Union nations that do not meet the European "adequacy" standard for privacy protection. Although the United States and the European Union (EU) share the goal of enhancing privacy protection for their citizens, the United States takes a different approach to privacy from that taken by the EU. The United States uses a sectoral approach that relies on a mix of legislation, regulation, and self-regulation. The EU, however, relies on comprehensive legislation that, for example, requires creation of government data protection agencies, registration of databases with those agencies, and in some instances prior approval before personal data processing may begin. As a result of these different privacy approaches, the Directive could have significantly hampered the ability of U.S. companies to engage in many transatlantic transactions.

In order to bridge these different privacy approaches and provide a streamlined means for U.S. organizations to comply with the Directive, the U.S. Department of Commerce in consultation with the European Commission developed a "safe harbor" framework. The Safe Harbor Program—approved by the EU in 2000—is an important way for U.S. companies to avoid experiencing interruptions in their business dealings with the EU or facing prosecution by European authorities under European privacy laws. Certifying to the Safe Harbor will assure that EU organizations know that a U.S. company provides "adequate" privacy protection, as defined by the Directive.

Organizations that participate in the Safe Harbor Program, which is voluntary, must comply with the Safe Harbor requirements and must publicly declare their adherence. To do so, an organization self-certifies annually to the Department of Commerce in writing that it agrees to adhere to the Safe Harbor Program's requirements. It must also state in its published privacy policy statement that it adheres to the Safe Harbor Program.

To qualify for the Safe Harbor Program, an organization can (1) join a self-regulatory program that adheres to the Safe Harbor's requirements and certify to the Department of Commerce or (2) develop its own self-regulatory privacy policy that conforms to the Safe Harbor and certify its adherence to the Department of Commerce.

The Safe Harbor Program consists of seven privacy principles:

1. **Notice.** This involves the purposes for which a company collects and uses information and how individuals can contact the organization with inquiries, the types of third parties that may receive the information, and the choices and means the organization offers for limiting its use and disclosure.

2. **Choice.** Choose (opt-out) whether personal information will be disclosed to a third party or used for a purpose incompatible with its original or authorized purpose. For sensitive information, affirmative or explicit (opt-in) choice must be given if the information is to be disclosed to a third party or used for another purpose.

3. **Onward transfer.** This is the transfer of information only to third parties who comply with Safe Harbor principles or with whom the organization has a written agreement requiring the third party to provide at least the same level of privacy protection.

4. **Access.** Individuals must have access to personal information about them and be able to correct or delete information that's inaccurate (except where the burden would be disproportionate to the risks of the individual's privacy or where the rights of other persons would be violated).

5. **Security.** Reasonable precautions must be taken to protect information from loss, misuse, unauthorized access, disclosure, alteration, and destruction.

6. **Data integrity.** Personal information must be relevant for the purposes for which it is to be used. An organization should take reasonable steps to ensure that data is reliable for its intended use, accurate, complete, and current.

7. **Enforcement.** Must have mechanisms for assuring compliance, and sanctions must be sufficiently vigorous to ensure compliance.[22]

Ethics and Professionalism

Today's business ethics are actually a subset of the values held by society as a whole. The values that underlie marketing decisions have been acquired through family, educational, and religious institutions, and social movements (for example, women's rights, environmental protection). A marketing researcher with a mature set of ethical values accepts personal responsibility for decisions that affect the community. Considerations include the following:

- Employees' needs and desires and the long-range best interests of the organization
- The long-range goodwill and best interests of people who are directly affected by company activities (a bonus: good publicity for the firm)
- The societal values and conditions that provide the basis for the social structure in which the company exists

High standards of ethics and professionalism go hand in hand. Good ethics provide a solid foundation for professionalism, and striving for a lofty level of professionalism requires ethical behavior on the part of researchers.

Fostering Professionalism   Because of the specialized knowledge and expertise they possess, members of a profession have influence and power over those for whom they provide a particular service. The tools of a doctor or lawyer cannot easily be obtained and sold in the marketplace; these professions guard their knowledge and control who has access to it. Although marketing researchers and marketers wield power and influence over their customers and even society, the marketing industry does not have a credentialing process or high entry barriers. The argument can be made that the marketers who most need to think, believe, and behave with professionalism are those in marketing research.

The distinction between a profession and professionalism is important: a **profession** and membership in it are objectively determined (for example, by medical board exams), whereas **professionalism** is evaluated on more personal and subjective levels. A study designed to measure the level of professionalism in marketing research found that researchers had autonomy in their jobs, were permitted to exercise judgment, and were recognized for their level of expertise and ability to work independently. These characteristics are marks of professionalism. However, most researchers did not readily identify the contribution that marketing makes to society, nor did most firms tend to reward researchers' participation in professional organizations. These characteristics do not indicate a high level of professionalism.

Several steps have been taken recently to improve the level of professionalism in the marketing research industry. For example, CASRO has sponsored symposia dealing with ethical issues in survey research. CASRO also has created a code of ethics that has been widely disseminated to research professionals. The CASRO board has worked with groups such as the Marketing Research Association (MRA) to provide input to legislatures considering antimarketing research legislation. The MRA has also created its own code of ethics. Selected provisions are summarized in Exhibit 2.7.

A profession and membership in it are objectively determined; professionalism is evaluated on more personal and subjective levels.

profession
Organization whose membership is determined by objective standards, such as an examination.

professionalism
Quality said to be possessed by a worker with a high level of expertise, the freedom to exercise judgment, and the ability to work independently.

Researcher Certification   Today, it is far too easy to begin practicing marketing research. We have seen several "fast talkers" convince unwary clients that they are qualified researchers. Unfortunately, relying on poor information to make major decisions has resulted in loss of market share, reduction in profits, and, in some cases, bankruptcy.

Certification has generated a great deal of debate among members of the marketing research industry. It should be noted that certification is not licensing. *Licensing* is a mandatory procedure administered by a governmental body that allows one to practice a profession. *Certification* is a voluntary program administered by a nongovernmental body that provides a credential for differentiation in the marketplace. The issue of certification is sensitive because it directly affects marketing researchers' ability to practice their profession freely.

The MRA has launched a Professional Researcher Certification program. The objectives, according to the MRA, are "to encourage high standards within the profession in order to raise competency, establish an objective measure of an individual's knowledge and proficiency, and to encourage continued professional development."[23] The program allows for certification as a research user, supplier, or data collector. The process requires a series of continuing education credits and then passing an exam. To date, over 1,500 people have become certified.

| EXHIBIT 2.7 | A Partial Listing of the Marketing Research Association Code of Marketing Research Standards |

1. Will ensure that each study is conducted according to the agreement with the client.

2. Will never falsify or omit data for any reason at any phase of a research study or project.

3. Will protect and preserve the confidentiality of all research techniques and/or methodologies and of information considered confidential or proprietary.

4. Will report research results accurately and honestly.

5. Will protect the rights and privacy of respondents.

6. Will treat respondents in a professional manner.

7. Will take all reasonable precautions that respondents are in no way directly harmed or adversely affected as a result of their participation in a marketing research project.

8. Will not misrepresent themselves as having qualifications, experience, skills, resources or other facility locations that they do not possess.

9. Will not use research information to identify respondents without the permission of the respondent. The following are exceptions:
    a. Respondent identification information may be used in processing the data and merging data files.
    b. Respondent identification information may be used to append client or third-party data to a survey-based data file.
    c. Respondent identification information may be revealed in compliance with a court order or other legal demand from a competent and recognized legal authority (e.g. discovery phase of a pending legal case).

10. Will respect the respondent's right to withdraw or to refuse to cooperate at any stage of the study and will not use any procedure or technique to coerce or imply that cooperation is obligatory.

11. Will ensure that respondents are informed at the outset if the interview/discussion is being audio or video recorded by any means and will, if required, obtain written consent if the recorded interview/discussion will be
    • viewed by a third party
    • reproduced for outside use

12. Will consider all research materials provided by the client or generated as a result of materials provided by the client to be the property of the client. These materials will be retained or disposed of as agreed upon with the client at the time of the study.

13. For Internet research, will not use any data in any way contrary to the provider's published privacy statement without permission from the respondent. *Data shall not be captured without respondent's consent. Doing so is in direct violation of the privacy rights stated in the Code and may violate the laws of a particular jurisdiction.*

14. For Internet research, will not send unsolicited e-mail to those who have opted out.

15. Will compile, maintain and utilize Internet samples of only those individuals who have provided their permission to be contacted (opt-in) and who have a reasonable expectation that they will receive Internet invitations for opinion and marketing research purposes.

16. Will, upon request, identify the appropriateness of the sample methodology itself and its ability to accomplish research objectives.

17. Will offer respondents the choice with each survey to be removed (opt-out) for future Internet invitations.

Source: MRA, 2010.

SUMMARY

The marketing research industry consists of (1) information users (consumer and industrial goods and services producers; federal, state, and local governments; media companies; retailers and wholesalers), (2) marketing research suppliers (custom research firms' syndicated research firms, online tracking firms, and limited function research firms), and (3) marketing research supplier service firms.

Users of marketing research can be further categorized as external or internal to the firm. External users include company vendors and franchisees. The primary internal user of marketing research is the marketing department, which seeks data for decision making in such areas as logistics, sales, promotions, new product development, brand management, and pricing. Other internal groups and departments using marketing research are senior management, product engineers, finance, manufacturing, human resources management, and legal.

The marketing research industry was hurt by the recent recession. Sales and employment dropped for the first time in many years. Client organizations began insourcing to save money. At the same time, clients were also seeking strategic partnerships with research suppliers. This has led many client firms to reduce the number of suppliers they use.

Ethics are moral principles or values generally governing the conduct of an individual or group. The deontology theory says that a person will follow his or her obligations to another individual or society because upholding one's duty is what is considered ethically correct. In contrast, utilitarian ethical theory maintains that a choice yielding the greatest benefit to the greatest number of people is the choice that is ethically correct. The casuist theory holds that a decision should be made by comparing a current ethical dilemma with examples of similar ethical dilemmas and their outcomes.

Unethical practices by some suppliers include low-ball pricing, allowing subjectivity into the research, abusing respondents, selling unnecessary research, violating client confidentiality, and using black box branding. Unethical practices performed by some research clients include requesting bids when a supplier has been predetermined, requesting bids to gain free advice or methodology, making false promises, and issuing unauthorized requests for proposals. Marketing research field services have used professional respondents, which is unethical. The growing amounts of data collected by online tracking firms has resulted in demands by many consumers for stronger privacy laws.

Respondents have certain rights, including the right to choose whether to participate in a marketing research project, the right to safety from physical and psychological harm, and the right to be informed of all aspects of the research task. They should know what is involved, how long it will take, and what will be done with the data. Respondents also have the right to privacy.

The level of professionalism in the marketing research industry can be raised through the efforts of organizations such as CASRO and CMOR, as well as socially concerned marketing research firms. Researcher certification is available through the MRA.

KEY TERMS & DEFINITIONS

custom research firms Companies that carry out customized marketing research to address specific projects for corporate clients.

syndicated service research firms Companies that collect, package, and sell the same general market research data to many firms.

research panel A group of individuals who agree to participate in a series of research studies over time.

field service firms Companies that only collect survey data for corporate clients or research firms.

strategic partnership An alliance formed by two or more firms with unique skills and resources to offer a new service for clients, provide strategic support for each firm, or in some other manner create mutual benefits.

ethics Moral principles or values, generally governing the conduct of an individual or group.

low-ball pricing Quoting an unrealistically low price to secure a firm's business and then using some means to substantially raise the price.

profession Organization whose membership is determined by objective standards, such as an examination.

professionalism Quality said to be possessed by a worker with a high level of expertise, the freedom to exercise judgment, and the ability to work independently.

QUESTIONS FOR REVIEW & CRITICAL THINKING

1. Compare and contrast custom and syndicated marketing research firms.
2. What is the role of field service firms in marketing research?
3. Describe the marketing research industry.
4. List several key characteristics of corporate marketing research departments.
5. Discuss the various project offerings of syndicated service firms.
6. Divide the class into groups of five. Each group should select one section of the city in which the course is being taught (or the closest large city) and determine the zip codes for this section of the city. Next, go to *http://www.claritas.com* and follow the instructions for getting Prizm profiles by zip code. Each group should then discuss the marketing profile for its section of the city.
7. What do you see as the role of a code of ethics within an organization? What can be done to ensure that employees follow this code of ethics?
8. Who would you say has the greatest responsibility within the marketing research industry to raise the standards of ethics—marketing research suppliers, marketing research clients, or field services?
9. What role should the federal government play in establishing ethical standards for the marketing research industry? How might such standards be enforced?
10. If respondents consent to interviews after being told they will be paid $50 for their opinions, do they forfeit all respondent rights? If so, what rights have been forfeited?
11. What is the relationship between ethics and professionalism? What do you think can be done to raise the level of professionalism within the marketing research industry?
12. Explain the Safe Harbor Program and its importance.
13. Are online tracking firms gathering too much information about people? Why or why not?

WORKING THE NET

1. Compare the offerings of two marketing research firms, DSS Research and Burke Incorporated, by visiting their Web sites at *http://dssresearch.com* and *http://www.burke.com.*

2. The Kantar Group, is a major international marketing research firm, with offices in 54 countries. Go to its Web site at *http://www.kantar.com* and report on its global research capabilities.

3. Interviewers must take special care when interviewing children or young people. The informed consent of the parent or responsible adult first must be obtained for interviews with children. Parents or responsible adults must be told some specifics about the interview process and special tasks, such as audio or video recording, taste testing, and respondent fees before permission is obtained. All researchers must adhere to all federal and state regulations regarding the interviewing of children 13 years of age or younger. All interviews conducted online must adhere to the Children's Online Privacy Protection Act (COPPA). Use the Internet to gather more information about interviewing children and report the results to the class.

4. Go to *http://www.mra-net.org/ga* for a discussion of the latest issue regarding government affairs.

REAL-LIFE RESEARCH • 2.1

Respondent Recruiters—Clean Up Your Act

Mark Goodin is president of Aaron-Abrams Field Services, Las Vegas. The firm specializes in delivering respondents to qualitative marketing researchers. Below he discusses problems he sees in the respondent recruitment business. When he discusses "supplies," he is referring to firms that recruit respondents. Thus, respondent suppliers may be recruiting for a research supplier, as discussed in the chapter, or a research client, such as a manufacturer like Frito-Lay, which is doing their own qualitative research.

Over the past few years, I have witnessed a couple of disturbing trends in qualitative research. And I have to believe that if this is happening to me on such a large and consistent basis, then it's happening to other research buyers in the industry as well—they're just not talking about it. These trends are not good for the future of qualitative research:

- The trend of respondent recruiters accepting projects and then forcing changes in vital aspects of the project's original design once recruiting is underway.

- The trend among recruiters to recruit unqualified respondents and then charge for the recruiting and incentive.

My belief is that many suppliers simply shut up, take the project, and let the problems unfold. I believe they have adopted the attitude that clients can ask for the moon but in the end they're going to get what they get. More often than not, that's what happens once a project goes into the field.

I've never seen so many projects that are accepted by respondent recruiters as-is— without sharing their concerns or issuing any warnings—only to say later, "We're not finding what you're looking for, you'll need to make relaxations in the qualifications of the type of person that you are looking for." Or, "We've reached our budget, and we'll need more money if you want us to continue."

What's more, it's even less palatable to accept respondent suppliers' need for relaxations or additional money when, along the way, they've delivered substandard service. For example:

- recruiting progress reports aren't delivered when requested;
- recruiting progress reports contain errors and misspellings;
- respondents don't qualify when rescreened or revalidated;
- screeners have been incorrectly administered;
- discrepancies in the screener have been overlooked or ignored;
- instructions have not been followed; and
- recruiting hours have been put into the job, but not enough contacts—or calls—have been made.

Must Stop Today

The practice of respondent suppliers charging for respondents who don't fit the qualifying criteria must stop today. If the respondent isn't qualified and cannot be used in the research, we should not be charged for the respondent. Period. It's time for respondent suppliers to stop recruiting unqualified or marginally qualified respondents and hiding behind a myriad of excuses. Recruiters are entirely responsible for respondent accuracy. Period. If recruiters cannot stand behind the product they deliver, they should find another line of work. Our firm has a simple policy that third-party recruiting suppliers know about prior to the start of a project: We will not pay recruiting fees or the incentives for any respondents who do not qualify at rescreening or at the time of the actual research. We actively encourage all researchers to do the same.[24]

Questions

1. Why is it important for respondents to meet the exact qualifications specified for the research project?
2. Have you ever participated in a research project where you knew that you were marginally qualified to participate? Did you tell the researcher?
3. Is it unethical for respondent suppliers to charge their clients for unqualified respondents?
4. Would it be unethical if a recruiter was seeking current cat owners and you said "no but I had a cat when I was growing up," to which the recruiter replied, "That will work, just tell them that you still have a cat".

REAL-LIFE RESEARCH • 2.2

Budget Rent a Car Drives a Message Home

As part of the global Budget organization, Budget Rent a Car in South Africa operates a large network of over 80 branches located throughout South Africa, Namibia, and Botswana. In-terminal branches at all major airports ensure that no matter how customers choose to reach their destination, Budget Rent a Car is never far away.

In the highly competitive car rental business, Budget strives to consistently deliver world-class customer service and continuously find ways to further improve the experiences of its customers. With the relative ease of moving to a competitor, the need to retain existing customers and build brand loyalty is critical for success.

It is especially important to immediately identify customers who are dissatisfied with Budget and to rapidly address their concerns. Budget caters primarily to the business traveler, so the lifetime value of each customer is substantial.

As most travelers are busy and in a hurry to get to their next destination, Budget strives to minimize the time it takes customers to collect or return a car. As an example, the Budget Fastbreak program removes the necessity for the customer to sign any documentation at the time of vehicle collection. On arrival, the customer simply proceeds directly to the Fastbreak dedicated counter, where the keys are handed over. "Unfortunately these and other programs limit the opportunity to interact with customers at a personal level and obtain feedback about their experiences with the car or service they received," says Bev Vorster, Budget business support manager. "Customers who have had a negative experience, in most instances, do not have a channel to complain and simply move to a competitor the next time they hire a car while sharing their negative experience with friends and colleagues."

Low Response Rate

To get customer feedback, Budget in the past had used prepaid reply survey cards. However, the effectiveness of this method in capturing and immediately responding to customer issues was very poor, and the overall response rate very low. It typically took up to 3 months for a customer to get a reply to a complaint as the survey cards had to be delivered to a central point at the head office, manually captured into a computer system, assessed by a customer service representative, sorted in terms of type of complaint, and then an appropriate response had to be formulated. In most cases the customer simply received a form letter from the Budget CEO advising that the issue was being looked into and steps were being taken to avoid a recurrence. This delayed and impersonal method of communication had the potential of further alienating customers and driving them to competitors.

In 2004 the Budget corporate customer service management team was introduced to the customer feedback management system developed by South Africa-based research firm Touchwork. The system captures and provides customer feedback using cell phone-based text messaging, letting Budget immediately act on negative feedback and address customer concerns. Budget realized that this approach would resolve many of the shortcomings of the reply card process and enable it to further differentiate itself from competitors.

With the widespread use of cell phones across all sectors of the population and the growing use of text messaging, Budget also wanted to be seen as an innovator in using new technologies to further enhance its reputation as a leader in its space.

Core Part

The ongoing customer satisfaction campaign was launched in May 2004 and forms a core part of Budget's customer satisfaction and performance management initiatives.

Budget determined that the following six survey questions represented the most critical issues related to a customer's experience. A simple yes/no response to each question was deemed adequate to identify service delivery issues and initiate follow-up action.

Q.1 Did you receive fast and courteous service when you rented your car?

Q.2 Did you receive fast and courteous service when you returned your car?

Q.3 Were our people neat in appearance and pleasing in attitude?

Q.4 Was your car clean inside and out?

Q.5 Was your car in good mechanical condition?

Q.6 Would you rent from Budget again?

In addition to these responses, customers had to provide a branch code and could include additional comments.

These questions, along with simple instructions on how to send a response, are printed on a hanger (Exhibit 2.8), which is placed on the rearview mirror of every car. This placement ensures that the customer will notice the survey, as the hanger must be removed before driving the car. Posters were also created for display within each branch.

As an incentive to submit a response, customers are guaranteed 50 miles with the Voyager frequent flyer program provided by South African Airways (SAA). As Budget caters primarily to business travelers and has a partnership with SAA, the majority of its customers are SAA Voyager members and the 50 miles was deemed to be a meaningful incentive, one representing the equivalent of miles that could be earned via a $100 credit card purchase.

Budget branch personnel are not required to do anything more except to bring the campaign to the attention of customers. Branch managers are instantly notified by an SMS text message whenever a negative response is received and are asked to immediately follow up with the customer. Regional and corporate managers are also notified via e-mail.

Fivefold Increase

Since the launch of the campaign, there has been a fivefold increase in the number of responses versus the number that were obtained using the prepaid reply cards. It is anticipated that as customers become even more familiar with text messaging, the response rate will increase further.

All responses are stored in the database and are available 24/7 on a secure Web site. A range of management reports is provided to identify trends and determine a customer satisfaction index for corporate reporting purposes. These are shown graphically as bar, pie, and line graphs and include response counts by branch, region as well as totals; general overview and question breakdown; negative feedback weekly, monthly, and total; and negative response spread by question. Exhibit 2.9 shows a typical summary report of all negative responses by question over a 6-month period.

GIVE US YOUR COMMENTS
AND STAND A CHANCE TO WIN
1000 VOYAGER MILES – EVERY MONTH
PLUS Guaranteed 50 free Voyager Miles
if you reply via SMS

Standard rate cost for SMS - NOT premium rate!
depending on the type of car rental, the SMS cost will range from 1% to a maximum of 75%

Thank you for renting from Budget. It is our goal to provide you with complete satisfaction with each rental experience. To achieve this, your feedback is important to us. Would you therefore spare about a moment, to tell us about your rental experience, and in so doing, put yourself in line to win 1000 Voyager Miles in our monthly draw. To send us your feedback, you may post your entry or hand it in at your nearest Budget office. But, if you send your reply via SMS, you will automatically earn 50 free Voyager Miles, as well as be added into the monthly draw.

How to send your SMS and automatically earn 50 Voyager Miles.
Submit your comments via SMS to 0027 83 406 6969 as follows:
1. Reply to questions One to Six. 2. Enter the branch code. 3. Enter the Budget car registration number. 4. Enter your SAA Voyager number. 5. (Optional) Enter your text message.
EXAMPLE: If you were happy with the services and would choose Budget again, your message would be as follows (in one' message):

Question 1 to 6	Branch code	Registration No.	SAA Voyager No.	Text message
999 999	JS	ABC123GP	12345	Great Service

Note: The above branch code is an example only. Please see below for the branch code of this branch. Soaces may be added between numbers. Only one SMS per rental.

	No	Yes
1. Did you receive fast and continuous service when you rented your car?	0	9
2. Did you receive fast and continuous service when you returned your car?	0	9
3. Were our people neat in appearance and pleasing in attitude?	0	9
4. Was your car clean inside and out?	0	9
5. Was your car in good mechanical condition?	0	9
6. Would you rent from Budget again?	0	9

Please insert this branch code if sending via SMS **JS**

Please complete the following if posting your entry

Any other comments _____

Name _____ e-mail _____
Telephone _____ Fax _____
Company _____
Rental Agreement number or your rental vehicle registration number _____

Customers can't help but notice the survey invitation as it hangs from the rearview mirror of their car.

Exhibit 2.8

Budget's Survey Hanger Courtesy of Budget Car Rental, Inc.

Over 90 percent of responses have indicated that customers are completely satisfied with their experience and have included comments such as:

- "Very impressive service."
- "Superb as always."
- "Excellent service and good rate. Many thanks."
- "My couple of complaints handled promptly."
- "Nicely done!"
- "1st class."
- "Efficient and helpful."

Responses with negative ratings have given Budget quantitative information regarding areas requiring attention. This includes both overall issues that must be addressed at a corporate level, such as improving certain processes and procedures, and issues at specific branches.

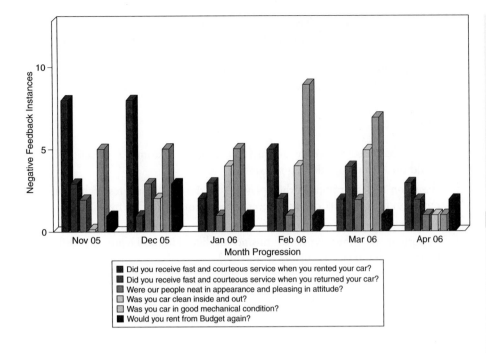

Exhibit 2.9

A Typical Summary
Report of Negative
Responses over a
6-Month Period
Courtesy of Budget
Car Rental, Inc.

Examples of comments received with negative responses include:

- "Car struggled to turn over every time I started it!"
- "Nice quick friendly service, but the parking bays need to be open so the trolley can fit thru when returning the car."
- "Ensure more staff on Fridays!"

Core Tools

Based on the success of the campaign to date, Budget plans to continue to use the ESP system to obtain customer feedback, Vorster says. "It forms one of the core tools Budget uses in its quest for service excellence and has greatly assisted our customer retention and satisfaction initiatives."

Budget's assessment and conclusions regarding the use of the ESP system for its customer satisfaction campaign are as follows:

- Text messaging is providing an additional channel to communicate with customers and help build relationships.
- The immediate notification of branch, regional, and head-office management ensures full visibility of customer issues.
- Areas for improvement are highlighted.
- Underperforming branches can be identified, enabling Budget corporate to take corrective action.
- Store managers are immediately notified of dissatisfied customers and can take appropriate steps to address the issues and prevent recurrences.
- Branch managers can compare their performance with that of the national average in an objective manner and identify areas for improvement.

"The most significant benefit has been the total surprise and positive reaction of customers when, after submitting a negative response, they are immediately contacted by a manager to address their issues," says Vorster. "In almost every case, customers who had indicated that they would not again rent from Budget were converted into repeat customers with a much-enhanced perception of Budget as a company."[25]

Questions

1. Budget has used marketing research to measure customer satisfaction. How else could the firm use marketing research?

2. Based on a description of the "players" in the marketing research industry, discussed in the first part of the chapter, what is Touchwork? Why?

3. Why is customer feedback so important to a company like Budget? Is it just as important to other types of businesses like Home Depot or Duke Energy Corporation (an electric utility company)?

Problem Definition, Exploratory Research, and the Research Process

LEARNING OBJECTIVES

→ **1.** To understand the problem definition process.

→ **2.** To learn the steps involved in the marketing research process.

→ **3.** To understand the components of the research request.

→ **4.** To learn the advantages and disadvantages of survey, observation, and experiment research techniques.

→ **5.** To become familiar with how the marketing research process is initiated.

Conducting marketing research involves a series of logical steps, beginning with problem definition and research objectives. What are the steps in the marketing research process? How is the research process initiated? These are the issues we will address in this chapter.

Critical Importance of Correctly Defining the Problem

Recognize the problem or opportunity

↓

Find out why the information is being sought

↓

Understand the decision-making environment (the industry, company, products, and target market)

↓

Use the symptoms to help clarify the problem

↓

Translate the management problem into a marketing research problem

↓

Determine whether the information already exists

↓

Determine whether the question really can be answered

↓

State the research objectives

Exhibit 3.1

Problem Definition Process

Correctly defining the problem is the crucial first step in the marketing research process. If the research problem is defined incorrectly, the research objectives will also be wrong, and the entire marketing research process will be a waste of time and money. A large consumer packaged goods company wanted to conduct a study among a brand's heavy users in order to understand the brand's equity. More specifically, it wanted to expand that equity into new products. The brand had very low penetration, so the company needed new products to meet the upcoming fiscal year's volume goal of double-digit growth. Notice the absence of tying research learning—understanding the brand's equity—to the business objective.

The brand had a small base from which to grow, so simply investigating the brand's equity among its most loyal users wouldn't help decision makers reach a double-digit growth rate. Upon reflection, the business objective focused on identifying marketing levers that would increase brand penetration—and thus growth. Accordingly, the research objectives transformed into understanding barriers to current brand purchase and identifying bridges that would motivate category users to buy the brand.

Study results showed that the brand chiefly suffered from awareness problems. Both brand and category users liked the product, but didn't use it as often as others in the category because they simply forgot about the brand. Reminders—in the form of advertising, incentives, and new products—became the levers that could improve brand penetration and growth. Conducting an equity study among heavy users clearly wouldn't have caught this.[1]

The process for defining the problem is shown in Exhibit 3.1. Note that the ultimate goal is to develop clear, concise, and meaningful marketing research objectives. Researching such objectives will yield precise decision-making information for managers.

Recognize the Problem or Opportunity

The marketing research process begins with the recognition of a marketing problem or opportunity. As changes occur in the firm's external environment, marketing managers are faced with the questions "Should we change the existing marketing mix?" and, if so, "How?" Marketing research may be used to evaluate products and services, promotion, distribution, and pricing alternatives. In addition, it may be used to find and evaluate new opportunities, in a process called **opportunity identification**.

> → **opportunity identification**
> Using marketing research to find and evaluate new opportunities.

Let's look at an example of opportunity identification. By 2015 there will likely be a major shift to online video. Perhaps half of all videos will be viewed online. This estimate might be quite conservative when one considers the historical adoption of other, related technologies. For example, DVD players were in 70 percent of American TV households by 2004—only 6 years after their commercial introduction.[2]

There are several different ways the transition could play out, but the outcome is the same: Internet-enabled TVs will find their way into most American homes. In one scenario, large numbers of viewers will learn to use the built-in Internet capabilities available in most new TVs in a way that complements their consumption of broadcast video. Alternatively, the aggressive new breed of video providers, such as Apple TV and Netflix, may win oiver American consumers with their promises of free, on-demand video. Most likely, however, cable operators and alternative delivery systems, in a concerted effort to preempt this onslaught and retain their subscription businesses, will rapidly replace today's set top boxes with units that combine broadcast, DVR, and online video in a single box.

One reason for this production is that Generation Y, born between 1979 and 1994, already watches a growing amount of video online. In 2010, 29 percent of consumers under 25 did, according to Research Now. But over the next 5 years, this group will mature and make up a growing portion of U.S. households.[3]

Second, the user interface on set top boxes will vastly improve by automatically recommending content and making it easier for all viewers—including the less tech-savvy Baby Boomers—to choose online video over broadcast. Imagine the scenario: When a person turns on the TV, they see a welcome screen that includes an option to watch, immediately, on demand, the next episode of their favorite show. Or they could spend a half an hour trolling the broadcast channels in hopes of finding something they like. Which one's the more likely outcome?

Online can represent a great opportunity to Netflix and even Dish Network, but a successful marketing strategy is required to be successful. This requires an understanding of the marketplace, the rate of adoption of online video, online video watcher market segments (Gen Yers will probably use it differently from Baby Boomers), and so forth. From a different perspective, a major advertiser, like Procter and Gamble, which now spends mostly on targeted online ads and traditional media like radio and broadcast TV, must understand the trend toward online video and adjust its media mix accordingly.

Of course, marketing research doesn't always deal with opportunities. Managers may want to know, for example, "Why are we losing marketing share?" or "What should we do about Ajax Manufacturing lowering its prices by 10 percent?" In these instances, marketing researchers can help managers solve problems.

Find Out Why the Information Is Being Sought

Large amounts of money, effort, and time are wasted because requests for marketing information are poorly formulated or misunderstood. For example, managers may not have a clear idea of what they want or may not phrase their questions properly. Therefore, marketing researchers often find the following activities helpful:

- Discuss what the information will be used for and what decisions might be made as a result of the research. Work through detailed examples to help clarify the issue.
- Try to get the client or manager to prioritize their questions. This helps sort out central questions from those of incidental interest.
- Rephrase the questions in several slightly different forms and discuss the differences.
- Create sample data and ask if such data would help answer the questions. Simulate the decision process.
- Remember that the more clear-cut you think the questions are and the more quickly you come to feel that the questions are straightforward, the more you should doubt that you have understood the real need.

Understand the Decision-Making Environment with Exploratory Research

situation analysis
Studying the decision-making environment within which the marketing research will take place.

Once researchers understand the motivation for conducting the research, often they need additional background information to fully comprehend the problem. This may mean simply talking to brand managers or new product managers, reading company reports, visiting production facilities and retail stores, and perhaps talking with suppliers. If the industry has a trade association, researchers might peruse its Web site for information published by the association. The better the marketing researcher understands the decision-making environment, including the industry, the firm, its products or services, and the target market, the more likely it is that the problem will be defined correctly. This step may be referred to as conducting a **situation analysis**.

exploratory research
Preliminary research conducted to increase understanding of a concept, to clarify the exact nature of the problem to be solved, or to identify important variables to be studied.

Sometimes informed discussions with managers and suppliers and on-site visits aren't enough. **Exploratory research** may be conducted to obtain greater understanding of a concept or to help crystallize the definition of a problem. It is also used to identify important variables to be studied. Exploratory research is preliminary research, not the definitive research used to determine a course of action.

Exploratory research can take several forms: pilot studies, experience surveys, secondary data analysis, pilot studies case analysis, and focus groups. **Pilot studies** are surveys using a limited number of respondents and often employing less rigorous sampling techniques than are employed in large, quantitative studies.

pilot studies
Surveys using a limited number of respondents and often employing less rigorous sampling techniques than are employed in large, quantitative studies.

Nickelodeon, for example, was well aware of the new baby boom and wanted to know what it meant for the network. Exploratory research found that a long-held assumption about kids' attitudes was not accurate: the belief that female images in TV programming generally work with girls but alienate boys. The exploratory research consisted of a small-scale pilot study on the Internet and focus groups in which children were brought together to discuss their attitudes toward television. Like Nickelodeon's research, much exploratory research is highly flexible, with researchers following ideas, clues, and hunches as long as time and money constraints permit. Often ideas are obtained from so-called experts in the field. Nickelodeon, for example, could have spoken with child psychologists.

As the researcher moves through the exploratory research process, a list of marketing research problems and subproblems should be developed. The investigator should identify all factors that seem to be related to the problem area, as these are probable research topics. This stage of problem definition requires a brainstorming-type approach, but one guided by the previous stage's findings. All possibilities should be listed without regard to the feasibility of addressing them via research. Nickelodeon ultimately decided to define the marketing research problem as determining whether a live-action show with girls as the protagonists would appeal to both sexes. Quantitative marketing research results showed that such a program would have dual appeal. Managerial action taken as a result yielded a program where the star was female, but the audience was 53 percent male.[4]

Experience Surveys Analysis   A second form of exploratory research is experience surveys. **Experience surveys** involve talking with knowledgeable individuals, both inside and outside the organization, who may provide insights into the problem. Rarely do experience surveys include a formal questionnaire. Instead, the researcher may simply have a list of topics to be discussed. The survey, then, is much like an informal discussion. For example, if Jet Blue is redesigning the interior of its aircraft, it may use experience surveys to speak with interior designers, frequent flyers, flight attendants, and pilots.

> ➤ **experience surveys**
> Discussions with knowledgeable individuals, both inside and outside the organization, who may provide insights into the problem.

Secondary Data Analysis   Secondary data analysis is another form of exploratory research. Because secondary data analysis is covered extensively in Chapter 4, we will touch on it only lightly here. *Secondary data* are data that have been gathered for some purpose other than the one at hand. Today, marketing researchers can use the Internet to access countless sources of secondary data quickly and at minimal expense. There are few subjects that have not been analyzed at one time or another. With a bit of luck, the marketing researcher can use secondary data to help precisely define the problem.

Case Analysis   Case analysis represents the fourth form of exploratory research. The purpose of **case analysis** is to review information from a few other situations that are similar to the present research problem. For example, electric utilities across America are scrambling to adopt the marketing concept and to become customer-oriented; these utilities are conducting market segmentation research, customer satisfaction studies, and customer loyalty surveys. To better understand the deregulation of the electric utility industry, marketing researchers are examining case studies on the deregulation of the airline industry. Researchers, however, must always take care to determine the relevancy of any case study to the present research problem.

> ➤ **case analysis**
> Reviewing information from situations that are similar to the current one.

Focus Groups   Focus groups are in-depth discussions, usually consisting of 8 to 12 participants, which are led by a moderator and are generally limited to one particular concept, idea, or theme. The general idea is to have what one person says generate thoughts and comments by others, therefore creating group dynamics. That is, the interplay of responses will yield more information than if the same number of persons had contributed in individual interviews. Focus groups are the primary topic of discussion in Chapter 5, so they will be lightly covered here. We mention them now because they are probably the most popular form of exploratory research.

Focus groups can, and do, cover just about any topic imaginable. Your authors, unlike all other marketing research text authors, have conducted over 3,000 focus group sessions. When used in exploratory research, focus groups are used to help clarify and understand the problem and issues involved. A few examples of topics that we have covered include: what creates the Harley-Davidson mystique, what happens when you discover head lice in your children, whether having a tequila made in America is a problem, what kitchen item is most difficult to clean, and the list goes on.

Using Intranets for Exploratory Research   The computer can be a very powerful tool for doing exploratory research. In very large organizations with intranets, the researcher has the capability of determining whether needed or relevant information is available somewhere inside the organization. The corporate marketing research department at Texas Instruments (TI), for example, has developed a powerful intranet application that permits TI managers worldwide to search for past research studies and those currently in progress on the basis of key words. They have immediate online access to a brief description of each study and can send e-mail seeking permission to view the full text of reports on old projects. Permission can be granted electronically via e-mail by the owner of the report (the person who paid for it), and the full text can be accessed online.

More and more organizations are developing similar systems to permit much more effective managerial use of information resources. In large organizations, it is not uncommon for a group in one part of the organization to conduct a research project that might have great value to managers in another part of the organization. Too often, there is no way for one group to find out what another group has already done. Intranet systems like the one at Texas Instruments will help organizations get the most mileage out of their research dollars.

While intranets provide easy access to internal data, the Internet is an invaluable resource for searching tens of millions of external sources for the information needed. At the exploratory stage, a researcher might use any one or several of the online search engines to find information needed. This type of search not only is much faster than a traditional library search but also provides access to an incredible array of information that is not available in any library. The researcher can perform an Internet search and point out or download the desired information in a matter of hours rather than the days or weeks a standard library search might require. Finally, the researcher can identify a range of discussion or special-interest groups on the Internet that may be relevant to a research project.

Completing Exploratory Research   The end of exploratory study comes when the marketing researchers are convinced that they have found the major dimensions of the problem. They may have defined a set of questions that can be used as specific guides to a detailed research design. Or they may have developed a number of potential ideas about possible causes of a specific problem of importance to management. They may also have determined that certain other factors are such remote possibilities that they can be safely ignored in any further study. Finally, the researchers may end exploration because they feel that further research is not needed or is not presently possible due to time, money, or other constraints.

Bonnie Sisenfeld, a Philadelphia-based independent marketing research consultant discusses exploratory research and obectives in the Practicing Marketing Research box on next page.

Use the Symptoms to Clarify the Problem

Marketing researchers must be careful to distinguish between symptoms and the real problem. A symptom is a phenomenon that occurs because of the existence of something else. For example, managers often talk about the problem of poor sales, declining profits, increased customer complaints, or defecting customers. Each of these is a symptom of a deeper problem. That is, something is causing a company's customers to leave. Is it lower prices offered by the competition? Or is it better service? Focusing on the symptoms and not the true problem is often referred to as the *iceberg principle*. Approximately 10 percent of an iceberg rises out of the ocean; the remaining 90 percent is below the surface. Preoccupied with the obstacle they can see, managers may fail to comprehend and confront the deeper problem, which remains submerged. Marketing researchers Terry

PRACTICING MARKETING RESEARCH

What Do You Need to Know

Are you trying to explore a topic, or are you trying to measure something? The best approach is to explore first and then measure. You can miss a lot of information if you skip the exploratory stage. In many instances where exploratory research was skipped, the questionnaire for the measurement phase neglected to ask the most important questions. In addition, the multiple response choices did not include some of the most important answers.

As an example, a company had just installed an employee software platform and wanted to measure employee satisfaction with it. The IT managers were about to jump in and ask people how satisfied they were with different elements of the software and postpone asking any questions about training and support. Luckily the marketing research team was able to persuade the IT managers to conduct some exploratory in-depth interviews first.

Findings from these exploratory interviews showed that training and support were primary concerns. The quantitative research phase was then designed to measure satisfaction with those two elements and to uncover any suggestions for improvement.

Eventually, the findings led to greatly improved levels of support and more tailored training methods for segments of the employee population.[5]

Questions

1. Do researchers always need to conduct exploratory research? If not, when is it not necessary?

2. If exploratory research seems to answer the management problem, is there any reason to do more research?

Grapentine, president of Grapentine Company and Diane, owner of Strategy Resource Company, discuss the role of marketing researchers in problem definition in the Practicing Marketing Research box on page 65.

Ensuring that the true problem has been defined is not always easy. Managers and marketing researchers must use creativity and good judgment. Cutting through to the heart of a problem is a bit like peeling an onion—you must take off one layer at a time. One approach to eliminating symptoms is to ask "What caused this to occur?" When the researcher can no longer answer this question, the real problem is at hand. For example, when a Saint Louis manufacturer of pumps faced a 7 percent decline in sales from the previous year, managers asked, "What caused this?" A look at sales across the product line showed that sales were up or about the same on all items except large, heavy-duty submersible pumps, whose sales were down almost 60 percent. They then asked, "What caused this?" Sales of the pump in the eastern and central divisions were about the same as in the previous year. However, in the western region, sales were zero! Once again they asked, "What caused this?" Further investigation revealed that a Japanese manufacturer was dumping a similar submersible pump in Western markets at about 50 percent of the Saint Louis manufacturer's wholesale price. This was the true problem. The manufacturer lobbied the Justice Department to fine the Japanese company and to issue a cease-and-desist order.

Whenever possible top management should be involved in defining the problem. This topic is discussed in the Practicing Marketing Research box that appears on page 65.

Translate the Management Problem into a Marketing Research Problem

Once the true management decision problem has been identified, it must be converted into a marketing research problem. The **marketing research problem** specifies what information is needed to solve the problem and how that information can be obtained efficiently and effectively. The **marketing research objective**, then, is the goal statement, defining the specific information needed to solve the marketing research problem. Managers must combine this information with their own experience and other related information to make a proper decision.

In contrast to the marketing research problem, the **management decision problem** is action-oriented. Management decision problems tend to be much broader in scope and far more general than marketing research problems, which must be narrowly defined and specific if the research effort is to be successful. Sometimes several research studies must be conducted to solve a broad management decision problem.

> **marketing research problem**
> A statement specifying the type of information needed by the decision maker to help solve the management decision problem and how that information can be obtained efficiently and effectively.

> **marketing research objective**
> A goal statement, defining the specific information needed to solve the marketing research problem.

> **management decision problem**
> A statement specifying the type of managerial action required to solve the problem.

Determine Whether the Information Already Exists

It often seems easier and more interesting to develop new information than to delve through old reports and data files to see whether the required information already exists. There is a tendency to assume that current data are superior to data collected in the past, as current data appear to be a "fix on today's situation." And because researchers have more control over the format and comprehensiveness of fresh data, they promise to be easier to work with. Yet, using existing data can save managers time and money if such data can answer the research question.

Research objectives must be as specific and unambiguous as possible. Remember that the entire research effort (in terms of time and money) is geared toward achieving the objectives. When the marketing researcher meets with a committee to learn the goals of a particular project, committee members may not fully agree on what is needed. We have learned from experience to go back to a committee (or the individual in charge) with a written list of research objectives. The researcher should then ask the manager, "If we accomplish the objectives on this list, will you have enough information to make informed decisions about the problem?" If the reply is yes, the manager should be asked to sign off on the objectives. The researcher should then give the manager a copy and keep a copy for the research files. Putting the agreed-on objectives in writing prevents the manager from saying later, "Hey, this is not the information I wanted." In a busy and hectic corporate environment, such misunderstandings happen more frequently than one might imagine.

Avoiding the Nice-to-Know Syndrome Even after conducting exploratory research, managers often tend to discuss research objectives in terms of broad areas of ignorance. They say, in effect, "Here are some things I don't know." A Starbucks executive might wonder: "You know, we already sell fresh-baked goods in our stores. . . . I wonder if people would buy frozen Starbucks pastries and rolls in supermarkets?" Maybe I'll ask this question on our out-of-home advertising media study. Unfortunately, this scenario usually leads to disappointment. There is nothing wrong with interesting findings, but they must also be *actionable*. That is, the findings must provide decision-making information. Accomplishment of a research objective has to do more than reduce management's level of ignorance. Unless all the research is exploratory, it should lead to a decision. Perhaps the best way to assure that research is actionable is to determine how the research results will be implemented. Asking a single question about purchase intent of Starbucks frozen baked goods in a grocery store is not actionable. So much more would have to be known—for example, type of goods, price points, packaging design, and so forth. Numerous taste tests would also have to be conducted.

Determine Whether the Question Can Be Answered

When marketing researchers promise more than they can deliver, they hurt the credibility of marketing research. It is extremely important for researchers to avoid being impelled—either by overeagerness to please or by managerial a machismo—into an effort that they know has a limited probability of success. In most cases, you can discern in advance the likelihood of success by identifying the following:

- Instances in which you know for certain that information of the type required exists or can be readily obtained.
- Situations in which you are fairly sure, based on similar prior experiences, that the information can be gathered.
- Cases in which you know that you are trying something quite new and there is a real risk of drawing a complete blank.

PRACTICING MARKETING RESEARCH

Importance of Top Management's Definition of the Management Problem

Researchers report that they receive incomplete, and even incorrect, answers if the person who commissions the study is not the ultimate decision maker. In one case, the commissioning agent (a midlevel manager) said the research was being conducted to learn about the market. In reality, the senior decision maker wanted to know whether version A or B would gain a bigger share of the market. The research did a great job of exploring the boundaries of the market, defining customer segments and their needs, and identifying likely competitors. But the senior decision maker found the research largely irrelevant because it did not tell him whether to go with version A or B.

While senior decision makers may say they are too busy to talk or insist on delegating the task to someone junior, researchers who have stood firm and insisted on talking to the senior person report the effort is worth it. "First, I asked to meet the [CEO] to discuss the firm's mission and strategy and how the research would help him make better decisions. When that wasn't an option, I wrote up a one-page description of the situation and the research objectives and asked to have the CEO approve it before I designed the research. When he didn't have time to look at it, I said I couldn't waste the firm's resources by starting without clear goals. *Then* I got his full attention. We met and, believe me, the CEO's needs were quite different from what I had been told. I was really glad I had insisted. If I'd waited until the research was done, I'd never have gotten his attention, and the research would have been largely irrelevant."[6]

Questions

1. Should top management always be involved in defining the management problem?
2. What tactics might marketing researchers use to get top management involved in problem definition?

State the Research Objectives

The culmination of the problem definition process is a statement of the research objectives. These objectives are stated in terms of the precise information necessary to address the marketing research problem/opportunity. Well-formulated objectives serve as a road map in pursuing the research project. They also serve as a standard that later will enable managers to evaluate the quality and value of the work by asking "Were the objectives met?" and "Do the recommendations flow logically from the objectives and the research findings?"

Research Objectives as Hypotheses   Often researchers state a research objective in the form of a hypothesis. A **hypothesis** is a conjectural statement about a relationship between two or more variables that can be tested with empirical data; it is considered to be plausible, given the available information. A good hypothesis will contain clear implications for testing stated relationships. For example, based on exploratory research, a researcher might hypothesize that a doubling of expenditures for billboards in cities of 300,000 or more population will increase the sales of Starbucks summer drinks by 15 percent. Alternatively, a second hypothesis might be that spending $30,000 for vehicle wraps in cities of 300,000 or more will have no significant impact on the sales of Starbucks' summer drinks.

> **hypothesis**
> A conjectural statement about a relationship between two or more variables that can be tested with empirical data.

Marketing Research Process

We have just discussed the first step in the marketing research process: identifying the problem/opportunity and stating the marketing research objectives. The other steps in the process are creating the research design, choosing the method of research, selecting the sampling procedure, collecting the data, analyzing the data, writing and presenting the report, and following up on any recommendations that were made as a result of the report (see Exhibit 3.2). The overview of the process in this section forms the foundation for the remainder of the text. The following chapters examine specific aspects of the marketing research process.

Creating the Research Design

The **research design** is a plan for addressing the research objectives or hypotheses. In essence, the researcher develops a structure or framework to answer a specific research problem/opportunity. There is no single best research design. Instead, different designs offer an array of choices, each with certain advantages and disadvantages. Ultimately, trade-offs are typically involved. A common trade-off is between research costs and the quality of the decision-making information provided. Generally speaking, the more precise and error-free the information obtained, the higher the cost. Another common trade-off is between time constraints and the type of research design selected. Overall, the researcher must attempt to provide management with the best information possible, subject to the various constraints under which he or she must operate. The researcher's first task is to decide whether the research will be descriptive or causal.

> **research design**
> The plan to be followed to answer the marketing research objectives.

> **descriptive studies**
> Research studies that answer the questions who, what, when, where, and how.

Descriptive Studies   **Descriptive studies** are conducted to answer who, what, when, where, and how questions. Implicit in descriptive research is the fact that management already knows or understands the underlying relationships among the variables in the problem. A **variable** is simply a symbol or concept that can assume any one of a set of values.

A descriptive study for Starbucks might include demographic and lifestyle characteristics of typical, light, and heavy patronizers of Starbucks stores, purchasers of Starbucks

> **variable**
> A symbol or concept that can assume any one of a set of values.

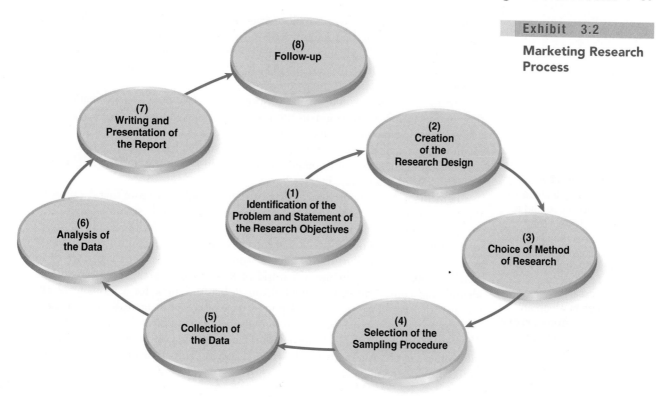

baked goods, purchasers of Starbucks sandwiches, and buyers of coffee to take home. Other questions might determine drive time from work or home to the nearest Starbucks and if purchasers pay by cash or credit.

Descriptive research can tell us that two variables, such as advertising and sales, seem to be somehow associated, but it cannot provide convincing evidence that high levels of advertising cause high sales. Because descriptive research can shed light on associations or relationships, it helps the researcher select variables for a causal study.

Causal Studies

In **causal studies**, the researcher investigates whether the value of one variable causes or determines the value of another variable, in an attempt to establish linkage between them. Experiments (see Chapter 8) often are used to measure causality. A **dependent variable** is a symbol or concept expected to be explained or affected by an independent variable. In contrast, an **independent variable** is a variable that the market researcher can, to some extent, manipulate, change, or alter. An independent variable in a research project is a presumed cause of or influence on the dependent variable, the presumed effect. For example, Starbucks would like to know whether the level of advertising (independent variable) determines the level of sales (dependent variable).

A causal study for Starbucks might involve changing one independent variable (for example, the number of direct mailings offering a 10 percent discount on a 1-pound bag of coffee over a 6-month period to target customers) and then observing the effect on coffee sales. Here, there is an appropriate causal order of events, or **temporal sequence**; the effect follows closely the hypothesized cause. Temporal sequence is one criterion that must be met for causality.

A second criterion for causality is **concomitant variation**—the degree to which a presumed cause (direct-mail promotion) and a presumed effect (coffee sales) occur together or vary together. If direct-mail promotions are a cause of increased coffee sales,

causal studies
Research studies that examine whether the value of one variable causes or determines the value of another variable.

dependent variable
A symbol or concept expected to be explained or influenced by the independent variable.

independent variable
A symbol or concept over which the researcher has some control and that is hypothesized to cause or influence the dependent variable.

temporal sequence
An appropriate causal order of events.

concomitant variation
The degree to which a presumed cause and a presumed effect occur or vary together.

then when the number of direct-mail promotions is increased, coffee sales should go up, and when the number of promotions is decreased, sales should fall. If, however, an increase in direct-mail promotions does not result in an increase in coffee sales, the researcher must conclude that the hypothesis about the relationship between direct-mail promotions and coffee sales is not supported.

An ideal situation would be one in which sales of coffee increased markedly every time Starbucks increased its e-mail promotions (up to a saturation level). But, alas, we live in a world where such perfection is rarely achieved. One additional saturation e-mail might bring a small increase in sales and the next e-mail a larger increment, or vice versa. And during the next 6-month period, an increase in e-mail promotions might produce no increase or even a decline in sales.

Remember, even perfect concomitant variation would not prove that A causes B. All the researcher could say is that the association makes the hypothesis more likely.

An important issue in studying causality is recognizing the possibility of **spurious association**, in which other variables are actually causing changes in the dependent variable. In an ideal situation, the researcher would demonstrate a total absence of other causal factors. However, in the real world of marketing research, it is very difficult to identify and control all other potential causal factors. Think for a moment of all the variables that could cause sales of 1-pound bags of coffee to increase or decrease—for example, prices, newspaper and television advertising, coupons, discounts, and weather. The researcher may be able to lower spurious associations by trying to hold constant these other factors. Alternatively, the researcher may look at changes in sales in similar socioeconomic areas.

> **spurious association**
> A relationship between a presumed cause and a presumed effect that occurs as a result of an unexamined variable or set of variables.

> **survey research**
> Research in which an interviewer (except in mail and Internet surveys) interacts with respondents to obtain facts, opinions, and attitudes.

> **observation research**
> Typically, descriptive research that monitors respondents' actions without direct interaction.

Choosing a Basic Method of Research

A research design, either descriptive or causal, is chosen based on a project's objectives. The next step is to select a means of gathering data. There are three basic research methods: (1) survey, (2) observation, and (3) experiment. Survey research is often descriptive in nature but can be causal. Observation research is typically descriptive, and experiment research is almost always causal.

Surveys **Survey research** involves an interviewer (except in mail and Internet surveys) who interacts with respondents to obtain facts, opinions, and attitudes. A questionnaire is used to ensure an orderly and structured approach to data gathering. Face-to-face interviews may take place in the respondent's home, a shopping mall, or a place of business.

Observations **Observation research** is examining patterns of behavior as opposed to asking consumers why they do what they do. This may involve people watching consumers or the use of a variety of machines. Kimberly-Clark, the maker of Huggies, Kleenex, and other household staples, outfits consumers with mini video cameras mounted to visors and linked to a recording device. Paid participants wear the somewhat strange-looking eye gear, known internally as the Consumer Vision System (CVS), while doing chores or shopping.

Under the system, K-C discovered that mothers who used Huggies Baby Wash, a bathing lotion, had trouble holding the bottle and needed two hands to open and

Scanning bar code information is a means of observation research that is widely used today.

dispense its contents. "[Moms] almost always have to have one hand on the baby at one time," said Becky Walter, K-C director-innovation, design and testing.[7]

K-C redesigned the product with a grippable bottle and a large lid that could easily be lifted with a thumb. The result was a significant increase in market share. Observation research is discussed in detail in Chapter 7.

Experiments **Experiments** are the third method researchers use to gather data. Experiment research is distinguished by the researcher's changing one or more independent variables—price, package, design, shelf space, advertising theme, or advertising expenditures—and observing the effects of those changes on a dependent variable (usually sales). The objective of experiments is to measure causality. The best experiments are those in which all factors other than the ones being manipulated are held constant. This enables the researcher to infer with confidence that changes in sales, for example, are caused by changes in the amount of money spent on advertising.

Holding all other factors constant in the external environment is a monumental and costly, if not impossible, task. Factors such as competitors' actions, weather, and economic conditions in various markets are beyond the control of the researcher. One way researchers attempt to control factors that might influence the dependent variable is to use a laboratory experiment—that is, an experiment conducted in a test facility rather than in the natural environment. Researchers sometimes create simulated supermarket environments, give consumers scrip (play money), and then ask them to shop as they normally would for groceries. By varying package design or color over several time periods, for example, the researcher can determine which package is most likely to stimulate sales. Although laboratory techniques can provide valuable information, it is important to recognize that the consumer is not in a natural environment; how people act in a test facility may differ from how they act in an actual shopping situation. Experiments are discussed in detail in Chapter 8.

> **experiments**
> Research to measure causality, in which the researcher changes one or more independent variables and observes the effect of the changes on the dependent variable.

Selecting the Sampling Procedure

A sample is a subset from a larger population. Although the basic nature of the sample is specified in the research design, selecting the sampling procedure is a separate step in the research process. Several questions must be answered before a sampling procedure is selected. First, the population or universe of interest must be defined. This is the group from which the sample will be drawn. It should include all the people whose opinions, behaviors, preferences, attitudes, and so on will yield information needed to answer the research problem—for example, all persons who eat Mexican food at least once every 60 days.

After the population has been defined, the next question is whether to use a probability sample or a nonprobability sample. A **probability sample** is a sample for which every element in the population has a known nonzero probability of being selected. Such samples allow the researcher to estimate how much sampling error is present in a given study. All samples that cannot be considered probability samples are nonprobability samples. **Nonprobability samples** are those in which the chances of selection for the various elements in the population are unknown. Researchers cannot statistically calculate the reliability of a nonprobability sample; that is, they cannot determine the degree of sampling error that can be expected. Sampling is the topic of Chapter 13.

> **probability sample**
> A subset of a population where every element in the population has a known nonzero chance of being selected.

> **nonprobability sample**
> A subset of a population in which the chances of selection for the various elements in the population are unknown.

Collecting the Data

Most survey-based data are now collected on the Internet. Interviewer-based data collection is done by marketing research field services. Field service firms, found throughout the country, specialize in collecting data through personal and telephone interviewing on a subcontract basis. A typical interviewer-based research study involves data collection in several cities and requires working with a comparable number of field service firms. To ensure that all subcontractors do everything exactly the same way, detailed field instructions should be developed for every job. Nothing should be left to chance; in particular, no interpretations of procedures should be left to the subcontractors.

In addition to doing interviewing, field service firms often provide group research facilities, mall intercept locations, test product storage, and kitchen facilities for preparing test food products. They may also conduct retail audits (counting the amount of product sold from retail shelves).

Analyzing the Data

After the data have been collected, the next step in the research process is data analysis. The purpose of this analysis is to interpret and draw conclusions from the mass of collected data. The marketing researcher may use a variety of techniques, beginning with simple frequency analysis and culminating in complex multivariate techniques. Data analysis will be discussed later in the text.

Writing and Presenting the Report

After data analysis is completed, the researcher must prepare the report and communicate the conclusions and recommendations to management. This is a key step in the process because a marketing researcher who wants project conclusions acted on must convince the manager that the results are credible and justified by the data collected.

The researcher usually will be required to present both written and oral reports on a project. The nature of the audience must be kept in mind when these reports are being prepared and presented. The oral report should begin with a clear statement of the research objectives, followed by an outline of the methodology. A summary of major findings should come next. The report should end with a presentation of conclusions and recommendations for management. In today's fast-paced world of marketing research, long, elaborately written reports are virtually a thing of the past. Decision makers today typically want only a copy of the PowerPoint presentation.

Judging the Quality of a Report   Because most people who enter marketing become research users rather than research suppliers, it is important to know what to look for in a research report. The ability to evaluate a research report is crucial. As with many other items we purchase, the quality of a research report is not always readily apparent. Nor does paying a high price for a project necessarily guarantee superior quality. The basis for measuring a report's quality lies in the research proposal. Does the report meet the objectives established in the proposal? Has the methodology outlined in the proposal been followed? Are the conclusions based on logical deductions from the data analysis? Do the recommendations seem prudent, given the conclusions?

Using the Internet to Disseminate Reports   It is becoming increasingly commonplace for research suppliers and clients to publish reports directly to the Web. Most companies, such as Texas Instruments, locate this material not in public areas on the Web but on corporate intranets or in password-protected locations on Web sites. Publishing reports on the Web has a number of advantages:

1. The reports become immediately accessible to managers and other authorized and interested parties worldwide.

2. The reports can incorporate full multimedia presentation, including text, graphs, various types of animation, audio comments, and video clips.

3. The reports are fully searchable. Suppose a manager is interested in any material relating to advertising. Instead of manually scanning a long and detailed report for such mentions, he or she can search the report for comments relating to advertising.

Following Up

After a company has spent a considerable amount of effort and money on marketing research and the preparation of a report, it is important that the findings be used. Management should determine whether the recommendations were followed and, if not, why not. As you will learn in the next section, one way to increase the likelihood that research conducted by a corporate marketing department will be used is to minimize conflict between that department and other departments within the company.

Managing the Research Process

The Research Request

Before conducting a research project, a company such as Microsoft® might require approval of a formal research request. Moderate- and large-size retailers, manufacturers, and nonprofit organizations often use the **research request** as a basis for determining which projects will be funded. Typically, in larger organizations there are far more requests by managers for marketing research information than monies available to conduct such research. Requiring a research request is a formalized approach to allocating scarce research dollars.

> ➤ **research request**
> An internal document used by large organizations that describes a potential research project, its benefits to the organization, and estimated costs; it must be formally approved before a research project can begin.

It is very important for the brand manager, new product specialist, or whoever is in need of research information to clearly state in the formal research request why the desired information is critical to the organization. Otherwise, the person with approval authority may fail to see why the expenditure is necessary.

In smaller organizations, the communication link between brand managers and marketing researchers is much closer. Their day-to-day contact often removes the need for a formal research request. Instead, decisions to fund research are made on an ad hoc basis by the marketing manager or the director of marketing research.

Completion and approval of the request represent a disciplined approach to identifying research problems and obtaining funding to solve them. The degree of effort expended at this step in the research process will be reflected in the quality of the information provided to the decision maker because a well-conceived research request will guide the design, data-gathering, analysis, and reporting processes toward a highly focused objective. The sections of a formal research request are as follows:

1. *Action.* The decision maker should describe the action to be taken on the basis of the research. This will help the decision maker focus on what information should be obtained and guide the researcher in creating the research design and in analyzing the results.

2. *Origin.* The decision maker should state the events that led to a need for a decision. This will help the researcher understand more deeply the nature of the management decision problem.

3. *Information.* The decision maker should list the questions that she or he needs to have answered to take action. Carefully considering the questions will improve the efficiency of the research.

4. *Use.* This section should explain how each piece of information will be used to help make the actual decision. By giving logical reasons for each part of the research, it will ensure that the questions make sense in light of the action to be taken.

5. *Target groups and subgroups.* By describing those from whom information must be gathered to address the research problem, this section will help the researcher design the sample procedure for the research project.

6. *Logistics.* Time and budget constraints always affect the research technique chosen for a project. For this reason, approximations of the amount of money available and the amount of time left before results are needed must be included as a part of the research request.

7. *Comments.* Any other comments relevant to the research project must be stated so that, once again, the researcher can fully understand the nature of the problem.

Request for Proposal

The research request is an internal document used by management to determine which projects to fund. A **request for proposal (RFP)** is a solicitation sent to marketing research suppliers inviting them to submit a formal proposal, including a bid. The RFP is the lifeblood of a research supplier. Receiving it is the initial step in getting new business and, therefore, revenue.

A typical RFP provides background data on why a study is to be conducted, outlines the research objectives, describes a methodology, and suggests a time frame. In some

> ➤ **request for proposal (RFP)**
> A solicitation sent to marketing research suppliers inviting them to submit a formal proposal, including a bid.

PRACTICING
MARKETING RESEARCH

Where Do I Send the RFP?

For most companies, it's best to pinpoint suppliers through extensive research or professional referrals, Linda Stevenson says. "I like to go through the networking route," she says. "I can pick up the phone and say, 'Who would you use for this project?'

Maryanne Spillane McInturf recommends honing in on a very select group of suppliers to target. "Start with a manageable number of firms you want to approach," she says. "It can get overwhelming if you do a dozen." By pinpointing five or six suppliers who offer the specific services you're looking for or have completed similar projects in the past, "you're not wasting their time, and they're not wasting your time," she says.

"I try to get the company that's doing the written proposal to also come in and do a presentation, if it's possible," Spillane McInturf says. The more information the supplier has from you and the more information you have from your supplier, the better the match—and the results—can be.[8]

Questions

1. Each year Quirks publishes the Researcher Source Book that lists suppliers by state, alphabetically. Each listing describes the specialties of the firm. Would this be a good starting point for finding suppliers to include in an RFP mailing list?

2. Do you think that the best way to get the lowest price for a project is to send out as many RFPs as possible?

RFPs, the supplier is asked to recommend a methodology or even help develop the research objectives. Most RFPs also ask for (1) a detailed cost breakdown, (2) the supplier's experience in relevant areas, and (3) references. Usually, a due date for the proposal will be specified.

Maryanne Spillane McInturf, director of marketing and communications at Boston College's Carroll School of Management and Linda M. Stevenson, president of Lucidity Works, a Rochester, New York-based provider of search, retrieval, and report generation software, discusses where to send the RFP after it is completed in the Practicing Marketing Research box below.

Suppliers must exercise care in preparing their proposals in response to the RFP. More than one client has said, "We find the quality of the proposals indicative of the quality of work produced by the firm." Thus, a research supplier that doesn't have the necessary time to adequately prepare a proposal should simply not submit a bid.

The Marketing Research Proposal

When marketing research suppliers receive an RFP, they respond to the potential client with a research proposal. The **research proposal** is a document that presents the research objectives, research design, time line, and cost of a project. We have included an actual proposal (disguised) prepared by two project managers at Decision Analyst (a large international marketing research firm) in Appendix 3-A. Most research proposals today are short (3 to 5 pages) and are transmitted back to the potential client as an e-mail attachment. A proposal for the federal government can run 50 pages or longer. The federal proposal will include a number of standard forms mandated by the government.

> **research proposal**
> A document developed, usually in response to an RFP, that presents the research objectives, research design, time line, and cost of a project.

Most proposals contain the following elements:

I. Title Page

    This includes the title of the project from the RFP, the names of the preparers of the proposal, and contact information; who the proposal is being prepared for; and the date.

II. Statement of the Research Objectives.

    These are often stated in the RFP. If not, they must be determined as described earlier in the chapter.

III. Study Design

    This presents a statement of how the data will be gathered and who will be sampled and the sample size.

IV. Areas of Questioning

    This is not found in all proposals, but in our experience we have found it to be very helpful. It is a tentative list of survey topics based on the research objectives.

V. Data Analysis

    This states which techniques will be used to analyze the data.

VI. Personnel Involved

    This provides a complete list of all supervisory and analytical personnel who will be involved in the project and a short vita of each. Each person's responsibility is also outlined. This element is typically not included when the client and supplier have an ongoing relationship. It is mandatory in most government work.

VII. Specifications and Assumptions

Most RFPs are relatively short and don't spell out every detail. In order to make certain that the supplier and potential client are on the same page, it is a good idea to list the specifications and assumptions that were made when creating the proposal (see Appendix 3-A).

Exhibit 3.3 details the benefits of a good proposal to both the client and the supplier.

VIII. Services

This spells out exactly what the research supplier will do (see Appendix 3-A). For example, who is designing the questionnaire? Is it the client, the supplier, or is it a joint effort? Again, the purpose is to make sure that the client and the research supplier operate from the same set of expectations.

IX. Cost

This specifies the cost and payment schedule.

X. Timing

This states when various phases of the project will be completed and provides a final completion date.

Preparing proposals may be the most important function a research supplier performs inasmuch as proposals, and their acceptance or rejection, determine the revenue of the firm. If a research firm's proposals are not accepted, the company will have no funds and will ultimately go out of business! Moreover, if the price that is quoted is too low, the researcher may get the job but lose money. If the price is too high, the proposal may be outstanding, but the researcher will lose the work to a competitor.

EXHIBIT 3.3	Benefits of a Good Proposal
Client	**Supplier**
Serves as a road map for the project	Serves as a road map for the project
<ul><li>specifies research methodology</li><li>specifies time line</li><li>specifies deliverables</li><li>specifies projected costs</li><li>allows for planning-team member involvement and resource allocation</li></ul>	<ul><li>identifies specific responsibilities of the vendor</li><li>identifies the role the client has in fielding the research</li><li>allows for planning-team member involvement and resource allocation</li></ul>
Ensures that competing vendors carefully consider:	Serves as a valuable tool for managing client expectations, especially when the client:
<ul><li>project specifications</li><li>research design/methodology</li><li>project cost</li></ul>	<ul><li>contributes to delays or revises project time line</li><li>mandates changes to project scope</li><li>requests additional or alternative deliverables</li><li>cancels the project</li></ul>
Ensures that the selected vendor has an explicit understanding of business decisions the research will affect	Provides an objective method for clients to examine vendor qualifications
Prompts the client to consider unique capabilities that individual firms offer, which might contribute to project success	

Source: Matthew Singer, "Writer's Lock," *Marketing Research* (Fall 2006), p. 38.

What to Look for in a Marketing Research Supplier

Market Directions, a Kansas City marketing research firm, asked marketing research clients around the United States to rate the importance of several statements about research companies and research departments. Replies were received from a wide range of industries, resulting in the following top 10 list of desirable qualities in marketing researchers:

1. Maintains client confidentiality.
2. Is honest.
3. Is punctual.
4. Is flexible.
5. Delivers against project specifications.
6. Provides high-quality output.
7. Is responsive to the client's needs.
8. Has high-quality control standards.
9. Is customer-oriented in interactions with client.
10. Keeps the client informed throughout a project.[9]

The two most important qualities, confidentiality and honesty, are ethical issues; the remaining factors relate to managing the research function and maintaining good communications.

Good communications are a necessity. Four of the qualities on the top 10 list—flexibility, responsiveness to clients' needs, customer orientation, and keeping the client informed—are about good communications. A successful marketing research organization requires good communications both within the research company and with clients.

How important is communication? Consider this: Managers spend at least 80 percent of every working day in direct communication with others. In other words, 48 minutes of every hour are spent in meetings, on the telephone, or talking informally. The other 20 percent of a typical manager's time is spent doing desk work, most of which is communication in the form of reading and writing.[10] Communications permeate every aspect of managing the marketing research function.

What Motivates Decision Makers to Use Research Information?

When research managers communicate effectively, generate quality data, control costs, and deliver information on time, they increase the probability that decision makers will use the research information they provide. Yet academic research shows that political factors and preconceptions can also influence whether research information is used. Specifically, the determinants of whether or not a manager uses research data are (1) conformity to prior expectations, (2) clarity of presentation, (3) research quality, (4) political acceptability within the firm, and (5) lack of challenge to the status quo.[11] Managers and researchers both agree that technical quality is the most important determinant of research use. However, managers are less likely to use research that does not conform to preconceived notions or is not politically acceptable. This does not mean, of course, that researchers should alter their findings to meet management's preconceived notions.

Marketing managers in industrial firms tend to use research findings more than do their counterparts in consumer goods organizations.[12] This tendency among industrial managers is attributed to a greater exploratory objective in information collection, a greater degree of formalization of organizational structure, and a lesser degree of surprise in the information collected.

SUMMARY

The process for correctly defining the research problem consists of a series of steps: (1) recognize the problem or opportunity, (2) find out why the information is being sought, (3) understand the decision-making environment, (4) use the symptoms to help clarify the problem, (5) translate the management problem into a marketing research problem, (6) determine whether the information already exists, (7) determine whether the question can really be answered, and (8) state the research objectives. If the problem is not defined correctly, the remainder of the research project will be a waste of time and money.

The steps in the market research process are as follows:

1. Identification of the problem/opportunity and statement of the marketing research objectives

2. Creation of the research design

3. Choice of the method of research

4. Selection of the sampling procedure

5. Collection of data

6. Analysis of data

7. Preparation and presentation of the research report

8. Follow-up

In specifying a research design, the researcher must determine whether the research will be descriptive or causal. Descriptive studies are conducted to answer who, what, when, where, and how questions. Causal studies are those in which the researcher investigates whether one variable (independent) causes or influences another variable (dependent). The next step in creating a research design is to select a research method: survey, observation, or experiment. Survey research involves an interviewer (except in mail and Internet surveys) interacting with a respondent to obtain facts, opinions, and attitudes. Observation research, in contrast, monitors respondents' actions and does not rely on direct interaction with people. An experiment is distinguished by the fact that the researcher changes one or more variables and observes the effects of those changes on another variable (usually sales). The objective of most experiments is to measure causality.

A sample is a subset of a larger population. A probability sample is one for which every element in the population has a known nonzero probability of being selected. All samples that cannot be considered probability samples are nonprobability samples. Any sample in which the chances of selection for the various elements in the population are unknown can be considered a nonprobability sample.

In larger organizations, it is common to have a research request prepared after the statement of research objectives. The research request generally describes the action to be taken on the basis of the research, the reason for the need for the information, the questions management wants to have answered, how the information will be used, the target groups from whom information must be gathered, the amount of time and money available to complete the project, and any other information pertinent to the request. The request for proposal (RFP) is the document used by clients to solicit proposals from marketing research suppliers.

Marketing research proposals are developed in response to an RFP. In some cases, the proposals are created based on an informal request such as in a telephone conversation between a client and research supplier. The research proposal gives the research objectives, research design, time line, and cost. Research proposals are the tool that generates revenue for the research firm.

Good communications are the foundation of research management and the basis for getting decision makers to use research information. The information communicated to a decision maker depends on the type of research being conducted.

KEY TERMS & DEFINITIONS

opportunity identification Using marketing research to find and evaluate new opportunities.

situation analysis Studying the decision-making environment within which the marketing research will take place.

exploratory research Preliminary research conducted to increase understanding of a concept, to clarify the exact nature of the problem to be solved, or to identify important variables to be studied.

pilot studies Surveys using a limited number of respondents and often employing less rigorous sampling techniques than are employed in large, quantitative studies.

experience surveys Discussions with knowledgeable individuals, both inside and outside the organization, who may provide insights into the problem.

case analysis Reviewing information from situations that are similar to the current one.

marketing research problem A statement specifying the type of information needed by the decision maker to help solve the management decision problem and how that information can be obtained efficiently and effectively.

marketing research objective A goal statement, defining the specific information needed to solve the marketing research problem.

management decision problem A statement specifying the type of managerial action required to solve the problem.

hypothesis A conjectural statement about a relationship between two or more variables that can be tested with empirical data.

research design The plan to be followed to answer the marketing research objectives.

descriptive studies Research studies that answer the questions who, what, when, where, and how.

variable A symbol or concept that can assume any one of a set of values.

causal studies Research studies that examine whether the value of one variable causes or determines the value of another variable.

dependent variable A symbol or concept expected to be explained or influenced by the independent variable.

independent variable A symbol or concept over which the researcher has some control and that is hypothesized to cause or influence the dependent variable.

temporal sequence An appropriate causal order of events.

concomitant variation The degree to which a presumed cause and a presumed effect occur or vary together.

spurious association A relationship between a presumed cause and a presumed effect that occurs as a result of an unexamined variable or set of variables.

survey research Research in which an interviewer (except in mail and Internet surveys) interacts with respondents to obtain facts, opinions, and attitudes.

observation research Typically, descriptive research that monitors respondents' actions without direct interaction.

experiments Research to measure causality, in which the researcher changes one or more independent variables and observes the effect of the changes on the dependent variable.

probability sample A subset of a population where every element in the population has a known nonzero chance of being selected.

nonprobability sample A subset of a population in which the chances of selection for the various elements in the population are unknown.

research request An internal document used by large organizations that describes a potential research project, its benefits to the organization, and estimated costs; it must be formally approved before a research project can begin.

request for proposal (RFP) A solicitation sent to marketing research suppliers inviting them to submit a formal proposal, including a bid.

research proposal A document developed, usually in response to an RFP, that states the research objectives, research design, time line, and cost.

QUESTIONS FOR REVIEW & CRITICAL THINKING

1. The definition of the research problem is one of the critical steps in the research process. Why? Who should be involved in this process?

2. What role does exploratory research play in the marketing research process? How does exploratory research differ from other forms of marketing research?

3. Give some examples of symptoms of problems and then suggest some underlying real problems.

4. Give several examples of situations in which it would be better to take a census of the population than a sample.

5. Critique the following methodologies and suggest more appropriate alternatives:

   a. A supermarket is interested in determining its image. Cashiers drop a short questionnaire into the grocery bag of each customer prior to bagging the groceries.

   b. To assess the extent of its trade area, a shopping mall stations interviewers in the parking lot every Monday and Friday evening. After people park their cars, interviewers walk up to them and ask them for their zip codes.

   c. To assess the potential for new horror movies starring alien robots, a major studio invites people to call a 900 number and vote yes if they would like to see such movies or no if they would not. Each caller is billed a $2 charge.

6. You have been charged with determining how to attract more business majors to your school. Outline the steps you would take, including sampling procedures, to accomplish this task.

7. What can researchers do to increase the chances that decision makers will use the marketing research information they generate?

8. Explain the critical role of the research proposal.

9. [Team exercise] Divide the class into teams of four or five. Half of the teams should prepare short RFPs on the following topics:
   a. Food on campus
   b. Role of fraternities and sororities on campus
   c. Entertainment in your city
   d. Your university Web site
   e. Role of student internships in education
   f. Online purchasing of school supplies
   g. Purchasing music on the Internet

The RFPs should state clearly and precisely the research objectives and other pertinent information. The remaining teams should create proposals in response to the RFPs.

WORKING THE NET

1. Go to the Internet and search on "intranet 3 future." Report your findings to the class.
2. Describe how putting research reports on the Web can benefit managers.
3. Go to a search engine and type "writing RFPs." Explain what kind of help is available to prepare RFPs.

REAL-LIFE RESEARCH • 3.1

Let's Go Out to Eat!

In retail environments, creating positive customer experiences can make any customer more valuable to the business, sometimes increasing the average transaction amount up to 50 percent. However, in a restaurant environment, because customers are rarely in a position to order and eat twice as much as they planned, there is less opportunity to increase the transaction amount by providing a great experience. Still, creating a positive experience for the customer and executing service standards has been shown to effect at least some increase in average ticket amounts.

Although the results are not as dramatic as those for retail, customers who have a highly satisfying experience in a restaurant spend slightly more money than those who were just satisfied (Figure 1). Part of this increase can be attributed to up-sell effects when a

Figure 1

**"Highly Satisfied"
Guests Spend
Slightly More than
"Satisfied" Guests**

▶ Drive-thru guests show the largest difference in average ticket amount

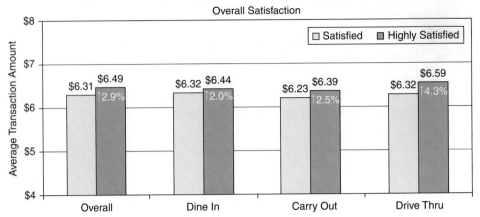

SMG quick-service restaurant client

server mentions a particular appetizer or menu item (Figure 2). However, higher average ticket amounts are not merely the result of suggestive selling; restaurant staff can increase average check amounts by creating a great dining experience that customers want to enhance and make longer by sampling additional menu items. The immediate effect on sales from providing a great customer experience may be small, but it makes a big impact on the business when multiplied over thousands of transactions for an individual restaurant or restaurant chain.

Pretty Intuitive

Customers who have a highly satisfying experience tell us time and again that they are going to return to that restaurant more often than those who don't have a highly satisfying experience. That's pretty intuitive, right? What may not be as intuitive is the difference between a good experience and a great experience. When the restaurant is working well—the server is friendly and knowledgeable, the food tastes great, and the atmosphere is humming—that's when you create a loyal guest. On average, results show that when comparing those who say they had an exceptional experience to those who were merely satisfied, twice as many who had the exceptional experience are likely to return and

Figure 2

**"Offered Refills" and
"Suggested Menu
Items" Show Largest
Difference in
Average Spend**

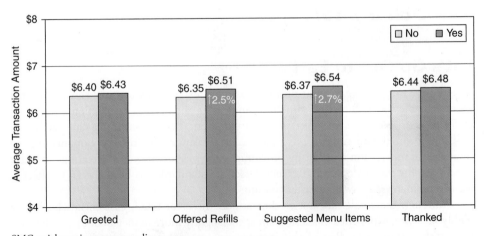

SMG quick-service restaurant client

▶ Guests are three times as likely to recommend to others and twice as likely to return if they were "Highly Satisfied" vs. "Satisfied" with their experience

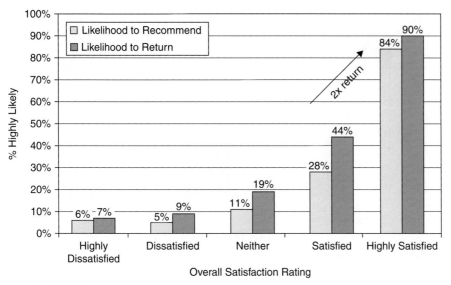

SMG fast-food client

three times as many are likely to recommend that restaurant to their friend and family (Figure 3). This pattern is true for restaurants at all ends of the service spectrum, from quick-serivce to white-tablecloth. Simply put, creating a great customer experience creates loyal customers.

Just because someone says they are going to do something, they may not necessarily follow through. When someone says that they are loyal to a restaurant, does that mean they really are? Maybe they say they are going to come back more often, but will they really do it? This can be measured by tying customer satisfaction results to credit-card or loyalty-club data. For one casual-dining concept, customers who said they were highly likely to come back in the next 30 days did so at almost twice the rate of customers who said they were likely to return in the next 30 days (Figure 4). Imagine the impact on traffic and revenue if restaurants could provide the kind of experience that would convert just 5 or 10 percent of their guests from having good experiences to having the kind of experience that would engender this kind of loyalty.

Spend More Money

One interesting finding is that when customers visit a restaurant because of a recommendation or a previous positive experience, they actually spend more money. This is in sharp contrast to the people who visited primarily because of a promotion or advertisement. Those people actually spent less than people who visited for any other reason. In one quick-service restaurant (QSR) example, it was found that customers who visited because of a positive recommendation from a trusted friend or family member spent approximately 14 percent more than those who visited because of a promotion or advertisement.

Servers Are the Key

How do restaurants build those positive experiences that customers want to repeat and recommend to others? It starts at the front line. Servers are the key to converting a

Figure 4

Intent to Return Mirrors Actual Return in Next 30 Days

▶ Customers who say they are "Highly Likely to Return" actually return at twice the rate

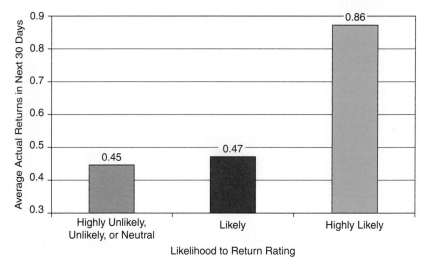

SMG casual-dining client

customer from merely satisfied to loyal. Executing a simple set of service standards can have a big impact on driving guest satisfaction with their experience. Figure 5 illustrates that by simply greeting guests, checking back with them regularly, thanking them for their business, and ensuring that a manager is visible in the dining room, restaurants can nearly quadruple guest satisfaction compared to a guest who receives zero or just one of those behaviors. So although retaining the best servers is the most effective way to drive satisfaction and loyalty, ensuring that simple service behaviors are consistently executed may be the most attainable way to improve the guests' experiences.

Figure 5

Less Than Half of Your Customers Experience All of Your Basic Service Standards

▶ Overall satisfaction increases significantly with each additional standard that is delivered

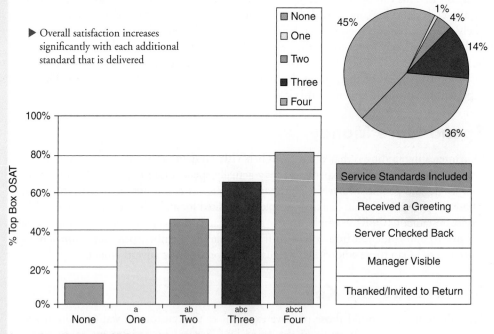

Comparison groups: ABCDE
Lowercase letters represent significantly lower scores at the 95% confidence level

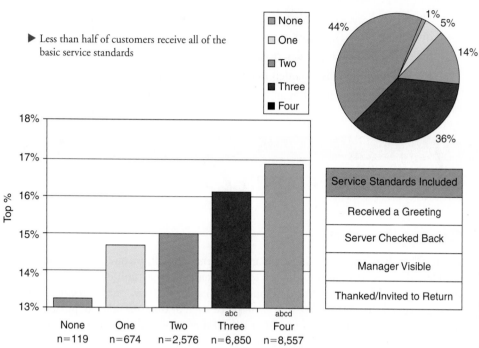

▶ Less than half of customers receive all of the basic service standards

Service Standards Experienced

Legend: None, One, Two, Three, Four

Pie chart: 44%, 1%, 5%, 14%, 36%

Service Standards Included
Received a Greeting
Server Checked Back
Manager Visible
Thanked/Invited to Return

None n=119	One n=674	Two n=2,576	Three n=6,850 abc	Four n=8,557 abcd

Lowercase letters represent significantly lower scores at the 95% confidence level

Figure 6

Tip Percentage Increases Significantly When More Than Three Service Standards Are Delivered

One way managers and executives can create buy-in from servers is to go back to the data and show them the kind of impact their actions can have on their own income. By again tying guest feedback to transaction information, it can be shown that guests who experienced all of the prescribed service behaviors are not only more loyal to the restaurant but they really do tip their servesrs better. In fact, for one casual dining concept there was a marked increase in tip value when guests experienced all of the service behaviors instead of just one (Figure 6). Everyboldy in the restaurant wins when service becomes the focus.[13]

▶ Restaurants with a greater percentage of customers saying they are 'Highly Likely to Recommend' have better comp sales

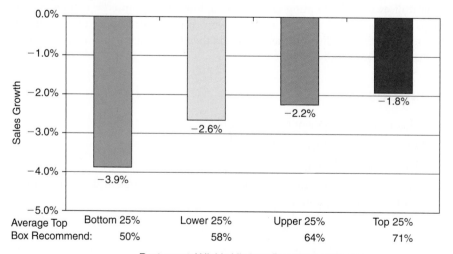

Bar chart — Sales Growth:

	Bottom 25%	Lower 25%	Upper 25%	Top 25%
Sales Growth	−3.9%	−2.6%	−2.2%	−1.8%
Average Top Box Recommend:	50%	58%	64%	71%

Restaurants' Highly Likely to Recommend Scores

Note: SMG refers to Service Management Group, a Kansas City, MO marketing research firm.

Figure 7

Higher Customer Loyalty Can Help Reduce the Impact of a Difficult Economic Environment

Questions

1. Would you say that this was an exploratory study? If not, what are the research questions?
2. Is this research causal or descriptive? Why?
3. Explain how the Olive Garden might use this information; McDonald's.
4. What might be included in an RFP to do further research?

REAL-LIFE RESEARCH • 3.2

Cessna Aircraft

Cessna Aircraft is one of the largest manufacturers of small, private-business airplanes in the United States. It is always looking for new market opportunities, which may involve cultivating existing segments or developing and exploiting new ones. Recent research by Cessna revealed that although a very small percentage of the total adult population enrolls in private pilot-training programs, about half of the individuals who enter a training program complete it. And the number of people with pilot's licenses is increasing. Eventually, about one out of five people with a private pilot's license buys a private airplane. Thus, pilot training is an important part of the total market for Cessna and its competitors.

A small percentage of pilots are women. Similarly, a small percentage of the students in training programs are women; this figure has shown only a slight increase in recent years. Moreover, there are very few women instructors in pilot-training programs. A substantial number of women have the necessary skills, time, and income to enroll in and complete the basic training program. Cessna is interested in learning why more women don't enter the program and how the program and/or promotional materials could appeal to and motivate more women to consider or inquire about such programs.

There may be several specific market segments worthy of examination. These include wives of pilots, businesswomen, women who have the income and desire to travel for pleasure, and young women who seek future employment as corporate aircraft pilots. Cessna realizes that the limiting factor may be low levels of interest or motivation and perhaps attitudes toward the desirability of women pilots. But opportunities for women are increasing in many different fields. Cessna therefore believes that a vital market may exist that is not being fully exploited.

Questions

1. What is the management decision problem?
2. Define the marketing research problem(s).
3. Develop the marketing research objectives.
4. Explain how a marketing researcher should use the problem definition process to answer the above questions.

APPENDIX 3A
A MARKETING RESEARCH PROPOSAL

Decision Analyst, Inc.
Proposal to Conduct
a Brand Equity Study

Prepared For:
Fun City Gaming, Inc.

Prepared by:
Kathi McKenzie & Sally Danforth
January 2013

Background

Fun City Gaming, Inc. currently operates a multilevel dockside riverboat casino and a land-based pavilion with three restaurants and a hotel, all located on the Arlen River. The casino offers 1,500 slot machines and 70 table games, and is the "flagship" of the Fun City franchise. The Fun City Casino has four primary competitors currently operating in the area, all within a roughly 30-mile radius of the Fun City. The Fun City Casino ranks second in revenue but first in profit among these competitors. In addition to these competitors, additional competition will be provided by the planned "River Wild" casino, which will likely begin construction in about a year. This casino will be located in Saint George, minutes from the Fun City Casino.

Fun City is currently undergoing a large redevelopment, involving construction of a completely new gaming vessel, significant upgrades to the pavilion, addition of new restaurants, and a new parking garage. The gaming vessel will feature 2,500 slot machines, 84 table games, high-limit gaming areas, and upgraded décor. The new Fun City will offer superior features to the current product as well as to primary competitors.

In order to be financially feasible, this project must increase business from current customers as well as attract customers from competitive casinos, some of whom may have to travel past competitive casinos to arrive at Fun City. In addition, the new offering should be especially attractive to premium casino players.

Objectives

The overall objective of this study would be to help management position the new Fun City offering. Key questions to be addressed include:

- What should be the positioning of the new casino?
- Should the Fun City name be used, or should it be rebranded?
- If rebranded, what name should be used?

Study Design

This study would be conducted using a targeted telephone survey among 800 gamblers within a 100-mile radius of the Fun City Casino location. Specifically, we will survey 400 within the Arlen Valley portion of this area and 400 in the area eastward, where the majority of current/future competition lies. Respondents will be screened based on past 12-month casino usage.

Areas of Questioning

Decision Analyst would work closely with Fun City Gaming in developing the questionnaire. Assuming that we have three to four potential positionings to test, tentative survey topics would include:

- Current casino usage and gambling behavior.
- Awareness and overall rating for the Fun City name, as well as names of key competitors and other names owned by Fun City Gaming which might be used for the new casino.
- Rating of the Fun City and key competitors on several (8 to 10) image attributes.

- Exposure to brief description of the "new" (redeveloped) casino. Each respondent would be exposed to the description with *one* of the potential positionings. This will result in a readable sample size for each positioning.
- Overall rating and rating on key image attributes for the "new" casino.
- Rating of the Fun City name and other potential names on overall appeal and fit with this description.
- Projected use of new casino; effect on gambling habits and share of casino visits.

Data will be analyzed both by area of residence and by gambling value (high/medium/low value gamblers).

Data Analysis

Factor analysis will be conducted, and the factors that are most related to the overall rating of the casino will be identified. On the basis of these factors, a perceptual map will be created to show visually the relationship between the current Fun City and competitive brands, based on brand image. The image projected by the new casino description will also be shown on this map, and a gap analysis conducted to highlight possible differences in image projected by each of the three to four positionings.

Personnel Involved

This project will be supervised by Kathi McKenzie and Sally DanGorth. Kathi will be the overall supervisor and Sally will be responsible for the data analysis and presentation. (*Note:* A short bio of each person would normally be attached.)

Specifications/Assumptions

The cost estimate is based on the following assumptions:

- Number of completed interviews = 800
- Average interview length = 20 minutes
- Average completion rate = 0.62
- Complete per hour Assumed incidence = 25%
- No open-ended questions
- Type of sample: targeted random digit
- Up to two banners of statistical tables in Word format
- Factor analysis, two perceptual maps (total sample and high-value gambler), and gap analysis
- Report Personal presentation, if desired

Services

Decision Analyst, Inc. would:

- Develop the questionnaire, in conjunction with Fun City Gaming management.
- Generate sample within the target area.
- Program the survey.

■ Manage and administer the project.
■ Monitor and oversee all telephone interviewing.
■ Process data, specify cross-tabulations, and compile statistical tables.
■ Analyze the data and prepare presentation-style report, if desired.

Cost

The cost to conduct this study, as described, would be $61,900, plus or minimum a 10 percent contingency fee, which would only be spent with specific prior approval of Fun City Gaming. This cost estimate does not include the cost of any travel outside of the Dallas-Fort Worth area. Any overnight deliveries or travel expenses would be billed at cost at the end of the study.

Decision Analyst would closely monitor data collection. If the actual data collection experience differed from the stated specifications and assumptions, we would notify you immediately to discuss the options available.

Timing

After approval of the final questionnaire, the project would require approximately five to six weeks, as outlined below:

Survey programming and quality control	3–4 days
Data collection	3 weeks
Final data tabulations	3 days
Final report	1–2 weeks

Secondary Data and Databases

LEARNING OBJECTIVES

→ **1.** To understand how firms create an internal database.

→ **2.** To learn about the advantages of creating a database from Web site visitors.

→ **3.** To become familiar with data mining.

→ **4.** To understand the advantages and disadvantages of using secondary data.

→ **5.** To understand the role of the Internet in obtaining secondary data.

→ **6.** To learn about types of information management systems.

What is secondary data and its advantages and disadvantages? How is data mining used by managers to extract insights from data bases? Most importantly, how do managers manage the huge flow of information they have available? You will learn the answers to these questions in chapter four.

Nature of Secondary Data

→ **secondary data**
Data that have been previously gathered.

→ **primary data**
New data gathered to help solve the problem under investigation.

Secondary data consist of information that has already been gathered and might be relevant to the problem at hand. **Primary data**, in contrast, are survey, observation, and experiment data collected to solve the particular problem under investigation. It is highly unlikely that any marketing research problem is entirely unique or has never occurred before. It also is probable that someone else has investigated the problem or one similar to it in the past. Therefore, secondary data can be a cost-effective and efficient means of obtaining information for marketing research. There are two basic sources of secondary data: the company itself (internal databases, like Bud Net) and other organizations or persons (external databases).

Secondary information originating within the company includes annual reports, reports to stockholders, sales data, customer profiles, purchase patterns, product testing results (perhaps made available to the news media), and house periodicals composed by company personnel for communication to employees, customers, or others. Often all this information is incorporated into a company's internal database.

Outside sources of secondary information include innumerable government (federal, state, and local) departments and agencies that compile and publish summaries of business data, as well as trade and industry associations, business periodicals, and other news media that regularly publish studies and articles on the economy, specific industries, and even individual companies. When economic considerations or priorities within the organization preclude publication of summaries of the information from these sources, unpublished summaries may be found in internal reports, memos, or special-purpose analyses with limited circulation. Most of these sources can be found on the Internet.

Advantages of Secondary Data

Marketing researchers use secondary information because it can be obtained at a fraction of the cost, time, and inconvenience associated with primary data collection. Additional advantages of using secondary information include the following:

■ *Secondary data may help to clarify or redefine the problem during the exploratory research process* (see Chapter 3). Consider the experience of a local YMCA. Concerned about a stagnant level of membership and a lack of participation in traditional YMCA programs, it decided to survey members and nonmembers. Secondary data revealed that there had been a tremendous influx of young single persons into the target market, while the number of "traditional families" had remained constant. The problem was redefined to examine how the YMCA could attract a significant share of the young single adult market while maintaining its traditional family base.

■ *Secondary data may actually provide a solution to the problem.* It is highly unlikely that the problem is unique; there is always the possibility that someone else has addressed the identical problem or a very similar one. Thus, the precise information desired may have been collected, but not for the same purpose.

Many states publish a directory of manufacturers (typically available online) that contains information on companies: location, markets, product lines, number of plants, names of key personnel, number of employees, and sales levels. When a consulting company specializing in long-range strategic planning for members of

PRACTICING MARKETING RESEARCH

Would you pull off the road to fill your gas tank if you could already see that the needle was showing full? Probably not. However, we have found that many companies are essentially doing just that by executing surveys to gather data on questions for which they already have the answers.

A major hotel chain found that it successfully delivered clean bathrooms 99.6 percent of the time. To monitor their continued success, rather than survey 10,000 people to get back 1,000 surveys four weeks later, of which four would have bathroom complaints, the chain chose to put a sticker in the bathroom and on the room desk highlighting the guest services hotline. Customers' call rates would let the chain know if quality had slipped.

In another situation, a bank was surveying customers on their satisfaction with the uptime of the ATMs. However, the bank already had internal IT metrics that measured ATM uptime to four decimal places.

In summary, make sure the data do not already exist. We have found that departments often operate in silos, unaware of the research being done or data being collected by their co-workers. Sharing existing research and internal metrics not only gives immediate access to actionable data but does so without incurring the costs of conducting surveys.[1]

Questions

1. What can companies do to make sure that the data do not already exist?

2. How can an intranet help avoid duplicate research?

---

the semiconductor industry needed a regional profile of its potential clients, it used individual state directories to compile the profile; no primary data collection was necessary. John Goodman and David Beinhacker of TARP, an Arlington, Virginia, marketing research firm, note in the above Practicing Marketing Research box that secondary data may help companies save a lot of money by not conducting unnecessary surveys.

■ *Secondary data may provide primary data research method alternatives.* Each primary data research endeavor is custom-designed for the situation at hand; consequently, the marketing researcher should always be open to sources that suggest research alternatives. For example, when we started work on a research project for a large southwestern city's convention and visitor's bureau, we obtained a research report prepared by *Meeting and Convention Planners* magazine. In designing our questionnaire, we used a series of scales from the magazine's questionnaire. Not only were the scales well designed, but results from our study could be compared with the magazine's data.

■ *Secondary data may alert the marketing researcher to potential problems and/or difficulties.* In addition to alternatives, secondary information may divulge potential dangers. Unpopular collection methods, sample selection difficulties, or respondent hostility may be uncovered. For example, examination of a study of anesthesiologists by a researcher planning to conduct a study of their satisfaction with certain drugs discovered a high refusal rate in a telephone survey. The researcher had planned to use a telephone study but instead switched to a mail questionnaire with a response incentive.

■ *Secondary data may provide necessary background information and build credibility for the research report.* Secondary information often yields a wealth of background data for planning a research project. It may offer a profile of potential buyers versus non-buyers, industry data, desirable new product features, language used by purchasers to describe the industry, and the advantages and disadvantages of existing products. Language used by target consumers can aid in phrasing questions that will be meaningful to respondents. Sometimes background data can satisfy some of the research objectives, eliminating the need to ask certain questions; shorter questionnaires typically have higher completion rates. And secondary data can enrich research findings by providing additional insights into what the data mean or by corroborating current findings. Finally, secondary data can serve as a reference base for subsequent research projects.

■ *Secondary data may provide the sample frame.* If a company, such as UPS, wants to track its levels of customer satisfaction each quarter, the names of customers must come from its database. Thus, the customer list is the sample frame, and the sample frame is the list or device from which a sample is drawn.

Limitations of Secondary Data

Despite the many advantages of secondary data, they also pose some dangers. The main disadvantages of secondary information are lack of availability, lack of relevance, inaccuracy, and insufficiency.

Lack of Availability   For some research questions, there are simply no available data. Suppose Kraft General Foods wants to evaluate the taste, texture, and color of three new gourmet brownie mixes. No secondary data exist that can answer these questions; consumers must try each mix and then evaluate it. If McDonald's wants to evaluate its image in Phoenix, Arizona, it must gather primary data. If BMW wants to know the reaction of college students to a new two-seater sports car design, it must show prototypes to the students and evaluate their opinions. Of course, secondary data may have played a major role in the engineer's design plan for the car.

Lack of Relevance   It is not uncommon for secondary data to be expressed in units or measures that cannot be used by the researcher. For example, Joan Dermott, a retailer of oriental rugs, determined that the primary customers for her rugs were families with a total household income of $40,000 to $80,000. Higher-income consumers tended to purchase pricier rugs than those Dermott carried. When she was trying to decide whether to open a store in another Florida city, she could not find useful income data. One source offered class breakdowns of $30,000 to $50,000, $50,000 to $70,000, $70,000 to $90,000, and so forth. Another secondary source broke down incomes into less than $15,000, $15,000 to $30,000, and more than $30,000. Even if the given income brackets had met Joan's needs, she would have faced another problem: outdated information. One study had been conducted in 1995 and the other in 2001. In Florida's dynamic markets, the percentages probably were no longer relevant. This is often the case with U.S. Census data, which are nearly a year old before they become available.

Inaccuracy   Users of secondary data should always assess the accuracy of the data. There are a number of potential sources of error when a researcher gathers, codes, analyzes, and presents data. Any report that does not mention possible sources and ranges of error should be suspect.

Using secondary data does not relieve the researcher from attempting to assess their accuracy. A few guidelines for determining the accuracy of secondary data are as follows:

1. *Who gathered the data?* The source of the secondary data is a key to their accuracy. Federal agencies, most state agencies, and large commercial marketing research firms generally can be counted on to have conducted their research as professionally as possible. Marketing researchers should always be on guard when examining data in which a hidden agenda might be reflected. A chamber of commerce, for instance, is always going to put its best foot forward. Similarly, trade associations often advocate one position over another.

2. *What was the purpose of the study?* Data are always collected for some reason. Understanding the motivation for the research can provide clues to the quality of the data. A chamber of commerce study conducted to provide data that could be used to attract new industry to the area should be scrutinized with a great deal of caution. There have been situations in which advertising agencies have been hired by clients to assess the impact of their own advertising programs. In other words, they have been asked to evaluate the quality of the job they were doing for their clients!

3. *What information was collected?* A researcher should always identify exactly what information was gathered and from whom. For example, in a dog food study, were purchasers of canned, dry, and semimoist food interviewed, or were just one or two types of dog food purchasers surveyed? In a voters' survey, were only Democrats or only Republicans interviewed? Were the respondents registered voters? Was any attempt made to ascertain a respondent's likelihood of voting in the next election? Were self-reported data used to infer actual behavior?

4. *When was the information collected?* A shopping mall study that surveyed shoppers only on weekends would not reflect the opinions of "typical" mall patrons. A telephone survey conducted from 9:00 A.M. to 5:00 P.M. would vastly underrepresent working persons. A survey of Florida visitors conducted during the summer probably would reveal motivations and interests different from those of winter visitors.

5. *How was the information collected?* Were the data collected by mail, telephone, Internet, or personal interview? Each of these techniques offers advantages and disadvantages. What was the refusal rate? Were decision makers or their representatives interviewed? In short, the researcher must attempt to discern the amount of bias injected into the data by the information-gathering process. A mail survey with a 1 percent response rate (that is, only 1 percent of those who received the survey mailed it back) probably contains a lot of self-selection bias.

6. *Is the information consistent with other information?* A lack of consistency between secondary data sets should dictate caution. The researcher should delve into possible causes of the discrepancy. Differences in the sample, time frame, sampling methodology, questionnaire structure, and other factors can lead to variations in studies. If possible, the researcher should assess the validity of the different studies as a basis for determining which, if any, study should be used for decision making.

Insufficiency A researcher may determine that available data are relevant and accurate but still not sufficient to make a decision or bring closure to a problem. For example, a manager for Wal-Mart may have sufficient secondary data on incomes, family sizes, number of competitors, and growth potential to determine in which of five Iowa towns Wal-Mart wishes to locate its next store. But if no traffic counts exist for the selected town, primary data will have to be gathered to select a specific site for the store.

Internal Databases

For many companies, a computerized database containing information about customers and prospects has become an essential marketing tool. An internal database is simply a collection of related information developed from data within the organization.

→ **internal database**
A collection of related information developed from data within the organization.

Creating an Internal Database

A firm's sales activities can be an excellent source of information for creating an internal database. A traditional starting point has been the firm's sales or inquiry processing and tracking system. Typically, such a system is built on salespersons' "call reports." A call report provides a blueprint of a salesperson's daily activities. It details the number of calls made, characteristics of each firm visited, sales activity resulting from the call, and any information picked up from the client regarding competitors, such as price changes, new products or services, credit term modifications, and new product or service features.

An internal marketing database built on sales results and customer preferences can be a powerful marketing tool. While large companies build mammoth internal databases Ben & Jerry's uses databases to maintain the highest quality ice creams as discussed in the following Practicing Marketing Research feature.

PRACTICING MARKETING RESEARCH

Looking for Intelligence in Ice Cream

Just beyond the souvenir shop and down the relic-filled hallways in the Ben & Jerry's factory in Waterbury, Vermont, massive pipes pump out 190,000 pints of ice cream each day. Throughout the day, tractor trailers pull up, pick up the mountains of Cherry Garcia or Chunky Monkey pints, and deliver them to depots. From there, the ice cream is shipped out to 50,000 grocery stores in the United States and 12 other countries. Once it's on the freezer shelves, it has the magical effect of curing a broken heart, satiating a sweet tooth, or possibly just heightening someone's cholesterol level.

For Ben & Jerry's, that's only the start of the journey. At the company's headquarters in Burlington, Vermont, just miles from where the founders opened their first shop 25 years ago, the life of each pint—from ingredients to sale—is tracked in a database. Once the pint is stamped and sent out, Ben & Jerry's stores its tracking number in a database; then it puts it under the microscope. Using software from a company called Business Objects, the sales team can check to see if Chocolate Chip Cookie Dough is gaining ground on Cherry Garcia for the coveted No. 1 sales position. Down the hall in the marketing department, the company checks to see whether orders online require Ben & Jerry's to make a donation to one of its philanthropies. The finance people pop the number into their journals to show results. Since they started using the software, they've sharply cut the time it takes to close their monthly books. And probably most important to a company focused on customer loyalty, the consumer affairs staff matches up the pint with the 225 calls and e-mails received each week, checking to see if there were any complaints, and if so, which supplier's milk, eggs, or cherries didn't meet the company's near obsession with quality.

Ben & Jerry's may cultivate a down-home image, but as a unit of $47-billion-a-year Unilever, it depends just as heavily on the statistics for its success. And to get those figures, it relies on business intelligence, or BI, software: a name for programs that crunch huge quantities of data in a database in search of trends, problems, or new business opportunities.

Typical BI applications first pull information out of giant databases into so-called data marts—smaller clusters of similar information that can keep financial data in one area, inventory data in another. Then the software is ready for the hunt. When a Lands' End product manager wants to know, say, what the hottest-selling turtleneck has been in the last month, the BI software first runs the request through a so-called semantic layer, which translates the query into database-speak (at Lands' End, white turtlenecks go by the number "66780," for example). Then it uses the terms to gather the relevant data from the right data mart, organize it, analyze it, translate it back, and offer an answer.

The employee sees only the last part. Just about every company now offers stand-alone or browser-based software that the industry calls "dashboards," which presents graphical displays of inventory levels, sales info, and other urgent gauges of day-to-day business.

Companies are using BI software to mine their databases not to just better understand trends and solve problems but also to eliminate false assumptions. Ben & Jerry's noticed a swell in complaints from Cherry Garcia ice cream customers, most of whom were irritated that the product had too few cherries. The company matched the complaints against the shipment records and analyzed them using Business Objects. First it eliminated the chance that this was a regional problem—complaints were coming from all over the country. Then it queried information on the manufacturing process; the recipe and ingredients all turned out to be normal. Finally, after nixing just about every possibility, the company discovered the problem: The photo on the ice-cream-pop box was not of the ice cream but of frozen yogurt—a product more laden with cherries than the paler-pink ice-cream treat. Ben & Jerry's changed the image on the box, and the complaints melted away.[4]

Questions

1. Could your university use a "dashboard?" How?

2. How can databases improve customer service?

Growing Importance of Internal Database Marketing

Perhaps the fastest growing use of internal databases is database marketing. Database marketing relies on the creation of a large computerized file of customers' and potential customers' profiles and purchase patterns to create a targeted marketing mix. A recent study found that 94 percent of the large companies in America have a marketing database.[2]

In the 1950s, network television enabled advertisers to "get the same message to everyone simultaneously." Database marketing can get a customized, individual message to everyone simultaneously through direct mail. This is why database marketing is sometimes called *micromarketing.* Database marketing can create a computerized form of the old-fashioned relationship that people used to have with the corner grocer, butcher, or baker. "A database is sort of a collective memory," says Richard G. Barlow, president of Frequency Marketing, Inc., a Cincinnati-based consulting firm. "It deals with you in the same personalized way as a mom-and-pop grocery store, where they knew customers by name and stocked what they wanted."[3]

→ **database marketing**
Marketing that relies on the creation of a large computerized file of customers' and potential customers' profiles and purchase patterns to create a targeted marketing mix.

The size of some databases is impressive: Ford Motor Company's is about 50 million names; Kraft General Foods, 30 million; Citicorp, 30 million; and Kimberly Clark, maker of Huggies diapers, 10 million new mothers. American Express can pull from its database all cardholders who made purchases at golf pro shops in the past 6 months, who attended symphony concerts, or who traveled to Europe more than once in the past year, as well as the very few people who did all three.

The San Diego Padres baseball team used database marketing to attract 60,000 new fans and collected about $400,000 in revenues from new season ticket sales. This was accomplished by marrying the database with customer relationship marketing (CRM) software. New, powerful CRM software is helping marketers enhance their recruitment of new customers and also keep current clients.

Aided by technology, sports-specific strategies are helping marketers reconnect with their fans. Even when a team is winning and stadiums are packed, CRM helps identify those fans most likely to buy season tickets or ticket packages in advance by creating databases on fan attendance. A team can then target these prospects for season tickets the following year. Advance ticket sales are extremely valuable to sports teams since they guarantee a certain revenue level for the season.

"Club cards," similar to ATM cards, are at the heart of fan loyalty programs these days. Although programs vary slightly from team to team, the idea is pretty much the same: Each time fans use their card, they rack up attendance points redeemable for promotional coupons or items such as food, drinks, and souvenirs. The more points they compile, the more "rewards" they receive. In return, the teams get a database filled with information on their fans, which could lead to additional revenue streams.[5]

A few tips on database design are offered in the Practicing Marketing Research box that follows.

PRACTICING MARKETING RESEARCH

Database Design and Implementation

With both an MBA and an undergraduate degree in computer science, Mike Foytik, chief technology officer for information science for DSS Research, exemplifies the new breed of marketing service managers with a strong background in computers. He is a proponent of the use of relational databases. He has designed dozens for DSS clients in direct marketing and retailing.

He notes that there are many advantages to using a relational database instead of the traditional database approach, sometimes referred to as the flat-file method. In a relational database, data are stored in several small structures, or files, rather than in a single large one. Each of the small files in a relational database contains key information that allows individual records in the database to be linked to associated data in other individual files that make up the entire database structure.

For example, a customer database might contain one file that includes customer information such as name, mailing address, and Social Security number. This information is updated occasionally. Products purchased by each customer would go into another file that is updated frequently (every time the customer buys something). The two files might be linked by the customer's Social Security number.

With each new order, a record is created that includes the product purchased, the price, other relevant information concerning the purchase, and the buyer's Social Security number. Under the traditional, flat-file approach, all this information (the product purchase information and the buyer's personal information) would have to be entered with each product purchase. Relational databases have a number of distinct advantages:

- *Less data storage space is required.* There is very little redundant information in a relational database. Data such as addresses are stored only once for each customer rather than being stored with every new purchase that is added. Foytik notes that "we have achieved 75 percent storage space reductions for some of our clients."

- *The database is more flexible.* Relational databases offer much greater flexibility and efficiency with respect to changes in the way data are stored and used. With flat-file databases, every time a new data field is added to the database, the database must be re-created in order to add the new data field to every record in the database. With a relational database, new information is stored in a new file and, therefore, has no effect on existing data in other files in the database.

- *Restricting access to sensitive information is easier.* Relational databases can be easily designed to restrict user access to certain areas of the database via the use of special passwords or codes while still allowing more general access to less sensitive areas. In flat-file databases, this sort of restricted access to some parts of the database is all but impossible. Users must have either total access or no access.

- *The database can easily be designed to accommodate many users.* Foytik notes that "most of our clients have a number of different departments with very different informational needs accessing customer data." With flat files, separate copies of the database must be created and modified to meet the needs of different users. With relational databases, the physical data remain unchanged, while the data or reports seen by the different user groups (sometimes called the logical data) can be varied.

Finally, he notes, all these advantages come at some cost. First, relational databases require much more sophisticated software and more sophisticated people to program them. Second, relational databases require much more up-front planning if the company is to reap the full benefits of this type of data. Finally, relational databases tend to require more processor horsepower. This is becoming less of an issue with the price/performance ratio of computers constantly improving and numerous off-the-shelf software programs that can help even computer novices establish relational databases.[6]

Questions

1. Why are more firms creating relational databases?

2. What are the primary drawbacks of relational databases?

Data Mining

American Express uses a neural network to examine the hundreds of millions of entries in its database that tell how and where individual cardholders transact business. A **neural network** is a computer program that mimics the processes of the human brain and thus is capable of learning from examples to find patterns in data. The result is a set of *purchase propensity scores* for each cardholder. Based on these scores, AmEx matches offers from affiliated merchants to the purchase histories of individual cardholders and encloses these offers with their monthly statements. The benefits are reduced expenses for AmEx and information of higher value for its cardholders; American Express is engaged in data mining.

Data mining is the use of statistical and other advanced software to discover nonobvious patterns hidden in a database. The objective is to identify patterns that marketers can use in creating new strategies and tactics to increase a firm's profitability. Camelot

→ **neural network**
A computer program that mimics the processes of the human brain and thus is capable of learning from examples to find patterns in data.

→ **data mining**
The use of statistical and other advanced software to discover nonobvious patterns hidden in a database.

Music Holdings used data mining to identify a group of high-spending, 65-plus customers (members of its frequent shopper club) who were buying lots of classical and jazz music and movies. Further data mining revealed that a large percentage were also buying rap and alternative music; these were grandparents buying for the grandkids. Now, Camelot tells the senior citizens what's hot in rap and alternative music, as well as in traditional music.

Data mining involves searching for interesting patterns and following the data trail wherever it leads. The discovery process often requires sifting through massive quantities of data; electronic point-of-sale transactions, inventory records, and online customer orders matched with demographics can easily use up hundreds of gigabytes of data storage space. Probability sampling, descriptive statistics, and multivariate statistics are all tools of data mining that make the task manageable. (Probability sampling was discussed in Chapter 3; descriptive statistics programs and multivariate statistics will be covered in Chapters 14 through 18.) Other more advanced data mining tools, such as genetic algorithms and case-based reasoning systems, must be left for an advanced text.

Data mining has many potential uses in marketing. Those with widest application include the following:

■ *Customer acquisition.* In the first stage of a two-stage process, direct marketers apply data mining methods to discover customer attributes that predict their responses to special offers and communications such as catalogues. In the second stage, attributes that the model indicates make customers most likely to respond are matched to the attributes appended to rented lists of noncustomers in order to select noncustomer households most likely to respond to a new offer or communication.

■ *Customer retention.* In a typical marketing application, data mining identifies those customers who contribute to the company's bottom line but who are likely to leave and go to a competitor. With this information, the company can target the vulnerable customers for special offers and other inducements not available to less vulnerable customers.

■ *Customer abandonment.* Some customers cost more than they contribute and should be encouraged to take their business elsewhere. At Federal Express, customers who spend a lot with little service and marketing investment get different treatment

Farmers Group Insurance used data mining to find out that, as long as a sports car wasn't the only vehicle in a household, the accident rate for sports cars wasn't much greater than that for regular cars. This information led to lower insurance rates for sports cars in this category.

from, say, those who spend just as much but cost more to keep. If their shipping volume falters, "good" clients can expect a phone call, which can head off defections before they occur. As for the "bad" clients—those who spend but are expensive to the company—FedEx is turning them into profitable customers, in many cases, by charging higher shipping prices. And the "ugly" clients, those customers who spend little and show few signs of spending more in the future? They can catch the TV ads. "We just don't market to them anymore," says Sharanjit Singh, managing director for marketing analysis at FedEx. "That automatically brings our costs down."[7]

■ *Market basket analysis.* By identifying the associations among product purchases in point-of-sale transactions, retailers and direct marketers can spot product affinities and develop focused promotion strategies that work more effectively than traditional one-size-fits-all approaches. The American Express strategy of selectively stuffing offers in monthly statements is an example of how market basket analysis can be employed to increase marketing efficiency.

The Farmers Group has used data mining to better understand its customers. A few years ago, owning a Porsche or a Corvette almost guaranteed that you would pay more for car insurance. Conventional wisdom and decades of data collected by insurers suggested that drivers of high-performance sports cars were more likely to have accidents than were other motorists. But, by using data mining, the Farmers Group discovered something interesting: as long as the sports car wasn't the only vehicle in a household, the accident rate actually wasn't much greater than that for a regular car. Based on that information, Farmers changed its policy that had excluded sports cars from its lowest-priced insurance rates. By eliminating that rule, "we figured out that we could almost double our sports-car market," says Melissa McBratney, vice president of personal lines at the Los Angeles insurer.[8] Farmers estimates that just letting Corvettes and Porsches into its "preferred premium" plan could bring in an additional $4.5 million in premium revenue over the next 2 years, without a significant rise in claims. The pattern Farmers discovered isn't intuitive—it had eluded most insurance veterans.

Behavioral Targeting

Behavioral targeting is the use of online and offline data to understand a consumer's habits, demographics, and social networks in order to increase the effectiveness of online advertising. As the Internet has matured, nontargeted advertising has decreased in efficiency. One study found that only 4 percent of Internet users account for 67 percent of all display ad clicks. Another recent study by DoubleClick reported an average click-through rate of just 0.1 percent. Translated, that means that only one out of a thousand people actually click through the average display ad. Behavioral targeting attempts to change the odds in favor of the advertiser. In fact, recent research confirms that targeted ad click-throughs and conversion rates are significantly higher than nontargeted ads.[9]

EXelate Media, a research firm that collects and sells Web data, announced an alliance with A. C. Nielsen, one of America's largest marketing research firms. The deal tied eXelate's data on more than 150 million Internet users to Nielsen's database on 115 million American households to provide more detailed profiles of consumers.

EXelate gathers online consumer data through deals with hundreds of Web sites. The firm determines a consumer's age, sex, ethnicity, marital status, and profession by scouring Web-site registration data. It pinpoints, for example, which consumers in the market to buy a car are fitness buffs, based on their Internet searches and the sites they frequent. It gathers and stores the information using tracking cookies, or small strings of data that are placed on the hard drive of a consumer's computer when that

> **behavioral targeting**
> The use of online and offline data to understand a consumer's habits, demographics, and social networks in order to increase the effectiveness of online advertising

consumer visits a participating site. A more detailed discussion of the tracking process can be found in Chapter 8.

An auto maker, for instance, could use EXelate and Nielsen's databases to target ads promoting a sports car to people who visit auto blogs, search online for sports cars, and fit into a group Nielsen calls the "young digerati." This group includes tech-savvy, affluent consumers who live in trendy apartments or condos, are 25 to 44 years old, make about $88,000 a year, and typically read *The Economist*.[10]

The addition of social networking data has been a huge boost to behavioral targeting. Users of Facebook and other social sites reveal interests, connections, and tastes like never before. In the past, online advertisers have found it very effective to promote to persons who have either bought from them, visited their site, or interacted with an ad. The problem comes in with generating demand among people who may not even know the product. This is where social data comes into play. Companies like Media 6° takes an advertiser's customer data and links it to social user information it licenses from social networking sites. The technology matches a prospect with his or her closest friends. So a remessaging campaign can target the original customer plus his or her friends. Instead of reaching one prospect, the campaign may reach 8 or 10 million prospects. It is the idea that "birds of a feather flock together."[11]

Lotame and 33across are among the other companies aiming to mine social networking data for advertisers. Lotame attempts to use social data to get at influencers. It trolls social networks, blogs, and message boards for users who have created content about specific topics. Then it expands the circle by adding in people who consumed that user-generated content. Finally, it adds people who look like those content creators and consumers.[12]

Both EBay and Spring have used 33across to improve their online advertising effectiveness.

Battle over Privacy

There is a downside to behavioral targeting: consumer privacy. The researchers say that their data contains no personally identifiable information. In one survey, only 24 percent said that they were comfortable with advertisers using their browsing history to deliver more relevant ads.[13] How much tracking actually goes on? *The Wall Street Journal* picked 50 Web sites that account for about 40 percent of all U.S. page views. The 50 sites installed a total of 3,180 tracking cookies on a test computer used to conduct the study. Only one site, Wikipedia.org, installed none. Twelve sites, including Comcast.net and MSN.com, installed more than 100 tracking tools apiece. Dictionary.com installed 168 tracking tools that didn't let users decline to be tracked and 121 tools that, according to privacy statements, didn't rule out collecting financial or health data.[14]

Congress is considering laws to limit tracking. The Federal Trade Commission is developing privacy guidelines for the industry. If "you were in the Gap, and the sales associate said to you, 'OK, from now on, since you shopped here today, we are going to follow you around the mall and view your consumer transactions,' no person would ever agree to that," Senator George LeMieux of Florida said in a Senate hearing on Internet privacy.[15]

The computer consultant Tom Owad has published the results of an experiment that provided a lesson in just how easy it is to extract sensitive personal data from the Net. Mr. Owad wrote a simple piece of software that allowed him to download public wish lists that Amazon.com customers post to catalog products that they plan to purchase or would like to receive as gifts. These lists usually include the name of the list's owner and his or her city and state.

Using a couple of standard-issue PCs, Mr. Owad was able to download over 250,000 wish lists over the course of a day. He then searched the data for controversial or politically sensitive books and authors, from Kurt Vonnegut's *Slaughterhouse-Five* to the Koran. He then used Yahoo People Search to identify addresses and phone numbers for many of the list owners.

Mr. Owad ended up with maps of the United States showing the locations of people interested in particular books and ideas, including George Orwell's *1984*. He could just as easily have published a map showing the residences of people interested in books about treating depression or adopting a child. "It used to be," Mr. Owad concluded, "you had to get a warrant to monitor a person or a group of people. Today, it is increasingly easy to monitor ideas. And then track them back to people.

What Mr. Owad did by hand can increasingly be performed automatically, with data mining software that draws from many sites and databases. One of the essential characteristics of the Net is the interconnection of diverse stores of information. The "*openness*" of databases is what gives the system much of its power and usefulness. But it also makes it easy to discover hidden relationships among far-flung bits of data.[16]

An emerging technique that is upsetting many privacy advocates is called "scraping." Firms offer to harvest online conversations and collect personal details from social networking sites, resumé sites, and online forums, where people might discuss their lives. (Scraping is discussed in more detail in Chapter 8.)

Recently, the Web site PatientsLikeMe.com noticed suspicious activity on its "Mood" discussion board. There, people exchange highly personal stories about their emotional disorders, ranging from bipolar disease to a desire to cut themselves.[17]

It was a break-in. A new member of the site, using sophisticated software, was "scraping," or copying, every single message off PatientsLikeMe's private online forums.

PatientsLikeMe managed to block and identify the intruder: Nielsen Co., the privately held New York media research firm. Nielsen monitors online "buzz" for clients, including major drug makers, which, Nielsen says, buy data gleaned from the Web to get insight from consumers about their products.

"I felt totally violated," says Bilal Ahmed, a 33-year-old resident of Sydney, Australia, who used PatientsLikeMe to connect with other people suffering from depression.[18] He used a pseudonym on the message boards, but his PatientsLikeMe profile linked to his blog, which contains his real name.

After PatientsLikeMe told users about the break-in, Mr. Ahmed deleted all his posts, plus a list of drugs he uses. "It was very disturbing to know that your information is being sold," he says. Nielsen says it no longer scrapes data from private message boards.[19]

Behavioral tracking has become the foundation of the $25 billion plus online advertising industry. Online advertising is why a company like Google can spend millions and millions of dollars on free services like its search engine, Gmail, mapping tools, Google Groups, and more.

And it's not just Google. Facebook, Yahoo, MSN, and thousands of blogs, news sites, and comment boards use advertising to support what they do. And personalized advertising is more valuable than advertising aimed at just anyone. Marketers will pay more to reach you if you are likely to use their products or services.

A new system designed to police privacy abuses by companies that track consumers' Web-surfing habits for ad targeting will be launched in coming months by groups whose members include heavy users of this type of information—Internet companies such as Yahoo Inc. and Microsoft Corp. and advertising companies such as WPP PLC.

The system is part of a broader push by Madison Avenue and the Internet industry to develop stricter self-regulation, in part to ward off federal regulation of the online advertising industry. A coalition of trade groups, including the Council of Better Business Bureaus and Direct Marketing Association trade group, is leading the effort.[20]

EXHIBIT 4.1	How to Cover Your Tracks Online

Simple Steps

Major browsers including Microsoft Corp.'s Internet Explorer, Mozilla Foundation's Firefox, Google Inc.'s Chrome, and Apple Inc.'s Safari have privacy features. To have the highest privacy option, upgrade to the latest version of the browser you use.

Check and Delete Cookies: All popular browsers let users view and delete cookies installed on their computer. Methods vary by browser.

For instance, on Internet Explorer 8 (the most widely used browser), go to the "Tools" menu, pull down to "Internet Options," and under the "General" tab there are options for deleting some or all cookies.

Adjust Browser Settings: Once you've deleted cookies, you can limit the installation of new ones. Major browsers let you accept some cookies and block others. To maintain logins and settings for sites you visit regularly, but limit tracking, block "third-party" cookies. Safari automatically does this; other browsers may be set manually.

No major browsers let you track or block beacons (a beacon is a file that keeps track of your navigation through a Web site or a series of Web sites), without installing extra software known as "plug-ins."

Turn on "Private" Browsing: All major browsers offer a "private browsing" mode to limit cookies. Chrome calls it "Incognito," Internet Explorer calls it "InPrivate Browsing." But this option is available only in the latest version, IE8.

Private browsing doesn't block cookies. It deletes cookies each time you close the browser or turn off private browsing, effectively hiding your history.

Monitor "Flash Cookies": Another kind of cookie uses Adobe Systems Inc.'s popular Flash program to save information on your computer. Flash is the most common way to show video online. As with regular cookies, Flash cookies can be useful for remembering preferences, such as volume settings for videos. But marketers also can use Flash cookies to track what you do online.

To identify the Flash cookies on your computer and adjust your settings, you need to go to an Adobe Web site: *www.macromedia .com/support/documentation/en/flashplayer/help/settings_manager.html.* You can delete Flash cookies stored on your computer and specify whether you want to accept future third-party Flash cookies.

Advanced Steps

Install Privacy "Plug-ins": Small programs called "add-ons" or "plug-ins" can help maintain privacy. Some let you monitor trackers that can't be seen through the browser; others allow you to delete cookies on a regular schedule.

Not all browsers can use all plug-ins. And some plug-ins can be tricky to set up. With those caveats, some plug-ins may be worth a look:

Better Privacy: This plug-in offers control over Flash cookies. It doesn't block them, but lets you set rules for deleting them—a distinction that can be helpful if you frequent sites that require you to use third-party Flash cookies to see their content. Better Privacy (available only for Firefox) is at addons.mozilla.org/en-US/firefox/addon/6623/.

Ghostery: Available at ghostery.com, it helps control beacons. It alerts you when there's a beacon on a page you're viewing, tells you who placed it, and details the company's privacy policy. With Internet Explorer or Firefox, you can then block the beacon from capturing information on your computer.

Source: Jennifer Valentino DeVries, "How to Avoid the Prying Eyes," *The Wall Street Journal* (July 31–August 1, 2010), p. W3.

Exhibit 4.1 details several ways that you can limit prying eyes.

The concept of privacy is changing radically as a result of our new computer-based lives. Privacy used to be achieved through the sheer friction of everyday life: distance, time, and lack of records. Information didn't travel well, and most people who wanted to escape their past could simply move to a new location. Now the picture has changed. People can escape their surroundings through the Internet, but their actions can easily catch up with them. And it's not just the Internet; it's electronic toll roads (exactly when did you leave that party?), credit card transactions (we know what hotel you went to), vendor databases (and what book you bought), cell phone records (and whom you called), and more. At work, employee arrival and departure times may be recorded, along with their Web searches, e-mail messages, and sick days.

What makes all this troubling to privacy advocates is the growing ability of technology to combine information: the products you bought from a variety of different merchants; your sick days plus someone else's hotel bills. It's not the routine use of this information for marketing purposes that people find troubling; it's the way someone with an agenda might put the pieces together.

Identity Theft   People have a right to be concerned. Identity theft cost $55 billion annually.[21] One company that has come under fire is ChoicePoint. Since spinning off from the credit bureau Equifax in 1997, it has been buying up databases and data mining operations. Businesses, individuals, even the FBI, now rely on its storehouse. Other customers: Nigerian scammers who apparently used the data to steal people's identities.

The problem was unreliable safeguards. To ensure that only certain businesses had access to its data, ChoicePoint set up certain requirements that potential customers must meet. A man named Olatunji Oluwatosin—and possibly others—used fake names and a Hollywood copy shop fax machine to create fictitious small businesses requesting ChoicePoint service. Before Oluwatosin was caught—after someone at ChoicePoint grew suspicious about one of his applications—he accessed at least 145,000 names. (Oluwatosin pleaded no contest to felony identity theft in California in February 2005; he served a 16-month sentence.)[22] ChoicePoint announced in 2005 that it will no longer sell consumer data that includes drivers license numbers and Social Security numbers.[23]

In many cases, finding Social Security and credit card numbers or medical records on the Internet doesn't require much computer expertise. Instead, such information is accessible to anyone who knows where to look.

A file containing names, Social Security numbers, and home phone numbers of about 1,000 current and former Atlanta Fire Rescue employees was discovered online by city officials.

Social Security and driver's license numbers of hundreds of people associated with Edward Waters College in Jacksonville, Fla., were on the Internet and indexed by search engines.[24]

Eric Johnson, a professor at Dartmouth College's Tuck School of Business, has found files containing names, Social Security, and health insurance numbers belonging to thousands of individuals exposed by so-called peer-to-peer software.

The software, such as LimeWire, which allows computers to connect directly to one another, is most often used to trade music and video files, but is capable of transmitting any data, including workplace documents and spreadsheets.

By entering basic search terms like hospital names into the software, Mr. Johnson said he turned up a 1,718-page document containing insurance details and diagnoses leaked by a medical-testing lab. He said he also found spreadsheets from a hospital system that contained contact information and Social Security numbers for more than 20,000 patients.

"There's no hacking or anything like that going on," he said. "We were just searching."[25]

Mr. Johnson said he contacts the organizations, but even if they remove the peer-to-peer software from employee computers, copies of the shared files may still be available online.

In many cases files containing sensitive personal information are downloaded by known cyber criminals, said Rick Wallace, a researcher at Tiversa Inc., a security company that looks for leaked files on behalf of corporate clients. Tiversa found more than 13 million leaked files that contained information about its customers in one 12-month period.

Cyber criminals often sell the credit card numbers and other personal information they find in hacker chat rooms that aren't secret but can only be found by people in the know—although anyone who types "fullz" and "cvv2" into Google's search engine can see a sampling.

Often data comes from breaches where hackers have bypassed weak security systems, said Steven Peisner, president of Sellitsafe Inc., which helps merchants avoid processing fraudulent purchases. He estimates he sees about 15,000 or so stolen accounts being published each month in these dark corners of the Internet.[26]

Governmental Actions   Three key laws (one a state law) have been passed to protect consumers from identity theft. These are:

Federal Laws

Gramm-Leach-Bliley Act (Financial Services Modernization Act): aimed at financial companies. Requires those corporations to tell their customers how they use their personal information and to have policies that prevent fraudulent access to it. Partial compliance has been required since 2001.

Health Insurance Portability and Accountability Act: aimed at the healthcare industry. Limits disclosure of individuals' medical information and imposes penalties on organizations that violate privacy rules. Compliance has been required for large companies since 2003.

The Fair Credit Reporting Act (FCRA): enforced by the Federal Trade Commission, promotes accuracy in consumer reports, and is meant to ensure the privacy of the information in them.

The Children's Online Privacy Protection Act (COPPA): aims to give parents control over what information is collected from their children online and how such information may be used.

The Rule applies to:

- Operators of commercial Web sites and online services directed to children under 13 that collect personal information from them.
- Operators of general audience sites that knowingly collect personal information from children under 13.
- Operators of general audience sites that have a separate children's area and that collect personal information from children under 13.

The Rule requires operators to:

- Post a privacy policy on the homepage of the Web site and link to the privacy policy on every page where personal information is collected.
- Provide notice about the site's information collection practices to parents and obtain verifiable parental consent before collecting personal information from children.
- Give parents a choice as to whether their child's personal information will be disclosed to third parties.
- Provide parents access to their child's personal information and the opportunity to delete the child's personal information and opt out of future collection or use of the information.
- Not condition a child's participation in a game, contest, or other activity on the child's disclosing more personal information than is reasonably necessary to participate in that activity.
- Maintain the confidentiality, security and, integrity of personal information collected from children.

State Laws

California's Notice of Security Breach Law: if any company or agency that has collected the personal information of a California resident discovers that nonencrypted information has been taken by an unauthorized person, the company or agency must tell the resident. Compliance has been required since 2003. (Some 30 other states are considering similar laws.)

Getting Paid to Give Up Your Privacy   A number of marketing research firms are paying people to participate in online surveys, to track their click streams, or to evaluate Web sites. This, of course, is legitimate research. Usually, consumers are willing to give up their right to privacy quite cheaply. A recent Jupiter report said that 82 percent of respondents would give personal information to new shopping sites to enter a $100 sweepstakes.[27] There is also a dark side to getting paid for online surveys. Many Web sites, such as Express Paid Surveys, Get Cash for Surveys, and Opinion Paycheck, promise money for taking surveys. The catch is that you must first pay a membership fee; such fees range from $25 to $37. Donna Gillin and Jane Sheppard, both directors of the Council for Marketing and Opinion Research, discuss the membership fee in the Practicing Marketing Research box below.

PRACTICING MARKETING RESEARCH

Have you recently received e-mail that offers to pay you for your opinions, "turn your opinions into cash," or the like? If the answer to this question is yes, you're not alone. Many in the survey research industry have received and expressed concern over similar e-mails with offers to pay members of the public for their opinions (usually for a membership fee). In reality, these Web sites sell their "members" a database of industry members they claim will "pay" respondents for their opinions. This type of offer raises several concerns. First, a legitimate survey researcher (focus group or otherwise) never asks respondents to pay to become research participants. Second, with the publicity of these offers, respondents may become uniformly accustomed to being "paid for their opinions," rather than, in some cases, being paid as an incentive or a thank you for participation by legitimate industry members.

Moreover, although incentives may be used in focus groups, mall studies, customer satisfaction studies, Web surveys, or others, incentives normally are not used in telephone studies where telephone numbers have been randomly generated by a computer. Since telephone studies make up a considerable amount of the survey research conducted in our industry, the respondent is left with an unrealistic expectation of being offered or receiving an incentive whenever he or she participates in survey research. In addition, given the reality that all potential respondents won't fit the desired demographic for all studies, the materials (generally) don't clearly notify potential respondents that they may never be chosen to participate in any survey research and therefore may never be provided with an incentive to participate in the research process.

Lastly, as industry members have reported, one net effect of such "offers" is the creation of "professional respondents" or "professional survey takers." Such individuals who frequent group discussions have views that may not be wholly representative of the group and are more familiar with group discussion practice—which may result in uncharacteristic and unrepresentative behavior.[28]

Questions

1. Do you think that it is ethical to pay for someone's opinion?

2. How can paying for opinions influence data quality?

Marketing Research Aggregators

➜ **marketing research aggregator**
A company that acquires, catalogs, reformats, segments, and resells reports already published by large and small marketing research firms.

The **marketing research aggregator** industry is a $100 million business that is growing about 6 percent a year. Companies in this field acquire, catalog, reformat, segment, and resell reports already published by large and small marketing research firms. Even Amazon.com has added a marketing research aggregation area to its high-profile e-commerce site.

The role of aggregator firms is growing because their databases of research reports are getting bigger and more comprehensive—and more useful—as marketing research firms get more comfortable using resellers as a sales channel. Meanwhile, advances in Web technology are making the databases easier to search and deliveries speedier. And aggregators are slicing and repackaging research reports into narrower, more specialized sections for resale to better serve small- and medium-sized clients who often cannot afford to commission their own studies or buy full reports—essentially nurturing a new target market for the information.

Research aggregators are indirectly tapping new markets for traditional research firms. Selling smaller chunks of data at a lower price point is putting big research firms' results into the hands of small- and medium-sized business clients, who often cannot afford to spend more than a few hundred dollars for a report.

Prior to the emergence of research aggregators, a lot of marketing research was only available as premium-priced subscription services. For example, a $2,800 report from Wintergreen Research, Inc. (based in Lexington, Massachusetts) was recently broken up and sold (on AllNetResearch.com) for $350 per chapter for the report's 17 chapters, significantly boosting the overall revenue generated by the report.

In addition to AllNetResearch.com, other major aggregators are Profound.com, Bitpipe.com, USADATA.com, and MarketResearch.com.

Information Management

Computerized databases, secondary data published or posted on the Internet, and internal databases are important parts of an organization's information system. Intelligent decision making is always predicated on having good information. The problem today is how to manage all the information available. It was sometime after the middle of the 20th century that—for the first time in human history—we began to produce information faster than we could process it. Various innovations—computers, microwave transmissions, television, satellites, and the like—have pushed us from a state of information scarcity to a state of information surplus in a very short time.

The need to make better decisions requires that emphasis move from the problems of data acquisition to the problems of effectively managing and utilizing the vast sea of data available. Everyone who has been faced with a decision recognizes that information is the single most important input influencing the quality of that decision. Information is necessary to define the problem, to determine its scope and magnitude, and to generate and evaluate alternatives. Poor decisions are usually the result of using incorrect information, making invalid assumptions, or inappropriately analyzing the information available.

Today, most managers in large and medium-size organizations and progressive smaller ones are bombarded with information. The concern at firms such as American Airlines, Pfizer, and Citicorp has shifted from the generation of information to the shaping and evaluation of information to make it useful to decision makers.

Meineke uses geographic information systems to map its stores and competitors in relation to its customer base. Go to http://www.meineke.com to find out how it positions its Web site based on customer information.

Geographic Information System

A geographic information system (GIS) provides both a means of maintaining geographic databases and a tool capable of complex spatial analysis to provide information for a decision support system. Spatial analysis is the analysis of phenomena distributed in space and having physical dimensions (the location of, proximity to, or orientation of objects, such as stores, with respect to one another). A geographic database can store and provide access to corporate data, such as customer locations, facilities, logistic routes, and competitors. As a spatial analysis tool, this corporate data can be immersed with secondary demographic data and digitized maps to analyze and maximize the effects of locations. Utilities, oil companies, large retailers, and government agencies have long used these systems. Today the technology accounts for several billion dollars a year in hardware, software, and consulting sales. There are three reasons for this boom. The cost of a GIS has fallen dramatically, the ease of use for business-related analysis has improved, and GIS data can now be transmitted over the Internet fairly easily. GIS is now one of the hottest business information tools. Companies as diverse as Chase Manhattan, Domino's Pizza, Ace Hardware, Gold's Gym, and Subaru America have embraced mapping as an easier and more powerful way to manage geographic data than mind-numbing printouts, spreadsheets, and charts. GIS offers researchers, managers, and clients an intuitive way to organize data and to see relationships and patterns.[29]

Recently, Avon Products, Inc.'s sales rose 29 percent. One reason for this success could be its extensive use of GIS software to identify sales opportunities, manage market penetration, and realign territory. Avon uses a GIS product called Territory Manager from Tactician Corporation. This software assists Avon in identifying new sales opportunities by combining secondary demographic data with their internal corporate sales data to segment the U.S. market. For example, the software helped Avon to pinpoint a growing Asian American population in the Southeast. The maps produced are then used to further penetrate the market and to identify new sales representatives. After using the

> **geographic information system (GIS)**
> Computer-based system that uses secondary and/or primary data to generate maps that visually display various types of data geographically.

Territory Manager software, some sales areas saw recruitment increase up to 138 percent over of the previous year during the same time period. The GIS is then used to create maps ranking sales territories to optimize the distribution and alignment of sales areas. These maps are made available to sales representatives over the Internet.[30]

GIS analysts and geographers talk about lines, points, and polygons (areas), while marketing researchers talk about roads, stores, and sales territories. But lines, points, and polygons are how business data is represented within a geographic database. Applications using lines include finding the quickest truck routes for long-haul freight companies and the shortest routes for local delivery trucks. Sears Roebuck calculates daily delivery routes, based on "estimated travel times, in-home time, truck capacity, optimal stop sequence." GPS (global positioning system) receivers in the vehicles can communicate with a GIS to receive real-time weather and road conditions to the drivers. Applications involving points focus on finding the best potential sites for retail bank branches and devising the best strategy for a network of miniwarehouses. Applications involving areas range from finding the best markets for hardware sales to identifying the best location for a new Taco Bell. A GIS can also answer detailed marketing questions. If a marketing researcher for Target wants to know how many of the company's high-performance stores have trading areas that overlap by at least 50 percent with trading areas for Wal-Mart, a GIS analyst can run a spatial query on a geographic database to address the question.

Aftermarket auto repair is a highly competitive $90 billion-a-year business in which dealerships have improved their services and market share. To stay ahead of the competition, Meineke Discount Muffler Corporation has turned to GIS. Meineke's 900 franchisees continuously send detailed customer and service records to Meineke headquarters in Charlotte, North Carolina. Records include customer's name and home address; vehicle make, model, and year; work performed; and payment method. They also explain how the customer learned about Meineke. This data is integrated with demographics, average commute times, market area incomes, and the like, within a geographic database. Meineke can then map its stores, competitors, and other retail outlets in relation to its customer base. GIS analysis is used to compute site selection, market share analysis, and inventory management.

Using TargetPro GIS software from MapInfo Corporation, Meineke analysts have developed GIS models (geographic formulas), allowing them to specify an actual or proposed retail location and then create an easy to understand report. Meineke can customize trade areas as it sees fit. If marketing research shows that some customers will not cross a river or a state boundary to get to the nearest outlet but will drive 2 miles farther to another Meineke franchise in a different zip code, the company can use TargetPro to create a map that reflects those shopping patterns. Meineke uses GIS to determine optimal inventory levels by analyzing demographics, commute times, and historical sales figures, which can point to short- and long-term potential business.

"We can place a store on the map, draw a radius around it, then ask the system how many vehicles are in the area," said Paul Baratta, director of real estate and international development for Meineke. "There might be 75,000 cars in a given neighborhood, but another layer of data might show that 65,000 of those are Lexus brands. How many people are going to put mufflers on a car that they're trading in every two years? [GIS] looks at the information in a different way."[31]

MapInfo is now combining GIS, data mining, and predictive analysis software to predict not only which markets offer the best potential for expansion—down to specific intersections—but also how each new store will affect revenue across the chain, generating color-coded maps of the best locales. For example, in the fast-food business, clustering with similar merchants is often beneficial because diners typically will drive only 5 minutes for quick food and tend to go where they have myriad options. But as Arby's learned, specific products can affect behavior. MapInfo discovered that diners drove as much as 20 percent farther for an Arby's roast beef sandwich than for the chain's chicken offering. The reason? Shoppers could get chicken elsewhere but considered roast beef a "destination" product.[32]

Decision Support Systems

A **decision support system (DSS)** is designed to support the needs and styles of individual decision makers. In theory, a DSS represents something close to the ultimate in data management. We say "in theory" because, for the most part, the ideal has not been realized in practice. However, there have been some notable exceptions that have provided a glimpse of how a DSS can truly support the decision-making process. Characteristics of a true DSS are as follows:

■ *Interactive.* The manager gives simple instructions and sees results generated on the spot. The process is under the manager's direct control; no computer programmer is needed, and there is no need to wait for scheduled reports.

■ *Flexible.* It can sort, regroup, total, average, and manipulate data in a variety of ways. It will shift gears as the user changes topics, matching information to the problem at hand. For example, the chief executive can see highly aggregated figures, while the marketing analyst can view detailed breakouts.

■ *Discovery-oriented.* It helps managers probe for trends, isolate problems, and ask new questions.

■ *Easy to learn and use.* Managers need not be particularly knowledgeable about computers. Novice users can elect a standard, or default, method of using the system, bypassing optional features to work with the basic system immediately. The opportunity to gradually learn about the system's possibilities minimizes the frustration that frequently accompanies use of new computer software.

Managers use a DSS to conduct sales analyses, forecast sales, evaluate advertising, analyze product lines, and keep tabs on market trends and competitors' actions. A DSS not only allows managers to ask "what if" questions but enables them to view any given slice of the data.

Here's a hypothetical example of using a DSS provided by a manager of new products:

> To evaluate sales of a recently introduced new product, we can "call up" sales by the week, then by the month, breaking them out at [the vice president's] option by, say, customer segments. As he works at his terminal, his inquiries could go in several directions depending on the decision at hand. If his train of thought raises questions about monthly sales last quarter compared to forecasts, he wants his decision support system to follow along and give him answers immediately.
>
> He might see that his new product's sales were significantly below forecast. Forecasts too optimistic? He compares other products' sales to his forecasts and finds that the targets were very accurate. Something wrong with the product? Maybe his sales department is getting insufficient leads, or is not putting leads to good use? Thinking a minute about how to examine that question, he checks ratios of leads converted to sales, product by product. The results disturb him. Only 5 percent of the new product's leads generate orders compared to the company's 12 percent all-product average. Why? He guesses that the sales force is not supporting the new product vigorously enough. Quantitative information from the DSS perhaps could provide more evidence to back that suspicion. But already having enough quantitative knowledge to satisfy himself, the VP acts on his intuition and experience and decides to have a chat with his sales manager.

→ **decision support system (DSS)**
An interactive, personalized information management system, designed to be initiated and controlled by individual decision makers.

SUMMARY

Secondary data are previously gathered information that might be relevant to the problem at hand. They can come from sources internal to the organization or external to it. Primary data are survey, observation, or experiment data collected to solve the particular problem under investigation.

A database is a collection of related data. A traditional type of internal marketing database is founded on customer information. For example, a customer database may have demographic and perhaps psychographic information about existing customers and purchase data such as when the goods and services were bought, the types of merchandise procured, the dollar amount of sales, and any promotional information associated with sales. A database can even be created from recorded conversations. An internal database also may contain competitive intelligence, such as new products offered by competitors and changes in competitors' service policies and prices.

Data mining has dramatically increased users' ability to get insightful information out of databases. It can be used to acquire new customers, retain existing customers, abandon accounts that are not cost-effective, and engage in market-based analyses.

The proliferation of databases on and off the Internet and behavioral targeting have raised consumer and government concerns over privacy. Several laws have been passed to protect our privacy. These include the Gramm-Leach-Bliley Act, the Health Insurance Portability and Accountability Act, the Fair Credit Reporting Act, the Children's Online Privacy Act, and California's Notice of Security Breach Law.

Using secondary data has several advantages. Secondary data may (1) help to clarify or redefine the problem during the exploratory research process, (2) actually provide a solution to the problem, (3) provide primary data research method alternatives, (4) alert the marketing researcher to potential problems and difficulties, and (5) provide necessary background data and build credibility for the research report. The disadvantages of using secondary data include lack of availability, lack of relevance, inaccuracy, and insufficient data.

Geographic information systems, which consist of a demographic database, digitized maps, and software, enable users to add primary data from a current study (or secondary corporate data) to the mix. The result is computer-generated maps that can reveal a variety of strategic findings to marketing managers; for example, a map may indicate an optimal location for a new retail store.

Decision support systems are designed from the individual decision maker's perspective. DSS systems are interactive, flexible, discovery-oriented, and easy to learn; they can offer many benefits to small and large firms alike.

KEY TERMS & DEFINITIONS

secondary data Data that have been previously gathered.

primary data New data gathered to help solve the problem under investigation.

internal database A collection of related information developed from data within the organization.

database marketing Marketing that relies on the creation of a large computerized file of customers' and potential customers' profiles and purchase patterns to create a targeted marketing mix.

neural network A computer program that mimics the processes of the human brain and thus is capable of learning from examples to find patterns in data.

data mining The use of statistical and other advanced software to discover nonobvious patterns hidden in a database.

behavioral targeting The use of online and offline data to understand a consumer's habits, demographics, and social networks in order to increase the effectiveness of online advertising.

marketing research aggregator A company that acquires, catalogs, reformats, segments, and resells reports already published by large and small marketing research firms.

geographic information system (GIS) A system that provides both a means of maintaining geographic databases and a tool capable of complex spatial analysis to provide information for a decision support system.

decision support system (DSS) An interactive, personalized information management system, designed to be initiated and controlled by individual decision makers.

QUESTIONS FOR REVIEW & CRITICAL THINKING

1. Why should companies consider creating an internal marketing database? Name some types of information that might be found in this database and the sources of this information.

2. Why has data mining become so popular with firms such as United Airlines, American Express, and Ford Motor Company?

3. What are some of the keys to ensuring the success of an internal database?

4. Why are secondary data often preferred to primary data?

5. What pitfalls might a researcher encounter in using secondary data?

6. Why has behavioral targeting become so popular with marketers? Why is it controversial?

7. In the absence of company problems, is there any need to conduct marketing research or develop a decision support system?

8. What is a marketing research aggregator? What role does it play in marketing research?

9. Divide the class into groups of four or five. Each team should go to the Internet and look up database marketing. Each team should then report to the class on how a specific company is effectively using databases to improve their marketing efficiency.

(Team Exercise)

WORKING THE NET

1. What makes vendors' Web sites a desirable tool for creating an internal database?

2. Go to *http://www.yankelovich.com*. Explain to the class the nature and scope of the Yankelovich MONITOR. How can marketing researchers use the data from this research?

3. Go to the National Opinion Research Center at *www.norc.uchicago.edu.* and describe what new reports are available for researchers.

4. You are interested in home-building trends in the United States, as your company, Whirlpool, is a major supplier of kitchen appliances. Go to *http://www.nahb.com* and describe what types of information at this site might be of interest to Whirlpool.

5. Go to *http://www.claritas.com*. Describe types of secondary data available at this site.

6. Go to *www.marketresearch.com* and explain what types of reports are available.

7. Go to *www.comscore.com* and explain what they offer their customers.

8. Go to *www.Nielsen.com* and read about BuzzMetrics. Explain how it works and why it is a valuable tool to some marketers.

REAL-LIFE RESEARCH • 4.1

Sanitized to Perfection

Marketing research firm Yankelovich's *Monitor Minute* newsletter has been tracking a growing segment of the American population it has dubbed "Neatniks"—those who agree that "having a clean, spotless home is important in personal life today." The group comprised 35 percent of those surveyed; Non-Neatniks made up 63 percent.

But consumers are seeking more from the act of cleaning than simply streak-free windows. Yankelovich examined the deeper dimensions today's consumers associate with cleaning, and how cleaning satisfies their emotional needs.

"As people increasingly look to gain control over what they can in the world, there is a growing minority of consumers focusing on the importance of maintaining a clean house," the report stated. "Cleaning today fills a multidimensional role in people's lives."

In other words, average American citizens can't create a cure for the bird flu; they do, however, have dominion over dust bunnies.

Being clean has taken on a more elevated status in maintaining one's overall well-being in the minds of consumers, who believe good grooming is a crucial component to staying healthy: The *Yankelovich Preventive Health and Wellness in America* study reports that two-thirds of respondents (68 percent) cited "personal hygiene and cleanliness" as the best way to maintain one's good health.

Three-quarters (72 percent) of the population said housecleaning is a regular physical activity, even when it's a drag. A year earlier, 63 percent of parents with kids under age 18 said keeping up with housework caused a fair amount to a great deal of stress in their lives.

While Neatniks may believe cleanliness is next to Godliness, it's more of an aspiration than an actual exertion for many of them. Only 22 percent of Americans surveyed said they have a clean and spotless home, and less than half (45 percent) of so-called Neatniks said this accurately describes the state of their domicile.[33]

I Clean, Therefore I Am (Stylish, Self-Reliant)[34]

In order to provide the biggest payoff from consumers' investment of time and elbow grease, Yankelovich suggests that marketers position cleaning tools as fulfilling a lot of other needs in their lives. Products and services that satisfy these higher-level cravings can gain a competitive advantage.

Neatniks' lives aren't solely about dusting and polishing the surfaces, but research suggests that such tasks may represent deeper themes. For example, the propensity for one to value cleaning correlates with a high premium on self-reliance. And Neatniks are more concerned than Non-Neatniks about how others view their personal style and in-the-know status. Here are partial results from the Yankelovich study.

Being as self-reliant as possible is important in my personal life today	**Neatniks 81%** **Non-Neatniks 66%**
Extremely/very important for others to see me as:	
Having a sense of style	**Neatniks 50%** **Non-Neatniks 31%**
Someone with "the inside scoop"	**Neatniks 39%** **Non-Neatniks 25%**
Concerned with buying products that express my own style and personality	**Neatniks 34%** **Non-Neatniks 30%**

Questions

1. Is the Yankelovich study primary or secondary data? Why?
2. How might some firms like Procter & Gamble use this information? Hoover (vacuum cleaners)?
3. Are psychographic data as helpful to marketers as demographic data?
4. What other sources might a company like Hoover use to help develop new products/product modifications, identify target customers, and develop a promotional strategy?

REAL-LIFE RESEARCH • 4.2

The Changing Face of Motherhood

Today's mothers of newborns are older, better educated, less likely to be white, and less likely to be married than their counterparts were in 1990.

There were more births to teenagers in 1990 than to women ages 35 and older. By 2008 (the latest date for which data is available), things had changed: 14 percent of births were to older women and 10 percent were to teens. Across all major race and ethnic groups, the rate of births to women ages 35 and older grew 64 percent between 1990 and 2008.

Another study on fertility attitudes and trends found:

- 35 percent of parents cited the reason "It wasn't a decision; it just happened" as very important and 12 percent as somewhat important in the decision to have their first or only child.

- Women (51 percent) were somewhat more likely than men (42 percent) to say that "it just happened" was somewhat or very important.

- Forty-six percent said two children was the ideal number for a family; 26 percent said three; 9 percent said four; and 3 percent each said zero, one, or five or more. Among parents of three or more children, 33 percent said two was ideal.

- Nearly two-thirds of Americans (65 percent) said the growing number of single women having babies is bad for society. Only a minority disapproved of more women having babies after age 40 (33 percent), more women undergoing fertility treatment in order to have a baby (28 percent), and more women not ever having children (38 percent).

- Most adults said they knew at least one woman who had a baby while she was not married and one man who fathered a child while he was not married. A third said they knew a woman who had fertility treatment in order to get pregnant.

There are fewer women in the prime childbearing years now than in 1990, as the youngest Baby Boomers have aged into their mid-40s. But changes in the racial and ethnic makeup of young women—mainly, the growth of the Hispanic population, which has higher birth rates that other groups—have helped keep birth numbers relatively level.

Another influence on births is the nation's growing number of immigrants, who tend to have higher birth rates than the native-born (although those rates have declined in recent years). The share of births to foreign-born mothers—15 percent of U.S. births in 1990—grew as least 60 percent through 2004. Births to foreign-born women in 2004 accounted for the majority of Hispanic (61 percent) and Asian (83 percent) births.

Eighty-two percent of the nation's population growth through 2050 will be accounted for by immigrants who arrived in the United States after 2005 and their descendants, assuming current trends continue. Of the 142 million people added to the population from 2005 to 2050, the projections say, 50 million will be the children or grandchildren of the new immigrants.

The average age for U.S. mothers who had their first baby in 2008 was 25, a year older than the average first-time mother in 1990. Among all women who had a baby in 2008, the average age is 27, up from 26 in 1990. The prime childbearing years remain 29–34—three-quarters of mothers of newborns are in this age range. Birth rates peak among women in their late 20s.

Since 1990, birth rates have risen for all women ages 30 and older. Although in some cases the number of births is small, the rate increases have been sharpest for women in the oldest age groups—47 percent for women ages 35–39 and 80 percent for women ages 40–44, for example.

Dual Factors

The delay in age of motherhood is associated with delay in age of marriage and with growing educational attainment, the report notes. The more education a woman has, the later she tends to marry and have children. Birth rates also have risen for the most educated women—those with at least some college education—while staying relatively stable for women with less education. These dual factors have worked together to increase the education levels of mothers and newborns.

Among mothers under age 50 and fathers under age 60, 82 percent say they plan to have no more children. When those parents, as well as parents beyond the childbearing ages, were asked why they decided to limit the number of children they had, the only reason cited as "very important" by most parents (64 percent) was that they wanted to devote time to the children they already had. A total of 76 percent described this reason as very important or somewhat important. A total of 72 percent said the cost of having another child was very or somewhat important to them in deciding to limit their family size.

Cited by smaller groups of respondents as very or somewhat important were the stress of raising children (49 percent), the wishes of their spouse or partner for no more children (46 percent), their age (42 percent), and their desire to have time for other interests (40 percent).[35]

Questions

1. Is this information primary or secondary data?
2. How might Gerber use this information? Would it need to follow up with primary research?
3. Cite examples of how promotion may need to change to reach new mothers.
4. If Disney World considers adding a new theme area to its Orlando park, what clues might they pull from the above case? Suggest areas of follow-up research.

Qualitative Research

LEARNING OBJECTIVES

→ **1.** To define qualitative research.

→ **2.** To explore the popularity of qualitative research.

→ **3.** To learn about focus groups and their tremendous popularity.

→ **4.** To gain insight into conducting and analyzing a focus group.

→ **5.** To learn about other forms of qualitative research.

What is qualitative research and what are the advantages and disadvantages? Why are focus groups so popular and what are the trends in focus group research? What other qualitative tools are available to marketing researchers? These are the areas that will be covered in chapter five.

Nature of Qualitative Research

Qualitative research is a term used loosely to refer to research whose findings are not subject to quantification or quantitative analysis. A quantitative study may determine that a heavy user of a particular brand of tequila is 21 to 35 years of age and has an annual income of $25,000 to $40,000. While **quantitative research** might be used to find statistically significant differences between heavy and light users, qualitative research could be used to examine the attitudes, feelings, and motivations of the heavy user. Advertising agencies planning a campaign for tequila might employ qualitative techniques to learn how heavy users express themselves and what language they use—essentially, how to communicate with them.

The qualitative approach was derived from the work of the mid-18th-century historian Giambattista Vico. Vico wrote that only people can understand people and that they do so through a faculty called *intuitive understanding*. In sociology and other social sciences, the concept of *Verstehen*, or the intuitive experiment, and the use of empathy have been associated with major discoveries (and disputes).

> **qualitative research**
> Research whose findings are not subject to quantification or quantitative analysis.

> **quantitative research**
> Research that uses mathematical analysis.

Qualitative Research versus Quantitative Research

Exhibit 5.1 compares qualitative and quantitative research on several levels. Perhaps most significant to managers is the fact that qualitative research typically is characterized by small samples—a trait that has been a focal point for criticism of all qualitative techniques. In essence, many managers are reluctant to base important strategy decisions on small-sample research because it relies so greatly on the subjectivity and interpretation of the researcher. They strongly prefer a large sample, with results analyzed on a computer

EXHIBIT 5.1	Qualitative versus Quantitative Research	
	Qualitative Research	**Quantitative Research**
Types of questions	Probing	Limited probing
Sample size	Small	Large
Amount of information from each respondent	Substantial	Varies
Requirements for administration	Interviewer with special skills	Interviewer with fewer special skills or no interviewer
Type of analysis	Subjective, interpretive	Statistical, summation
Hardware	Sound recorders, projection devices, video recorders, pictures, discussion guides	Questionnaires, computers, printouts, mobile devices
Degree of replicability	Low	High
Researcher training	Psychology, sociology, social psychology, consumer behavior, marketing, marketing research	Statistical, decision models, decision support systems, computer programming, marketing, marketing research
Type of research	Exploratory	Descriptive or causal

and summarized into tables. These managers feel comfortable with marketing research based on large samples and high levels of statistical significance because the data are generated in a rigorous and scientific manner.

Popularity of Qualitative Research

Companies are now spending over $4.3 billion annually on qualitative research.[1] Why does the popularity of qualitative research continue to grow? First, qualitative research is usually much cheaper than quantitative research. Second, there is no better way to understand the in-depth motivations and feelings of consumers. When, in a popular form of qualitative research, product managers unobtrusively observe from behind a one-way mirror, they obtain firsthand experiences with flesh-and-blood consumers. Instead of plodding through a computer printout or consultant's report that requires them to digest reams of numbers, the product manager and other marketing personnel observe consumers' reactions to concepts and hear consumers discuss their own and their competitors' products at length, in their own language. Sitting behind a one-way mirror can be a humbling experience for a new product-development manager when the consumer begins to tear apart product concepts that were months in development in the sterile laboratory environment.

A third reason for the popularity of qualitative research is that it can improve the efficiency of quantitative research. Reckitt Benckiser PLC, the maker of Woolite and Lysol, knew women were not happy with how glasses were cleaned in a dishwasher. Focus groups learned that, over time, glasses washed in a dishwasher tended to become cloudy and stained. The company decided to embark on a major quantitative study to determine the extent of the perceived "staining" problem among households with dishwashers. The quantitative study verified that consumers were indeed unhappy with how their glasses looked after numerous rounds in the dishwasher. They also were willing to pay a reasonable price to find a solution. Reckitt Benckiser recently introduced Finish Glass Protector, a dishwasher detergent that protects glassware from mineral corrosion. Thus qualitative research led to a well-conceived quantitative study that verified demand for the new product.

It is becoming more common for marketing researchers to combine qualitative and quantitative research into a single study or a series of studies. The Finish Glass example showed how qualitative research can be used prior to quantitative research; in other research designs, the two types of research are conducted in the reverse order. For instance, the patterns displayed in quantitative research can be enriched with the addition of qualitative information on the reasons and motivations of consumers. One major insurance company conducted a quantitative study in which respondents were asked to rank the importance of 50 service characteristics. Later, focus groups were conducted in which participants were asked to define and expound on the top 10 characteristics. Most of these characteristics dealt with client–insurance agent interactions. From these focus groups the researchers found that "agent responds quickly" may mean either a virtually instantaneous response or a response within a reasonable time; that is, it means "as soon as is humanly possible for emergencies" and "about 24 hours for routine matters." The researchers noted that had they not conducted focus groups after the quantitative study, they could only have theorized about what "responds quickly" means to customers.

In the final analysis, all marketing research is undertaken to increase the effectiveness of decision making. Qualitative research blends with quantitative measures to provide a more thorough understanding of consumer demand. Qualitative techniques involve open-ended questioning and probing. The resulting data are rich, human, subtle, and often very revealing.

Limitations of Qualitative Research

Qualitative research can and does produce helpful and useful information—yet it is held in disdain by some researchers. One drawback relates to the fact that marketing successes and failures many times are based on small differences in attitudes or opinions about a marketing mix, and qualitative research does not distinguish those small differences as well as large-scale quantitative research does. However, qualitative research is sometimes able to detect problems that escape notice in a quantitative study. For example, a major manufacturer of household cleaners conducted a large quantitative study in an effort to learn why its bathroom cleanser had lackluster sales when in fact its chemical compound was more effective than those used by leading competitors. The quantitative study provided no clear-cut answer. The frustrated product manager then turned to qualitative research, which quickly found that the muted pastel colors on the package did not connote "cleansing strength" to the shopper. In light of this finding and the finding that a number of people were using old toothbrushes to clean between their bathroom tiles, the package was redesigned with brighter, bolder colors and with a brush built into the top.

A second limitation of qualitative studies is that they are not necessarily representative of the population of interest to the researcher. One would be hard-pressed to say that a group of 10 college students was representative of all college students, of college students at a particular university, of business majors at that university, or even of marketing majors! Small sample size and free-flowing discussion can lead qualitative research projects down many paths. Because the subjects of qualitative research are free to talk about what interests them, a dominant individual in a group discussion can lead the group into areas of only tangential interest to the researcher. It takes a highly skilled researcher to get the discussion back on track without stifling the group's interest, enthusiasm, and willingness to speak out.

The Importance of Focus Groups

Focus groups had their beginnings in group therapy used by psychiatrists. Today, a **focus group** consists of 8 to 12 participants who are led by a moderator in an in-depth discussion on one particular topic or concept. The goal of focus group research is to learn and understand what people have to say and why. The emphasis is on getting people to talk at length and in detail about the subject at hand. The intent is to find out how they feel about a product, concept, idea, or organization; how it fits into their lives; and their emotional involvement with it.

> **focus group**
> Group of 8 to 12 participants who are led by a moderator in an in-depth discussion on one particular topic or concept.

Focus groups are much more than merely question-and-answer interviews. A distinction is made between *group dynamics* and *group interviewing*. The interaction associated with **group dynamics** is essential to the success of focus group research; this interaction is the reason for conducting research with a group rather than with individuals. One idea behind focus groups is that a response from one person will become a stimulus for another person, thereby generating an interplay of responses that will yield more information than if the same number of people had contributed independently.

> **group dynamics**
> Interaction among people in a group.

The idea for group dynamics research in marketing came from the field of social psychology, where studies indicated that, unknown to themselves, people of all walks of life and in all occupations would talk more about a topic and do so in greater depth if they were encouraged to act spontaneously instead of reacting to questions. Normally, in group dynamics, direct questions are avoided. In their place are indirect inquiries that stimulate free and spontaneous discussions. The result is a much richer base of information, of a kind impossible to obtain by direct questioning.

Popularity of Focus Groups

The terms *qualitative research* and *focus groups* are often used as synonyms by marketing research practitioners. Popular writing abounds, with examples of researchers referring to qualitative research in one breath and focus groups in the next. Although focus groups are but one aspect of qualitative research, the overwhelming popularity of the technique has virtually overshadowed the use of other qualitative tools.

How popular are focus groups? Most marketing research firms, advertising agencies, and consumer goods manufacturers use them. Today, most of all marketing research expenditures for qualitative research is spent on focus groups. The majority of focus research projects in the United States take place in over 750 focus facilities and are directed by over 1,000 moderators. The most common formats of qualitative research are focus groups and individual depth interviews (IDIs).

Focus group research is a globally accepted form of marketing research. It is estimated that over 550,000 focus groups are conducted worldwide each year. Approximately 255,000 focus group sessions take place in the United States annually.[2]

Focus groups tend to be used more extensively by consumer goods companies than by industrial goods organizations, as forming industrial groups poses a host of problems not found in consumer research. For example, it is usually quite easy to assemble a group of 12 homemakers; however, putting together a group of 10 engineers, sales managers, or financial analysts is far more costly and time-consuming.

Lewis Stone, former manager of Colgate-Palmolive's Research and Development Division, says the following about focus groups:

If it weren't for focus groups, Colgate-Palmolive Co. might never know that some women squeeze their bottles of dishwashing soap, others squeeeeeze them, and still others squeeeeeeeeze out the desired amount. Then there are the ones who use the soap "neat." That is, they put the product directly on a sponge or washcloth and wash the dishes under running water until the suds run out. Then they apply more detergent.

Stone was explaining how body language, exhibited during focus groups, provides insights into a product that are not apparent from reading questionnaires on habits and practices. Focus groups represent a most efficient way of learning how one's products are actually used in the home. By drawing out the panelists to describe in detail how they do certain tasks . . . you can learn a great deal about possible need-gaps that could be filled by new or improved products, and also how a new product might be received.[3]

Thus, an "experiencing" approach represents an opportunity to learn from a flesh-and-blood consumer. Reality in the kitchen or supermarket differs drastically from that in most corporate offices. Focus groups allow the researcher to experience the emotional framework in which the product is being used. In a sense, the researcher can go into a person's life and relive with him or her all the satisfactions, dissatisfactions, rewards, and frustrations experienced when the product is taken home.

Robert L. Wehling, senior vice president of global marketing and consumer knowledge at the Procter & Gamble Company, issued the following mandate to researchers: "Know the individual consumer's heart and you will own the future! Get to know this changing consumer personally. Not as an average but as a person."[4]

Conducting Focus Groups

On the following pages, we will consider the process of conducting focus groups, illustrated in Exhibit 5.2. We devote considerable space to this topic because there is much potential for researcher error in conducting focus groups.

Exhibit 5.2

Steps in Conducting a Focus Group

Setting Focus groups are usually held in a **focus group facility**. The setting is often a conference room, with a large one-way mirror built into one wall. Microphones are placed in an unobtrusive location (usually the ceiling) to record the discussion. Behind the mirror is the viewing room, which holds chairs and note-taking benches or tables for the clients. The viewing room also houses the recording or videotaping equipment. The photo in Exhibit 5.3 illustrates a focus group in progress.

Some research firms offer a living-room setting as an alternative to the conference room. It is presumed that the informality of a living room (a typical homelike setting) will make the participants more at ease. Another variation is to televise the proceedings to a remote viewing room rather than use a one-way mirror. This approach offers clients the advantage of being able to move around and speak in a normal tone of voice without being heard through the wall. On more than one occasion, focus groups have been dis-

focus group facility
Research facility consisting of a conference room or living room setting and a separate observation room with a one-way mirror or live audiovisual feed.

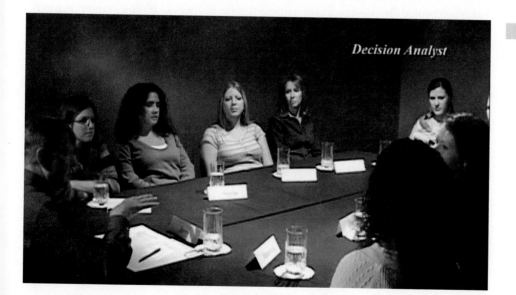

Exhibit 5.3

A Focus Group in Progress

tracted by a flash seen through the mirror when a client moved too suddenly while watching the group.

Participants   Participants for focus groups are recruited from a variety of sources. Two traditional procedures are mall-intercept interviewing and random telephone screening. (Both methods are described in detail in Chapter 6.) Researchers normally establish criteria for the group participants. For example, if Quaker Oats is researching a new cereal, it might request as participants mothers who have children between 7 and 12 years old and who have served cold cereal, perhaps of a specific brand, in the past 3 weeks.

Some progressive focus group researchers are now combining psychographics and demographics to recruit group participants. For example, RoperASW in New York City has studied a consumer segment it calls "the Influentials"—the one American in every 10 who has significant word-of-mouth clout. Drawing on a database of more than 10,000 questions and interviews with more than 50,000 Influentials and 500,000 other Americans, RoperASW uses its knowledge of this segment to help its clients recruit candidates for qualitative research, says RoperASW CEO Ed Keller.[5]

"Influentials are two to five years ahead of the curve in their involvement with new trends and new products and lifestyle choices. They have this bellwether nature to them," explains Keller. Recruiting Influentials is particularly useful when a marketer is trying to determine how to launch a new product or how a product's use is changing over time, he says. "We'd never say that this is a panacea for every eventuality, but to the extent that you're looking for people knowledgeable, informed and open-minded, and ahead of the curve, Influentials are very appropriate to study in qualitative research," adds Keller.[6]

Other focus group recruiters go to where the target market is to find qualified respondents. This type of recruiting means going to nursery schools to find moms with kids, health clubs to find people with active lifestyles, the home improvement center to find do-it-yourselfers, supermarkets to find primary food shoppers, and community centers to find senior citizens.

Usually, researchers strive to avoid repeat, or "professional," respondents in focus groups. Professional respondents are viewed by many researchers as actors or, at the very least, less than candid participants. Questions also may be raised regarding the motives of the person who would continually come to group sessions. Is she or he lonely? Does she or he really need the respondent fee that badly? It is highly unlikely that professional respondents are representative of many, if any, target markets. Unfortunately, field services find it much easier to use repeat respondents than to recruit a new group of individuals each time. Sample screening questions to identify repeat respondents are shown in Exhibit 5.4.

Although there is no ideal number of participants, a typical group will contain 8 participants. If the group contains more than 8 people, group members will have little time to express their opinions. Rarely will a group last more than 2 hours; an hour and a half is more common. The first 10 minutes is spent on introductions and an explanation of procedures. This leaves about 80 useful minutes in the session, and up to 25 percent of that time may be taken by the moderator. With 10 people in the group, an average of only 6 minutes per individual is left for actual discussion. If the topic is quite interesting or of a technical nature, fewer than 8 respondents may be needed. The type of group will also affect the number recruited.

Why do people agree to participate in focus groups? Research shows that the number one reason is money.[7] Other motivations, in rank order, are (2) the topic was interesting, (3) it was a convenient time, (4) focus groups are fun, (5) respondent knew a lot about the product, (6) curiosity, and (7) focus groups offer an opportunity to express opinions. The study also found that participants who came only for the money were less committed to research and tended to fulfill their roles in a more perfunctory way.

1. Past Participation Series

Sometimes it is important to talk with people who have participated in previous research because they have experience talking about certain topics. At other times, it is important to talk with people who have never participated in an opinion study. Often we are looking for a mix of different experiences. What type of opinion studies, if any, have you ever participated in? (DO NOT READ LIST.)

	CIRCLE ALL MENTIONS
One-on-one in-person depth interview	1
Group interview with two or more participants	2
Mock jury or trial	3
Product placement test with a follow-up interview	4
Mail interview	5
Internet survey	6
Phone survey	7
Other (SPECIFY)	8
None	9

1A. When was the last time you participated in a

_____ Group interview with two or more participants

_____ (LIST ANOTHER TYPE OF RESEARCH YOU MIGHT CONSIDER INAPPROPRIATE.)

IF WITHIN THE LAST SIX MONTHS, THANK AND TERMINATE.

1B. What were the topics of all of the group interviews in which you have participated?

_____

_____

IF ONE OF THE TOPICS LISTED BELOW IS MENTIONED, THANK AND TERMINATE.

(   ) MP3 Players

(   ) Camera Cell Phones

1C. Are you currently scheduled to participate in any type of market research study?

	CIRCLE
Yes	1→ (THANK AND TERMINATE)
No	2 → (CONTINUE)

Source: Merril Shugoll and Nancy Kolkebeck, "You Get What You Ask For," *Quirk's Marketing Research Review* (December 1999), pp. 61–65. Reprinted by permission.

Exhibit 5.4

Sample Screening Questions for Identifying Professional Focus Group Participants

Moderator   Having qualified respondents and a good focus group moderator are the keys to a successful focus group. A **focus group moderator** needs two sets of skills. First, the moderator must be able to conduct a group properly. Second, he or she must have good business skills in order to effectively interact with the client. Key attributes for conducting a focus group include the following:

1. Genuine interest in people, their behavior, emotions, lifestyles, passions, and opinions.

2. Acceptance and appreciation for the differences in people, especially those whose lives vary greatly from your own.

3. Good listening skills: the ability both to hear what is being said and to identify what is not being said.

focus group moderator
Person hired by the client to lead the focus group; this person should have a background in psychology or sociology or, at least, marketing.

4. Good observation skills: the ability to see in detail what is happening or not happening and to interpret body language.

5. Interest in a wide range of topics and the ability to immerse yourself in the topic and learn the necessary knowledge and language quickly.

6. Good oral and written communication skills: the ability to clearly express yourself and to do so confidently in groups of all types and sizes.

7. Objectivity: the ability to set your personal ideas and feelings aside and remain open to the ideas and feelings of others.

8. Sound knowledge of the basic principles, foundations, and applications of research, marketing, and advertising.

9. Flexibility, ability to live with uncertainty, make fast decisions, and think on your feet (or the part of your anatomy that is seated in the moderator's chair).

10. Good attention to detail and organizational ability.[8]

Rapport is the medium that makes research work. Rapport means to be in a close or sympathetic relationship. A moderator develops a free and easy sense of discourse about anything with respondents. These strangers meet and are helped to a common ground through the ease of rapport. In a comfortable, nonthreatening, lively place, they can talk about anything at all—about sausage, insurance, tires, baked goods, magazines. In research the moderator is the bridge builder, and rapport is the bridge between people's everyday lives and the client's business interest.

Naomi Henderson, CEO of Riva Marketing Research, talks about how she builds rapport in the following Practicing Marketing Research box.

PRACTICING MARKETING RESEARCH

Building a Strong Bond with Focus Group Participants

I have found, over the years, that rapport is a multilayered process. While it doesn't take long to create, it isn't composed of just one activity. It reminds me of the act of walking. It's not something I think about when I'm doing it, but, when you break it down, it's composed of many different activities that involve so much more than just the feet.

Once rapport is created, there's an unspoken agreement to engage in conversation. The moderator has created a safe space for respondents to answer a wide variety of questions. The moderator has demonstrated a nonjudgmental listening style, and respondents step up to answer because they know they'll be listened to and respected. Moderators know they'll obtain responses because they have established guidelines for behavior, and they have also demonstrated an open manner and attentive attitude.

Tools, Tips and Techniques

Smile. First of all, smile as soon as you see respondents, and be sure it is genuine. Also, during ground rules and each respondent self-introduction, make eye contact lasting at least 20 seconds with each participant to form a bond or connection in a group. In those 20 seconds, there is no one in the room except the moderator and the respondent. Group reactions and interactions will come later in the interview.

Get physical. It's also a good idea to imagine that you are making a physical connection with each participant during introductions like a handshake when you meet someone. As you greet them and say hello, picture handing them one end of a silk thread while you hold the other end in your hand. Asking a follow-up question to their introduction or referencing a similarity in your life (e.g., "I have a dog, too.") is when they accept their end of the silken thread, via dialogue. During the session, keep checking the threads to make sure none have gone slack. Picture taking the threads back for closure.

Turn on the charm. Make an extra effort to respond warmly to each respondent when round-robin introductions are made. Make comments like "Welcome," "Glad you could make it," and "Thank you for coming."

Offer empathy. If some participants have problems or concerns as they arrive at the group, address these issues, either on your own or by enlisting facility staff help, before starting the group itself. People will appreciate your concern and will reciprocate by doing their best to help you.

Be real. Find a way to be fully sincere in the actions suggested. If you remain "authentic" and "appropriate" without phoniness or lies, you set the example and imply that the same behavior is desired from the respondents. It is during the first 3 minutes of a group that participants form their first opinions about me, and this is where the platform for rapport is built. Without rapport, discussion can take place, but will invariably lack the richness of groups where it is present and may well affect the level of candor achieved. I know it is my job, as a moderator, to establish and manage rapport as early as I can and be willing to rebuild rapport at any state of the group as needed.

Mind the details. Include logistics with your introductory statements. Mention food and drink and where bathrooms are located and ask if everyone is comfortable with the temperature. All these add to the group's impression of you as a caring person, not just a "taker" of information. Questions like these build rapport: "I can hear you clearly, can you hear me?" and "Do you want water or something to sip on in case you get thirsty?"

Come to complete closure. Even if the comments are brief, make them final. There are times when rapport is so strong that the group does not want to leave, or individuals want to stay in touch beyond the research setting. Learn to say a firm goodbye. Don't leave people hanging. A good way to bring closure in a focus group is to stand up, go to room exit, and say, "I'll shake your hand on your way out—and then you'll see the front desk for your stipend."[9]

Questions

1. Is it necessary to have rapport in order to have an effective focus group?

2. What other techniques might a moderator use to create rapport?

In the past few years, there has been an increase in the number of formal moderator training courses offered by advertising agencies, research firms, and manufacturers with large marketing research departments. Most programs are strictly for employees, but a few are open to anyone. Also, there is the Qualitative Research Consultants Association that promotes professionalism in a qualitative research. The association has a quarterly publication, *QRCAViews*, that features ideas and tools for qualitative research. In addition, the organization holds an annual conference dedicated to improving qualitative research. You can learn more at *www.qrca.org*.

Discussion Guide Regardless of how well trained and personable the moderator is, a successful focus group requires a well-planned discussion guide. A **discussion guide** is

> ➤ **discussion guide**
> Written outline of topics to be covered during a focus group discussion.

a written outline of the topics to be covered during the session. Usually the guide is generated by the moderator based on the research objectives and client information needs. It serves as a checklist to ensure that all salient topics are covered and in the proper sequence. For example, an outline might begin with attitudes and feelings toward eating out, then move to fast foods, and conclude with a discussion of the food and decor of a particular chain. It is important to get the research director and other client observers, such as a brand manager, to agree that the topics listed in the guide are the most important ones to be covered. It is not uncommon for a team approach to be used in generating a discussion guide.

The guide tends to lead the discussion through three stages. In the first stage, rapport is established, the rules of group interactions are explained, and objectives are given. In the second stage, the moderator attempts to provoke intensive discussion. The final stage is used for summarizing significant conclusions and testing the limits of belief and commitment.

Exhibit 5.5 shows an actual discussion guide for diet breads by a Decision Analyst moderator. The groups were held in several cities around the country.

Focus Group Length   Many managers today prefer shorter (around an hour) focus groups. Yet the average group today is still about 90 minutes. Although shorter groups may be the trend, there is much to be said for longer focus groups. By a longer group we mean 2 hours or longer. A long group helps managers get more things done in a single session, and it also allows the respondents to get more involved, participate in more time-consuming tasks, and interact more extensively.

The issue of group length is not an isolated one; rather, it is intertwined with a second key factor: the number of questions in the discussion guide. One of the biggest problems with focus groups today, in our opinion, is the tendency to prepare discussion guides that pose far too many questions, which virtually precludes any depth of coverage or any significant group interactions. Managers want to get their money's worth, so it makes sense for them to ask every possible question. The "focus group" turns into a group interrogation or survey but without the controls and statistical power of scientific surveys.

In order to think more explicitly and logically about the number of questions to ask, managers should examine the interactions between the length of the focus group and the size of the discussion guide. As illustrated in Exhibit 5.6, more questions and less time combine to create a research environment that elicits responses that are mere survey-like sound bites. Also, moderators who have to plow through 40 questions in 90 minutes are likely to feel rushed, unable to probe interesting responses, and inclined to be abrupt with long-winded or slow individuals. As we move up and to the right in the table, these pressures and constraints diminish. With fewer questions and more time, respondents can elaborate their answers, moderators can probe more effectively, and the pace becomes more relaxed, natural, and humanistic.[10]

The Client's Role   The client, of course, selects the supplier and sometimes the moderator as well.[11] The client typically selects the markets where the groups will be held and specifies the characteristics of the group respondents. Sometimes the client will hand a finished discussion guide to the moderator, and, in other circumstances, the moderator and the client work together to create a final guide.

The client should go over not only the discussion guide with the moderator but the product or service being discussed as well. For example, a moderator was doing a group on new earpieces, and the client had not shown the moderator how they worked. The moderator was not told that, if you wore glasses, the frames would interfere with putting on the earpieces. When the moderator attempted to demonstrate the earpieces, they would not fit in his hears. Obviously, this created a negative impression among group participants.[12]

I. Introduction
- A. Recording/observers
- B. Casual, relaxed, informal
- C. No right or wrong answers
- D. Be honest. Tell the truth
- E. Discussion rules
  - Talk one at a time
  - Don't dominate the discussion
  - Talk in any order
  - Listen to others

II. General Attitudes toward Bread
- A. Eating more or less bread now, compared to two years ago? Explore reasons.
- B. Advantages of bread, compared to other foods?
- C. Disadvantages of bread, compared to other foods?
- D. Words/mental images associated with great tasting bread?
- E. Foods bread goes with best? Why?

III. Usage/Purchase of Bread
- A. When and where is bread consumed most often?
- B. How does bread usage vary by household member? Why?
- C. Types of bread used most frequently?
- D. Likes/dislikes of each type of bread?
- E. Brands preferred? Why these brands? Vary by family member?

IV. Bread Consumption When Dieting
- A. Changes in bread consumption related to dieting? Why?
- B. Types of bread eaten when dieting, if any reasons?
- C. Role of bread in dieting?

V. Attitudes toward Diet Breads
- A. Awareness of diet breads/brands?
- B. Experiences with diet breads/brands?
- C. Satisfaction with each brand? Why like or not like? Brand perceptions?
- D. Important factors/product attributes associated with preferred brands?

VI. The Perfect Diet Bread
- A. Product characteristics?
  - Taste
  - Texture
  - Color
  - Crust
- B. Nutritional benefits?
- C. Packaging preferences?

VII. Show and Discuss Advertising Concepts
- A. Overall reactions to each concept?
- B. Likes/dislikes for each concept?
- C. Main idea for each concept?
- D. Believability?

VIII. Reactions to Diet Bread Samples
- A. Overall reactions to each bread?
- B. Reactions to taste?
- C. Reactions to texture and mouth feel?
- D. Reaction to slice shape and thickness?
- E. Reaction to loaf shape and size?
- F. Reaction to color?
- G. Reaction to feel in hand?

Exhibit 5.5

Decision Analyst, Inc. Discussion Outline Diet Breads

EXHIBIT 5.6	Response Time per Question per Respondent		
	Focus Group Length		
Number of Questions	**75 min.**	**90 min.**	**120 min.**
15	:30	:36	:48
20	:23	:27	:36
25	:18	:22	:29
30	:15	:18	:24
35	:13	:15	:21
40	:11	:14	:18

Note: The analysis assumes a group comprising 10 respondents.

Source: Dennis Rook, "Out of Focus Groups," *Marketing Research* (Summer 2003), p. 13.

→ **instant analysis**
Moderator debriefing, offering a forum for brainstorming by the moderator and client observers.

Focus Group Report   Typically, after the final group in a series is completed, there will be a moderator debriefing, sometimes called **instant analysis**. This tradition has both pros and cons. Arguments for instant analysis include the idea that it serves as a forum for combining the knowledge of the marketing specialists who viewed the group with that of the moderator. It gives the client an opportunity to hear and react to the moderator's initial perceptions, and it harnesses the heightened awareness and excitement of the moment to generate new ideas and implications in a brainstorming environment.

The shortcomings include the possibility of biasing future analysis on the part of the moderator with this "hip-shooting commentary," conducted without the benefit of time to reflect on what transpired. Instant analysis will be influenced by recency, selective recall, and other factors associated with limited memory capabilities; it does not allow the moderator to hear all that was said in a less than highly involved and anxious state. There is nothing wrong with a moderator debriefing as long as the moderator explicitly reserves the right to change her or his opinion after reviewing the tapes.

Today, a formal focus group report is typically a PowerPoint presentation. The written report is nothing more than a copy of the PowerPoint slides.

Jacob Brown of In-Depth Research discusses conducting focus groups in the accompanying Global Research box.

Focus Group Trends

Video Transmissions   A very popular trend in focus group research is conducting the groups online. This topic is discussed in detail in Chapter 7. Even when focus groups are conducted in traditional focus group facilities there is a growing tendency for clients to watch the sessions online. The advantage to the client is that they can avoid the time and expense of traveling to a distant city. Over 25 percent of all focus groups conducted in traditional facilities involve video transmissions.

Focus Group Panels   Typically, a screening question for participating in a focus group is: "Have you participated in a focus group within the last six months?" If the answer is "yes," they are disqualified. The notion is that clients don't want professional respondents but want "fresh participants." A different model now being used by some firms is a focus group panel. The idea is to establish a group of about 8 to 12 qualified respondents who agree to participate in a series of interviews on a given product, service,

GLOBAL RESEARCH

Planning Global Focus Groups

Consistency is best achieved by building a well-defined research template that clearly communicates research guidelines but still allows each moderator to adapt the process to fit local culture and individual style. Clearly articulating these ground rules will eliminate much of the ambiguity and reduce opportunities for misunderstanding. Some simple suggestions include the following.

- Start the research in your home country (we'll assume you're a U.S.-based company). That way all the stakeholders have a chance to attend the groups and agree on how the research "should" look before you fan out across the globe.

- Send copies of the U.S. videotapes to each foreign moderator. Remember that you may need to convert the tapes to the appropriate video format for each country and pay to have a translator watch the video with the moderator.

- Have the U.S. moderator schedule conference calls with each moderator to discuss the research process and answer questions—after they have watched the videos.

- If your budget allows it, have the U.S. moderator travel to each country. The U.S. moderator can manage the process locally, give consistent direction to each moderator, and ensure that the research doesn't get off course.

Internationally, most moderators have a more passive moderating style. They generally like a more leisurely pace and a more open group environment. As a result, you may not be able to cover as many topics as you might in the United States, nor will you be able to drill down quite as deeply.

Tips for Some Major Countries

Here are a few facts about conducting research in some of the major markets.

Japan

Scheduling a large number of B2B groups can be a challenge in Japan since you can only do one focus group each night, not two as we do in the United States. Professionals have long commutes, they work late, and they can't leave early or do a lunch group. However, they are willing to come in and do groups or interviews on the weekend. So, if you need to do six groups, think of doing three on Saturday and three on Sunday. But remember that there's a lot of competition for space at facilities on the weekend, so book early.

Germany

When doing any research in Germany, be aware that the privacy laws are probably the most restrictive in the world. Your ability to get names from e-mail lists, publication lists, or other databases can be severely constrained. Even using names from your own company database may be an issue.

France

Paris is famous for strikes, especially among the transportation workers. Check with the recruiter to see if there are any strikes on the horizon. If strikes have been in the news, make sure you schedule enough replacements and expect some delays. If a transportation strike is expected, you can still do the research, but have the recruiter check with each respondent about his or her ability to get to the facility if there is a strike. And make sure your hotel is within walking distance of the facility.

England

There is a wide mix of educational levels among UK businesspeople. Leaving school early is not uncommon in England, and many successful businesspeople have relatively little formal education. If a degree is important, make sure to include it in the screener—don't assume it the way you would in the United States. Conversely, don't require a degree in the screener unless you really feel it's important.

Scandinavia

Companies often overlook the Scandinavian countries when planning European research. But remember: Scandinavia has the best technology infrastructure and the most educated and fluent English-speaking professionals in Europe.[13]

Questions

1. Can focus groups be conducted the same all over the world?

2. How might culture impact a focus group?

---

or topic. Once recruited, the same group of respondents would then agree to meet once a month for approximately a six-month period.

One advantage of the panel is that a variety of topics can be addressed and then revisited if necessary. For example, assume that a consumer packaged-goods company is seeking to launch a new line of salad dressings. Its qualitative panel starts out first with the seeds of new ideas for a line of salad dressings. The next session refines those ideas to the point where packaging, graphics and flavor concepts are developed. And before the subsequent session, advertising stimuli boards can be created with positioning statements and potential names generated. This, ultimately, can save clients time and money.

The key advantages of focus group panels are as follows.

- Consumer panels can be significantly less expensive versus recruiting the same number of separate groups over the same time period. Because the same people are used each month, there are no additional recruiting costs—only simple reminder calls are required. This more streamlined design can result in a 25 to 30 percent reduction in cost to clients.

- Because quick feedback is critical, and the entire process is so fluid, the company doesn't require a full report. A topline summary works well and can be delivered just a few days after the panel convenes.

- Companies also appreciate the discipline that consumer panels can impose in the process. They know that each month they need to meet with marketing, packaging and R&D to determine what issued still exist. Meanwhile, the various internal departments welcome the concept of having a voice in the panel content each month.[14]

Adding Marketing Professionals as Repondents When the product or service concept warrants it, marketing professionals (e.g., advertising executives, new product development managers, marketing officers) are mixed in with typical consumers. These professionals are referred to as "prosumers." British Airways was looking to challenge American Airlines and Virgin Atlantic for dominance of business-class related travel on the airlines' transatlantic routes. The qualitative research being conducted with consumers was not getting the research team the kind of insights they were seeking. They decided they would need to shake things up if they were going to achieve any breakthroughs that would help British Airways differentiate its business-class travel experience.

The research team took an unusual step. They set up focus groups that involved the usual target—regular business travelers. But they added product-development and marketing professionals who frequently traveled from New York to London—precisely the kind of professional that would typically be intentionally screened out.

After a joint focus group that included both consumers and these "prosumers," the prosumers group joined British Airways' leadership team for a gloves-off creative session that incorporated what was learned in the focus group, but also took into account the prosumers' understanding of the types of informed, innovative thinking the research team was seeking.

One of those prosumers, a research and development director at Unilever, shared the confidence that when she travels, she likes a seat that fully reclines but does not like to be sleeping in full-recline mode next to strangers or business associates. And she presumed that many women travelers would probably agree with her. From that observation, an idea was born. And now, seats that cradle passengers and pullout privacy panels are designed into almost all international business-travel sections.

"Her professional experience—understanding demographics, knowing that we were looking for breakthrough ideas—and her ability to express her ideas in a useful way to the research team made her a key part of the process," says Christopher Miller, founder of Lancaster, Pennsylvania-based Innovation Focus, Inc. "That creative tension, where respondents speak both personally and as a professional, has become the foundation of this process.[15]

The marketing team at WD-40 Company got precisely that—breakthroughs—when they used the process to help with their product development efforts. Their project involved WD-40 Company professionals, two prosumers and a small group of consumers. In the creative session following the focus groups, it was a prosumer who wondered whether the lubricant could be put in a handheld pen format. That outside-the-box idea is now known as the No-Mess Pen. And another prosumer who needed to cover a very large piece of equipment with WD-40 tossed out the question of whether the product could be put into a bug spray-style fogger. The answer was yes. That business-to-business product is now called Big Blast Can.[16]

Benefits and Drawbacks of Focus Groups

The benefits and drawbacks of qualitative research in general also apply to focus groups. But focus groups have some unique pros and cons that deserve mention.

Advantages of Focus Groups

The interactions among respondents can stimulate new ideas and thoughts that might not arise during one-on-one interviews. And group pressure can help challenge respondents to keep their thinking realistic. Energetic interactions among respondents also make it likely that observation of a group will provide firsthand consumer information to client observers in a shorter amount of time and in a more interesting way than will individual interviews.

Another advantage focus groups offer is the opportunity to observe customers or prospects from behind a one-way mirror, video feed, or online. In fact, there is growing use of focus groups to expose a broader range of employees to customer comments and views. "We have found that the only way to get people to really understand what customers want is to let them see customers, but there are few people who actually come in contact with customers," says Bonnie Keith, corporate market research manager at

Hewlett-Packard. "Right now, we are getting people from our manufacturing and engineering operations to attend and observe focus groups."

Another advantage of focus groups is that they can be executed more quickly than many other research techniques. In addition, findings from groups tend to be easier to understand and to have a compelling immediacy and excitement. "I can get up and show a client all the charts and graphs in the world, but it has nowhere near the impact of showing 8 or 10 customers sitting around a table and saying that the company's service isn't good," says Jean-Anne Mutter, director of marketing research at Ketchum Advertising.

Disadvantages of Focus Groups Unfortunately, some of the strengths of focus groups also can become disadvantages. For example, the immediacy and apparent understandability of focus group findings can cause managers to be misled instead of informed. Mutter says, "Even though you're only getting a very small slice, a focus group gives you a sense that you really understand the situation." She adds that focus groups can strongly appeal to "people's desire for quick, simple answers to problems, and I see a decreasing willingness to go with complexity and to put forth the effort needed to really think through the complex data that will be yielded by a quantitative study."

Gary Willets, director of marketing research for NCR Corporation, echoes this sentiment. He notes, "What can happen is that you will do the focus group, and you will find out all of these details, and someone will say, 'OK, we've found out all that we need to know.' The problem is that what is said in a focus group may not be all that typical. What you really want to do is do a qualitative study on the front end and follow it up with a quantitative study." Focus groups, like qualitative research in general, are essentially inductive in approach. The research is data-driven, with findings and conclusions being drawn directly from the information provided. In contrast, quantitative studies generally follow a deductive approach, in which formulated ideas and hypotheses are tested with data collected specifically for that purpose.

Other disadvantages relate to the focus group process. For example, focus group recruiting may be a problem if the type of person recruited responds differently to the issues being discussed than do other target segments. White middle-class individuals, for example, participate in qualitative research in numbers disproportionate to their presence in the marketplace. Also, some focus group facilities create an impersonal feeling, making honest conversation unlikely. Corporate or formal settings with large boardroom tables and unattractive or plain decor may make it difficult for respondents to relax and share their feelings.

The greatest potential for distortion is during the group interview itself. As a participant in the social interaction, the moderator must take care not to behave in ways that prejudice responses. The moderator's style may contribute to bias. For example, an aggressive, confronting style may lead respondents to say whatever they think the moderator wants them to say, to avoid attack. Or "playing dumb" may create the perception that the moderator is insincere or phony and cause respondents to withdraw.

Respondents also can be a problem. Some individuals are simply introverted and do not like to speak out in group settings. Other people may attempt to dominate the discussion. These are people who know it all—or think they do—and answer every question first, without giving others a chance to speak. A dominating participant may succeed in swaying other group members. If a moderator is abrupt with a respondent, it can send the wrong message to other group members—"You'd better be cautious, or I will do the same thing to you." Fortunately, a good moderator can stifle a dominant group member and not the rest of the group. Simple techniques used by moderators include avoiding eye contact with a dominant person; reminding the group that "we want to give everyone a chance to talk;" saying "Let's have someone else go first;" or if someone else is speaking and the dominant person interrupts, looking at the initial speaker and saying, "Sorry, I cannot hear you."

Other Qualitative Methodologies

Most of this chapter has been devoted to focus groups because of their pervasive use in marketing research. However, several other qualitative techniques are also used, albeit on a much more limited basis.

Individual Depth Interviews

Individual depth interviews (IDI) are relatively unstructured one-on-one interviews. The interviewer is thoroughly trained in the skill of probing and eliciting detailed answers to each question. Sometimes psychologists are used as depth interviewers: They may employ nondirective clinical techniques to uncover hidden motivations. IDIs are the second most popular form of qualitative research.

> ➤ **individual depth interviews** One-on-one interviews that probe and elicit detailed answers to questions, often using nondirective techniques to uncover hidden motivations.

The direction of a depth interview is guided by the responses of the interviewee. As the interview unfolds, the interviewer thoroughly probes each answer and uses the replies as a basis for further questioning. For example, a depth interview might begin with a discussion of snack foods. The interviewer might follow each answer with "Can you tell me more?" "Would you elaborate on that?" or "Is that all?" The interviewer might then move into the pros and cons of various ingredients, such as corn, wheat, and potatoes. The next phase could delve into the sociability of the snack food. Are Fritos, for example, more commonly eaten alone or in a crowd? Are Wheat Thins usually reserved for parties? When should you serve Ritz crackers?

The advantages of depth interviews over focus groups are as follows.

1. Group pressure is eliminated, so the respondent reveals more honest feelings, not necessarily those considered most acceptable among peers.

2. The personal one-on-one situation gives the respondent the feeling of being the focus of attention—that his or her thoughts and feelings are important and truly wanted.

3. The respondent attains a heightened state of awareness because he or she has constant interaction with the interviewer and there are no group members to hide behind.

4. The longer time devoted to individual respondents encourages the revelation of new information.

5. Respondents can be probed at length to reveal the feelings and motivations that underlie statements.

6. Without the restrictions of cultivating a group process, new directions of questioning can be improvised more easily. Individual interviews allow greater flexibility to explore casual remarks and tangential issues, which may provide critical insights into the main issue.

7. The closeness of the one-on-one relationship allows the interviewer to become more sensitive to nonverbal feedback.

8. A singular viewpoint can be obtained from a respondent without influence from others.

9. The interview can be conducted anywhere, in places other than a focus group facility.

10. Depth interviews may be the only viable technique for situations in which a group approach would require that competitors be placed in the same room. For example, it might be very difficult to do a focus group on systems for preventing bad checks with managers from competing department stores or restaurants.

11. When the research objective is to understand individual decision processes or individual responses to marketing stimuli (e.g., Web sites), IDIs are typically the choice. IDIs allow detailed exploration of a single respondent's reactions without contamination. They are particularly valuable when researchers want individual reactions placed in the context of the individual's experiences.

12. If the topic is highly sensitive (e.g., serious illnesses), use of IDIs is indicated. Subjects that are highly personal (e.g., bankruptcy) or very detailed (e.g., divorce decrees) are best probed deeply with IDIs.

The disadvantages of depth interviews relative to focus groups are as follows:

1. The total cost of depth interviews can be more expensive than focus groups, but not on a cost per respondent minute (see the next heading below).

2. Depth interviews do not generally get the same degree of client involvement as focus groups. It is difficult to convince most client personnel to sit through multiple hours of depth interviews so as to benefit firsthand from the information.

3. Because depth interviews are physically exhausting for the moderator, they do not cover as much ground in one day as do focus groups. Most moderators will not do more than four or five depth interviews in a day, whereas they can involve 20 people in a day in two focus groups.

4. Focus groups are called for when consensus or debate is required to explore disparate views. Groups generate opportunities for point-counterpoint discussion and resolutions.

5. Focus groups give the moderator an ability to leverage the dynamics of the group to obtain reactions that might not be generated in a one-on-one session.[17]

The success of any depth interview depends mainly on the skills of the interviewer. Most IDIs are conducted smoothly and without problems. Yet, inevitably, some respondents present a real challenge to the interviewer. Consider the following:

The Digresser

Problem: *The Digresser could not stay on-topic if his or her life depended on it. One moment the Digresser will be talking about the challenges he faces in taking his asthma medication and the next moment he will start talking about Aunt Betsy and how she has difficulties remembering to brush her teeth in the morning. It takes enormous patience on the part of the moderator to keep these respondents on-topic.*

Solution: *As soon as the interviewer senses that this person may be a Digresser, he or she should try to nip the problem in the bud. But do so in a diplomatic way! Say, "Herbert, I appreciate your willingness to talk with us today, but I have to say that we have a very limited amount of time here, and I'll need you to keep your answers as brief and to-the-point as possible."*

In addition, it may be a good idea to explain to such respondents that they will benefit from keeping their responses bried: "Herbert, I don't want to keep you longer than necessary, and if you can try to limit your answers to 30 seconds or less, I'll be able to let you out of here.

The Withholder

Problem: *The Withholder is at the opposite end of the spectrum from the Digresser. Rather than talking too much, this respondent will provide one- or two-word answers whenever possible. The interviewer might say, "Please tell me your thoughts about the advertisement you see in front of you," and the Withholder will say, "It's fine."*

Solution: *Probing, probing and more probing! This is where the good interviewer gets to show off his or her probing prowess. Rather than letting the respondent say nothing, the moderator needs to seize the opportunity to follow up and probe as much as possible. Examples might be, "Lori, what leads you to say this advertisement is 'fine?'" . . . "What elements of this ad do you like?" . . . "Why do you like those elements?" . . . "What else, if anything, do you like in this advertisement?"*

The Ruminator

Problem: *The Ruminator takes every question asked and spends several minutes digesting it and coming up with a response. This can try the patience of even the most tolerant moderator, particularly when the discussion guide is over five pages long and the interviewer has barely an hour in which to cover everything.*

Solution: *Chances are that the respondent is a slow, methodical thinker who is not accustomed to answering questions in rapid-fire succession. He or she is almost always well-intentioned and attempting to provide the most accurate or useful information possible. In fact, this type of person is generally going to give very helpful responses; it's just that these responses take a while to be formulated.*

To alleviate this situation, an approach similar to that taken with the Digresser can be used. Explain to the respondent, as early as possible in the interview, that time is limited and that there are a lot of questions to be covered. (In some cases it can be helpful to quickly show the respondent all of the pages of questions in the discussion guide or to point out the large stack of materials that they will need to provide feedback on. This can provide the interviewee with a sobering perspective on how much ground needs to be covered in one hour's time.) In addition, the interviewer can reinforce his or her plea by asking questions quickly.[18]

Good depth interviewers, whether psychologists or not, are hard to find and expensive. A second factor that determines the success of depth research is proper interpretation. The unstructured nature of the interview and the clinical nature of the analysis increase the complexity of the task. Small sample sizes, the difficulty of making comparisons, the subjective nature of the researcher's interpretations, and high costs have all contributed to the lack of popularity of depth interviewing. Classic applications of depth interviews include:

- Communication checks (for example, review of print, radio, or TV advertisements or other written materials)
- Sensory evaluations (for example, reactions to varied formulations for deodorants or hand lotions, sniff tests for new perfumes, or taste tests for a new frosting)
- Exploratory research (for example, defining baseline understanding or a product, service, or idea)
- New product development, prototype stage
- Packaging or usage research (for example, when clients want to "mirror" personal experience and obtain key language descriptors)[19]

A variation of the depth interview is called customer care research (CCR). The basic idea is to use depth interviewing to understand the dynamics of the purchase process. The following seven questions are the basis for CCR:

1. What started you on the road to making this purchase?
2. Why did you make this purchase now?
3. What was the hardest part of this process? Was there any point where you got stuck?
4. When and how did you decide the price was acceptable?

5. Is there someone else with whom I should talk to get more of the story behind this purchase?

6. If you've purchased this product before, how does the story of your last purchase differ from this one?

7. At what point did you decide you trusted this organization and this person to work with in your best interests?[20]

Cost of Focus Groups versus IDI

In a standard, eight-person, 90-minute focus group, there are nine people (eight participants plus moderator) sharing the floor. On average, therefore, each respondent is allotted 10 minutes of talk time across those 90 minutes (90 minutes divided by nine people).

The cost of a focus group of this type is about $10,000. That number includes everything: recruiter, moderator, participant stipend, food, facility, report write-up, and the cost of getting a few observers to the event. Divide 80 minutes of participant talk time (the moderator doesn't count) into the $10,000 expense, and your cost per respondent minute in this case is $125 ($10,000/80).

If, however, a typical in-depth interview runs 30 minutes and costs between $600 and $800 (including recruiting, interviewing, participant stipend, and reporting), the cost per respondent minute is in the range of $20 to $27. The big difference results from the amount of time the respondent spends talking, which is typically about 20 to 25 of those 30 minutes in an in-depth phone interview.

Thus, when considering the cost per respondent minute, in-depth interviews can provide much greater value.[21] Of course, the quality of both the focus groups and the IDI determines the real value of the research.

Using Hermeneutics

Some IDI researchers use a technique called hermeneutic research to achieve their goals. **Hermeneutic research** focuses on interpretation as a basis of understanding the consumer. Interpretation comes about through "conversations" between the researcher and the participant. In hermeneutic research, the researcher answers the participant's questions and, as in the traditional method, the researcher only questions the respondent. There are no predetermined questions, but questions arise spontaneously as the conversation unfolds.

> ➤ **hermeneutic research**
> research that focuses on
> interpretation through
> conversations

For example, a researcher and consumer in conversation about why that individual purchased a high-end home theater system may discuss the reasons for making the purchase, such as holding movie parties, enjoying a stay-at-home luxury, or immersing oneself in sporting events. The researcher may interpret "holding movie parties" as a reason for purchase to mean that without the system, the consumer would not hold the parties at all, and so the researcher will return to the consumer for additional information. Upon reviewing the data and talking more, the researcher and consumer determine that why the item was purchased and why it is used (which may or may not be the same) are not as telling as how the product makes its owner feel. In this case, the owner may feel confident as an entertainer, more social, powerful, wealthy, relaxed, or rejuvenated. Talking and probing more about the use of the home theater, the researcher uncovers both new data and new issues to address or consider moving forward.[22]

Writing an IDI report, whether or not hermeneutics are used, is quite different from writing a quantitative report.

Using the Delphi Method

The Delphi Method is often used in new product development when firms are looking for creative new ideas to incorporate in products or services. The term *Delphi* has its roots in Greek history. The city of Delphi was a hub of activity, combining culture, religion, and perspective into one highly populated area of information. Delphi was also home to the Oracle of Pythia, a woman believed to offer great insight into the future. The Oracle was a great influence to visitors, who believed this knowledge of the future would help them succeed in life.

Typically, the Delphi Method relies on people who are experts in some area. It may be product development researchers, marketing managers, professional people (MDs, engineers, etc.), magazine editors, executives, priests, and so forth. Obviously, the type of experts used depends on the objectives of the Delphi session. If one is looking for more efficient ways to handle materials management in a warehouse, the experts may simply be the workers in the warehouse.

The Delphi Method involves a number of rounds of data collection. In the classical Delphi procedure, the first round is unstructured, in order to allow individual experts relative freedom to identify and elaborate the pertinent issues from their point of view. These issues are then consolidated by the researcher(s) into a structured questionnaire.

This questionnaire is subsequently used to elicit the opinions and judgments of the panel of experts in a quantitative form. The responses are analyzed and statistically summarized and presented back to the panelists for further consideration. Respondents are then given the opportunity to alter prior opinions on the basis of feedback. The number of rounds varies from two to ten, but seldom goes beyond one or two iterations.

The key characteristics of Delphi are anonymity, iteration, feedback, and aggregation of group responses. The objective is to obtain the most reliable consensus of opinion via a series of intensive questionnaires, interspersed with opinion feedback.

The purpose of anonymity in a Delphi study is to exclude group interaction, which can cause a number of problems, such as group conflict and individual dominance. Delphi relies on a structured, indirect approach to group decision making; that is, participants don't meet, relying instead on statistical aggregation of individual predictions and ideas.

Controlled feedback, developed from the results of a round, is presented back to the panel of experts at the start of the next round. The form of the feedback varies depending on the topic. It may simply be an aggregation of ideas, or, if the group is estimating sales of a proposed new product, then quantitative estimates, for example, medians, may be given. Sometimes the Delphi Method creates scenarios—for example, how can we create a better customer relationship management (CRM) software that will enable us to take market share from the two market leaders? Scenarios can be used to answer two types of questions: (1) Precisely how might some hypothetical situation come about, step by step? And (2) what alternatives exist, for each actor, at each step, for preventing, diverting, or facilitating the process?

The iteration, controlled feedback, and aggregation of group responses aim to produce as many high-quality responses and opinions as possible on a given issue(s) from a panel of experts to enhance decision making. By feeding back responses from the panel to each member in the group, through a series of iterations, experts are able to adjust their estimates on the basis of others' comments.[23]

Projective Tests

Projective techniques are sometimes incorporated into depth interviews. The origins of projective techniques lie in the field of clinical psychology. In essence, the objective of any **projective test** is to delve below surface responses to obtain true feelings, meanings, and motivations. The rationale behind projective tests comes from the knowledge that people are often reluctant or unable to reveal their deepest feelings. In some instances, they are unaware of those feelings because of psychological defense mechanisms.

projective test
Technique for tapping respondents' deepest feelings by having them project those feelings into an unstructured situation.

Projective tests are techniques for penetrating a person's defense mechanisms to allow true feelings and attitudes to emerge. Generally, a respondent is presented with an unstructured and nebulous situation and asked to respond. Because the situation is ill-defined and has no true meaning, the respondent must impose her or his own frame of reference. In theory, the respondent "projects" personal feelings into the unstructured situation, bypassing defense mechanisms because the respondent is not referring directly to herself or himself. As the individual talks about something or someone else, her or his inner feelings are revealed.

Why is projection important? Consumers (or doctors, voters, managers, or whomever we are studying) may not tell us everything that influences them. Three obstacles stand in the way:

1. Respondents may be unconscious or unaware of a particular influence.

2. They may be aware of an influence, but feel it is too personal or socially undesirable to admit (e.g., prestige image or racial bias).

3. They may be aware that they perceive a product a particular way, but they may not bother to mention this because, in their view, it is not a logical, rational reason for buying or not buying the product. Some doctors, for example, are adamant that what they prescribe has nothing to do with the sound of a drug's name or the attractiveness of the manufacturer's logo, and is based solely on decision-making factors such as research findings, clinical experience, and patient compliance.[24]

Most projective tests are easy to administer and are tabulated like other open-ended questions. They are often used in conjunction with nonprojective open- and closed-ended questions. A projective test may gather "richer," and perhaps more revealing, data than do standard questioning techniques. Projective techniques are used often in image questionnaires and concept tests, and occasionally in advertising pretests. It is also common to apply several projective techniques during a depth interview.

The most common forms of projective techniques used in marketing research are word association tests, sentence and story completion tests, cartoon tests, photo sorts, consumer drawings, storytelling, and third-person techniques. Other techniques, such as psychodrama tests and the Thematic Apperception Test (TAT), have been popular in treating psychological disorders but of less help in marketing research.

word association test
Projective test in which the interviewer says a word and the respondent must mention the first thing that comes to mind.

Word Association Tests   **Word association tests** are among the most practical and effective projective tools for marketing researchers. An interviewer reads a word to a respondent and asks him or her to mention the first thing that comes to mind. Usually, the individual will respond with a synonym or an antonym. The words are read in quick succession to avoid allowing time for defense mechanisms to come into play. If the respondent fails to answer within 3 seconds, some emotional involvement with the word is assumed.

Word association tests are used to select brand names, advertising campaign themes, and slogans. For example, a cosmetic manufacturer might ask consumers to respond to the following words as potential names for a new perfume: infinity, encounter, flame, desire, precious, erotic. One of these words or a synonym suggested by respondents might then be selected as the brand name.

analogy
Drawing a comparison between two items in terms of their similarities.

Analogies   Slightly different from word associations, **analogies** draw a comparison between two items in terms of their similarities. For example, a researcher investigating consumers' perceptions of Ford automobiles may ask: "I'm going to read you a list of stores, and then I'd like you to tell me which of these is most similar to Ford cars. If possible, try to give the first answer that comes to mind. The stores are: Neiman Marcus,

Wal-Mart, Macy's, JC Penney, Kmart, Nordstrom, Target, and Lord & Taylor." As a follow-up, the researcher would then ask: "What is it about [Store X] that is most similar to Ford cars? How are the qualities of Ford cars similar to this store?" This line of questioning induces the respondent to talk (indirectly) about his or her perceptions of Ford cars.

The use of analogies in this instance is not to determine which store(s) people associate with Ford cars but rather to get people to talk about their perceptions of Ford cars in ways they might otherwise be unable to do. Because perceptions of stores vary, some respondents may choose Store A, and some may choose Store B. The researcher should be less concerned with identifying the store(s) that respondents tend to select and more concerned with determining the reasons respondents give for the choices they make. Person A may select a different store from Person B, but this is of little significance if these two individuals share similar perceptions of the stores they chose, and hence of the Ford brand.[25]

Personification   A technique similar to analogies, **personification** involves drawing a comparison between a product and a person. To continue with the example from above, the researcher might say, "Think about the Ford brand, and imagine it were a person. Who would this brand be? How would you describe this person? What personality characteristics would this person have? In what ways do you associate this person with the brand?"

During this type of exercise, the researcher should encourage the participant to discuss such things as the person's values, beliefs, goals, lifestyle, appearance, age, occupation, socioeconomic status, hobbies, and interests. All of these can speak volumes about the respondent's attitudes toward the brand and can go significantly beyond the output of standard lines of questioning.[26]

> **personification**
> Drawing a comparison between a product and a person.

Sentence and Story Completion Tests   **Sentence and story completion tests** can be used in conjunction with word association tests. The respondent is furnished with an incomplete story or group of sentences and asked to complete it. A few examples of incomplete sentences follow:

1. Best Buy is . . .
2. The people who shop at Best Buy are . . .
3. Best Buy should really . . .
4. I don't understand why Best Buy doesn't . . .

Here's an example of a story completion test:

> **sentence and story completion test**
> Projective test in which respondents complete sentences or stories in their own words.

Sally Jones just moved to Chicago from Los Angeles, where she had been a salesperson for IBM. She is now a district manager for the Chicago area. Her neighbor Rhonda Smith has just come over to Sally's apartment to welcome her to Chicago. A discussion of where to shop ensues. Sally notes, "You know, I've heard some things about Best Buy. . . ." What is Rhonda's reply?

As you can see, story completion tests provide a more structured and detailed scenario for the respondent. Again, the objective is for the interviewees to put themselves in the role of the imaginary person mentioned in the scenario.

Some researchers consider sentence and story completion tests to be the most useful and reliable of all the projective tests. Decision Analyst is now offering both online sentence completion and online word association research to its clients.

Cartoon Tests   The typical **cartoon test** consists of two characters with balloons, similar to those seen in comic books; one balloon is filled with dialogue, and the other balloon is blank (see Exhibit 5.7). The respondent is asked to fill in the blank balloon.

> **cartoon test**
> Projective test in which the respondent fills in the dialogue of one of two characters in a cartoon.

Exhibit 5.7

Cartoon Test

Note that the cartoon figures in Exhibit 5.7 are left vague and without expression so that the respondent is not given clues regarding a suggested type of response. The ambiguity is designed to make it easier for the respondent to project his or her feelings into the cartoon situation.

Cartoon tests are extremely versatile and highly projective. They can be used to obtain differential attitudes toward two types of establishments and the congruity or lack of congruity between these establishments and a particular product. They can also be used to measure the strength of an attitude toward a particular product or brand, or to ascertain what function is being performed by a given attitude.

Photo Sorts With **photo sorts**, consumers express their feelings about brands by manipulating a specially developed photo deck depicting different types of people, from business executives to college students. Respondents connect the individuals in the photos with the brands they think they would use.

BBDO Worldwide, one of the country's largest advertising agencies, has developed a trademarked technique called Photosort. A Photosort conducted for General Electric found that consumers thought the brand attracted conservative, older, business types. To change that image, GE adopted the "Bring Good Things to Life" campaign. A Photosort for Visa found the credit card to have a wholesome, female, middle-of-the-road image in customers' minds. The "Everywhere You Want to Be" campaign was devised to interest more high-income men.

Another Photosort technique, entitled Pictured Aspirations Technique (PAT), was created by Grey Advertising, a large New York advertising agency. The technique attempts to uncover how a product fits into a consumer's aspirations. Consumers sort a deck of photos according to how well the pictures describe their aspirations. In research done for Playtex's 18-hour bra, this technique revealed that the product was out of sync with the aspirations of potential customers. The respondents chose a set of pictures that depicted "the me they wanted to be" as very energetic, slim, youthful, and vigorous. But the pictures they used to express their sense of the product were a little more old-fashioned, a little stouter, and less vital and energetic looking. Out went the "Good News for Full-Figured Gals" campaign, with Jane Russell as spokesperson, and in came the sexier, more fashionable concept of "Great Curves Deserve 18 Hours."

photo sort
Projective technique in which a respondent sorts photos of different types of people, identifying those people who she or he feels would use the specified product or service.

Consumer Drawings   Researchers sometimes ask consumers to draw what they are feeling or how they perceive an object. **Consumer drawings** can unlock motivations or express perceptions. For example, the McCann-Erickson advertising agency wanted to find out why Raid roach spray outsold Combat insecticide disks in certain markets. In interviews, most users agreed that Combat is a better product because it kills roaches without any effort on the user's part. So the agency asked the heaviest users of roach spray—low-income women from the southern United States—to draw pictures of their prey (see Exhibit 5.8). The goal was to get at their underlying feelings about this dirty job.

All of the 100 women who participated in the agency's interviews portrayed roaches as men. "A lot of their feelings about the roach were very similar to the feelings that they had about the men in their lives," said Paula Drillman, executive vice president at McCann-Erickson. Many of the women were in common-law relationships. They said that the roach, like the man in their life, "only comes around when he wants food." The act of spraying roaches and seeing them die was satisfying to this frustrated, powerless group. Setting out Combat disks may have been less trouble, but it just didn't give them the same feeling. "These women wanted control," Drillman said. "They used the spray because it allowed them to participate in the kill."

> **consumer drawings**
> Projective technique in which respondents draw what they are feeling or how they perceive an object.

Exhibit   5.8

Consumer Drawings That Helped Identify Respondents' Need for Control
Source: Courtesy of McCann-Erickson, New York.

"One night I just couldn't take the horror of these bugs sneaking around in the dark. They are always crawling when you can't see them. I had to do something. I thought wouldn't it be wonderful if when I switch on the light the roaches would shrink up and die like vampires to sunlight. So I did, but they just all scattered. But I was ready with my spray so it wasn't a total loss. I got quite a few . . . continued tomorrow night when nighttime falls."

"A man likes a free meal you cook for him; as long as there is food he will stay."

"I tiptoed quietly into the kitchen, perhaps he wasn't around. I stretched my arm up to turn on the light. I hoped I'd be alone when the light went on. Perhaps he is sitting on the table I thought. You think that's impossible? Nothing is impossible with that guy. He might not even be alone. He'll run when the light goes on I thought. But what's worse is for him to slip out of sight. No, it would be better to confront him before he takes control and 'invites a companion'."

➡️ **storytelling**
Projective technique in which respondents are required to tell stories about their experiences, with a company or product, for example; also known as the *metaphor technique*.

Storytelling   As the name implies, **storytelling** requires consumers to tell stories about their experiences. It is a search for subtle insights into consumer behavior.

Gerald Zaltman, a Harvard Business School professor, has created a metaphor laboratory to facilitate the storytelling process. (A metaphor is a description of one thing in terms that are usually used to describe another; it can be used to represent thoughts that are tacit, implicit, and unspoken.) Zaltman elicits metaphors from consumers by asking them to spend time over several weeks thinking about how they would visually represent their experiences with a company. To help them with the process, he asks them to cut out magazine pictures that somehow convey those experiences. Then, consumers come to his lab and spend several hours telling stories about all of the images they chose and the connections between the images and their experiences with the firm.

One metaphor study was conducted on pantyhose. "Women in focus groups have always said that they wear them because they have to, and they hate it," says Glenda Green, a marketing research manager at DuPont, which supplies the raw material for many pantyhose manufacturers. "We didn't think we had a completely accurate picture of their feelings, but we hadn't come up with a good way to test them."[27] DuPont turned to storytelling for better insights. Someone brought a picture of a spilled ice cream sundae, capturing the rage she feels when she spots a run in her hose. Another arrived with a picture of a beautiful woman with baskets of fruit. Other photos depicted a Mercedes and Queen Elizabeth. "As we kept probing into the emotions behind the choice of these photos, the women finally began admitting that hose made them feel sensual, sexy, and more attractive to men," says Green. "There's no way anyone would admit that in a focus group." Several stocking manufacturers used this information to alter their advertising and package design.

Tom Neveril, Managing Partner at Storybook Consulting, discusses how to set up storytelling research in the following Practicing Marketing Research box.

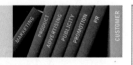

PRACTICING MARKETING RESEARCH

Getting Consumers to Tell Their Stories

Storytelling is not easy because it requires respondents to probe their memories. Therefore, it's important to use an interview structure that will contribute to recall. Chronological ordering of topics is ideal. For example, a market researcher might explore how customers behave during the typical time line of brand experience: gaining awareness, shopping, consideration, selection, purchase, and usage.

Once a format has been determined, how might a researcher evoke stories?

Set the stage for storytelling. Storytelling can be conducted on site or in a traditional research facility setting. In either situation, it's important to take advantage of the fact that sounds, products, scents, and flavors can stir up memories. The senses are critical to putting your target customers at ease, so they can think, feel, talk and—most importantly—behave in an authentic way.

Know how to identify a good story. Before embarking on a customer storytelling project, it's important to know the basic elements of a useful, compelling story. From the grandest novel to the urban myth to a simple joke, all powerful stories have four elements. The first element is plot—a sequence of related events. That's a no-brainer.

Second, on top of plot, all good stories have conflict. Conflict is only possible when we have a protagonist with humanlike motivations, who takes actions that are in conflict with an antagonist.

Plot and conflict naturally occur in the everyday experience of being a consumer. Conflict occurs as people move toward a specific brand, and then competitors or other influencers attempt to steer them in a different direction. To gather plot and conflict, it is crucial to understand the need the consumer was attempting to satisfy and the people or personalities that stood in the way.

Useful stories also contain surprise, the third element. The definition of surprise is the situation produced when an expectation about life comes into conflict with reality. When listening to someone's experiences, keep in mind that it's not necessary that we as researchers are surprised, although we often are. Rather, it must be plausible that the customer has experienced a surprising situation.

The function of surprise in a story is to illuminate the fourth element: lesson, also called theme or moral. A lesson is what the protagonist learns at the conclusion of the conflict. It is possible only when we have the preceding elements of plot, conflict and surprise. But it doesn't need to be philosophical or complex. For example, the simple lesson of the typical FedEx customer is that using FedEx eliminates risk.

Evoke good stories by focusing on their "markers." While every useful story has all four elements, researchers don't have to look for all four. The fast track to evoking good stories is by asking about surprises and lessons. They are far more memorable than the zillions of plots, conflicts, and boring chronologies floating through our minds.

Here's an example of a question that might evoke a good story: "Do you remember a time when you were surprised by Brand X's customer service?" The answer will likely reveal plenty about someone's experience in the category. For example, I put that question to a frequent business traveler several years ago, and he replied by recounting the following memorable experience in a foreign hotel: "I'd been on a business trip, staying at the hotel for several weeks. I kept on missing calls from my family. I was so frustrated. The hotel concierge took it upon himself to call my secretary, get a photo of my family, frame it and put it in my room. And next to it was a faxed note from my youngest daughter that said, 'Miss you, Daddy.' I'll always go back to that hotel."[28]

Questions

1. When would storytelling be more appropriate than IDIs?

2. Do you think that focus group moderators usually would also be good at conducting storytelling research? Why?

Third-Person Technique   Perhaps the easiest projective technique to apply, other than word association, is the **third-person technique**. Rather than directly asking respondents what they think, researchers couch the question in terms of "your neighbor," "most people," or some other third party. Rather than asking a mother why she typically does not fix a nutritionally balanced breakfast for her children, a researcher might ask, "Why don't many people provide their families nutritionally balanced breakfasts?" The third-person technique is often used to avoid questions that might be embarrassing or evoke hostility if posed directly to a respondent.

> **third-person technique**
> Projective technique in which the interviewer learns about respondents' feelings by asking them to answer for a third party, such as "your neighbor" or "most people."

Future of Qualitative Research

The rationale behind qualitative research tests is as follows:

1. The criteria employed and the evaluations made in most buying and usage decisions have emotional and subconscious content, which is an important determinant of buying and usage decisions.

2. Such content is adequately and accurately verbalized by the respondent only through *indirect* communicative techniques.

To the extent that these tenets remain true or even partially correct, the demand for qualitative applications in marketing research will continue to exist. But the problems of small sample sizes and subjective interpretation will continue to plague some forms of qualitative research. Inability to validate and replicate qualitative research will further deter its use.

On the positive side, the use of focus groups will grow. Focus group research can provide data and insights not available through any other techniques. Low cost and ease of application will lend even greater impetus to use online focus groups. Finally, the qualitative–quantitative split will begin to close as adaptations and innovations allow researchers to enjoy the advantages of both approaches simultaneously.

SUMMARY

Qualitative research refers to research whose findings are not subject to quantification or quantitative analysis. It is often used to examine consumer attitudes, feelings, and motivations. Qualitative research, particularly the use of focus groups, continues to grow in popularity for three reasons. First, qualitative research is usually cheaper than quantitative studies. Second, it is an excellent means of understanding the in-depth motivations and feelings of consumers. Third, it can improve the efficiency of quantitative research.

Qualitative research is not without its disadvantages. Sometimes, qualitative research does not distinguish small differences in attitudes or opinions about a marketing mix as well as large-scale quantitative studies do. Also, respondents in qualitative studies are not necessarily representative of the population of interest to the researcher. And the quality of the research may be questionable, given the number of individuals who profess to be experts in the field, yet lack formal training.

Focus groups are the most popular type of qualitative research. A focus group typically consists of 8 to 12 paid participants who are led by a moderator in an in-depth discussion on a particular topic or concept. The goal of the focus group is to learn and understand what people have to say and why. The emphasis is on getting people to talk at length and in detail about the subject at hand. The interaction associated with group dynamics is essential to the success of focus group research. The idea is that a response from one person will become a stimulus for another person, thereby generating an interplay of responses that will yield more information than if the same number of people had contributed independently.

Most focus groups are held in a group facility, which is typically set up in a conference room, with a large one-way mirror built into one wall. Microphones are placed in unobtrusive locations to record the discussion. Behind the mirror is a viewing room. The moderator plays a critical role in the success or failure of the group and is aided in his or her efforts by a well-planned discussion guide.

A number of other qualitative research methodologies are used but on a much more infrequent basis. One such technique is depth interviews. Individual depth interviews are unstructured one-on-one interviews. The interviewer is thoroughly trained in the skill of probing and eliciting detailed answers to each question. He or she often uses nondirective clinical techniques to uncover hidden motivations. Other qualitative techniques are hermeneutics and the Delphi Method. The use of projective techniques represents another form of qualitative research. The objective of any projective test is to delve below the surface responses to obtain true feelings, meanings, or motivations. Some common forms of projective techniques are word association tests, analogies, personification sentence and story completion tests, cartoon tests, photo sorts, consumer drawings, storytelling, and third-person techniques.

KEY TERMS & DEFINITIONS

qualitative research Research findings that are not subject to quantification or quantitative analysis.

quantitative research Research that uses mathematical analysis.

focus group Group of 8 to 12 participants who are led by a moderator in an in-depth discussion on one particular topic or concept.

group dynamics Interaction among people in a group.

focus group facility Research facility consisting of a conference room or living room setting and a separate observation room with a one-way mirror or live audio-visual feed.

focus group moderator Person hired by the client to lead the focus group; this person should have a background in psychology or sociology or, at least, marketing.

discussion guide Written outline of topics to be covered during a focus group discussion.

instant analysis Moderator debriefing, offering a forum for brainstorming by the moderator and client observers.

individual depth interviews One-on-one interviews that probe and elicit detailed answers to questions, often using nondirective techniques to uncover hidden motivations.

hermeneutic research Research that focuses on interpretation through conversations.

Delphi Method Rounds of individual data collection from knowledgeable people. Results are summarized and returned to the participants for further refinement.

projective test Technique for tapping respondents' deepest feelings by having them project those feelings into an unstructured situation.

word association test Projective test in which the interviewer says a word and the respondent must mention the first thing that comes to mind.

analogy Comparison of two items based on similarities.

personification Drawing a comparison between a product and a person.

sentence and story completion test Projective test in which respondents complete sentences or stories in their own words.

cartoon test Projective test in which the respondent fills in the dialogue of one of two characters in a cartoon.

photo sort Projective technique in which a respondent sorts photos of different types of people, identifying those people who she or he feels would use the specified product or service.

consumer drawings Projective technique in which respondents draw what they are feeling or how they perceive an object.

storytelling Projective technique in which respondents are required to tell stories about their experiences, with a company or product, for example; also known as the *metaphor technique.*

third-person technique A projective technique in which the interviewer learns about respondents' feelings by asking them to answer for a third party, such as "your neighbor" or "most people."

QUESTIONS FOR REVIEW & CRITICAL THINKING

1. What are the major differences between quantitative and qualitative research?

2. What are some of the possible disadvantages of using focus groups?

3. Create a story completion test for downloading music from the Internet.

4. What can the client do to get more out of focus groups?

5. What is the purpose of a projective test? What major factors should be considered in using a projective technique?

6. Divide the class into groups of four and eight. The groups of four will select a topic below (or one suggested by your instructor) and create a discussion guide. One of the four will then serve as the group moderator. One of the groups of eight will serve as participants in the focus group. The groups should last at least 20 minutes and be observed by the remainder of the class. Suggested topics:
   a. New video games
   b. Buying a hybrid gasoline/electric car
   c. Student experiences at the student union
   d. The quality of existing frozen dinners and snacks and new items that would be desired by students
   e. How students spend their entertainment dollars and what additional entertainment opportunities they would like to see offered

7. What are some major issues in conducting international focus groups?

8. Take a consumer drawing test—draw a typical Pepsi drinker and a typical Coke drinker. What do the images suggest about your perceptions of Coke and Pepsi drinkers?

9. Use the metaphor technique to tell a story about going to the supermarket.

WORKING THE NET

Go to *http://www.researchconnections.com*. Under "Demos," look at the information available at Virtual Focus Facility. Report your findings to the class.

REAL-LIFE RESEARCH • 5.1

Repositioning Scotland

The proliferation of low-cost air carriers and the expansion of their pan-European route network means European consumers now have a greater choice of vacation destinations than ever before. Consequently, the need for established tourist destinations to market themselves appropriately, and to communicate their unique "reasons to visit" clearly and effectively to their audience, has become requisite.

As tourist destinations face up to increased competition for market share, VisitScotland, Scotland's national tourism agency, approached UK-based Nunwood Consulting to develop and instigate a qualitative research program. The research was intended to determine consumer wants and current brand perceptions within the three key markets of France, Germany, and Spain. The resulting insights would then be used to adapt and refine the group's future marketing and creative communications strategy, with the ultimate goals of repositioning the brand "Scotland" within the tourism sector and reigniting consumer interest within the three stated key territories.

The Process

Nunwood carried out a series of in-depth, qualitative workshops (focus groups) at six different locations within the three countries. The research utilized existing imagery of Scotland to elicit spontaneous responses based on emotional experience. Overall, it could be broken down into a series of key questions:

- What are the current consumer perceptions of the brand "Scotland"?
- Which aspects of the country are most appealing/would motivate a person to visit?
- Which of these aspects then appeal specifically to each of their market target countries, and thus, would a generic, pan-European communications strategy be feasible? (This would represent a huge cost saving.)

Unmet Needs

Once the research was completed, the debrief—in this case, a facilitated workshop-style process with a carefully constructed audience—yielded remarkable insight and identified three core and as-yet-unmet consumer needs:

- *Social engagement/cultural immersion*. Ad executions should advance from traditional, purely landscape-oriented messages to create the expectation within a visitor that they'll experience high levels of social interaction with the archetypal friendly, welcoming, indigenous people.
- *Discovery and learning*. The brand should communicate feelings of unique discovery, surprise, and the capacity for personal learning.
- *Flexibility and independence*. Future communications should appeal to more spontaneous, proactive, "flexible" tourists with few preordained plans.

Another important piece of information to emerge from the data was that these needs were consistent across all of the defined national markets, allowing for the generic, pan-European campaign that VisitScotland had hoped for.

The Rebrand

The next step was to utilize these findings to develop and refine a new, effective, and creative promotional compaign. The old campaign was based on a traditional and generic approach to advertising vacation/short-break destinations: a simple but heart-stoppingly beautiful picture of the destination, plus an image of a calm and relaxed vacationer. The new campaign, called "the white line concept," answered the brief, as defined by the research recommendations. Any engaging creative for VisitScotland needed to underline elements of sociability and cultural immersion, discovery and learning, and freedom and

Scotland, Welcome to
Our Life.

independence. Nunwood tested the creative mock-ups across the three nations in a second wave of qualitative workshops several months later and made final edits based on this. The designs and the concept researched remarkably well, with the friendly and informal tone really appealing to the tourist segment.

"White lines" consist of a series of panoramic, visually rich landscape/scenery shots, featuring the tagline "Scotland, Welcome to Our Life." While the comparison of these images hints at the wealth of things to discover in Scotland, a white, hand-drawn line runs through the scene, tracing the path a visitor could take. Short, scribbled stories, written in the first-person tense and dotted at points on the line, are indicative of the situations a visitor could experience during their time in Scotland.

Story examples include:

"I spoke to a lovely lady, thought she was the gardener, but turned out she owns the castle."

"Got stuck in a herd of sheep—the Scottish way to slow down your life."

Well Received

To substantiate initial positive feedback, and to make sure that this line of creative was on-track, on-brand, and effectively delivering the key messages all parties had agreed upon, Nunwood conducted a series of one-on-one conversation studies in France, Germany, and Spain in order to gauge direct consumer response on the new campaign. With the exception of a few small refinements, the creative was very well received and the new campaign was promptly rolled out across all three European markets.[33]

Questions

1. The rebranding used focus groups and individual depth interviews. What other qualitative techniques could have been used?

2. Was the qualitative research done here sufficient to make decisions regarding the rebranding campaign?

3. What else could the researchers have determined if they had done a quantitative study?

4. How might one measure the success of the campaign?

REAL-LIFE RESEARCH • 5.2

Steering Midas in the Right Direction

Midas, Inc. is one of the best-known providers of automotive services, offering brakes, maintenance, tires, exhaust, steering, and suspension repairs at nearly 2,400 franchised, licensed and company-owned Midas shops in 16 countries, including more than 1,600 in the United States and Canada. Although he works for Midas Inc., Garry Rosenfeldt is the first to admit that some of his company's customers could have the same uneasy feelings about visiting a Midas shop. "As an industry, we are typically not known for warm and fuzzy customer service," says Rosenfeldt, the firm's director of marketing research.

But car owners may soon begin looking at Midas in a different way. Rosenfeldt has used two large-scale qualitative research projects to help show the company's franchisees how bad things are in the auto service realm and, more importantly, how good things could get if shop managers started adhering to a set of basic service guidelines and behaviors that have not become a fundamental component of a broader retail operating model called the Midas Way. When initial discussions were held about undertaking a project to research and document the state of customer service in the car repair business, Rosenfeldt knew that the edicts to improve service would perhaps be better received internally if they were in the consumers' own words rather than those of Midas's corporate chiefs. "It occurred to me that the best way to get franchisees on board is to have somebody else basically say what they should be doing and hey, wouldn't it be great if that 'somebody else' happened to be real, live customers?"

The best way to accomplish this was to enable consumers to do the talking to video cameras in the privacy of their own homes. For the first project, Rosenfeldt recruited all of the respondents himself. He went to an electronics retailer and bought 150 video cameras and sent them out with instruction packets.

The goal was to learn about the ideal car repair service, not just at a Midas location but anywhere, so respondents had to complete a handful of tasks. For the first assignment, they were asked to look at scores of photos that represented many of the things that would happen in an auto service experience and expres their thoughts—have they experienced the same thing, what did they think about it, and so on.

Next they were asked to make an appointment for some kind of car service—an oil change, new brakes, and the like—at any service provider of their choosing and explain why they chose the shop they did, whether they had been there before, what they expected to happen, and how they expected to be treated. After the service, the consumers gave a wrap-up of how things went, including what was good, what was bad, and what could have been better.

Rosenfeldt edited the hundreds of hours of videotape down to the most important, impactful responses and set about distributing the video to franchisees over the Midas corporate Web portal, on DVDs in the mail, and via various road shows to explore and explain the results to internal audiences.

The franchisees' response? "We found that it was among the best, most effective research projects we've ever done."

The next step was to say, "We heard what you said. Here is what we have done. Is it correct? Are we doing the right thing?" Midas used the initial research to adopt new service protocols. This second phase was conducted by QualVu, an online video-based qualitative research firm. The company recruited respondents and distributed cameras. Both Midas customers and noncustomers were selected. Respondents were asked to have their cars serviced at Midas and report back.

Midas learned that it got the service model correct. "Customers did in fact notice a huge difference in the way the stores operated. Three main components of the Midas service model are greet, explain, and thank. "When you are a shop manager and a customer walks in the door, you need to do three things: greet them, explain what you are doing and thank them," Rosenfeldt says. "It sounds ridiculously simple, but it almost never happens in this industry. We have found that when shops are able to execute those behaviors consistently, our customer satisfaction goes way up and people come back and they purchase more services from me.[29]

Questions

1. We discussed a number of different types of qualitative research in this chapter. What type of research was conducted by Midas?

2. Could this data have been gathered by other forms of qualitative research? If so, which ones?

3. How did this form of research facilitate getting "buy-in" from the franchisees?

4. Should quantitative research play a role in the future for Midas? If so, how?

Traditional Survey Research

LEARNING OBJECTIVES

→ **1.** To understand the reasons for the popularity of survey research.

→ **2.** To learn about the types of errors in survey research.

→ **3.** To learn about the types of surveys.

→ **4.** To gain insight into the factors that determine the choice of particular survey methods.

Survey research is the use of a questionnaire to gather facts, opinions, and attitudes; it is the most popular way to gather primary data. What are the various types of survey research? As noted previously, not everyone is willing to participate in a survey. What kinds of errors does that create? What are the other types of errors encountered in survey research? Why has Internet survey research become so popular, and what are its drawbacks? These questions are answered in this chapter.

Popularity of Survey Research

Some 126 million Americans have been interviewed at some point in their lives. Each year, about 70 million people are interviewed in the United States, which is the equivalent of over 15 minutes per adult per year. Surveys have a high rate of usage in marketing research compared to other means of collecting primary data, for some very good reasons.

- *The need to know why.* In marketing research, there is a critical need to have some idea about why people do or do not do something. For example, why did they buy or not buy a particular brand? What did they like or dislike about it? Who or what influenced them? We do not mean to imply that surveys can prove causation, only that they can be used to develop some idea of the causal forces at work.

- *The need to know how.* At the same time, the marketing researcher often finds it necessary to understand the process consumers go through before taking some action. How did they make the decision? What time period passed? What did they examine or consider? When and where was the decision made? What do they plan to do next?

- *The need to know who.* The marketing researcher also needs to know who the person is, from a demographic or lifestyle perspective. Information on age, income, occupation, marital status, stage in the family life cycle, education, and other factors is necessary for the identification and definition of market segments.

A new survey of marketing research professionals found that the most common source of market research information is survey data, used by 94 percent of companies surveyed. Other sources include syndicated research (78 percent); focus groups (74 percent); company sales data (67 percent); and scanner data (16 percent). Also, 88 percent of corporations use online methods to conduct survey-based market research. Sixty-five percent of those surveyed agree that the speed of online research has helped accelerate the pace of their business. More than half of all online research dollars are spent on projects transitioning from traditional (i.e., telephone, mail, mall) research methods.[1]

Types of Errors in Survey Research

When assessing the quality of information obtained from survey research, the manager must determine the accuracy of those results. This requires careful consideration of the research methodology employed in relation to the various types of errors that might result (see Exhibit 6.1).

Sampling Error

Two major types of errors may be encountered in connection with the sampling process. They are random error and systematic error, sometimes referred to as bias.

Surveys often attempt to obtain information from a representative cross section of a target population. The goal is to make inferences about the total population based on the

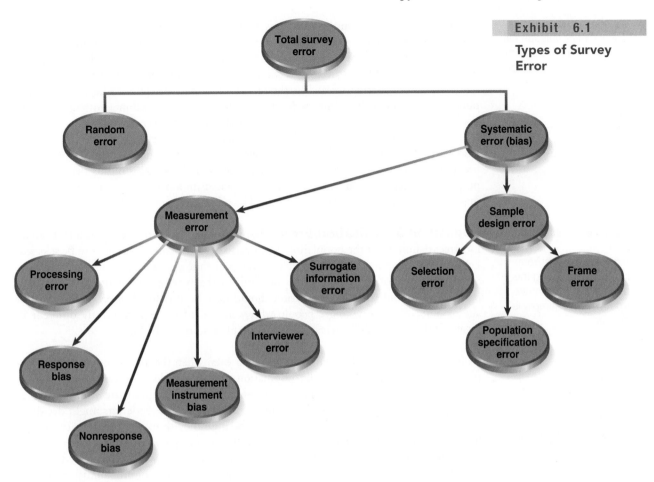

Exhibit 6.1

Types of Survey Error

responses given by respondents sampled. Even when all aspects of the sample are investigated properly, the results are still subject to a certain amount of **random error** (or **random sampling error**) because of chance variation. **Chance variation** is the difference between the sample value and the true value of the population mean. This error cannot be eliminated, but it can be reduced by increasing the sample size. It is possible to estimate the range of random error at a particular level of confidence. Random error and the procedures for estimating it are discussed in detail in Chapters 13 and 14.

Systematic Error

Systematic error, or **bias**, results from mistakes or problems in the research design or from flaws in the execution of the sample design. Systematic error exists in the results of a sample if those results show a consistent tendency to vary in one direction (consistently higher or consistently lower) from the true value of the population parameter. Systematic error includes all sources of error except those introduced by the random sampling process. Therefore, systematic errors are sometimes called *nonsampling errors*. The nonsampling errors that can systematically influence survey answers can be categorized as *sample design error* and *measurement error*.

Sample Design Error   **Sample design error** is a systematic error that results from a problem in the sample design or sampling procedures. Types of sample design errors include frame errors, population specification errors, and selection errors.

> **random error, or random sampling error**
> Error that results from chance variation.

> **chance variation**
> The difference between the sample value and the true value of the population mean.

> **systematic error, or bias**
> Error that results from problems or flaws in the execution of the research design; sometimes called *nonsampling error*.

> **sample design error**
> Systematic error that results from an error in the sample design or sampling procedures.

sampling frame
The list of population elements or members from which units to be sampled are selected.

frame error
Error resulting from an inaccurate or incomplete sampling frame.

population specification error
Error that results from incorrectly defining the population or universe from which a sample is chosen.

selection error
Error that results from incomplete or improper sample selection procedures or not following appropriate procedures.

Frame Error The **sampling frame** is the list of population elements or members from which units to be sampled are selected. **Frame error** results from using an incomplete or inaccurate sampling frame. The problem is that a sample drawn from a list that is subject to frame error may not be a true cross section of the target population. A common source of frame error in marketing research is the use of a published telephone directory as a sampling frame for a telephone survey. Many households are not listed in a current telephone book because they do not want to be listed or are not listed accurately because they have recently moved or changed their telephone number. Research has shown that those people who are listed in telephone directories are systematically different from those who are not listed in certain important ways, such as socioeconomic levels. This means that if a study purporting to represent the opinions of all households in a particular area is based on listings in the current telephone directory, it will be subject to frame error.

Population Specification Error **Population specification error** results from an incorrect definition of the population or universe from which the sample is to be selected. For example, suppose a researcher defined the population or universe for a study as people over the age of 35. Later, it was determined that younger individuals should have been included and that the population should have been defined as people 20 years of age or older. If those younger people who were excluded are significantly different in regard to the variables of interest, then the sample results will be biased.

Selection Error Selection error can occur even when the analyst has a proper sampling frame and has defined the population correctly. **Selection error** occurs when sampling procedures are incomplete or improper or when appropriate selection procedures are not properly followed. For example, door-to-door interviewers might decide to avoid houses that do not look neat and tidy because they think the inhabitants will not be agreeable to doing a survey. If people who live in messy houses are systematically different from those who live in tidy houses, then selection error will be introduced into the results of the survey. Selection error is a serious problem in nonprobability samples, a subject discussed in Chapter 13.

A population must be defined before research can begin. Errors can occur if a population is not defined correctly or if selection procedures are not followed properly.

Measurement Error Measurement error is often a much more serious threat to survey accuracy than is random error. When the results of public opinion polls are given in the media and in professional marketing research reports, an error figure is frequently reported (say, plus or minus 5 percent). The television viewer or the user of a marketing research study is left with the impression that this figure refers to total survey error. Unfortunately, this is not the case. This figure refers only to random sampling error. It does not include sample design error and speaks in no way to the measurement error that may exist in the research results. **Measurement error** occurs when there is variation between the information being sought (true value) and the information actually obtained by the measurement process. Our main concern in this text is with systematic measurement error. Various types of error may be caused by numerous deficiencies in the measurement process. These errors include surrogate information error, interviewer error, measurement instrument bias, processing error, nonresponse bias, and response bias.

Surrogate Information Error **Surrogate information error** occurs when there is a discrepancy between the information actually required to solve a problem and the information being sought by the researcher. It relates to general problems in the research design, particularly failure to properly define the problem. A few years ago, Kellogg spent millions developing a line of 17 breakfast cereals that featured ingredients that would help consumers cut down on their cholesterol. The product line was called Ensemble. It failed miserably in the marketplace. Yes, people want to lower their cholesterol, but the real question was whether they would purchase a line of breakfast cereals to accomplish this task. This question was never asked in the research. Also, the name "Ensemble" usually refers to either an orchestra or something you wear. Consumers didn't understand either the product line or the need to consume it.

Interviewer Error **Interviewer error, or interviewer bias**, results from the interviewer's influencing a respondent—consciously or unconsciously—to give untrue or inaccurate answers. The dress, age, gender, facial expressions, body language, or tone of voice of the interviewer may influence the answers given by some or all respondents. This type of error is caused by problems in the selection and training of interviewers or by the failure of interviewers to follow instructions. Interviewers must be properly trained and supervised to appear neutral at all times. Another type of interviewer error occurs when deliberate cheating takes place. This can be a particular problem in door-to-door interviewing, where interviewers may be tempted to falsify interviews and get paid for work they did not actually do. The procedures developed by the researcher must include safeguards to ensure that this problem will be detected (see Chapter 15).

Measurement Instrument Bias **Measurement instrument bias** (sometimes called *questionnaire bias*) results from problems with the measurement instrument or questionnaire (see Chapter 12). Examples of such problems include leading questions or elements of the questionnaire design that make recording responses difficult and prone to recording errors. Problems of this type can be avoided by paying careful attention to detail in the questionnaire design phase and by using questionnaire pretests before field interviewing begins.

Processing Error **Processing errors** are primarily due to mistakes that occur when information from survey documents is entered into the computer. For example, a document may be scanned incorrectly.

Nonresponse Bias Ideally, if a sample of 400 people is selected from a particular population, all 400 of those individuals should be interviewed. As a practical matter, this

measurement error Systematic error that results from a variation between the information being sought and what is actually obtained by the measurement process.

surrogate information error Error that results from a discrepancy between the information needed to solve a problem and that sought by the researcher.

interviewer error, or interviewer bias Error that results from the interviewer's influencing—consciously or unconsciously—the answers of the respondent.

measurement instrument bias Error that results from the design of the questionnaire or measurement instrument; also known as *questionnaire bias*.

processing error Error that results from the incorrect transfer of information from a survey document to a computer.

nonresponse bias
Error that results from a systematic difference between those who do and those who do not respond to a measurement instrument.

will never happen. Response rates of 5 percent or less are common in mail surveys. The question is "Are those who did respond to the survey systematically differ in some important way from those who did not respond?" Such differences lead to **nonresponse bias**. We recently examined the results of a study conducted among customers of a large savings and loan association. The response rate to the questionnaire, included in customer monthly statements, was slightly under 1 percent. Analysis of the occupations of those who responded revealed that the percentage of retired people among respondents was 20 times higher than in the local metropolitan area. This overrepresentation of retired individuals raised serious doubts about the accuracy of the results.

Obviously, the higher the response rate, the less the possible impact of nonresponse because nonrespondents then represent a smaller subset of the overall picture. If the decrease in bias associated with improved response rates is trivial, then allocating resources to obtain higher response rates might be wasteful in studies in which resources could be used for better purposes.

Nonresponse error occurs when the following happens:

- A person cannot be reached at a particular time.
- A potential respondent is reached but cannot or will not participate at that time (for example, the telephone request to participate in a survey comes just as the family is sitting down to dinner).
- A person is reached but refuses to participate in the survey. This is the most serious problem because it may be possible to achieve future participation in the first two circumstances.

refusal rate
Percentage of persons contacted who refused to participate in a survey.

The **refusal rate** is the percentage of persons contacted who refused to participate in a survey. Today, the overall refusal rate is approximately 60 percent—up from 52 percent in 1992, according to the Council for Marketing and Opinion Research (CMOR). Most refusals (68 percent) occur before the survey introduction (initial refusals); only one-quarter (26 percent) occur after the introduction is read (qualified refusals). Few (6 percent) terminate once the survey is under way. While most individuals (71 percent) express a willingness to participate in future surveys, this willingness is lukewarm (nearly three times as many are "fairly willing" compared to "very willing").[2] While these percentages are based on a study by the CMOR and are not necessarily reflective of the entire industry, they do reflect the significant increase in the refusal rate.

response bias
Error that results from the tendency of people to answer a question incorrectly through either deliberate falsification or unconscious misrepresentation.

Response Bias. If there is a tendency for people to answer a particular question in a certain way, then there is **response bias**. Response bias can result from deliberate falsification or unconscious misrepresentation.

Deliberate falsification occurs when people purposefully give untrue answers to questions. There are many reasons why people might knowingly misrepresent information in a survey. They may wish to appear intelligent, they may not reveal information that they feel is embarrassing, or they may want to conceal information that they consider to be personal.

For example, in a survey about fast-food buying behavior, the respondents may have a fairly good idea of how many times they visited a fast-food restaurant in the past month. However, they may not remember which fast-food restaurants they visited or how many times they visited each restaurant. Rather than answering "Don't know" in response to a question regarding which restaurants they visited, the respondents may simply guess.

Unconscious misrepresentation occurs when a respondent is legitimately trying to be truthful and accurate but gives an inaccurate response. This type of bias may occur because of question format, question content, or various other reasons.

Strategies for minimizing survey errors are summarized in Exhibit 6.2.

EXHIBIT 6.2	Types of Errors and Strategies for Minimizing Errors

I. Random error — This error can be reduced only by increasing sample size.

II. Systematic error — This error can be reduced by minimizing sample design and measurement errors.

    A. Sample design error

        Frame error — This error can be minimized by getting the best sampling frame possible and doing preliminary quality control checks to evaluate the accuracy and completeness of the frame.

        Population specification error — This error results from incorrect definition of the population of interest. It can be reduced or minimized only by more careful consideration and definition of the population of interest.

        Selection error — This error results from using incomplete or improper sampling procedures or not following appropriate selection procedures. It can occur even with a good sampling frame and an appropriate specification of the population. It is minimized by developing selection procedures that will ensure randomness and by developing quality control checks to make sure that these procedures are followed in the field.

    B. Measurement error

        Surrogate information error — This error results from seeking and basing decisions on the wrong information. It results from poor design and can be minimized only by paying more careful attention to specification of the types of information required to fulfill the objectives of the research.

        Interviewer error — This error occurs because of interactions between the interviewer and the respondent that affect the responses given. It is minimized by careful interviewer selection and training. In addition, quality control checks should involve unobtrusive monitoring of interviewers to ascertain whether they are following prescribed guidelines.

        Measurement instrument bias — Also referred to as *questionnaire bias*, this error is minimized only by careful questionnaire design and pretesting.

        Processing error — This error can occur in the process of transferring data from questionnaires to the computer. It is minimized by developing and following rigid quality control procedures for transferring data and supporting quality control checks.

        Nonresponse bias — This error results from the fact that those people chosen for the sample who actually respond are systematically different from those who are chosen and do not respond. It is particularly serious in connection with mail surveys. It is minimized by doing everything possible (e.g., shortening the questionnaire, making the questionnaire more respondent friendly, doing callbacks, providing incentives, contacting people when they are most likely to be at home) to encourage those chosen for the sample to respond.

        Response bias — This error occurs when something about a question leads people to answer it in a particular way. It can be minimized by paying special attention to questionnaire design. In particular, questions that are hard to answer, might make the respondent look uninformed, or deal with sensitive issues should be modified (see Chapter 12).

Types of Surveys

Asking people questions is the essence of the survey approach. But what type of survey is best for a given situation? The non-Internet survey alternatives discussed in this chapter are door-to-door interviews, executive interviews, mall-intercept interviews, telephone interviews, self-administered questionnaires, and mail surveys.

Door-to-Door Interviews

Door-to-door interviews, in which consumers are interviewed in person in their homes, were at one time thought to be the best survey method. This conclusion was based on a number of factors. First, the door-to-door interview is a personal, face-to-face interaction

> **door-to-door interviews**
> Interviews conducted face to face with consumers in their homes.

with all the attendant advantages—immediate feedback from the respondent, the ability to explain complicated tasks, the ability to use special questionnaire techniques that require visual contact to speed up the interview or improve data quality, and the ability to show the respondent product concepts and other stimuli for evaluation. Second, the participant is at ease in a familiar, comfortable, secure environment.

Door-to-door interviews began a steep decline in the early 1970s and have now virtually disappeared altogether from the U.S. marketing research scene. The primary reason is the cost of paying an interviewer's travel time, mileage, and survey time as well as ever-rising refusal rates. The method is still used in some government research. For

GLOBAL RESEARCH

Conducting Marketing Research in China

Data collection in China has traditionally given significant weight to face-to-face interviewing, in consumer and B2B research alike. In 2000, marketing research firms conducted about 90 percent of all research interviews in China this way. Since then, the role of face-to-face interviewing has decreased; current estimates are at just more than 60 percent. Of course, this is considerably higher than most Western research firms, which conduct less than 10 percent of all interviews face-to-face.

Face-to-face interviewing is prominent in relation to certain target respondent groups. In B2B research, the more senior the respondent, the more likely he or she will require a meeting to discuss his or her views on the market. Middle- to senior-level managers and government officials are the main respondent groups in the face-to-face category. This is partly due to respondents' natural curiosity about to whom they are giving information. But it's also due to a cultural perception that high-level discussions merit a face-to-face meeting. This perception is often as prominent within the research firms as it is among respondents.

The main reason for the trend away from face-to-face interviews is the growing understanding and acceptance of market research among Chinese target respondents; they are increasingly willing to discuss business and other matters over the telephone. And in contrast to Western markets, access to respondents is increasing.

Marketing research firms use the focus group methodology in China, albeit less than in Western markets. There's an almost unanimous view that Chinese respondents—particularly businesspeople—prefer to provide information on a one-to-one basis rather than in groups. The exact reason for this preference is unclear, although the balance of opinion suggests that this is more a cultural than a confidentiality issue. When researchers conduct focus groups, they commonly do so in a "mini-group" format of three or four people; groups of six to eight people are also fairly common. Groups of more than eight are very rare.

Although Chinese agencies are extremely technologically savvy, they tend to lag behind their Western counterparts in their use of online data-collection techniques. Currently, online surveys are limited to certain groups such as IT managers and teenagers, and online focus groups are being introduced to audiences.[3]

The move toward more telephone-based fieldwork will continue—as acceptance increases among the target market and clients alike and as demand for research grows outside of the main cities. Face-to-face interviewing will remain significant, as it is entrenched in China's culture of research.

The emergence of the Internet as a viable means of data collection is happening based on the acceptability of this method to both clients and respondents. The high demand for large-sample projects within China means that the Web survey will be the most widespread of these techniques, with substantial growth predicted.[3]

example, some of the most recent U.S. Census was done door-to-door. Door-to-door interviewing is also used in developing countries. Matthew Harrison, a director of B2B International, an English marketing research firm, talks about door-to-door and other forms of marketing research in the accompanying Global Research box.

Executive Interviews

Marketing researchers use **executive interviews** as the industrial equivalent of door-to-door interviews. This type of survey involves interviewing businesspeople at their offices concerning industrial products or services. For example, if Hewlett-Packard wants information about user preferences for features that might be offered in a new line of office printers, it needs to interview prospective user-purchasers of the printers. It would thus be appropriate to locate and interview these people at their offices.

    This type of interviewing is expensive. First, individuals involved in the purchasing decision for the product in question must be identified and located. Sometimes lists can be obtained from various sources, but more frequently screening must be conducted over the telephone. A particular company may indeed have individuals of the type being sought, but locating them within a large organization can be expensive and time-consuming. Once a qualified person is located, the next step is to get that person to agree to be interviewed and to set a time for the interview. This is not usually as hard as it might seem because most professionals seem to enjoy talking about topics related to their work.

    Finally, an interviewer must go to the particular place at the appointed time. Long waits are frequent; cancellations are common. This type of survey requires highly skilled interviewers because they are frequently interviewing on topics they know little about. Executive interviews have essentially the same advantages and disadvantages as door-to-door interviews. More and more executive interviews are moving online.

> **executive interviews**
> Industrial equivalent of door-to-door interviewing.

Mall-Intercept Interviews

Mall-intercept interviews are a popular survey method for conducting personal interviews. This survey approach is relatively simple. Shoppers are intercepted in public areas of shopping malls and either interviewed on the spot or asked to come to a permanent interviewing facility in the mall. Approximately 500 malls throughout the country have permanent survey facilities operated by marketing research firms. An equal or greater number of malls permit marketing researchers to interview on a daily basis. Many malls do not permit marketing research interviewing, however, because they view it as an unnecessary nuisance to shoppers.

    Mall surveys are less expensive than door-to-door interviews because respondents come to the interviewer rather than the other way around. Interviewers spend more of their time actually interviewing and less of their time hunting for someone to interview. Also, mall interviewers do not have the substantial travel time and mileage expenses associated with door-to-door interviewing. In addition to low-cost, mall-intercept interviews have many of the advantages associated with door-to-door interviews in that respondents can try test products on the spot.

    However, a number of serious disadvantages are associated with mall-intercept interviewing. First, it is virtually impossible to get a sample representative of a large metropolitan area from shoppers at a particular mall. Even though malls may be large, most of them draw shoppers from a relatively small local area. In addition, malls tend to attract certain types of people, based on the stores they contain. Studies also show that some people shop more frequently than others and therefore have a greater chance of being selected. Finally, many people refuse mall interviews. In summary, mall-intercept

> **mall-intercept interviews**
> Interviews conducted by intercepting mall shoppers (or shoppers in other high-traffic locations) and interviewing them face to face.

interviewing cannot produce a good or representative sample except in the rare case in which the population of interest is coincident with or is a subset of the population that shops at a particular mall.

Second, the mall environment is not always viewed as a comfortable place to conduct an interview. Respondents may be ill at ease, in a hurry, or preoccupied by various distractions outside the researcher's control. These factors may adversely affect the quality of the data obtained. Even with all its problems, the popularity of mall-intercept interviews has only slightly declined in recent years.

Rather than interview in the public areas of malls, some researchers are conducting surveys in stores at the point-of-purchase. Firms such as Marketing Research Services, Inc. (*www.mrsi.com*), specialize in in-store interviewing. The company notes:

When a consumer reaches for a product on a store shelf, the eye of market research should be wide open. This is the only time and place that consumers' purchase interest and motivations are well defined and readily expressed. The moment of purchase is the most critical point in the entire marketing cycle. It is the moment when shoppers best recall why they made the choice to put a particular item in their shopping cart.[4]

Various companies, including Procter & Gamble, General Mills, Starbucks, McDonald's, and Walgreens, currently conduct in-store studies.

Telephone Interviews

Until 1990, telephone interviewing was the most popular form of survey research. The advantages of telephone interviewing are compelling. First, telephoning is a relatively inexpensive way to collect survey data. Second, the telephone interview has traditionally produced a high-quality sample. Ninety-five percent of all Americans have some type of phone. *Random-digit sampling*, or *random-digit dialing*, is a frequently used sampling approach (see Chapter 13). The basic idea is simple: Instead of drawing a sample from the phone book or other directory, researchers use telephone numbers generated via a random-number procedure. This approach ensures that people with unlisted numbers and those who have moved or otherwise changed their telephone numbers since the last published phone book are included in the sample in the correct proportion.

Predictive Dialing   Today, random digit dialing has been merged with sophisticated software to create predictive dialing. One provider of predictive dialing is SPSS, Incorporated, which also provides the statistical software that is provided with each new copy of this test. The company has launched SPSS mrDialer 4.0 with Voice Over Internet Protocol (VoIP), a product designed to deliver faster completion of projects, allow lower staff costs, and give market researchers more control over survey projects.

Since VoIP uses broadband connections instead of analog phone lines, SPSS mrDialer 4.0 is intended to support virtual call centers where interviewers are dispersed over a wide geographic space, either in separate offices or working from their homes. MrDialer 4.0 is designed to allow market researchers to centralize control of the call center, operate around the clock, and scale resources without significant cost escalation.

SPSS mrDialer uses predictive dialing algorithms to identify busy, unanswered, or unobtainable numbers. It is also designed to be adaptable to new rules and dialing methodologies that can be updated with a graphical user interface.

SPSS mrDialer 4.0 is designed to offer market researchers the ability to record interviews for quality assurance and capture responses; analyze busy signals and unanswered, modem and fax calls; prioritize recalls to meet a preset appointment time; simultaneously run multiple interviewing projects; deliver real-time reporting of numbers dialed and attempted, along with completed, interviews; and monitor the interview screen and voices from any station.[5]

Cell Phone Interviewing   Today, almost 40 percent of American households can only be reached on a cell phone or smart phone.[6] Remember, in this chapter, we are speaking about traditional telephone interviews—that is, when an interviewer asks a series of questions to a respondent. The respondent may answer on a traditional telephone, cell phone, or smart phone. Smart phones, of course, can be used to reply to Web surveys. Mobile Internet surveys are covered in Chapter 7.

Cell phone interviewing enables researchers to access people otherwise unreachable for a telephone interview. Yet, cell phone interviewing tends to substantially drive up costs. Each completed interview can cost double or triple that of a landline interview.[7] Federal law requires interviewers to hand dial cell phone numbers rather than using auto dialers. Researchers also pay $1 to $10 or more to the respondents to cover the cost of the minutes. Also, it takes more calls to achieve a completed interview. People may not answer their cell phone when their usage isn't free, so they may defer the call when driving or in a public place.

A new Federal Communication Commission (FCC) proposal allows automatic dialers but will require "prior written consent" from the respondent. The Market Research Association has complained to the FCC that the new proposal will result in decreased response rates, add to the cost of research, increase the time required to complete studies, and decrease the representativeness of survey and opinion research. The association also claims that the proposed rule will impose serious recordkeeping burdens on researchers and increase risks to security and confidentiality.[8]

Besides the cell phone problems, the telephone survey approach has several inherent disadvantages. First, respondents cannot be shown anything in a traditional telephone interview. This shortcoming ordinarily eliminates the telephone survey as an alternative in situations that require respondents to comment on visual product concepts, advertisements, and the like. Of course, smart phone surveys overcome this problem.

A second disadvantage of the telephone interview is that it limits the quantity and types of information that can be obtained. A respondent's patience wears thin more easily over the phone, and it is easy to hang up the phone. The telephone is also a poor vehicle for conducting a depth interview or a long interview with many open-ended questions.

A third disadvantage of telephone interviewing is associated with the increased use of screening devices. These include answering machines, do-not-call lists, call blocking, caller ID, and distinctive ringing. On the average, for every hour an interviewer spends on the phone, 30 minutes is spent just trying to find a person who will agree to be surveyed. This, of course, drives up the cost of telephone surveys.

Today, nearly all telephone interviews are central-location call center interviews. In some cases, firms are further centralizing the process by conducting completely automated telephone surveys but only from landlines.

Call Center Telephone Interviews   **Call center telephone interviews** are conducted from a facility set up for that purpose. The reason for the popularity of call center phone interviews is fairly straightforward—in a single word, control. First, the interviewing process can be monitored; most call center telephone interviewing facilities have unobtrusive monitoring equipment that permits supervisors to listen in on interviews as they are being conducted. Interviewers who are not doing the interview properly can be corrected, and those who are incapable of conducting a proper interview can be terminated. One supervisor can monitor from 10 to 20 interviewers. Ordinarily, each interviewer is monitored at least once per shift. Second, completed interviews are edited on

> **call center telephone interviews**
> Interviews conducted by calling respondents from a centrally located marketing research facility.

the spot as a further quality control check. Interviewers can be immediately informed of any deficiencies in their work. Finally, interviewers' working hours are controlled.

Virtually all research firms have computerized the call center telephone interviewing process. In **computer-assisted telephone interviews (CATI)**, each interviewer is seated in front of a computer terminal or a personal computer. When a qualified respondent gets on the line, the interviewer starts the interview by pressing a key or series of keys on the keyboard. The questions and multiple-choice answers appear on the screen one at a time. The interviewer reads the question and enters the response, and the computer skips ahead to the appropriate next question. For example, the interviewer might ask whether the respondent has a dog. If the answer is yes, there might be a series of questions regarding what type of dog food the person buys. If the answer is no, those questions would be inappropriate. The computer takes into account the answer to the dog ownership question and skips ahead to the next appropriate question.

In addition, the computer can help customize questionnaires. For example, in the early part of a long interview, a respondent is asked the years, makes, and models of all the cars he or she owns. Later in the interview, questions might be asked about each specific car owned. The question might come up on the interviewer's screen as follows: "You said you own a 2011 GMC truck. Which family member drives this vehicle most often?" Other questions about this vehicle and others owned would appear in similar fashion.

Another advantage of CATI is that computer tabulations can be run at any point in the study. Based on preliminary tabulations, certain questions might be dropped, saving time and money in subsequent interviewing. If, for example, 98.3 percent of those interviewed answer a particular question in the same manner, there is probably no need to continue asking the question. Tabulations may also suggest the need to add questions to the survey. If an unexpected pattern of product use is uncovered in the early stages of interviewing, questions can be added that delve further into this behavior. Finally, management may find the early reporting of survey results useful in preliminary planning and strategy development.

Gaining respondent cooperation is the key to a successful telephone interview. Amanda Durkee, senior project manager for Zanthus Research, Portland, Oregon, talks about the importance of a good first impression in the next Practicing Marketing Research box.

> → **computer-assisted telephone interviews (CATI)**
> Call center telephone interviews in which interviewers enter respondents' answers directly into a computer.

PRACTICING MARKETING RESEARCH

Picture yourself sitting at work. Your phone rings. On the other end, a voice tentatively says, "Hi, this is Bob from Masterful Research. I'm conducting a survey today on widgets. Is this a good time for me to ask you a few questions?"

What Would You Do?

For many purchase decision makers at businesses, such as IT managers, this type of call is an everyday occurrence. Unless there's a compelling reason to participate from the very beginning, it's

very likely that they'll pass on the opportunity. The following are some guidelines to increase the persuasiveness of your survey introduction.

- *Keep the intro short and natural.* Interviewers are trained to read introductions and questions verbatim, so keep the scripted introduction short and simple.

- *Make sure to say why you're calling.* Identifying the subject of the survey will not only help generate interest but also avoid confusion and result in more direct, informed responses.

- *Tell the respondent how much time you need.* If the survey is under 20 minutes, disclose the length upfront. A survey conducted by the Marketing Research Association shows that cooperation rates drop off sharply after 20 minutes, so if your survey is longer you may want to consider shortening it!

- *Offer an incentive.* If the length is over 15 or 20 minutes and/or if the audience has a particularly low incidence among the population, it is very possible that you will need an incentive to gain participation.

- *Distinguish yourself from telemarketers in a non-salesy way.* An example introduction is, "We are very interested in the opinions of companies like yours so that manufacturers of [product] can continually improve the products and services they provide. Would you help me with my research?"

- *Identify the client, if possible.* Tell respondents who is conducting the survey, particularly if you or your client is a well-established, well-regarded brand and if disclosing sponsorship won't bias answers.

- *Offer confidentiality and respect for respondents.* Last but certainly not least, remind respondents that their responses will be held in confidence and that they will not be placed on any mailing lists or receive any sales solicitations as a result of their participation.

Remind them also that their opinions are valuable![9]

Questions

1. Can you think of any other ways to get people to participate?
2. Do you usually agree to be interviewed in telephone surveys? Why or why not?

Self-Administered Questionnaires

The self-administered and mail survey methods explained in this section have one thing in common. They differ from the other survey methods discussed in that no interviewer—human or computer—is involved. The major disadvantage of **self-administered questionnaires** is that no one is present to explain things to the respondent and clarify responses to open-ended questions. For example, if someone were asked via an open-ended question why he or she does not buy a particular brand of soft drink, a typical answer might be "because I don't like it." From a managerial perspective, this answer is useless. It provides no information that can be used to alter the marketing mix and thereby make the product more attractive. An interviewer conducting the survey, however, would "probe" for a response—after receiving and recording the useless response, the interviewer would ask the respondent what it was that he or she did not like about the product. The interviewee might then indicate a dislike for the taste. Next, the interviewer would ask what it was about the taste that the person did not like. Here the interviewer might finally get something useful, with the respondent indicating

Kiosk-based computer interviewing is a relatively new and successful way of capturing data on consumers' recent experiences. Go to *www.intouchsurvey.com* to find out more about the kiosk-based offerings of In-Touch Survey Systems, Inc.

➜ **self-administered questionnaires**
Questionnaires filled out by respondents with no interviewer present.

that the product in question was, for example, "too sweet." If many people give a similar response, management might elect to reduce the sweetness of the drink. The point is that, without probing, management would have only the useless first response.

Some have argued that the absence of an interviewer is an advantage in that it eliminates one source of bias. There is no interviewer whose appearance, dress, manner of speaking, or failure to follow instructions may influence respondents' answers to questions.

Self-administered interviews are often used in malls or other central locations where the researcher has access to a captive audience. Airlines, for example, often have programs in which questionnaires are administered during the flight. Passengers are asked to rate various aspects of the airline's services, and the results are used to track passenger perceptions of service over time. Many hotels, restaurants, and other service businesses provide brief questionnaires to patrons to find out how they feel about the quality of service provided (see Exhibit 6.3).

A recent development in the area of direct computer interviewing is kiosk-based computer interviewing. Kiosks are developed with multimedia, touch-screen computers contained in freestanding cabinets. These computers can be programmed to administer complex surveys, show full-color scanned images (products, store layouts), and play sound and video clips. Kiosks have been used successfully at trade shows and conventions and are now being tested in retail environments, where they have many applications. From a research standpoint, kiosk-based interviewing can be used in place of exit interviews to capture data on recent experiences. Kiosks have other definite advantages: This form of interviewing tends to be less expensive, and people tend to give more honest answers than they would to a human interviewer, and internal control is higher because the survey is preprogrammed.[10]

Mail Surveys

➜ **ad hoc mail surveys**
Questionnaires sent to selected names and addresses without prior contact by the researcher; sometimes called *one-shot mail surveys*.

➜ **mail panels**
Precontacted and pre-screened participants who are periodically sent questionnaires.

Two general types of mail surveys are used in marketing research: ad hoc mail surveys and mail panels. In **ad hoc mail surveys** (sometimes called *one-shot mail surveys*), the researcher selects a sample of names and addresses from an appropriate source and mails questionnaires to the people selected. Ordinarily, there is no prior contact, and the sample is used only for a single project. However, the same questionnaire may be sent to nonrespondents several times to increase the overall response rate. In contrast, **mail panels** operate in the following manner:

1. A sample group is precontacted by letter. In this initial contact, the purpose of the panel is explained, and people are usually offered a gratuity.

2. As part of the initial contact, consumers are asked to fill out a background questionnaire on the number of family members, their ages, education level, income, types of pets, types of vehicles and ages, types of appliances, and so forth.

3. After the initial contact, panel participants are sent questionnaires from time to time. The background data collected on initial contact enable researchers to send questionnaires only to appropriate households. For example, a survey about dog food usage and preferences would be sent only to dog owners.

➜ **longitudinal study**
Study in which the same respondents are resampled over time.

A mail panel is a type of longitudinal study. A **longitudinal study** is one that questions the same respondents at different points in time. Several companies, including Synovate, NPD Research, and The Gallop Panel, operate large (more than 100,000 households) consumer mail panels.

On first consideration, mail appears to be an attractive way to collect survey data. There are no interviewers to recruit, train, monitor, and pay. The entire study can be sent out and administered from a single location. Hard-to-reach respondents can be readily surveyed. Mail surveys appear to be convenient, efficient, and inexpensive. The promise of anonymity is another benefit. While personal and telephone interviews may indicate

GATWICK EXPRESS

Customer Survey

Self-Administered Questionnaire: Airport Travel
Please fill out the following questionnaire. Check the appropriate boxes and write your answers in the space provided.

Exhibit 6.3

Customer Survey

Source: Courtesy of Accent Marketing & Research, Ltd., London.

1. Where are you flying from? Where are you going? Please list the departure and arrival times of your flights as well as the airline you are flying with.
   - Departure Location: _____
     - Departure Time: _____
     - Airline/Flight Number: _____
   - Arrival Locations _____
     - Arrival Time: _____
     - Airline/Flight Number: _____

2. Which class are you sitting in?
   - First Class ○
   - Coach ○

3. Are your flights direct? If not, where is your layover? How long is your layover?
   _____

4. Where do you live?
   _____

5. What is your age, gender, and yearly household income?
   - Age _____
   - Gender _____
   - Income _____

6. How many adults are in your party? How many children?
   - Adults _____
   - Children _____

7. Why are you flying today? Check all that apply.
   - Business ○
   - Vacation ○
   - Visiting friends or relatives ○
   - Other ○

8. How many times have you flown in the last 12 months?
   _____

9. How did you book your flight?
   - Online ○
   - Through a travel agency ○
   - Over the phone ○

10. How did you first hear about the airline you are flying with today?
    _____

11. Did you consider alternative modes of transportation? If so, which ones? And why did you ultimately choose to fly with the airline you chose?

12. Please comment on your travel experience today with your particular airline.
    Comments:
    _____

Thank you for completing today's airline travel questionnaire. Enjoy your flight!

that all information collected will be kept confidential, blind mail surveys absolutely guarantee it. This is particularly important to someone who may be asked to provide information of a confidential or personal nature.[11]

Like self-administered questionnaires, mail surveys of both types encounter the problems associated with not having an interviewer present. In particular, no one is there to probe responses to open-ended questions, a real constraint on the types of information that can be sought. The number of questions—and, consequently, the quantity of obtainable information—is usually more limited in mail surveys than in surveys involving interviewers.

EXHIBIT 6.4	Tactics Employed to Increase Mail Survey Response Rates

- ■ Advance postcard or telephone call alerting respondent to survey
- ■ Follow-up postcard or phone call
- ■ Monetary incentives (half-dollar, dollar)
- ■ Premiums (pencil, pen, keychain, etc.)
- ■ Postage stamps rather than metered envelopes
- ■ Self-addressed, stamped return envelope
- ■ Personalized address and well-written cover letter
- ■ Promise of contribution to favorite charity
- ■ Entry into drawings for prizes
- ■ Emotional appeals
- ■ Affiliation with universities or research institutions
- ■ Personally signed cover letter
- ■ Multiple mailings of the questionnaire
- ■ Reminder that respondent participated in previous studies (for mail panel participants)

Ad hoc mail surveys suffer from a high rate of nonresponse and attendant systematic error. Nonresponse in mail surveys is not a problem as long as everyone has an equal probability of not responding. However, numerous studies have shown that certain types of people—such as those with more education, those with high-level occupations, women, those less interested in the topic, and students—have a greater probability of not responding than other types. Response rates in ad hoc mail surveys may run anywhere from less than 5 percent to more than 50 percent, depending on the length of the questionnaire, its content, the group surveyed, the incentives employed, and other factors. Those who operate mail panels claim response rates in the vicinity of 70 percent.

Many strategies designed to enhance response rates have been developed. Some of the more common ones are summarized in Exhibit 6.4. The question must always be, "Is the cost of the particular strategy worth the increased response rate generated?" Unfortunately, there is no clear answer to this question that can be applied to all procedures in all situations.

Mail surveying is declining in popularity in commercial marketing research. Today, many research projects that, in the past, would have been conducted by mail are now being moved to the Internet.

Non-Internet survey alternatives discussed in this section are summarized in Exhibit 6.5.

Determination of the Survey Method

A number of factors may affect the choice of a survey method in a given situation. The researcher should choose the survey method that will provide data of the desired types, quality, and quantity at the lowest cost. The major considerations in the selection of a survey method are summarized in Exhibit 6.6.

Sampling Precision

The required level of sampling precision is an important factor in determining which survey method is appropriate in a given situation. Some projects by their very nature require a high level of sampling accuracy, whereas this may not be a critical consideration in other projects. If sampling accuracy were the only criterion, the appropriate data-collection

EXHIBIT 6.5	Non-Internet Forms of Survey Research
Type of Interview	**Description**
Door-to-door interviews	Interviews are conducted in respondents' homes (rarely used today in the United States).
Executive interviews	Interviews of industrial product users (e.g., engineers, architects, doctors, executives) or decision makers are conducted at their place of business.
Mall-intercept interviews	Interviews with consumers are conducted in a shopping mall or other high-traffic location. Interviews may be done in a public area of the mall, or respondents may be taken to a private test area.
Call center telephone interviews	Interviews are conducted from a telephone facility set up for that purpose. These facilities typically have equipment that permits supervisors to unobtrusively monitor the interviewing while it is taking place. Many of these facilities do national sampling from a single location. An increasing number have computer-assisted interviewing capabilities. At these locations, the interviewer sits in front of a computer terminal with a personal computer. The questionnaire is programmed into the computer, and the interviewer uses the keyboard to directly enter responses.
Self-administered questionnaires	Self-administered questionnaires are most frequently employed at high-traffic locations such as shopping malls or in captive audience situations such as classrooms and airplanes. Respondents are given general information on how to fill out the questionnaire and are expected to fill it out on their own. Kiosk-based point-of-service touch screens provide a way to capture information from individuals in stores, health clinics, and other shopping or service environments.
Ad hoc (one-shot) mail surveys	Questionnaires are mailed to a sample of consumers or industrial users, without prior contact by the researcher. Instructions are included; respondents are asked to fill out the questionnaire and return it via mail. Sometimes a gift or monetary incentive is provided.
Mail panels	Questionnaires are mailed to a sample of individuals who have been precontacted. The panel concept has been explained to them, and they have agreed to participate for some period of time, in exchange for gratuities. Mail panels typically generate much higher response rates than do ad hoc mail surveys.

technique would probably be call center telephone interviewing, an online survey of a sample drawn from a huge Internet panel, or some other form of polling of a sample drawn from customer lists. The appropriate survey method for a project not requiring a high level of sampling accuracy might be the mail approach or some type of mall survey.

The trade-off between the call center telephone survey, Internet panel, and the mail survey methods in regard to sampling precision is one of accuracy versus cost. A call center telephone survey employing a random-digit dialing sampling procedure that includes cell

EXHIBIT 6.6	Factors That Determine the Selection of a Particular Survey Method
Factor	**Comment**
Sampling precision	If the need for accuracy in the study results is not great, less rigorous and less expensive sampling procedures may be appropriate.
Budget	It is important to determine how much money is available for the survey portion of the study.
Need to expose respondent to various stimuli and have respondent perform specialized tasks	Taste tests and prototype usage tests usually require face-to-face contact. Card sorts, certain visual scaling methods, and the like require either face-to-face contact or the Internet.
Quality of data required	It is important to determine how accurate the results of the study need to be.
Length of questionnaire	Long questionnaires are difficult to do by mail, over the phone, or in a mall.
Incidence rate	Are you looking for people who make up 1 percent of the total population or 50 percent of the population? If you are looking for a needle in a haystack, you need an inexpensive way to find it. The Internet is probably the best source.
Degree of structure of questionnaire	Highly unstructured questionnaires may require data collection by personal interview.
Time available to complete survey	There may not be time to wait for responses via snail-mail. The Internet is the fastest way to go.

phone and smart phones might produce a better sample than the mail survey method. However, the mail survey will most likely cost less. In some cases, Internet samples will provide both lower cost and greater accuracy.

Budget

The commercial marketing researcher frequently encounters situations in which the budget available for a study has a strong influence on the survey method used. For example, assume that for a particular study the budgetary constraint for interviewing is $10,000 and the sample size required for the necessary accuracy is 1,000. If the cost of administering the questionnaire using the mall-intercept method is $34.50 per interview and the cost of administering it via Internet survey is $1.50 per interview, the choice is fairly clear—assuming that nothing about the survey absolutely requires face-to-face contact.

Requirements for Respondent Reactions

In some studies, the marketing researcher needs to get respondent reactions to various marketing stimuli—perhaps product prototype usage (a new style of PC keyboard) or a taste test. In these cases, the need to get respondent reactions to stimuli normally requires personal contact between interviewer and respondent.

Taste tests are most often conducted in a controlled environment because of their unique requirements. Can you imagine conducting this type of research through a mail survey?

Taste tests typically require food preparation. This preparation must be done under controlled conditions so that the researcher can be certain that each person interviewed is responding to the same stimulus. The only viable survey alternative for tests of this type is the mall-intercept approach or some variant. One variant, for example, is recruiting people to come to properly equipped central locations, such as community centers, to sample products and be interviewed.

Some surveys require face-to-face interviewing because of the need to use special measurement techniques or obtain specialized forms of information. The tasks are so complex that the interviewer must be available to explain the tasks and ascertain whether the respondents understand what is required of them.

Quality of Data

The quality of data required is an important determinant of the survey method. Data quality is measured in terms of validity and reliability. (These two concepts are discussed in detail in Chapter 10.) *Validity* refers to the degree to which a measure reflects the characteristic of interest. In other words, a valid measure provides an accurate reading of whatever the researcher is trying to measure. *Reliability* refers to the consistency with which a measure produces the same results with the same or comparable populations.

Many factors beyond the interviewing method affect data quality. Sampling methods, questionnaire design, specific scaling methods, and interviewer training are a few of them. However, each of the various interviewing methods has certain inherent strengths and weaknesses in terms of data quality. These strengths and weaknesses are summarized in Exhibit 6.7.

The important point here is that the issue of data quality may override other considerations such as cost. For example, although the least expensive way to get responses to a long questionnaire with many open-ended questions might be via a mall-intercept interview, the data obtained by this method might be so biased—because of respondent fatigue, distraction, and carelessness—that the results would be worthless at best and misleading at worst.

EXHIBIT 6.7	Strengths and Weaknesses of Selected Data-Collection Methods in Terms of Quality of Data Produced	
Method	**Strengths**	**Weaknesses**
Mall-intercept interview	Interviewer can show, explain, and probe.	Many distractions are inherent in the mall environment; respondent may be in a hurry, not in proper frame of mind to answer survey questions; there is more chance for interviewer bias; nonprobability sampling problems arise.
Call center telephone interview	Supervisor can monitor the interviewing process easily; excellent samples can be obtained; interviewer can explain and probe.	Respondent may be distracted by things going on at their location; problems arise in long interviews and interviews with many open-ended questions. Many refuse to participate.
Self-administered questionnaire	Interviewer and associated biases are eliminated; respondent can complete the questionnaire when convenient; respondent can look up information and work at own pace.	There is no interviewer to show, explain, or probe; sample may be poor because of nonresponse; who actually completes the questionnaire cannot be controlled.
Mail survey	Same strengths as for self-administered method.	Same weaknesses as for self-administered questionnaire; sample quality is better with mail panel.

Length of the Questionnaire

The length of the questionnaire—the amount of time it takes the average respondent to complete the survey—is an important determinant of the appropriate survey method to use. If the questionnaire for a particular study takes an hour to complete, the choices of survey method are extremely limited. Telephone, mall-intercept, and most other types of surveys, with the exception of personal interviews, will not work. People shopping at a mall ordinarily do not have an hour to spend being interviewed. Terminations increase and tempers flare when interviewers must try to keep respondents on the phone for an hour. Response rates plummet when people receive through the mail questionnaires that take an hour or more to complete. The trick is to match the survey technique to the length of the questionnaire.

SurveySpot, SSI's huge Internet panel, asked its panel members what was the ideal survey length. The responses were as follows:[12]

- Less than 2 minutes   2%
- 2 to 5 minutes   21%
- 6 to 10 minutes   44%
- 11 to 15 minutes   21%
- 16 to 25 minutes   3%
- 26 minutes or more   0%
- No ideal length   8%
- Not sure   1%

Incidence Rate

Recall that the incidence rate refers to the percentage of people, households, or businesses in the general population that would qualify as interviewees in a particular study. Search costs, which correlate with the time spent trying to locate qualified respondents, sometimes exceed the costs of interviewing. In situations where the researcher expects incidence rates to be low and search costs high, it is important to select the method or combination of methods that will provide the desired survey results at a reasonable cost.

Doing a low-incidence rate study in a mall would be very expensive. This approach should be taken only if there is some compelling reason for doing so—a long in-depth interview, for example. The lowest-cost survey alternative for the low-incidence study is probably the Internet panel, assuming that this approach meets the other data-collection requirements of the study. One advantage of the Internet panel is that it can be pre-screened; people can be asked a number of questions, usually including some on product usage. For example, if panel members were asked during prescreening whether anyone in their household participated in downhill or alpine skiing, the Internet panel operator could—at very low cost—pull out only those households with one or more skiers for a survey of Alpine skiers.

Structure of the Questionnaire

In addition to the length of the questionnaire, the degree of structure required in the questionnaire may be a factor in determining which survey method is most appropriate for a given study. *Structure* refers to the extent to which the questionnaire follows a set sequence or order, has a predetermined wording of questions, and relies on closed-ended (multiple-choice) questions. A questionnaire that does all these things would be structured; one that deviates from these set patterns would be considered unstructured. A questionnaire with little structure is likely to require a face-to-face interview. Very brief, highly structured questionnaires do not require face-to-face contact between interviewer and respondent. Mail, telephone, self-administered, and online surveys are viable options for studies of this type.

Time Available to Complete the Survey

If the client needs to have survey results quickly, the Internet is the best choice. Generally, call center telephone and mall-intercept interviews can also be completed in a timely manner.

Marketing Research Interviewer

No discussion of survey research in marketing would be complete without considering the person who actually does the interviewing. As noted in Chapter 2, most marketing research in-person interviewing is still done under the direct supervision of field service firms. The actual interviewing is conducted, to a large extent, by individuals who work part-time for relatively low wages. A new, totally inexperienced interviewer works at a rate somewhere between minimum wage and minimum wage plus 20 percent. It is unusual to find even the most experienced interviewers earning more than minimum wage plus 50 percent. The pay is not good, and fringe benefits are minimal. Ordinarily, an interviewer's involvement with an interviewing assignment begins when he or she is asked by a supervisor at a field service firm to work on a particular job. If the interviewer accepts the assignment, he or she will be given a date and time for a briefing about the job. At the briefing, the questionnaire for the study and all deadlines and requirements for the job are discussed.

Interviewers are typically the main interface with consumers and are, therefore, a vital link to consumer cooperation. Their skill level and pay level are areas of concern now being addressed by the Marketing Research Association, which has several suggestions for developing and strengthening interviewers' consumer interaction skills: good training programs that cover ways to establish consumer rapport and a basic understanding of "cooperation turning points," frequent monitoring of interviewers' interaction skills to evaluate their impact on consumer cooperation, and feedback to interviewers on monitoring results.

SUMMARY

Surveys are popular for several reasons. First, managers need to know why people do or do not do something. Second, managers need to know how decisions are made. Third, managers need to know what kind of person, from a demographic or lifestyle perspective, is making the decision to buy or not to buy a product.

There are two major categories of errors in survey research: random error and systematic error, or bias. Systematic error can be further broken down into measurement error and sample design error. Types of sample design error include selection, population specification, and frame errors. Frame error results from the use of an incomplete or inaccurate sampling frame. Population specification error results from an incorrect definition of the universe or population from which the sample is to be selected. Selection error results from adopting incomplete or improper sampling procedures or not properly following appropriate selection procedures.

The second major category of systematic error is measurement error. Measurement error occurs when there is a discrepancy between the information being sought (true value) and the information actually obtained by the measurement process. Measurement error can be created by a number of factors, including surrogate information error, interviewer error, measurement instrument bias, processing error, nonresponse bias, and response bias. Surrogate information error results from a discrepancy between the information actually required to solve a problem and the information sought by the researcher. Interviewer error occurs when an interviewer influences a respondent to give untrue or inaccurate answers. Measurement instrument bias is caused by problems within the questionnaire itself. Processing error results from mistakes in the transfer of information from survey documents to the computer. Nonresponse bias occurs when a particular individual in a sample cannot be reached or refuses to participate in the survey. Response bias arises when interviewees tend to answer questions in a particular way, whether out of deliberate falsification or unconscious misrepresentation.

There are several types of traditional surveys. Mall-intercept interviews are conducted with shoppers in public areas of shopping malls, either by interviewing them in the mall or by asking them to come to a permanent interviewing facility within the mall. Executive interviews are the industrial equivalent of door-to-door interviews; they involve interviewing professional people at their offices, typically concerning industrial products or services. Call center telephone interviews are conducted from a facility set up for the specific purpose of doing telephone survey research. Computer-assisted telephone interviewing (CATI) is a form of call center interviewing. Each interviewer is seated in front of a computer terminal or personal computer. The computer guides the interviewer and the interviewing process by exhibiting appropriate questions on the computer screen. The data are entered into the computer as the interview takes place. A self-administered questionnaire is filled out by the respondent. The big disadvantage of this approach is that probes cannot be used to clarify responses. Mail surveys can be divided into ad hoc, or one-shot, surveys and mail panels. In ad hoc mail surveys, questionnaires are mailed to potential respondents without prior contact. The sample is used for only a single survey project. In a mail panel, consumers are precontacted by letter and are offered an incentive for participating in the panel for a period of time. If they agree, they fill out a background questionnaire. Then, periodically, panel participants are sent questionnaires.

The factors that determine which survey method to use include the degree of sampling precision required, budget size, whether respondents need to react to various stimuli or to perform specialized tasks, the quality of data required, the length of the questionnaire, the degree of structure of the questionnaire, and the time available to complete the survey.

KEY TERMS & DEFINITIONS

random error, or random sampling error Error that results from chance variation.

chance variation Difference between the sample value and the true value of the population mean.

systematic error, or bias Error that results from problems or flaws in the execution of the research design; sometimes called non-sampling error.

sample design error Systematic error that results from an error in the sample design or sampling procedures.

sampling frame List of population elements or members from which units to be sampled are selected.

frame error Error resulting from an inaccurate or incomplete sampling frame.

population specification error Error that results from incorrectly defining the population or universe from which a sample is chosen.

selection error Error that results from incomplete or improper sample selection procedures or not following appropriate procedures.

measurement error Systematic error that results from a variation between the information being sought and what is actually obtained by the measurement process.

surrogate information error Error that results from a discrepancy between the information needed to solve a problem and that sought by the researcher.

interviewer error, or interviewer bias Error that results from the interviewer's influencing—consciously or unconsciously—the respondent.

measurement instrument bias Error that results from the design of the questionnaire or measurement instrument; also known as questionnaire bias.

processing error Error that results from the incorrect transfer of information from a survey document to a computer.

nonresponse bias Error that results from a systematic difference between those who do and those who do not respond to a measurement instrument.

refusal rate Percentage of persons contacted who refused to participate in a survey.

response bias Error that results from the tendency of people to answer a question incorrectly through either deliberate falsification or unconscious misrepresentation.

door-to-door interviews Interviews conducted face-to-face with consumers in their homes.

executive interviews Industrial equivalent of door-to-door interviewing.

mall-intercept interviews Interviews conducted by intercepting mall shoppers (or shoppers in other high-traffic locations) and interviewing them face-to-face.

call center telephone interviews Interviews conducted by calling respondents from a centrally located marketing research facility.

computer-assisted telephone interviews (CATI) Call center telephone interviews in which interviewers enter respondents' answers directly into a computer.

self-administered questionnaires Questionnaires filled out by respondents with no interviewer present.

ad hoc mail surveys Questionnaires sent to selected names and addresses without prior contact by the researcher; sometimes called one-shot mail surveys.

mail panels Precontacted and prescreened participants who are periodically sent questionnaires.

longitudinal study Study in which the same respondents are resampled over time.

QUESTIONS FOR REVIEW & CRITICAL THINKING

1. The owner of a hardware store in Eureka, California, is interested in determining the demographic characteristics of people who shop at his store versus those of people who shop at competing stores. He also wants to know what his image is relative to the competition. He would like to have the information within three weeks and is working on a limited budget. Which survey method would you recommend? Why?

2. Discuss this statement: "A mall-intercept interview is representative only of people who shop in that particular mall. Therefore, only surveys that relate to shopping patterns of consumers within that mall should be conducted in a mall-intercept interview."

3. A colleague is arguing that the best way to conduct a study of attitudes toward city government in your community is through a mail survey because it is the cheapest method. How would you respond to your colleague? If time were not a critical factor in your decision, would your response change? Why?

4. Discuss the various types of sample design errors and give examples of each.

5. Why is it important to consider measurement error in survey research? Why is this typically not discussed in professional marketing research reports?

6. What types of error might be associated with the following situations?
   a. Conducting a survey about attitudes toward city government, using the telephone directory as a sample frame.
   b. Interviewing respondents only between 8:00 A.M. and 5:00 P.M. on features they would like to see in a new condominium development.
   c. Asking people if they have visited the public library in the past two months.
   d. Asking people how many tubes of toothpaste they used in the past year.
   e. Telling interviewers they can probe using any particular example they wish to make up.

REAL-LIFE RESEARCH • 6.1

Yes, Teens Love Their Mobile Phones!

Cell phone texting has become the preferred channel of basic communication between teens and their friends, and cell calling is a close second. Some 75 percent of 12- to 17-year-olds own cell phones, up from 45 percent in 2004. Those phones have become indispensable tools in teen communication patterns. Fully 72 percent of all teens—or 88 percent of teen cell phone users—are text-messengers. That is a sharp rise from the 51 percent of teens who were texters in 2006. More than half of teens (54 percent) are daily texters.

Among all teens, the frequency of use of texting has now overtaken the frequency of every other common form of interaction with their friends.

Fully two-thirds of teen texters say they are more likely to use their cell phones to text their friends than talk to them by cell phone.

One in three teens sends more than 100 text messages a day, or 3,000 texts a month.

Daily text messaging by teens to friends has increased rapidly since early 2008. Some 38 percent of teens were daily texters in February 2008, and that has risen to 54 percent of teens who use texting in September 2009. Of the 75 percent of teens who own cell phones, 87 percent use text messaging at least occasionally. Among those texters:

- Half of teens send 50 or more text messages a day, or 1,500 texts a month, and one in three send more than 100 texts a day, or more than 3,000 texts a month.
- 15 percent of teens who are texters send more than 200 texts a day, or more than 6,000 texts a month.
- Boys typically send and receive 30 texts a day; girls typically send and receive 80 messages per day.
- Teen texters, ages 12–13, typically send and receive 20 texts a day.
- 14- to 17-year-old texters typically send and receive 60 text messages a day.
- Older girls who text are the most active, with 14- to 17-year-old girls typically sending 100 or more messages a day, or more than 3,000 texts a month.
- However, while many teens are avid texters, a substantial minority are not. One-fifth of teen texters (22 percent) send and receive just 1–10 texts a day, or 30–300 a month.

Calling is still a central function of the cell phone for teens, and for many teens, voice is the primary mode of conversing with parents.

Among cell-owning teens, using the phone for calling is a critically important function, especially when it comes to connecting with their parents. But teens make and receive far fewer phone calls than text messages on their cell phones.

Teens typically make or receive 5 calls a day. White teens typically make or receive 4 calls a day, or around 120 calls a month, while African American teens exchange 7 calls a day, or about 210 calls a month, and Hispanic teens typically make and receive 5 calls a day, or about 150 calls a month.

Girls more fully embrace most aspects of cell phone-based communication.

As we see with other communicative technologies and applications, girls are more likely than boys to use both text messaging and voice calling and are likely to do each more frequently.

- Girls typically send and receive 80 texts a day; boys send and receive 30.
- 86 percent of girls text message friends several times a day; 64 percent of boys do the same.
- 59 percent of girls call friends on their cell phone every day; 42 percent of boys call friends daily on their cell phones.

Girls are also more likely than boys to text for social reasons, to text privately, and to text about school work.

- 59 percent of girls text several times a day to "just say hello and chat"; 42 percent of boys do so.

- 84 percent of girls have long text exchanges on personal matters; 67 percent of boys have similar exchanges.
- 76 percent of girls text about school work, while 64 percent of boys text about school work.

Cell phones are not just about calling or texting—with expanding functionality, phones have become multimedia recording devices and pocket-sized Internet-connected computers. Among teen cell phone owners:

Teens who have multipurpose phones are avid users of those extra features. The most popular are taking and sharing pictures and playing music.

- 83 percent use their phones to take pictures.
- 64 percent share pictures with others.
- 60 percent play music on their phones.
- 46 percent play games on their phones.
- 32 percent exchange videos on their phones.
- 31 percent exchange instant messages on their phones.
- 27 percent go online for general purposes on their phones.
- 23 percent access social network sites on their phones.
- 21 percent use e-mail on their phone.
- 11 percent purchase things via their phones.[13]

Questions

1. How might Verizon use this information?
2. This study was conducted by the Pew Research Center. What would you want to ask the Pew researchers about the data and the methods used to collect the data before purchasing the complete report?
3. What are the various survey methods that could have been used to collect this data? What are the advantages and disadvantages of each?

REAL-LIFE RESEARCH • 6.2

The NFL Is King!

Professional football continues to surge in popularity as one-third (33 percent) of U.S. adults who follow at least one sport say it is their favorite sport. This is up three points from 2004. Baseball slipped slightly in 2005, dropping to 14 percent, down one point from 2004. Coming close on the heels of baseball is college football (13 percent) followed by auto racing (11 percent). These are the results of a nationwide survey conducted online by Harris Interactive, Rochester, New York, between December 8 and 14, 2005 among 1,961 U.S. adults, of whom 1,402 follow at least one sport.

In the past 20 years, professional football and baseball have seen the most dramatic changes in popularity. Since 1985, professional football has risen nine points in popularity (from 25 to 33 percent), while baseball has dropped the same amount (from 23 to 14 percent). The next largest change in popularity is in auto racing, which has risen six points since 1985, from 5 to 11 percent. Men's tennis has seen a drop in popularity of four points in this same time period down to 1 percent from 5 percent in 1985.

The survey also finds some sizable differences between different segments of the population. Pro football is most popular among African Americans (47 percent), those with household incomes of $50,000 to under $75,000 (41 percent) and $35,000 to under $50,000 (40 percent), and among Generation X—those aged 28 to 39—(30 percent). Those with a postgraduate education are least likely (23 percent) to call professional football their favorite sport.

Baseball does best among Hispanics (20 percent) and Echo Boomers—those aged 18 to 27—(21 percent). African Americans are least likely to say baseball is their favorite sport (6 percent).

College football is particularly popular among Republicans and those with postgraduate degrees (both 20 percent). Five percent of those with household incomes of less than $15,000 cite professional football as their favorite sport.

Auto racing (which includes NASCAR) is most popular among those with a high school education or less (19 percent) and Baby Boomers (15 percent), while it fares worst among those with a postgraduate degree (2 percent) and among members of Generation X (4 percent). For more information, visit www.harrisinteractive.com.[14]

Questions

1. This survey was conducted online, which is covered in detail in Chapter 7. Suggest three ways that these data might have been gathered and the advantages and disadvantages of each.

2. Assume that we are interested in a detailed understanding of why GenXers are so enthralled with pro football. How might we gather the data?

3. What are four types of errors that could be present in this survey? What can be done to minimize each?

Google

business news

business news
business news **articles**
business news **network**
business news **daily**
business news **americas**
newspapers

Online Marketing Research

LEARNING OBJECTIVES

→ **1.** To understand the online world as it applies to marketing research.

→ **2.** To learn about using the Internet to gather secondary data for marketing research.

→ **3.** To appreciate Internet search strategies.

→ **4.** To understand the popularity and types of online focus groups.

→ **5.** To gain insights into survey research on the Internet.

→ **6.** To appreciate the importance of panel management in maintaining data quality.

Chapter 7 explores the ever-increasing role of the Internet in secondary data searches, qualitative research, and survey research. Online observation research, another form of research growing at a sizzling pace, is covered in Chapter 8.

The Online World

The world's Internet population will total almost 2 billion users by the time you read this paragraph. That's right, about one-fifth of the world's population is online. In the United States and Canada, over 77 percent of the population is online, spanning every ethnic, socioeconomic, and educational divide. Since the year 2000, while online growth in the United States and Canada has grown by almost 150 percent, the growth in Africa and the Middle East is in excess of 2,000 percent![1] It is no wonder then that most managers accept the idea that online research can, under appropriate conditions, accurately represent U.S. consumers as a whole.[2] Nonadopters of the Internet tend to be older, low-income consumers (aged 65+ and with household incomes less than $30,000).[3] These consumers are not the target market for many companies' goods and services.

The popularity of online research continues to grow, with the vast majority of America's marketing research companies conducting some form of online research.[4] Today, online survey research has replaced computer-assisted telephone interviewing (CATI) as the most popular mode of data collection.[5] Internet data collection is also rated as having the greatest potential for further growth. Having made this observation, we must also report that there is no sign that paper surveys are disappearing as two-thirds of market research companies are still relying on them.[6]

Using the Internet for Secondary Data

Recall from Chapter 4 that secondary data can play a key role early in the marketing research process. It can clarify the problem, perhaps suggest a methodology for approaching the problem, and, if you are really lucky, provide a solution so that the time and cost of primary research are avoided.

Sites of Interest to Marketing Researchers

Exhibit 7.1 details a number of different sites where researchers can go to obtain secondary information, including competitive intelligence. You will note that a rich variety of data are available on many different topics. Although a lot of information is free, some, such as that offered by Claritas International, must be purchased.

Periodical, Newspaper, and Book Databases   Several excellent periodical, newspaper, and book databases are available to researchers. We have also posted these on our Web site at *www.wiley.com/college/McDaniel*. Some can be directly accessed via the Internet and others through your local library's Web site.

Newsgroups

A primary means of communicating with other professionals and special-interest groups on the Internet is through newsgroups. With an Internet connection and newsreader software, you can visit any newsgroup supported by your service provider. If your service provider does not offer newsgroups or does not carry the group in which you are interested, you can find one of the publicly available newsgroup servers that does carry the group you'd like to read.

EXHIBIT 7.1	Secondary Data Available Online for Marketing Researchers	
Organization	URL	Description
American Marketing Association	www.marketingpower.com	Enables users to search all of the AMA's publications by using keywords.
American Fact Finder	www.factfinder.census.gov	Provides ongoing data collected by the Census Bureau.
BLS Consumer Expenditure Surveys	www.bls.gov/cex	Provides information on the buying habits of consumers, including data on their expenditures, income, and credit ratings.
Bureau of Economic Analysis	www.bea.gov	Offers a wide range of economic statistics.
Bureau of Transportation Statistics	www.bts.gov	Serves as a comprehensive source for a wide range of statistics on transportation.
American City Business Journals	www.bizjournals.com	Offers a wealth of articles, reports, news, and data on everything from ratings of America's best small cities to statistics on men's and women's salaries. Current articles and reports, as well as an extensive archive dating back to 1994, provide insight and analysis of key business and economic trends.
Center for International Earth Science Network	www.ciesin.org	Serves as an excellent source of demographic information concerning the United States.
Centers for Disease Control/National Center for Health Statistics	www.cdc.gov/nchs	Maintains data on vital events, health status, lifestyle, exposure to unhealthy influences, onset and diagnosis of illness and disability, and use of health–care, through the National Center for Health Statistics. The NCHS, a subdivision of the Centers for Disease Control and Prevention, is the federal government's principal agency for vital and health statistics.
Clickz.com	www.clickz.com	Provides statistics on Internet research: weekly usage statistics, online populations, browser statistics and more.
The Dismal Scientist	www.dismal.com	Provides timely economic information, with comprehensive data and analyses at the metro, state, and national levels. This authoritative site also has data and analyses of global issues, including situations facing Asia, South America, and Europe. Visitors can rank states and metro areas on more than 100 economic, socioeconomic, and demographic categories.
Easy Analytic Software, Inc./The Right Site	www.easidemographics.com	Offers demographic site reports, or three-ring studies, including current estimates for population and households. Each three-ring study has census estimates for race, ethnicity, age distribution, and income distribution, as well as weather data.
EconData.net	www.econdata.net	Enables users to access a tremendous number of links to government, private, and academic data sources. Check out the list of top 10 data sources at this premier site for researchers interested in economics and demographics.
FreeDemographics	www.freedemographics.com	Offers free demographic market analysis reports.
Harris InfoSource	www.harrisinfo.com	Provides business-to-business data on American manufacturers and key decision makers.
Hoovers	www.hoovers.com	Gives company descriptions and industry information.
Internet Public Library	www.ipl.org/div/aon	Offers a collection of over 1,100 Internet sites providing information about a wide variety of professional and trade associations.
Marketing Research Association	www.mra-net.org	Offers causes and solutions of "declining respondent cooperation" and links to research suppliers.
Mediamark Research/Top-Line Reports	www.mediamark.com/mri/docs/toplinereports.html	Allows marketers and researchers to access demographic data on magazines, cable TV, and 53 different product or service categories. Top-Line Reports breaks down cable TV networks' viewers according to age, sex, and income. Magazines are listed by total audience, circulation, readers per copy, median age, and income.

(continued)

EXHIBIT 7.1	(Continued)	
Organization	**URL**	**Description**
Opinion Research (ORC International)	www.opinionresearch.com	Offers consulting and research services. Their Web site claims expertise in a broad range of industries, including information technology and telecommunications, healthcare, financial services, public services, energy and utilities market research, and more.
Population Reference Bureau	www.prb.org	Source of demographic information on population issues.
Quirks	www.quirks.com	Magazine for market researchers.
Service Intelligence	www.serviceintelligence.com	Has an area devoted to customer stories of unpleasant experiences with airlines, banks, restaurants, and other service businesses. However, "hero" stories are also included.
Social Security Administration	www.socialsecurity.gov/policy	Provides a range of government statistics about social security beneficiaries.
U.S. Census Bureau	www.census.gov	Serves as the source for all federal census data.
U.S. Department of Agriculture/Economic Research Service	www.ers.usda.gov	Offers a wide range of agricultural statistics.
USAData	www.usadata.com	Provides access to consumer lifestyle data on a local, regional, and national basis.
U.S. Government	www.fedstats.gov	Serves as a source for statistics and reports for more than 100 government agencies. Also links to other sources of relevant information. Highly recommended site but you may have to dig a little.
Valuation Resources	www.valuationresources.com	Offers a directory of resources that address subjects such as industry overview, issues, trends, and outlook, industry financial information and financial ratios, and compensation and salary surveys for a wide variety of industries.
Wikipedia	www.wikipedia.org	Functions as the free encyclopedia that anyone can edit.
World Fact Book	www.cia.gov/library/publications/the-world-factbook	Provides detailed information about countries of the world, including political and economic aspects.
WorldOpinion	www.worldopinion.com	Offers thousands of marketing research reports. This is perhaps the premier site for the marketing research industry.

newsgroup
An Internet site where people can read and post messages devoted to a specific topic.

Newsgroups function much like bulletin boards for a particular topic or interest. A newsgroup is established to focus on a particular topic. Readers stop by that newsgroup to read messages left by other people, post responses to others' questions, and send rebuttals to comments with which they disagree. Generally, there is some management of the messages to keep discussions within the topic area and to remove offensive material. However, readers of a newsgroup are free to discuss any issue and communicate with anyone in the world who visits that group. Images and data files can be exchanged in newsgroups, just as they can be exchanged via e-mail.

With over 250,000 newsgroups currently in existence and more being added every day, there is a newsgroup for nearly every hobby, profession, and lifestyle. Most browsers come with newsgroup readers. If you do not already have a newsgroup reader, you can go to one of the search engines and search for a freeware or shareware newsgroup reader. These newsgroup readers function much like e-mail programs. To find a particular newsgroup, follow these steps:

1. Connect to the Internet in your usual way.
2. Open your newsreader program.

3. Search for the topic of interest. Most newsreaders allow you to search the names of the newsgroups for key words or topics. Some newsreaders, like Microsoft Internet Explorer, also allow you to search the brief descriptions that accompany most newsgroups.

4. Select the newsgroup of interest.

5. Begin scanning messages. The title of each message generally indicates its subject matter.

Newsgroup messages look like e-mail messages. They contain a subject title, author, and message body. Unlike normal e-mail messages, however, newsgroup messages are threaded discussions. This means that any reply to a previous message will appear linked to that message. Therefore, you can follow a discussion between two or more people by starting at the original message and following the links (or threads) to each successive reply. Images, sound files, and video clips can be attached to messages for anyone to download and examine.

Blogs

The traditional definition of a blog, or Web log, was a frequent, chronological publication of personal thoughts and Web links. Now companies are also using blogs to communicate directly with customers and other businesses. More recently market researchers have used blogs to monitor brands, track trends, profile customers, and identify unmet needs. Blogs are growing to be an important tool in the exploratory research stage of many formal survey projects.[7]

Companies also use blogs to talk to customers and to other businesses. Blogging gained popularity with the introduction of automated published systems, most notably at *bloggeratblogger.com*. Marketing researchers are finding blogs to be an important source of information on just about any topic imaginable. Researchers have used them to recruit respondents for surveys. Although blogs can be found on most search engines, several engines such as blogsearchengine.com are dedicated to blog searches.

Internet Search Strategies

There is perhaps no single best way to search the Web, but we recommend a five-step strategy.[8]

Step One: Analyze your topic to decide where to begin. A suggested worksheet is shown in Exhibit 7.2.

Step Two: Test run a word or phrase in a search engine such as Google. Consider synonyms or equivalent terms.

Step Three: Learn as you go and vary your approach with what you learn. Don't assume that you know what you want to find. Look at the search results and see what else you might use in addition to what you thought of.

Step Four: Don't get bogged down in any strategy that doesn't work. Consider using a subject directory. A few of the best are the Librarian's Index, *lii.org*; Infomine, *infomine.ucr.edu*; Academic Info, *www.academicinfo.net*; Google Directory, *directory.google.com*; About.com, *www.about.com*; and Yahoo Directory, *dir.yahoo.com*. Many researchers switch back and forth between directories and search engines.

Step Five: If you haven't found what you want, go back to earlier steps better informed.

EXHIBIT 7.2	Internet Search Topic Worksheet

Jot down a topic or subject you'd like to explore on the Web:

BEGIN THE PRE-SEARCHING ANALYSIS

1. **What UNIQUE WORDS, DISTINCTIVE NAMES, ABBREVIATIONS, or ACRONYMS are associated with your topic?**
These may be the place to begin because their specificity will help zero in on relevant pages.

2. **Can you think of societies, organizations, or groups that might have information on your subject via their pages?**
Search these as a "phrase in quotes," looking for a homepage that might contain links to other pages, journals, discussion groups, or databases on your subject. You may require the "phrase in quotes" to be in the documents' titles by preceding it by **title** (no space)

3. **What other words are likely to be in ANY Web documents on your topic?**
You may want to require these by joining them with **AND** or preceding each by + (no space)

4. **Do any of the words in 1, 2, or 3 belong in phrases or strings—together in a certain order, like a cliché?**
Search these as a "phrase in quotes" (e.g., "observation research" or "marketing research aggregator").

5. **For any of the terms in #4, can you think of synonyms, variant spellings, or equivalent terms you would also accept in relevant documents?**
You may want to allow these terms by joining them by **OR** and including each set of equivalent terms in parentheses (e.g., surveys or interviews).

6. **Can you think of any extraneosus or irrelevant documents these words might pick up?**
You may want to exclude terms or phrases with—**[no space] before each term,** or **AND NOT** (e.g., surveys or interviews—job).

7. **What BROADER terms could your topic be covered by?**
When browsing subject categories or searching sites of webliographies or databases on your topic, try broader categories (e.g., marketing research).

Evaluating Web Pages   Once you have found what you were looking for, the next step is to evaluate the quality. Things are not always as they seem. For example, recall the Web sites that want you to pay a membership fee to become an online survey respondent. There is a Web site that supposedly ranks Web sites that provide an entrée to earning cash through completing interviews. All of the sites ranked required a membership fee, and no real marketing research firms, such as Greenfield Online or Harris Interactive, were included. Of course, legitimate researchers don't charge a fee to become a panel member. The ranking site was probably created by one of the sites that charge a membership fee. No criteria were given for how the rankings were determined.

Techniques for evaluating Web pages are detailed in Exhibit 7.3.

EXHIBIT 7.3 | How to Evaluate Web Pages

1. What can the URL tell you?
Techniques for Web Evaluation:
1. Before you leave the list of search results—before you click and get interested in anything written on the page—glean all you can from the URLs of each page.
2. Then choose pages most likely to be reliable and authentic.

Questions to ask:
Is it somebody's *personal page*?
- Read the URL carefully:
  - Look for a personal name (e.g., jbarker or barker) following a tilde (~), a percent sign (%), or the words "users," "members," or "people."
  - Is the server a commercial *ISP* * or other provider mostly of Web page hosting (like aol.com or geocities.com)

What are the implications?
Personal pages are not necessarily "bad," but you need to investigate the author very carefully. For personal pages, there is no publisher or domain owner vouching for the information in the page.

Look for appropriateness and fit. What kind of information source do you think is most reliable for your topic?

What type of *domain* does it come from?
(educational, nonprofit, commercial, government, etc.)
- Is the domain appropriate for the content?
  - Government sites: look for .gov, .mil, .us, or other country code
  - Educational sites: look for .edu

2. Scan the perimeter of the page, looking for answers to these questions.
Techniques for Web Evaluation:
1. Look for links that say **"About us," "Philosophy," "Background," "Biography," "Who am I,"** etc.
2. If you cannot find any links like these, you can often find this kind of information if you truncate back the URL.

    INSTRUCTIONS for Truncating back a URL: In the top Location Box, delete the end characters of the URL stopping just before each / (leave the slash). Press enter to see if you can see more about the author or the origins/nature of the site providing the page. Continue this process, one slash (/) at a time, until you reach the first single / which is preceded by the domain name portion. This is the page's server or "publisher."

3. Look for the date "last updated"—usually at the bottom of a Web page. Check the date on all the pages on the site. Do not rely on a date given in browser file properties or page information displays. These dates can be automatically kept current and are useless in critical evaluation.

Questions to ask:
Who wrote the page?
- Look for the name of the author, or the name of the organization, institution, agency, or whatever, who is responsible for the page
  - An e-mail contact is not enough.
- If there is no personal author, look for an agency or organization that claims responsibility for the page.
  - If you cannot find this, locate the publisher by truncating back the URL (see technique above). Does this publisher claim responsibility for the content? Does it explain why the page exists in any way?

What are the implications?
Web pages are all created with a purpose in mind by some person or agency or entity. They do not simply "grow" on the Web like mildew grows in moist corners. You are looking for someone who claims accountability and responsibility for the content. An e-mail address with no additional information about the author is not sufficient for assessing the author's credentials. If this is all you have, try e-mailing the author and asking politely for more information about him or her.

3. Look for indicators of quality information:
Techniques for Web Evaluation:
1. Look for a link called "links," "additional sites," "related links," etc.
2. In the text, if you see little footnote numbers or links that might refer to documentation, take the time to explore them. What kinds of publications or sites are they? reputable? scholarly? Are they real? On the Web (where no publisher is editing most pages), it is possible to create totally fake references.
3. Look at the publisher of the page (first part of the URL). Expect a journal article, newspaper article, and some other publications that are recent to come from the original publisher if the publication is available on the Web. Look at the bottom of such articles for copyright information or permissions to reproduce.

(continued)

EXHIBIT 7.3	(Continued)

Question to ask:
Are sources documented with footnotes or links?

- Where did the author get the information?
    - As in published scholarly/academic journals and books, you should expect documentation.
- If there are links to other pages as sources, are they to reliable sources?
- Do the links work?

What are the implications?
In scholarly/research work, the credibility of most writings is proven through footnote documentation or other means of revealing the sources of information. Saying what you believe without documentation is not much better than just expressing an opinion or a point of view.

4. What do others say?
Techniques for Web Evaluation:
1. Find out what other Web pages link to this page.
    a. Use *alexa.com* URL information:
    Simply paste the URL into alexa.com's search box.
    You will see, depending on the volume of traffic to the page:
    - Traffic rank
    - Subjective reviews
    - "Site statistics" including some page history, sites that link to the page
    - Contact/ownership information for the domain name

5. Does it all add up?
Techniques for Web evaluation:
1. Step back and think about all you have learned about the page. Listen to your gut reaction. Think about why the page was created, the intentions of its author(s).
    If you have doubts, ask your instructor or come to one of the library reference desks and ask for advice.
2. Be sensitive to the possibility that you are the victim of irony, spoof, fraud, or other falsehood.
3. Ask yourself if the Web is truly the best place to find resources for the research you are doing.

Questions to ask:
Why was the page put on the Web?
- Inform, give facts, give data?
- Explain, persuade?
- Sell, entice?
- Share?
- Disclose?

So what? What are the implications?
These are some reasons to think of. The Web is a public place, open to all. You need to be aware of the entire range of human possibilities of intentions behind Web pages.

Creating a Database from a Web Site— A Marketer's Dream[9]

If a person today were opening, say, a wine shop, which of the following would give the owner the best opportunity to build a database—a traditional store or a Web retailer such as wine.com?

A Web merchant like wine.com has access to data about its clients that would make its physical-world counterparts very envious. A customer's conduit to an online store is a two-way electronic link, allowing the online merchant to gather all sorts of information, particularly if that customer has shopped with that merchant before.

Getting the customer's name, address, and purchasing history is only the beginning. A Web merchant can record the customer's actions as he or she moves through the merchant's site, taking note not only of purchases but also of window shopping. The end result is a file that allows the merchant to determine what that customer is most likely to purchase next—and then offer inducements to make it happen.

Meanwhile, back in the physical world, the wine store owner sits behind the register, eyeing the anonymous customer who just went out empty-handed. Had the customer visited the store before? If so, what did he or she buy? Did the customer even see the new Chardonnay that just came in? Unfortunately, the owner was too busy to ask those questions (and the customer would have been offended if the owner had). Maybe the customer will come back—maybe not.

Preview Travel Inc., an online travel agency based in San Francisco, determined that Las Vegas, Orlando, and Cancun were the top three vacation spots among its customers.

The firm quickly purchased key words for the three destinations on several Internet directory sites; when a Web surfer performs a search for any of the three vacation spots, a Preview Travel advertising banner accompanies the list of results. Karen Askey, senior vice president of consumer marketing at Preview Travel, says traditional travel agencies could employ the same promotional tactics, but she doubts they could spot top destinations as quickly. "When you're online, the speed at which you can get that data is basically instantaneous," she says.

Once Web surfers start clicking around the virtual aisles of an online store, merchants can monitor their every move. The best known method of doing so involves a **cookie**, a text file that sits on a user's computer and identifies that user when she or he revisits a Web site.

Even some privacy advocates admit that cookies have beneficial uses. For instance, they can store passwords, sparing users the hassle of having to identify themselves every time they go to a Web site, and they allow online shopping carts to work. Despite what some Net users believe, a site can read only the cookie that site put on the user's system, not any other cookies the user has collected from other Web sites.

Cookies are a powerful device for monitoring a user's behavior within a site, one that can tell a merchant whether the user lingers in lingerie or lawn chairs. "What it's like," says Nick Donatiello, president of Odyssey, a marketing research firm based in San Francisco, "is every time you walk into Macy's, they put a little tracker on you that follows you everywhere you go, how long you look at perfume and blue jeans."[10]

Cookies give Web merchants an advantage over their competitors in traditional retailing. Web merchants can follow window shoppers and then use the information they obtain to target promotions to them on return visits. And, unlike their traditional counterparts, an online merchant can rearrange the entire layout of a store in real time, sticking an advertisement for, say, parkas, on the front door when an avid skier comes calling.

> **cookie**
> A text file placed on a user's computer in order to identify the user when she or he revisits the Web site.

Online Qualitative Research

The primary form of online qualitative research is focus groups. These come in two categories in the online world: *traditional*, sometimes referred to as synchronous groups, and *online bulletin boards*, sometimes referred to as asynchronous groups. You will learn that online focus groups can take several forms. Traditional online groups are what the name implies. The goal is to get 8 to 10 participants online at the same time, for a moderator to send questions to the participants, and the participants to provide their comments. Special software from companies such as Itracks (see *www.itracks.com/qual*) provides the environment for these groups. Online bulletin boards are a new form of qualitative research that takes advantage of the online medium. In these groups, questions are posted for participants each day, and they have all day to provide their responses. They usually run for two to three days, sometimes longer. The moderator answers questions from participants throughout the day. Questions for the next day can be modified based on what participants have to say. Probing questions can be sent to individual participants or to all. Supporting software can permit participants to see what others had to say after they respond. An even newer twist on online focus groups are Web communities, which we will also examine in this section. We conclude with a brief look at online individual depth interviewing.

The Popularity of Online Focus Groups

➜ **online focus groups**
Focus groups conducted via the Internet.

Perhaps the hottest area in qualitative research today is **online focus groups**. Many marketing researchers, such as NFO Interactive, and Harris Black International, believe that Internet focus groups can replace face-to-face focus groups, although they acknowledge that online research has limitations. Others that are moving aggressively into online marketing research, such as Millward Brown International and Digital Marketing Services (DMS), were slower to use online focus groups.

Advantages of Online Focus Groups   Marketers who have used online focus groups, and the marketing researchers conducting them, say that the benefits far outweigh the limitations. Those benefits include much lower costs (about half as much), faster turnaround time, respondents, ability to be geographically separate and be located anywhere, and intangibles such as increased openness on the part of respondents when they do not have a moderator staring them in the face.

"I think [the panelists] were more definite about things they didn't like than they'd be in front of a moderator," said Lisa Crane, vice president of sales and marketing for Universal Studios Online, which used an online focus group to test a redesigned site it's developing for Captain Morgan Original Spiced Rum, a brand of its parent company, Seagram Company. Rudy Nadilo, president and CEO of Greenfield Online, which conducted the online focus groups for Universal, said they are meant "to complement, not replace" traditional panels.[11] Not only are the costs lower for online focus groups, but there are substantial travel savings for the client as well. Expenditures for round-trip airline tickets to distant cities, meals, hotels, and taxis are avoided. Clients merely log on in their own office, or even at home, to observe the research in progress.

Another advantage of online focus groups lies in access to the hard-to-reach target population. Online, it's possible to reach populations that are traditionally inaccessible because of time or professional constraints—groups such as physicians, lawyers, and senior business executives. Chances are higher that they will be available to participate, too, since they do not need to take time from their busy schedules to visit a focus group facility but, rather, can participate from the privacy of their own homes.

Another advantage claimed for online focus groups is efficient moderator–client interaction. During the traditional focus group, the client observes the discussion from behind a one-way glass; communication with the moderator is impossible without interfering with the discussion. An online focus group, however, offers a remarkable opportunity for two-way interaction between the moderator and the client. This direct interaction, while the moderator conducts the group, has become a necessity in operating a fully effective online focus group discussion and can facilitate the probing of sensitive personal topics.[12] Rather than sneaking into the room with a note scribbled on a piece of paper, the client can address the moderator directly, clearly, and efficiently, without interrupting the group dynamic.

Traditional focus groups always include "natural talkers," who dominate the discussion, despite a good moderator's attempt to equalize participant contributions. Other participants will be less comfortable voicing opinions in a group; they may express themselves more freely when not face to face with their peers. The online focus group has a built-in leveling effect, in the sense that shy participants can express themselves as freely as more outgoing participants. One participant points out why he likes participating in online focus groups, explaining, "I can be honest without the face-to-face peer pressure of focus groups"; another offers, "I get to express my opinion without having to hear someone's reaction."[13] At least in terms of honesty and willingness to offer genuine ideas and opinions, respondents tend to feel more comfortable participating from the privacy of their own homes.

Advantages of the online approach for B2B research are discussed in the following Practicing Marketing Research feature.

PRACTICING MARKETING RESEARCH

Advantages of Online Focus Groups in B2B research[14]

Recently, online focus groups have been emerging as a means of obtaining qualitative information. In an online focus group, participants access a secure Web site and answer questions in the form of an online questionnaire. Every participant can see the responses of everyone else. As the discussion develops, the moderator probes to set further information or to explore areas of interest. Online focus groups typically last for a set time period. Some online focus groups are run over a two-day period, allowing respondents to enter the discussion at different times.

Here are 13 advantages to using online B2B focus groups:

1. *Volume of information*—In online focus groups run by B2B International over a two-day span, respondents contributed about 2 hours worth of comments each. Compare that to a typical 8-person, 90-minute, face-to-face focus group in which each respondent will average 10 minutes of comments.

2. *Information depth and quality*—Online focus groups offer opportunities to explore issues where more detail is needed just as well as face-to-face groups do. Also, people often consider what they say in writing more than when speaking.

3. *Reflection time*—Online focus groups can be performed over a longer time span than face-to-face focus groups, allowing respondents more time to consider questions.

4. *Accuracy and granularity*—Researchers receive individual respondent answers in

written form, which can then be sorted into various categories.

5. *Inclusiveness*—The online focus group format creates greater opportunity for less vocal individuals to participate.

6. *Honesty of respondents*—Results from numerous online focus groups indicate that respondents will be more open as a result of the perceived anonymity of Web-based interaction.

7. *A better spread of respondents*—Online groups are not subject to logistical and geographic limitations, allowing researchers to draw from a much broader pool.

8. *Incorporating different geographies and time zones*—Similarly, the longer duration of online focus groups eliminates the restrictiveness of using respondents in different time zones.

9. *Researching senior respondents*—The flexibility of online focus groups makes it easier for heads of businesses to incorporate participation into their busy schedules.

10. *Participation rates*—Costs of recruiting respondents are lower, and respondents are less likely to pull out at the last minute due to extenuating circumstances.

11. *Introducing stimuli into the conversation*—Online focus groups are especially good for introducing electronic stimuli into discussions, such as images, videos, Web site links, and other documents.

12. *Everyone has an equal say*—Respondents who would typically be more vocal in face-to-face groups are less likely to dominate in online groups. Also, it is much easier for

a moderator to manage larger groups of people online.

13. *Client participation*—Clients can easily view results of the online focus group as it is going on and ask the moderator to direct the conversation to areas of particular interest.

Online focus groups are certainly not the best fit for every situation, though. Online focus groups are limited in their ability to present physical stimuli. They can also be more difficult when dealing with nontechnical participants. Much like with face-to-face groups, recruitment can be difficult and expensive as well.

Expenditures for online research, however, are expected to triple over the next 3 years, and many of these advantages should make online focus groups a more prominent tool in the online research department.

Questions

1. Do you think an online focus group would be more effective with consumer research or B2B research? Why do you think as you do?

2. Would you rather participate in an online or a traditional focus group? Why?

Disadvantages of Online Focus Groups   Critics say that the research community does itself an injustice by calling qualitative research sessions conducted over the Internet "focus groups." Their criticisms include the following:

Group Dynamics   One of the key reasons for using traditional focus groups is to view the interactions among the group participants, as they can provide excellent insights.

In cyberspace, it is difficult, if not impossible, to create any real group dynamics, particularly when the participants are reading from computer screens rather than interacting verbally. *Note:* new systems such as these offered by M2 overcome this problem.

Nonverbal Inputs   Experienced moderators use nonverbal inputs from participants while moderating and analyzing sessions. It is not always possible to duplicate the nonverbal input in an online environment.

Client Involvement   Many organizations use the focus group methodology because it gives clients an opportunity to experience direct interface with consumers in an objective environment. Nothing can replace the impact of watching focus groups from behind a one-way mirror, no matter how good the videotapes, remote broadcast facilities, streaming video, or reports written by moderators.

Exposure to External Stimuli   A key use of focus groups is to present advertising copy, new product concepts, prototypes, or other stimuli to the participants in order to get their reactions. In an online chat situation, it is almost impossible to duplicate the kind of exposure to external stimuli that occurs in the live focus group environment. As a result, the value of the input received online is more questionable than that of input coming from a live environment.

Role and Skill of the Moderator   Most marketing professionals agree that the most important factor in the quality of traditional focus group research is the skill of the moderator. Experienced moderators do more than simply ask questions of participants. A good moderator uses innovative techniques to draw out quiet or shy participants, energize a slow group, and delve a little deeper into the minds of the participants. The techniques available to a moderator sitting at a computer terminal are not the same as face-to-face involvements.

EXHIBIT 7.4	Advantages and Disadvantages of Traditional and Online Focus Groups	
	Traditional Focus Groups	**Online Focus Groups**
Basic costs	More expensive.	Cheaper.
Participants	Participants are locally based because of travel time and expense.	Anyone in the world with a computer and modem can participate.
Time commitment	Approximately 3½-hour time commitment. Busy respondents are less likely to be available.	No driving to facility, approximately 60-minute time commitment. Busy respondents are more likely to be available.
Openness of respondents	Some respondents are intimidated and afraid to speak openly in a face-to-face group setting.	Lack of direct face-to-face contact may lead respondents to express true feelings in writing if no Web cam is available.
Group dynamics	What one person says and does (gestures and expressions) can lead others to react.	None, according to critics.
Nonverbal communication	Body language can be observed.	Body language can only be observed if Web cameras are used.
Transcripts	Transcript is time-consuming and expensive to obtain; often not in complete sentences or thoughts.	Word-for-word transcripts are available almost immediately; usually in complete sentences/thoughts.
Respondent recruiting	Recruiting certain types of respondents (e.g., physicians, top managers) is difficult.	It is easier to obtain all types of respondents.
Client travel costs	Very expensive when client must go to several cities for one or two days each.	None.
Communication with moderator	Observers can send notes into focus group room.	Observers can communicate privately with moderator on a split screen.
Respondent security	Participants are accurately identified.	It is sometimes more difficult to ascertain who is participating.
Client involvement	Client can observe flesh-and-blood consumers interacting.	Client can observe via Web cameras.
Exposure to external stimuli	Package designs, advertising copy, and product prototypes with demonstrations can be shown to participants.	Ability to show stimuli is somewhat limited.

Exhibit 7.4 summarizes the advantages and disadvantages of traditional and online focus groups.

Using Channel M2 to Conduct Online Focus Groups Channel M2 provides market researchers with user-friendly virtual interview rooms, recruiting, and technical support for conducting virtual qualitative research efficiently and effectively. By using Channel M2, the moderator and client can see and hear every respondent. You can see a demo at *www.channelM2.com*.

Focus group recruiting at M2 uses a blend of e-mail recruitment (from a global panel with access to over 15 million online consumers) and telephone verification and confirmation. Specifically, e-mails elicit involvement and direct participants to an online qualification questionnaire to ensure that each meets screening criteria. Telephone follow-up confirms that respondents qualify. Prior to the interview, respondents know they must show photo ID on camera so as to verify identity. Specifically, respondents are directed to show their driver's license to their Web cam.

Channel M2 focus groups begin by the participants logging onto a Web page where everyone sees and hears each other, and communicates in a group setting. Participants are recruited using traditional methods and are then sent a Web camera so that both verbal and nonverbal reactions can be recorded. Installation of the Web cam is simple, aided by Channel M2 tech support 1 to 2 days prior to the interview.

Participants are then provided instructions via e-mail, including a link to the Channel M2 interviewing room and a toll-free teleconference number to call. Upon clicking on the link, participants sign on and see the Channel M2 interview room, complete with live video of the other participants, text chat, screen or slide sharing, and whiteboard.

Once the focus group is underway, questions and answers occur in "real time" in a lively setting. Participants comment spontaneously, both verbally or via text messaging, yet the moderator can provide direction exactly as they would in a traditional setting.[15]

Types of Online Focus Groups　Decision Analyst, one of America's most progressive firms in applying Internet technology to marketing research, offers two types of online focus groups:

1. **Real-Time Online Focus Groups.** These are live, interactive sessions with four to six participants and a moderator in a chat room format. The typical session lasts no longer than 45 to 50 minutes. The technique is best for simple, straightforward issues that can be covered in a limited time. The results tend to be superficial compared to in-person focus groups—but this is acceptable for certain types of projects.

   Typically, three to four groups are recommended as a minimum. Clients can view the chat room as the session unfolds and communicate with the moderator.

2. **Time-Extended Online Focus Groups.** These sessions, sometimes called Bulletin Board Focus Groups, follow a message board format and usually last 5 to 10 days. The 15 to 20 participants must comment at least two or three times per day and spend 15 minutes a day logged in to the discussion. The moderator reviews respondents' comments several times per day (and night) and probes or redirects the discussion as needed. This technique provides three to four times as much content as the average in-person focus group. Time-extended online focus groups, also called asynchronous focus groups, give participants to reflect, to talk to others, to visit a store, or time to check the pantry. This extra time translates into richer content and deeper insights. Clients can view the online content as it is posted and may communicate with the moderator at any time.

Using the Web to Find Focus Group Participants　The Internet is proving to be an excellent tool to locate group participants that fit a very specific set of requirements. Researchers are tapping online bulletin boards such as Craigslist, which attracts 5 million visitors each month to its classified advertisements. The site is most useful "when you're trying to find niche users to a small population of users that is hard to find," says Tim Plowman, an anthropologist who works at Cheskin, a marketing consulting firm.

Point Forward, Inc., a Redwood City, California, marketing research firm, has used Craigslist to find people who fit very specific categories, such as people who travel frequently between the United States and Mexico, says Vice President Michael Barry.

A recent Craigslist posting by a different marketing research firm offered $350 to $900 to New York residents willing to give researchers a tour of their liquor cabinets, take them on a liquor-shopping trip, or make a video-based documentary of a social event they were planning.

Screening questions included: "When you are out for drinks or purchasing alcohol in a store, do people tend to ask for your advice on which brands of liquor to buy? If yes, how often does that happen?"[16]

web community
Carefully selected group of consumers who agree to participate in an ongoing dialogue with a corporation.

Web Community Research[17]　A **Web community** is a carefully selected group of consumers who agree to participate in an ongoing dialogue with a particular corporation.

All community interaction takes place on a custom-designed Web site. During the life of the community—which may last anywhere from 6 months to a year or more—community members respond to questions posed by the corporation on a regular basis. These discussions, which typically take the form of qualitative "dialogues," are augmented by the ability of community members to talk to one another about topics that are of interest to them as well.

The popularity and power of Web communities initially came from several key benefits. Web communities

- Engage customers in a space where they are most comfortable, allowing clients to interact with them on a deeper level.

- Uncover "exciters" and "eureka moments," resulting in customer-derived innovations.

FROM THE FRONT LINE

Eight Tips for Conducting Successful Bulletin Board Focus Groups

Ryan Larson, formerly Project Manager, DSS Research

The online focus group methodology is a new frontier of qualitative marketing research. One specific model of online focus groups is the bulletin board focus group (BBFG). The bulletin board approach to focus groups has been around since 1999 and is becoming a more popular online qualitative research option. While a traditional focus group is a 90-minute session that consists of 6–12 participants, a BBFG can run for 2–5 days and accommodate anywhere from 15–40 participants. Furthermore, unlike a traditional focus group, multiple BBFGs can be run simultaneously. This leaves the moderator with a greater responsibility to familiarize and engage with more people, and creates a longer commitment of time in moderating the group. Typically, new primary questions are posted each day, and participants are instructed to log in to the group at least twice a day, at their convenience. Participants will answer the primary questions that are posted, and then also have an opportunity to respond to the moderator's follow-up probing questions and the other participants' responses that are posted underneath each primary question.

In my tips that follow, you will see that BBFGs and traditional focus groups still have much in common, but take note of the subtle differences that will increase the success of administering and moderating a BBFG.

1. **Stay safe and over-recruit the group.** Just because a BBFG increases the convenience of participation does not mean that 100 percent of the individuals you recruited will join the group. For consumers, you should recruit approximately 20 percent more than you want to participate. For a business-to-business study, recruit 30 percent extra.

2. **Be welcoming and give clear instructions.** Most respondents who join a BBFG are participating for the first time. As with anything new, there can be apprehension on the part of participants. To deal with this problem, the moderator has to immediately establish a comfortable rapport with the participants. Let the respondent know who the moderator is right away. The moderator should also immediately begin to add her or his own responses so participants see the moderator is online with them. After welcoming participants, it is vital to provide clear instructions and supporting details to the group. Because clients are often new to this type of research, it is equally as important to keep them informed on group progress. The client will not be observing the BBFGs constantly. The moderator will have the sole responsibility for catering to both the participants

and client continuously for the duration of the group.

3. **The primary questions will dictate the value of responses.** In general, participants will match their contributions to the questions asked. Therefore, avoid simple questions that will yield short, valueless responses. If the questions are simple, group them together as a primary question, as long as they are related. Grouping questions develops fuller answers from participants and is consistent with the way a moderator operates in traditional focus groups. Not every question may get answered, but the moderator will learn which topics are the most important to the participants.

4. **Keep the primary questions formal, but the conversation casual.** Be casual with the interaction among participants. Even though the primary questions should be formally stated, the rest of the conversation and probing questions do not have to so formal. The moderator should type comments and probes in the same fashion as she or he would speak. Casual conversation helps to open up participants and show them that the moderator is a real person and not a computer. In fact, feel free to use an emoticon: or ☺, ☹.

5. **Encourage the efforts participants make in the group.** When reading through the question responses, the moderator should make comments of encouragement as appropriate. If a participant gives an insightful answer, let her or him (as well as the rest of the group) know that you appreciate the thought that went into the response. Be sure not to offer any agreement or a specific opinion on a response because it could bias subsequent answers about the research topic. Finally, try to avoid making too many of these comments to just a few of the participants. Spread the encouragement.

6. **Accept the fact that some people will "cut and run."** Not every participant in a BBFG is going to write Pulitzer prize-winning prose in responses. Some BBFG participants will do their best in making the smallest effort to give the group as little information as possible in their responses. Be sure to engage and probe these participants, but do not waste too much time with them. The moderator's efforts are best spent probing and conversing with the participants who are giving valuable information.

7. **Simply put . . . Probe!** Remember, this is qualitative, exploratory research. As in traditional groups, the moderator looks for interesting comments and expands on them with follow-up questions. Unlike traditional groups, each probe does not necessarily move the conversation. The moderator can probe individual participants or the group as a whole. It is important to specifically address the person or people who are intended to answer the probe. As noted above, most respondents will be new to this process, and while the BBFG program will notify participants of new postings, participants may not know if they should answer a question posted in a primary question's conversation string. Finally, probing is the best way to engage participants and develop a positive, friendly relationship. The client will greatly appreciate this kind of involvement and effort.

8. **Watch for participation peak times.** The moderator's best chance to get answers to probing questions, or for the moderator to address any issues, is when the moderator and participant are both logged in. However, it is understandable that the moderator simply cannot be logged in to a BBFG for 72 hours straight during a three-day BBFG session, even though participants are free to log in at any time during the three days. The best way to avoid moderator absence is to look for patterns as to when people log in. Participants tend to be consistent in the times of day they log in. Some will always join the group in the mornings before work, while others will log in every day during their lunch breaks. Being alert to when participants log in and being responsive to their patterns enable the moderator to be online at the right times and to be more engaged with the group.

- Establish brand advocates who are emotionally invested in a company's success.
- Offer real-time results, enabling clients to explore ideas that normal time constraints prohibit.
- Create a forum in which natural dialogue allows customers to initiate topics important to them.[18]

In addition, Web communities help companies create a customer-centered organization by putting employees into direct contact with consumers from the comfort of their own desks.

Since communities provide advantages in speed, flexibility, and 24/7 access to consumers, they let the organization be agile in its research decision making and prudent in its spending.

By adding a research focus to the Web community environment, this holistic perspective deepens as the community becomes a way to

- Map the psyche of consumer segments.
- Brainstorm new ideas.
- Co-create and test new products.
- Observe natural consumer behavior.
- Rally the company around a customer-centered perspective.[19]

Beyond that, communities provide even greater value when the insights gained can be quickly shifted from the community space to the traditional market research space. This tight integration with more mainstream research approaches ensures that the community is both feeding new research initiatives and being fueled by insights gained from traditional research projects.

This type of cross-pollination takes another step toward a new research paradigm, one that integrates Web communities and traditional research. This new paradigm offers the potential to

- Increase the efficiency of research by quickly finding the most appropriate forum for exploration of new insights.
- Reduce costs by using the community to follow up on questions left unanswered from ad hoc research studies.
- Improve the way consumer insights and implications are shared across organizational departments.[20]

Online Individual Depth Interviewing   Depth interview projects can be very expensive when done in person. Although depth interviews can be conducted by phone, they must be recorded and transcribed. A few marketing research firms are experimenting with online individual depth interviews (IDIs). After respondents are recruited, via a secured chat platform, each participant is given a private blog where they can create their online journal for the project. Over a period of days, the respondents are given a series of questions to ponder in their blogs. The result is an immediate perfect transcription.[21] A second phase of the research may feature a telephone, e-mail, or bulletin board in-depth discussion. The discussion topics are derived from the blogs.

Online depth interviews are appropriate when group dynamics are not important to generating responses. Advantages of these time-extended depth interviews include (1) an effective method for interviewing high-level persons like physicians and busy executives, (2) richer content and deeper insights per respondent, and (3) ability to view transcripts at any time and make adjustments in the process by communicating with moderators.[22]

New innovative solutions for qualitative research are described in the following Practicing Marketing Research feature.

PRACTICING MARKETING RESEARCH

Have Technology, Will Investigate: Innovative Online Solutions for Qualitative[23]

New technologies offer significant improvements in online research over the original online platforms and provide many different tools marketers can use. When incorporating these online tools, however, a researcher must remember they are only part of the project design. A few options that researchers might consider looking into further are as follows:

Text-message posting to discussion boards

Respondents can post answers to these question via smartphone anytime and from anywhere. This tool is especially effective at getting in-the-moment reactions from respondents. Such responses might encourage reactions from other discussion board respondents as well.

In-situ *narrations*

Questions are sent to the respondent via e-mail or text and the respondent leaves a recorded answer on an answering machine. This method also allows the researcher to acquire substantial in-the-moment insights.

Word-and-picture diaries

Respondents answer questions in online diaries that can include photos and videos as well. This method can effectively capture evolving impressions of a product over time.

Wireless Webcams

The Webcam is set up to observe a particular activity the respondent is engaged in (such as using a new convection oven). This offers a more complete account of the experience than a written log would. Researchers must take time, however, to make sure they understand the respondent's environment and that setup of the Webcam is done correctly. Offering the Webcam to the respondent as compensation is a common practice.

"Mark-up" tools

Respondents are shown a print ad, concept sketch, or other stimulus, and then use the interface's editing tools to mark up the item with rough drawings, likes, dislikes, and comments. The moderator can control how much of each other's commentary respondents can see. This is a highly engaging method for getting feedback on ad mock-ups.

Private virtual communities

Respondents create profiles in a private virtual community which the researcher creates around her specific project. Respondents can interact with other community members while engaging with the researcher's study questions. Less suited for shorter projects, virtual communities can provide a means of keeping respondents involved and invested in long-term projects.

Video-editing tools

Video supplements are becoming much easier to include in research reports. Researchers can incorporate prerecorded questions with answer videos from individual respondents or real-time video discussions between a group of respondents and the researcher.

Questions

1. Which innovative method for collecting primary data would you most like to try?

2. Rank the new online tools from most beneficial to least beneficial to a company. Why did you rank the choices as you did?

Online Survey Research

The Internet has forever changed the way we conduct survey research. As noted earlier, a vast majority of all U.S. research firms are now conducting online research. In the United States, the online population is now closely tracking the U.S. population in most key demographic areas. Moreover, the number of Internet users around the world continues to explode. As the number of users grows worldwide, characteristics of a country's population and Internet user characteristics tend to meld. The reason for the phenomenal growth of online research is straightforward. The advantages far outweigh the disadvantages.

Advantages of Online Surveys

Most companies today face shorter product life cycles, increased competition, and a rapidly changing business environment. Management decision makers are having to make complex, rapid-fire decisions, and Internet research can help by providing timely information. The specific advantages of online surveys include the following:[24]

- **Rapid deployment, real-time reporting** Online surveys can be broadcast to thousands of potential respondents simultaneously. Respondents complete surveys and the results are tabulated and posted for corporate clients to view as the returns arrive. Thus, Internet survey results can be in the decision maker's hands in significantly less time than traditional survey results.

- **Reduced costs** The use of electronic survey methods can cut costs by 25 to 40 percent and provide results in half the time it takes to do traditional telephone surveys. Data-collection costs account for a large proportion of any traditional marketing research budget. Telephone surveys are labor-intensive efforts incurring training, telecommunications, and management costs. Online surveys eliminate these costs almost completely. Although the costs of traditional survey techniques rise in proportion to the number of interviews desired, electronic solicitations can grow in volume with less increase in project costs.

- **Ready personalization** Internet surveys can be highly personalized for greater relevance to each respondent's own situation, thus speeding up the response process. Respondents appreciate being asked only pertinent questions, being able to pause and then resume the survey as needed, and having the ability to see previous responses and correct inconsistencies.

- **High response rates** Busy respondents may be growing increasingly intolerant of "snail mail" or telephone-based surveys. Online surveys take less time to complete than phone interviews do, can be accomplished at the respondent's convenience (after work hours), and are much more stimulating and engaging. Graphics, interactivity, links to incentive sites, and real-time summary reports make the interview more enjoyable. The result: much higher response rates.

- **Ability to contact the hard-to-reach** Certain groups are among the most difficult to reach (doctors, high-income professionals, CIOs in Global 2000 firms). Most of these groups are well represented online. Internet surveys provide convenient anytime/anywhere access that makes it easy for busy professionals to participate.

- **Simplified and enhanced panel management** Internet panels are electronic databases, linked via the Internet, that are committed to providing feedback and counsel to research firms and their clients. They may be large or small, syndicated or proprietary, and they may consist of customers, potential customers, partners, or employees. Internet panels can be built and maintained at less cost and time required for traditional panels. Once a panel is created and a questionnaire is finalized, surveys can be deployed, data are collected, and top-level results are reported within days.

A sophisticated database tracks panelist profile data and survey responses, facilitating longitudinal studies and data mining to yield insights into attitudes and behaviors over time and across segments. Response rates are high, typically 20 to 60 percent, because respondents have agreed in advance to participate in the survey. These participants tend to provide more detailed and thoughtful answers than do those in traditional surveys, because they don't have to give demographic and lifestyle information (it's already been captured) and because they become engaged in the panel over time.

■ ***External Internet panels simplify life for research suppliers*** The availability of huge Internet panels maintained by firms such as Harris Interactive, SSI, Greenfield Online, Research Now, and Decision Analyst makes the sampling process much easier for research companies that utilize these panels. We will discuss these panels in detail later in the chapter. Moreover, the cost to use the panels has dropped as the number of panel suppliers has increased.

Advantages of online research in key global markets, such as Russia, are discussed in the following Global Research feature.

GLOBAL RESEARCH

Research in Russia[25]

Over the past decade, the Russian economy has emerged from the chaos of the 1990s and made dramatic steps toward stability and prosperity. One of the biggest indicators of growth has been the rise in disposable income, which has increased on average by 27 percent each year since 2000. Multinational companies and their marketing departments are taking notice too, especially as growth in many developed markets has slowed.

As Lyudmila Krokhina, a market research director for Wrigley, the candy and gum company, says, "There is an increased importance of market research overall and more decisions are based on consumer feedback." Luckily, Russian consumers are generally open to interacting with researchers and are eager to share their opinions on growing consumer choices. Still, researchers in Russia face several challenges.

One of those challenges is determining an appropriate representative sample of the Russian market. Russia covers a wide span of territories, so a true representative sample should cover all eight regions or, more specifically, all 89 federal districts. The sample would also need to account for typical demographic variables, such as age, gender, and socioeconomic status.

Despite the need for such a broad representative sample, most research focuses on major cities because that's where the majority of disposable income is located. Typically, market entry into Russia begins in Moscow and, increasingly, Saint Petersburg and other large cities. The need for marketing research throughout Russia has grown rapidly over the past decade. The challenge is how to collect data.

Face-to-face interviews are difficult because of the country's size and because telephone surveyors have to navigate the inefficiencies of the government-controlled telecommunications system. Online marketing research is only a recent development as Internet access has grown. Roughly 12 to 17.5 percent of the 142 million Russians have Internet access; however, these numbers are growing quickly at about 27 percent year-over-year. Larger cities like Moscow and Saint Petersburg tend to have higher penetration rates.

Even though online research has several advantages over other collection methods, it also has downsides. Certain demographics tend to be underrepresented in online research. Response rates of people over age 40 tend to be lower, as do those of women. Young, wealthy, educated males are the easiest group of Russians to access. Timing can be another issue for online researchers, as internal debate over the best approach to take with this market can drag out the research process. To make the most of online methods in Russia, researchers can consider converting standard studies into online studies. Conducting parallel studies both online and offline is also a good strategy.

As the Russian market continues to grow, understanding the Russian consumer will become increasingly important to firms looking to operate there as they try to create a sustainable competitive advantage.

Questions

1. How are the challenges facing researchers in Russia similar to those faced by researchers in other developed nations? How do you think they differ?

2. If most of Russia's disposable income is located in major metropolitan areas, why should a researcher concern himself with getting a sample that includes remote, less affluent regions?

Disadvantages of Online Surveys

The most common complaint about the use of online surveys traditionally was that Internet users are not representative of the population as a whole. As mentioned earlier, this comment has largely disappeared in the United States. Harris Interactive and DSS Research have conducted over 300 surveys using parallel modes (telephone and Internet) and found that the research produced similar results. In all of the studies, it was rare to find a statistically significant difference between the sampling modes.[26] DSS concluded that the Internet panel methodology offered the best alternative for market share measurement and competitive benchmarking objectives based on cost (half the cost of telephone), speed (can be completed in less than half the time of telephone), and accuracy of measurement.

Lee Smith, COO of Insight Express, conducted a side-by-side comparison of online research and mail surveys. He found that online research delivered data of the same quality as using mail surveys in one-eighth the time and at one-eighth the cost.[27] Other research has shown that in most countries where the Internet penetration rate exceeds 20 percent, online surveys tend to yield results similar to those found in traditional methods such as telephone or paper-and-pencil survey research.[28]

A second problem exists when an **unrestricted Internet sample** is set up on the Internet. This means anyone who wishes to complete the questionnaire can do so. It is fully self-selecting and probably representative of no one except Web surfers. The problem gets worse if the same Internet user can access the questionnaire over and over. For example, the first time *InfoWorld*, a computer user magazine, conducted its Readers' Choice survey on the Internet, the results were so skewed by repeat voting for one product that the entire survey was publicly abandoned and the editor had to ask for readers' help to avoid the problem again. All responsible organizations conducting surveys over the Internet easily guard against this problem by providing unique passwords to those individuals they invite to participate. These passwords permit one-time access to the survey.

A third problem is that the sample frame needed may not be available on the Internet. Assume that Guido's, a popular Italian restaurant in Dayton, Ohio, wanted to know how its customers perceived the food quality and service compared with that of the

> **unrestricted Internet sample** Self-selected sample group consisting of anyone who wishes to complete an Internet survey.

big chains, such as Olive Garden. A large Internet panel, such as Greenfield Online, is probably not going to have enough members in Dayton, Ohio, that patronize Guido's to give a representative sample. If Guido's doesn't have customer e-mail addresses, then an Internet sample isn't feasible.

Other problems include a lack of "callback" procedures to clarify open-end responses, potential for questionnaire programming errors, and a lack of bandwidth (some potential respondents can't complete the survey or download photos and video quickly). Some companies may view Internet research as fast and simple, and software to conduct basic surveys is readily available. However, some research companies don't have the technical expertise to conduct Internet research properly.

PRACTICING MARKETING RESEARCH

The Primacy of Online Research[29]

When the 2009 Globalpark Annual Market Research Software Survey released its findings, many trends emerged, but two were notable. First, although many market researchers are eager to get behind mobile research, they have yet to achieve real consensus on its viability. Second, despite attracting much attention, successful online research communities in practice are still few and far between.

The Globalpark survey asks respondents about the types of research their firms offer. In 2009, 94 percent of respondents said their firms offered Web research, making it far and away the most popular research mode. Regarding mobile research, respondents overall thought that mobile Web surveys had the most potential, although large companies slightly favored surveys via applets. Large companies tended to be more optimistic about all mobile research methodologies in general.

Regarding technical or operational challenges facing mobile research, about two-thirds of respondents said the small format limits usable question types. The second biggest challenge cited was the difficulty in obtaining a sample, followed by support for different devices and complex cost structures of the many telecommunications networks.

Only about 17 percent of companies surveyed were operating online communities, and over half reported plans to start online communities. Most existing online communities are in the early-adoption stage. While substantial technology exists to facilitate online communities, the industry appears to be generally hesitant to initiate in this area.

A surprising number of respondents, especially during a recession, were either planning to change their software (32 percent) or were considering it (26 percent). Over the last 4 years, a clear trend has emerged as companies shift toward using an integrated software platform for multiple research methodologies. In 2009, 59 percent reported using an integrated platform. Online sample sources varied widely by company and region, but overall, panels made up 61 percent of sources and 24 percent came from client samples.

Demand for online reporting systems appeared strong, with almost no respondents forecasting declines. Larger companies generally forecasted higher demand increases than smaller ones, particularly in more high-tech areas such as portals.

Questions

1. Why do you think researchers have not come to consensus about the viability of mobile research?

2. In future Globalpark surveys, how do you think market researchers will respond about delivering research through tablet applications, such as the iPad?

Methods of Conducting Online Surveys

There are several basic methods for conducting online surveys: Web survey software, survey design Web sites, and Web hosting.

Web Survey Software   Web survey software includes software systems specifically designed for Web questionnaire construction and delivery. In a typical use, the questionnaire is constructed with an easy-to-use edit feature, using a visual interface, and then automatically transmitted to a Web server system. The Web server distributes the questionnaire and files responses in a database. The user can query the server at any time for completion statistics, descriptive statistics on responses, and graphical displays of data. Several popular online survey research software packages are SPSS Quanquest, Inquisite, Sawtooth CiW, Infopoll, Designer, and SurveyGold.

Gaining Survey Completions   Do-it-yourself software, such as SPSS Quanquest, requires that you offer the respondent a good experience if you expect the person to complete the survey. The more engaged respondents are, the better quality insights they will provide. The following tips can help create a better experience for the interviewee:

- As with any questionnaire, use language that is less "research-ese" and more conversational.
- Be honest and upfront about the time required to complete a study.
- Provide more opportunities for participants to provide open-ended answers and truly express themselves.
- Ensure that all possible answer choices are given; avoid overuse of "other."
- Keep survey to less than 20 minutes in length and provide participants with progress information as they advance through the survey.
- Consider using graphics when possible or appropriate to make the experience more visually engaging.
- Explore new ways to facilitate interaction between respondents and a researcher.
- Make studies more informative—participants are particularly motivated by acquiring new knowledge and information about a product or topic.
- Offer participants the opportunity to be contacted again to receive updates on projects of products being tested.[30]

How important are incentives in online research? And does the cosmetic appearance of the questionnaire have an impact on completion rates? Decipher Inc. conducted an online study to address these questions.[31] It conducted a survey using a domestic customer list provided by eBay Inc. Over 1,900 eBay members participated in a 7-minute online survey. The recruits were sent an e-mail invitation containing a link that directed them to the survey. The study employed four parallel cells:

	Survey Design	Incentive
Cell 1	Plain	None
Cell 2	Fancy	None
Cell 3	Fancy	1 in 500 chance to win $1,000
Cell 4	Fancy	Guaranteed $2 cash to first 500 qualified completes

As can be seen from the setup, a comparison between Cell 1 and Cell 2 measured the effect of a plain versus fancy survey design. Color, the use of tables, and the right-aligned buttons distinguished the fancy from the plain survey design (see Exhibit 7.5).

Exhibit 7.5

Does a Fancy Survey Design Matter?

Source: Jamin Brazil, Aaron Jue, Chandra Mullins, and Jamye Plunkett, "Capture Their Interest," *Quirk's Marketing Research Review* (July/August 2006), p. 48.

Privacy Policy • Help

Survey project for consumers

Approximately how many items have you <u>bought</u> here in the <u>last 12 months</u>?

Select one

◯   None
◯   1 to 5
◯   6 to 10
◯   11 to 25
◯   25 to 50
◯   51 to 100
◯   More than 100

[Continue]

Figure 1 - Plain

Privacy Policy • Help

Approximately how many items have you <u>bought</u> here in the <u>last 12 months</u>?

Select one

None	&#9711;
1 to 5	&#9711;
6 to 10	&#9711;
11 to 25	&#9711;
26 to 50	&#9711;
51 to 100	&#9711;
More than 100	&#9711;

Figure 1 - Fancy [Continue]

A comparison between Cells 2 and 3 or Cells 2 and 4 measured incentive effects. Finally, a comparison between Cells 3 and 4 measured the effects of the different types of incentive: a cash prize drawing or a smaller, guaranteed cash incentive.

The appearance of the survey had no measurable impact on the completion rate (in both instances about 77 percent completed the survey). Nor did the type of incentive affect completion rates. However, either incentive boosted completion rates about 10 percent. For all four cells, dropouts occurred primarily over the first 90 seconds after a respondent entered the survey. Persons offered an incentive were significantly less likely to drop out during this period.[32] Another issue involving Internet surveys is whether timing is important in sending out survey invitations. It is in the United Kingdom, as explained in the Global Research box on page 202

Survey Design and Web Hosting Sites

Many Web sites allow the researcher to design a survey online without loading design software. The survey is then administered on the design site's server. Some offer tabulation and analysis packages as well. Popular sites that offer Web hosting are WebSurveyor, Perseus Survey Monkey, Research Now, and Zoomerang.

Commercial Online Panels

Many researchers turn to commercial online panel providers to assist in the process of completing a market research study, often by hosting a survey on their Web site. Commercial online panels are not created for the exclusive use of any one specific company or for any one particular project. Instead, **commercial online panels** are created for the use of multiple projects by many different companies. The companies providing access to the online panels have invested in the pre-recruitment of people who opt to participate in online market research surveys. Some online panels are for use by a specific industry, such as construction, medical, or technology industries, and may have a few thousand panel members, while the large commercial online panels have millions of people who have opted to participate in online surveys of varying topics. When people join most online panels, they answer an extensive profiling questionnaire that records demographic, lifestyle, and psychographic information, typically with hundreds of dimensions. This profiling information enables the panel provider to record detailed information on every panel member. Using this information, the panel provider can then target research efforts to panel members who meet specific criteria.

> **commercial online panels**
> Group of individuals who have agreed to receive invitations to do online surveys from a particular panel company such as eRewards or SSI. The panel company charges organizations doing surveys for access to the panel. Charges are usually so much per survey depending on survey length and the type of people being sought for the survey. The panel company controls all access to the members of its panel.

Panel Management

While online panels are quite effective at reducing costs and field time, the quality of the data is dependent on how well the panel is managed. Several factors influence the quality of an online panel. These include the recruitment methods, respondent participation, panel management practices, and types of incentives offered.

Panel Recruitment

The method of recruitment of panel members is critical to the quality of the panel. If the panel is to meet a researcher's needs for a study requiring a general audience of consumers, it is important to evaluate whether the panel's recruitment method draws from a representative audience of consumers. Likewise, if a researcher's project requires business professionals, the panel's recruitment methods should draw from a universe of business professionals. Ideally, a panel should represent a diverse sampling of the population under study. Panel member recruitment methodology is a key distinction among online panels. There are essentially two methods for recruiting for an online panel: open source and by invitation only.

Intercepting people as they surf the Internet through ads is known as open recruitment. **Open online panel recruitment** allows any person who has access to the Internet to "self-select" and enroll in a market research panel. This provides the benefit of building a panel quickly with people who are Internet-savvy and responsive to online advertising.

A key drawback is the lack of control over who is recruited. A panel with open recruitment may sign up millions of Web surfers who share similar characteristics, but may include only people who are responsive to Web ads and/or "seek out" an

> **open online panel recruitment**
> Any person with Internet access can self-select to be in a research panel.

GLOBAL RESEARCH

Timing Is Everything in Survey Invitations

Although respondents to online surveys can choose when to complete surveys, the time at which the invitation is sent can have a major impact on the number of responses, according to findings from London-based Lightspeed Research.

The firm sent out invitations to an online survey to 7,440 of its panelists in Great Britain at different times during the week. Overall, the results showed that invitations sent on a Monday afternoon achieved the best response rates, at up to 39 percent. Surveys sent at 5:30 P.M. on Friday afternoon resulted in relatively low response rates of 28 percent for women and 29 percent for men.

In addition, the research showed that external events could have a dramatic impact on response rates for online surveys. A major soccer game on Wednesday night had an impact on response rates, in particular among male respondents. Only 11 percent of male invitees from the Wednesday 5:30 P.M. invitation group responded to the survey, compared to 31 percent of women.

The research also showed that the majority of responders are likely to respond in the first 24 hours, with only around a third responding after this period. In other words, if the response rate is quite low within the first 24 hours, it is unlikely to recover in the following days. Invitations sent on Monday at 5:30 P.M. achieved a response rate of 26 percent within the first 24 hours and ended with a total response rate of 38 percent after six days. On the other hand, an invitation sent on Wednesday at 5:30 P.M. achieved only a 14 percent response rate after 24 hours and a total rate of 22 percent after six days.[33]

A research study may focus on people who meet a specific criterion such as golfing once a week.

opportunity to join an online panel by using search engines. This leaves out a large percentage of the general population.

In many cases, open recruitment leads to an overabundance of panel members who participate in many different panels and complete an inordinate amount of surveys. These are known in the industry as "professional survey takers"—people who sign up to take hundreds of surveys in order to enter into sweepstakes drawings or other types of incentives. The primary concerns associated with professional survey takers are that (1) they can give false or misleading information in an attempt to get through a survey quickly without regard to providing well-considered responses; (2) they tend to go through surveys in a perfunctory manner, which shows up in the time they take to complete the survey; and (3) they can make up a disproportionate amount of survey responders, leading to biased and unrepresentative research data. To the detriment of Internet marketing research, some Web sites have been developed to recruit people to sign up for several panels at one time. One study found that more than 30 percent of all online surveys are completed by less than 1 percent of the population. The study also found that professional survey takers respond to an average of 80 surveys over a 90-day period—with some taking several surveys per day.[34] However, it is important to consider that not all online panels are made up of professional survey takers. This is why it is so important to understand the recruitment methods used by an online panel before employing them in the research process.

The other method used for recruiting respondents to an online panel, the by-invitation-only method, was first used by Research Now, one of America's largest commercial online panel providers. **Closed online panel recruitment**, or by invitation only, invites only prevalidated individuals, or individuals who share known characteristics, to enroll in a market research panel. Most often, this is accomplished by inviting customers from large, highly trusted leading brands who collectively have a large, diverse base of customers in a given population (i.e., general consumers or business professionals). In recruiting for its consumer panel, for example, Research Now has partnered with large, well-known companies that have large, diverse customer bases. Similarly, in recruiting for its panel of business professionals, they have partnered with major airlines, hotels, and car rental companies. There is some natural overlap in the recruiting since business professionals who travel are also consumers, but Research Now pays close attention to panelist enrollment to ensure there isn't panelist duplication.

The "by-invitation-only" method enables a panel researcher to recruit people with specific demographics into the panel in order to meet a client's needs for a representative sample of the understudy population, or to meet specific needs. For example, in order to recruit affluent panel members, the panel provider may recruit customers from upscale retailers to join the panel. To recruit teenagers, a panel provider may recruit customers of specific clothing retailers that specialize in the teen market. To recruit business decision makers, a panel provider may recruit customers from companies that cater to businesspeople, such as airlines, hotels, car rental companies, and subscribers to business publications.

Using a "by-invitation-only" recruitment method gives a panel provider greater control over who is invited to the panel and greatly reduces the likelihood of professional survey takers. One particular area that requires attention with this approach is that the panel composition is dependent on the people who are invited to join the panel and may be biased by customers of a specific recruitment source. Thus, it is important that a "by-invitation-only" panel have a large number of diverse recruitment sources by working with companies in many different areas to ensure balanced representation in the panel.

> **closed online panel recruitment**
> Inviting only prevalidated individuals or those with shared known characteristics to enroll in a research panel.

Open versus Closed Recruitment

Research Now conducted a study of recruitment methods to compare "open" versus "closed" recruitment. During a 6-month test, Research Now, which recruits exclusively with a closed-loop recruitment approach termed *by invitation only*, enrolled 38,162 panel members into an experimental consumer panel using an open enrollment methodology. They then conducted a parallel tracking experiment that compared closed-sourced panelists to these open-sourced panelists (see Exhibit 7-6).

The experiment revealed that open-sourced panelists are often quite different from closed-sourced panelists. Open-sourced panelists were much more likely to be homemakers, retired people, students, and unemployed. They were also more likely to exhibit the behaviors of professional survey takers, including enrollment in multiple panels, a preference for multiple surveys each week, and a tendency to complete surveys more quickly, indicating a lack of thoughtful participation.

Respondent Cooperation

Respondent participation is critical to the success of the research process in order to minimize nonresponse bias. Therefore, it is important to understand the panel management practices and incentives employed by an online panel. Response rates for online surveys can vary dramatically, with some populations having average response rates less than 5 percent, others with response rates closer to 30 percent, and sometimes well over 60 percent for prescreened individuals, who have been alerted to expect to receive a survey at a

EXHIBIT 7.6	Open versus Closed Panel ("by-invitation-only") Recruitment Methods	
	Open Recruitment	**Closed Recruitment**
Percent working outside of the home	45.6%	77.0%
Percent homemaker	15.7%	4.4%
Percent female	73.7%	47.5%
Percent participate in multiple survey panels	87.3%	39.5%
Percent participate in five or more panels	55.2%	19.6%
Mean number of online panels joined	5.4	1.4
Mean time to take survey	8 min: 22 sec	9 min: 45 sec

Source: Research Now 2008.

specific time or date. The diminishing response rates observed with telephone interviewing have played a key role in the increased usage of online panels.

Ensuring participation is a function of several factors, including to what extent panel members are engaged in the research process, their experience with surveys and the panel in general, and the topic of the research. Of course, one of the primary drivers of participation is the incentive program.

Generally, online panels use two incentive models: the sweepstakes model and the pay-all model. The sweepstakes model offers survey participants a chance to be entered into a drawing for a prize, often hundreds or thousands of dollars, albeit with extremely low odds of winning. Pay-all incentive models pay each respondent a small incentive for their time and participation each time they take part in a survey.

The choice of incentive model is not trivial. A sound incentive model influences not only survey response rates, but also retention rates for panel members—which becomes very important when there is a need to use profiling information for targeting a specific type of respondent. Panel members who do not feel adequately compensated for their time and effort are much less likely to participate in research studies.

A study conducted by Research Now in 2006, using a third-party online panel, compared sweepstakes and pay-all incentive methods. For a 3-minute survey about books and music with 100 percent qualifying incidence, 40,000 people were invited to complete the survey in order to be entered into a sweepstakes drawing of $2,500 for one winner. An additional 4,000 people were invited to complete the same survey in exchange for $2.00 in cash. Both groups were selected randomly and then invited on the same day of the week and at the same time of day (Wednesday afternoon), and both were given 7 days to complete the survey.

The study found that the pay-all model was much more effective than the sweepstakes method (see Exhibit 7-7). People who were offered the pay-all incentive responded more quickly, and the response rate for the pay-all incentive group was 58 percent higher than that of the sweepstakes group (19.3 percent response rate vs. 12.2 percent response rate). While response rate is not the only measure of the quality of an online panel, it is a key metric.

Controlling the Panel

In addition to effective panel recruitment and respondent cooperation programs, online panel providers must have effective ongoing management of their panel to

Response Rates by Day

Exhibit 7.7

Pay-all versus Sweepstakes

Source: Research Now, 2007.

ensure a high level of quality. Panels must continually see that that their participants have positive experiences with every research project. Among other components, good panel management includes frequency controls to see that panel members are not surveyed too little or too much. Panel members should be given enough survey opportunities to stay effectively engaged in the research process, but not surveyed too much as to be burdened with survey invitations. Other keys to guaranteeing a positive panel member's experience is providing respondent privacy, safeguarding personal information, and protecting members from bogus research that attempts to use online surveys as a sales channel (this is the practice of "sugging"—selling under the guise of research).

Panel providers are continually recruiting new members to keep up with the growth in demand for online samples, as well as replace any panel members who may drop out. Even with exceptional panel member retention, some panel members will become less active in responding to surveys. In addition, panels will often recruit new members to assist in growing certain hard-to-reach segments and/or balancing the panel to have maximum representation of the overall population. Ensuring a growing supply of engaged, active panel members is a constant goal of every panel provider.

Finally, panel management includes ensuring panel freshness. As panel members change, their profiles must be updated. A single, 25-year-old college student with an annual income of $12,000 from last year may now be a married 26-year-old accountant with a new baby and a household income of $45,000. Updating profiles ensures that panel providers are able to consistently target qualified people for surveys.

When evaluating the quality of an online panel, there are several key drivers that contribute toward a panel's overall methodologies. If a panel does not have well-defined guiding principles to help deliver the highest level of quality, a sample purchaser should beware of the potential negative implications for the quality of the data. Research Now, for example, utilizes its *15 Points of Quality Differentiation* (see Exhibit 7-8) to see that every aspect of their panel's operation delivers the highest level of quality.

Mobile Internet Research—The Next Step

In 2010 the mobile Web grew 110 percent in the United States and 148 percent worldwide. Forty-seven million Americans or 38 percent of the mobile Internet users access the Internet from their mobile phones daily. With regard to age, 65 percent of users 18–29 go online from their phones versus 43 percent of those aged 30–49. The highest rates of usage of cell phones accessing the Internet are college graduates and persons earning more than $75,000 per year. Despite this rapid growth, mobile Web accounted for only 1.26 percent of total Web consumption in the United States.[35]

While global online penetration continues to increase, mobile phones have quickly become the preferred mode of communication for many consumers. Mobile phones share the characteristics of the four traditional quantitative methodologies—face-to-face, postal, telephone, and online—but benefit particularly from location and immediacy of results. Furthermore, as the infrastructure supporting mobile usage has grown, and global trends of mobile usage and mobile ad spending continue to accelerate, mobile phone-based interviewing is quickly emerging as a fifth research methodology.

One prevailing assumption has been that mobile research methods are only useful for short, simple surveys. Early on, researchers cited the high cost of text messaging, difficulties in getting people to divulge mobile contact information, and data security concerns as critical challenges to using mobile research to a fuller extent. Many of the early obstacles to mobile research have since been overcome, however, and mobile research can actually accommodate a wide variety of question-and-answer features beyond basic SMS messages and wireless application protocol mobile device surveys:

- Pictures and videos
- Time/date stamps on responses
- GPS locations
- Anonymity for respondents
- Personalized surveys
- And more

When combined with the other four methodologies, mobile research can create a variety of new research options, such as point-of-sale customer satisfaction queries, continuous real-time event feedback, brand and advertising tracking and feedback, and live product concept testing—to name a few.

For mobile research to be effective, however, researchers must still apply general principles of good research. For those who do, opportunities are numerous to capitalize on the mobile research revolution and to engage consumers on the cutting edge of communication.[36]

Mobile research offers:

- An alternative way to conduct research with hard-to-reach groups.
- Increased respondent cooperation from all demographic groups.
- Immediate feedback on research questions concerning marketing campaigns, ad testing, and more.
- Cost savings—faster reply to surveys, shorter project completion time.
- Use as a mobile recruiting tool to direct respondents to online surveys.
- Another way of reaching people on the go.[37]

A few disadvantages of mobile Internet surveys are as follows.

- Lightspeed found that the response rate decreased with age due to lower usage of mobile Internet services among older people. Thus, the profile doesn't reflect the average consumer.
- Questionnaires must be short.

- Question types are limited, as is the length of questions.
- Higher incentives must be offered to remove the financial burden of receiving and completing mobile surveys from the respondent.[38]

Mobile Internet technologies provide an exciting new channel for marketing researchers. However, their limitations will mean that traditional online marketing research will be the channel of choice for most survey research. Additional perspectives on mobile surveys are provided in the accompanying Practicing Marketing Research feature.

PRACTICING
MARKETING RESEARCH

Mobile Research Is Right Now

The recent economic crisis put significant pressure on the market research industry to make significant changes in how it did things. Demand for better, faster, and cheaper research methods led researchers to explore new research avenues such as proprietary panels and social media outlets.

Mobile research (namely, mobile phone-based survey response via mobile Web, SMS, or MMS) has demonstrated strong potential as a research platform, boasting high rates of mobile phone adoption and coverage, growing functionality, and broad penetration. Adoption rates have risen swiftly, especially in emerging markets like China, India, and Africa. Furthermore, online surveys designed for desktop access are increasingly being accessed via mobile devices.

Respondent convenience is the most compelling advantage of mobile research. In addition, it offers three other major benefits: access, speed, and enriched insights. Mobile platforms offer marketing researchers access to key demographics such as 14- to 49-year-olds or harder-to-reach audiences like B2B professionals. Respondents can be reached while on the move and can be reached at the point of experience. For marketers looking for instant feedback, mobile can deliver as well.

In tests run on mobile platforms, two sets of research found that 85 to 90 percent of respondents had returned their surveys within 1 to 2 hours of distribution. Mobile also offers enriched insights. Beyond in-the-moment feedback, mobile respondents are more open to respond to personal and private questions or send photos and videos.

The research community is still divided on the value and efficacy of mobile, but at the least, it appears that this methodology will be growing in the future. Before mobile research is more fully adopted, researchers need to address some key issues around data integration, combining research results from different methodologies, and compatibility between Web-based and mobile-based research tools among others.

Although mobile research is still an emerging platform, it has established a solid foundation. Many practical applications of mobile research already exist, and those who adopt this mode of research will find numerous opportunities beyond mere data collection.

Questions

1. Why do you think respondents are more likely to answer more personal questions using a mobile phone than other devices?

2. Is faster information always better information? Why do you think as you do?

FROM THE FRONT LINE

Why Isn't All Data Collection Moving to the Internet?

Elizabeth Anderson, formerly Research Analyst, DSS Research

As discussed in the text, the Internet has proven to be an efficient and fast way to collect reliable data. The reliability and, to a lesser extent, the validity (which is harder to demonstrate) of the data produced by Internet surveys have been demonstrated in a number of studies.

Recently, we conducted a study involving 56,000 Internet surveys, and we completed it in about 10 days. The cost was approximately one-third of what it would have cost to do the survey by telephone, and it was completed in a fraction of the time a telephone study would have taken. Comparison of the results with previous waves of the same research conducted by telephone showed a high level of consistency and no apparent differences due to the change in mode of data collection.

So, given all these wonderful advantages, why don't we collect all our surveys by Internet? There are a number of reasons why this is not advisable or feasible:

- Generally, except in very special cases, the Internet does not work for customer satisfaction surveys because in the vast majority of instances clients do not have any e-mail addresses for customers; or, if they do, it is not a comprehensive list of customer e-mail addresses. This may change in the future, but it is not the case today and it will not be the case in the near future.
- The Internet does not work for many surveys of business decision makers, especially if we are looking at a narrow geography (i.e., metro area, region of a state with a smaller population). Yes, there are business-to-business panels out there, and they are often feasible for national studies of certain types of business decision makers. The problem comes when we

are looking for individuals in organizations who make decisions to purchase certain specialized products or services. None of the panels has consistently accurate information on realms of decision making for different panelists. This means that we cannot specifically target them by e-mail invitation but must screen huge numbers of panelists to try to find them the old-fashioned way.

- Studies where you need to measure unaided awareness can be a problem. Questions such as "name all the makes and models of cars that you can think of" present problems because the list is likely to be long and requires a lot of typing by the respondent. In a telephone study, you would just name the cars and an interviewer would check them off of a list. In an Internet poll, however, it's unlikely a respondent will want to, or have the patience, to type out 40 to 50 different car makes and models, nor can you give them the list of cars because the goal is to check their unaided awareness and giving them the list directly aids them.
- Any study focusing on a narrow geography (smaller market or portion of a market) can be a problem because the Internet panel company you are using may not have enough panelists to produce the number of interviews you need.
- Low-incidence populations (e.g., people who have purchased MP3 players made by a certain manufacturer in the last 2 weeks) can also present a problem for Internet panels because they simply don't have enough people in their panel who meet the required qualifications. Combine low incidence with narrow geography and the problem is compounded. These types of studies can, of course, present problems for any interviewing method.
- Surveys with subpopulations, such as those over 65 years of age who are less likely to be Internet users, may be difficult to complete via Internet and may produce biased samples. These samples may be biased because those in the subpopulation who are online may be systematically different from those not online.

SUMMARY

Almost 30 percent of the world's population is online. In the United States and Canada the figure is over 77 percent. Over 90 percent of America's research firms are conducting online research. Secondary data can play a key role in the marketing research process. It can clarify a problem, suggest a particular research methodology, or sometimes actually provide a solution to the problem. Exhibit 7.1 offers an extensive list of online sources of secondary data. The Internet has, in many ways, revolutionized the gathering of secondary data. Now, rather than wait for replies from government agencies or other sources, users can find millions of pieces of information on the Internet. Trips to the library may become a thing of the past for many researchers. Search engines and directories contain links to millions of documents throughout the world. Special-interest discussion groups and blogs on the Internet can also be valuable sources of secondary data.

A five-step approach to searching the Internet is presented. This is followed by a detailed procedure that explains how to evaluate the quality of Web pages. Geographic information systems, which consist of a demographic database, digitized maps, and software, enable users to add primary data from a current study (or secondary corporate data) to the mix. The result is computer-generated maps that can reveal a variety of strategic findings to marketing managers; for example, a map may indicate an optimal location for a new retail store.

Web site databases can produce important insights. A Web merchant can track a person as he or she clicks through a site. The merchant can examine what was looked at and what was bought. The screen the customer will see first on the next visit to the site can be tailored to the customer's past purchase and browsing behavior. Cookies are an important tool for monitoring a user's behavior within a site.

More and more focus groups are being conducted online because online focus groups are fast and cost effective; they also reach populations that are typically inaccessible. However, there are several problems associated with online focus groups. Channel M2 provides virtual focus group interview rooms where respondents participate via a webcam. Questions and answers occur in real time, thus simulating a traditional focus group. Asynchronous focus groups are time-extended focus groups conducted much like an online chat group. Web community research is where a group of consumers agree to participate in an ongoing dialogue with a company. The discussion may last a year or more, and participants respond to questions that are regularly posted to the community. Insights from the community can be used as a basis for traditional marketing research.

Some firms are experimenting with individual depth interviews online. Each participant creates an online journal based on a series of questions provided by the researcher.

Internet surveys offer rapid deployment and real-time reporting, dramatically reduced costs, ready personalization, high response rates, ability to reach low-incidence respondents, simplified and enhanced panel management, and profitability for survey research firms. The disadvantages are the potential nonrepresentativeness of Internet users, lack of callback procedures to clarify open-end responses, bandwidth problems, and the fact that the sample frame needed may not be available on the Internet.

A number of tips are given for improving completion rates for online surveys. One study found that appearance had no impact, but financial incentives did improve completions. When formatting a survey, radio buttons should be used with a predetermined set of options. Drop-down boxes are appropriate when respondents are familiar with the categories, such as the state where you live. Fill-in boxes require clear, concise directions. They should be used sparingly because they have a high skip rate.

Commercial online panels are used for multiple projects by many different companies. While panels reduce cost and field time, the quality of the data requires good panel management. Panel recruitment can be by open source or "by invitation only." The by-invitation-only method is highly preferred for quality purposes. Good panel management requires the blocking of professional survey takers. Typically, Internet panels use either a "pay-all" or a sweepstakes strategy to gain respondent cooperation. Pay-all tends to be much more effective. Mobile Internet technologies will probably be the next platform in Internet survey research.

KEY TERMS & DEFINITIONS

newsgroup An Internet site where people can read and post messages devoted to a specific topic.

cookie A text file placed on a user's computer in order to identify the user when she or he revisits the Web site.

online focus groups Focus groups conducted via the Internet.

web community Carefully selected group of consumers who agree to participate in an ongoing dialogue with a corporation.

unrestricted Internet sample Self-selected sample group consisting of anyone who wishes to complete an Internet survey.

commercial online panel Group of individuals who have agreed to receive invitations to do online surveys from a particular panel company such as eRewards or SSI. The panel company charges organizations doing surveys for access to the panel. Charges are usually so much per survey depending on survey length and the type of people being sought for the survey. The panel company controls all access to the members of its panel.

open online panel recruitment Any person with Internet access can self-select to be in a research panel.

closed online panel recruitment Inviting only prevalidated individuals or those with shared known characteristics to enroll in a research panel.

QUESTIONS FOR REVIEW & CRITICAL THINKING

1. Do you think that eventually all marketing research will be done on the Internet? Why or why not?

2. Explain the relationship between blogs and marketing research.

3. How can a researcher evaluate the quality of a Web page?

4. How can a company benefit from building an internal database from its Web site visitors? Is there an advantage that a Web retailer might have over a traditional store?

5. Discuss the advantages and disadvantages of online focus groups.

6. Explain the differences between real-time focus groups and asynchronous focus groups.

7. Do you think that a company such as Caterpillar could benefit from Web community research? Ford? United Airlines?

8. Discuss the popularity of online survey research. Why is it so popular?

9. What are some techniques for increasing survey completion rates?

10. Describe some ways to recruit for online panels.

11. How does one avoid professional survey takers with online panels?

12. Is panel management a critical task for a quality online panel?

WORKING THE NET

Go to Exhibit 7.1 and, using it as a resource, determine the 10 highest income counties in the United States; where the highest ratio of pickup trucks per capita is found; the oldest median age zip code in America; a list of key decision makers in the U.S. steel industry; a reader profile on *Time* magazine; where most avocados are grown; and this week's Internet usage in the United States.

Compare and contrast the offerings of *www.surveysampling.com*; *www.zommerang .com*; *www.researchnow.com*; and *www.surveymonkey.com*.

REAL-LIFE RESEARCH • 7.1

Good Things Come to Brands That Give

In Kenya, Coca-Cola is helping teach children how to test drinking water for contamination. The company also is providing water-purification systems for some of the country's most poverty-stricken areas.

In India, Starbucks is addressing sanitation-related health problems by donating $1 million to WaterAid. Coca-Cola and Starbucks have taken the initiative to illustrate the good they are doing for the 1.1 billion people who lack access to clean drinking water.

Such efforts are applauded not only from a humanitarian standpoint, but also from a branding perspective. Sixty percent of U.S. adults over the age of 18 said "knowing a company is mindful of its impact on the environment and society makes me more likely to buy their products and services," according to findings in the Lifestyles of Health & Sustainability (LOHAS) *Consumer Trends Database* by the Natural Marketing Institute in Harleysville, Pennsylvania.

The company surveyed 2,000 adults via the Web to gauge their perceptions of how companies are dealing with social and environmental issues as well as how those perceptions impact their buying decisions.

Fifty-seven percent of consumers said they feel more loyal to companies that are socially responsible, and about half (52 percent) said they were more likely to talk to their friends and families about such mindful corporations.

More than a third (38 percent) said they'd be willing to pay extra for products produced by socially responsible companies, and 35 percent said they were more likely to buy stock in such corporations. "Consumers are more likely to be brand loyal and less likely to be price sensitive," said Steve French, managing partner at the Natural Marketing Institute, which was founded in 1990.

Despite that, the study found that many companies that do good, do a bad job of promoting the fact. "There's a big disconnect between what companies are doing and what consumer perceptions are," said French.[39]

Questions

1. Given the general nature of this survey, would an open panel be an acceptable source for a sample? Why or why not?

2. If a researcher was going to place restrictions on who might participate in this survey, what might those be? Age was already mentioned as a qualifier.

3. Could this survey have been done just as easily by mail? Why or why not?

4. How might a firm like McDonald's or Microsoft use this information?

REAL-LIFE RESEARCH • 7.2

Weiner World

Weiner World has been running a tracking study to assess awareness, usage, and attitudes toward their brand and competitive brands on a national basis since 1986. The study provides key input and guidance for their marketing plans.

Over the last 5 years their research supplier has reported declining response rates for the telephone survey, and analysis of the demographic profile of their sample has shown that it is skewing toward older consumers (proportionally more older people than is true for the population according to the most recent Census) and underrepresenting those under 35. In addition, given the lower response rate, the cost of the telephone approach has increased dramatically.

Hans Walder, head of the Market Insights (formerly Marketing Research) at Weiner World, has been discussing the issues and possible solutions with other members of his team and senior management. Several of his colleagues have suggested that they consider replacing the telephone approach with an online survey using an Internet panel. A number of concerns have been expressed by both the marketing research team and senior managers in marketing regarding comparability of the results generated by the two different approaches.

Questions

1. Why do you think the sample is skewing older?

2. Why do you feel response rates for the traditional telephone methodology have fallen?

3. Do you believe the Internet panel approach will address the age skew issue? Why do you say that?

4. How about comparability of data? Will the telephone and Internet panel approaches produce comparable data? Explain your reasoning.

5. How could you test the comparability issue? Describe the approach.

6. What do you think Weiner World should do? Explain your reasoning.

Primary Data Collection: Observation

LEARNING OBJECTIVES

→ **1.** To develop a basic understanding of observation research.

→ **2.** To learn the approaches to observation research.

→ **3.** To understand the advantages and disadvantages of observation research.

→ **4.** To explore the types of human observation.

→ **5.** To understand the types of machine observation and their advantages and disadvantages.

→ **6.** To explore the tremendous impact of scanner-based research on the marketing research industry.

→ **7.** To learn about observation research on the Internet.

Whnography and why is it so popular? Observation research has exploded on the Internet. Why? Why is Internet observation research so controversial? What are the machines that can be used in observation research and what kind of data do they produce? We will answer these questions in chapter eight.

Nature of Observation Research

→ **observation research**
Systematic process of recording patterns of occurrences or behaviors without normally communicating with the people involved.

Instead of asking people questions, as a survey does, observation research depends on watching what people do. Specifically, **observation research** can be defined as the systematic process of recording patterns of occurrences or behaviors without normally questioning or communicating with the people involved. (Mystery shopping is an exception.) A marketing researcher using the observation technique witnesses and records events as they occur or compiles evidence from records of past events. The observation may involve watching people or watching phenomena, and it may be conducted by human observers or by machines. Exhibit 8.1 gives examples of some common observation situations.

Conditions for Using Observation

Three conditions must be met before observation can be successfully used as a data-collection tool for marketing research:

1. The needed information must be either observable or inferable from behavior that is observable. For example, if a researcher wants to know why an individual purchased a new Toyota Sequoia rather than a Ford, observation research will not provide the answer.

2. The behavior of interest must be repetitive, frequent, or in some manner predictable. Otherwise, the costs of observation may make the approach prohibitively expensive.

3. The behavior of interest must be of relatively short duration. Observation of the entire decision-making process for purchasing a new home, which might take several weeks or months, is not feasible.

Approaches to Observation Research

Researchers can choose from a variety of observation approaches. They are faced with the task of choosing the most effective approach for a particular research problem, from the standpoint of cost and data quality. The dimensions along which observation approaches vary are (1) natural versus contrived situations, (2) open versus disguised observation, (3) human versus machine observers, and (4) direct versus indirect observation.

EXHIBIT 8.1	**Observation Situations**
Situations	**Example**
People watching people	Observers stationed in supermarkets watch consumers select frozen Mexican dinners, with the purpose of seeing how much comparison shopping people do at the point of purchase.
People watching phenomena	Observers stationed at an intersection count vehicles moving in various directions to establish the need for a traffic light.
Machines watching people	Movie or video cameras record consumers selecting frozen Mexican dinners.
Machines watching phenomena	Traffic-counting machines monitor the flow of vehicles at an intersection.

Natural versus Contrived Situations   Counting how many people use the drive-in window at a particular bank during certain hours is a good example of a completely natural situation. The observer plays no role in the behavior of interest. Those being observed should have no idea that they are under observation. At the other extreme is recruiting people to do their shopping in a simulated supermarket (rows of stocked shelves set up in a field service's mall facility) so that their behavior can be carefully observed. In this case, the recruited people must be given at least some idea that they are participating in a study. The participants might be given grocery carts and told to browse the shelves and pick out items that they might normally use. The researchers might use alternative point-of-purchase displays for several products under study. To test the effectiveness of the various displays, the observers would note how long the shopper paused in front of the test displays and how often the product was actually selected. Today, many firms, such as Frito-Lay and Procter & Gamble, use online simulated environments.

A contrived environment enables the researcher to better control extraneous variables that might have an impact on a person's behavior or the interpretation of that behavior. Use of such an environment also tends to speed up the data-gathering process. The researcher does not have to wait for natural events to occur but instead instructs the participants to perform certain actions. Because more observations can be collected in the same length of time, the result will be either a larger sample or faster collection of the targeted amount of data. The latter should lower the costs of the project.

The primary disadvantage of a contrived setting is that it is artificial, and thus the observed behavior may be different from what would occur in a real-world situation. The more natural the setting, the more likely it is that the behavior will be normal for the individual being observed.

Open versus Disguised Observation   Does the person being observed know that he or she is being observed? It is well known that the presence of an observer may have an influence on the phenomena being observed. Two general mechanisms work to bias the data. First, if people know they are being observed (as in **open observation**), they may behave differently. Second, the appearance and behavior of the observer offer potential for bias similar to that associated with the presence of an interviewer in survey research.

> **open observation**
> Process of monitoring people who know they are being watched.

Disguised observation is the process of monitoring people who do not know they are being watched. A common form of disguised observation is observing behavior from behind a one-way mirror. For example, a product manager may observe respondent reactions to alternative package designs from behind a one-way mirror during a focus group discussion.

> **disguised observation**
> Process of monitoring people who do not know they are being watched.

Human versus Machine Observers   In some situations, it is possible and even desirable to replace human observers with machines—when machines can do the job less expensively, more accurately, or more readily. Traffic-counting devices are probably more accurate, definitely cheaper, and certainly more willing than human observers. It would not be feasible, for example, for Nielsen Company to have human observers in people's homes to record television viewing habits. Movie cameras and audiovisual equipment record behavior much more objectively and in greater detail than human observers ever could. Finally, the electronic scanners found in most retail stores provide more accurate and timely data on product movement than human observers ever could.

Direct versus Indirect Observation   Much of the observation carried out for marketing research is direct observation of current behavior or artifacts. For example, the contents of 100 women's purses in Portland, Oregon and Plano, Texas were examined as part of an observational study. Nearly every participant (99 percent) had something of a financial nature such as a credit or debit card, checkbook or wallet. Women who were married, college educated, and with high incomes carried the most cards. Ninety-eight percent of the women carried reward and membership cards. Office supplies, like paper and pens, were found in 93 percent of the purses. Other items discovered, in rank order, were: beauty and hair care, identification, receipts, cell phones and accessories, insurance cards, food and candy, healthcare products, coupons, glasses, photos, trash, nail care products, feminine care products, tissues, hand sanitizers, food/drink supplies such as napkins and toothpicks, oral care products, religious items, weapons, keepsakes, and cameras. Only 8 percent carried a camera.[1]

In some cases, past behavior must be observed. To do this, the researcher must turn to some record of the behavior. Archaeologists dig up sites of old settlements and attempt to determine the nature of life in early societies from the physical evidence they find. **Garbologists** sort through people's garbage to analyze household consumption patterns. Marketing research usually is much more mundane. In a product prototype test, it may be important to learn how much of the test product the consumer used. The most accurate way to find this out is to have the respondent return the unused product so that the researcher can see how much is left. If a study involved the in-home use of a laundry soil and stain remover, it would be important to know how much of the remover each respondent actually used. All of the respondents' answers to questions would be considered from this usage perspective.

Pictures can also be used to see what people have done in certain situations. For example, a global study conducted by New York-based GfK NOP created a massive visual database with the goal of better understanding global consumers. Part of that research was photographing people's kitchens, which in many cultures is the "heart of the home." Examples of the kind of understanding the researchers gleaned from the photos are shown in Exhibit 8.2.

> **garbologists**
> Researchers who sort through people's garbage to analyze household consumption patterns.

Advantages of Observation Research

Watching what people actually do rather than depending on their reports of what they did has one very significant and obvious advantage: Firsthand information is not subject to many of the biasing factors associated with the survey approach. Specifically, the researcher avoids problems associated with the willingness and ability of respondents to

Exhibit 8.2

Pictures Can Help Understand Global Consumers

answer questions. Also, some forms of data are gathered more quickly and accurately by observation. Letting a scanner record the items in a grocery bag is much more efficient than asking the shopper to enumerate them. Similarly, rather than asking young children which toys they like, major toy manufacturers prefer to invite target groups of children into a large playroom and observe via a one-way mirror which toys are chosen and how long each holds the child's attention.

Disadvantages of Observation Research

The primary disadvantage of observation research is that only behavior and physical personal characteristics usually can be examined. The researcher does not learn about motives, attitudes, intentions, or feelings. Also, only public behavior is observed; private behavior—such as dressing for work or committee decision making within a company—is beyond the scope of observation research. A second problem is that present observed behavior may not be projectable into the future. The fact that a consumer purchases a certain brand of milk after examining several alternatives does not mean that he or she will continue to do so in the future.

Observation research can be time-consuming and costly if the observed behavior occurs rather infrequently. For example, if observers in a supermarket are waiting to watch the purchase behavior of persons selecting Lava soap, they may have a long wait. And if the choice of consumers to be observed is biased (for example, shoppers who go grocery shopping after 5:00 P.M.), distorted data may be obtained.

Human Observation

As noted in Exhibit 8.1, people can be employed to watch other people or certain phenomena. For example, people can act as mystery shoppers, observers behind one-way mirrors, or recorders of shopper traffic and behavior patterns.

Ethnographic Research

Ethnographic research comes to marketing from the field of anthropology. The popularity of the technique in commercial marketing research is increasing. **Ethnographic research**, or the study of human behavior in its natural context, involves observation of behavior and physical settings. Ethnographers directly observe the population they are studying. As "participant observers," ethnographers can use their intimacy with the people they are studying to gain richer, deeper insights into culture and behavior—in short, what makes people do what they do. Over $400 million annually is spent on ethnographic research.[2] Today, corporations, such as Procter & Gamble and Microsoft, have their own in-house ethnographers. Procter & Gamble conducted ethnographic research in Mexico City among lower-middle-class families. The research led to Downy Single Rinse, a fabric softener that removed a step from the less mechanized laundry process there. Ethnographic studies can cost anywhere from $5,000 to as much as $800,000, depending on how deeply a company wants to delve into its customers' lives.

One of the first uses of ethnographic research in an informal manner goes back to the Spanish Civil War in the 1930s. Forrest Mars Sr., when he wasn't dodging bullets, was observing soldiers coating their chocolate with sugar. The result of this observational or ethnographic research? M&M's, named for Mars and business associate Bruce Murrie.[3]

> **ethnographic research**
> Study of human behavior in its natural context, involving observation of behavior and physical setting.

Advantages of Ethnographic Research
Both focus groups and individual depth interviews rely on retrospection. That is, they ask respondents to recall their behavior and the behavior of others. Human memory, of course, can sometimes be faulty.

In addition, respondents sometimes reply in a socially desirable manner. A man may be reading adult magazines but claims to be reading *Fortune* and *BusinessWeek*.

Ethnographic research offers a number of advantages. These include the following:

- Ethnography is reality-based. It can show exactly how consumers live with a product, not just what they say about it or how they remember using it.
- It can reveal unexpressed needs and wants.
- It can discover unexploited consumer benefits.
- It can reveal product problems.
- It can show how, when, why and where people shop for brands—and how they perceive it compared to competitive products.
- It can show who in the family actually uses a product and perhaps uncover a whole new potential demographic target.
- It takes advantage of consumers' experience with the category and their hands-on creativity as they demonstrate their ideas for new products and product improvements.
- It can test new products in a real context.
- It can reveal advertising execution ideas that derive directly from consumer experience.
- It can help form a better relationship with your consumers, based on an intimate knowledge of their lifestyles.[4]

Because individuals generally acclimate to an observer's presence over time (often quickly), their behavior becomes relatively unbiased by the observer—resulting in a more accurate characterization of behavior.

Although the ethnographic researcher's principal activity is observing behavior, active interviews or discussion with respondents is a key component. Getting respondents' perspectives on actions, through dialogue, is informative. Furthermore, the ethnographic data can be utilized in mixed method studies, for comparing and contrasting it with data from other sources. For example, a research manager could leverage observational data of the sales reps interacting with customers and prospects, and compare it with information from in-depth district and regional sales manager interviews—identifying any disconnects between what's being done and what's expected.

Conducting Ethnographic Research   The first step is to find participants. Afterward, the observation process can begin. A highly skilled ethnographer is typically trained in anthropology. The research begins with systematic observation and inquiry. The ethnographer is trained to examine human culture: symbols, codes, myths, rituals, beliefs, values, rules for social interaction, and conceptual categories and perceptions. Many so-called ethnographists' interviews occur over a 90-minute period, too brief for close environmental observation and questioning. (Three to four hours per ethnographic observation and interview is far more productive.)

In a study on how consumers think about and use home printers, a highly trained ethnographer would ask:

- What are the meanings and processes of printing in their most elemental senses, as if the ethnographer had never seen a printer?
- Can we understand the symbolism of printing by exploring how respondents classify nonprinted versus printed matter?
- Anthropologists use a construct called binary opposition:

Binary Opposition	
Nonprinted Matter	**Printed Matter**
Intangible	Tangible
Fleeting	Lasting
Public	Private

- What are the consumer myths, stories, and beliefs about printing versus not printing and about different brands of printers?
- How do printing rituals serve as rites of passage that transform consumers from one state of being into another?
- Are people who print and save hard copies different in a "tribal" way from people who see printing as antiquated and wasteful?
- Are there social or business situations that demand or deny printing choices and, if so, why?

These questions and observations would undoubtedly enrich new-product development and marketing communications, helping shape product design, brand positioning, and advertising content.[5] In contrast to the above, ethnography-lite would consist of limited observations (under an hour) and a few individual depth interviews. This form of research is often conducted by persons without advanced training in anthropology or sociology. Unfortunately, a number of studies are conducted in this manner, which often yield very few insights.

The next step is to analyze and interpret all of the data collected to find themes and patterns of meaning. This is no simple task. Hours and hours of audio and video must be transcribed and re-studied. Even for the well-trained and experienced ethnographer, the amount of data can at times be overwhelming. But through careful and thorough analysis of the data, themes and categories emerge and applicable findings become clear. Ethnographers usually create frameworks to help companies think about their consumers and understand what it all means.

Triangulation—the process of checking findings against what other people say and against similar research already conducted—is a way to verify the accuracy of collected data. While traditional ethnography stops with the description of the group studies, this is not sufficient for businesses. They need actionable guidelines, recommendations, and an outline of strategy. The findings must be presented in a fashion that will enable companies to create innovative and successful solutions.

For managers at Cambridge SoundWorks, it was a perplexing problem: In retail outlets across the country, men stood wide-eyed when sales reps showed off the company's hi-fi, "blow-your-hair-back" stereo speakers. So why didn't such unabashed enthusiasm for the product translate into larger—and bigger ticket—sales?

To find out, the Andover, Massachusetts, manufacturer and retailer of stereo equipment hired research firm Design Continuum, in West Newton, Massachusetts, to follow a dozen prospective customers over the course of 2 weeks. The researchers' conclusion: The high-end speaker market suffered from something referred to as "the spouse acceptance factor." While men adored the big black boxes, women hated their unsightly appearance. Concerned about the way the speakers would "look" in the living room, women would talk their husbands out of buying a cool but hideous and expensive piece of stereo equipment. Even those who had purchased the product had trouble showing it off: Men would attempt to display the loudspeakers as trophies in living rooms, while women would hide them behind plants, vases, and chairs. "Women would come into the store, look at the speakers and say, 'that thing is ugly,'" says Ellen Di Resta, principal at Design Continuum. "The men would lose the argument and leave the store without a stereo. The solution was to give the target market what men and women *both* wanted: a great sound system that looks like furniture so you don't have to hide it."

Armed with this knowledge, Cambridge SoundWorks unveiled a new line. The furniture-like Newton Series of speakers and home theater systems comes in an array of colors and finishes. The result: The Newton Series is the fastest growing and best-selling product line in the firm's 14-year history.

Marriott hired IDEO, Inc., to rethink the hotel experience for an increasingly important customer: the young, tech-savvy road warrior. "This is all about looking freshly at business travel and how people behave and what they need," explains Michael E. Jannini, Marriott's executive vice president for brand management.[6]

To better understand Marriott's customers, IDEO dispatched a team of seven consultants, including a designer, anthropologist, writer, and architect, on a six-week trip. Covering 12 cities, the group hung out in hotel lobbies, cafés, and bars, and asked guests to graph what they were doing hour by hour.

This is what they learned: Hotels are generally good at serving large parties but not small groups of business travelers. Researchers noted that hotel lobbies tend to be dark and better suited to killing time than conducting casual business. Marriott lacked places where guests could comfortably combine work with pleasure outside their rooms. IDEO consultant and Marriott project manager Dana Cho recalls watching a female business traveler drink wine in the lobby while trying not to spill it on papers spread out on a desk. "There are very few hotel services that address [such] problems," says Cho.[7]

Having studied IDEO's findings, in January Marriott announced plans to reinvent the lobbies of its Marriott and Renaissance Hotels, creating for each a social zone, with small tables, brighter lights, and wireless Web access, that is better suited to meetings. Another area will allow solo travelers to work or unwind in larger, quiet, semiprivate spaces where they won't have to worry about spilling coffee on their laptops or papers.

Jim Stengel, Procter & Gamble's chief marketing officer, notes, "I'm a big observational guy." So he has urged the P&G marketers to spend lots of time with consumers in their homes, watching the ways they wash their clothes, clean their floors, and diaper their babies, and asking them about their habits and frustrations. Back in 2000, the typical brand marketer spent less than 4 hours a month with consumers. Says Stengel: "It's at least triple that now."[8]

Ethnography and Focus Groups Of course, both ethnography and focus groups are forms of qualitative research. Yet most research clients see the two techniques playing different roles in the overall research process. Sometimes both methodologies are used on the same project:

- Ethnography for strategic understanding, exploratory research at the beginning of the creative/innovation process.
- Focus groups/IDIs for tactical issues—reactions to stimuli (ads, visuals, concepts, etc.), often ones that have been developed in the first phase. In a sense, these methods have been repositioned in some clients' minds.

I think of focus groups to get narrow things. If I have eight concepts, [I want to know] what's working better than another, what language is working better, etc. When I'm trying to get something deeper and something I didn't know how to ask, I would use one-on-ones. If I have the choice and the time—there's time and money associated with ethnography—I'd opt for ethnography hands-down every time. (pharmaceutical client)

Focus groups still have their place for consensus-building and culling down ideas. For innovation, I do think ethnography has an advantage. (consultant)

It's rare that we do a study that doesn't have both ethnography and focus groups. They both have their purposes. We try [ideas] out in the focus groups based on earlier insights and ideas drawn from the ethnography. Focus groups yield time and efficiency that can lead to tighter and more effective surveys." (financial services client)[9]

Martha Rivera, with Doyle Research Associates, Chicago, talks about how ethnography complements and expands other forms of research in the accompanying Global Research box.

GLOBAL RESEARCH

Ethnography Is an Enriching Process

Some of the insights resulting from the use of ethnography as a key element of consumer insights research are as follows.

- *No person can fully report his or her own unconscious behavior.* During a research study conducted in Venezuela, in an ordinary bathroom I saw a large multicolored, perfectly round sphere made of small bits of body soap. The interviewee explained that he usually compressed together these bits

of body soap when they had become too small. None of the previous interviewees had reported something like that, but all subsequent participants were asked what they regularly did with the last pieces of their body soap. Most of them automatically placed the old small piece onto the new soap bar without another thought. Supplementary questions revealed that the flat form of the client's soap bar was thought to facilitate this, and that these consumers actually looked for that particular brand for that reason. Hence the client abandoned its plan to change the shape of its soap.

- *People's reports of their own behavior always contain at least a small portion of biases and inaccuracies.* While testing a new type of package for pre-prepared meat, Mexican housewives claimed that they would readily buy any pre-prepared food item because it offered the convenience that they reportedly expected from all types of products. However, it was observed that their refrigerators were filled exclusively with fresh food items, thus suggesting that these housewives habitually prepared their meals from scratch and did not consume any form of pre-prepared food. Further questions about such apparent incongruity confirmed this inference.

- *Researchers' unfamiliarity with the product makes it hard to interpret verbal reports from consumers.* We were commissioned to investigate the general mind-set of Venezuelan truck drivers in regards to air filters, and so short in-truck trips were performed. The truck drivers were requested to teach the ethnographers about the replacement of an external air filter on the truck's exhaust system. As a result, the researchers were able to remove the air filters from their cases and to identify the right moment to replace them. Most drivers used their air filters far longer than recommended by the manufacturer. The truckers waited until the filters got to a particular tone of gray, which we were able to reproduce for the written report. The manufacturer was able to prepare a simple sheet correlating the different degrees of gray with increasingly adverse consequences for the truck's performance.[10]

Jerry Thomas, CEO of Decision Analyst, discusses "online ethnography" in the accompanying Practicing Marketing Research box.

Mystery Shoppers

mystery shoppers
People who pose as consumers and shop at a company's own stores or those of its competitors to collect data about customer–employee interactions and to gather observational data; they may also compare prices, displays, and the like.

Mystery shoppers are used to gather observational data about a store (for example, are the shelves neatly stocked?) and to collect data about customer–employee interactions. In the latter case, of course, there is communication between the mystery shopper and the employee. The mystery shopper may ask, "How much is this item?" "Do you have this in blue?" or "Can you deliver this by Friday?" The interaction is not an interview, and communication occurs only so that the mystery shopper can observe the actions and comments of the employee. Mystery shopping is, therefore, classified as an observational marketing research method, even though communication is often involved. It is estimated that 70 percent of America's national retailers use the technique: Wal-Mart, McDonald's, Starbucks, Blockbuster, Jiffy Lube, Rite Aid, PF Chang's restaurants, and Whole Foods Markets are some of the big-name clients that rely on mystery shoppers.

"The No. 1 thing we're trying to do is reinforce a company's training," explains David Rich, president of ICC/Decision Services, which deploys mystery shoppers for such clients as Levi's and Godiva.[12] Mystery shopping gives managers nearly instant feedback on whether their workers are smiling when they ought to, making customers feel at ease, or inviting them to get fries with that. Many companies tie bonuses to performance on mystery inspections, giving employees an incentive to be nice.

The mystery shopping concept has four basic levels, which differ in the depth and type of information collected:

- *Level 1*—The mystery shopper conducts a mystery telephone call. Here, the mystery shopper calls the client location and evaluates the level of service received over the phone, following a scripted conversation.

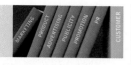

PRACTICING MARKETING RESEARCH

Taking Ethnography Online

Online ethnography begins by pulling a sample that is representative of the target market, typically from an online panel. One of the advantages here is that panel members are accustomed to surveys and therefore are more likely to participate than the average man or woman on the street. Moreover, since no one is visiting their homes or offices, a higher share of potential subjects will agree to participate, which creates a more representative sample.

Beyond the sampling advantages, another benefit of this approach is that the online environment promotes a sense of anonymity and safety, which encourages a high level of self-disclosure. In the online environment, participants feel comfortable expressing their feelings. With guidance from experienced moderators, respondents can explore and describe all the behaviors, routines, thoughts, feelings, and experiences they believe are most relevant to their purchasing decisions.

The respondents' normal routines are not disrupted. They can provide their detailed responses at a convenient time and over a span of several days (or sometimes weeks). This expanse of time also gives the respondents an opportunity to reflect on the questions posed and to give detailed descriptions of their thoughts, feelings, and experiences.

So, how does online ethnography work? How is it conducted? The exact design of the project and its execution depend on the product or service category and the objectives of the research.

As a general rule, some or all of the following steps are involved:

- *Respondents might be asked to keep diaries* (either online or offline) to record their behaviors, routines, thoughts, and observations related to the purposes of the study.

- *Participants might be asked to take digital pictures* related to the focus of the study (it could be photos of their refrigerators, pantries, backyards, or bedrooms). And with the spread of digital cameras (even cell phones now have digital cameras), digital photos are relatively easy for most people to take and send (with the moderator subsequently uploading the pictures for discussion).

- *One member of the household could be asked to take photos or videos* of other members of the household at certain times or to record specific behaviors, events, and so on.

- *Participants' stories or explanations typically accompany the photos*, telling us what is in the picture, who is in the picture, what is happening, and perhaps even what it means to the respondent.

- *Projective techniques can be employed* as well (for example, respondents might search and select online photos or be instructed to take photos that represent the personality of a brand, or that bring to mind memories of the brand).

Typically, the digital photos or videos are sent to the moderator via e-mail for review and uploading to the online depth interview. The diaries and photos are studied by the analyst and then used as stimulus in conducting the follow-up online depth interviews. These are typically described as "time-extended" depth interviews since the project unfolds over a period of several days (5 to 10 days, but longer time periods are possible). In fact, the term *time-extended* should be used to describe the whole online ethnography process. Indeed, this is one of the major advantages of the method: the respondent's concentration on a topic for a period of several days sensitizes her to the subject and reveals her own feelings and motives related to the topic.

Example of an Online Ethnography Project

Decision Analyst conducted an online ethnographic project on health and beauty products among women and men from the United States, the United Kingdom, and France. All participants were medium to heavy users of skin-care products.

Study Methodology

■ Respondents were asked to take *digital pictures of their skin-care products and other health and beauty products* in their normal storage place. They were also asked to add stories of "what's in the pictures" to accompany the pictures.

■ To record *daily diary entries* of their morning/evening routines when using health and beauty products.

■ *To provide detailed descriptions* of their experiences from a regular shopping occasion for health and beauty products.

■ To keep a *log of advertising* they noticed related to health and beauty.

Follow-up *depth interviews* focused on the following types of questions: How do you define beauty? What motivates your interest in skin beauty? How would you feel if your favorite skin-care lotion should vanish from the marketplace? How much time do you spend daily caring for your skin? What are your favorite brands, and why?

Some Comments and Pictures from One Participant, Sally, in Chicago:

Obviously my medicine cabinet is filled with a variety of products at various price points. I admit that I like to try the high-end brands, but I'm on a budget and also take advantage of the less pricey products one finds at drugstores and stores like Body Shop. So that's why Crème de la Mer is elbowing for room with Olay, and Kinerase is cheek-and-jowl with Ponds.

Once all of the photos, diaries, stories, and interview transcripts are finished, the next step is the analysis, which is the most time-consuming and brain-intensive part of the process. There are no shortcuts. The analyst must comb and re-comb through all of the raw data (photos, videos, diaries, transcripts) and try to understand what it all means. Certainly, some understanding of cultural anthropology is helpful to the analyst, as is some knowledge of psychology, sociology, economics, history, and so on. The most important background, however, is knowledge of the target industry, the product category, and previous experience with marketing and marketing research related to the product or service. If all of these knowledge sets can be integrated, the analysis is apt to be much better than an analysis based on a single academic discipline.[11]

Questions

1. Which do you think reveals the most insights—traditional ethnography or online ethnography?

2. Which is most difficult to conduct?

3. Would you rather participate in an online or traditional ethnographic study?

■ *Level 2*—The mystery shopper visits an establishment and makes a quick purchase; little or no customer–employee interaction is required. For example, in a Level 2 mystery shop, a mystery shopper purchases an item (for example, gas, a hamburger, or a lottery ticket) and evaluates the transaction and image of the facility.

■ *Level 3*—The mystery shopper visits an establishment and, using a script or scenario, initiates a conversation with a service and/or sales representative. Level 3 mystery shopping usually does not involve an actual purchase. Examples include discussing different cellular telephone packages with a sales representative, reviewing services provided during an oil change, and so forth.

■ *Level 4*—The mystery shopper performs a visit that requires excellent communication skills and knowledge of the product. Discussing a home loan, the process for purchasing a new car, or visiting apartment complexes serve as examples. The "HotelSpy" in the Practicing Market Research box in page 000 is another example of Level 4 mystery shopping.

Mystery shopping can have one or several objectives. As mentioned earlier, a common objective is measuring employee training. Other objectives are:

- Enabling an organization to monitor compliance with product/service delivery standards and specifications.
- Enabling marketers to examine the gap between promises made through advertising/sales promotion and actual service delivery.
- Helping monitor the impact of training and performance improvement initiatives on compliance with or conformance to product/service delivery specifications.
- Identifying differences in the customer experience across different times of day, locations, product/service types, and other potential sources of variation in product/service quality.[13]

One mystery shopping firm that specializes in chain, midpriced restaurants gathers the following types of data:

- Telephone skills/hostess services
- Guest experience
- Food quality and temperature
- Facility conditions
- Cleanliness of restroom facilities
- Parking lot condition
- Dress code compliance
- Visibility and interaction of management staff
- Compliance with franchise agreement.[14]

Understanding a restaurant's service and environment is critical to the success of Fridays, Olive Garden, and Chili's. For example, one survey of 4,000 diners in midpriced chains found that when food delivery was less than 10 minutes, 57 percent stated that they "definitely would return." That percentage dropped to 17 percent when delivery was longer than 15 minutes.[15]

One-Way Mirror Observations

The discussion of focus groups in Chapter 5 noted that focus group facilities almost always provide **one-way mirror observation**, which allows clients to observe the group discussion as it unfolds. New product development managers, for example, can note consumers' reactions to various package prototypes as they are demonstrated by the moderator. (One researcher spent 200 hours watching mothers change diapers to gather information for the redesign of disposable diapers.) In addition, the clients can observe the degree of emotion exhibited by the consumer as he or she speaks. One-way mirrors are also sometimes used by child psychologists and toy designers to observe children at play. At the Fisher-Price Play Lab some 3,500 children per year pass through. It is set up like a preschool classroom. On the other side of the glass is a narrow carpeted room with about 10 chairs and two video cameras. Nearly all Fisher-Price toys have been taken for a spin in the Play Lab at some point in their development.

The lighting level in the observation room must be very dim relative to that in the focus group room. Otherwise, the focus group participants can see into the observation room. Several years ago, we (the authors) were conducting a focus group of orthopedic surgeons in St. Louis, Missouri. One physician arrived approximately 20 minutes early and was ushered into the group room. A young assistant product manager for the pharmaceutical manufacturer was already seated in the observation room. The physician, being alone in the group room, decided to take advantage of the large framed mirror on

> **one-way mirror observation** Practice of watching behaviors or activities from behind a one-way mirror.

PRACTICING MARKETING RESEARCH

Undercover with a Hotel Spy

J. C. Schaefer unscrews a light bulb from a bedside lamp in the posh Windsor Court Hotel in New Orleans and begins violently whacking it against the bedspread. He shakes the light bulb to make sure the filament inside is broken and then carefully screws it back into the lamp.

Mr. Schaefer isn't your average hotel guest. In fact, he isn't even J. C. Schaefer. His real name is David Richey, and he's a hotel spy who uses a variety of aliases to check out luxury hotels all over the world. Over 2 days, he'll employ an extensive bag of tricks to see if the Windsor Court—rated as the top hotel in the world in a *Condé Nast Traveler* magazine poll—is as good as its reputation. The "burnt-out light bulb" test is one of the toughest. Only 11 percent of hotels tested by Mr. Richey's Chevy Chase, Maryland, firm, Richey International, detect the burnt-out bulb on the housekeeping staff's first pass.

The Windsor Court is a member of Preferred Hotels & Resorts Worldwide, a group of 120 independent luxury hotels that share a common reservations system. Preferred requires that all its hotels meet at least 80 percent of its standards in a test conducted annually by Richey International.

After checking in, Mr. Richey heads off to lunch while his room is being prepared. The Windsor Court has a five-star dining room, but the mystery shopper decides to eat at the hotel bar, the Polo Club Lounge. Mr. Richey orders crab cakes from the menu, then orders french fries to see if the bar readily accommodates off-menu orders. It does.

The food is good, and the service is friendly. But the waiters get marked down for not making eye contact and for not busing away the ketchup after the meal is done. "They're nice guys," Mr. Richey says, "But they're not real polished."

A little after 2 P.M. Mr. Richey walks into a sprawling $295-a-night suite at the Windsor Court. He pulls out a disposable camera and begins taking pictures. Overall, the room gets high marks for cleanliness and creature comforts. But Mr. Richey spots scuff marks on the baseboard and a snag in one of the curtains.

Then it's on to the bathroom. "Forty percent of hotels have hair in either the sink, the tub or on the floor," Mr. Richey announces as he begins his inspection. This room, it turns out, does not.

Before leaving for dinner, Mr. Richey sets up a test to see how well the housekeeping staff will pick up the room when they turn down the covers on the bed later that evening. He leaves some magazines askew in the magazine rack, puts a cup of pistachio shells on the table and disables the light bulb.

After dinner, Mr. Richey heads downstairs for another test. "I have changed my travel plans and will be going to New York tomorrow," Mr. Richey informs the concierge. "Can you make reservations for me?" "Unfortunately we can't do that," the concierge replies. "You either have to do it yourself or call a travel agent." Mr. Richey, as always, takes the news calmly. "That was awful," he says later. "I'm sure the general manager will be horrified." Back in the room, Mr. Richey finds a neatly turned-down bed. However, the housekeeper hasn't done a very good job of tidying the room. And the defective light bulb hasn't been replaced. Mr. Richey takes copious photos. It's 10 P.M., but Mr. Richey will be up for another couple of hours preparing his report.[16]

Questions

1. Do you think that mystery shopping is beneficial to the Windsor Court? Why?

2. Do you think that Mr. Richey's observations would be meaningful to Motel 6? Why?

the wall for some last-minute grooming. He walked over to the mirror and began combing his hair. At the same time, the assistant product manager, sitting about a foot away on the other side of the mirror, decided to light a cigarette. As the doctor combed his hair, there was suddenly a bright flash of light, and another face appeared through the mirror. What happened next goes beyond the scope of this text. In recent years, the trend has been to inform participants of the one-way mirror and to explain who is in the other room watching and why.

Machine Observation

The observation methods discussed so far have involved people observing things or consumers. Now we turn our attention to observation by machines, including traffic counters, physiological measurement devices, opinion and behavior management devices, and scanners.

Traffic Counters

Among the most common and popular machines in observation research are **traffic counters**. As the name implies, traffic counters measure vehicular flow over a particular stretch of roadway. Outdoor advertisers rely on traffic counts to determine the number of exposures per day to a specific billboard. Retailers use the information to ascertain where to locate a particular type of store. Convenience stores, for example, require a moderately high-traffic volume to reach target levels of profitability.

> **traffic counters** Machines used to measure vehicular flow over a particular stretch of roadway.

Physiological Measurement Devices

When an individual is aroused or feels inner tension or alertness, his or her condition is referred to as *activation*. Activation is stimulated via a subcortical unit called the *reticular activation system* (*RAS*), located in the human brain stem. The sight of a product or advertisement, for example, can activate the RAS. When the arousal processes in the RAS are directly provoked, the processing of information increases. Researchers have used a number of devices to measure the level of a person's activation.

Electroencephalograph An **electroencephalograph** (**EEG**) is a machine that measures electric pulses on the scalp and generates a record of electrical activity in the brain. Although electroencephalography probably is the most versatile and sensitive procedure for detecting arousal, it involves expensive equipment, a laboratory environment, and complex data analysis requiring special software programs. Using EEG technology developed by NASA to monitor astronauts' alertness levels, Capita Corporation has begun measuring respondents' reactions to advertisements. Capita uses a headset that reads electrical signals coming from a subject's scalp five times per second, as the person interacts with media such as a television program, a commercial, a Web page, or a banner ad. These brain waves are converted into a scrolling graph synchronized with the visual stimuli on the screen, giving the marketer a play-by-play view of which segments excite the viewer and which ones don't.

> **electroencephalograph (EEG)** Machine that measures electrical pulses on the scalp and generates a record of electrical activity in the brain.

Recently, Capita, with the help of U.S. Interactive, an Internet services company that tracks Web ads, tested the system's reliability. Capita monitored the brain waves of 48 respondents as they confronted four banner ads with strong click-through rates and four ads with low rates. In three of four tests, Capita's measure correctly identified the "strong" banners.[17]

A UCLA academic study used a magnetic resonance imaging machine (MRI) instead of an EEG to study advertising effectiveness. The researchers found that some participants had increased activity in the medical prefrontal cortex region of the brain while viewing a public service announcement on the importance of using sunscreen. This brain region is located in the front of the brain between the eyebrows. It is associated with self-reflection thinking about what we like and dislike and also motivations and desires. Those with increased brain activity were much more likely to increase their use of sunscreen than those without increased brain activity.[18]

In a taste test sponsored by PepsiCo, pitting Pepsi against Coke, 67 people had brain scans using an MRI while testing the two soft drinks. After analysis, it was concluded that, based on the taste test, Pepsi should command 50 percent of the soft-drink market. As Pepsi clearly didn't have that kind of market share, and the results seemed to show that people were choosing Coca-Cola due to branding, it allowed Pepsi to divert funds earmarked to improve taste into improving the Pepsi brand.[19]

The ability to accurately translate the data is what troubles one cable network executive. "An ad might get someone to perspire or their eyes to dilate or their brain waves to peak, but the resounding issue is, what does that really tell you?" he says. "Just because the needles are moving does not mean that it will affect their behavior, get them to purchase something, or improve their brand awareness."[20]

galvanic skin response (GSR)
Change in the electric resistance of the skin associated with activation responses; also called *electrodermal response*.

Galvanic Skin Response   **Galvanic skin response (GSR)**, also known as *electrodermal response*, is a change in the electric resistance of the skin associated with activation responses. A small electric current of constant intensity is sent into the skin through electrodes attached to the palmar side of the fingers. The changes in voltage observed between the electrodes indicate the level of stimulation. Because the equipment is portable and not expensive, measuring GSR is the most popular way to assess emotional reaction to a stimulus. GSR is used primarily to measure stimulus response to advertisements but is sometimes used in packaging research.

Inner Response, Incorporated uses GSR to evaluate commercials. In tests of an Eastman Kodak Company digital photo processing ad, Inner Response determined that viewers' interest levels built slowly in the opening scenes, rose when a snapshot of an attractive young woman was shown, but spiked highest when a picture appeared of a smiling, pigtailed girl. Knowing which scenes had the highest impact helped Kodak in making changes in the spot's content and cutting its length.[21]

Eye Tracking   There has been a surge in the use of eye-tracking research as the equipment has gotten more sophisticated. Tobii Technology has introduced glasses that look and feel like modern eyewear and allows subjects to walk around freely in a real-world environment. They can browse in stores, use a computer, try out a new product, or read an advertisement.[22] Companies like Unilever, Kimberly-Clark, Con Agra, Heinz, and Kellogg all use eye-tracking research. Tobii creates virtual store shelves for Procter & Gamble to test the pulling power of new package designs. A sample of eye tracking on a virtual store shelf is shown in Exhibit 8.3.

Much eye-tracking research is being conducted to improve Web sites and is it providing insights into user interaction with a screen between clicks. This research yields valuable information on which features are the most eye-catching, which features cause confusion, and which ones are ignored altogether. In the realm of Web site usability and online advertising, here are some of the major lessons learned from eye-tracking research:

1. Ads in the top and left portions of a homepage receive the most eye fixations. Ads in the right column are treated by users as an afterthought area. Ads at the bottom of the page are typically only seen by a small percentage of people.

Exhibit 8.3

Eye Tracking at Work

Source: Elaine Wong, "Eye Tracking Sees Growth in Hyper-Competitive Market," Brand Week, June 7, 2010, p. 8.

2. Close proximity to popular editorial content helps ads get noticed. When an ad is separated from editorial matter either by white space or a rule, the ad receives fewer fixations than when there is no such barrier.

3. Of all types of ads tested, text ads are viewed most intently. On average, text ads are viewed for about 7 seconds, and the best display-type ads are only looked at for 1 to 2 seconds.

4. When it comes to ads, size matters. Bigger ads have a better chance of being seen. Small ads on the right side of homepages are viewed about a third of the time. Small ads on the rest of the page rarely attract attention, but this may not equate to the relative costs of these different advertising formats.

5. Larger images hold the eye longer than smaller images. Interestingly enough, people often click on photos, even if clicking doesn't take them anywhere or lead to any significant information.

6. Clean, clear faces in images attract more eye fixations on homepages.

7. People are more likely to recall facts, names, and places correctly when they were presented with that information in a text format. New, unfamiliar, conceptual information is more accurately recalled when participants receive it in a multimedia graphic format.

8. Shorter paragraphs perform better than longer ones and generally receive twice as much eye fixation as those with longer paragraphs.

9. On a Web site, eyes most often fixate first in the upper left of the page, then hover in that area before going left to right. Only after perusing the top portion of the page for some time do eyes explore further down the page.[23]

Exhibit 8.4

Which One Is Blowing Smoke?

Dan Hill, president of Sensory Logic, says that some of the consumers who tell you they like what you're selling don't really mean it. Here he shows us how to tell who's being genuine and who's just making nice.

Facial Action Coding Service (FACS) Researchers at the University of California at San Francisco identified the 43 muscle movements responsible for all human facial expression (see Exhibit 8.4). They spent seven years categorizing roughly 3,000 combinations of such movements and the emotions they convey—the "eyelid tightener" expresses anger, for instance, and the "nasolabial fold deepener" manifests sadness. The system has proved to be highly accurate; the FBI and CIA reportedly use the FACS method to determine the emotions of suspects during interrogations.[24]

Sensory Logic, a Saint Paul, Minnesota, research firm, uses FACS to get to the "truth." The firm's clients include Target, Nextel, General Motors, and Eli Lilly, according to Don Hill, the firm's president (see *www.sensorylogic.com*). To measure initial gut reactions to a commercial or ad, Hill first attaches electrodes to the side of a subject's mouth (monitoring the zygomatic muscle, for smiles), above the eyebrow (corrugator muscle, for frowns), and on two fingers (for sweat). He says the facial muscle movements reflect appeal, whereas perspiration translates into what he calls "impact"—emotional power. After Hill takes initial readings, he removes the electrodes and he videotapes an interview with each subject. Later, his FACS-trained team reviews the video, second by second, cataloguing emotions.

Even some of Hill's happy customers say that face reading has limitations. For one thing, not everyone believes that pitches have to aim for the heart. "A lot of the advertising we do is a more rational sell," a General Motors researcher says, "so emotional research doesn't apply."[25]

Gender and Age Recognition Systems NEC Electronics of Japan has developed technology to recognize gender and approximate age of consumers. It has married this system with digital signs that can be placed in malls, airports, and other heavily trafficked public areas. Mall retailers, for example, can tailor their message to a person as they walk by. The system can also count the number of persons who walked past the flat-panel digital signs during any specific time period. The program uses an algorithm that draws on a database on thousands of faces as a reference. It looks at distinguishing points of the face, from the shape of the ears and eyes to hair color, to determine the age. The database expands as more people walk past the camera, allowing the program to make better judgment calls with time.

The People Reader, an opinion and behavior measurement device developed by the PreTesting Company, unobtrusively records reading material and readers' eye activity to determine readers' habits as well as the stopping power and brand-name recall associated with different-sized ads. Go to *www.pretesting.com* to learn about the products and services this company offers.

NEC also has installed the recognition system in vending machines in Japan. When a person stands in front of a vending machine, the system reads a consumer's profile. It then recommends snacks and drinks that fit the person's profile.

Consumers, meanwhile, may object to getting their faces scanned, without their knowledge. Likewise, retailers may not want to involve themselves in what some may perceive as a violation of privacy. To date, the systems have not been installed in the United States.[26]

People Reader The PreTesting Company has invented a device called the **People Reader**, which looks like a lamp. When respondents sit in front of it, they are not aware that it is simultaneously recording both their reading material and the activity of their eyes. The self-contained unit is totally automatic and can record any respondent—with or without glasses—without the use of attachments, chin rests, helmets, or special optics. It allows respondents to read any size magazine or newspaper and lets them spend as much time as they want reading and rereading the publication. Through use of the People Reader and specially designed hidden cameras, the PreTesting Company has been able to document both reading habits and the results of different-sized ads in terms of stopping power and brand-name recall. The company's research has found the following:

> **People Reader**
> Machine that simultaneously records the respondent's reading material and eye reactions.

- Nearly 40 percent of all readers either start from the back of a magazine or "fan" a magazine for interesting articles and ads. Fewer than half the readers start from the very first page of a magazine.

- Rarely does a double-page ad provide more than 15 percent additional top-of-mind awareness than a single-page ad. Usually, the benefits of a double-page spread are additional involvement and communication, not top-of-mind awareness.

- In the typical magazine, nearly 35 percent of each ad receive less than 2 seconds' worth of voluntary examination.

- The strongest involvement power recorded for ads has been three or more successive single-page ads on the right-hand side of a magazine.

■ Because most ads "hide" the name of the advertisers and do not show a close-up view of the product package, brand-name confusion is greater than 50 percent on many products such as cosmetics and clothing.

■ A strong ad that is above average in stopping power and communication will work regardless of which section in the magazine it is placed. It will also work well in any type of ad or editorial environment. However, an ad that is below average in stopping power and involvement will be seriously affected by the surrounding environment.[27]

Television Audience Measurement and the Portable People Meter

For the past decade or so, watching television in America has been defined by the families recruited by Nielsen Media Research who have agreed to have an electronic meter attached to their televisions or to record in a diary what shows they watch. Traditional "people meters" are electronic TV-set-top boxes that continually record which channel is tuned in. Today, the trend is away from traditional people meters to direct measurement from "set-top boxes" (STB). These are the boxes installed by the likes of Direct TV, Dish Network, and the cable companies to enable you to watch television programs. As the technology develops, researchers will be able to tap second-by-second viewing habits of millions of households. In contrast, Nielsen's national people meter panel consists of only 18,000 people.

Despite the advantage of a huge sample in STB audience measurement, there are many technological and methodological challenges. Set-top boxes were never designed to collect and process viewing data. Not only are the internal workings of the cable boxes different system to system, but there are also multiple generations deployed within each system. That leads to a long list of issues that need to be addressed, not the least of which is figuring out if the TV set attached to the box is on or off. According to Nielsen, 10 percent of STBs never get turned off over any month long period; about 30 percent of boxes remain on for 24 hours on any given day.[28] Even if the TV is on the question becomes, "who, if anyone, is watching it?" Also, the only demographic data currently available would be at the household level.

Recently Nielsen entered into an agreement with Charter Communications that gives Nielsen access to viewing information from 330,000 homes in the Los Angeles area. One of its first clients was the National Geographic Channel. Early on, the channel found that viewers were changing the channel 10 to 20 seconds before the show would break for ads. National Geographic made a number of changes, including how the show uses story recaps and teasers (about what is coming next). These changes boosted viewership of the channel's commercials.[29]

The Portable People Meter Arbitron has counted radio listeners—and, at various times, television viewers—since the late 1940s. It has harnessed new technology to measure audiences. Participants wear or carry a plastic box that looks like a pager, 3 inches by 2 inches by ½ inch, whose circuitry is roughly as complex as that of a cell phone. The device is called the **portable people meter**, or the PPM.

portable people meter
Device worn by people that measures the radio and TV programming to which the participant was exposed during the day.

Participants clip the PPM to their belts, or put it in a pocket and wear it throughout their waking hours. Before going to bed, they dock the PPM in a cradle so that overnight it can automatically send its data to a computer center in Maryland, where marketing researchers can download and review the information. Arbitron gathers information from approximately 70,000 consumers in 48 markets. The PPM detects radio, television, smart phone viewing, and even cinema advertising. The technology can measure audiences for out-of-home (OOH) TV viewing: watching a sports program at a friend's home, viewing a news network in an airport, or seeing a health show at the gym or doctor's office.

Arbitron has found that many younger consumers multitask. For example, in the last Winter Olympics, many people watching the Olympics on NBC were also online at NBC's Winter Olympics Web site. Other viewers tended to switch back and forth between the two.[30]

Symphony IRI Consumer Network

The Symphony IRI Consumer Network is a continuous household purchase panel that receives purchasing data from the National Consumer Panel (NCP), a joint venture between Symphony IRI and the Nielsen Companies. Households are recruited to the NCP and given incentives to record all of their UPC-based purchases, with a hand-held in-home scanning device.

The data available from the panel includes the following:

- Average amount of product purchased by each household during a specific period.
- Total projected category or product volume sold in the specific period.
- Projected number of households that purchased the category or product within the specific period.
- The average number of shopping trips when the product was purchased.
- The average volume sold for the product per purchase occasion.[31]

Observation Research on the Internet

At the time this text was published, the courts had ruled that tracking across Web sites was legal, comparing the practice to allowing someone to listen in on a phone conversation as long as one person involved in the call authorized it. As a result, online tracking has become the foundation of the $25 billion online advertising industry. The industry claims that tracking tools help subsidize content, allowing many Web sites to be free to users.[32]

Internet tracking is fundamentally another form of observation research. A cookie is a piece of text stored by a user's Web browser. It can be used for authentication, storing site preferences, shopping cart contents, and other useful functions. Cookies can also be used for tracking the Internet user's Web browsing habits. A "flash cookie" is a cookie placed on a computer via Adobe System's popular Flash program. Flash is the most common way to show video online.

Online tracking has come a long way since the now defunct Netscape created the first cookies. For example, Lotame Solutions, Inc., a New York company, uses sophisticated software called a "beacon" to capture what people are typing on a Web site—their comments on monies, say, or their interest in parenting and pregnancy. Lotame packages that data into profiles about individuals, without determining a person's name and sells the profiles to companies seeking customers.

Perhaps the most controversial monitoring comes from "third-party cookies." They work like this: The first time a site is visited, it installs a tracking file, which assigns the computer a unique ID number. Later, when the user visits another site affiliated with the same tracking company, it can take note of where that user was before and where he is now. This way, over time the company can build a robust profile.

The new technologies are transforming the Internet economy. Advertisers once primarily bought ads on specific Web pages—a car ad on a car site. Now, advertisers are paying a premium to follow people around the Internet, wherever they go, with highly specific marketing messages.

Blue Kai, a collector of Internet user data, recently followed a Web surfer as he browsed for electronics on EBay, searched for cruises, and checked out snowboards. It also tracked when a Web surfer researched Chevrolet Sport Utility vehicles on auto site Autobytel and priced flights to Durham, North Carolina, at travel site Expedia.

After collecting that kind of information, Blue Kai groups Web visits into categories of consumers. It then immediately auctions off the data from some of the sites to marketers and Internet companies, which in turn use it for consumer research and ad personalization. Blue Kai regularly records information on more than 160 million unique monthly visitors shopping on retail, travel and auto Web sites.[33]

Blue Kai and other trackers sell their information at data exchanges, which are like stock exchanges for online information. Web sites then put ad space up for auction, and ad agencies, armed with demographic and behavioral data about the people who visit those sites, bid to place ads for their client's campaigns. Google, Yahoo, Microsoft, and others run ad auctions.

How popular is online tracking? The *Wall Street Journal* examined the 50 most popular U.S. Web sites, which account for about 40 percent of the Web pages viewed by Americans. It then analyzed the tracking files and programs these sites downloaded onto a test computer.

As a group, the top 50 sites placed 3,180 tracking files in total on the *Journal*'s test computer. Nearly a third of these were innocuous, deployed to remember the password to a favorite site or tally most-popular articles. But over two-thirds—2,224—were installed by 131 companies, many of which are Internet tracking companies.[34] One tracking company not only tracks people online but also stores their names in their databases. This enables the company to merge online behavior with sources such as voter registration, real estate records, shopping histories, and social networking activities to build a very detailed profile of individual consumers. Rapleaf, a tracking software company, says that it never discloses people's names to clients for online advertising.[35] If you want to find out if there is tracking software on your computer, go to *www.ghostery.com*.

comScore   comScore approaches Internet tracking using a different methodology. The firm has created a panel of over 2 million Internet users who have given comScore permission to capture their browsing and purchase behavior. Panel members receive gift certificates or other compensation.[36] comScore provides audience data that many advertisers use for making online advertising purchase decisions. Small Web sites like Digg and Yelp claim that comScore undercounts their audience size. CNBC says that their audience number is also incorrect. CNBC argues that their audience is relatively wealthy. As a result, they are less motivated to join a panel when offered gift certificates or petty cash incentives. Despite the problems, comScore is still the leader in online audience measurement.[37]

Scraping   During July 2010, users spent 1,181,194,905 hours on Facebook.[38] Some portion of this time was spent saying good and bad things about companies and brands. During the same month, Twitter averaged 65 million Tweets per day.[39] In addition to social media and Twitter, community groups, product and service reviews, discussion boards, and bloggers also comment about specific products and services. User-generated content (UGC) is typically honest and candid and can also be very thoughtful and passionate. Marketers need to understand what is being said about their offerings and then adapt the marketing mix accordingly. The sheer volume of online conversations is overwhelming, and marketers look for tools to help focus their efforts. One popular solution is to "scrape" the Web and use text analytic tools to automate the analysis (see

Chapter 4). How does scraping work? The researcher selects a number of search terms, much like a search engine, and then the tool crawls the Web in search of UGC relating to these search terms. All positive hits are then aggregated in a database, Next, a text analytic tool counts how frequently a product, feature, brand, and so on, is mentioned and makes an attitudinal assessment (e.g., positive, neutral, negative) for each statement.[40]

Context is essential to understand meaning. It is also extremely difficult to automate since contextual clues are constantly evolving alongside language and are often very subtle (e.g., discerning Apple the company from apple the food). While text analytic and Web-scraping tools are improving in their ability to understand context, it is certain that any Web-scraped database still includes many irrelevant search results and excludes some relevant ones.[41]

Here are some examples that highlight the contextual confusion issue. Most of today's text analytic tools would classify the following statement as a negative comment about the Toyota Scion: "With the supercharger included on my Scion, it is one bad machine"—not being able to recognize the slang use of the word bad to actually mean good. Similarly, most of the technology would classify the following statement as being positive for Scion: "I loved my Scion; then I had to replace the transmission twice in the past two years."[42]

Observation Research and Virtual Shopping

Advances in computer technology have enabled researchers to simulate an actual retail store environment on a computer screen. Depending on the type of simulation, a shopper can "pick up" a package by touching its image on the monitor and rotate it to examine all sides. Like buying on most online retailers, the shopper touches the shopping cart to add an item to the basket. During the shopping process, the computer unobtrusively records the amount of time the consumer spends shopping in each product category, the time the consumer spends examining each side of a package, the quantity of product the consumer purchases, and the order in which items are purchased.

Computer-simulated environments like this one offer a number of advantages over older research methods. First, unlike focus groups, concept tests, and other laboratory approaches, the virtual store duplicates the distracting clutter of an actual market. Consumers can shop in an environment with a realistic level of complexity and variety. Second, researchers can set up and alter the tests very quickly. Once images of the product are scanned into the computer, the researcher can make changes in the assortment of brands, product packaging, pricing, promotions, and shelf space within minutes. Data collection is also fast and error-free because the information generated by the purchase is automatically tabulated and stored by the computer. Third, production costs are low because displays are created electronically. Once the hardware and software are in place, the cost of a test is largely a function of the number of respondents, who generally are given a small incentive to participate. Fourth, the simulation has a high degree of flexibility. It can be used to test entirely new marketing concepts or to fine-tune existing programs. The simulation also makes it possible to eliminate much of the noise that exists in field experiments.[43]

Kimberly-Clark has refined the virtual shopping experience even more. Located in Appleton, Wisconsin, the firm's virtual testing lab has a woman standing in a room surrounded by three screens showing a store aisle, a retina-tracking device recording her every glance.

Asked by a Kimberly-Clark researcher to find a "big box" of Huggies Natural Fit diapers in size three, the woman pushed forward on a handle like that of a shopping cart, and the video simulated her progress down the aisle. Spotting Huggies' red packages, she turned the handle to the right to face a dizzying array of diapers. After pushing a button to get a kneeling view of the shelves, she reached forward and tapped the screen to put the box she wanted in her virtual cart.

Kimberly-Clark hopes these virtual shopping aisles will provide better understanding of consumer behavior and make the testing of new products faster, more convenient, and more precise.[44]

Kimberly-Clark's lab also features a U-shaped floor-to-ceiling screen that re-creates in vivid detail interiors of the big retailers that sell the company's products—a tool that the company will use in presentations to executives in bids to win shelf space. A separate area is reserved for real replicas of store interiors, which can be customized to match the flooring, light fixtures, and shelves of retailers such as Target Corp. and Wal-Mart Stores, Inc.

Kimberly-Clark says its studio allows researchers and designers to get a fast read on new product designs and displays without having to stage real-life tests in the early stages of development. Doing the research in a windowless basement, rather than an actual test market, also avoids tipping off competitors early in the development process.

"We're trying to test ideas faster, cheaper, and better," says Ramin Eivaz, a vice president at Kimberly-Clark focusing on strategy. Formerly, new product testing typically took 8 months to 2 years. Now, that time is cut in half, he says. Projects that test well with the virtual-reality tools will be fast-tracked to real-store trials, Mr. Eivaz says.[45]

Virtual-shopping research is growing rapidly as companies such as Frito-Lay, Goodyear, Procter & Gamble, General Mills, and Coca-Cola realize the benefits from this type of observation research. About 40,000 new consumer package goods are introduced in the United States each year. All are vying for very limited retail shelf space. Any process, such as virtual shopping, that can speed product development time and lower costs is always welcomed by manufacturers.

To sell retailers on new products, manufacturers are revealing more about their product pipelines to drum up interest early on. Over the past several months, Kimberly-Clark says it has brought in executives from major chains, including Target, Wal-Mart, and Kroger, to see the Appleton facility. Kimberly-Clark uses the data from its virtual-reality tests with consumers to tout the performance of products in development.

"It no longer works to show up on a retailer's doorstep with your new product and say, 'Isn't this pretty?'" Mr. Eivaz says. "We need to be an indispensable partner to our retailers and show we can do more for them."[46]

SUMMARY

Observation research is the systematic process of recording patterns of occurrences or behaviors without questioning or normally communicating with the people involved. For observation to be used successfully, the needed information must be observable and the behavior of interest must be repetitive, frequent, or in some manner predictable. The behavior of interest also should be of a relatively short duration. There are four dimensions along which observation approaches vary: (1) natural versus contrived situations, (2) open versus disguised observation, (3) human versus machine observers, and (4) direct versus indirect observation.

The biggest advantage of observation research is that researchers can see what people actually do rather than having to rely on what they say they did, thereby avoiding many biasing factors. Also, some forms of data are more quickly and accurately gathered by observation. The primary disadvantage of this type of research is that the researcher learns nothing about motives, attitudes, intentions, or feelings.

People watching people or objects can take the form of ethnographic research, mystery shopping, one-way mirror observations (for example, child psychologists might watch children play with toys), and shopper pattern and behavior studies.

Machine observation may involve traffic counters, physiological measurement devices, opinion and behavior measurement devices, or scanners. Symphony IRI employs hand-held scanners with its National Consumer Panel to scan all household purchases with UPC codes. This data is then used to measure consumer shopping patterns and sales by product category and brand.

Observation research on the Internet originally focused on tracking the surfing patterns of Internet users. Firms track consumer online behavior via cookies, flash cookies, and beacons. Beacons are the most intrusive because they can capture what people are typing on a Web site. Some firms are blending online data with offline information to build detailed consumer profiles. The objective is to increase the efficiency of targeted online advertising. Advertisers used to buy online advertising based on the Web site's content. Today, they buy based on the profiles of a person's Web activity, demographics, and psychographics.

Virtual shopping using advanced computer technology to create a simulated shopping environment is a rapidly growing form of observation research. It reduces the cost and time it takes to bring new products to the market.

KEY TERMS & DEFINITIONS

observation research Systematic process of recording patterns of occurrences or behaviors without normally communicating with the people involved.

open observation Process of monitoring people who know they are being watched.

disguised observation Process of monitoring people who do not know they are being watched.

garbologists Researchers who sort through people's garbage to analyze household consumption patterns.

ethnographic research Study of human behavior in its natural context, involving observation of behavior and physical setting.

mystery shoppers People who pose as consumers and shop at a company's own stores or those of its competitors to collect data about customer–employee interactions and to gather observational data; they may also compare prices, displays, and the like.

one-way mirror observation Practice of watching behaviors or activities from behind a one-way mirror.

traffic counters Machines used to measure vehicular flow over a particular stretch of roadway.

electroencephalograph (EEG) Machine that measures electrical pulses on the scalp and generates a record of electrical activity in the brain.

galvanic skin response (GSR) Change in the electric resistance of the skin associated with activation responses; also called *electro-dermal response*.

People Reader Machine that simultaneously records the respondent's reading material and eye reactions.

portable people meter Device worn by people that measures the radio and TV programming to which the participant was exposed during the day.

QUESTIONS FOR REVIEW & CRITICAL THINKING

1. You are charged with the responsibility of determining whether men are brand conscious when shopping for racquetball equipment. Outline an observation research procedure for making that determination.

2. Fisher-Price has asked you to develop a research procedure for determining which of its prototype toys is most appealing to 4- and 5-year-olds. Suggest a methodology for making this determination.

3. What are the biggest drawbacks of observation research?

4. Compare the advantages and disadvantages of observation research with those of survey research.

5. It has been said that "people buy things not for what they will do, but for what they mean." Discuss this statement in relation to observation research.

6. You are a manufacturer of a premium brand of ice cream. You want to know more about your market share, competitors' pricing, and the types of outlets where your product is selling best. What kind of observation research data would you purchase? Why?

7. How might a mystery shopper be valuable to the following organizations?
   a. JetBlue Airlines
   b. Macy's Department Store
   c. H&R Block

8. Use ethnographic research to evaluate the dining experience at your student center. What did you learn?

9. Do you think that tracking beacons should be outlawed? Why or why not?

10. Describe how tracking research can benefit an online retailer.

11. Do you think that virtual shopping will replace other forms of marketing research? Why or why not?

12. Divide the class into teams of five. Each team should select a different retailer (services are okay for mystery shopping). Two members of the team should prepare a list of 10 to 15 questions to be answered. A sample of questions for an Eye Care Clinic is shown below. The remaining three members of the team should become mystery shoppers with the goal of answering the questions created by the team. After the shopping is complete, the team should combine their findings and make a report to the class. *(Team Exercise)*

Sample Mystery Shopping Questions for an Eye Care Clinic

1. Was the phone answered within three rings?

2. How long did you have to wait for an appointment?

3. Were you given clear directions to the office?

4. Did you receive a new patient packet in the mail?

5. Were signs directing you to the office clear and visible?

6. Did the receptionist greet you when you entered the office?

7. How long did you wait before being taken into a room for the pre-exam?

8. Did all staff members have a name tag on?

9. Was the facility clean?

10. Were your eyes dilated before you saw the doctor?

11. Were exam procedures explained clearly?

12. Were you given an opportunity to ask the doctor questions?

13. Were your questions answered promptly and respectfully?

14. Were you directed to the optical shop after your exam?

15. Were your glasses/contacts ready when promised?

WORKING THE NET

1. Go to *www.symphonyiri.com* **and** *www.nielsen.com* and report what types of observation research are being conducted by the two research firms.

2. Go to *www.doubleclick.com* and read its latest research findings. Make an oral presentation to your class.

3. Go to *www.mysteryshop.org* to learn more about mystery shopping.

REAL-LIFE RESEARCH • 8.1

A Glad Trash Bag Breakthrough

Previous innovation in the $1.03 billion trash bag category has focused on the act of tying: First there was the twist tie, then there were plastic ties, then bags with longer flaps that you could tie, and, finally, the drawstring. Other enhancements, such as bags that absorbed or limited smells, haven't sparked much consumer interest. And while companies have made stronger bags that could carry larger loads, "there hadn't been much focus on tensile strength," said Ken Harris of Cannondale Associates, Evanston, Illinois.

The problem was that, as bags got stronger and thicker, they also got less flexible and more likely to tear. And that is where Glad found its, pardon the phrase, opening.

Glad Products (a subsidary of Clorox, Oakland, California) launched ForceFlex, a bag that stretches to accommodate the bulky items that consumers tend to throw away. The *New York Times* called ForceFlex "the Mercedes of trash bags." Subsequent sales confirmed that Glad had a winner on its hands.

With a price tag of $6.50–$7.99 for a 28-count with drawstring (versus $4.50–$6.00 for the regular product), ForceFlex cleaned up with $108.4 million in sales for the year ended August 13, posting a 38.9 percent increase in unit sales in the same period, per Information Resources. ForceFlex's performance was no small marketing feat, given that consumers don't usually contemplate their trash bags longer than it takes to haul out the garbage. "If you are actually spending time with your trash, there's something wrong," said Audy Baack, marketing manager for Glad Trash.

To avoid a "trash disaster" (i.e., a broken bag), companies had made bags that were thicker, heavier, and stronger, said Alan Savicki, Glad's group manager for trash business R&D. "They needed to be, because the trash composition was heavily laden with big glass bottles and cardboard boxes. So we're saying we ought to look at the design of our bag," said Savicki. "Is it meeting today's consumer needs?"

Glad went straight to the source for answers by conducting ethnographic studies, which Baack said was every bit as odd as it sounds. "You go to peoples' homes and say, 'Can I ask you about your trash?' and you get some funny looks."

Nevertheless, researchers found that consumers were putting more items into their trash bags that were leaky, including food leftovers, or were big but light, such as pizza boxes and hangers. Because those latter objects tend to have sharp points and edges, they easily punctured the bags—creating a sticky situation. Armed with enough evidence, Glad turned to a partner with the scientific expertise necessary to implement a new technology.

Enter Procter & Gamble, which owned a 10 percent stake in Glad and was trying to figure out what to do with a new, stretchable plastic it had developed for some of its baby products. "P&G had some interesting ideas it didn't know what to do with," said Baack. "Glad had the marketing and category expertise to turn some of those into [trash bag] products."[47]

Questions

1. How else might the decision-making information have been gathered besides ethnographics?
2. What are the disadvantages to Glad if they only used ethnographics?
3. Could this research have been done using virtual reality? Why or why not?
4. Could the location of the ethnographic research influence the research outcome? Explain.

REAL-LIFE RESEARCH • 8.2

Stovetops and Laptops

Every year On-Site Research conducts a cross-country ethnographic study called Cyber Census. Members of the research team drive an RV across 20 states to track a core group of 150 Americans and their use of and interaction with Web-based and other technology.

The interviews are designed to allow the researchers to embed themselves in the consumer's real life, from a few hours to days spent living with the study participant. Researchers also conduct a full exploration of the consumer's online life via a surf-along, which lets them experience their cyber lives.

The research shows that people are increasingly looking for a space in the home, most often the kitchen or family room, where they can interact with people and media in both physical and cyberspace. They want a highly interactive room that lets them socialize in physical space while using their hand-held devices and computers to access their virtual environments.

This trend has manifested itself in a number of ways: In some homes, dining rooms are rarely used for dining; computers are migrating out of the home office; and technology of all types has moved to the family kitchen.

These observations led the researchers to the acronym HIVE (highly interactive + virtual environment) and the associated term *hiving*, which is our way of characterizing this trend. People report hiving for many reasons, but the most common reason is that they don't want to be isolated from others. The home office/den filled with technology may give you the ability to communicate with others online, but it does little to connect you with the actual people in the home. Consumers report "catching grief" from spouses because they spend too much time on the computer away from the family, especially during dinner time. Parents are concerned about monitoring their children while they use the computer for homework and other activities. And parents of older children really worry about all the time their teens spend alone on the computer and hand-held devices.

Another factor driving hiving is Americans' addiction to multitasking. Multitasking in the HIVE is what the HIVE is all about. In a well-equipped HIVE, you can make dinner, talk on your phone via Bluetooth, help your kids on the computer do their homework, charge your hand-held devices, download and sync your media, check your e-mail, watch television, check your stocks, pay bills and still feel that you are a part of the social activity in the home. The laptop has become as common as the toaster oven in the kitchen. And electric cords and chargers clutter countertops, making a different kind of spaghetti.[48]

Questions

1. How might this type of research benefit GE, Viking, or Jenn Air?
2. Should qualitative research be undertaken before any actual strategies are developed? Why?
3. What other types of research could have been used to gather this information?
4. This research was conducted in less than half of the states. Might this bias the survey findings? If so, how?

Primary Data Collection: Experimentation and Test Markets

LEARNING OBJECTIVES

→ 1. To understand the nature of experiments.

→ 2. To gain insight into requirements for proving causation.

→ 3. To learn about the experimental setting.

→ 4. To examine experimental validity.

→ 5. To learn the limitations of experimentation in marketing research.

→ 6. To compare types of experimental designs.

→ 7. To gain insight into test marketing.

In this chapter, we cover issues related to the use of experiments for data collection in marketing research. Field experiments, laboratory experiments and test markets are the major experimental approaches covered. We also present the things you have to show to prove that one thing caused another (not easy), different types of designs and sources of error in experiments.

What Is an Experiment?

Research based on experimentation is fundamentally different from research based on surveys or observation.[1] In the case of both survey and observation research, the researcher is, in essence, a passive assembler of data. The researcher asks people questions or observes what they do. In experimental research, the situation is very different: The researcher becomes an active participant in the process.

In concept, an **experiment** is straightforward. The researcher changes or manipulates one thing (called an *experimental, treatment, independent,* or *explanatory variable*) to observe the effect on something else (referred to as a *dependent variable*). In marketing experiments, the dependent variable is frequently some measure of sales, such as total sales or market share; experimental variables are typically marketing mix variables, such as price, amount or type of advertising, and changes in product features.

> **experiment**
> Research approach in which one variable is manipulated and the effect on another variable is observed.

Demonstrating Causation

Experimental research is often referred to as **causal** (not casual) **research** because it is the only type of research that has the potential to demonstrate that a change in one variable *causes* some predictable change in another variable. To demonstrate causation (that *A* likely caused *B*), one must be able to show three things:

1. Concomitant variation (correlation)
2. Appropriate time order of occurrence
3. Elimination of other possible causal factors

> **causal research**
> Research designed to determine whether a change in one variable likely caused an observed change in another.

Please note that we are using the terms *causation* and *causality* in the scientific sense.[2] The scientific view of causation is quite different from the popular view, which often implies that there is a single cause of an event. For example, when someone says in everyday conversation that *X* is the cause of some observed change in *Y*, he or she generally means that *X* is the only cause of the observed change in *Y*. But the scientific view holds that *X* is only one of a number of possible determining conditions that caused the observed change in *Y*.

In addition, the everyday view of causality implies a completely deterministic relationship, while the scientific view implies a probabilistic relationship. The popular view is that if *X* is the cause of *Y*, then *X* must always lead to *Y*. The scientific view holds that *X* can be a cause of *Y* if the presence of *X* makes the occurrence of *Y* more probable or likely.

Finally, the scientific view holds that one can never definitively prove that *X* is a cause of *Y* but only infer that a relationship exists. In other words, causal relationships are always inferred and never demonstrated conclusively beyond a shadow of a doubt. Three types of evidence—concomitant variation, appropriate time order of occurrence, and elimination of other possible causal factors—are used to infer causal relationships.

Concomitant Variation

To provide evidence that a change in *A* caused a particular change in *B*, one must first show that there is **concomitant variation**, or correlation, between *A* and *B*; in other

> **concomitant variation**
> Statistical relationship between two variables.

words, *A* and *B* must vary together in some predictable fashion. This might be a *positive* or an *inverse* relationship. Two variables that might be related in a positive manner are advertising and sales. They would be positively related if sales increased by some predictable amount when advertising increased by a certain amount. Two variables that might be related in an inverse manner are price and sales. They would be inversely (negatively) related if sales increased when price decreased and decreased when price increased. The researcher can test for the existence and direction of statistical relationships by means of a number of statistical procedures, including chi-square analysis, correlation analysis, regression analysis, and analysis of variance to mention a few. All of these statistical procedures are discussed later in the text (chi-square, correlation analysis, and regression analysis in Chapter 16 and analysis of variance in Chapter 17).

However, concomitant variation by itself does not prove causation. Simply because two variables happen to vary together in some predictable fashion does not prove that one causes the other. For example, suppose you found a high degree of correlation between sales of a product in the United States and the GDP (gross domestic product) of Germany. This might be true simply because both variables happened to be increasing at a similar rate. Further examination and consideration might show that there is no true link between the two variables. To infer causation, you must be able to show correlation—but correlation alone is not proof of causation.

Appropriate Time Order of Occurrence

appropriate time order of occurrence
Change in an independent variable occurred before an observed change in the dependent variable.

The second requirement for demonstrating that a causal relationship likely exists between two variables is showing that there is an **appropriate time order of occurrence**. To demonstrate that *A* caused *B*, one must be able to show that *A* occurred before *B* occurred. For example, to demonstrate that a price change had an effect on sales, you must be able to show that the price change occurred before the change in sales was observed. However, showing that *A* and *B* vary concomitantly and that *A* occurred before *B* still does not provide evidence strong enough to permit one to conclude that *A* is the likely cause of an observed change in *B*.

Elimination of Other Possible Causal Factors

elimination of other possible causal factors
Hard to prove that something else did not cause change in *B*.

The most difficult thing to demonstrate in marketing experiments is that the change in *B* was not caused by some factor other than *A*. For example, suppose a company increased its advertising expenditures and observed an increase in the sales of its product. Correlation and appropriate time order of occurrence are present. But has a likely causal relationship been demonstrated? The answer is "no." It is possible that the observed change in sales is due to some factor other than the increase in advertising. For example, at the same time advertising expenditures were increased, a major competitor may have decreased advertising expenditures, or increased price, or pulled out of the market. Even if the competitive environment did not change, one or a combination of other factors may have influenced sales. For example, the economy in the area might have received a major boost for some reason that has nothing to do with the experiment. For any of these reasons, or many others, the observed increase in sales might have been caused by some factor or combination of factors other than or in addition to the increase in advertising expenditures. Much of the discussion in this chapter is related to designing experiments so as to eliminate or adjust for the effects of other possible causal factors.

Experimental Setting

Experiments can be conducted in a laboratory or a field setting.[3] Most experiments in the physical sciences are conducted in a laboratory setting; many marketing experiments are field experiments.

Laboratory Experiments

Laboratory experiments provide a number of important advantages.[4] The major advantage of conducting experiments in a laboratory is the ability to control extraneous causal factors—temperature, light, humidity, and so on—and focus on the effect of a change in A on B. In the lab, the researcher can effectively deal with the third element of proving causation (elimination of other possible causal factors) and focus on the first two elements (concomitant variation and appropriate time order of occurrence). This additional control strengthens the researcher's ability to infer that an observed change in the dependent variable was caused by a change in the experimental, or treatment, variable. As a result, laboratory experiments are viewed as having greater internal validity (discussed in greater detail in the next section). On the other hand, the controlled and possibly sterile environment of the laboratory may not be a good analog of the marketplace. For this reason, the findings of laboratory experiments sometimes do not hold up when transferred to the marketplace. Therefore, laboratory experiments are seen as having greater problems with external validity (see the next section). However, laboratory experiments are probably being used to a greater extent in marketing research today than in the past because of their many advantages. Laboratory experiments have an important place in marketing as illustrated in the Practicing Marketing Research feature below.

→ **laboratory experiments**
Experiments conducted in a controlled setting.

PRACTICING MARKETING RESEARCH

What's It Like to Be Old?[5]

Traditionally, many industries have neglected actively marketing to the 65 and over age demographic, preferring to focus on young, more culturally attractive demographics. Some institutions, however, like the Oregon Health & Science University, the Massachusetts Institute of Technology's AgeLab, and Stanford, are taking a different approach to this demographic: Design products and services for the elderly that promote wellness, autonomy, and social engagement.

Organizations like these are taking innovative approaches to the research and testing parts of their work as well. For instance, the AgeLab developed the Age Gain Now Empathy System (AGNES), a modified jumpsuit designed to help wearers better understand the basic challenges that many elderly people experience daily. Tension cords stretch from a pelvic harness to the arms, legs, and a helmet on the head, constricting limb and joint movement and cramping the neck and spine. Shoes with uneven padded soles disrupt balance. Extra

thick gloves limit manual dexterity. Yellow tinted goggles cloud vision. AgeLab uses tools like AGNES to provide insight into the wants and needs of elderly people and to test new products to see how they can be designed to better serve this market.

One of the biggest takeaways from AgeLab has been simply that elderly people don't like being marketed to as if they are elderly. Products like big-button phones that scream "You're old!" don't go over well. Through its testing programs, AgeLab's goal is to find ways of making products that appeal to a broader demographic but address specific needs of the elderly. For example, a hands-free parallel parking system, which AgeLab is testing for Ford Motor, could greatly benefit older drivers who have trouble turning their necks to look back but could also appeal to any driver who loves smart tech.

As researchers and testers strive to create products enabling health, wellness, independence, and connectivity for seniors, some organizations are even redefining concepts as basic as the traditional testing laboratory. The real-estate developer Pacific Retirement Services and the Oregon Center for Aging & Technology (Orcatech) have teamed up to create the Mirabella, a $130 million luxury high-rise retirement community in downtown Portland. Residents have been encouraged to take part in a "living laboratory" program. Wireless motion sensors track residents' mobility and send the data to Orcatech for monitoring. The monitoring system is undergoing tests itself in the "lab" that is the Mirabella, as Orcatech researchers look to find out how to effectively monitor residents' health status in real time and respond to problems like falls and social withdrawal more quickly—or even prevent them entirely.

The Mirabella also offers a real-life testing ground for other products being studied at Orcatech, like electronic pillboxes and social networking programs for residents. The original design of the building itself even underwent feedback-based changes in response to potential residents asking for space in the garage to stow their kayaks. Like most traditional testing programs, however, the Mirabella is not cheap.

The monitoring system costs $1,000 per resident to set up, and $2,600 per year for technical and research support.

Although prospects look promising right now, many of these methods have yet to prove themselves. Still, as the 65-and-older population continues to grow, one thing is for sure: Researchers must innovate both in products and in the testing methods themselves if they want to tap the potential of this market.

Questions

1. The Mirabella is being used as a kind of test market. How do you think this program affects the way products and services are test-marketed there?

2. Experiments like those discussed here are typically costly. Do you think those costs are worth it, or do you think researchers might be better off finding a cheaper method entirely?

Field Experiments

> **field experiments**
> Tests conducted outside the laboratory in an actual environment, such as a marketplace.

Field experiments are conducted outside the laboratory in an actual market environment. Test markets, discussed later in this chapter, are a frequently used type of field experiment. Field experiments solve the problem of the realism of the environment but open up a whole new set of problems. The major problem is that in the field the researcher cannot control all the spurious factors that might influence the dependent variable, such as the actions of competitors, the weather, the economy, societal trends, and the political climate. Therefore, field experiments have more problems related to internal validity, whereas lab experiments have more problems related to external validity.

Experimental Validity

Validity is defined as the degree to which an experiment actually measures what the researcher was trying to measure (see Chapter 10). The validity of a measure depends on the extent to which the measure is free from both systematic and random error. Two specific kinds of validity are relevant to experimentation: internal validity and external validity.

> **internal validity**
> Extent to which competing explanations for the experimental results observed can be ruled out.

Internal validity refers to the extent to which competing explanations for the experimental results observed can be ruled out. If the researcher can show that the experimental, or treatment, variable actually produced the differences observed in the dependent variable, then the experiment can be said to be internally valid. This kind of validity requires evidence demonstrating that variation in the dependent variable was caused by exposure to the treatment variable and not other possible causal factors.

External validity refers to the extent to which the causal relationships measured in an experiment can be generalized to outside persons, settings, and times.[6] The issue here is how representative the subjects and the setting used in the experiment are of other populations and settings to which the researcher would like to project the results. As noted earlier, field experiments offer a higher degree of external validity and a lower degree of internal validity than do laboratory experiments.

> ➜ **external validity**
> Extent to which causal relationships measured in an experiment can be generalized to outside persons, settings, and times.

PRACTICING MARKETING RESEARCH

Know Your Potential Customers, Psychologically Speaking

Put aside demographics; a better way to know test market customers in advance might be psychographics, based on real-life psychological and lifestyle portraits. Researchers at Wayne State University in Detroit, Michigan, used a random sample of 1,000 applicants for various bank services to come up with what they thought would be a "superior predictor" of market behavior, combining the benefits of demographics with "the richness and dimensionality of psychological characteristics" of target customers. Product-specific psychological profiles, they report, increase marketers' ability to predict customer behavior by getting a more refined analysis of its people makeup.

Out of 1,000 people polled, 350 filled out the researchers' special questionnaires, which queried respondents on standard demographic variables and 53 psychographic items. The questions were presented in 10 categories, such as price consciousness, dynamic leadership, credit use, and innovation, with typical questions such as: "I usually shop a lot for 'specials.'" Or "I often try new brands before my friends and neighbors do." The results were calculated using discriminant analysis to show how "relatively stable" consumer characteristics (the psychographics) were linked to and thereby predictive of service usage, in this case, bank credit cards. These results then gave marketers solid data on *exactly who* the users of the intended services are and how best to service them.

The researchers discovered that lifestyle variables, culled from the 53 psychographic inventory questions, proved to be excellent predictors of user patterns. In all, 55 to 56 percent of credit card users were correctly classified and predicted this way. Heavy credit card users, contrasted with light and medium users, scored highest in the categories of fashion consciousness, income level, dynamic leadership, and financial satisfaction; second lowest in community mindedness; and lowest in price consciousness. In summary, the researchers found that heavy credit card users had much higher incomes and self-confidence levels than people who used their cards less.[7]

Questions

1. In developing an experimental design and identifying key variables to manipulate, how could you take maximum advantage from the fact that heavy credit card users are not concerned with price?

2. Identify several factors among heavy credit card users that contradict the psychographic findings and reduce the degree to which they match the profile presented (e.g., the correlation of heavy credit card usage with personal debt and bankruptcy).

Experimental Notation

In our discussion of experiments, we will use a standard system of notation, described as follows:

- ▪ *X* is used to indicate the exposure of an individual or a group to an experimental treatment. The experimental treatment is the factor whose effects we want to measure and compare. Experimental treatments may be factors such as different prices, package designs, point-of-purchase displays, advertising approaches, or product forms.
- ▪ *O* (for observation) is used to refer to the process of taking measurements on the test units. *Test units* are individuals, groups of individuals, or entities whose response to the experimental treatments is being tested. Test units might include individual consumers, groups of consumers, retail stores, total markets, or other entities that might be the targets of a firm's marketing program.
- ▪ Different time periods are represented by the horizontal arrangement of the *X*'s and *O*'s. For example,

$$O_1 \; X \; O_2$$

would describe an experiment in which a preliminary measurement O_1 was taken of one or more test units, then one or more test units were exposed to the experimental variable *X*, and then a measurement O_2 of the test units was taken. The *X*'s and *O*'s can be arranged vertically to show simultaneous exposure and measurement of different test units. For example, the following design involves two different groups of test units:

$$X_1 \; O_1$$
$$X_2 \; O_2$$

The two groups of test units received different experimental treatments at the same time (X_1 and X_2), and then the two groups were measured simultaneously (O_1 and O_2)[8]

Extraneous Variables

In interpreting experimental results, the researcher would like to be able to conclude that the observed response is due to the effect of the experimental variable. However, many things stand in the way of the ability to reach this conclusion. In anticipation of possible problems in interpretation, the researcher needs to design the experiment so as to eliminate as many extraneous factors as possible as causes of the observed effect.

Examples of Extraneous Variables

Examples of extraneous factors or variables that pose a threat to experimental validity are history, maturation, instrument variation, selection bias, mortality, testing effects, and regression to the mean.[9]

➤ **history**
Intervention, between the beginning and end of an experiment, of outside variables or events that might change the dependent variable.

History **History** refers to the intervention, between the beginning and end of the experiment, of any variable or event—other than those manipulated by the researcher (experimental variables)—that might affect the value of the dependent variable. Early tests of Prego spaghetti sauce by the Campbell Soup Company provide an example of a possible problem with extraneous variables. Campbell executives claim that Ragu, a competing brand, greatly increased its advertising levels and use of cents-off deals during their Prego tests. They believe that this increased marketing activity was designed to get shoppers to stock up on Ragu and make it impossible for Campbell to get an accurate reading of potential sales for its Prego product.

Maturation
Maturation refers to changes in subjects during the course of the experiment that are a function of time; it includes getting older, hungrier, more tired, and the like. Throughout the course of an experiment, the responses of people to a treatment variable may change because of these maturation factors and not because of the treatment variable. The likelihood that maturation will be a serious problem in a particular experiment depends on the length of the experiment. The longer the experiment runs, the more likely it is that maturation will present problems for interpreting the results.

> **maturation**
> Changes in subjects occurring during the experiment that are not related to the experiment but that may affect subjects' response to the treatment factor.

Instrument Variation
Instrument variation refers to any changes in measurement instruments that might explain differences in the measurements taken. It is a serious problem in marketing experiments where people are used as interviewers or observers to measure the dependent variable. If measurements on the same subject are taken by different interviewers or observers at different points in time, differences between measurements may reflect variations in the way the interviewing or observation was done by different interviewers or observers. On the other hand, if the same interviewer or observer is used to take measurements on the same subject over time, differences may reflect the fact that the particular observer or interviewer has become less interested and is doing a sloppier job.

> **instrument variation**
> Changes in measurement instruments (e.g., interviewers or observers) that might affect measurements.

Selection Bias
The threat to validity posed by **selection bias** is encountered in situations where the experimental or test group is systematically different from the population to which the researcher would like to project the experimental results or from the control group. In projecting the results to a population that is systematically different from the test group, the researcher may get results very different from those we got in the test because of differences in the makeup of the two groups. Similarly, an observed difference between a test group and an untreated control group (not exposed to the experimental variable) may be due to differences between the two groups and not to the effect of the experimental variable. Researchers can ensure equality of groups through either randomization or matching. *Randomization* involves assigning subjects to test groups and control groups at random. *Matching* involves what the name suggests—making sure that there is a one-to-one match between people or other units in the test and control groups in regard to key characteristics (e.g., age). Specific matching procedures are discussed later in this chapter.

> **selection bias**
> Systematic differences between the test group and the control group due to a biased selection process.

Mortality
Mortality refers to the loss of test units during the course of an experiment. It is a problem because there is no easy way to know whether the lost units would have responded to the treatment variable in the same way as those units that remained throughout the entire experiment. An experimental group that was representative of the population or that matched a control group may become nonrepresentative because of the systematic loss of subjects with certain characteristics. For example, in a study of music preferences of the population, if nearly all the subjects under the age of 25 were lost during the course of the experiment, then the researcher would likely get a biased picture of music preferences at the end of the experiment. In this case, the results would lack external validity.

> **mortality**
> Loss of test units or subjects during the course of an experiment, which may result in a nonrepresentativeness.

Testing Effects
Testing effects result from the fact that the process of experimentation may produce its own effect on the responses observed. For example, measuring attitude

> **testing effect**
> Effect that is a by-product of the research process itself.

toward a product before exposing subjects to an ad may act as a treatment variable, influencing perception of the ad. Testing effects come in two forms:

- *Main testing effects* are the possible effects of earlier observations on later observations. For example, students taking the GMAT for the second time tend to do better than those taking the test for the first time, even though the students have no information about the items they actually missed on the first test. This effect also can be reactive in the sense that responses to the first administration of an attitude test have some actual effect on subjects' attitudes that is reflected in subsequent applications of the same test.
- *Interactive testing effect* is the effect of a prior measurement on a subject's response to a later measurement. For example, if subjects are asked about their awareness of advertising for various products (pre-exposure measurement) and then exposed to advertising for one or more of these products (treatment variable), postmeasurements would likely reflect the joint effect of the pre-exposure and the treatment condition.

regression to the mean
Tendency of subjects with extreme behavior to move toward the average for that behavior during the course of an experiment.

Regression to the Mean   **Regression to the mean** refers to the observed tendency of subjects with extreme behavior to move toward the average for that behavior during the course of an experiment. Test units may exhibit extreme behavior because of chance, or they may have been specifically chosen because of their extreme behavior. The researcher might, for example, have chosen people for an experimental group because they were extremely heavy users of a particular product or service. In such situations, their tendency to move toward the average behavior may be interpreted as having been caused by the treatment variable when in fact it has nothing to do with the treatment variable.

Controlling Extraneous Variables

Causal factors that threaten validity must be controlled in some manner to establish a clear picture of the effect of the manipulated variable on the dependent variable. Extraneous causal factors are ordinarily referred to as *confounding variables* because they confound the treatment condition, making it impossible to determine whether changes in the dependent variable are due solely to the treatment conditions.

randomization
Random assignment of subjects to treatment conditions to ensure equal representation of subject characteristics.

Four basic approaches are used to control extraneous factors: randomization, physical control, design control, and statistical control.

Randomization is carried out by randomly assigning subjects to treatment conditions so that extraneous causal factors related to subject characteristics can reasonably be assumed to be represented equally in each treatment condition, thus canceling out extraneous effects.

physical control
Holding constant the value or level of extraneous variables throughout the course of an experiment.

Physical control of extraneous causal factors may involve somehow holding constant the value or level of the extraneous variable throughout the experiment. Another approach to physical control is matching respondents in regard to important personal characteristics (e.g., age, income, lifestyle) before assigning them to different treatment conditions. The goal is to make sure there are no important differences between characteristics of respondents in the test and control groups.

design control
Use of the experimental design to control extraneous causal factors.

Design control is the control of extraneous factors by means of specific types of experimental designs developed for this purpose. Such designs are discussed later in this chapter.

statistical control
Adjusting for the effects of confounded variables by statistically adjusting the value of the dependent variable for each treatment condition.

Finally, **statistical control** can be used to account for extraneous causal factors if these factors can be identified and measured throughout the course of the experiment. Procedures such as analysis of covariance can adjust for the effects of a confounded variable on the dependent variable by statistically adjusting the value of the dependent variable for each treatment condition.

PRACTICING MARKETING RESEARCH

Data Use: The Insidious Top-box and Its Effects on Measuring Line Share[10]

Consumers have limited budgets and consumption capacities, so when companies want to make changes to a product line, managers want to know how those changes would affect the choices people make within the category. To find out, marketers often use the "top-box" measurement tool of purchase intent. A survey using top-box presents a given product that respondents will rate on a scale typically ranging from "definitely will buy" to "definitely will not buy." A clear response would seem to provide the information a manager would need.

Even though the response from the survey participant is clear, the answer for the company is not. One potential line extension may rate higher in a top-box scenario, but the top-box comparison offers no indication of whether the higher-rated option will steal share from competitors or pull from other products in the line. Top-box is also known for producing inflated results. Again, this is because it measures desire, not actual choice. It often fails to make distinctions within a broad spectrum of desire, and, as shown in Figure 1, is less able to produce results that clearly demonstrate perceived differences among various product concepts.

Marketers would benefit from using alternative methods, such as conjoint analyses and discrete choice, that measure choice, not simply model it. Researchers should create equivalent test groups from the sample, establishing a control group using a full set of relevant competing products, including those they currently offer, and systematically introduce the test product altering a single different variable for each other test group. This is essentially an application of the scientific method. This approach allows experimenters to manipulate any variable within the test sample or element within the marketing mix. Experimenters can even compare different strategies, such as a product adaptation versus a line extension.

For the marketer who is concerned with growing business and acquiring relevant information on product interaction and line share, rethinking the tools used to gather this data is a worthwhile exercise.

Questions

1. Do you think top-box measurement would be more accurate if only one option were presented rather than multiple options? Why or why not?

2. Do you think any marketing research method can accurately predict action rather than simply assess desire?

Figure 1

Sensitivity: Top Box v. Choice Experiment

% Top Box
n = 250 per concept

Controlled Experiment
Strategy Share
n = 250 per concept

Concept A — 19.8 | 7.8
Concept B — 19.0 | 3.1
Concept C — 20.0 | 4.8

No significant differentiation among concepts | Highly significant differentiation among concepts

Experimental Design, Treatment, and Effects

experimental design
Test in which the researcher has control over and manipulates one or more independent variables.

In an **experimental design**, the researcher has control over and manipulates one or more independent variables. In the experiments we discuss, typically only one independent variable is manipulated. Nonexperimental designs, which involve no manipulation, are often referred to as ex post facto (after the fact) research—an effect is observed, and then some attempt is made to attribute this effect to some causal factor.

An experimental design includes four factors:

1. The *treatment,* or experimental, *variable* (independent variable) that is manipulated
2. The *subjects* who participate in the experiment
3. A *dependent variable* that is measured
4. Some *plan or procedure* for dealing with extraneous causal factors

treatment variable
Independent variable that is manipulated in an experiment.

The **treatment variable** is the independent variable that is manipulated. *Manipulation* refers to a process in which the researcher sets the levels of the independent variable to test a particular causal relationship. To test the relationship between price (independent variable) and sales of a product (dependent variable), a researcher might expose subjects to three different levels of price and record the level of purchases at each price level. As the variable that is manipulated, price is the single treatment variable, with three treatment conditions or levels.

An experiment may include a test, or treatment, group, and a control group. A *control group* is a group in which the independent variable is not changed during the course of the experiment. A *test group* is a group that is exposed to manipulation (change) of the independent variable.

experimental effect
Effect of the treatment variable on the dependent variable.

The term **experimental effect** refers to the effect of the treatment variable on the dependent variable. The goal is to determine the effect of each treatment condition (level of treatment variable) on the dependent variable. For example, suppose that three different markets are selected to test three different prices, or treatment conditions. Each price is tested in each market for 3 months. In Market 1, a price 2 percent lower than existing prices for the product is tested; in Market 2, a price 4 percent lower is tested; and in Market 3, a price 6 percent lower is tested. At the end of the 3-month test, sales in Market 1 are observed to have increased by less than 1 percent over sales for the preceding 3-month period. In Market 2, sales increased by 3 percent; and in Market 3, sales increased by 5 percent. The change in sales observed in each market is the experimental effect.

Limitations of Experimental Research

As the preceding discussion shows, experiments are an extremely powerful form of research—the only type of research that can truly explore the existence and nature of causal relationships between variables of interest. Given these obvious advantages over other research designs for primary data collection, you might ask why experimental research is not used more often. There are many reasons, including the cost of experiments, the issue of security, and problems associated with implementing experiments.

High Cost of Experiments

To some degree, when making comparisons of the costs of experiments with the costs of surveys or observation-based research, we are comparing apples to oranges. Experiments can be very costly in both money and time. In many cases, managers may anticipate that the costs of doing an experiment would exceed the value of the information gained. Consider, for example, the costs of testing three alternative advertising campaigns in three different geographic areas. Three different campaigns must be produced; airtime must be purchased in all three markets; the timing in all three markets must be carefully coordinated; some system must be put into place to measure sales before, during, and after the test campaigns have run; measurements of other extraneous variables must be made; extensive analysis of the results must be performed; and a variety of other tasks must be completed in order to execute the experiment. All of this will cost a bare minimum of $1 million for a low-profile product and as much as tens of millions for a high-profile brand.

Security Issues

Conducting a field experiment in a test market involves exposing a marketing plan or some key element of a marketing plan in the actual marketplace. Undoubtedly, competitors will find out what is being considered well in advance of full-scale market introduction. This advance notice gives competitors an opportunity to decide whether and how to respond. In any case, the element of surprise is lost. In some instances, competitors have actually "stolen" concepts that were being tested in the marketplace and gone into national distribution before the company testing the product or strategy element completed the test marketing.

Implementation Problems

Problems that may hamper the implementation of an experiment include difficulty gaining cooperation within the organization, contamination problems, differences between test markets and the total population, and the lack of an appropriate group of people or geographic area for a control group.

It can be extremely difficult to obtain cooperation within the organization to execute certain types of experiments. For example, a regional marketing manager might be very reluctant to permit her market area to be used as a test market for a reduced level of advertising or a higher price. Quite naturally, her concern would be that the experiment might lower sales for the area.

Contamination occurs when buyers from outside the test area come into the area to purchase the product being tested, thereby distorting the results of the experiment. Outside buyers might live on the fringes of the test market area and receive TV advertisements—intended only for those in the test area—that offer a lower price, a special rebate, or some other incentive to buy a product. Their purchases will indicate that the particular sales-stimulating factor being tested is more effective than actually is the case.

In some cases, test markets may be so different, and the behavior of consumers in those markets so different, that a relatively small experimental effect is difficult to detect. This problem can be dealt with by careful matching of test markets and other similar strategies designed to ensure a high degree of equivalency of test units.

Finally, in some situations, no appropriate geographic area or group of people may be available to serve as a control group. This may be the case in a test of industrial products, whose very small number of purchasers are concentrated geographically. An attempt to test a new product among a subset of such purchasers would almost certainly be doomed to failure.

> **contamination**
> Inclusion in a test of a group of respondents who are not normally there; for example, buyers from outside the test market who see an advertisement intended only for those in the test area and enter the area to purchase the product being tested.

Selected Experimental Designs

This section presents examples of pre-experimental, true experimental, and quasi-experimental designs.[11] In outlining these experimental designs, we will use the system of notation introduced earlier.

Pre-Experimental Designs

Pre-experimental designs are research designs that do not include basic elements required in a true experimental design. Because of their simplicity, they may make sense in certain situations, but they may be difficult to interpret. Studies using **pre-experimental designs** generally are difficult to interpret because such designs offer little or no control over the influence of extraneous factors. As a result, these studies often are not much better than descriptive studies when it comes to making causal inferences. With these designs, the researcher has little control over aspects of exposure to the treatment variable (such as to whom and when) and measurements. However, these designs frequently are used in commercial test marketing because they are simple and inexpensive. They are useful for suggesting new hypotheses but do not offer strong tests of existing hypotheses. The reasons for this will be clear after you review the discussion of pre-experimental designs that follows.

> **pre-experimental designs**
> Designs that offer little or no control over extraneous factors.

One-Shot Case Study Design The **one-shot case study design** involves exposing test units (people or test markets) to the treatment variable for some period of time and then taking a measurement of the dependent variable. Using standard notation, the design is shown as follows:

$$X\ O_1$$

> **one-shot case study design**
> Pre-experimental design with no pretest observations, no control group, and an after measurement only.

There are two basic weaknesses in this design. No pretest observations are made of the test units that will receive the treatment, and no control group of test units that did not receive the treatment is observed. As a result of these deficiencies, the design does not deal with the effects of any of the extraneous variables discussed previously. Therefore, the design lacks internal validity and, most likely, external validity as well. This design is useful for suggesting causal hypotheses but does not provide a strong test of such hypotheses. Many test markets for new products (not previously on the market) are based on this design because it is simpler and less costly.

One-Group Pretest–Posttest Design The **one-group pretest–posttest design** is the design employed most frequently for testing changes in established products or marketing strategies. The fact that the product was on the market before the change provides the basis for the pretest measurement (O_1). The design is shown symbolically as follows:

> **one-group pretest–posttest design**
> Pre-experimental design with pre- and postmeasurements but no control group.

$$O_1\ X\ O_2$$

Pretest observations are made of a single group of subjects or a single test unit (O_1) that then receives the treatment. Finally, a posttest observation is made (O_2). The treatment effect is estimated by $O_2 - O_1$.

History is a threat to the internal validity of this design because an observed change in the dependent variable might be caused by an event that took place outside the experiment between the pretest and posttest measurements. In laboratory experiments, this threat can be controlled by insulating respondents from outside influences. Unfortunately, this type of control is impossible in field experiments.

Maturation is another threat to this type of design. An observed effect might be caused by the fact that subjects have grown older, smarter, more experienced, or the like between the pretest and the posttest.

This design has only one pretest observation. As a result, the researcher knows nothing of the pretest trend in the dependent variable. The posttest score may be higher because of an increasing trend of the dependent variable in a situation where this effect is not the treatment of interest.

Bias can creep into any design as discussed next in the Global Research box.

GLOBAL RESEARCH

What Happens When Your Selection Bias Is the Interviewer's Gender?

In creating an experimental design to test variables in a market research strategy, selection bias usually means a threat to validity because the test group is too different from the desired target population the researcher wants to probe. But what if the selection bias starts with the market researcher's gender? What impact might that have on the experimental validity? Recently, German researchers found that surveys sent by women or with women's names get better responses than men's.

Stefan Althoff is a marketing researcher manager for Lufthansa Technik in Hamburg, Germany. In 2004, his department started an online customer survey. They received a very low response. A week later they sent out reminders, but the writer signing the letter was named Julia. The response rate jumped to 30 percent. For many of the subsequent online surveys, Lufthansa Technik had women sign their e-mail surveys and reminders, and anecdotally the researchers had the impression respondents read and completed the surveys faster than before when men had signed them. They called this the Anita Effect—the impact of a sender's gender on response.

In January 2006, Althoff and colleagues ran an in-house employee survey at Lufthansa Technik regarding intranet usage. Their sample was two groups of 105 men each in which one group got a mailed invitation to participate from a female, one from men. The response rate for the 210 men was 80 percent, but for the men receiving invitations from the female sender, it was 83.9 percent and from men, it was only 74.3 percent.

In March 2006, Althoff and his associates tested the Anita Effect again, this time with a survey of registered users of UNIpark and associated with the academic market. Althoff split 460 users into four groups and asked them to evaluate UNIpark's Web site homepage and the utility of Globalpark's online survey software. Althoff and crew (which included a woman researcher) varied the gender of the e-mail invitations, but the results were significant: "The response rate was higher from the group that received an invitation mailed from a female sender," Althoff commented.[12]

Questions

1. What types of possible (even if subtle) bias might result from male respondents answering an e-mail survey sent or signed by a female?

2. Althoff planned to test the impact of different women's names on response rate. Consider which three female names might be the most attractive and least attractive to male respondents.

True Experimental Designs

In a **true experimental design**, the experimenter randomly assigns treatments to randomly selected test units. In our notation system, the random assignment of test units to treatments is denoted by (R). Randomization is an important mechanism that makes the results of true experimental designs more valid than the results of pre-experimental designs. True experimental designs are superior because randomization takes care of many extraneous variables. The principal reason for choosing randomized experiments over other types of research designs is that they clarify causal inference.[13] Two true experimental designs are discussed in this section: before and after with control group design and after-only with control group design.

> **true experimental design** Research using an experimental group and a control group, to which test units are randomly assigned.

Before and After with Control Group Design The **before and after with control group design** can be presented symbolically as follows:

Experimental Group:	(R)	O_1	X	O_2
Control Group:	(R)	O_3		O_4

Because the test units in this design are randomly assigned to the experimental and control groups, the two groups can be considered equivalent. Therefore, they are likely to be subject to the same extraneous causal factors, except for the treatment of interest in the experimental group. For this reason, the difference between the pre- and postmeasurements of the control group $(O_4 - O_3)$ should provide a good estimate of the effect of all the extraneous influences experienced by each group. The true impact of the treatment variable X can be known only when the extraneous influences are removed from the difference between the pre- and postmeasurements of the experimental group. Thus, the true impact of X is estimated by $(O_2 - O_1) - (O_4 - O_3)$. This design generally controls for all but two major threats to validity: mortality and history.

Mortality is a problem if units drop out during the study and these units differ systematically from the ones that remain. This results in a selection bias because the experimental and control groups are composed of different subjects at the posttest than at the pretest. History will be a problem in those situations where factors other than the treatment variable affect the experimental group but not the control group, or vice versa. Examples of this design and the after-only with control group design are provided in Exhibit 9.1.

After-Only with Control Group Design The **after-only with control group design** differs from the static-group comparison design (the pre-experimental design with nonequivalent groups) in regard to the assignment of the test units. In the

---

EXHIBIT 9.1 | **Examples of True Experimental Designs**

Situation: California Tan wants to measure the sales effect of a point-of-purchase display. The firm is considering two true experimental designs.

After-Only with Control Group Design	Before and After with Control Group Design

After-Only with Control Group Design

Basic design:

Experimental Group:	(R)	X	O_1
Control Group:	(R)		O_2

Sample: Random sample of stores that sell their products. Stores are randomly assigned to test and control groups. Groups can be considered equivalent.
Treatment (X): Placing the point-of-purchase display in stores in the experimental group for 1 month.
Measurements (O_1, O_2): Actual sales of company's brand during the period that the point-of-purchase displays are in test stores.
Comments:
Because of random assignment of stores to groups, the test group and control group can be considered equivalent. Measure of the treatment effect of X is $O_1 - O_2$. If $O_1 = 125,000$ units and $O_2 = 113,000$ units, then treatment effect = 12,000 units.

Before and After with Control Group Design

Basic design:

Experimental Group:	(R)	O_1	X	O_2
Control Group:	(R)	O_3		O_4

Sample: Same as after-only design.
Treatment (X): Same as after-only design.
Measurements (O_1 to O_4):
O_1 and O_2 are pre- and postmeasurements for the experimental group;
O_3 and O_4 are the same for the control group.
Results:
$O_1 = 113,000$ units
$O_2 = 125,000$ units
$O_3 = 111,000$ units
$O_4 = 118,000$ units
Comments:
Random assignment to groups means that the groups can be considered equivalent.
Because groups are equivalent, it is reasonable to assume that they will be equally affected by the same extraneous factors.
The difference between pre- and postmeasurements for the control group $(O_4 - O_3)$ provides a good estimate of the effects of all extraneous factors on both groups. Based on these results, $O_4 - O_3 = 7,000$ units. The estimated treatment effect is $(O_2 - O_1) - (O_4 - O_3) = (125,000 - 113,000) - (118,000 - 111,000) = 5,000$ units.

static-group comparison design, test units are not randomly assigned to treatment groups. As a result, it is possible for the groups to differ in regard to the dependent variable before presentation of the treatment. The after-only with control group design deals with this shortcoming; it can be shown symbolically as follows:

Experimental Group: (R) X O_1

Control Group: (R) O_2

Notice that the test units are randomly (R) assigned to experimental and control groups. This random assignment should produce experimental and control groups that are approximately equal in regard to the dependent variable before presentation of the treatment to the experimental group. It can reasonably be assumed that test unit mortality (one of the threats to internal validity) will affect each group in the same way.

Considering this design in the context of the sun tan lotion example described in Exhibit 9.1, we can see a number of problems. Events other than the treatment variable may have occurred during the experimental period in one or a few stores in the experimental group. If a particular store in the experimental group ran a sale on certain other products and, as a result, had a larger than average number of customers in the store, sun tan lotion sales might have increased because of the heavier traffic. Events such as these, which are store-specific (history), may distort the overall treatment effect. Also, there is a possibility that a few stores may drop out during the experiment (mortality threat), resulting in selection bias because the stores in the experimental group will be different at the posttest.

Quasi-Experiments

When designing a true experiment, the researcher often must create artificial environments to control independent and extraneous variables. Because of this artificiality, questions are raised about the external validity of the experimental findings. Quasi-experimental designs have been developed to deal with this problem. They generally are more feasible in field settings than are true experiments.

In **quasi-experiments**, the researcher lacks complete control over the scheduling of treatments or must assign respondents to treatments in a *nonrandom* fashion. These designs frequently are used in marketing research studies because cost and field constraints often do not permit the researcher to exert direct control over the scheduling of treatments and the randomization of respondents. Examples of quasi-experiments are interrupted time-series designs and multiple time-series designs.

> **quasi-experiments**
> Studies in which the researcher lacks complete control over the scheduling of treatments or must assign respondents to treatments in a nonrandom manner.

Interrupted Time-Series Designs **Interrupted time-series designs** involve repeated measurement of an effect both before and after a treatment is introduced that "interrupts" previous data patterns. Interrupted time-series experimental designs can be shown symbolically as follows:

$$O_1 \quad O_2 \quad O_3 \quad O_4 \quad X \quad O_5 \quad O_6 \quad O_7 \quad O_8$$

> **interrupted time-series design**
> Research in which repeated measurement of an effect "interrupts" previous data patterns.

A common example of this type of design in marketing research involves the use of consumer purchase panels. A researcher might use such a panel to make periodic measurements of consumer purchase activity (the O's), introducing a new promotional campaign (the X) and examining the panel data for an effect. The researcher has control over the timing of the promotional campaign but cannot be sure when the panel members were exposed to the campaign or whether they were exposed at all.

This design is very similar to the one-group pretest–posttest design

$$O_1 \quad X \quad O_2$$

However, time-series experimental designs have greater interpretability than the one-group pretest–posttest design because the many measurements allow more understanding of extraneous variables. If, for example, sales of a product were on the rise and a new promotional campaign were introduced, the true effect of this campaign could not be estimated if a pretest–posttest design were used. However, the rising trend in sales would be obvious if a number of pretest and posttest observations had been made. Time-series designs help determine the underlying trend of the dependent variable and provide better interpretability in regard to the treatment effect.

The interrupted time-series design has two fundamental weaknesses. The primary weakness is the experimenter's inability to control history. Although maintaining a careful log of all possibly relevant external happenings can reduce this problem, the researcher has no way of determining the appropriate number and timing of pretest and posttest observations.

The other weakness of this design comes from the possibility of interactive effects of testing and evaluation apprehension resulting from the repeated measurements taken on test units. For example, panel members may become "expert" shoppers or simply become more conscious of their shopping habits. Under these circumstances, it may be inappropriate to make generalizations to other populations.

Multiple Time-Series Designs   If a control group can be added to an interrupted time-series design, then researchers can be more certain in their interpretation of the treatment effect. This design, called the **multiple time-series design**, can be shown symbolically as follows:

> ➤ **multiple time-series design**
> Interrupted time-series design with a control group.

Experimental Group: O_1 O_2 O_3 O_4 O_5 O_6

Control Group: O_1 O_2 O_3 O_4 O_5 O_6

The researcher must take care in selecting the control group. For example, if an advertiser were testing a new advertising campaign in a test city, that city would constitute the experimental group and another city that was not exposed to the new campaign would be chosen as the control group. It is important that the test and control cities be roughly equivalent in regard to characteristics related to the sale of the product (e.g., competitive brands available).

Test Markets

The development of products and services goes through a sequence of rather predictable steps, beginning with idea generation, screening of ideas, concept testing, business analysis, prototype development, test marketing, and commercialization. Probably the least predictable of the development steps is test marketing. Marketers may or may not rest market a product or service depending on its expected rate of diffusion, the degree to which it is different from existing competitive offerings, and a host of other factors. It is a crucial step since it represents the last step before the company's offering is commercialized.

Test marketing is a common form of experimentation used by marketing researchers. The term **test market** is used rather loosely to refer to any research that involves testing a new product or change in an existing marketing strategy (e.g., product, price, place promotion) in a single market, group of markets, or region of the country through the use of experimental or quasi-experimental designs.[14]

> ➤ **test market**
> Real-world testing of a new product or some element of the marketing mix using an experimental or quasi-experimental design.

New product introductions play a key role in a firm's financial success or failure. The conventional wisdom in the corporate world is that new products will have to be more profitable in the future than they were in the past because of higher levels of competition and a faster pace of change. Estimates of new-product failure rates vary all over the place and range to more than 90 percent.

As you probably already recognize, test market studies have the goal of helping marketing managers make better decisions about new products and additions or changes to existing products or marketing strategies. A test market study does this by providing a real-world test for evaluating products and marketing programs. Marketing managers use test markets to evaluate proposed national programs with many separate elements on a smaller, less costly scale. The basic idea is to determine whether the estimated profits from rolling the product out on a national basis justify the potential risks. Test market studies are designed to provide information in regard to the following issues:

- Estimates of market share and volume.
- The effects that the new product will have on sales of similar products (if any) already marketed by the company. This is referred to as the *cannibalization rate*.
- Characteristics of consumers who buy the product. Demographic data will almost surely be collected, and lifestyle, psychographic, and other types of classification data may also be collected. This information is useful in helping the firm refine the marketing strategy for the product. For example, knowing the demographic characteristics of likely purchasers will help in developing a media plan that will effectively and efficiently reach target customers. Knowing the psychographic and lifestyle characteristics of target customers will provide valuable insights into how to position the product and the types of promotional messages that will appeal to them.
- The behavior of competitors during the test. This may provide some indication of what competitors will do if the product is introduced nationally.

Types of Test Markets

The vast majority of test markets can be categorized into four types—traditional, scanner or electronic, controlled, and simulated.[15] The *traditional or standard test market* involves testing the product and other elements of the marketing mix through a firm's regular channels of distribution. Traditional test markets take a relatively long time (6 months or more), are costly, and immediately tip one's hand to the competition. Some have argued that the traditional test market provides the best read on how a product and the associated marketing mix will actually do if introduced because it provides the best analog of the real marketplace. However, some of the other options, discussed in this section, may provide very good estimates at a fraction of the cost, more quickly and without giving the competition advance warning regarding what a company is planning to do.

Scanner or electronic test markets are markets where scanner panel research firms have panels of consumers who carry scannable cards for use in buying particular products, especially those sold through grocery stores. These panels permit us to analyze the characteristics of those consumers who buy and those who don't buy the test products. Purchase/nonpurchase by individual panel participants can be related to their detailed demographic data, past purchase history, and, in some cases, media viewing habits. Firms offering scanner panels include ACNielsen and Information Resources. This approach offers speed, lower cost, and some degree of security regarding the marketing strategy or changes in strategy we are considering. The major criticism of this approach to test marketing relates to what some argue is its unrepresentative sampling: Those who agree to participate in these panels may not be representative of the broader populations of consumers in these and other markets.

Lifestyle data are often collected to find out about the characteristics of possible consumers. This information helps a firm refine the marketing strategy for its product. What might lifestyle data reveal about consumers who would purchase this iPhone?

Controlled test markets are managed by research suppliers who ensure that the product is distributed through the agreed upon types and numbers of distributors. Research suppliers who offer controlled test markets, such as ACNielsen, pay distributors to provide the required amount of shelf space for test products. Research suppliers carefully monitor sales of the product in these controlled test markets. They enable companies to get their products into test markets more quickly, often supply more realistic levels of distribution, and provide better monitoring of product movement. Some test markets are more popular than others, as discussed in the following Global Research box.

GLOBAL RESEARCH

What Makes a Good Test Market? How about Calgary?

Every so many years a demographer or other research group will publish a list of "best test markets" for a given area, usually a country like the United States or Canada. Typically, these studies look at cities whose demographic characteristics most closely approximate those of the country in question. This type of broad classification of test market cities can sometimes be misleading. The real key to the selection of a good test market city is to find one whose purchase behavior most closely approximates the purchase behavior and demographics for the category of product or service in question for a given geographic area. In the following example, I doubt that Calgary would rate as the "all-Canadian city," but for the product in question, because its demographic characteristics are linked to the product in question, it was selected as a test market.

If you're trying to reach smart, affluent, 30-something females comfortable with and even adept in new technologies, Calgary in Alberta, Canada, is your place. Calgary is growing, in terms of both population and business. According to the 2009 Canadian population estimates, Calgary's population was 1,230,248, up 14 percent since the 2006 census and outpacing all population growth throughout Canada.[16] Who's there?

The average person living in Calgary is age 35, and there are slightly more women than men, especially in the 35- to 49-year-old bracket, a hotly pursued age group. They're highly educated (73 percent attended college), have one of

Canada's highest per-capita incomes ($40,021), and their income is growing 4.5 percent yearly. They have surplus money, and they dare to try new things, especially high-tech products. People in Calgary, the demographics reveal, are a tech-savvy population, technically adept and comfortable with new technologies. Even better, Calgary is geographically isolated from other major cities, making it desirable for uncontaminated consumer testing.[17]

Because of these favorable demographic trends, at least five major companies have test-marketed products in Calgary in recent years. In May 2005, Labatt selected Calgary and Edmonton as test markets for its new Brazilian Brahma beer. In June that year, Podere Castorani, a winery in Italy, targeted Calgary for its all-Canadian product launch. Shell Canada debuted its Easy Pay tag (an electronic swipe payment method) in 1999, premiering it in Calgary. A few years before that, Shoppers Drug Mart tried out its loyalty program there and in January 2005, Canada Post tested its Fetch, a personalized technology similar to Blackberry that lets people access cell phone and e-mail information in private.

Questions

1. Determine three new consumer products developed in the United States, such as prepared foods, that would not be suitable to try in Calgary.

2. Develop a demographics and psychological profile for the typical person, age 35, who is a member of this new "hotly pursued age group."

STMs (simulated test markets) are just what the name implies—simulations of the types of test markets noted above. They can normally be conducted more quickly than the other two approaches, at a lower cost, and produce results that are, in most cases, highly predictive of what will actually happen. In these simulated test markets, a more limited amount of information is used in conjunction with mathematical models that include estimates of the effects of different marketing variables that can be adjusted to fit the situation. A number of different companies, including ACNielsen (Bases), Harris Interactive (Litmus), and Synovate (MarkeTest), offer these services and each one has special features. However, they all share the following elements:

- A sample of consumers is selected based on the expected or known characteristics of the target consumer for the test product.
- Consumers sampled are recruited to come to a central location testing facility to view commercials for the test product and competitive products.
- Consumers are then given the opportunity to purchase the test product in the actual marketplace or in a simulated store environment.
- Purchasers are contacted after they have had time to use the product. They are asked how likely they are to repurchase and for their evaluations of the product.
- The above information is used with the proprietary model of the STM company to generate estimates of sales volume, market share, and other key market metrics.[18]

Costs of Test Marketing

Test marketing is expensive. A simple two-market test can cost a bare minimum of $1 million and probably much more. A long-running, more complex test can cost in the tens of millions of dollars. These estimates refer only to direct costs, which may include the following:

- Production of commercials
- Payments to an advertising agency for services
- Media time, charged at a higher rate because of low volume
- Syndicated research information
- Customized research information and associated data analysis
- Point-of-purchase materials
- Coupons and sampling
- Higher trade allowances to obtain distribution[19]

Many *indirect costs* are also associated with test marketing, including the following:

- Cost of management time spent on the test market
- Diversion of sales activity from existing products
- Possible negative impact of a test market failure on other products with the same family brand
- Possible negative trade reactions to products if the firm develops a reputation for not doing well
- Cost of letting competitors know what the firm is doing, thereby allowing them to develop a better strategy or beat the firm to the national market[20]

Test markets are expensive, and, as a result, they should be used only as the last step in a research process that has shown the new product or strategy has potential. In some situations, it may be cheaper to go ahead and launch the product, even if it fails.

Decision to Conduct Test Marketing

From the preceding discussion, you can see that test markets offer at least two important benefits to the firm conducting the test.[21]

■ First and foremost, the test market provides a vehicle by which the firm can obtain a good estimate of a product's sales potential under realistic market conditions. A researcher can develop estimates of the product's national market share on the basis of these test results and use this figure to develop estimates of future financial performance for the product.

■ Second, the test should identify weaknesses of the product and the proposed marketing strategy for the product and give management an opportunity to correct any weaknesses. It is much easier and less expensive to correct these problems at the test market stage than after the product has gone into national distribution.

These benefits must be weighed against a number of costs and other negatives associated with test markets.[22] The financial costs of test markets are not insignificant. And test markets give competitors an early indication of what the firm is planning to do. They thus share the opportunity to make adjustments in their marketing strategy; or, if the idea is simple and not legally protected, they may be able to copy the idea and move into national distribution faster than the original firm can.

Four major factors should be taken into account in determining whether to conduct a test market:

1. Weigh the cost and risk of failure against the probability of success and associated profits. If estimated costs are high and you are uncertain about the likelihood of success, then you should lean toward doing a test market. On the other hand, if both expected costs and the risk of product failure are low, then an immediate national rollout without a test market may be the appropriate strategy.

2. Consider the likelihood and speed with which competitors can copy your product and introduce it on a national basis. If the product can be easily copied, then it may be appropriate to introduce the product without a test market.

3. Consider the investment required to produce the product for the test market versus the investment required to produce the product in the quantities necessary for a national rollout. In cases where the difference in investment required is very small, it may make sense to introduce the product nationally without a test market. However, in cases where a very large difference exists between the investment required to produce the product for test market and that required for a national rollout, conducting a test market before making a decision to introduce the product nationally makes good sense.

4. Consider how much damage an unsuccessful new product launch would inflict on the firm's reputation. Failure may hurt the firm's reputation with other members of the channel of distribution (retailers) and impede the firm's ability to gain their cooperation in future product launches.

Steps in a Test Market Study

Once the decision has been made to conduct test marketing, a number of steps must be carried out if we are to achieve a satisfactory result.

Step One: Define the Objective
As always with these kinds of lists, the first step in the process is to define the objectives of the test. Typical test market objectives include the following:

- Develop share and volume estimates.
- Determine the characteristics of people who are purchasing the product.
- Determine the frequency and purpose of purchase.
- Determine where (retail outlets) purchases are made.
- Measure the effect of sales of the new product on sales of similar existing products in the line.

Step Two: Select a Basic Approach After specifying the objectives of the test market exercise, the next step is to decide on the appropriate type of test market, given the stated objectives.

Earlier in the chapter, we discussed the characteristics, advantages, and disadvantages of four types of test markets:

- Traditional or standard test market
- Scanner or electronic test market
- Controlled test market
- Simulated test market (STM) (See Global Research on page 268 for more discussion of STMs.)

The decision regarding which type of test market to use in a given situation depends on how much time you have, how much budget you have, and how important it is to keep the competition in the dark about what you are planning to do.

Step Three: Develop Detailed Test Procedures After the objectives and a basic approach for the test have been developed, the researcher must develop a detailed plan for conducting the test. Manufacturing and distribution decisions must be made to ensure that adequate product is available and that it is available in most stores of the type that sell that particular product class. In addition, the detailed marketing plan to be used for the test must be specified. The basic positioning approach must be selected, the actual commercials must be developed, a pricing strategy must be chosen, a media plan must be developed, and various promotional activities must be specified.

 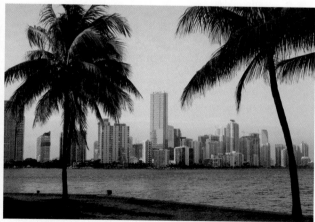

Selecting markets for a test is an important decision. Significant regional differences should be considered in choosing cities as test markets. To find some readily apparent regional differences between Seattle and Miami, visit *www.ci.seattle.wa.us* and *www.miami.com*.

GLOBAL RESEARCH

Best Global Test Markets? Danes Are Quick, Koreans Love Tech

If you want to reach the world's most innovative customers, try Denmark for your next test market in global marketing, says the Danish weekly, *Mandag Morgen*.

The claim is supported by the findings of a major market research initiative of European markets conducted by American and European universities, whose numbers included Professor Gerard Tellis, a prominent market researcher at the University of Southern California. Danish consumers are quicker to adopt new products than all other Europeans and even Americans or Chinese, the study found. The Danes are also more open to new ideas, an essential foundation for trying new products.

It takes only 3.3 years from product launch to widespread sales and market entrenchment in Denmark, compared to Germany, France, or England, where it might take two to three times longer, or up to 9.3 years in Portugal, the study said. Companies that release new products in Denmark's climate of quick uptake have the advantage of being able to improve or adjust them faster based on results there before committing themselves to an expensive multination product rollout.[23]

If it's brand-new wireless, Internet services and applications, or equipment and services pertaining to the telecom infrastructure, South Korea, the most wired nation in Asia and the hotbed for digital or online innovations, is *the* test market for high tech, says *BusinessWeek*. Two-thirds of the population's 16 million households have broadband Internet service, and 68 percent already have advanced cell phones capable of high-speed data transmission. Korea offers global test marketers a "rapid uptake" of the newest types of wireless and Internet products and a "mass" of consumers already versed in this technology and in formats that are not even that familiar to high-tech Americans. As with Denmark, uptake and consumer response for new tech products promise to be delivered fast in digitized South Korea.[24]

Denmark may be an all-purpose test marketing bellwether and South Korea may be the tech marketer's paradise, but you'll still need to tailor your approach to local customs, language, habits of perception, and cultural preferences for success. Mary Beth Lake, chief of global product design and development for Synovate of Chicago, a major marketing research firm, stresses that companies engaged in global marketing need to "localize their product offerings in ways that are culturally acceptable." She has three recommendations in this regard.

First, study and master the particularities of the country's language usage. She calls this *vocabulary elicitation* and advises market researchers to compile a dictionary on how consumers in the target country use and define products. What is "creaminess in the mouth" for a North American to describe a beverage's taste impact is "milk feel" to the Japanese. The North American term does not compute in Japanese food experience, just as "milk feel" may leave us speechless.

Second, perform a one-on-one analysis at the level of individual consumers. Study the reaction of the potential customers to the product in conditions approximating how it will be when they actually use it on their own, says Lake. Take software marketed for children or elementary school use. Testing here involves interviewing the students, observing them on closed-circuit television, and evaluating their experience as they follow directions for using the software in a real classroom.

Third, Lake adds, don't overlook traditional qualitative analysis. Interview groups of potential consumers to find out how they perceive and describe the products; look into whether your proposed imagery and message style will work in that specific cultural context, and if not, find ways to adjust it to fit the cognitive framework. Modify the packaging if necessary to reinforce the adjusted message. Follow these three steps, says Lake, to fine-tune your culture-specific test marketing.[25]

Questions

1. Identify and discuss other examples of culture-specific references that are taken for granted in the United States but that would seem strange or incomprehensible in other countries.

2. Identify three cutting-edge high-tech products (e.g., in the category of new products like iPhone, Kindle, or flat-screen televisions) and devise a test market approach for Danish customers.

Step Four: Select Test Markets   The selection of markets for the test is an important decision. A number of factors must be taken into account in making this decision. First, there are the overall standards[26]:

■ There should be a minimum of two test markets, in addition to a control market, for an existing national brand or a minimum of three markets for testing a new brand.

■ The markets selected should be geographically dispersed; if the brand is a regional brand, the markets should cover several dispersed markets within that region.

■ Markets should be demographically representative of the United States, unless, for instance, a pronounced ethnic skew is desirable for a specific brand.

■ Depending on the product purchase cycle, the test should be run for at least 6 months, up to 12 months, before the results can be considered reliably projectable. If the product is purchased infrequently, it is advisable to run the test for even longer than a year.

■ The market must have a variety of media outlets, including at least four television stations, cable penetration no more than 10 percent above or below the U.S. average, at least four radio stations, a dominant local newspaper with daily and Sunday editions, a Sunday supplement with a syndicated edition, or a local supplement of similar quality.

■ There should be a dominant newspaper in the market or a dominant newspaper in each city the market encompasses.

■ The market should be as reflective as possible of the U.S. population or regional population if that is more appropriate for the particular test.

See the Global Marketing Research on page 264 for discussion of what makes a good global test market.

Step Five: Execute the Plan   Once the plan is in place, the researcher can begin execution. At this point, a key decision has to be made: how long should the test run? The average test runs for 6 to 12 months. However, shorter and longer tests are not uncommon. The test must run long enough for an adequate number of repeat purchase cycles to be observed in order to provide a measure of the "staying power" of a new product or marketing program. The shorter the average period is, the shorter the test needs to be. Cigarettes, soft drinks, and packaged goods are purchased every few days, whereas such products as shaving cream and toothpaste are purchased only every few months. The latter products would require a longer test. Whatever the product type, the test must be continued until the repeat purchase rate stabilizes. The percentage of people making repeat purchases tends to drop for some period of time before reaching a relatively

General Mills used the "rolling rollout" when it introduced MultiGrain Cheerios to the public. Visit *www.generalmills.com* to find out what new products the company may be introducing.

constant level. Repeat purchase rate is critical to the process of estimating ultimate sales of the product. If the test is ended too soon, sales will be overestimated.

Two other considerations in determining the length of the test relate to the expected speed of competitor reaction and the costs of running the test. If there is reason to expect that competitors will react quickly to the test marketing (introduce their own versions of the new product), then the test should be as short as possible. Minimizing the length of the test reduces the amount of time competitors have to react. Finally, the value of additional information to be gained from the test must be balanced against the cost of continuing to run the test. At some point, the value of additional information will be outweighed by its cost.

Step Six: Analyze the Test Results The data produced by an experiment should be evaluated throughout the test period. However, after completion of the experiment, a more careful and thorough evaluation of the data must be performed. This analysis will focus on four areas:

- *Purchase data.* The purchase data are often the most important data produced by an experiment. The levels of initial purchase (trial) throughout the course of the experiment provide an indication of how well the advertising and promotion program worked. The repeat rate (percentage of initial triers who made second and subsequent purchases) provides an indication of how well the product met the expectations created through advertising and promotion. Of course, the trial and repeat purchase results provide the basis for estimating sales and market share if the product was distributed nationally.

- *Awareness data.* How effective were the media expenditures and media plan in creating awareness of the product? Do consumers know how much the product costs? Do they know its key features?

PRACTICING
MARKETING RESEARCH

Quick Scans of Product-Specific Test Markets

Some locations just seem to specialize in favorable conditions for selected test market trials, such as for high-end beer, premium vodkas, or Brazilian steakhouses.

Miller Brewing Company of Milwaukee, Wisconsin, decided to test market three kinds of low-calorie, craft-style light beers in only four cities starting in 2008: Minneapolis, Minnesota; Charlotte, North Carolina; San Diego, California; and Baltimore, Maryland. Their goal was to establish a new category for light craft-style beers and to capitalize on three noticeable trends in the beer industry: the shift toward lighter beers (fewer calories and carbohydrates), more variety, and the, so-called premiumization–high-end, quality-perceived offerings. It's a solid idea because craft beer sales for 2006 were up 17.8 percent and those four cities have the right combination of demographics to warrant the test market.[27]

Fuller's, a London brewery founded in 1711, selected Denver, Colorado, as the premium United States locale to test market its high-end London Pride beer. Why Denver? The area is home to a hefty quantity of beer drinkers who prefer the high-end brews and presumably won't mind spending $8 for a London Pride six-pack. People there, research has found, are "friendly" to premium or craft-style beers. Even better, craft beer commands a 10 percent market share in Colorado, putting it third in the nation. Fuller's marketing approach included radio ads that trolled for the golf and outdoors-focused types who are more the "microbrew set," the company said.[28] Anheuser-Busch is test-running its Purus vodka, distilled in Italy and fetching $35 a bottle retail, in Boston, New York, Washington, and Annapolis. Why there? The company wants to attract the "modern luxury connoisseur" to their organic wheat-based Purus, and they want to test-position it in those cities' most exclusive lounges and restaurants as well as in a handful of specialty groceries and liquor stores. Again, there's evidence of sober thinking behind the approach: U.S. sales of upper-end or ultra-premium vodkas more than doubled between 2003 and 2006. Typical consumers? Young drinkers, aged 21 to 30, who care more about image than price.[29]

What U.S. city did International Restaurant Concepts of Lakewood, Colorado, select to test market its Tucanos Brazilian Grill steakhouse? Provo, Utah. At first glance, Provo's demographics would seem against it: of its 100,000 residents, 87 percent are white and only 10 percent Hispanic, so where's the market for Tucanos's *churrascaria*? It turns out that because Provo is the home of Brigham Young University and runs a missionary training center for the Church of the Latter-Day Saints, many of the thousands of Mormon students sent out in the field have been posted to Brazil. In addition, the university population comprises many international students—all of which generates an ethnically diverse and language-rich community and good test market.[30]

Questions

1. What characteristics do the cities of Minneapolis, Charlotte, San Diego, and Baltimore possess that make them good markets for introducing premium-level beers?

2. How would you tailor a test market experimentation for Brazilian cuisine in a Mormon-saturated region whose members, nonetheless, are well-traveled and versed in Brazilian foods?

GLOBAL RESEARCH

Using Simulated Test Markets in Global Markets

Simulated test markets (STMs) are frequently used to predict success for product introductions in global markets, but interpretation of the data from different countries is tricky and can have a big impact on the reliability of the forecasts. Normally, STM researchers figure an accuracy margin of 320 percent; an erroneous interpretation of the data could increase that figure to anywhere from 57 to 354 percent, a new study shows.

According to Jim Miller, senior vice president of ACNielsen BASES, the intelligent design of multicountry research using STMs must address three crucial considerations. First, as a market researcher, should you believe what consumers say about their future buying behavior? Yes, but not fully, says Miller. His research shows that consumers in a given country will not follow their own predicted behavior to the letter but only approximately. Thus, beware of the gap between claimed intentions and actual behaviors. See Graph 1 below.

Second, does this gap differ from country to country? Yes, Miller says, and it's a function of demographics, particularly education. He found that consumers with more education had less of a tendency to overstate their future purchasing

behaviors than did those with less education. Further complicating the picture is the fact that overstatement levels vary by country, so it is necessary to assess what overstatement level is representative of a given country before drawing any reliable marketing conclusions from STM results. Differences are illustrated in Graph 2 on the next page.

Third, given the cultural differences in overstatement tendencies, will this consideration materially affect volume forecast based on STM research? Yes. The differences are big enough "to have enormous impact on forecasting volume," explains Miller. He uses the following case study to make his point.

Miller's firm was testing receptivity to a confection concept and product for a major consumer packaged goods manufacturer and wanted to try it out in Argentina, Mexico, Canada, and the United States. Miller's company conducted a full test in each country and used this test to generate a multicountry forecast. Unadjusted consumer scores led to the conclusion that Mexicans liked the product concept the best, far more than Americans did. Yet once Miller adjusted the data to accommodate each country's "unique level of overstatement," he found that consumer interest in Mexico was about equal to that of the United States.

(continued)

Graph 1

Consumers consistently overstate their purchase behavior . . .

Visions—Global Research: Evaluating new products globally;
Using consumer research to predict success

Consumers "Claimed Intentions" vs. "Actual Behaviors"

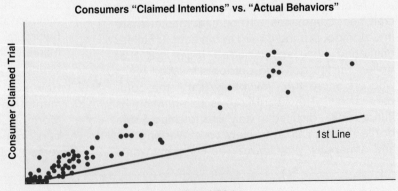

Graph 2

. . . But consumers don't all overstate to the same degree

For example, consumers with more education are less likely to overstate their purchasing behavior

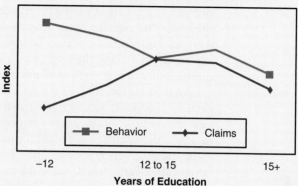

This same process of adjusting the data to remove country overstatement bias yielded another valuable set of data. When you identify and remove the different degrees of cultural overstatement, then you can see genuine differences in consumer interest in each country under study. Initially, the research showed that the level of consumer interest in the products in Argentina and Mexico, both before and after product use, was similar. After adjustment for overstatement, however, interest in Argentina was far stronger than that in Mexico.

Miller adjusted the data in the other countries so that individual country forecasts could be combined to make a four-country regional forecast. He cautions that if he had not made these adjustments for overstatement, the product sales volume estimates would have ranged, erroneously, from 57 to 354 percent. If you don't take the overstatement issue into consideration, compounded by the inherent 320 percent inaccuracy of STM data, your market estimates based on lead-country forecasts could end up being "essentially meaningless."

As for which approach—country-specific versus lead-country—is the most accurate, the country-specific may be the most accurate but it generally costs too much, whereas the lead country can produce very misleading results. The solution, Miller proposes, is to conduct the full test in the true lead country (or countries) combined with a reduced-base testing in the other targeted countries. This research design saves money and increases accuracy, and it captures important cultural differences in consumer responses, with only a small degree of forecasting variance within the accepted 320 percent range of error.[31]

- *Competitive response.* Ideally, the responses of competitors should be monitored during the period of the test market. For example, competitors may try to distort test results by offering special promotions, price deals, and quantity discounts. Their actions may provide some indication of what they will do if the product moves into national distribution and some basis for estimating the effect of these actions on their part.

- *Source of sales.* If the product is a new entry in an existing product category, it is important to determine where sales are coming from. In other words, which brands did the people who purchased the test product previously purchase? This information provides a true indication of real competitors. If the firm has an existing brand in the market, it also indicates to what extent the new product will take business from existing brands and from the competition.

Based on the evaluation, a decision will be made to improve the marketing program or the product, drop the product, or move the product into national or regional distribution.

Other Types of Product Tests

In addition to traditional test marketing and STMs, there are other means by which companies can gauge a product's potential. One alternative is a *rolling rollout*, which usually follows a pretest. A product is launched in a certain region rather than in one or two cities. Within a matter of days, scanner data can provide information on how the product is doing. The product can then be launched in additional regions; ads and promotions can be adjusted along the way to a national introduction. General Mills has used this approach for products such as MultiGrain Cheerios.

Another alternative is to try a product out in a foreign market before rolling it out globally. Specifically, one or a few countries can serve as a test market for a continent or even the world. This *lead country strategy* has been used by Colgate-Palmolive Company. In 1991, the company launched Palmolive Optims shampoo and conditioner in the Philippines, Australia, Mexico, and Hong Kong. Later, the products were rolled out in Europe, Asia, Latin America, and Africa.

Some marketers think that classic test marketing will make a comeback. It may be that, for totally new products, more thorough testing will be necessary, whereas for other types of product introductions, such as line extensions, an alternative approach is more appropriate.

SUMMARY

Experimental research provides evidence of whether a change in an independent variable causes some predictable change in a dependent variable. To show that a change in A likely caused an observed change in B, one must show three things: concomitant variation, appropriate time order of occurrence, and the elimination of other possible causal factors. Experiments can be conducted in a laboratory or a field setting. The major advantage of conducting experiments in a laboratory is that the researcher can control extraneous factors. However, in marketing research, laboratory settings often do not appropriately replicate the marketplace. Experiments conducted in the actual marketplace are called field experiments. The major difficulty with field experiments is that the researcher cannot control all the other factors that might influence the dependent variable.

In experimentation, we are concerned with internal and external validity. Internal validity refers to the extent to which competing explanations of the experimental results observed can be ruled out. External validity refers to the extent to which causal relationships measured in an experiment can be generalized to other settings. Extraneous variables are other independent variables that may affect the dependent variable and thus stand in the way of the ability to conclude that an observed change in the dependent variable was due to the effect of the experimental, or treatment, variable. Extraneous factors include history, maturation, instrument variation, selection bias, mortality, testing effects, and regression to the mean. Four basic approaches are used to control extraneous factors: randomization, physical control, design control, and statistical control.

In an experimental design, the researcher has control over and manipulates one or more independent variables. Nonexperimental designs, which involve no manipulation, are referred to as ex post facto research. An experimental design includes four elements: the treatment, subjects, a dependent variable that is measured, and a plan or procedure for dealing with extraneous causal factors. An experimental effect is the effect of the treatment variable on the dependent variable.

Experiments have an obvious advantage in that they are the only type of research that can demonstrate the existence and nature of causal relationships between variables of interest. Yet the amount of actual experimentation done in marketing research is limited because of the high cost of experiments, security issues, and implementation problems. There is evidence to suggest that the use of experiments in marketing research is growing.

Pre-experimental designs offer little or no control over the influence of extraneous factors and are thus generally difficult to interpret. Examples include the one-shot case study design and the one-group pretest–posttest design. In a true experimental design, the researcher is able to eliminate all extraneous variables as competitive hypotheses to the treatment. Examples of true experimental designs are the before and after with control group design and the after-only with control group design.

In quasi-experiments, the researcher has control over data-collection procedures but lacks complete control over the scheduling of treatments. The treatment groups in a quasi-experiment normally are formed by assigning respondents to treatments in a non-random fashion. Examples of quasi-experimental designs are the interrupted time-series design and the multiple time-series design.

Test marketing involves testing a new product or some element of the marketing mix by using experimental or quasi-experimental designs. Test markets are field experiments and they are extremely expensive to conduct. The steps in conducting a test market study include defining the objectives for the study, selecting a basic approach to be used, developing detailed procedures for the test, selecting markets for the test, executing the plan, and analyzing the test results.

KEY TERMS & DEFINITIONS

experiment Research approach in which one variable is manipulated and the effect on another variable is observed.

causal research Research designed to determine whether a change in one variable likely caused an observed change in another.

concomitant variation Statistical relationship between two variables.

appropriate time order of occurrence Change in an independent variable occurring before an observed change in the dependent variable.

elimination of other possible causal factors Hard to prove that something else did not cause change in B.

laboratory experiments Experiments conducted in a controlled setting.

field experiments Tests conducted outside the laboratory in an actual environment, such as a marketplace.

internal validity Extent to which competing explanations for the experimental results observed can be ruled out.

external validity Extent to which causal relationships measured in an experiment can be generalized to outside persons, settings, and times.

history Intervention, between the beginning and end of an experiment, of outside variables or events that might change the dependent variable.

maturation Changes in subjects occurring during the experiment that are not related to the experiment but that may affect subjects' response to the treatment factor.

instrument variation Changes in measurement instruments (e.g., interviewers or observers) that might affect measurements.

selection bias Systematic differences between the test group and the control group due to a biased selection process.

mortality Loss of test units or subjects during the course of an experiment, which may result in nonrepresentativeness.

testing effect Effect that is a by-product of the research process itself.

regression to the mean Tendency of subjects with extreme behavior to move toward the average for that behavior during the course of an experiment.

randomization Random assignment of subjects to treatment conditions to ensure equal representation of subject characteristics.

physical control Holding constant the value or level of extraneous variables throughout the course of an experiment.

design control Use of the experimental design to control extraneous causal factors.

statistical control Adjusting for the effects of confounded variables by statistically adjusting the value of the dependent variable for each treatment condition.

experimental design Test in which the researcher has control over and manipulates one or more independent variables.

treatment variable Independent variable that is manipulated in an experiment.

experimental effect Effect of the treatment variable on the dependent variable.

contamination Inclusion in a test of a group of respondents who are not normally there—for example, buyers from outside the test market who see an advertisement intended only for those in the test area and who enter the area to purchase the product being tested.

pre-experimental designs Designs that offer little or no control over extraneous factors.

one-shot case study design Pre-experimental design with no pretest observations, no control group, and an after measurement only.

one-group pretest–posttest design Pre-experimental design with pre- and postmeasurements but no control group.

true experimental design Research using an experimental group and a control group, to which test units are randomly assigned.

before and after with control group design True experimental design that involves random assignment of subjects or test units to experimental and control groups and pre- and postmeasurements of both groups.

after-only with control group design True experimental design that involves random assignment of subjects or test units to experimental and control groups, but no premeasurement of the dependent variable.

quasi-experiments Studies in which the researcher lacks complete control over the scheduling of treatments or must assign respondents to treatments in a nonrandom manner.

interrupted time-series design Research in which repeated measurements of an effect "interrupts" previous data patterns.

multiple time-series design An interrupted time-series design with a control group.

test market Testing of a new product or some element of the marketing mix using an experimental or quasi-experimental design.

QUESTIONS FOR REVIEW & CRITICAL THINKING

1. Divide the class into as many as six groups, as appropriate. Each group will have the task of recommending a test market design and addressing the associated questions for one of the following scenarios.

(Team Exercise)

- Design a test of a new pricing strategy for orange juice concentrate. The brand is an established brand, and we are only interested in testing the effect of a 5 percent price increase and a 5 percent decrease. All other elements of the marketing mix will remain the same.

- A soft-drink company has determined in taste tests that consumers prefer the taste of their diet product when sweetened with Splenda® in comparison to Equal®. Now they are interested in determining how the new sweetener will play in the marketplace. Design a test market that will achieve this goal.

- A national pizza chain wants to test the effect on sales of four different discount coupons. Design a test that will do this in a way that gives a clear read. Your focus should be on the effect on sales volume. Financial analysis after the test results are in will address the revenue and profit impact.

- A national value-priced hotel chain needs to understand the business impact of including a free buffet-style breakfast to guests. Design and justify a test that will do this.

- A credit card company needs to test its strategy for attracting college students to its card. It is going to continue using booths in student unions and other high-traffic campus locations. It has been offering free CDs from a list to those who sign up for its card, but since other card companies are using this approach, the company wants to try some alternatives. It is considering free MP3 downloads from iTunes and t-shirts featuring popular music groups. Design a test that will tell the company which option to choose if its goal is to increase signups by the largest amount.

2. Tico Taco, a national chain of Mexican fast-food restaurants, has developed the "Super Sonic Taco," which is the largest taco in the market and sells for $1.19. Tico Taco has identified its target customers for this new product as men under 30 who are not concerned about health issues, such as fat content or calories. It wants to test the product in at least four regional markets before making a decision to introduce it nationally. What criteria would you use to select test cities for this new product? Which cities would you recommend using? Why would you recommend those cities?

3. Of the primary data-collection techniques available to the researcher (survey, observation, experiment), why is the experiment the only one that can provide conclusive evidence of causal relationships? Of the various types of experiments, which type or types provide the best evidence of causation or noncausation?

4. What are some important independent variables that must be dealt with in an experiment to test consumer reactions to a pilot for a new TV series? Explain why those variables are important.

5. Managers of the student center at your university or college are considering three alternative brands of frozen pizza to be offered on the menu. They want to offer

only one of the three and want to find out which brand students prefer. Design an experiment to determine which brand of pizza the students prefer.

6. Night students at the university or college are much older than day students. Introduce an explicit control for day versus night students in the preceding experiment.

7. Why are quasi-experiments much more popular in marketing research than true experiments?

8. How does history differ from maturation? What specific actions might you take to deal with each in an experiment?

9. A manufacturer of microwave ovens has designed an improved model that will reduce energy costs and cook food evenly throughout. However, this new model will increase the product's price by 30 percent because of extra components and engineering design changes. It decides to test market the new oven in a market area with an extremely high household income level. In addition, the producer offers a discount coupon to facilitate product sales. The company wants to determine what effect the new model will have on sales of its microwave ovens. Do you see any potential problems with a sales forecast based on the results of the test market sales? What would you do differently?

10. Discuss various methods by which extraneous causal factors can be controlled.

11. Discuss the alternatives to traditional test marketing. Explain their advantages and disadvantages.

WORKING THE NET

1. Visit *www.questionpro.com/akira/showLibrary.do?categoryID=16&mode=1* to take a psychographics profile with 269 focused questions distributed into 15 categories. What kind of consumer are you? How would you design a test market to attract a customer like yourself?

2. Consult *www.city-data.com* Research city demographics for Cedar Rapids, Iowa; Eau Claire, Wisconsin; and Grand Junction, Colorado, to evaluate why *Advertising Age* (2005) ranked them among the top seven most popular test market sites in the United States for matching the average American demographic profile.

REAL-LIFE RESEARCH • 9.1

Texas Red Soft Drinks

Texas Red is the oldest soft-drink company in Texas. During the 1980s, the company went through bankruptcy because of its inability to compete with the big national soft-drink brands. In 2003, a group of investors purchased the brand name from the bankruptcy court and reincarnated it with distribution primarily through specialty grocery stores and selected theme restaurants. The company is currently available in 267 grocery stores and 123 restaurants across Texas.

The "new" Texas Red has experienced solid growth and financial performance over its almost 8-year history. However, the competitive environment remains tough with the big national brands at one end of the spectrum and other specialty soft-drink producers at the other end. It is critical that Texas Red spend its limited marketing budget in the most efficient manner to drive business to its retail and restaurant locations.

In recent months, the management team at Texas Red has been divided in regard to the best marketing strategy for the company. One contingent wants to pursue a strategy based on a low price relative to other specialty soft drinks. The other group wants to focus on enhancing awareness and image of the brand with a focus on its long history in the state of Texas and the unique aspects and high quality of its products. The difference of opinion between the two factions has become heated and somewhat divisive. Furthermore, time is running out to get their marketing strategy in place for the coming year.

Toby Newbern, director of marketing, knows that it is important to make the right decision and to break the deadlock quickly so that the company can move on with its plans and business development activities. He wants to design a test that will settle the issue once and for all in a scientific manner. Texas Star has always focused on an upscale demographic target. Toby's research plan calls for testing the price-oriented campaign in one market and the image-oriented campaign in another. The impact on sales in the respective markets will indicate the effectiveness of the two approaches. He faces a number of decisions. First, he needs to choose the markets for the test. Second, there is the question of how long to run the test. Finally, it is necessary to sort out what happens in the two test markets from the general trend for Texas Red.

Questions

1. Is the test market approach the best way to tackle this problem, all things considered? Are there other viable options and, if so, what are the options?

2. Which of the experimental designs discussed in the chapter would be most feasible for this project? Why that design?

3. How many markets should be used for the test? What should be the characteristics of these markets?

4. What sort of evidence, from the test, would definitively break the deadlock between the two groups with different visions as the company?

CHAPTER

The Concept of Measurement

LEARNING OBJECTIVES

1. To understand the concept of measurement.

2. To learn about the measurement process and how to develop a good measurement scale.

3. To understand the four levels of scales and their typical usage.

4. To explore the concepts of reliability and validity.

What is the nature of measurement? Describe the steps which are involved. Explain the three levels of measurement and their differences. What are the notions of validity and reliability? Why are they so critically important to the concept of measurement? These are the topics of chapter ten.

Measurement Process

Measurement is the process of assigning numbers or labels to persons, objects, or events in accordance with specific rules for representing quantities or qualities of attributes. Measurement, then, is a procedure used to assign numbers that reflect the amount of an attribute possessed by a person, object, or event. Note that it is not the person, object, or event that is being measured, but rather its attributes. A researcher, for example, does not measure a consumer per se but rather measures that consumer's attitudes, income, brand loyalty, age, and other relevant factors.

The concept of rules is key to measurement. A **rule** is a guide, a method, or a command that tells a researcher what to do. For example, a rule of measurement might state, "Assign the numbers 1 through 5 to people according to their disposition to do household chores. If they are extremely willing to do any and all household chores, assign them a 1. If they are not willing to do any household chores, assign them a 5." The numbers 2, 3, and 4 would be assigned based on the *degree* of their willingness to do chores, as it relates to the absolute end points of 1 and 5.

A problem often encountered with rules is a lack of clarity or specificity. Some things are easy to measure because rules are easy to create and follow. The measurement of gender, for example, is quite simple, as the researcher has concrete criteria to apply in assigning a 1 for a male and a 2 for a female. Unfortunately, many characteristics of interest to a marketing researcher—such as brand loyalty, purchase intent, and total family income—are much harder to measure because of the difficulty of devising rules to assess the true value of these consumer attributes. The steps a researcher should take to measure a phenomenon appear in Exhibit 10.1.

→ **measurement**
Process of assigning numbers or labels to persons, objects, or events in accordance with specific rules for representing quantities or qualities of attributes.

→ **rule**
Guide, method, or command that tells a researcher what to do.

Exhibit   10.1

Measurement Process

Step One: Identify the Concept of Interest

The measurement process begins with identification of the concept of interest. A *concept* is an abstract idea generalized from particular facts. It is a category of thought used to group sense data together "as if they were all the same." All perceptions regarding a stop light at the intersection of South and Main streets form a category of thought, though a relatively narrow one. Perceptions of all stoplights, regardless of location, would be a broader concept, or category of thought.

Step Two: Develop a Construct

constructs
Specific types of concepts that exist at higher levels of abstraction.

Constructs are specific types of concepts that exist at higher levels of abstraction than do everyday concepts. Constructs are invented for theoretical use and thus are likely to cut across various preexisting categories of thought. The value of specific constructs depends on how useful they are in explaining, predicting, and controlling phenomena, just as the value of everyday concepts depends on how helpful they are in everyday affairs. Generally, constructs are not directly observable. Instead, they are inferred by some indirect method from results such as findings on a questionnaire. Examples of marketing constructs include brand loyalty, high-involvement purchasing, social class, personality, and channel power. Constructs aid researchers by simplifying and integrating the complex phenomena found in the marketing environment.

Step Three: Define the Concept Constitutively

constitutive definition
Statement of the meaning of the central idea or concept under study, establishing its boundaries; also known as *theoretical*, or *conceptual*, *definition*.

The third step in the measurement process is to define the concept constitutively. A **constitutive** (or *theoretical*, or *conceptual*) **definition** is a statement of the meaning of the central idea or concept under study, establishing its boundaries. Constructs of a scientific theory are defined constitutively. Thus, all constructs, to be capable of being used in theories, must possess constitutive meaning. Like a dictionary definition, a constitutive definition should fully distinguish the concept under investigation from all other concepts, making the study concept readily discernible from very similar but different concepts. A vague constitutive definition can cause an incorrect research question to be addressed. For instance, to say that researchers are interested in studying marital roles would be so general as to be meaningless. To say that they want to examine the marital roles of newlyweds (married less than 12 months) from 24 to 28 years of age with 4 years of college may not even suffice. While one researcher may be interested in communication patterns as partners assume certain roles, a second researcher may be interested in parenting roles.

Step Four: Define the Concept Operationally

operational definition
Statement of precisely which observable characteristics will be measured and the process for assigning a value to the concept.

A precise constitutive definition makes the operational definition task much easier. An **operational definition** specifies which observable characteristics will be measured and the process for assigning a value to the concept. In other words, it assigns meaning to a construct in terms of the operations necessary to measure it in any concrete situation.

Because it is overly restrictive in marketing to insist that all variables be operationally defined in directly measurable terms, many variables are stated in more abstract terms and measured indirectly, based on theoretical assumptions about their nature. For example, it is impossible to measure an attitude directly, because an attitude is an abstract concept that refers to things inside a person's mind. It is possible, nonetheless, to give a clear theoretical definition of an attitude as an enduring organization of motivational, emotional, perceptual, and cognitive processes with respect to some aspect of the environment. On the basis of this definition, instruments have been developed for measuring attitudes indirectly, by asking questions about how a person feels, what the person believes, and how the person intends to behave.

In summary, an operational definition serves as a bridge between a theoretical concept and real-world events or factors. Constructs such as "attitude" and "high-involvement purchasing" are abstractions that cannot be observed. Operational definitions transform such constructs into observable events. In other words, they define or give meaning to a construct by spelling out what the researcher must do to measure it. There are many different potential operational definitions for any single concept, regardless of how exact the constitutive definition may be. The researcher must choose the operational definition that fits most appropriately with the objectives of the research.

An example of a constitutive definition, a corresponding operational definition, and a resultant measurement scale are shown in Exhibit 10.2. The operational definition of role ambiguity was developed by two marketing professors for use with salespeople and customer service personnel. The theoretical notion is that role ambiguity leads to job stress and impedes a worker's ability to improve performance and obtain job-based rewards, leading to job dissatisfaction.

Construct equivalence deals with how people see, understand, and develop measurements of a particular phenomenon. The problem confronting the global marketing researcher is that, because of sociocultural, economic, and political differences, construct

EXHIBIT 10.2	Constitutive and Operational Definitions of Role Ambiguity
Constitutive Definition	Role ambiguity is a direct function of the discrepancy between the information available to the person and that which is required for adequate performance of a role. It is the difference between a person's actual state of knowledge and the knowledge that provides adequate satisfaction of that person's personal needs and values.
Operational Definition	Role ambiguity is the amount of uncertainty (ranging from very uncertain to very certain on a 5-point scale) an individual feels regarding job-role responsibilities and expectations from other employees and customers.
Measurement Scale	The measurement scale consists of 45 items, with each item assessed by a 5-point scale with category labels *1* = very certain, *2* = certain, *3* = neutral, *4* = uncertain, *5* = very uncertain. Samples of the 45 items follow:

- How much freedom of action I am expected to have
- How I am expected to handle nonroutine activities on the job
- The sheer amount of work I am expected to do
- To what extent my boss is open to hearing my point of view
- How satisfied my boss is with me
- How managers in other departments expect me to interact with them
- What managers in other departments think about the job I perform
- How I am expected to interact with my customers
- How I should behave (with customers) while on the job
- If I am expected to lie a little to win customer confidence
- If I am expected to hide my company's foul-ups from my customers
- About how much time my family feels I should spend on the job
- To what extent my family expects me to share my job-related problems
- How my co-workers expect me to behave while on the job
- How much information my co-workers expect me to convey to my boss

Source: Adapted from Jagdip Singh and Gary K. Rhoads, "Boundary Role Ambiguity in Marketing-Oriented Positions: A Multidimensional, Multi-faceted Operationalization," *Journal of Marketing Research*, 28 (August 1991), pp. 328–338. Reprinted by permission of the American Marketing Association.

perspectives may be neither identical nor equivalent. The examples provided in the Global Research feature on page 282 highlight the construct equivalence problem faced by global marketing researchers.

Step Five: Develop a Measurement Scale

→ **scale**
Set of symbols or numbers so constructed that the symbols or numbers can be assigned by a rule to the individuals (or their behaviors or attitudes) to whom the scale is applied.

Exhibit 10.2 includes a scale that ranges from "very certain" to "very uncertain." A **scale** is a set of symbols or numbers so constructed that the symbols or numbers can be assigned by a rule to the individuals (or their behaviors or attitudes) to whom the scale is applied. The assignment on the scale is indicated by the individual's possession of whatever the scale is supposed to measure. Thus, a salesperson who feels he knows exactly how he is supposed to interact with customers would mark *very certain* for that item on the scale in Exhibit 10.2.

Creating a measurement scale begins with determining the level of measurement that is desirable or possible. Exhibit 10.3 describes the four basic levels of measurement: nominal, ordinal, interval, and ratio.

Nominal Level of Measurement

→ **nominal scales**
Scales that partition data into mutually exclusive and collectively exhaustive categories.

Nominal scales are among those most commonly used in marketing research. A nominal scale partitions data into categories that are mutually exclusive and collectively exhaustive, implying that every bit of data will fit into one and only one category and that all data will fit somewhere on the scale. The term *nominal* means "name-like," indicating that the numbers assigned to objects or phenomena are naming or classifying them but have no true number value; that is, the numbers cannot be ordered, added, or divided. The numbers are simply labels or identification numbers and nothing else. Examples of two nominal scales follow:

EXHIBIT 10.3	The Four Basic Levels of Measurement			
Level	**Basic Empirical Description***	**Operations**	**Typical Usage**	**Typical Descriptive Statistics**
Nominal	Uses numerals to identify objects, individuals, events, or groups	Determination of equality/inequality	Classification (male/ female; buyer/ nonbuyer)	Frequency counts, percentages/modes
Ordinal	In addition to identification, provides information about the relative amount of some characteristic possessed by an event, object, etc.	Determination of greater or lesser	Rankings/ratings (preferences for hotels, banks, etc.; social class; ratings of foods based on fat content, cholesterol)	Median (mean and variance metric)
Interval	Possesses all the properties of nominal and ordinal scales plus equal intervals between consecutive points	Determination of equality of intervals	Preferred measure of complex concepts/ constructs (temperature scale, air pressure scale, level of knowledge about brands)	Mean/variance
Ratio	Incorporates all the properties of nominal, ordinal, and interval scales plus an absolute zero point	Determination of equality of ratios	Preferred measure when precision instruments are available (sales, number of on-time arrivals, age)	Geometric mean/ harmonic mean

*Because higher levels of measurement contain all the properties of lower levels, higher level scales can be converted into lower level ones (i.e., ratio to interval or ordinal or nominal, or interval to ordinal or nominal, or ordinal to nominal).
Source: Adapted from S. S. Stevens, "On the Theory of Scales of Measurement," *Science*, 103 (June 7, 1946), pp. 677–680.

Gender:	(1) Male	(2) Female	
Geographic area:	(1) Urban	(2) Rural	(3) Suburban

The only quantifications in numerical scales are the number and percentage of objects in each category—for example, 50 males (48.5 percent) and 53 females (51.5 percent). Computing a mean of 2.4 for geographic area would be meaningless; only the mode, the value that appears most often, would be appropriate.

Ordinal Level of Measurement

Ordinal scales have the labeling characteristics of nominal scales plus an ability to order data. Ordinal measurement is possible when the transitivity postulate can be applied. (A *postulate* is an assumption that is an essential prerequisite to carrying out an operation or line of thinking.) The *transitivity postulate* is described by the notion that "if *a* is greater than *b*, and *b* is greater than *c*, then *a* is greater than *c*." Other terms that can be substituted for *is greater than* are *is preferred to*, *is stronger than*, and *precedes*. An example of an ordinal scale follows:

> ordinal scales
> Scales that maintain the labeling characteristics of nominal scales and have the ability to order data.

> Please rank the following online dating services from 1 to 5, with 1 being the most preferred and 5 the least preferred.
>
> www.spark.com   _____
> www.eharmony.com   _____
> www.match.com   _____
> www.greatexpectations.com   _____
> www.friendfinder.com   _____

Ordinal numbers are used strictly to indicate rank order. The numbers do not indicate absolute quantities, nor do they imply that the intervals between the numbers are equal. For example, a person ranking fax machines might like HP only slightly more than Canon and view Sharp as totally unacceptable. Such information would not be obtained from an ordinal scale.

Because ranking is the objective of an ordinal scale, any rule prescribing a series of numbers that preserves the ordered relationship is satisfactory. In other words, Spark could have been assigned a value of 30; eharmony, 40; Match, 27; GreatExpectations, 32; and FriendFinder, 42. Or any other series of numbers could have been used, as long as the basic ordering was preserved. In the case just cited, FriendFinder is 1; eHarmony 2; GreatExpectations 3; Spark 4; and Match 5. Common arithmetical operations such as addition and multiplication cannot be used with ordinal scales. The appropriate measure of central tendency is the mode or the median. A percentile or quartile measure is used for measuring dispersion.

A controversial (yet rather common) use of ordinal scales is to rate various characteristics. In this case, the researcher assigns numbers to reflect the relative ratings of a series of statements, then uses these numbers to interpret relative distance. Recall that the marketing researchers examining role ambiguity used a scale ranging from *very certain* to *very uncertain*. The following values were assigned:

(1)	(2)	(3)	(4)	(5)
Very Certain	**Certain**	**Neutral**	**Uncertain**	**Very Uncertain**

If a researcher can justify the assumption that the intervals are equal within the scale, then the more powerful parametric statistical tests can be applied. (Parametric statistical tests will be discussed in Chapters 16 and 17.) Indeed, some measurement scholars argue that equal intervals should be normally assumed.

GLOBAL RESEARCH

Construct Equivalence Problems Often Occur in Global Marketing Research

Construct equivalence problems in global marketing research may relate to functional equivalence, conceptual equivalence, or definitional equivalence. Some examples of each type of problem follow.

Functional Equivalence. In England, Germany, and Scandinavia, beer is generally perceived as an alcoholic beverage. In Mediterranean lands, however, beer is considered akin to soft drinks. Therefore, a study of the competitive status of beer in northern Europe would have to build in questions on wine and liquor. In Italy, Spain, or Greece, the comparison would have to be with soft drinks.

In Italy, it's common for children to have a bar of chocolate between two slices of bread as a snack. In France, bar chocolate is often used in cooking. But a German housewife would be revolted by either practice.

Conceptual Equivalence. A researcher using the concepts "out-group" and "in-group" would be dealing with very different groups in the United States and Greece. In the United States, the in-group includes people from one's own country, and the out-group includes foreigners. In Greece, the out-group includes countrymen with whom

one is not closely associated. (When Athenians were asked to help fellow Greeks and foreigners mail letters, the Greeks received worse treatment than did the foreigners.)

Personality traits such as aggressiveness or assertiveness may not be relevant in all countries or cultures. The concept may be absent from the culture and language, or it may have an entirely different meaning.

As a final example, Japanese and Western concepts of decision making differ considerably. Whereas the Westerner sees decision making as a discrete event, the Japanese cannot make that distinction.

Definitional Equivalence. In France, fragrance is measured on a hot–cold continuum. In the United States and the United Kingdom, hot and cold are not attributes assigned to fragrances. That is, an attribute used to categorize product classes may vary from one country or culture to another.

Perceptions of beer, as cited under functional equivalence, also provide an example of problems in achieving definitional equivalence. In the United Kingdom, beer would be classified as an alcoholic drink. In Mediterranean cultures, it would be classified as a soft drink.[1] Questions: 1. Why is construct equivalence important in global research? 2. Do you think that a researcher should worry about construct equivalence between the United States and Canada?

The best procedure would seem to be to treat ordinal measurements as though they were interval measurements but to be constantly alert to the possibility of gross inequality of intervals. As much as possible about the characteristics of the measuring tools should be learned. Much useful information has been obtained by this approach, with resulting scientific advances in psychology, sociology, and education. In short, it is unlikely that researchers will be led seriously astray by heeding this advice, if they are careful in applying it.[2]

> **interval scales**
> Scales that have the characteristics of ordinal scales, plus equal intervals between points to show relative amounts; they may include an arbitrary zero point.

Interval Level of Measurement

Interval scales contain all the features of ordinal scales with the added dimension that the intervals between the points on the scale are equal. The concept of temperature is based on equal intervals. Marketing researchers often prefer interval scales over ordinal scales because they can measure how much of a trait one consumer has (or does not have) over another. An interval scale enables a researcher to discuss differences separating two objects. The scale possesses properties of order and difference but with an arbitrary zero point. Examples are the Fahrenheit and Celsius scales; the freezing point of water is zero on one scale and 32 degrees on the other.

The arbitrary zero point of interval scales restricts the statements that a researcher can make about the scale points. One can say that 80°F is hotter than 32°F or that 64°F is 16° cooler than 80°F. However, one cannot say that 64°F is twice as warm as 32°F. Why? Because the zero point on the Fahrenheit scale is arbitrary. To understand this point, consider the transformation of the two Fahrenheit temperatures to Celsius using the formula Celsius 3 $(F - 32)(5/9)$; 32°F equals 0°C, and 64°F equals 17.8°C. The statement we made about the Fahrenheit temperatures (64° is twice as warm as 32°) does not hold for Celsius. The same would be true of rankings of online dating services on an interval scale. If Match had received a 20 and GreatExpectations a 10, we cannot say that Match is liked twice as much as GreatExpectations, because a point defining the absence of liking has not been identified and assigned a value of zero on the scale.

Interval scales are amenable to computation of an arithmetic mean, standard deviation, and correlation coefficients. The more powerful parametric statistical tests such as t tests and F tests can be applied. In addition, researchers can take a more conservative approach and use nonparametric tests if they have concern about the equal intervals assumption.

Ratio Level of Measurement

Ratio scales have all the characteristics of those scales previously discussed as well as a meaningful absolute zero or origin. Because there is universal agreement as to the location of the zero point, comparisons among the magnitudes of ratio-scaled values are acceptable. Thus, a ratio scale reflects the actual amount of a variable. Physical characteristics of a respondent such as age, weight, and height are examples of ratio-scaled variables. Other ratio scales are based on area, distance, money values, return rates, population counts, and lapsed periods of time.

Because some objects have none of the property being measured, a ratio scale originates at a zero point with absolute empirical meaning. For example, an investment (albeit a poor one) can have no rate of return, or a census tract in New Mexico could be devoid of any persons. An absolute zero implies that all arithmetic operations are possible, including multiplication and division. Numbers on the scale indicate the actual amounts of the property being measured. A large bag of McDonald's french fries weighs 8 ounces, and a regular bag at Burger King weighs 4 ounces; thus, a large McDonald's bag of fries weighs twice as much as a regular Burger King bag of fries.

Commonly used temperature scales are based on equal intervals and an arbitrary zero point. Marketing researchers often prefer interval scales because they can measure how much more of a trait one consumer has than another.

Step Six: Evaluate the Reliability and Validity of the Measurement

An ideal marketing research study would provide information that is accurate, precise, lucid, and timely. Accurate data imply accurate measurement, or $M = A$, where M refers to measurement and A stands for complete accuracy. In marketing research, this ideal is rarely, if ever, achieved. Instead,

$$M = A + E$$
$$\text{where} \quad E = \text{errors}$$

Errors can be either random or systematic, as noted in Chapter 6. Systematic error results in a constant bias in the measurements caused by faults in the measurement instrument or process. For example, if a faulty ruler (on which one inch is actually one

→ **ratio scales**
Scales that have the characteristics of interval scales, plus a meaningful zero point so that magnitudes can be compared arithmetically.

FROM THE FRONT LINE

Making Sure You Have the Right Level of Scaling

Dave Nixon, Account Executive, DSS Research

The level of scaling—nominal, ordinal, interval, or ratio—is a critical consideration because, as you will see in later chapters in the text, different kinds of analytical techniques require different levels of scaling. Your objectives may require that you do a particular type of analysis, but if you do not seek the required information in the appropriate manner in the questionnaire, when you get to the analysis phase you will be out of luck.

We usually simplify the four categories listed above into two with nominal and ordinal scales referred to as non-metric and interval and ratio scales referred to as metric. As noted above, you've got to be sure you're going to end up with data scaled at the level required for the analysis specified.

If you only need cross tabulations, they can be produced with any level of scaling. However, if your plan calls for more powerful multivariate procedures, such as regression analysis then you need metric data (interval or ratio). For example, if you need to have respondents indicate the importance of different product or service characteristics and you need to use the results as predictor variables in a regression analysis, then metric data are needed. This means that if you are considering having respondents rate or rank each item then you should go the rating route in this instance.

Ranking data are non-metric and cannot be used in most multivariate procedures such as regression analysis. Rating data are generally considered to be metric (there is some debate on this point) and are normally considered appropriate for regression analysis. You need metric data for the analysis planned.

And then there is the question of the number of scale points, 1 to 5, 1 to 7, 1 to 10, 1 to 100, etc. These issues are discussed in detail in the chapter. From an analytical standpoint, we would like to have more scale points. From a practical standpoint, respondents can only discriminate so much between options. At a minimum you want to see 5-point scales, 7- and 10-point scales are common. Going beyond that you're kidding yourself.

and a half inches) is used in Pillsbury's test kitchens to measure the height of chocolate cakes baked with alternative recipes, all cakes will be recorded at less than their actual height. *Random error* also influences the measurements but not systematically. Thus, random error is transient in nature. A person may not answer a question truthfully because he is in a bad mood that day.

Two scores on a measurement scale can differ for a number of reasons.[3] Only the first of the following eight reasons does not involve error. A researcher must determine whether any of the remaining seven sources of measurement differences are producing random or systematic error.

1. *A true difference in the characteristic being measured.* A perfect measurement difference is solely the result of actual differences. For example, John rates McDonald's service as 1 (excellent) and Sandy rates its service as 4 (average), and the variation is due only to actual attitude differences.

2. *Differences due to stable characteristics of individual respondents,* such as personality, values, and intelligence. Sandy has an aggressive, rather critical personality, and she gives no one and nothing the benefit of the doubt. She actually was quite pleased

Two scores on a measurement scale can differ for a number of reasons. McDonald's may score higher on one person's survey than on another person's because of real differences in perceptions of the service or because of a variety of random or systematic errors. The reliability and validity of the type of measurement should always be checked.

with the service she received at McDonald's, but she expects such service and so gave it an average rating.

3. *Differences due to short-term personal factors,* such as temporary mood swings, health problems, time constraints, or fatigue. Earlier on the day of the study, John had won $400 in a "Name That Tune" contest on a local radio station. He stopped by McDonald's for a burger after he picked up his winning check. His reply on the service quality questionnaire might have been quite different if he had been interviewed the previous day.

4. *Differences caused by situational factors,* such as distractions or others present in the interview situation. Sandy was giving her replies while trying to watch her 4-year-old nephew, who was running amok on the McDonald's playground; John had his new fiancée along when he was interviewed. Replies of both people might have been different if they had been interviewed at home while no other friend or relative was present.

5. *Differences resulting from variations in administering the survey.* Interviewers can ask questions with different voice inflections, causing response variation. And because of such factors as rapport with the interviewee, manner of dress, sex, or race, different interviewers can cause responses to vary. Interviewer bias can be as subtle as a nodding of the head. One interviewer who tended to nod unconsciously was found to bias some respondents. They thought that the interviewer was agreeing with them when he was, in fact, saying, "Okay, I'm recording what you say—tell me more."

6. *Differences due to the sampling of items included in the questionnaire.* When researchers attempt to measure the quality of service at McDonald's, the scales and other questions used represent only a portion of the items that could have been used. The scales created by the researchers reflect their interpretation of the construct (service quality) and the way it is measured. If the researchers had used different words or if items had been added or removed, the scale values reported by John and Sandy might have been different.

7. *Differences due to a lack of clarity in the measurement instrument.* A question may be ambiguous, complex, or incorrectly interpreted. A survey that asked "How far do you live from McDonald's?" and then gave choices "(1) less than 5 minutes, (2) 5 to 10 minutes," and so forth, would be ambiguous; someone walking would undoubtedly take longer to get to the restaurant than a person driving a car or riding a bike. This topic is covered in much greater detail in Chapter 11.

8. *Differences due to mechanical or instrument factors.* Blurred questionnaires, lack of space to fully record answers, missing pages in a questionnaire, incorrect computer keystrokes, or a balky pen can result in differences in responses.

Martin Weinberger, executive vice president of Oxtoby-Smith, Incorporated, offers his perspectives on measurement in the Practicing Marketing Research feature on page 287.

Reliability

A measurement scale that provides consistent results over time is reliable. If a ruler consistently measures a chocolate cake as 9 inches high, then the ruler is said to be reliable. Reliable scales, gauges, and other measurement devices can be used with confidence and with the knowledge that transient and situational factors are not interfering with the measurement process. Reliable instruments provide stable measures at different times under different conditions. A key question regarding reliability is "If we measure some phenomenon over and over again with the same measurement device, will we get the same or highly similar results?" An affirmative answer means that the device is reliable.

> **reliability**
> Degree to which measures are free from random error and, therefore, provide consistent data.

Thus, **reliability** is the degree to which measures are free from random error and, therefore, provide consistent data. The less error there is, the more reliable the observation is, so a measurement that is free of error is a correct measure. A reliable measurement, then, does not change when the concept being measured remains constant in value. However, if the concept being measured does change in value, the reliable measure will indicate that change. How can a measuring instrument be unreliable? If your weight stays constant at 150 pounds but repeated measurements on your bathroom scale show your weight to fluctuate, the scale's lack of reliability may be due to a weak spring.

There are three ways to assess reliability: test–retest, the use of equivalent forms, and internal consistency.

> **test–retest reliability**
> Ability of the same instrument to produce consistent results when used a second time under conditions as similar as possible to the original conditions.

Test–Retest Reliability **Test–retest reliability** is obtained by repeating the measurement with the same instrument, approximating the original conditions as closely as possible. The theory behind test–retest is that if random variations are present, they will be revealed by differences in the scores between the two tests. **Stability** means that very few differences in scores are found between the first and second administrations of the test; the measuring instrument is said to be stable. For example, assume that a 30-item department store image measurement scale was administered to the same group of shoppers at two different times. If the correlation between the two measurements was high, the reliability would be assumed to be high.

> **stability**
> Lack of change in results from test to retest.

There are several problems with test–retest reliability. First, it may be very difficult to locate and gain the cooperation of respondents for a second testing. Second, the first measurement may alter a person's response on the second measurement. Third, environmental or personal factors may change, causing the second measurement to change.

Equivalent Form Reliability The difficulties encountered with the test–retest approach can be avoided by creating equivalent forms of a measurement instrument. For example, assume that the researcher is interested in identifying inner-directed versus

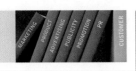

PRACTICING MARKETING RESEARCH

Truth about What Respondents Say

Martin Weinberger is executive vice president of Oxtoby-Smith, Incorporated, New York, one of America's largest and oldest marketing research companies. His 25 years of experience in the research industry has led him to develop certain perspectives regarding measurement in consumer research. Several of those perspectives are as follows.

1. **Sometimes Consumers Don't Tell the Truth; Sometimes They Are Willing to Reveal It.** Several years ago, a major catalogue company was having trouble with its boys' slacks—it was getting an unusually large number of returns. Consumers were writing that the reason for the return was that the slacks did not fit properly. On the basis of that information, the catalogue sales company believed something must be wrong with the diagrams and instructions it provided to consumers for ordering the right size slacks. Oxtoby-Smith was asked to find out what was wrong with the diagrams or the instructions so that the client could fix them. We were given the names of consumers who had returned the boys' slacks.

   We sent our interviewers into the field, carrying the heavy catalogue, with the diagrams and the instructions. What we found was not what we had expected to find. The consumers told us the slacks had fit perfectly well. The mothers had ordered three or four pairs of slacks for their teenage sons in the hope that the son would find *one* pair he would be willing to wear. Then the mother had to face returning the other two or three pairs. The mothers felt uncomfortable giving any explanation for the return of the slacks other than "poor fit." This finding indicated that the diagrams were not the problem. The instructions were not the problem. The catalogue company had to learn to live with the returns in the same way the mothers had to live with the habits of their teenage sons.

2. **Sometimes Consumers Claim More Than They Know; Sometimes They Are Just Confused.** It has been well established that consumers sometimes claim awareness of brands that do not exist. That is why it is important to include fictitious brand names in studies of brand awareness to see how much claiming is going on. In fact, I have done a study in which a fictitious brand name had *more* brand awareness than the client's brand and the client considered changing the name of its brand to the fictitious brand name!

3. **Sometimes Consumers Don't Know Why They Buy the Brands They Buy.** This section could be subtitled, "Why you should not ask why." I have conducted a large number of studies asking consumers, at the client's request, *why* they buy the products they buy, and I have looked at their answers to that question. At the same time, I have looked at their answers to other questions. I have found that consumers often do not really *know* why they buy the brands they buy.

   A simple case in point is a food or beverage product. Ask consumers why they buy a brand, and they usually will tell you "because it tastes good." If you give a consumer a blind product test, you may find out that this individual cannot differentiate between his or her preferred Brand X and Brand Y. If you use a double-blind paired comparison, in one paired blind test a consumer will prefer X and in another paired blind test the same individual will prefer Y.

4. **Consumers Not Only Have Opinions, They Have Passions.** Generally, consumers are very cooperative. They will answer almost any questions you ask them. But my experience teaches me that you need to know more than just their opinions; you need to know their passions.

For example, a manufacturer of toilet paper that is thinking of introducing a scented version might ask us to find out which of a series of scents is preferred by consumers. We could test the scents and tell them scent A is more widely preferred than scent B. However, we would be remiss in our job if we failed to find out whether consumers would be disposed toward toilet paper *with any scent at all* and what the scent preferences are of those who *like* the idea of scented toilet paper. Possibly those who are interested in toilet paper with scents prefer scent B over scent A, whereas scent A appeals to those who, in the marketplace, would be buying *unscented* paper.[4]

Questions

1. What can researchers do to determine whether the consumers' responses are true?

2. Do you think that the vast majority of respondents attempt to give true answers?

outer-directed lifestyles. Two questionnaires can be created containing measures of inner-directed behavior (see Exhibit 10.4) and measures of outer-directed behavior. These measures should receive about the same emphasis on each questionnaire. Thus, although the questions used to ascertain the lifestyles are different on the two questionnaires, the number of questions used to measure each lifestyle should be approximately equal. The recommended interval for administering the second equivalent form is 2 weeks, although in some cases the two forms are given one after the other or simultaneously. **Equivalent form reliability** is determined by measuring the correlation of the scores on the two instruments.

There are two problems with equivalent forms that should be noted. First, it is very difficult, and perhaps impossible, to create two totally equivalent forms. Second, if equivalence can be achieved, it may not be worth the time, trouble, and expense involved. The theory behind the equivalent forms approach to reliability assessment is the same as that of the test–retest. The primary difference between the test–retest and the equivalent forms

> **equivalent form reliability**
> Ability of two very similar forms of an instrument to produce closely correlated results.

EXHIBIT 10.4 | **Statements Used to Measure Inner-Directed Lifestyles**

I often don't get the credit I deserve for things I do well.
I try to get my own way regardless of others.
My greatest achievements are ahead of me.
I have a number of ideas that someday I would like to put into a book.
I am quick to accept new ideas.
I often think about how I look and what impression I am making on others.
I am a competitive person.
I feel upset when I hear that people are criticizing or blaming me.
I'd like to be a celebrity.
I get a real thrill out of doing dangerous things.
I feel that almost nothing in life can substitute for great achievement.
It's important for me to be noticed.
I keep in close touch with my friends.
I spend a good deal of time trying to decide how I feel about things.
I often think I can feel my way into the innermost being of another person.
I feel that ideals are powerful motivating forces in people.
I think someone can be a good person without believing in God.
The Eastern religions are more appealing to me than Christianity.
I feel satisfied with my life.
I enjoy getting involved in new and unusual situations.
Overall, I'd say I'm happy.
I feel I understand where my life is going.
I like to think I'm different from other people.
I adopt a commonsense attitude toward life.

methods is the testing instrument itself. Test–retest uses the same instrument, whereas the equivalent forms approach uses a different, but highly similar, measuring instrument.

Internal Consistency Reliability **Internal consistency reliability** assesses the ability to produce similar results when different samples are used to measure a phenomenon during the same time period. The theory of internal consistency rests on the concept of equivalence. *Equivalence* is concerned with how much error may be introduced by using different samples of items to measure a phenomenon; it focuses on variations at one point in time among samples of items. A researcher can test for item equivalence by assessing the homogeneity of a set of items. The total set of items used to measure a phenomenon, such as inner-directed lifestyles, is divided into two halves; the total scores of the two halves are then correlated. Use of the **split-half technique** typically calls for scale items to be randomly assigned to one half or the other. The problem with this method is that the estimate of the coefficient of reliability is totally dependent on how the items were split. Different splits result in different correlations when, ideally, they should not.

To overcome this problem, many researchers now use the *Cronbach alpha technique*, which involves computing mean reliability coefficient estimates for all possible ways of splitting a set of items in half. A lack of correlation of an item with other items in the scale is evidence that the item does not belong in the scale and should be omitted. One limitation of the Cronbach alpha is that the scale items require equal intervals. If this criterion cannot be met, another test called the KR-20 can be used. The *KR-20 technique* is applicable for all dichotomous or nominally scaled items.

> **internal consistency reliability**
> Ability of an instrument to produce similar results when used on different samples during the same time period to measure a phenomenon.

> **split-half technique**
> Method of assessing the reliability of a scale by dividing the total set of measurement items in half and correlating the results.

Validity

Recall that the second characteristic of a good measurement device is validity. **Validity** addresses the issue of whether what the researcher was trying to measure was actually measured. When Pontiac brought out the Aztek, research told them that the car would sell between 50,000 and 70,000 units annually despite the controversial styling. After selling only 27,000 cars per year, the model was discontinued in 2005. Unfortunately, the research measuring instrument was not valid. The validity of a measure refers to the extent to which the measurement instrument and procedure are free from both systematic and random error. Thus, a measuring device is valid only if differences in scores reflect true differences on the characteristic being measured rather than systematic or random error. You should recognize that a necessary precondition for validity is that the measuring instrument be reliable. An instrument that is not reliable will not yield consistent results when measuring the same phenomenon over time.

A scale or other measuring device is basically worthless to a researcher if it lacks validity because it is not measuring what it is supposed to. On the surface, this seems like a rather simple notion, yet validity often is based on subtle distinctions. Assume that your teacher gives an exam that he has constructed to measure marketing research knowledge, and the test consists strictly of applying a number of formulas to simple case problems. A friend receives a low score on the test and protests to the teacher that she "really understands marketing research." Her position, in essence, is that the test was not valid. She maintains that, rather than measuring knowledge of marketing research, the test measured memorization of formulas and the ability to use simple math to find solutions. The teacher could repeat the exam only to find that student scores still fell in the same order. Does this mean that the protesting student was incorrect? Not necessarily; the teacher may be systematically measuring the ability to memorize rather than a true understanding of marketing research.

Unlike the teacher attempting to measure marketing research knowledge, a brand manager is interested in successful prediction. The manager, for example, wants to know

> **validity**
> The degree to which what the researcher was trying to measure was actually measured.

if a purchase intent scale successfully predicts trial purchase of a new product. Thus, validity can be examined from a number of different perspectives, including face, content, criterion-related, and construct validity (see Exhibit 10.5).

→ face validity
Degree to which a measurement seems to measure what it is supposed to measure.

Face Validity

Face validity is the weakest form of validity. It is concerned with the degree to which a measurement seems to measure what it is supposed to measure. It is a judgment call by the researcher, made as the questions are designed. Thus, as each question is scrutinized, there is an implicit assessment of its face validity. Revisions enhance the face validity of the question until it passes the researcher's subjective evaluation. Alternatively, *face validity* can refer to the subjective agreement of researchers, experts, or people familiar with the market, product, or industry that a scale logically appears to be accurately reflecting what it is supposed to measure.[5] A straightforward question such as "What is your age?" followed by a series of age categories generally is agreed to have face validity. Most scales used in marketing research attempt to measure attitudes or behavioral intentions, which are much more elusive.

→ content validity
Representativeness, or sampling adequacy, of the content of the measurement instrument.

Content Validity

Content validity is the representativeness, or sampling adequacy, of the content of the measurement instrument. In other words, does the scale provide adequate coverage of the topic under study? Say that McDonald's has hired you to measure its image among adults 18 to 30 years of age who eat fast-food hamburgers at least once a month. You devise the following scale:

Modern building	1	2	3	4	5	Old-fashioned building
Beautiful landscaping	1	2	3	4	5	Poor landscaping
Clean parking lots	1	2	3	4	5	Dirty parking lots
Attractive signs	1	2	3	4	5	Unattractive signs

A McDonald's executive would quickly take issue with this scale, claiming that a person could evaluate McDonald's on this scale and never have eaten a McDonald's hamburger. In fact, the evaluation could be made simply by driving past a McDonald's. The executive could further argue that the scale lacks content validity because many important components of image—such as the quality of the food, cleanliness of the eating area and restrooms, and promptness and courtesy of service—were omitted.

EXHIBIT 10.5	Assessing the Validity of a Measurement Instrument
Face validity	The degree to which a measurement instrument seems to measure what it is supposed to, as judged by researchers.
Content validity	The degree to which measurement items represent the universe of the concept under study.
Criterion-related validity	The degree to which a measurement instrument can predict a variable that is designated a criterion.
	a. Predictive validity: The extent to which a future level of a criterion variable can be predicted by a current measurement on a scale.
	b. Concurrent validity: The extent to which a criterion variable measured at the same point in time as the variable of interest can be predicted by the measurement instrument.
Construct validity	The degree to which a measurement instrument confirms a hypothesis created from a theory based on the concepts under study.
	a. Convergent validity: The degree of association among different measurement instruments that purport to measure the same concept.
	b. Discriminant validity: A measure of the lack of association among constructs that are supposed to be different.

PRACTICING MARKETING RESEARCH

The Anonymity Gradient

Bill MacElroy, president of Socratic Technologies, San Francisco, discusses the concept of the importance of anonymous responses to respondents:

We feel that the privacy of the interviewee's environment may play a key role in the types of answers given because the change in the characteristics of answers doesn't stop when no specific interviewer is present. Even within self-administered interviewing situations, the degree to which the respondent feels "secure and alone" appears to produce more candor. We have called this observed phenomenon the anonymity gradient.

Over the past three years, we have had several opportunities to run side-by-side studies in which the same questions were asked using different modes of field methodology (e.g., one-on-one interviewing, CATI telephone, paper and pencil, disk-by-mail, and Web-based interviewing). As we examined the answers to identically worded questions, a curious pattern began to emerge. Increased human presence had the distinctive effect of producing kinder, less frank answers. This difference was also noted between paper and pencil surveys conducted with and without other people in the area.

The most candid answers (based on the degree to which people reported known problems, complained about service that was known to be a concern, and gave in-depth responses when probed for areas that needed improvement) came from people using their own personal computers. Researchers have reported that when people use computers, they tend to enter a "cool and immersive, womb-like environment" in which the level of engagement can produce exaggerated levels of perceived privacy. The anonymity gradient can be thought of as a pattern of candor that changes with the perceived level of privacy.

By itself, the anonymity gradient might be an interesting anomaly but without much practical value. We have, however, found some distinctive characteristics that may be helpful to people as they are planning conversions from certain forms of research to others. This is particularly important if your company has been tracking satisfaction, performance, problem resolution, and other similar topics using telephone, paper and pencil, or one-on-one interviewing techniques. There can be an unpleasant shock to the system when, after many periods of hearing from your customers that they are completely satisfied with no problems to report, you suddenly find out that they are less satisfied and have a whole list of demands for improvement. You may encounter this when converting traditional methodologies to newer technologies.

For example, most data related to purchase interest tends to be overstated when actual purchases are tallied. Although we haven't had the benefit of tracking actual results, we suspect that some data related to purchase interest collected using a more anonymous technology may be closer to what will really happen when the product actually ships.[6]

Questions

1. Do you think that respondents are more likely to give true answers in a group setting such as a focus group?

2. What about individual depth interviews?

The determination of content validity is not always a simple matter. It is very difficult, and perhaps impossible, to identify all the facets of McDonald's image. Content validity ultimately becomes a judgmental matter. One could approach content validity by first carefully defining precisely what is to be measured. Second, an exhaustive literature search and focus groups could be conducted to identify all possible items for inclusion on the scale. Third, a panel of experts could be asked their opinions on whether an item should be included. Finally, the scale could be pretested and an open-ended question asked that might identify other items to be included. For example, after a more refined image scale for McDonald's has been administered, a follow-up question could be "Do you have any other thoughts about McDonald's that you would like to express?" Answers to this pretest question might provide clues for other image dimensions not previously considered.

criterion-related validity
Degree to which a measurement instrument can predict a variable that is designated a criterion.

Criterion-Related Validity

Criterion-related validity examines the ability of a measuring instrument to predict a variable that is designated a criterion. Suppose that we wish to devise a test to identify marketing researchers who are exceptional at moderating focus groups. We begin by having impartial marketing research experts identify from a directory of researchers those they judge to be best at moderating focus groups. We then construct 300 items to which all the group moderators are asked to reply yes or no, such as "I believe it is important to compel shy group participants to speak out" and "I like to interact with small groups of people." We then go through the responses and select the items that the "best" focus group moderators answered one way and the rest of the moderators answered the other way. Assume that this process produces 84 items, which we put together to form what we shall call the Test of Effectiveness in Focus Group Moderating (TEFGM). We feel that this test will identify good focus group moderators. The criterion of interest here is the ability to conduct a good focus group. We might explore further the criterion-related validity of TEFGM by administering it to another group of moderators, each of whom has been designated as either "best" or "not as good." Then we could determine how well the test identifies the section to which each marketing researcher is assigned. Thus, criterion-related validity is concerned with detecting the presence or absence of one or more criteria considered to represent constructs of interest.

predictive validity
Degree to which a future level of a criterion variable can be forecast by a current measurement scale.

Two subcategories of criterion-related validity are predictive validity and concurrent validity. **Predictive validity** is the extent to which a future level of a criterion variable can be predicted by a current measurement on a scale. A voter-motivation scale, for example,

A politician is interested in what issues those likely to vote perceive as important. The predictive validity of the politician's measures may determine whether or not he or she is elected.

is used to predict the likelihood that a person will vote in the next election. A savvy politician is not interested in what the community as a whole perceives as important problems but only in what persons who are likely to vote perceive as important problems. These are the issues that the politician would address in speeches and advertising. Another example of predictive validity is the extent to which a purchase intent scale for a new Pepperidge Farm pastry predicts actual trial of the product.

Concurrent validity is concerned with the relationship between the predictor variable and the criterion variable, both of which are assessed at the same point in time—for example, the ability of a home pregnancy test to accurately determine whether a woman is pregnant right now. Such a test with low concurrent validity could cause a lot of undue stress.

concurrent validity
Degree to which another variable, measured at the same point in time as the variable of interest, can be predicted by the measurement instrument.

Construct Validity
Construct validity, though not often consciously addressed by many marketing researchers on a day-to-day basis, is extremely important to marketing scientists. Assessing construct validity involves understanding the theoretical foundations underlying the obtained measurements. A measure has **construct validity** if it behaves according to the theory behind the prediction. Purchase behavior can be observed directly; someone either buys product A or does not. Yet scientists have developed constructs on lifestyle, involvement, attitude, and personality that help explain why someone does or does not purchase something. These constructs are largely unobservable. Researchers can observe behavior related to the constructs—that is, the purchase of a product. However, they cannot observe the constructs themselves—such as an attitude. Constructs help scientists communicate and build theories to explain phenomena.[7]

construct validity
Degree to which a measurement instrument represents and logically connects, via the underlying theory, the observed phenomenon to the construct.

You might think of construct validity as a "labeling" issue. When you measure a notion (construct) called "high involvement," is that what you are really measuring? Viewed in a slightly different manner, when a researcher claims construct validity, he or she essentially has a theory of how phenomena, people, and measures relate to each other (and other theoretical terms). In other words, the researcher offers us a theoretical pattern. When the researcher claims construct validity, he or she is claiming that the observed pattern in a research project corresponds to the theoretical pattern. In this instance, how the researcher thought the world works is how it works.

Although construct validity is presented here with various other types of validity, it really stands above all others. Why? Because construct validity relates back to the very essence of what you are trying to measure. If your research lacks construct validity, little else matters.[8]

Two statistical measures of construct validity are convergent and discriminant validity. **Convergent validity** reflects the degree of correlation among different measures that purport to measure the same construct. **Discriminant validity** reveals the lack of—or low—correlation among constructs that are supposed to be different. Assume that we develop a multi-item scale that measures the propensity to shop at discount stores. Our theory suggests that this propensity is caused by four personality variables: high level of self-confidence, low need for status, low need for distinctiveness, and high level of adaptability. Furthermore, our theory suggests that propensity to shop at discount stores is not related to brand loyalty or high-level aggressiveness.

convergent validity
Degree of correlation among different measurement instruments that purport to measure the same construct.

Evidence of construct validity exists if our scale does the following:

■ Correlates highly with other measures of propensity to shop at discount stores, such as reported stores patronized and social class (convergent validity).

discriminant validity
Measure of the lack of association among constructs that are supposed to be different.

■ Has a low correlation with the unrelated constructs of brand loyalty and a high level of aggressiveness (discriminant validity).

All the types of validity discussed here are somewhat interrelated in both theory and practice. Predictive validity is obviously very important on a scale to predict whether a person will shop at a discount store. A researcher developing a discount store patronage

Exhibit 10.6

Illustrations of
Possible Reliability
and Validity
Situations in
Measurement

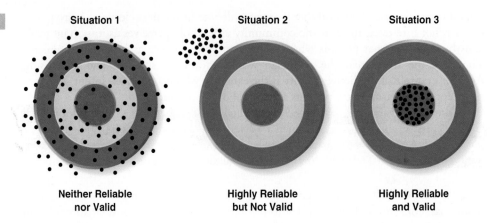

Situation 1 — Neither Reliable nor Valid

Situation 2 — Highly Reliable but Not Valid

Situation 3 — Highly Reliable and Valid

scale probably would first attempt to understand the constructs that provide the basis for prediction. The researcher would put forth a theory about discount store patronage—that, of course, is the foundation of construct validity. Next, the researcher would be concerned with which specific items to include on the discount store patronage scale and whether these items relate to the full range of the construct. Thus, the researcher would ascertain the degree of content validity. The issue of criterion-related validity could be addressed in a pretest by measuring scores on the discount store patronage scale and actual store patronage. Read more about measurement tips in the Practicing Marketing Research box below.

Reliability and Validity—A Concluding Comment

The concepts of reliability and validity are illustrated in Exhibit 10.6. Situation 1 shows holes all over the target, which could be caused by the use of an old rifle, being a poor shot, or many other factors. This complete lack of consistency means there is no reliability. Because the instrument lacks reliability, thus creating huge errors, it cannot be valid. Measurement reliability is a necessary condition for validity.

Situation 2 denotes a very tight pattern (consistency), but the pattern is far removed from the bull's-eye. This illustrates that an instrument can have a high level of reliability (little variance) but lack validity. The instrument is consistent, but it does not measure what it is supposed to measure. The shooter has a steady eye, but the sights are not adjusted properly. Situation 3 shows the reliability and validity that researchers strive to achieve in a measurement instrument; it is on target with what the researcher is attempting to measure.

PRACTICING
MARKETING RESEARCH

Tips for Managers on Putting Measurement to Work

Craig Bailey, president of Customer Centricity, Inc., was formerly manager of a customer care organization. The organization had been routinely sending out customer satisfaction surveys. One day,

when signing "thank you" letters to send to survey participants, he decided that something needed to change. He describes the situation, in his own words:

The reality was that the organization was investing resources in a process to perform customer satisfaction surveys and not getting the maximum value possible. And, worse, we were wasting our customers' time.

At such a juncture, you have two choices: stop the survey process (save your money and your customers' time) and throw the thank-you letters in the trash, or leverage the customer satisfaction survey results as a catalyst for continuous improvement. We selected option No. 2.

In order to make the customer survey information meaningful, we started at the beginning and examined what, for our purposes, we were measuring. We adopted the following principles to get the most out of customer surveys:

- **Any measurement that does not hold an individual responsible is not an effective metric.** While many companies adhere to one element of the first measurement principle (that of "measuring" customer satisfaction), managing it requires that an individual be held responsible for the customer satisfaction metrics. For example, a customer satisfaction survey program may be designed to produce feedback on customer service, account management, billing, and provisioning, for example. At the end of the day, the managers of these organizations are responsible for the customer satisfaction levels of their respective areas. As such, they should be fully engaged in your customer satisfaction survey program.

- **No one should ever be held responsible for a measurement that they cannot influence.** Too often, employees who deal with customers know that the firm is performing customer satisfaction surveys, but they don't know what the customers are saying in the results. This causes tremendous frustration, because front-line personnel want to know what they can do to improve customer satisfaction. Your program should be designed to include communications to them, so they know what they can do to improve customer satisfaction.

- **The importance of a measurement is determined by how high in an organization it is consistently reviewed.** Make no mistake, business is about numbers. In my opinion, there are two sets of numbers that every company must track and manage: the financials and customer satisfaction levels. If executives of a corporation only care about the financial indicators, the company will lose sight of their source of revenue—the customer. To be truly successful, companies must include customer satisfaction results on their list of key performance indicators that are reviewed by executive leadership on a monthly basis.

- **Every measurement must have clear and rational goals.** After establishing a baseline for its customer satisfaction levels, a company must set measurable and achievable goals in terms of where it wants to be. Many firms initially find that customers are totally satisfied in some areas of performance, while not satisfied in others. Often, companies focus their efforts only on areas of dissatisfaction, which is an appropriate step upon establishing a baseline. However, the customer satisfaction survey program needs to pay attention to all areas, because customer expectations are continuously changing. As such, areas in which customers are satisfied today may turn into areas of dissatisfaction, if a company doesn't remain progressive.

- **If a "carrot and stick" is not clear, measurement will fall into disuse.** Building on each of the above principles, it is not good enough to simply measure, manage, influence, promote visibility, and set goals for customer satisfaction results. Those personnel that can influence customer satisfaction, directly or indirectly, must benefit from reaching, and be affected by missing, customer satisfaction goals. To accomplish this, management must ensure the organization's compensation model is tied to customer satisfaction levels. This could be in the form of annual performance reviews in which merit increases would reflect the goals that were achieved, or missed. Alternatively, this could occur through a bonus program that is administered on a monthly, quarterly, or annual basis.[9]

Questions

1. Do you think that every manager's bonus in an organization should be based on measurement of customer satisfaction?

2. Some people say that all you need to measure customer satisfaction is one question: "Would you recommend our company to a friend?" Do you think that this is sufficient? (See Real-Life Research 10.2.)

SUMMARY

Measurement consists of using rules to assign numbers or labels to objects in such a way as to represent quantities or qualities of attributes. A measurement rule is a guide, a method, or a command that tells a researcher what to do. Accurate measurement requires rules that are both clear and specific.

The measurement process comprises the following steps: (1) identify the concept of interest, (2) develop a construct, (3) define the concept constitutively, (4) define the concept operationally, (5) develop a measurement scale, and (6) evaluate the reliability and validity of the scale. A constitutive definition is a statement of the meaning of the central concept under study, establishing its boundaries. An operational definition specifies which observable characteristics will be measured and the process for assigning a value to the concept.

There are four basic levels of measurement: nominal, ordinal, interval, and ratio. A nominal scale partitions data into categories that are mutually exclusive and collectively exhaustive. The numbers assigned to objects or phenomena have no true numerical meaning; they are simply labels. Ordinal scales have the labeling characteristics of nominal scales plus an ability to order data. Interval scales contain all the features of ordinal scales with the added dimension that the intervals between the points on the scale are equal. Interval scales enable the researcher to discuss differences separating two objects. They are amenable to computation of an arithmetic mean, standard deviation, and correlation coefficients. Ratio scales have all the characteristics of previously discussed scales as well as a meaningful absolute zero or origin, thus permitting comparison of the absolute magnitude of the numbers and reflecting the actual amount of the variable.

Measurement data consist of accurate information and errors. Systematic error results in a constant bias in the measurements. Random error also influences the measurements but is not systematic; it is transient in nature. Reliability is the degree to which measures are free from random error and therefore provide consistent data. There are three ways to assess reliability: test–retest, internal consistency, and use of equivalent forms. Validity addresses whether the attempt at measurement was successful. The validity of a measure refers to the extent to which the measurement device or process is free from both systematic and random error. Types of validity include face, content, criterion-related, and construct validity.

KEY TERMS & DEFINITIONS

measurement Process of assigning numbers or labels to persons, objects, or events in accordance with specific rules for representing quantities or qualities of attributes.

rule Guide, method, or command that tells a researcher what to do.

constructs Specific types of concepts that exist at higher levels of abstraction.

constitutive definition Statement of the meaning of the central idea or concept under study, establishing its boundaries; also known as *theoretical*, or *conceptual*, *definition*.

operational definition Statement of precisely which observable characteristics will be measured and the process for assigning a value to the concept.

scale Set of symbols or numbers so constructed that the symbols or numbers can be assigned by a rule to the individuals (or their behaviors or attitudes) to whom the scale is applied.

nominal scales Scales that partition data into mutually exclusive and collectively exhaustive categories.

ordinal scales Scales that maintain the labeling characteristics of nominal scales and have the ability to order data.

interval scales Scales that have the characteristics of ordinal scales, plus equal intervals between points to show relative amounts; they may include an arbitrary zero point.

ratio scales Scales that have the characteristics of interval scales, plus a meaningful zero point so that magnitudes can be compared arithmetically.

reliability Degree to which measures are free from random error and, therefore, provide consistent data.

test–retest reliability Ability of the same instrument to produce consistent results when used a second time under conditions as similar as possible to the original conditions.

stability Lack of change in results from test to retest.

equivalent form reliability Ability of two very similar forms of an instrument to produce closely correlated results.

internal consistency reliability Ability of an instrument to produce similar results when used on different samples during the same time period to measure a phenomenon.

split-half technique Method of assessing the reliability of a scale by dividing the total set of measurement items in half and correlating the results.

validity Degree to which what the researcher was trying to measure was actually measured.

face validity Degree to which a measurement seems to measure what it is supposed to measure.

content validity Representativeness, or sampling adequacy, of the content of the measurement instrument.

criterion-related validity Degree to which a measurement instrument can predict a variable that is designated a criterion.

predictive validity Degree to which a future level of a criterion variable can be forecast by a current measurement scale.

concurrent validity Degree to which another variable, measured at the same point in time as the variable of interest, can be predicted by the measurement instrument.

construct validity Degree to which a measurement instrument represents and logically connects, via the underlying theory, the observed phenomenon to the construct.

convergent validity Degree of correlation among different measurement instruments that purport to measure the same construct.

discriminant validity Measure of the lack of association among constructs that are supposed to be different.

QUESTIONS FOR REVIEW & CRITICAL THINKING

(Team Activity)

1. What is measurement?
2. Differentiate among the four types of measurement scales, and discuss the types of information obtained from each.

3. How does reliability differ from validity? Give examples of each.

4. Give an example of a scale that would be reliable but not valid. Also give an example of a scale that would be valid but not reliable.

5. What are three methods of assessing reliability?

6. What are three methods of assessing validity?

7. Divide the class into teams of four or five. Each team should go to the Internet and find the results of a survey with data. Each team should then determine the face validity and content validity of the research. Also, each team should suggest a method for assessing reliability of the survey.

WORKING THE NET

Go to a Web search engine and look up "validity and reliability." Describe to the class the new insights you gain into these important concepts.

REAL-LIFE RESEARCH • 10.1

Can Shopping Styles Be the Same around the World?

Global consumer packaged goods (CPG) shoppers should not be defined by their country but instead by their shopping attitudes and behavior—especially their attitudes toward price and their propensity to preplan their CPG purchases, according to a study conducted by Ipsos Marketing, a division of New York research company Ipsos North America.

Ipsos has identified five different types of CPG shoppers that can be found around the world in varying degrees. The five shopper segments are:

Brand Lovers (19 percent): The distinguishing trait of these shoppers is spending money on brands that may be more expensive than alternatives. These shoppers are the ones who are more influenced by store staff and place a greater value on convenience.

Price Driven (23 percent): With fixed budgets for grocery shopping, shoppers in this group are more likely to make a shopping list, compare prices, and go out of their way to find the stores with the lowest prices.

Indulgents (16 percent): The more impulsive group, this group is attracted to new products and is more likely to choose the good-tasting over the healthy option. They are happy to spend more to save time and don't mind paying more for branded products.

Responsible Planners (17 percent): Shoppers in this group are also on a fixed budget (like the Price-Driven shoppers) and always compare prices. They are the shoppers most likely to buy online and have changed their habits to shop in a more sustainable way.

Bargain Hunters (25 percent): Shoppers in this group also hunt for bargains but are less price-constrained and more impulsive. They can afford to buy in bulk and are less interested in shopping online.

These segments were developed based on a consumer survey conducted by Ipsos in 23 countries. The segmentation analysis revealed two important implications for CPG marketers. First, global CPG shoppers can be segmented based on their attitudes toward bargain-hunting, promotions, and price comparisons, and the degree to which they stick to their preplanned purchases versus buying on impulse. Second, country of residence is not a strong factor in trying to classify global shoppers into different segments. In fact, data suggests that consumers in different countries may exhibit similar shopping behavior even though they are geographically dispersed and at different stages of economic development.

"It's natural for marketers to try to customize their merchandising strategies to countries or geographies—there is an intuitive logic to doing that" says Donna Wydra, senior vice president, Ipsos Marketing, U.S. shopper and retail. "However, our findings demonstrate that retail strategies should align with shopping styles, which are not necessarily dictated by geography. For example, Brand Lovers dominate across China, India, Russia, and Turkey—therefore, marketers can take advantage of the opportunities that this provides as brands become more affordable in these growing economies. On the other hand, there is a need to continue to promote and meet the needs of the Bargain Hunters found in the United States, Canada, Great Britain, and Australia for whom smart shopping has become a way of life. The bottom line is that shopping strategies should align to shoppers, not countries."[10]

Questions

1. What is the construct in the research? Give a constitutive definition.
2. What level(s) of measurement could the researchers have used? Give examples.
3. What could the researchers have used to measure reliability?
4. How might the researchers approach the measurement of validity?
5. What can the researchers do to demonstrate construct validity?
6. Do you see this scale as having value to marketing researchers? Why?

REAL-LIFE RESEARCH • 10.2

Measuring Customer Satisfaction at GE

Not too long ago, Mark Dillon was fed up with General Electric Co. He had waited 6 months for GE's Capital Solutions group to approve a loan so that he could open an Applebee's restaurant in Wisconsin. When a survey firm called soon after and asked how likely, on a scale of 0 to 10, he would be to recommend the GE unit to a friend, Dillon responded, "one."

He wasn't alone. The survey revealed poor scores and stinging feedback from the unit's customers. In response, GE streamlined its loan process. Mr. Dillon recently tried GE again and closed a complex deal in 60 days. "Something changed," he says. "It was refreshing, to say the least."

To GE executives, Mr. Dillon's experience shows the value of the "net-promoter score," a tool for tracking customer sentiment that focuses on one question: "How likely are you to recommend us to a friend?"

Respondents are grouped into "proponents," "detractors," and "passives." Adherents say the concept, being promoted by consulting firm Bain & Co., allows them to track, and quickly address, customer concerns.

GE is using the concept in all of its businesses in an effort to reach customers from homeowners purchasing a refrigerator to hospitals buying medical equipment. Chief Executive Jeffrey Immelt highlights the net-promoter score as a key part of GE's growth formula. GE executives say the concept improves on past customer-tracking efforts, which are a patchwork of surveys and anecdotes.

"It's very hard to mobilize resources when you just have a comment here and there," says Paul Bossidy, chief executive of the Capital Solutions unit, which offers business loans and leases on products from printers to corporate jets.

Some users, however, caution against relying too much on the numerical scores. They are "not a silver bullet," says Steve Bennett, chief executive of software maker Intuit, Inc., which has used the net-promoter concept since 2002.

Bennett states that the surveys show taxpayers' preference for tax-preparation software, whether from Intuit or its rivals, rather than other methods of doing their taxes. But he finds the detailed customer comments more useful. For example, Bennett says Intuit eliminated rebates on its tax software after survey respondents reported that the paperwork was a hassle. Similarly, the company began offering 30 days of free assistance to small-business users of its accounting software. Changes are based "not only on a score but the insight you get from comments," Bennett notes.

At GE, Immelt has made the customer surveys a priority, telling managers that it would be a factor in their bonuses.

GE asks customers to rate on a scale of 0 to 10 how likely they would be to recommend the company to a friend. Those who rate GE a 9 or 10 are promoters, 7 or 8 passives, and 6 or lower detractors. To create a net-promoter score, the company subtracts the detractors from the promoters.

GE's diverse businesses have deployed the survey at different speeds with varied results. GE Capital Solutions has been surveying about 1,000 of its 1 million clients each month for the past year.

Mark Dillon was one of them. His Wisconsin Hospitality Group had relied on GE to finance most of its more than 120 Applebee's and Pizza Hut restaurants since the mid-1990s. In September 2004, Dillon applied for a loan to open a new Applebee's. Processing took 6 months when it should have taken no more than a week, he says.

Armed with scores and comments like Dillon's, GE's Paul Bossidy decided to focus on problems in the Capital Solutions unit that he previously understood only vaguely. Recently, he has made changes to speed loan processing and has hired analysts to help customers such as tugboat operators and construction-equipment makers.

Diane Cooper, head of the franchise-lending business, says her group reduced by one-third the steps—literally, footsteps—at its Scottsdale, Arizona office. Review teams now sit together, eliminating many trips across the sprawling office building. Cooper's group either dropped some processes or scheduled them to occur simultaneously. As a result, simple loans, such as the one for Mark Dillon's restaurant, are processed in 5 days or less, on average.[11]

Happy (and Not-So-Happy) Customers

General Electric is a big user of the net-promoter concept of customer satisfaction, popularized by Fred Reichheld of Bain & Co. Following are questions similar to those on which GE's Capital Solutions unit asks customers to rate the unit's performance on a 0 to 10 scale.

- How willing are you to recommend us to a friend or associate?
- How would you rate our ability to meet your needs?
- How would you rate our people?
- How would you rate our processes?
- What is your impression of our market reputation?
- How would you rate the cost of doing business with us?
- How would you rate the overall value of our product or service as being worth what you paid?

Source: General Electric Co.

Questions

1. What is the construct that GE is trying to measure?
2. How might GE assess construct validity?
3. Does "service recovery" play a big role in customer satisfaction?
4. What is the operational definition of the construct?
5. Does the scale adequately address the underlying construct?
6. What level of measurement is being used in the research? Could a higher level have been used?

Using Measurement Scales to Build Marketing Effectiveness

LEARNING OBJECTIVES

→ 1. To understand the linkage among attitudes, behavior, and marketing effectiveness.

→ 2. To become familiar with the concept of scaling.

→ 3. To learn about the various types of attitude scales.

→ 4. To examine some basic considerations in selecting a type of scale.

→ 5. To realize the importance of attitude measurement scales in management decision making.

What are the various ways to measure attitudes? Why is it useful to measure attitudes? What factors should be considered in creating an attitude scale? These questions will be addressed in this chapter.

Attitudes, Behavior, and Marketing Effectiveness

An attitude is a psychological construct, a way of conceptualizing an intangible. Attitudes cannot be observed or measured directly; their existence is inferred from their consequences. An **attitude** is an enduring organization of motivational, emotional, perceptual, and cognitive processes with respect to some aspect of a person's environment. In marketing research, it is a learned predisposition to respond in a consistently favorable or unfavorable manner toward an object or concept. Attitudes tend to be long lasting and consist of clusters of interrelated beliefs. They encompass a person's value system, which represents her or his standards of good and bad, right and wrong, and so forth. Thus, an individual may have a specific attitude toward Disney World, based on beliefs about a need for entertainment, cartoon characters, fantasy, crowds of people, waiting in lines, and many other things. Disney World also may be highly valued as good, clean, wholesome fun.

> **attitude**
> Enduring organization of motivational, emotional, perceptual, and cognitive processes with respect to some aspect of a person's environment.

Link between Attitudes and Behavior

The link between attitudes and behavior is complex. Predictions of future behavior for a group of consumers tend to be more accurate than those for a single consumer. Specifically, researchers have identified the following links:

1. The more favorable the attitude of consumers, the higher the incidence of product usage; the less favorable the attitude, the lower the incidence of product usage.

2. The less favorable people's attitudes toward a product, the more likely they are to stop using it.

Attitude measurement must be reliable, valid, and specific to the particular behavior. If the behavior is that of contributing to the American Cancer Society, the questions asked should refer to that charity. Go to *www.cancer.org* to find out what information is available to help in framing such questions.

3. The attitudes of people who have never tried a product tend to be distributed around the mean in the shape of a normal distribution.[1]

4. When attitudes are based on actually trying and experiencing a product, attitudes predict behavior quite well. Conversely, when attitudes are based on advertising, attitude–behavior consistency is significantly reduced.[2]

Some marketing researchers have become rather pessimistic about the ability of attitude research to predict behavior.[3] The present view of most researchers, however, is that one must learn to recognize the factors that influence the extent to which measured attitudes accurately predict behavior. Six factors should be considered in assessing whether attitude research findings will predict behavior:[4]

1. *Involvement of the consumer.* Attitudes are likely to predict purchase behavior only under conditions of high involvement.

2. *Attitude measurement.* The measure of attitude has to be reliable, valid, and at the same level of abstraction as the measure of behavior. For example, if the behavior involves contributing to a specific charity, such as the American Cancer Society, the attitude measure cannot ask less specific (i.e., more abstract) questions about consumers' attitudes toward charities in general. A similar consistency must be applied to the variable of time. If the behavior involves buying a new Porsche within the next 6 months, the measure should include a time parameter. The longer the time between attitude measurement and the behavior, the weaker the relationship is.

3. *Effects of other people.* The feelings of other people toward the purchase and the consumer's motivation to comply with these feelings influence the extent to which attitudes predict behavior.

4. *Situational factors.* If situational factors, such as holidays, time pressures, or sickness intervene, measured attitudes may fail to predict behavior well.

5. *Effects of other brands.* Even though a consumer's attitude toward a brand may be quite favorable, if that consumer's attitude toward another brand is even more favorable, the other brand will probably be purchased. One reason the "attitude toward the object" model is often unable to accurately predict behavior is that it fails to include measures of attitudes toward other objects.

6. *Attitude strength.* For an attitude to influence behavior, it must be held with sufficient strength and conviction to be activated in memory.[5] The degree of association between an attitude and an object varies across a continuum. At one end of the continuum is the nonattitude: The consumer has neither positive nor negative feelings about a particular brand. At the other end of the continuum is the extreme attitude: The consumer feels very strongly about the brand.

Enhancing Marketing Effectiveness

Attitudes are truly the essence of the "human change agent" that all marketers strive to influence. Marketing managers realize that there is not a perfect correlation between attitudes and behavior. Yet, in designing or modifying a marketing mix, managers know that attitude measures are often the best tool available for finding an effective mix. When Toyota is trying to decide which of three potential new designs will sell the most hybrid cars, it relies on attitude research. The implicit assumption is the design most preferred in attitude research testing will sell the most hybrids, all other things being equal. Thus, marketing managers measure attitudes in an attempt to predict behavior; correct predictions will enable managers to bring the "right" new product to the marketplace. This new product will be accompanied by the "right" marketing mix, again usually based to some extent on attitude research. Demographic data and past purchase patterns also are important data sources in deciding on a new marketing mix.

Scaling Defined

The term **scaling** refers to procedures for attempting to determine quantitative measures of subjective and sometimes abstract concepts. It is defined as a procedure for assigning numbers (or other symbols) to properties of an object in order to impart some numerical characteristics to the properties in question. Actually, numbers are assigned to *indicants* of the properties of objects. The rise and fall of mercury in a glass tube (a thermometer) is an indicant of temperature variations.

A scale is a measurement tool. Scales are either unidimensional or multidimensional. **Unidimensional scales** are designed to measure only one attribute of a concept, respondent, or object. Thus, a unidimensional scale measuring consumers' price sensitivity might include several items to measure price sensitivity, but combined into a single measure; all interviewees' attitudes are then placed along a linear continuum, called *degree of price sensitivity*. **Multidimensional scales** are based on the premise that a concept, respondent, or object might be better described using several dimensions. For example, target customers for Jaguar automobiles may be defined in three dimensions: level of wealth, degree of price sensitivity, and appreciation of fine motor cars.

> **scaling**
> Procedures for assigning numbers (or other symbols) to properties of an object in order to impart some numerical characteristics to the properties in question.

> **unidimensional scales**
> Scales designed to measure only one attribute of a concept, respondent, or object.

> **multidimensional scales**
> Scales designed to measure several dimensions of a concept, respondent, or object.

Attitude Measurement Scales

Measurement of attitudes relies on less precise scales than those found in the physical sciences and hence is much more difficult. Because an attitude is a construct that exists in the mind of the consumer, it is not directly observable—unlike, for example, weight in the physical sciences. In many cases, attitudes are measured at the nominal or ordinal level. Some more sophisticated scales enable the marketing researcher to measure at the interval level. One must be careful not to attribute the more powerful properties of an interval scale to the lower-level nominal or ordinal scales.

Graphic Rating Scales

Graphic rating scales offer respondents a graphic continuum, typically anchored by two extremes. Exhibit 11.1 depicts three types of graphic rating scales that might be used to evaluate La-Z-Boy recliners. Scale A represents the simplest form of a graphic scale. Respondents are instructed to mark their response on the continuum. After respondents have done so, scores are ascertained by dividing the line into as many categories as desired and assigning a score based on the category into which the mark has been placed. For example, if the line were 6 inches long, every inch might represent a category. Scale B offers the respondent slightly more structure by assigning numbers along the scale.

Responses to graphic rating scales are not limited to simply placing a mark on a continuum, as scale C illustrates. Scale C has been used successfully by many researchers to speed up self-administered interviews. Respondents are asked to touch the thermometer on the computer screen that best depicts their feelings.

Graphic rating scales can be constructed easily and are simple to use. They enable a researcher to discern fine distinctions, assuming that the rater has adequate discriminatory abilities. Numerical data obtained from the scales are typically treated as interval data.

One disadvantage of graphic rating scales is that overly extreme anchors tend to force respondents toward the middle of the scale. Also, some research has suggested that such scales are not as reliable as itemized rating scales.

> **graphic rating scales**
> Measurement scales that include a graphic continuum, anchored by two extremes.

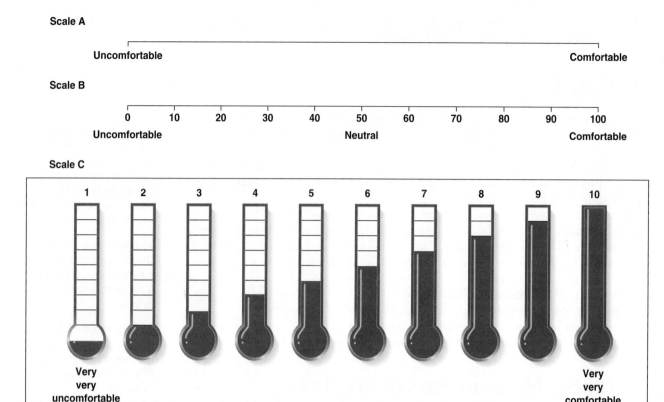

Scale A

Uncomfortable — Comfortable

Scale B

0 10 20 30 40 50 60 70 80 90 100

Uncomfortable — Neutral — Comfortable

Scale C

1 2 3 4 5 6 7 8 9 10

Very very uncomfortable — Very very comfortable

Exhibit 11.1

Three Types of Graphic Rating Scales

→ **itemized rating scales**
Measurement scales in which the respondent selects an answer from a limited number of ordered categories.

Itemized Rating Scales

Itemized rating scales are similar to graphic rating scales, except that respondents must select from a limited number of ordered categories rather than placing a mark on a continuous scale. (Purists would argue that scale C in Exhibit 11.1 is an itemized rating scale.) Exhibit 11.2 shows some examples of itemized rating scales taken from nation-wide marketing research surveys. Starting items are rotated on each questionnaire to eliminate the order bias that might arise from starting with the same item each time. Another example in the form of slider scales is discussed in the Practicing Marketing Research feature below.

PRACTICING MARKETING RESEARCH

Comparing the Traditional Likert Scale and Alternative Slider Scales[6]

Survey Sampling International ran a series of surveys designed to examine the differences between the performances of a "standard"

5-point Likert scale and a Flash-based slider scale. The two scales were assessed based on data collected, engagement, and respondent satisfaction with the instrument.

The experiment focused on two key ratings issues: equivalency of ratings and the spaces between ratings. In setting up the experiment, respondents were given a traditional Likert

	Disagree Strongly	Disagree Slightly	Neither/Nor	Agree Slightly	Agree Strongly
Traditional	12	40	105	231	201
Re-Scored Traditional	6	12	61	57	154
Labeled Slider	4	25	77	125	129
Mark Slider	1	17	92	88	114
Blank Slider	1	8	27	21	97
Slider with Score	4	10	51	47	124

Scale containing four statements and were asked at the end to rate how well they felt the instrument allowed them to express their true opinions. Respondents were then given a second scale on which they were allowed to rescore previous items on a scale up to 5 points in the direction of any adjacent ranks. While respondents generally expressed satisfaction with the accuracy of the traditional scale, a substantial portion chose to rerate, especially those posting ratings of agree/disagree slightly (as much as 75 percent). On the whole, the results indicated conclusively that the instrument did not offer a fine enough range of responses to precisely reflect respondents' opinions. In addition, items ranked the same could not be assumed to indicate equivalency of respondent opinions.

In the next stage of the experiment, respondents were asked to rate the statements again using a series of slider scales. Each of the four sliders was text anchored at the end and did not include any visual illustrative elements. The first slider offered the traditional labels; the second kept the hash-marks but removed the text; the third removed the marks; and the fourth added a numerical score between 1 and 5 to indicate the position of the slider. The following table offers an example of responses for all six ranking instruments. Responses were for the statement: The highest standards of morals and ethics is [sic] the most important thing in life.

Data distributions varied noticeably across the different designs, indicating that design did matter with regard to how respondents answered. In applying averages and mean scores, however, the data generally seemed to align across the scale designs. The clear takeaway was that the slider scales generally offered greater granularity in terms of response options. That granularity was reflected in respondent attitudes as, overall, respondents using slider scales reported higher satisfaction levels regardless of the slider design.

Questions

1. Using the following scale, assess the following statement: The assessment of the Likert scale in comparison to the slider scale is accurate.

2. Now given the opportunity, would you place your answer somewhere in between its current position and a position adjacent to it? Why or why not?

3. In answering the previous questions, do you think you have been able to accurately express your opinions regarding the given statement? Explain.

Scale A was used by a dot-com company in determining what features and services it should add to its Web site. Scale B was used in measuring satisfaction with an online travel site. Scale C was used by an e-commerce music retailer to better understand how people select a music Web site. Scale D was also an Internet survey, conducted by a producer of customer relationship management software. Examples of other itemized rating scales are shown in Exhibit 11.3.

If offered, how likely would you be to use the following areas on this site?

Scale A

a. Auctions
Not at all likely to use   o1   o2   o3   o4   o5   o6   o7   **Extremely likely to use**

b. Fee-based education tools
Not at all likely to use   o1   o2   o3   o4   o5   o6   o7   **Extremely likely to use**

c. Event registration
Not at all likely to use   o1   o2   o3   o4   o5   o6   o7   **Extremely likely to use**

d. Online shopping markets
Not at all likely to use   o1   o2   o3   o4   o5   o6   o7   **Extremely likely to use**

e. Recruiting
Not at all likely to use   o1   o2   o3   o4   o5   o6   o7   **Extremely likely to use**

f. Research subscription
Not at all likely to use   o1   o2   o3   o4   o5   o6   o7   **Extremely likely to use**

g. Trading community
Not at all likely to use   o1   o2   o3   o4   o5   o6   o7   **Extremely likely to use**

h. Training/seminars
Not at all likely to use   o1   o2   o3   o4   o5   o6   o7   **Extremely likely to use**

Scale B

Submitting a Request for a Hotel Reservation

We'd like to get your feedback regarding your experience in submitting a request for a hotel reservation at our Web site today. Please rate your satisfaction with each of the following aspects of *fasthotels.com* based on **your experience this visit**.

	Very Satisfied				Very Dissatisfied
	1	**2**	**3**	**4**	**5**
Ability to access the offer page	o	o	o	o	o
Ability to locate hotel information	o	o	o	o	o
Ability to locate city information	o	o	o	o	o
Clarity of how the bonus program works	o	o	o	o	o
Clarity of the purchase agreement	o	o	o	o	o

Please rate the extent to which you are satisfied that *Fasthotels.com* **has communicated** each of the following to you during this visit:

	Very Satisfied				Very Dissatisfied
	1	**2**	**3**	**4**	**5**
Your hotel reservation is/will be nonchangeable	o	o	o	o	o
Your hotel reservation is/will be nonrefundable	o	o	o	o	o

How **satisfied** would you say you were with **this visit** to *Fasthotels.com*?
- o   Very satisfied
- o   Satisfied
- o   Somewhat satisfied
- o   Neither satisfied nor dissatisfied
- o   Somewhat dissatisfied
- o   Dissatisfied
- o   Very dissatisfied

Scale C

What factors influence your choice of music Web sites? (Rate the importance of each item.)

	Not at All Important				Very Important
Customer benefits or rewards for shopping	o	o	o	o	o
Customer service or delivery options	o	o	o	o	o
Ease of use of Web site	o	o	o	o	o
Low prices	o	o	o	o	o
Real-time audio sampling of CDs	o	o	o	o	o
Reviews and artist information	o	o	o	o	o

Scale D

How interested would you be in obtaining additional information about this customer relationship management solution for your business?

o Extremely interested   o Somewhat interested   o Not at all interested
o Very interested   o Not very interested

How likely is it that your business will invest in this type of customer relationship management solution within the next 12 months?

o Extremely likely   o Somewhat likely   o Not at all likely
o Very likely   o Not very likely

Exhibit 11.2

Itemized Rating Scales Used in Internet and Mall Surveys (Continued)

EXHIBIT 11.3   Selected Itemized Rating Scales

Characteristic of Interest	Rating Choices				
Purchase Intent	Definitely will buy	Probably will buy	Probably will not buy	Definitely will not buy	
Level of Agreement	Strongly agree	Somewhat agree	Neither agree nor disagree	Somewhat disagree	Strongly disagree
Quality	Very good	Good	Neither good nor bad	Fair	Poor
Dependability	Completely dependable	Somewhat dependable	Not very dependable	Not dependable at all	
Style	Very stylish	Somewhat stylish	Not very stylish	Completely unstylish	
Satisfaction	Completely satisfied	Somewhat satisfied	Neither satisfied nor dissatisfied	Somewhat dissatisfied	Completely dissatisfied
Cost	Extremely expensive	Expensive	Neither expensive nor inexpensive	Slightly inexpensive	Very inexpensive
Ease of Use	Very easy to use	Somewhat easy to use	Not very easy to use	Difficult to use	
Color Brightness	Extremely bright	Very bright	Somewhat bright	Slightly bright	Not bright at all
Modernity	Very modern	Somewhat modern	Neither modern nor old-fashioned	Somewhat old-fashioned	Very old-fashioned

Although itemized rating scales do not allow for the fine distinctions that can be achieved in a graphic rating scale, they are easy to construct and administer. And the definitive categories found in itemized rating scales usually produce more reliable ratings.

When a researcher, for some reason, is interested in the most extreme position views, he or she may elect to use a two-stage format. Research has shown that a two-stage format can provide better data quality in detecting extreme views than a single-stage itemized rating scale. Following is an example of the two-stage approach.[7]

Traditional One-Stage Format

"How effective do you believe Senator Foghorn is in having your money stay in the community?"

Very effective	Somewhat effective	Somewhat ineffective	Very ineffective	Don't know
4	3	2	1	0

Two-Stage Format

"How effective do you believe Senator Foghorn is in having your money stay in the community?"

How *effective?*	Would that be very or *somewhat?*
☐ Effective	☐ Very
☐ Ineffective	☐ Somewhat
☐ No opinion	

Rank-Order Scales

→ **noncomparative scales**
Measurement scales in which judgment is made without reference to another object, concept, or person.

Itemized and graphic scales are considered to be **noncomparative scales** because the respondent makes a judgment without reference to another object, concept, or person. **Rank-order scales**, on the other hand, are **comparative scales** because the respondent is asked to compare two or more items and rank each item. Rank-order scales are widely used in marketing research for several reasons. They are easy to use and give ordinal measurements of the items evaluated. Instructions are easy to understand, and the process typically moves at a steady pace. Some researchers claim that rank-order scales force respondents to evaluate concepts in a realistic manner. Exhibit 11.4(A) illustrates a series of rank-order scales taken from a study on eye shadows. Exhibit 11.4(B) shows an online scale on automobile resale value percentage.

→ **rank-order scales**
Measurement scales in which the respondent compares two or more items and ranks them.

Rank-order scales possess several disadvantages. If all of the alternatives in a respondent's choice set are not included, the results could be misleading. For example, a respondent's first choice on all dimensions in the eye shadow study might have been Wet'n'Wild, which was not included. A second problem is that the concept being ranked may be completely outside a person's choice set, thus producing meaningless data. Perhaps a respondent doesn't use eye shadow and feels that the product isn't appropriate for any woman. Another limitation is that the scale gives the researcher only ordinal data. Nothing is learned about how far apart the items stand or how intensely the respondent feels about the ranking of an item. Finally, the researcher does not know why the respondent ranked the items as he or she did.

→ **comparative scales**
Measurement scales in which one object, concept, or person is compared with another on a scale.

Paired Comparisons

→ **paired comparison scales**
Measurement scales that ask the respondent to pick one of two objects in a set, based on some stated criteria.

Paired comparison scales ask a respondent to pick one of two objects from a set, based on some stated criteria. The respondent, therefore, makes a series of paired judgments between objects. Exhibit 11.5 shows a paired comparison scale used in a national study

Exhibit 11.4

Series of Rank-Order Scales Used to Evaluate Eye Shadows and Car Resale Values

Eye Shadow Scales

Please rank the following eye shadows, with 1 being the brand that best meets the characteristic being evaluated and 6 the worst brand on the characteristic being evaluated. The six brands are listed on card C. (HAND RESPONDENT CARD C.) Let's begin with the idea of having high-quality compacts or containers. Which brand would rank as having the highest quality compacts or containers? Which is second? (RECORD BELOW.)

	Q.48. Having High-Quality Container	Q.49. Having High-Quality Applicator	Q.50. Having High-Quality Eye Shadow
Avon	_____	_____	_____
Cover Girl	_____	_____	_____
Estee Lauder	_____	_____	_____
L'Oreal	_____	_____	_____
Natural Wonder	_____	_____	_____
Revlon	_____	_____	_____

Card C

Avon	Cover Girl	Estee Lauder
L'Oreal	Natural Wonder	Revlon

Car Resale Value Scale

Based on your personal experience or what you have seen, heard or read, please rank the following car brands according to the resale value percentage—that is, the brand that enables you to recover the largest dollar amount (percentage) of your original purchase price of the vehicle.

Place a "1" next to the brand that has the highest resale value percentage, a "2" next to the brand that has the next highest resale value percentage, and so forth. Remember, no two cars can have the same ranking.

_____	Chevrolet
_____	Toyota
_____	BMW
_____	Ford

for sun care products. Only part of the scale is shown; the data-collection procedure typically requires the respondent to compare all possible pairs of objects.

Paired comparisons overcome several problems of traditional rank-order scales. First, it is easier for people to select one item from a set of two than to rank a large set of data. Second, the problem of order bias is overcome; there is no pattern in the ordering of items or questions to create a source of bias. On the negative side, because all possible pairs are evaluated, the number of paired comparisons increases geometrically as the number of objects to be evaluated increases arithmetically. Thus, the number of objects to be evaluated should remain fairly small to prevent interviewee fatigue.

Constant Sum Scales

To avoid long lists of paired items, marketing researchers use **constant sum scales** more often than paired comparisons. Constant sum scales require the respondent to divide a given number of points, typically 100, among two or more attributes based on their importance to him or her. Respondents must value each item relative to all other items. The number of points allocated to each alternative indicates the ranking assigned to it by the respondent, as well as the relative magnitude of each alternative as perceived by the respondent. A constant sum scale used in a national study of tennis sportswear is shown in Exhibit 11.6. Another advantage of the constant sum scale over a rank-order or paired

constant sum scales
Measurement scales that ask the respondent to divide a given number of points, typically 100, among two or more attributes, based on their importance to him or her.

Exhibit 11.5

Paired Comparison Scale for Sun Care Products

Here are some characteristics used to describe sun care products in general. Please tell me which characteristic in each pair is more important to you when selecting a sun care product.

a. Tans evenly	b. Tans without burning
a. Prevents burning	b. Protects against burning and tanning
a. Good value for the money	b. Goes on evenly
a. Not greasy	b. Does not stain clothing
a. Tans without burning	b. Prevents burning
a. Protects against burning and tanning	b. Good value for the money
a. Goes on evenly	b. Tans evenly
a. Prevents burning	b. Not greasy

comparison scale is that if the respondent perceives two characteristics to have equal value, he or she can so indicate.

A major disadvantage of this scale is that the respondent may have difficulty allocating the points to total 100 if there are a lot of characteristics or items. Most researchers feel that 10 items is the upper limit on a constant sum scale.

Semantic Differential Scales

The semantic differential was developed by Charles Osgood, George Suci, and Percy Tannenbaum.[8] The focus of their original research was on the measurement of meaning of an object to a person. The object might be a savings and loan association and the meaning its image among a certain group of people.

The construction of a **semantic differential scale** begins with determination of a concept to be rated, such as the image of a company, brand, or store. The researcher selects dichotomous (opposite) pairs of words or phrases that could be used to describe the concept. Respondents then rate the concept on a scale (usually 1 to 7). The mean of the responses for each pair of adjectives is computed, and the means are plotted as a profile or image.

Exhibit 11.7 is an actual profile of an Arizona savings and loan association as perceived by noncustomers with family incomes of $80,000 and above. A quick glance shows that the firm is viewed as somewhat old-fashioned, with rather plain facilities. It is viewed as well-established, reliable, successful, and probably very nice to deal with. The institution has parking problems and perhaps entry and egress difficulties. Its advertising is viewed as dismal.

The semantic differential is a quick and efficient means of examining the strengths and weaknesses of a product or company image versus those of the competition. More importantly, however, the semantic differential has been shown to be sufficiently reliable and valid for decision making and prediction in marketing and the behavioral sciences.[9] Also, the semantic differential has proved to be statistically robust (generalizable from one group of subjects to another) when applied to corporate image research.[10] This makes possible the measurement and comparison of images held by interviewees with diverse backgrounds.

Although these advantages have led many researchers to use the semantic differential as an image measurement tool, it is not without disadvantages. First, the semantic differential suffers from a lack of standardization. It is a highly generalized technique that must be adapted for each research problem. There is no single set of standard scales; hence, the development of customized scales becomes an integral part of the research.

The number of divisions on the semantic differential scale also presents a problem. If too few divisions are used, the scale is crude and lacks meaning; if too many are used, the

semantic differential scales Measurement scales that examine the strengths and weaknesses of a concept by having the respondent rank it between dichotomous pairs of words or phrases that could be used to describe it; the means of the responses are then plotted as a profile or image.

Below are seven characteristics of women's tennis sportswear. Please allocate 100 points among the characteristics such that the allocation represents the importance of each characteristic to you. The more points that you assign to a characteristic, the more important it is. If the characteristic is totally unimportant, you should not allocate any points to it. When you've finished, please double-check to make sure that your total adds to 100.

Characteristics of Tennis Sportswear	Number of Points
Is comfortable to wear	_____
Is durable	_____
Is made by well-known brand or sports manufacturers	_____
Is made in the United States	_____
Has up-to-date styling	_____
Gives freedom of movement	_____
Is a good value for the money	_____
	100 points

Exhibit 11.6

Constant Sum Scale Used in Tennis Sportswear Study

Adjective 1			Mean of Each Adjective Pair					Adjective 2
	1	2	3	4	5	6	7	
Modern								Old-fashioned
Aggressive								Defensive
Friendly								Unfriendly
Well-established								Not well established
Attractive exterior								Unattractive exterior
Reliable								Unreliable
Appeals to small companies								Appeals to big companies
Makes you feel at home								Makes you feel uneasy
Helpful services								Indifferent to customers
Nice to deal with								Hard to deal with
No parking or transportation problems								Parking or transportation problems
My kind of people								Not my kind of people
Successful								Unsuccessful
Ads attract a lot of attention								Haven't noticed ads
Interesting ads								Uninteresting ads
Influential ads								Not influential

Exhibit 11.7

Semantic Differential Profile of an Arizona Savings and Loan Association

scale goes beyond the ability of most people to discriminate. Researchers have found the 7-point scale to be the most satisfactory.

Another disadvantage of the semantic differential is the *halo effect*. The rating of a specific image component may be dominated by the interviewee's overall impression of the concept being rated. Bias may be significant if the image is hazy in the respondent's mind. To partially counteract the halo effect, the researcher should randomly reverse scale adjectives so that all the "good" ones are not placed on one side of the scale and the "bad" ones on the other. This forces the interviewee to evaluate the adjectives before responding. After the data have been gathered, all the positive adjectives are placed on one side and the negative ones on the other to facilitate analysis.

GLOBAL RESEARCH

Cross-Cultural Segmentation: Accounting for Cross-Cultural Response Differences When Using Survey Rating Scales[11]

Marketers looking to develop a market segment on a global scale must take into account cultural differences in the way people respond to survey scale questions. While it may vary depending on the respondent group, three major trends tend to appear in the answers of respondents from different cultures.

1. Respondents offer high ratings for all questions.
2. Respondents offer low ratings for all questions.
3. Respondents bunch ratings at the ends of the scale.

As a result, marketing researchers have developed techniques to normalize survey responses across different cultures and countries of origin.

One technique is a Hierarchical Bayes scale usage model, which creates adjustments for individual respondents based on mean and standard deviation estimates. With these adjustments factored in, researchers combine data across countries and proceed with analysis as usual.

Another option is to choose a rating system other than scales, such as Maximum Difference or other choice modeling formats. In these sorts of formats, respondents might be given small groups of attributes and asked to select the one they think is most important and least important.

This type of most-least format offers two key benefits when dealing with cross-cultural segmentation. First, by forcing respondents to make discriminating choices between options, most-least surveys avoid the cultural biases that might appear in scale rankings. Second, the most-least survey is simpler than a full sort-and-rank survey, but it still demonstrates respondent preference.

Most-least surveys could be analyzed using Latent Class choice modeling to create customer segments with unique attribute importance scores or Hierarchical Bayes choice modeling to create unique attribute importance scores for every respondent.

Questions

1. In what kinds of situations do you think you would need a cross-cultural survey sample? Would it not be easier to simply segment your sample based on culture and respond individually to each culturally different market segment?
2. What, if any, weaknesses do you see in the methods described above when dealing with cross-cultural segments?

Stapel Scales

> **Stapel scales**
> Measurement scales that require the respondent to rate, on a scale ranging from +5 to –5, how closely and in what direction a descriptor adjective fits a given concept.

The **Stapel scale** is a modification of the semantic differential. A single adjective is placed in the center of the scale, which typically is a 10-point scale ranging from +5 to –5. The technique is designed to measure both the direction and the intensity of attitudes simultaneously. (The semantic differential, on the other hand, reflects how closely the descriptor adjective fits the concept being evaluated.) An example of a Stapel scale is shown in Exhibit 11.8.

The primary advantage of the Stapel scale is that it enables the researcher to avoid the arduous task of creating bipolar adjective pairs. The scale may also permit finer discrimination in measuring attitudes. A drawback is that descriptor adjectives can be phrased in a positive, neutral, or negative vein, and the choice of phrasing has been shown to affect the

+5	+5
+4	+4
+3	+3
+2	+2
+1	+1
Cheap Prices	Easy to Navigate
−1	−1
−2	−2
−3	−3
−4	−4
−5	−5

Select a "plus" number for words you think describe the Web site accurately. The more accurately you think the word describes the Web site, the larger the "plus" number you should choose. Select a "minus" number for words you think do not describe the Web site accurately. The less accurately you think the word describes the Web site, the larger the "minus" number you should choose. Therefore, you can select any number from 15 for words you think are very accurate all the way to −5 for words you think are very inaccurate.

Exhibit 11.8

Stapel Scale Used to Measure a Retailer's Web Site

scale results and the person's ability to respond.[12] The Stapel scale has never had much popularity in commercial research and is used less frequently than the semantic differential.

Likert Scales

The **Likert scale** is another scale that avoids the problem of developing pairs of dichotomous adjectives. The scale consists of a series of statements expressing either a favorable or an unfavorable attitude toward the concept under study. The respondent is asked to indicate the level of her or his agreement or disagreement with each statement by assigning it a numerical score. The scores are then totaled to measure the respondent's attitude.

Exhibit 11.9 shows two Likert scales for an Internet game site targeted toward teenagers. Scale A measures attitudes toward the registration process; scale B evaluates users' attitudes toward advertising on the Web site.

With the Likert scale, the respondent is required to consider only one statement at a time, with the scale running from one extreme to the other. A series of statements (attitudes) can be examined, yet there is only a single set of uniform replies for the respondent to choose from.

Rensis Likert created this scale to measure a person's attitude toward concepts (e.g., unions), activities (e.g., swimming), and so forth. He recommended the following steps in building the scale:

1. The researcher identifies the concept or activity to be scaled.

2. The researcher assembles a large number of statements (75 to 100) concerning the public's sentiments toward the concept or activity.

3. Each test item is classified by the researcher as generally "favorable" or "unfavorable" with regard to the attitude under study. No attempt is made to scale the items; however, a pretest is conducted that involves the full set of statements and a limited sample of respondents.

4. In the pretest, the respondent indicates agreement (or not) with *every* item, checking one of the following direction-intensity descriptors:
   a. Strongly agree
   b. Agree
   c. Undecided
   d. Disagree
   e. Strongly disagree

> **Likert scales**
> Measurement scales in which the respondent specifies a level of agreement or disagreement with statements expressing either a favorable or an unfavorable attitude toward the concept under study.

People's attitudes toward activities like snowboarding can be measured using Likert scales.

5. Each response is given a numerical weight (e.g., 5, 4, 3, 2, 1).

6. The individual's *total attitude score* is represented by the algebraic summation of weights associated with the items checked. In the scoring process, weights are assigned so that the direction of attitude—favorable to unfavorable—is consistent over items. For example, if 5 were assigned to "strongly agree" for favorable items, 5 should be assigned to "strongly disagree" for unfavorable items.

7. After seeing the results of the pretest, the researcher selects only those items that appear to discriminate well between high and low *total* scorers. This may be done by first finding the highest and lowest quartiles of subjects on the basis of *total* score and then comparing the mean differences on each *specific* item for these high and low groups (excluding the middle 50 percent of subjects).

8. The 20 to 25 items finally selected are those that have discriminated "best" (i.e., exhibited the greatest differences in mean values) between high and low total scorers in the pretest.

9. Steps 3 through 5 are then repeated in the main study.

Likert created the scale so that a researcher could look at a summed score and tell whether a person's attitude toward a concept was positive or negative. For example, the maximum favorable score on a 20-item scale would be 100; therefore, a person scoring 92 would be presumed to have a favorable attitude. Of course, two people could both score 92 and yet have rated various statements differently. Thus, specific components of their overall attitude could differ markedly. For example, if respondent A strongly agreed (5) that a particular bank had good parking and strongly disagreed (1) that its loan programs were the best in town and respondent B had the exact opposite attitude, both would have summed scores of 6.

In the world of marketing research, Likert-like scales are very popular. They are quick and easy to construct and can be administered by telephone or via the Internet. Commercial researchers rarely follow the textbook-like process just outlined. Instead, the scale usually is developed jointly by a client project manager and a researcher. Many times, the scale is created following a focus group.

Purchase Intent Scales

purchase intent scales
Scales used to measure a respondent's intention to buy or not buy a product.

Perhaps the single scale used most often in marketing research is the **purchase intent scale**. The ultimate issue for marketing managers is, will they buy the product or not? If so, what percentage of the market can I expect to obtain? The purchase intent question normally is asked for all new products and services and product and service modifications by manufacturers, retailers, and even nonprofit organizations.[13]

During new-product development, the purchase intent question is first asked during concept testing to get a rough idea of demand. The manager wants to quickly eliminate potential turkeys, take a careful look at those products for which purchase intent is moderate, and push forward the products that seem to have star potential. At this

Exhibit 11.9

Likert Scales Used by
an Internet Game Site

Scale A

How did you feel about the registration process when you became a new user?

	Strongly disagree	Somewhat disagree	Neutral	Somewhat agree	Strongly agree
The registration was simple.	O	O	O	O	O
The registration questions were "nonthreatening."	O	O	O	O	O
Registration here will protect my privacy.	O	O	O	O	O
The registration did not take a long time to complete.	O	O	O	O	O
The registration informed me about the site.	O	O	O	O	O

Scale B

How do you feel about the following statements?

	Strongly disagree	Somewhat disagree	Neutral	Somewhat agree	Strongly agree
Allowing companies to advertise on the Internet allows me to access free services.	O	O	O	O	O
I do not support advertising on this site even though it provides me with free entertainment.	O	O	O	O	O
There is extremely too much advertising on the Internet.	O	O	O	O	O
There is extremely too much advertising on this site.	O	O	O	O	O
It's easy for me to ignore the advertising on this site and just play the game.	O	O	O	O	O

stage, investment is minimal and product modification or concept repositioning is an easy task. As the product moves through development, the product itself, promotion strategy, price levels, and distribution channels become more concrete and focused. Purchase intent is evaluated at each stage of development and demand estimates are refined. The crucial go–no go decision for national or regional rollout typically comes after test marketing. Immediately before test marketing, commercial researchers have

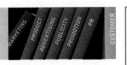

PRACTICING MARKETING RESEARCH

To Choose or Not to Choose? Are Choice Techniques the Right Choice?[14]

As marketers are expecting the research industry to deliver results that are predictive of the real world, choosing the right approach to research projects becomes increasingly important. This is especially true as the quality of data and collection methods are brought into question as well. One solution to this problem is to use research methodologies that reflect real-world decision-making processes, specifically by forcing people to make choices.

One example of these kinds of choices can be seen in political polls. Leading up to the presidential election in 2008, *Realclearpolitics.com* tracked 15 different polls from a wide variety of sources, using many different data-collection and screening methodologies. Surprisingly, the results of the polls were highly correlated and fell within an acceptable margin of error in relation to the actual election outcome. Such high correlation and accuracy levels are typical of political polls.

One of the major reasons for this is that the questions on political polls closely reflect the actual choice that voters have to make, for example, "Would you vote for Candidate A or Candidate B?" Often market research projects will ask questions that break down consumer preferences and perceptions, separating out all the decision-making factors individually. This deconstruction of preference complicates the consumer's actual decision-making process in ways that are not always true to real-world decision making and require the researcher to further determine which factors are most important.

With many choice techniques available—discrete choice, maximum difference, configurations, ranking—and the analytical tools to identify the reasons a respondent made a particular decision, it isn't always necessary to ask respondents to do the sorting-out themselves. Choice techniques may have some limitations compared to attribute ratings—when viewing answers to a poll, the researcher must still determine whether the response reflects the respondent's actual opinion or if it's just a matter of perception. Nonetheless, there is still great potential in using choice techniques that makes them worth consideration.

Questions

1. In what research situations do you think polls would be less effective? Why?
2. Compared to choice techniques, attribute batteries can be easier to set up and more familiar to the end users of the research. Do you think this ease of use could be a legitimate reason to choose attribute batteries over choice techniques?

---

another critical stage of evaluation. Here, the final or near-final version of the product is placed in consumers' homes in test cities around the country. After a period of in-home use (usually 2 to 6 weeks), a follow-up survey is conducted among participants to find out their likes and dislikes, how the product compares with what they use now, and what they would pay for it. The critical question near the end of the questionnaire is purchase intent.

Question 21 in Exhibit 11.10 is a purchase intent question taken from a follow-up study on in-home placement of a fly trap. The trap consisted of two 3-inch disks held

21. If a set of three traps sold for approximately $3.00 and was available in the stores where you normally shop, would you:

	(51)
definitely buy the set of traps	1
probably buy	2
probably not buy	3
definitely not buy	4

22. Would you use the traps (a) instead of or (b) in addition to existing products?

	(52)
instead of	1
in addition to	2

23. Would you recommend this product to your friends?

	(53)
definitely	1
probably	2
probably not	3
definitely not	4

Exhibit 11.10

Purchase Intent Scale and Related Questions for In-Home Product Placement of Fly Traps

---

about one-quarter inch apart by three plastic pillars; it looked somewhat like a large, thin yo-yo. The trap contained a pheromone to attract the flies and a glue that would remain sticky for 6 months. Supposedly, the flies flew in but never out. Centered on the back side of one of the disks was an adhesive tab so that the disk could be attached to a kitchen window. The concept was to eliminate flies in the kitchen area without resorting to a pesticide. Question 22 was designed to aid in positioning the product, and question 23 traditionally was used by the manufacturer as a double-check on purchase intent. If 60 percent of the respondents claimed that they definitely would buy the product and 90 percent said they definitely would not recommend the product to their friends, the researcher would question the validity of the purchase intent.

The purchase intent scale has been found to be a good predictor of consumer choice of frequently purchased and durable consumer products.[15] The scale is very easy to construct, and consumers are simply asked to make a subjective judgment of their likelihood of buying a new product. From past experience in the product category, a marketing manager can translate consumer responses on the scale to estimates of purchase probability. Obviously, everyone who "definitely will buy" the product will not do so; in fact, a few who state that they definitely will not buy actually will buy the product. The manufacturer of the fly trap is a major producer of both pesticide and nonpesticide pest control products. Assume that, based on historical follow-up studies, the manufacturer has learned the following about purchase intent of nonpesticide home-use pest-control products:

- 63 percent of the "definitely will buy" actually purchase within 12 months.
- 28 percent of the "probably will buy" actually purchase within 12 months.
- 12 percent of the "probably will not buy" actually purchase within 12 months.
- 3 percent of the "definitely will not buy" actually purchase within 12 months.

Suppose that the fly trap study resulted in the following:

- 40 percent—definitely will buy
- 20 percent—probably will buy
- 30 percent—probably will not buy
- 10 percent—definitely will not buy

Assuming that the sample is representative of the target market,

$$(0.4)(63\%) + (0.2)(28\%) + (0.3)(12\%) + (0.1)(3\%)$$
$$= 35.7\% \text{ market share}$$

Most marketing managers would be deliriously happy about such a high market share prediction for a new product. Unfortunately, because of consumer confusion, the product was killed after the in-home placement despite the high prediction.

It is not uncommon for marketing research firms to conduct studies containing a purchase intent scale in cases where the client does not have historical data to use as a basis for weighing the results. A reasonable but conservative estimate would be 70 percent of the "definitely will buy," 35 percent of the "probably will buy," 10 percent of the "probably will not buy," and zero of the "definitely will not buy."[16] Higher weights are common in the industrial market.

Some companies use the purchase intent scale to make go–no go decisions in product development without reference to market share. Typically, managers simply add the "definitely will buy" and "probably will buy" percentages and compare that total to a predetermined go–no go threshold. Combining "definitely" and "probably" is referred to as a top two box score. One consumer goods manufacturer, for example, requires a box score of 80 percent or higher at the concept testing stage and 65 percent for a product to move from in-home placement tests to test marketing.

Scale Conversions[17]

A considerable amount of voice-of-the-customer (VOC) data, also called customer satisfaction studies, is collected using tracking studies. Tracking studies simply follow changes in consumers' attitudes and purchase behavior over time. For example, VOC research may be conducted every quarter or every 6 months. Sometimes situations arise in firms, such as policy changes, that require changes in the VOC research methodology. One such change is moving from one scale (say, 5-point) to another scale (say, 10-point). There could be many reasons for that kind of change, but it raises the obvious question: How can data collected using the two scales be compared?

The objective is to aid the researcher in comparing data that are measured in different ways and make informed decisions. The underlying assumption here is that the scale wording is sufficiently comparable that scale conversions can be attempted. Although several techniques can be used for scale conversion, we will examine a simple, straightforward method here.

In the scale equivalence approach, no attempt is made to modify the data in any way. Instead, the focus is on identifying the appropriate way of reporting that would enable scores to become comparable. This wouldn't be applicable in all situations and is useful primarily in situations where "boxed" scores (top-two box, top-three box, etc.) are reported.

Consider four scales (in terms of scale points) that are commonly used in marketing research: 5-point, 7-point, 10-point, and 11-point scales. Often, the results of a study using these kinds of scales are reported using boxed scores. Questions then relate to how a study using a 5-point scale and reporting on "top-two box" scores can be translated when the new scale has, say, 7 points. In the approach of scale equivalence, we look at the proportion of a scale each scale point covers.

For example, each scale point on a 5-point scale covers 20 percent of the scale. That is, if we were generating completely random data to respond to this scale, we would expect approximately 20 percent of the responses to be 1, 20 percent to be 2, and so on. Therefore, a top-two box score would cover 40 percent of the scale points on a 5-point scale. Similarly, for a 7-point scale, each scale point accounts for approximately 14 percent of the scale, and top-two box scores would account for about 28 percent of the scale points. Exhibit 11.11 shows the box score distributions for the four scales.

EXHIBIT 11.11	Box Score Distributions for Four Scales				
Scale	Top 1	Top 2	Top 3	Top 4	Top 5
5-point	20%	40%			
7-point	14%	28%	42%		
10-point	10%	20%	30%	40%	
11-point	9%	18%	27%	36%	45%

The boxed numbers show, for example, that a top-two box score on a 5-point scale accounts for approximately the same proportion of the scale as a top-three box score on a 7-point scale, or a top-four box score on a 10-point scale (approximately 40 percent). Hence, when data using these scales are to be compared, the relevant number of top boxes could be used. More generally, Exhibit 11.12 provides (approximate) conversions for boxed scores among the four scales. A "?" indicates that a simple conversion is not available.

EXHIBIT 11.12	Approximate Conversions for Boxed Scores among Four Scales		
11-Point Scale	10-Point Scale	7-Point Scale	5-Point Scale
?	Top-4 Box	Top-3 Box	Top-2 Box
Top-3 Box	Top-3 Box	Top-2 Box	?
Top-2 Box	Top-2 Box	?	Top Box

Considerations in Selecting a Scale

Most nonimage studies include a purchase intent scale. But many other questions arise in selecting a scale. Considerations include the nature of the construct being measured, type of scale, balanced versus nonbalanced scale, number of scale categories, and forced versus nonforced choice.

The Nature of the Construct Being Measured

A basic check of the appropriateness of a scale is confirmation that it is drawn directly from the overall objective of the research study. The scope of the research objectives has a fundamental effect on the manner in which scales are used for survey measurement.

Type of Scale

Most commercial researchers lean toward scales that can be administered over the telephone or via the Internet, to save interviewing expense. Ease of administration and development also are important considerations. For example, a rank-order scale can be

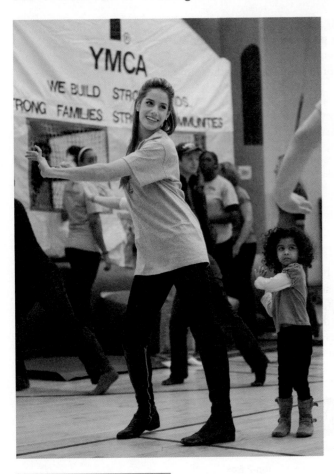

Past research has indicated that the YMCA has an overall positive image. This means that a nonbalanced scale with more positive gradients than negative can be used in future research about the YMCA. Go to www.ymca.com to see how the YMCA is using research to reach new customers.

→ **balanced scales**
Measurement scales that have the same number of positive and negative categories.

→ **nonbalanced scales**
Measurement scales that are weighted toward one end or the other of the scale.

quickly created, whereas developing a semantic differential (rating) scale is often a long and tedious process. The client's decision-making needs are always of paramount importance. Can the decision be made using ordinal data, or must the researcher provide interval information? Researchers also must consider the respondents, who usually prefer nominal and ordinal scales because of their simplicity. Ultimately, the choice of which type of scale to use will depend on the problem at hand and the questions that must be answered. It is not uncommon to find several types of scales in one research study. For example, an image study for a grocery chain might have a ranking scale of competing chains and a semantic differential to examine components of the chain's image.

Marketing researchers sometimes borrow scales directly from other studies or Internet sites. Many online survey sites have libraries of scales available. (See *surveymonkey.com*; *custominsight.com*; *surveysystem.com*; and *express.perseus.com*.) There are also several scale handbooks that facilitate the appropriate measures and encourage researchers to standardize on previously developed and validated measures.[18] This makes the research stream more cumulative. Marketing researchers often find that these borrowed scales work just fine. Sometimes, however, they don't work very well.

A marketing researcher should fully understand the nature of the construct that was measured, the scope of the measurement, and the content and phrasing of the scale items for relevance to a new population before borrowing a scale. In sum, the caveat is "borrow with caution."[19]

Balanced versus Nonbalanced Scale

A **balanced scale** has the same number of positive and negative categories; a **nonbalanced scale** is weighted toward one end or the other. If the researcher expects a wide range of opinions, then a balanced scale probably is in order. If past research or a preliminary study has determined that most opinions are positive, then using a scale with more positive gradients than negative ones will enable the researcher to ascertain the degree of positiveness toward the concept being researched. We have conducted a series of studies for the YMCA and know that its overall image is positive. Thus, we used the following categories to track the YMCA's image: (1) outstanding, (2) very good, (3) good, (4) fair, (5) poor.

Number of Scale Categories

The number of categories to be included in a scale is another issue that must be resolved by the marketing researcher. If the number of categories is too small—for example, good, fair, poor—the scale is crude and lacks richness. A 3-category scale does not reveal the intensity of feeling that, say, a 10-category scale offers. Yet, a 10-category scale may go beyond a person's ability to accurately discriminate among categories. Research has shown that rating scales with either 5 or 7 points are the most reliable.[20]

With an even number of scale categories, there is no neutral point. Without a neutral point, respondents are forced to indicate some degree of positive or negative feelings on an issue. Persons who are truly neutral are not allowed to express their neutrality. On the other hand, some marketing researchers say that putting a neutral point on a scale gives the respondent an easy way out, allowing the person with no really strong opinion to avoid concentrating on his or her actual feelings. Of course, it is rather unusual for any individual to be highly emotional about a new flavor of salad dressing, a package design, or a test commercial for a pickup truck!

Forced versus Nonforced Choice

As mentioned in the discussion of semantic differential scales, if a neutral category is included it typically will attract those who are neutral and those who lack adequate knowledge to answer the question. Some researchers have resolved this issue by adding a "Don't know" response as an additional category. For example, a semantic differential might be set up as follows:

Friendly	1	2	3	4	5	6	7	**Unfriendly**	Don't Know
Unexciting	1	2	3	4	5	6	7	**Exciting**	Don't Know

A "Don't know" option, however, can be an easy out for the lazy respondent.

If it has a neutral point, a scale without a "Don't know" option does not force a respondent to give a positive or negative opinion. A scale without a neutral point or a "Don't know" option forces even those persons with no information about an object to state an opinion. The argument for forced choice is that the respondent has to concentrate on his or her feelings. The arguments against forced choice are that inaccurate data are recorded and that some respondents may refuse to answer the question. A questionnaire that continues to require respondents to provide an opinion when, in fact, they lack the necessary information to do so can create ill will and result in early termination of the interview. The Practicing Marketing Research feature below discusses analysis of 7- and 10-point scales.

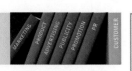

PRACTICING MARKETING RESEARCH

A Factor Analysis Case: The 10-Point Scale versus the 7-Point Scale[21]

Research indicates that a 10-point scale generally shows greater variability and is more effective when conducting multivariate analysis compared with a 7-point scale. But how do the 10-and 7-point scales compare with regard to factor analysis?

When respondents are given a long list of statements to rank, factor analysis helps distill them into their underlying conceptual dimensions. As such, well-defined rating scales are critical in factor analysis. If the rating scales do not effectively reflect these underlying dimensions, the factor analysis will be less efficient.

In 2006 and 2007, two comparable studies were performed to segment the telecom market based on consumer behaviors. The first was performed in 12 countries, using a 7-point scale; however, the resulting data was highly skewed. The study was repeated in 2007 across 18 countries, but this time a test run was performed in Australia to test the effectiveness of the 7-point scale against a 10-point scale. Respondents were directed to rank the importance of 50 potential category drivers over the scales ranging from "not important at all" to "very important."

First, any flatline results were removed before performing a factor analysis on the data. A principal component method was applied in the analysis based on a correlation matrix. Eleven factors were examined with respect to total variance, and for a 3-factor solution, which was determined to be most appropriate for these surveys, the 10-point scale, at 65 percent, explained 6 percent more variance than the 7-point scale. In a social research context, total variance results over 60 percent can generally be accepted. Generally, the cumulative variance of the 10-point scale proved greater than that of the 7-point scale, though the difference in variance tended to correlate inversely with the number of factors. As a split sample was used in the testing, the results would appear to be validated and might thus be projected to the general population.

The factor analysis performed on these tests did have its limitations. Needs statements tended to reflect emotional factors, which being subjective would tend toward greater variability. However, as the 10-point scale produced a better segmentation output in the test country, it was eventually adopted over the 7-point scale for use in the remaining 17 countries, producing satisfactory results with nine distinct segments included.

Questions

1. With only a difference of 6 percent for three factors, which would fall even further as the number of factors increases, do you think it really matters whether you use a 10-point scale rather than a 7-point scale?

2. How great of a factor do you think the choice of the test country was in the results? Do you think results might have been different if they had chosen a different test country?

Preferred Scale—Visual mode (paper, PC or Web-based, personal with "show card")

Overall, how satisfied were you with _____? Please check only one box

Not at All Satisfied	Slightly Satisfied	Somewhat Satisfied	Very Satisfied	Completely Satisfied
☐	☐	☐	☐	☐

Preferred Scale—Telephone or Mail Mode

Overall, how satisfied were you with _____? Would you say that you were not at all satisfied, slightly satisfied, somewhat satisfied, very satisfied, or completely satisfied? [RECORD ONE ANSWER.]

Attitude Measures and Management Decision Making

So far in this chapter we have discussed the nature of attitudes, various types of measurement scales, and some considerations in creating a scale. We now turn our attention to making attitude research more valuable for management decision making.

In the wide spectrum of features of a product or brand, there are some that predispose consumers to action (that is, to preference for the product, to actual purchase, to making recommendations to friends, and so on) and others that do not. Attitudes that are most closely related to preference or to actual purchase decisions are said to be **determinant attitudes**. Other attitudes—no matter how favorable—are not determinant. Obviously, marketers need to know which features lead to attitudes that "determine" buying behavior, for these are the features around which marketing strategy must be built.[22]

➤ **determinant attitudes**
Those consumer attitudes most closely related to preferences or to actual purchase decisions.

With reference to determinant attitudes, Nelson Foote, manager of the consumer and public relations research program for General Electric, commented: "In the electrical appliance business, we have been impressed over and over by the way in which certain characteristics of products come to be taken for granted by consumers, especially those concerned with basic functional performance or with values like safety."

"If these values are missing in a product, the user is extremely offended," he said. "But if they are present, the maker or seller gets no special credit or preference because, quite logically, every other maker and seller is assumed to be offering equivalent values. In other words, the values that are salient in decision making are the values that are problematic—that are important, to be sure, but also those which differentiate one offering from another."

In proprietary studies evaluating such automobile attributes as power, comfort, economy, appearance, and safety, for example, consumers often rank safety as first in importance. However, these same consumers do not see various makes of cars as differing widely with respect to safety; therefore, safety is not a determinant feature in the actual purchase decision. This fact should rightly lead the company to concentrate on raising its performance in features other than safety. However, if safety is totally ignored, the brand may soon be perceived as being so unsafe that it loses some of its share of the market. At this point, safety would achieve determinance, a quality it would hold until concentration on safety by the "unsafe" company brought its product back into line with those of other companies.

To identify determinant attitudes and discern their relative degree of determinance, researchers must go beyond the scaling of respondents' attitudes. The study design must include a methodology for measuring determinance, for it will not naturally develop in the course of scaling. There are three major approaches to identifying determinant attitudes: (1) direct questioning, (2) indirect questioning, and (3) observation.

Direct Questioning

The most obvious way to approach determinant attitudes is to ask consumers directly what factors they consider important in a purchasing decision. Through direct questioning, respondents may be asked to explain their reasons for preferring one product or brand over another. Or they may be asked to rate their "ideal brand" for a given product in terms of several product attributes so that a model profile can be constructed (see the discussion of semantic differential scales).

This approach has the appeal of seeming to get directly to the issue of "Why do you buy?" Unfortunately, it rests on two very questionable assumptions: (1) respondents know why they buy or prefer one product over another, and (2) they will willingly explain what these reasons are.

Another direct questioning approach is "dual questioning," which involves asking two questions concerning each product attribute that might be determinant. Consumers are first asked what factors they consider important in a purchasing decision and then asked how they perceive these factors as differing among the various products or brands.

Exhibits 11.13 and 11.14 illustrate this approach through ratings of attitudes toward savings and loan associations, given during a survey of the general public in the Los Angeles area. (The various benefits or claims are ranked in descending order in each exhibit so that comparisons between the exhibits can be made more easily.) Notice that some items are high in rated importance but are not thought to differ much among the various savings and loan associations (for example, safety of money, interest rate earned). Thus, while safety of

EXHIBIT 11.13	Importance Ratings of Savings and Loan Characteristics
Benefit or Claim	**Average Ratings***
Safety of money	1.4
Interest rate earned	1.6
Government insurance	1.6
Financial strength	2.0
Ease of withdrawing money	2.0
Management ability	2.0
Attitude of personnel	2.1
Speed/efficiency of service	2.2
Compounding frequency	2.2
Branch location convenience	2.3
Time required to earn interest	2.3
Parking convenience	2.4
Years in business	2.5
Other services offered	3.1
Building/office attractiveness	3.4
Premiums offered	4.0

*1—extremely important; 2—very important; 3—fairly important; 4—slightly important, etc.

Source: James Myers and Mark Alpert, "Determinant Buying Attitudes: Meaning and Measurement," *Marketing Management* (Summer 1997), p. 52. Reprinted by permission of the American Marketing Association.

EXHIBIT 11.14	Difference Ratings of Savings and Loan Characteristics			
Benefit or Claim	**Big Difference**	**Small Difference**	**No Difference**	**Don't Know**
Years in business	53 %	31%	10 %	6 %
Financial strength	40	32	22	6
Parking convenience	37	35	22	6
Safety of money	36	15	47	2
Management ability	35	26	27	12
Government insurance	35	11	51	3
Branch location convenience	34	36	28	2
Attitude of personnel	34	28	33	5
Interest rate earned	33	30	35	2
Speed/efficiency of service	32	28	35	5
Ease of withdrawing money	29	18	48	5
Compounding frequency	28	36	31	5
Time required to earn interest	26	34	33	7
Building/office attractiveness	24	44	30	2
Other services offered	21	34	29	16
Premiums offered	15	36	38	11

Source: James Myers and Mark Alpert, "Determinant Buying Attitudes: Meaning and Measurement," *Marketing Management* (Summer 1997), p. 53. Reprinted by permission of the American Marketing Association.

money is ranked first in importance, about half of all respondents feel there is no difference among savings and loan associations in terms of safety; therefore, safety of funds is probably not a determinant feature. Conversely, some items show big differences among the various associations but are considered to be of relatively little importance in determining the choice of a savings and loan (for example, years in business, parking convenience).

On the other hand, "interest rate earned" has a very high importance ranking, and far fewer respondents feel there is no difference among the various associations relative to interest rate. Financial strength is rated somewhat lower in importance but is second highest in terms of the difference between associations. Therefore, financial strength appears to be relatively determinant of attitudes. Similarly, the researcher can proceed through the rest of the ratings to identify those attitudes that seem to influence the choice among various savings and loans most strongly and thus, presumably, are determinant attitudes.

Indirect Questioning

Another approach to identifying determinant attitudes is indirect questioning, of which there are many forms. Recall from Chapter 5 that indirect questioning is any interviewing approach that does not directly ask respondents to indicate the reasons why they bought a product or service or which features or attributes are most important in determining choice.

Observation

A third technique for identifying buying motives is observation research (see Chapter 8). For example, in one study, supermarket shoppers were observed, and detailed reports were recorded of their movements and statements while interacting with certain products on display in several different stores. The authors drew conclusions concerning who does the shopping, the influence of children and adult males on purchasing decisions, the effect of pricing, where brand choices seem to be made, and how much package study is involved. One of the findings of this study was that shoppers seemed to reject certain candy packaging in favor of other packaging. This finding suggests that package design might be a determinant feature, though by no means the only one.[23] (The disadvantages of observation research were discussed in Chapter 8.)

Choosing a Method for Identifying Determinant Attitudes

Direct questioning, indirect questioning, and observation each have some limitations in identifying determinant attitudes. Therefore, the marketing researcher should use two or more of the techniques. Convergent findings will offer greater assurance that the attitudes identified are indeed determinant attitudes. Several statistical tools can aid the researcher in this process; they will be discussed in Chapters 15 to 18.

SUMMARY

An attitude is an enduring organization of motivational, emotional, perceptual, and cognitive processes with respect to some aspect of a person's environment. In marketing research, it is a learned predisposition to respond in a consistently favorable or unfavorable manner toward an object or concept.

The term *scaling* refers to procedures for attempting to determine quantitative measures of subjective and sometimes abstract concepts. It is defined as a procedure for assigning numbers or other symbols to properties of an object in order to impart some numerical characteristics to the properties in question. Scales are either unidimensional or multidimensional. A unidimensional scale is designed to measure only one attribute of a concept, respondent, or object. Multidimensional scaling is based on the premise that a concept, respondent, or object might be better described using several dimensions.

One type of scale is called a graphic rating scale. Respondents are presented with a graphic continuum, typically anchored by two extremes. Itemized rating scales are similar to graphic rating scales except that respondents must select from a limited number of categories rather than placing a mark on a continuous scale. A rank-order scale is a comparative scale because respondents are asked to compare two or more items with each other. Paired comparison scales ask the respondent to pick one of two objects from a set, based on some stated criteria. Constant sum scales require the respondent to divide a given number of points, typically 100, among two or more attributes, based on their importance to him or her. Respondents must value each item relative to all other items. The number of points allocated to each alternative indicates the ranking assigned to it by the respondent.

The semantic differential was developed to measure the meaning of an object to a person. The construction of a semantic differential scale begins with determination of a concept to be rated, such as a brand image; then the researcher selects dichotomous pairs of words or phrases that could be used to describe the concept. Respondents next rate the concept on a scale, usually 1 to 7. The mean of the responses is computed for each pair of adjectives, and the means are plotted as a profile or image. In the Stapel scale, a single adjective is placed in the center of the scale. Typically, a Stapel scale is designed to simultaneously measure both the direction and the intensity of attitudes. The Likert scale is another scale that avoids the problem of developing pairs of dichotomous adjectives. The scale consists of a series of statements expressing either a favorable or an unfavorable attitude toward the concept under study. The respondent is asked to indicate the level of his or her agreement or disagreement with each statement by assigning it a numerical score. Scores are then totaled to measure the respondent's attitude.

The scale that is used most often and perhaps is most important to marketing researchers is the purchase intent scale. This scale is used to measure a respondent's intention to buy or not buy a product. The purchase intent question usually asks a person to state whether he would definitely buy, probably buy, probably not buy, or definitely not buy the product under study. The purchase intent scale has been found to be a good predictor of consumer choice of frequently purchased consumer durable goods.

Sometimes it is necessary to do scale conversions in tracking studies when, over time, the number of points on a scale changes. Scale equivalence can be created when box scores are used as evaluation measures.

Several factors should be considered in selecting a particular scale for a study. The first is the type of scale to use: rating, ranking, sorting, or purchase intent. Next, consideration must be given to the use of a balanced scale versus a nonbalanced scale. The number of categories also must be determined. A related factor is whether to use an odd or even number of categories. Finally, the researcher must consider whether to use forced or nonforced choice sets.

Attitudes that predispose consumers to action are called determinant attitudes. Marketing researchers need to identify which attitudes, of all those measured, are determinant. This can be accomplished by direct questioning, indirect questioning, and observation research.

KEY TERMS & DEFINITIONS

attitude Enduring organization of motivational, emotional, perceptual, and cognitive processes with respect to some aspect of a person's environment.

scaling Procedures for assigning numbers (or other symbols) to properties of an object in order to impart some numerical characteristics to the properties in question.

unidimensional scales Scales designed to measure only one attribute of a concept, respondent, or object.

multidimensional scales Scales designed to measure several dimensions of a concept, respondent, or object.

graphic rating scales Measurement scales that include a graphic continuum, anchored by two extremes.

itemized rating scales Measurement scales in which the respondent selects an answer from a limited number of ordered categories.

noncomparative scales Measurement scales in which judgment is made without reference to another object, concept, or person.

rank-order scales Measurement scales in which the respondent compares two or more items and ranks them.

comparative scales Measurement scales in which one object, concept, or person is compared with another on a scale.

paired comparison scales Measurement scales that ask the respondent to pick one of two objects in a set, based on some stated criteria.

constant sum scales Measurement scales that ask the respondent to divide a given number of points, typically 100, among two or more attributes, based on their importance to him or her.

semantic differential scales Measurement scales that examine the strengths and weaknesses of a concept by having the respondent rank it between dichotomous pairs of words or phrases that could be used to describe it; the means of the responses are then plotted as a profile or image.

Stapel scales Measurement scales that require the respondent to rate, on a scale ranging from $+5$ to -5, how closely and in what direction a descriptor adjective fits a given concept.

Likert scales Measurement scales in which the respondent specifies a level of agreement or disagreement with statements expressing either a favorable or an unfavorable attitude toward the concept under study.

purchase intent scales Scales used to measure a respondent's intention to buy or not buy a product.

balanced scales Measurement scales that have the same number of positive and negative categories.

nonbalanced scales Measurement scales that are weighted toward one end or the other of the scale.

determinant attitudes Those consumer attitudes most closely related to preferences or to actual purchase decisions.

QUESTIONS FOR REVIEW & CRITICAL THINKING

1. Discuss some of the considerations in selecting a rating, ranking, or purchase intent scale.

2. What are some of the arguments for and against having a neutral point on a scale?

3. Compare and contrast the semantic differential scale, Stapel scale, and Likert scale. Under what conditions would a researcher use each one?

4. The local department store in your home town has been besieged by competition from the large national chains. What are some ways that target customers' attitudes toward the store could be changed?

5. Develop a Likert scale to evaluate the parks and recreation department in your city.

6. Develop a purchase intent scale for students eating at the university's cafeteria. How might the reliability and validity of this scale be measured? Why do you think purchase intent scales are so popular in commercial marketing research?

7. When might a researcher use a graphic rating scale rather than an itemized rating scale?

8. What is the difference between a rating and a ranking? Which is best for attitude measurement? Why?

9. Develop a rank-order scale for soda preferences of college students. What are the advantages and disadvantages of this type of scale?

10. What are determinant attitudes and why are they important?

11. Explain the concept of scale equivalence.

12. Discuss the relationship between customer satisfaction and profits.

13. Divide the class into teams. Each team should create five adjective pairs of phrases that could be used in a semantic differential to measure the image of your college or university. The instructor will then aggregate the suggestions into a single semantic differential. Each team member should then conduct five interviews with students not in the class. The data can then be analyzed later in the term when statistical analysis is covered.

(Team Exercise)

WORKING THE NET

SBI (Strategic Business Insights) is a spinoff of the Stanford Research Institute. One of its most popular products is called VALS (Values and Life Style Survey). SBI uses VALS to segment the marketplace on the basis of personality traits that drive consumer behavior. VALS is used in all phases of the marketing mix. The survey categorizes consumers into one of eight personality types. GEOVALS applies the power of VALS to local marketing efforts by identifying the concentration of the VALS consumer group residing within a specific block group or zip code.

Go to *www.strategicbusinessinsights.com*, then click on the VALS SURVEY link. Next, click on "Take the survey."

1. Explain the theory behind the creation of VALS.

2. Do you agree with your VALS classification? Learn more by going to "The VALS Types" link.

3. What kind of scale was used in the survey? Could other types of scales have been used?

4. Explain how a marketer could use GEOVALS.

REAL-LIFE RESEARCH • 11.1

Case Backhoe Enters the Global Market

There are the many types of construction equipment necessary for modern construction techniques. The most versatile and most often purchased of these is the loader backhoe.

How do engineers identify design advancements for the backhoe to keep the product line fresh and responsive to market needs? How do they make sure the design advancements are appropriate for the varied needs of a global marketplace? And how does marketing research pave the way for success in global construction equipment markets?

Corporate mergers, acquisitions, and joint ventures have brought Case together with other famous names in construction and agricultural equipment: New Holland, Kobelco, Hitachi, and Fiat—each brand a market success on its own. Recently these successful brands were given a new corporate identity in the form of CNH Global, which sells equipment in nearly every country in the world.

A frequent result of corporate mergers and acquisitions is that the newly merged corporation has multiple products competing in the same market. CNH Global is no exception. In particular, CNH Global has three strong brands competing in the global loader backhoe market.

As CNH Global plans for the future, the three loader backhoes will be differentiated in ways that create unique benefits for the customers of each brand while preserving the historic strengths of each brand. Engineering and marketing want advanced models of each brand to generate market share growth.

To design the next series of loader backhoe models, engineers were facing several key questions:

• How do loader backhoe operators view the various brands?

• What are the performance differences of each brand—whether grounded in real engineering design or perceived performance?

• What changes should be made in designing models for each of the CNH Global brands of loader backhoes to both bypass competition and differentiate the CNH brands?

• For answers to these questions, the global engineering team turned to marketing research.

Rigorous Field Tests

The first step was qualitative research, but traditional interviews or focus groups would not suffice. CNH chose field tests of each of five leading brands as the best way to level the playing field for brand experience and made the field tests grueling so that any real performance differences would be detected by equipment operators.

Following each test, operators rated the brand on an extensive list of performance attributes, and then were asked to give reasons for their ratings. Operators used their notes on "reasons" later in the day during in-depth discussions led by a moderator from the research supplier.

Scale Surprises

The field tests were also used to customize and pretest scales for later use in the quantitative stage of the marketing research. The intent was to develop scales that reflect the way operators think about loader backhoe performance. Researchers who routinely use symmetrical 7- or 9-point scales will be surprised by the findings.

Operators clearly identified four levels of satisfaction with loader backhoe performance attributes. They did not find four levels of dissatisfaction. So the symmetrical satisfaction scale often used in marketing research was not appropriate for the quantitative research.

They also found that use of the word *extremely*, as in "extremely satisfied," was inappropriate. While operators frequently said that more than one brand would be very effective for their job needs, they did not perceive anything "extremely" and never used a scale point with that adjective. So if a 7-point scale with the anchor points "extremely satisfied" and "extremely dissatisfied" had been used, as is often the practice in marketing research, it really would have been a 5-point scale from the operator's perspective.

CNH eventually determined that the scale that most effectively reflected the way operators think about their loader backhoes has four levels of satisfaction, a neutral point, and one level of dissatisfaction—a 6-point asymmetrical scale.

A scale with more levels would have introduced "noise" into the responses. Similarly, insisting that there be an equal number of levels of both satisfaction and dissatisfaction would have masked subtle differences in operator responses.

Global Implications

The results had a huge impact on advancing the engineering design of CNH loader backhoes. Operators indicated clear differences in performance among the brands. These findings are being used not only to better differentiate CNH brands from competitor brands but also to differentiate among the CNH brands.[24]

Questions

1. In addition to satisfaction-itemized rating scales, what other scales could have been used in the CNH marketing research?
2. Do you think that the decision to use an asymmetrical satisfaction scale was the right choice? Why or why not?
3. This study was conducted in many countries. Can scales be interpreted in the same manner around the world? For example, is a 2.1 the same in China as it is in Costa Rica?
4. Should purchase intent have been part of this questionnaire? Why or why not?

REAL-LIFE RESEARCH • 11.2

Frigidaire Refrigerators

Frigidaire Refrigerators was interested in comparing its image with the images of a number of other appliance corporations. Some of the questions used on the questionnaire follow.

Q.1 We are interested in your overall opinion of five companies that manufacture refrigerators. Please rank them from 1 to 5, with 1 being the best and 5 the worst. (READ LIST. WRITE IN NUMBER GIVEN FOR *EACH* COMPANY LISTED. BE SURE *ONE* ANSWER IS RECORDED FOR EACH COMPANY.)

Companies	Rank
General Electric	———
Westinghouse	———
Frigidaire	———
Sears	———
Whirlpool	———

Q.2 Now, I would like to have your opinion on a few statements that could be used to describe Frigidaire and the refrigerators it makes.

For each statement I read, please tell me how much you *agree* or *disagree* with the statement about Frigidaire. If you *agree completely* with the statement made, you should give it a *10* rating. If you *disagree completely* with the statement made, you should give it a *0* rating. Or, you can use any number in between which best expresses your opinion on each statement about Frigidaire. (READ LIST. BEGIN WITH STATEMENT CHECKED AND WRITE IN NUMBER GIVEN FOR *EACH* STATEMENT LISTED. BE SURE *ONE* ANSWER IS RECORDED FOR EACH.)

Statements	Rating
( ) They are a modern, up-to-date company.	———
( ) Their refrigerators offer better value than those made by other companies.	———
( ) Their refrigerators last longer than those made by other companies.	———
( ) They are a company that stands behind their products.	———
(√) Their refrigerators have more special features than those made by other companies.	———
( ) They are a well-established, reliable company.	———
( ) Their refrigerators are more dependable than those made by other companies.	———
( ) Their refrigerators offer higher-quality construction than those made by other companies.	———
( ) Their refrigerators have a better guarantee or warranty than those made by other companies.	———

Q.3 If you were buying a (READ APPLIANCE) today, what make would be your first choice? Your second choice? Your third choice? (DO *NOT* READ LIST. CIRCLE NUMBER BELOW APPROPRIATE APPLIANCE. *BEGIN WITH APPLIANCE CHECKED.*)

Brands	( ) Refrigerator			(√) Electric Range		
	First Choice	Second Choice	Third Choice	First Choice	Second Choice	Third Choice
General Electric	1	1	1	1	1	1
Westinghouse	2	2	2	2	2	2
Frigidaire	3	3	3	3	3	3
Sears	4	4	4	4	4	4
Whirlpool	5	5	5	5	5	5
Other (SPECIFY)						

Q.4 If you were in the market for a refrigerator today, how interested would you be in having the Frigidaire refrigerator that was described in the commercial in your home? Would you say you would be . . . (READ LIST)

	Very interested	1
1 (CIRCLE	Somewhat interested	2
2 ONE	Neither interested or disinterested	3
NUMBER)	Somewhat disinterested, or	4
	Very disinterested	5

Q.5 Why do you feel that way? (PROBE FOR COMPLETE AND MEANINGFUL ANSWERS.)

_____

_____

_____

_____

_____

Q.6 Now, I would like to ask you a few questions for statistical purposes only:

(A) Do you currently own any major appliances made by Frigidaire?
(CIRCLE ONE NUMBER)

Yes	1
No	2

(B) Is the head of household male or female?
(CIRCLE ONE NUMBER)

Male	1
Female	2

(C) Which letter on this card corresponds to your age group?

	A. Under 25	1
(CIRCLE	B. 25 to 34	2
ONE	C. 35 to 44	3
NUMBER)	D. 45 to 54	4
	E. 55 and over	5

Questions

1. What types of scales are represented in the questionnaire? What is the purpose of each scale? What other scales could have been substituted to obtain the same data?

2. Could a semantic differential scale have been used in this questionnaire? If so, what are some of the adjective pairs that might have been used?

3. Do you think the managers of Frigidaire have the necessary information now to evaluate the company's competitive position as perceived by consumers? If not, what additional questions should be asked?

Questionnaire Design

LEARNING OBJECTIVES

→ **1.** To understand the role of the questionnaire in the data-collection process.

→ **2.** To become familiar with the criteria for a good questionnaire.

→ **3.** To learn the process for questionnaire design.

→ **4.** To become knowledgeable about the three basic forms of questions.

→ **5.** To learn the necessary procedures for successful implementation of a survey.

→ **6.** To understand how software and the Internet are influencing questionnaire design.

→ **7.** To understand the impact of the questionnaire on data-collection costs.

At a high level, questionnaire design is more art than science. However, when dealing with questionnaire specifics, such as how to ask certain types of questions, there is plenty of science in the form of methodological research that has been conducted by academics and marketing research professionals. In this chapter, we will provide both overall guidance regarding questionnaire design and best practices for handling specific issues based on the findings of methodological research studies.

Role of a Questionnaire

> **questionnaire**
> Set of questions designed to generate the data necessary to accomplish the objectives of the research project; also called an *interview schedule* or *survey instrument*.

Every form of survey research relies on the use of a questionnaire, the common thread in almost all data-collection methods. A **questionnaire** is a set of questions designed to generate the data necessary to accomplish the objectives of the research project; it is a formalized schedule for collecting information from respondents. You have most likely seen or even filled out a questionnaire recently. Creating a good questionnaire requires both hard work and imagination.

A questionnaire standardizes the wording and sequencing of questions and imposes uniformity on the data-gathering process. Every respondent sees or hears the same words; every interviewer asks identical questions. Without such standardization, interviewers could ask whatever they wanted, and researchers would be left wondering whether respondents' answers were a consequence of interviewer influence or interpretation; a valid basis for comparing respondents' answers would not exist. The jumbled mass of data would be unmanageable from a tabulation standpoint. In a very real sense, then, the questionnaire is a control device, but it is a unique one, as you will see.

The questionnaire (sometimes referred to as an *interview schedule* or *survey instrument*) plays a critical role in the data-collection process. An elaborate sampling plan, well-trained interviewers, proper statistical analysis techniques, and good editing and coding are all for naught if the questionnaire is poorly designed. Improper design can lead to incomplete information, inaccurate data, and, of course, higher costs. The questionnaire is the production line of marketing research. It is here that the product, be it good or bad, is created. The questionnaire is the tool that creates the basic product (respondent information).

Exhibit 12.1 illustrates the pivotal role of the questionnaire. It is positioned between survey objectives (drawn from the manager's problem) and respondent information. In this position, it must translate the objectives into specific questions to solicit the required information from respondents.

Assume that Swatch is considering the development of a child's wristwatch. The timepiece would have a plastic casing with printed circuits inside. Swatch's engineering staff believes that it can come up with a watch that will withstand the potential abuse from the normal activities of a child between 8 and 13 years old. Preliminary marketing research is called for to determine the acceptability of the watch to the target market. One objective is to determine children's reactions to the watch. The marketing researchers must translate the objectives into language understandable to child

Exhibit 12.1

Questionnaire's Pivotal Role in the Research Process

respondents, as an 8-year-old child probably won't be able to respond to questions that use such terms as *acceptability*, *efficiency*, and *likelihood of purchase*.

This example illustrates the pivotal role of the questionnaire: It must translate the survey objectives into a form understandable to respondents and "pull" the requisite information from them. At the same time, it must recover their responses in a form that can be easily tabulated and translated into findings and recommendations that will satisfy a manager's information requirements. Questionnaires also play a key role in survey costs, which will be discussed in detail later in the chapter.

Criteria for a Good Questionnaire

To design a good questionnaire, the researchers must consider a number of issues: Does it provide the necessary decision-making information for management? Does it consider the respondent? Does it meet editing and coding, and data analysis requirements?

Does It Provide the Necessary Decision-Making Information?

The primary role of any questionnaire is to provide the information required for management decision making. Any questionnaire that fails to provide important insights for management or decision-making information should be discarded or revised. Therefore, the managers who will be using the data should always approve the questionnaire. By signing off on the questionnaire, the manager is saying, "Yes, this instrument will supply the data I need to reach a decision." If the manager does not sign off, then the marketing researcher must continue to revise the questionnaire.

Does It Consider the Respondent?

As companies have recognized the importance of marketing research, the number of surveys taken annually has mushroomed. Poorly designed, confusing, and lengthy surveys have literally turned off thousands of potential respondents.

The researcher designing a questionnaire must consider not only the topic and the type of respondent, but the interviewing environment and questionnaire length as well. Respondents will answer somewhat longer questionnaires when they are interested in the topic and when they perceive that they will have little difficulty in responding to the questions.

A questionnaire should be designed explicitly for the intended respondents. For example, although a parent typically is the purchaser of cold cereals, the child, either directly or indirectly, often makes the decision as to which brand. Thus, a taste test questionnaire about cold cereals should be formulated in children's language. On the other hand, a survey about *purchasing* cold cereals should be worded in language suitable for adult interviewees. One of the most important tasks of questionnaire design is to fit the questions to the prospective respondent. The questionnaire designer must strip away any marketing jargon and business terminology that may be misunderstood by the respondent. In fact, it is best to use simple, everyday language, as long as the result is not insulting or demeaning to the respondent.

Does It Meet Editing and Coding Requirements?

Once the information has been gathered, it will have to be coded for data analysis. A questionnaire should be designed with these later processes in mind.

A questionnaire should always fit the respondent. Although parents typically purchase cereal, children often make the decision about what kind to buy. A taste test questionnaire for children should be worded in language they can understand.

> **editing**
> Going through each questionnaire to ensure that skip patterns were followed and the required questions filled out.

> **skip pattern**
> Sequence in which questions are asked, based on a respondent's answer.

> **coding**
> The process of grouping and assigning numeric codes to the various responses to a question.

Editing refers to going through each questionnaire to make certain that skip patterns were followed and required questions were filled out. The **skip pattern** is the sequence in which questions are asked, based on a respondent's answer. Exhibit 12.2 shows a clearly defined skip pattern from question 4a to question 5a for persons who answer "No" to question 4a.

Most marketing research data analysis software automatically catches coding errors. Computer-aided telephone interviewing (CATI) and Internet software programs take care of skip patterns automatically. Flexibility is programmed into a questionnaire in two ways:

- Branching takes the participant to a different set of questions based on the answer that is given to a prior question. This could be a "simple skip," in which questions are skipped because they would not be relevant to the respondent, or could be "dynamic branching," in which one of many possible sets of questions is presented to the participant depending on the way that he or she responded to a question.
- Piping integrates responses from a question into later questions. A participant could be asked to type an answer to an open-ended question, and the text of that answer could be incorporated into the wording of the next question.

In mall, personal, telephone, and many Internet surveys, replies to all open-ended questions (which ask respondents to answer in their own words) are recorded verbatim by the interviewer or typed into the Internet survey by the respondent (see later discussion). Sometimes the responses are then **coded** manually by listing the answers from a number of randomly selected completed questionnaires; however, if at all possible, responses to open-ended questions should be precoded. Those responses occurring with the greatest frequency are listed on a coding sheet (such as the one in Exhibit 12.3), which the editor uses to code all other responses to the open-ended question. Today, sophisticated neural network systems and Internet survey software are decreasing the necessity for manually coding responses to open-ended questions.

4a. Do you usually use a cream rinse or a hair conditioner on your child's hair?
(1) ( ) No (SKIP to 5a)   (2) ( ) Yes (ASK Q. 4b)

4b. Is that a cream rinse that you pour on or a cream rinse that you spray on?
(1) ( ) Cream rinse that you pour on
(2) ( ) Cream rinse that you spray on

4c. About how often do you use a cream rinse or a hair conditioner on your child's hair? Would you say less than once a week, once a week, or more than once a week?
(1) ( ) Less than once a week
(2) ( ) Once a week
(3) ( ) More than once a week

5a. Thinking of the texture of your child's hair, is it. . . . (READ LIST)
(1) ( ) Fine   (2) ( ) Coarse   (3) ( ) Regular

5b. What is the length of your child's hair? (READ LIST)
(1) ( ) Long   (2) ( ) Medium   (3) ( ) Short

Exhibit 12.2

Example of a Questionnaire Skip Pattern

EXHIBIT 12.3	Coding Sheet for the Question "What Is Your Occupation?"

Category	Code
Professional/technical	1
Manager/official/self-employed	2
Clerical/sales	3
Skilled worker	4
Service worker	5
Unskilled laborer	6
Farm operator or rancher	7
Unemployed or student	8
Retired	9

In summary, a questionnaire serves many masters. First, it must accommodate all the research objectives in sufficient depth and breadth to satisfy the information requirements of the manager. Next, it must "speak" to the respondent in understandable language and at the appropriate intellectual level. Furthermore, it must be convenient for the interviewer to administer, and it must allow the interviewer to quickly record the respondent's answers. At the same time, the questionnaire must be easy to edit and check for completeness. It also should facilitate coding. Finally, the questionnaire must be translatable into findings that respond to the manager's original questions.

Tips for designing questionnaires to improve response rates are covered in the following Practicing Market Research feature.

Questionnaire Design Process

Designing a questionnaire involves a series of logical steps, as shown in Exhibit 12.4. The steps may vary slightly when performed by different researchers, but all researchers tend to follow the same general sequence. Committees and lines of authority can complicate the process, so it is wise to clear each step with the individual who has the ultimate

PRACTICING MARKETING RESEARCH

Tips for Maximizing User Response in Online Surveys

No other methodology now rivals the Internet for market research. You can target almost any kind of respondent group, and they can answer thoughtfully and thoroughly at their leisure. Here are 10 valuable tips for online survey development:

1. Make sure you would enjoy taking the survey. Put your screening and data management questions first. Use drop-down lists sparingly. Keep your directions clear. Go light on the number of product attributes, no more than 20. Give them an out, such as a "don't know" or "I prefer to not answer" option.

2. Don't forget the respondents are doing you a favor; find ways to make the experience enjoyable for them.

3. Make the attribute ratings easy on the viewer's eyes.

4. Keep the surveys as short as possible; long spells boredom or fatigue.

5. Be sensitive to special audiences and their needs or preferences, such as teenager studies (use snappy graphics; pose age-relevant questions).

6. Ensure the privacy of the respondent's answers on sensitive topics.

7. Use incentives, and make sure they're suitable to the target audience; for lengthy surveys, make sure you provide generous incentives.

8. Keep dropout trigger questions for the end of the survey.

9. Supplement e-mail surveys with telephone or interactive voice-response methodologies to increase and hold participation.

10. Take advantage of the prevalence of high-speed online interactivity through such technologies as Flash; these enable market researchers to sample consumer response to commercials or simulated shopping environments.[1]

What factors influence a person's decision to answer an online survey in the first place? According to Janet Westergaard, president of Esearch.com in Rolling Hills, California, here they are in order: (1) incentive offered, 66 percent; (2) available time when survey is presented, 56 percent; (3) survey topic, 37 percent; and (4) survey length, 30 percent.

Westergaard noted gender differences too. Males are more attracted to incentives, whereas women value their available time higher; the time factor is most critical for respondents aged 18 to 30 (72 percent said so) compared to people 31+ years old (50 percent said so). Men respond more strongly to the topic and survey length (46 percent) compared to women (31 percent). Overall, both men and women (47 percent) said incentive was the biggest factor, followed by whether they had the time to spare (27 percent). The actual topic was a determining factor to only 12.6 percent of respondents. The conclusion: Come up with a desirable incentive and choose your timing carefully for survey presentation.[2]

Still, don't discount the lure of an appealing topic. Researchers telephone-polled 2,300 adults and found that the chances of a person taking part in a survey rises by 40 percent if the topic holds great interest for them. The conclusion: If your topic is hot, divulge it early to secure respondents' interest.[3]

Questions

1. Draft three "hot" topics for a survey and find appealing ways to present the material in leading or early questions.

2. Consider the merits, or disadvantages, of three incentives that might be offered to potential survey respondents.

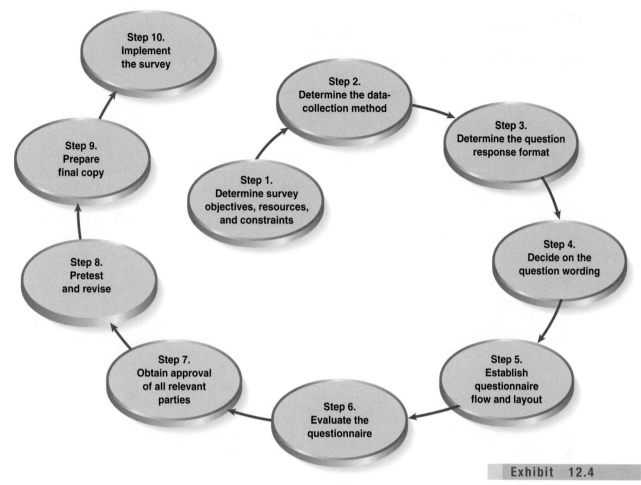

Exhibit 12.4

Questionnaire Design
Process

authority for the project. This is particularly true for the first step: determining survey objectives, resources, and constraints. Many work hours have been wasted because a researcher developed a questionnaire to answer one type of question and the "real" decision maker wanted something entirely different. It also should be noted that the design process itself—specifically, question wording and format—can raise additional issues or unanswered questions. This, in turn, can send the researcher back to step one for a clearer description of the information sought.

Step One: Determine Survey Objectives, Resources, and Constraints

The research process often begins when a marketing manager, brand manager, or new-product development specialist has a need for decision-making information that is not available. In some firms, it is the manager's responsibility to evaluate all secondary sources to make certain that the needed information has not already been gathered. In other companies, the manager leaves all research activities, primary and secondary, to the research department. The discussion of uses of marketing research in Chapter 2 covers this issue in more detail.

Although a brand manager may initiate the research request, everyone affected by the project—including the assistant brand manager, the group product manager, and even the marketing manager—should provide input into exactly what data are needed.

PRACTICING MARKETING RESEARCH

It's All about the Objectives

Every questionnaire has two overriding goals. The first is to keep respondents on-task—to hold their attention as they move through the questionnaire, keep them focused, and get them to answer each question honestly. The second is to generate data that fully addresses the study's objectives.

Achieving the second goal is the key. The sole purpose of achieving the first goal is to make achieving the second possible. How do you achieve both goals? By forging a questionnaire that is well-thought-out; that is clearly, logically, and succinctly written; that is constructed with the study's objectives in mind; that is always user-friendly; and that, if the stars align, has moments of ingenuity and imagination. The considerations that follow are intended to provide you with the tools and insights to construct questionnaires that satisfy these criteria.

1. **A study's objectives are its first and most important consideration.** They drive the research design, the construction of the questionnaire, and the analysis and interpretation of the data. Which is why this bears repeating: when constructing a questionnaire, the key question is always: Will this questionnaire generate data that fully addresses the objectives of this study? Keep asking yourself this question as you construct the questionnaire.

2. **Each question should be clearly written, in plain English, free of jargon and without ambiguity.** Any question that falls short of this requirement may lessen the validity of the questionnaire. Unfortunately, writing clearly is easier said than done. A key reason is the gap that usually exists between the clarity with which we think we write and the clarity with which we actually write. We can do several things to narrow, and possibly close, this gap:

- Be aware that it exists. It'll make you think more critically as you write, and it'll get you to review what you've written with a more discerning eye.

- Ask at least one person whose judgment about the written word you trust to look at your questionnaire and, as warranted, suggest changes.

- Personally administer your questionnaire to a few people. If you ask, they'll tell you whether the questions are easy to understand.

3. **Try to write questions the way you speak, in a conversational style.** It should make it easier for respondents to understand the questions and answer them, and it may help to keep them interested. One way to get an idea of how close you've come is to read it aloud and listen carefully to how it sounds— you want it to sound as if you're conversing with someone rather than reading aloud to them. Another way is to try it out on a few people and ask how easily it reads.

4. **Every questionnaire should have a logical flow to it and should make intuitive sense as the respondent moves from one question to the next.** One technique is to order them in a way that's consistent with how most people would approach the subject at hand. For example, if you're asking about a particular product, you might begin with questions about awareness, then move to questions about expectations, then to a purchase decision, then to reactions to the product, and finally to the likelihood of purchasing the product again. When you ask people how easily the questionnaire reads, ask them about its flow as well.

5. **The cost of wearing out your welcome is almost always high.** You're asking people to give you one of their more precious possessions—their time. If they feel that you're asking for too much, they may either stop in midstream and walk away or begin to answer

quickly and with little or no thought, which is an ugly compromise between feeling obligated to complete the questionnaire and not wanting to give it any more time and effort.

Accordingly, the time it takes to complete a questionnaire should always be reasonable. A key determinant is the respondents' level of involvement in the category. For example, you can probably get away with a longer questionnaire when you're interviewing people who ride motorcycles and asking questions about Harley-Davidsons than you can when you're asking people about toothpaste.

Another key determinant is how easy, or difficult, it is to get through the questionnaire. If there are no bumps in the road, no thorny patches, nothing to annoy or frustrate respondents, then a 15-minute questionnaire should be just fine. However, if there are questions that are less than clear, questions that involve rating and raking an overly long list of attributes, repetitive questions, and questions that don't make sense, then 15 minutes is going to seem like forever and respondents will react accordingly.[4]

Questions

1. Is there a problem with specifying the research objectives after the questionnaire has been designed? Why?

2. Why is questionnaire length an important issue in questionnaire design?

Survey objectives (outlining the decision-making information required) should be spelled out as clearly and precisely as possible. If this step is completed carefully and thoroughly, the rest of the process will follow more smoothly and efficiently.

Neil Kalt, president of Neil Kalt and Associates, talks about the importance of research objectives and the questionnaire. He also offers several tips on questionnaire design in the accompanying Practicing Marketing Research box.

➤ **survey objectives**
Outline of the decision-making information sought through the questionnaire.

Step Two: Determine the Data-Collection Method

Given the variety of ways in which survey data can be gathered, such as via the Internet, telephone, mail, or self-administration, the research method will have an impact on questionnaire design. An in-person interview in a mall will have constraints (such as a time limitation) not encountered with an Internet questionnaire. A self-administered questionnaire must be explicit and is usually rather short; because no interviewer will be present, respondents will not have the opportunity to clarify a question. A telephone interview may require a rich verbal description of a concept to make certain the respondent understands the idea being discussed. In contrast, an Internet survey can show the respondent a picture or video or demonstrate a concept.

Step Three: Determine the Question Response Format

Once the data-collection method has been determined, a decision must be made regarding the types of questions to be used in the survey. Three major types of questions are used in marketing research: open-ended, closed-ended, and scaled-response questions.

Ladders Can Sometimes Help   Infiniti recently won a "Best of What's New" award from *Popular Science* for its Around View Monitor (AVM). Cameras placed on every side of the vehivle reflect objects or other vehicles around the car. The AVM shows the surrounding environment in a composite bird's-eye perspective on a dashboard monitor. The AVM system was one of 25 advanced technology features Infiniti developers had on the table four years before its launch.

The decision to implement this feature came after literally hundreds of hours of employing a research technique called laddering. Laddering interviews are typically used to provide an in-depth understanding of how consumers relate to a brand by delving into hidden, preconscious factors that influence purchase. A desired outcome of the technique is often information that supports brand identity development and provides emotionally based direction to drive strategy (see Exhibit 12.5).[5]

Ladders can be developed using qualitative research and then examined in more detail in qualitative research. The ladder can be used as a guide for designing the survey questions. In Infiniti's case, laddering was the tool used to prioritize its technology roll-outs over several years. In this project, the goal was to identify the core value of individual technology features with the already known core values of the Infiniti brand.

Laddering, of course, is only useful when the tool lines up with the research objectives. Not all research objectives are attempting to uncover core values. In the Infiniti example, you can easily see how the research objectives led to laddering which, in turn, guided questionnaire development. An example of a ladder for a business-to-business survey is shown in Exhibit 12.6. Ladders can also be built for other research objectives and therefore serve as guidelines for questionnaire development.

➤ open-ended questions
Questions to which the respondent replies in her or his own words.

Open-Ended Questions   **Open-ended questions** are those to which the respondent replies in her or his own words. In other words, the researcher does not limit the response choices.

Exhibit 12.5

A Ladder for the Infiniti "Around-View Monitor"

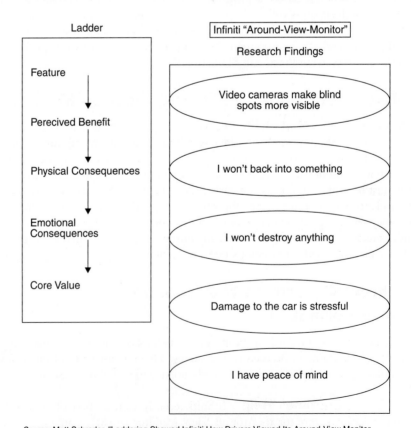

Source: Matt Schroder, "Laddering Showed Infiniti How Drivers Viewed Its Around-View Monitor Technology" *Quick's Marketing Research Review*, October 2009, p. 26

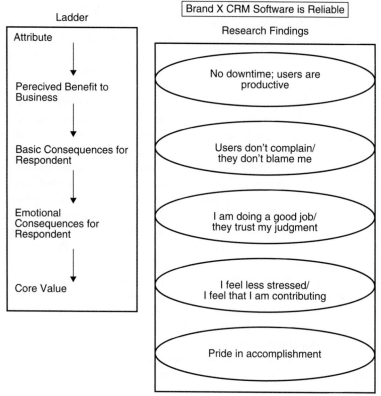

Exhibit 12.6

A Business Ladder for Customer Relationship Management (CRM) Software

Source: Adapted from: Bernadette DeLamar, "Get to the Point," *Quirk's Marketing Research Review,* March 2010, p. 53.

Open-ended questions offer several advantages to the researcher. They enable respondents to give their general reactions to questions like the following:

1. What advantages, if any, do you think ordering from an e-retailer company offers compared with buying from local retail outlets? (*Probe:* What else?)
2. Why do you have one or more of your rugs or carpets professionally cleaned rather than cleaning them yourself or having someone else in the household clean them?
3. What do you think is most in need of improvement here at the airport?
4. What is there about the color of _____ [product] that makes you like it the best? (*Probe:* What color is that?)
5. Why do you say that brand [the one you use most often] is better?

Each of the preceding questions was taken from a different nationwide survey covering five products and services. Note that open-ended questions 2 and 4 are part of a skip pattern. Before being asked question 2, the respondent has already indicated that he or she uses a professional carpet cleaning service and does not depend on members of the household.

Open-ended responses have the advantage of providing the researcher with a rich array of information. The respondent's answers are based on his or her personal frame of reference and described in real-world terminology rather than laboratory or marketing jargon. Often, this is helpful in designing promotion themes and campaigns; it enables copywriters to use the consumer's language. This rich array of information can also be captured in computer-assisted interviews and Internet surveys.

The inspection of open-ended responses also can serve as a means of interpreting closed-ended questions. Analysis often sheds additional light on the motivations or attitudes behind closed-ended response patterns. It is one thing to know that color ranks second in importance out of five product attributes—but it might be much more valuable to know why color is important. For example, a recent study of mobile home park residents identified a great deal of dissatisfaction with the trash pick-up service, but further inspection of the open-ended responses uncovered the reason: Neighbors' dogs were allowed to run free and were overturning the receptacles.

Similarly, open-ended questions may suggest additional alternatives not listed in a closed-ended response format. For example, a previously unrecognized advantage of using an e-retail company might be uncovered in responses to question 1. A closed-ended question on the same subject would not have this advantage.

One manufacturer for which the authors consult always ends product placement questionnaires with the following: "Is there anything else that you would like to tell us about the product that you have tried during the past three weeks?" This probe seeks any final tidbit of information that might provide additional insight for the researcher.

Alexa Smith, president of Research Department in New York City, suggests several open-ended questions that can be asked for greater insights in the Practicing Marketing Research box on page 348.

Open-ended questions are not without their problems. Editing and coding can consume great amounts of time and money if done manually. Editing open-ended responses requires collapsing the many response alternatives into some reasonable number. If too many categories are used, data patterns and response frequencies may be difficult to interpret. Even if a proper number of categories is used, editors may still have to interpret what the interviewer has recorded and force the data into a category. If the categories are too broad, the data may be too general and important meaning may be lost.

Probing Often, open-ended questions require probing. Probing means that an interviewer encourages the respondent to elaborate or continue the discussion.[6] Powerful probes will advance a discussion quickly away from top-of-mind responses and seat-of-the-pants answers—and access deeper information, allowing insight into the baseline thinking that drives behavior.

Probes fall into three distinct areas: proactive, reactive, and spontaneous. The last one is also called a "natural probe," since it just pops up instantly in the mind of a researcher who knows that deeper insights need to be expressed. For example, a respondent says: "I get upset when the line is too long at checkout." A natural probe has to be: "What upsets you?"

By contrast, a proactive probe is one that can be planned ahead of time, and it might look like the following:

The original question might be: "What were some key factors of importance to you when buying your last car?" And the proactive probe might be: "In reviewing those key factors in your mind, which one stands out as critical to buying decisions?" A proactive probing series can be planned ahead of time to lead the discussion to fertile areas for discussion, aimed at reaching the study purpose. And from time to time, a family of proactive probes might have a visitor from the "natural" probe family as well.

Reactive probes are almost like "natural probes," except that they are more "knee jerk" in character. The most common ones are: "What makes you say that?" Or: "What is the basis for that belief on your part?" Those kinds of probes question the baseline thinking of a respondent, rather than relying on a report of behavior. A few examples of probes are as follows.

Request for elaboration: "Tell me more about that." Give me an example of . . . ."

Request for word association: "What do you mean by . . . ? "What does the term _____ mean to you?"

Request for clarification: "How does that differ from . . . ?" "In what circumstances do you . . . ?"

Request for comparison: "How is _____ similar to _____?" Which costs more, X or Y?"

Request for classification: "Where does _____ fit?" "What else is in the category of _____?"

"**Silent" probe:** This is a nonverbal probe and is characterized by such actions as raised eyebrows or hand gestures such as moving the right hand in a rolling motion that signifies "Tell me more."[7]

Other examples of probing are shown in Exhibit 12.7.

EXHIBIT 12.7	The Nuances of Probing
Probing element	**Examples**
Comprehension Or Interpretation	– What does the term *outpatient* mean to you? – How do you refer to yourself—as a patient or as an outpatient??
Paraphrasing	– Can you repeat the question I just asked you in your own words?
Confidence Or Judgment	– How sure are you that your health insurance covers drug as well as alcohol treatment?
Recall	– How many times did you brush your teeth yesterday? – Follow-up probe: What were the reasons for each brushing? – How many times did you go to the bank to make a deposit in person in June? – Follow-up probes: Is June typical or not? If so, in what ways; if not, what are the reasons?
Assessing "self talk"	– You hesitated before answering… what was going on in your head in the pause?
Accessing "values/beliefs"	– What makes you think that cancer is America's most serious health problem?

Source: Naomi Henderson, *Marketing Research*, Winter 2007, p. 38.

If a food study on tacos asked, "What, if anything besides meat, do you normally add to a taco you have prepared at home?", coding categories would need to be determined to categorize answers to this open-ended question.

PRACTICING
MARKETING RESEARCH

Useful Open-Ended Questions

Here are some open-ended questions, often overlooked, that lead to greater insight:

- **What would it take to get you to use or buy a product or service?** Such a question is useful at the end of a focus group or in-depth interview. At minimum, it can provide a handy summation of the findings that have gone before. It can also serve as a forum for problems and issues that have not yet surfaced. In a study about children's magazines developed in Europe, for example, the respondents said the text would need to be simplified and the illustrations improved for the magazines to be acceptable for children in the United States.

- **What is the best thing about the product, service, or promotion?** This question yields far more than the typical "What do you like about it?" question and can be useful as an addition to the traditional "likes" question. A food company had developed a frozen breakfast item that did not seem to be winning any awards for quality and taste. But asking what respondents liked about the food item yielded little because respondents were dissatisfied with the product. By asking what the *best* thing about it was, however, the company found it was "the idea." Many of the participants in the study were working mothers and longed for a quick and convenient hot breakfast item they could provide for their families. Based on answers to a question on simple likes, the whole idea might have been thrown out, but based on "the best thing," the client knew the company was on to something and that the product just needed taste and quality improvements.

- **What is the worst thing about the product, service, or promotion?** The corollary to "the best thing," this question also often yields surprising answers. Respondents who talked about going to the dentist responded rationally to what they disliked, including pain, expense, and insecurity about their personal experience. When asked, "What is the worst thing that can happen when you go to the dentist?" many said, "You could die!" Dying in the dentist's chair is a rare occurrence, but the response taught the study's sponsor something about the level of fear people were dealing with.

- **Main idea registration.** At the least, the researcher needs to know if respondents have the correct understanding of an idea. Asking for main idea registration is often a good shortcut to identifying communications problems with a concept that would otherwise impede acceptance of an idea. Sometimes the executional elements of a concept can provide a sticking point that can be distracting. A quick fix may be either to verbally correct the misunderstanding or to rewrite the concepts in between focus groups or interviews. If respondents do not understand the intended message, they often find it difficult to answer a question about whether anything is confusing or hard to understand.

- **How would friends and close associates relate to this idea?** Sometimes an idea or a concept can be so blatant that it causes a consumer backlash. This can happen when a company tries to create an upscale, status-conscious image for its product or service. In this case, consumers will indicate something to the effect that they would never be so snobbish as to relate to the idea. When this happens, the merit of the strategy can become apparent if the question is moved into the third person, such as "Do you know friends and associates who would relate to this idea?" If respondents say "yes," then the researcher can determine what friends and associates would like about the idea. In telling how their friends and associates would relate to the idea, consumers are really talking about themselves in a more socially sanctioned way. A surprising number of clients are not aware of this and tend to pass the moderator admonishing notes about just wanting to know what respondents themselves think.

■ **What do you do just before you use a product or service?** Elderly women were asked this question in the context of reading their favorite magazine and how special the experience was when they explained that they take their shoes off, put on their favorite slippers, change into comfortable clothes, and go off by themselves to read the magazine. Reading the magazine was something they did entirely for themselves, and the publisher learned that the magazine was truly a valued companion to these women.[8]

Precoding open-ended questions can partially overcome these problems. Assume that this question was to be asked in a food study: "What, if anything, do you normally add to a taco that you have prepared at home, besides meat?" Coding categories for this open-ended question might be as follows:

Response	Code
Avocado	1
Cheese (Monterey Jack, cheddar)	2
Guacamole	3
Lettuce	4
Mexican hot sauce	5
Olives (black or green)	6
Onions (red or white)	7
Peppers (red or green)	8
Pimento	9
Sour cream	0
Other	X

These answers would be listed on the questionnaire, and a space would be provided to write in any nonconforming reply in the "Other" category. In a telephone interview, the question would still qualify as open-ended because the respondents would not see the categories and the interviewer would be instructed not to divulge them. Precoding necessitates that the researcher have sufficient familiarity with previous studies of a similar nature to anticipate respondents' answers. Otherwise, a pretest with a fairly large sample is needed.

Open-ended questions may be biased toward the articulate interviewee. A person with elaborate opinions and the ability to express them may have much greater input than a shy, inarticulate, or withdrawn respondent. Yet, both might be equally likely prospective consumers of a product.

Suppose an editor confronted the following responses to the taco question: "I usually add a green, avocado-tasting hot sauce." "I cut up a mixture of lettuce and spinach." "I'm a vegetarian; I don't use meat at all. My taco is filled only with guacamole." How should the editor code these?

A basic problem with open-ended questions lies in the interpretation-processing area. A two-phase judgment must be made. First, the researcher must decide on an appropriate set of categories, and then each response must be evaluated to determine into which category it falls.

A final difficulty with open-ended questions is their inappropriateness on some self-administered questionnaires. With no interviewer there to probe, respondents may give a shallow, incomplete, or unclear answer. On a self-administered questionnaire without precoded choices, answers to the taco question might read "I use a little bit of every-thing" or "I use the same things they use in restaurants." These answers would have vir-tually no value to a researcher.

> **closed-ended questions**
> Questions that require the respondent to choose from a list of answers.

Closed-Ended Questions   A **closed-ended question** requires the respondent to make a selection from a list of responses. The primary advantage of closed-ended questions is simply the avoidance of many of the problems associated with open-ended questions. Reading response alternatives may jog a person's memory and generate a more realistic response. Interviewer bias is eliminated because the interviewer is simply clicking a box, circling a category, recording a number, or punching a key. Because the option of expound-ing on a topic is not given to a respondent, there is no bias toward the articulate. Finally, coding and data entry can be done automatically with questionnaire software programs.

It is important to realize the difference between a precoded open-ended question and a multiple-choice question. A precoded open-ended question allows the respon-dent to answer in a freewheeling format; the interviewer simply checks coded answers as they are given. Probing is used, but a list is never read. If the answer given is not one of the precoded ones, it is written verbatim in the "Other" column. In contrast, a closed-ended question requires that a list of alternatives be read by the respondent or interviewer.

Traditionally, marketing researchers have separated closed-ended questions into two types: **dichotomous questions**, with a two-item response option, and **multiple-choice** (or multichotomous) **questions**, with a multi-item response option.

> **dichotomous questions**
> Closed-ended questions that ask the respondents to choose between two answers.

> **multiple-choice questions**
> Closed-ended questions that ask the respondent to choose among several answers; also called *multichotomous questions.*

Dichotomous Questions.   In a dichotomous question, the two response catego-ries are sometimes implicit. For instance, the implicit response options to the question "Did you buy gasoline for your automobile in the last week?" are "Yes" and "No." Even if the respondent says, "I rented a car last week, and they filled it up for me. Does that count?" the question would still be classified as dichotomous. A few examples of dichoto-mous questions follow:

1. Did you heat the Danish roll before serving it?
   Yes   1
   No   2

2. The federal government doesn't care what people like me think.
   Agree   1
   Disagree   2

3. Do you think that inflation will be greater or less than it was last year?
   Greater than   1
   Less than   2

Because the respondent is limited to two fixed alternatives, dichotomous questions are easy to administer and tabulate and usually evoke a rapid response. Many times, a neutral response option is added to dichotomous questions; if it is omitted, interviewers may jot down "DK" for "Don't know" or "NR" for "No response."

The "don't know" response has raised some concerns as telephone surveys have migrated to the Internet.

Dichotomous questions are prone to a large amount of measurement error. Because alternatives are polarized, the wide range of possible choices between the poles is omitted. Thus, appropriate wording is critical to obtaining accurate responses. Questions phrased in a positive form may well result in opposite answers from questions expressed in a negative form. For example, responses may depend on whether "Greater than" or "Less than" is listed first. These problems can be overcome by using a split ballot technique: One-half of the questionnaires have "Greater than" listed first, and the other half have "Less than" first. This procedure helps reduce potential order bias.

Another problem with the dichotomous question is that responses frequently fail to communicate any intensity of feeling on the part of the respondent. In some cases, like the gasoline purchasing example, the matter of intensity does not apply. But in some instances, strong feelings about an issue may be lost in the dichotomous response form. If the gasoline purchasing interview continued with the question "Would you purchase gasoline priced $1.00 per gallon above current prices if you were guaranteed twice the miles per gallon?" responses would likely range in intensity from "No; absolutely not" to "You bet!"

Multiple-Choice Questions.   With multiple-choice questions, replies do not have to be coded as they do with open-ended questions, but the amount of information provided is more limited. The respondent is asked to give one alternative that correctly expresses his or her opinion or, in some instances, to indicate all alternatives that apply. Some examples of multiple-choice questions follow:

1. I'd like you to think back to the last footwear of any kind that you bought. I'll read you a list of descriptions and would like for you to tell me into which category it falls.

Dress and/or formal	1	Specialized athletic shoes	4
Casual	2	Boots	5
Canvas-trainer-gym shoes	3		

2. Please check the age group to which you belong.

A. Under 17	1	D. 35–49 years	4
B. 17–24 years	2	E. 50–64 years	5
C. 25–34 years	3	F. 65 and over	6

3. In the last 3 months, have you used Noxzema Skin Cream . . . (CHECK ALL THAT APPLY)

as a facial wash?	1
for moisturizing the skin?	2
for treating blemishes?	3
for cleansing the skin?	4
for treating dry skin?	5
for softening skin?	6
for sunburn?	7
for making the facial skin smooth?	8

Question 1, from a mall intercept interview, may not cover all possible alternatives and, thus, may not capture a true response. Where, for example, would an interviewer record work shoes? The same thing can be said for question 3. Not only are all possible alternatives not included, but respondents cannot elaborate or qualify their answers. The problem could be easily overcome by adding an "Any other use?" alternative to the question.

The multiple-choice question has two additional disadvantages. First, the researcher must spend time generating the list of possible responses. This phase may require brainstorming or intensive analysis of focus group tapes or secondary data. Second, the researcher must settle on a range of possible answers. If the list is too long, the respondent may become confused or lose interest. A related problem with any list is *position bias*. Respondents typically will choose either the first or the last alternative, all other things being equal. When Internet questionnaire software and CATI systems are used, however, position bias is eliminated by automatically rotating response order.

Scaled-Response Questions   The last response format to be considered is **scaled-response questions**, which are closed-ended questions where the response choices are designed to capture intensity of feeling. Consider the following questions:

→ **scaled-response questions**
Closed-ended questions
in which the response
choices are designed to
capture the intensity of
the respondent's feeling.

1. Now that you have used the product, would you say that you would buy it or not? (CHECK ONE)
    Yes, would buy it
    No, would not buy it

2. Now that you have used the product, would you say that you . . . (CHECK ONE)
    definitely would buy it?
    probably would buy it?
    might or might not buy it?
    probably would not buy it?
    definitely would not buy it?

The first question fails to capture intensity. It determines the direction ("Yes" versus "No"), but it cannot compare with the second question in completeness or sensitivity of response. The latter also has the advantage of being ordinal in nature.

A primary advantage of using scaled-response questions is that scaling permits measurement of the intensity of respondents' answers. Also, many scaled-response forms incorporate numbers that can be used directly as codes. Finally, the marketing researcher can use much more powerful statistical tools with some scaled-response questions (see Chapter 17).

Sometimes scaling questions simply do not help in accomplishing the research objectives. For example, consider a 10-point scale that asks, "Please rate the timeliness of reports on the following 1–10 point scale." How would a researcher interpret a 6, 7, or 8? A simple way to accomplish the research objective is to ask, "Were you satisfied with the timeliness of the reports you received?" (Yes or No). This data will provide a clear answer to the objective.

Step Four: Decide on the Question Wording

Once the marketing researcher has decided on the specific types of questions and the response formats, the next task is the actual writing of the questions. Wording specific questions can require a significant investment of the researcher's time unless questionnaire software or a survey Web site like Perseus or Zoomerang is used. Four general guidelines about the wording of questions are useful to bear in mind: (1) The wording must be clear, (2) the wording must not bias the respondent, (3) the respondent must be able to answer the questions, and (4) the respondent must be willing to answer the questions.

Make Sure the Wording Is Clear   Once the researcher has decided that a question is absolutely necessary, the question must be stated so that it means the same thing to all respondents. Ambiguous terminology—for example, "Do you live within 5 minutes of here?" or "Where do you usually shop for clothes?"—should be avoided. The respondent's answer to the first question will depend on such factors as mode of transportation (maybe the respondent walks), driving speed, and perceptions of elapsed time. (The interviewer would do better to display a map with certain areas delineated and ask whether the respondent lives within the area outlined.) The second question depends on the type of clothing being purchased and the meaning of the word "Where."

Clarity also calls for the use of reasonable terminology. A questionnaire is not a vocabulary test. Jargon should be avoided, and verbiage should be geared to the target audience. The question "What is the level of efficacy of your preponderant dishwashing liquid?" probably would be greeted by a lot of blank stares. It would be much simpler to ask "Are you (1) very satisfied, (2) somewhat satisfied, or (3) not satisfied with your current brand of dishwashing liquid?" Words with precise meanings, universal usage, and minimal connotative confusion should be selected. When respondents are uncertain about what a question means, the incidence of "No response" answers increases.

A further complication in wording questions is the need to tailor the language to the target respondent group, whether it is lawyers or construction laborers. This advice may seem painfully obvious, but there are instances in which failure to relate to respondents' frames of reference has been disastrous. A case in point is the use of the word *bottles* (or *cans*) in this question: "How many bottles of beer do you drink in a normal week?" Because in some southern states beer is sold in 32-, 12-, 8-, 7-, 6-, and even 4-ounce bottles, a "heavy" drinker (defined as someone who consumes eight bottles of beer per week) may drink as little as 32 ounces while a "light" drinker (defined as someone who consumes up to three bottles) may actually drink as much as 96 ounces.

Clarity can be improved by stating the purpose of the survey at the beginning of the interview. To put the questions in the proper perspective, the respondent needs to understand the nature of the study and what is expected of him or her but not necessarily who is sponsoring the project.

Sometimes questions are asked with categories that are not mutually exclusive. For example:

What is your total yearly household income before taxes?

1. Under $40,000
2. $40,000–$60,000
3. $60,000–$80,000
4. Over $80,000

So if a respondent's family income is $60,000, does he or she pick answer 2 or 3? Here is a question with conflicting meaning:

Please indicate the product you use most often. Check all that apply.[9]

1. Cell phone
2. Toaster
3. Microwave
4. Vacuum cleaner

In this question, "use most often" and "check all that apply" are conflicting instructions.

Researchers must also be careful in determining when to allow multiple responses. The following question on an Internet survey allowed only one answer but should have been "check all that apply."

What time of the day do you like to check your e-mail?

- ■ Morning
- ■ Midday
- ■ Evening
- ■ Night
- ■ Check e-mail once per week or less
- ■ Do not use e-mail[10]

clarity in wording
Achieved by avoiding ambiguous terminology, using reasonable, vernacular language adjusted to the target group, and asking only one question at a time.

Researchers must allow all valid responses. The example below is quite obvious but, in some cases, response categories are much more subtle.

What is your favorite color?

- ■ Red
- ■ Green
- ■ Blue

To achieve clarity in wording, the researcher should avoid asking two questions in one, sometimes called a *double-barreled question*. For example, "How did you like the taste and texture of the coffee cake?" should be broken into two questions, one concerning taste and the other texture. Each question should address only one aspect of evaluation.

respondent biasing
Leading questions that give away the research goal or sponsor identity.

Avoid Biasing the Respondent Questions such as "Do you often shop at lower-class stores like Super Shop?" and "Have you purchased any high-quality Black & Decker tools in the past 6 months?" show an obvious bias. Leading questions, such as "Weren't you pleased with the good service you received last night at the Holiday Inn?" is also quite obviously biased. However, bias may be much more subtle than that illustrated in these examples.

Sponsor identification early in the interviewing process can distort answers. An opening statement such as "We are conducting a study on the quality of banking for Northeast National Bank and would like to ask you a few questions" should be avoided. Similarly, it will not take long, for example, for a person to recognize that the survey is being conducted for Miller beer if, after the third question, every question is related to this product.

respondent's question-answering ability
Factors affecting this ability include lack of required information, forgetfulness, or incomplete recall ability.

Consider the Respondent's Ability to Answer the Questions In some cases, a respondent may never have acquired the information needed to answer the question. For example, a husband may not know which brand of sewing thread is preferred by his wife, and respondents will know nothing about a brand or store that they have never encountered. A question worded so as to imply that the respondent should be able to answer it will often elicit a reply that is nothing more than a wild guess. This creates measurement error, since uninformed opinions are being recorded.

Another problem is forgetfulness. For example, you probably cannot remember the answers to all these questions: What was the name of the last movie you saw in a theater? Who were the stars? Did you have popcorn? How many ounces were in the container? What price did you pay for the popcorn? Did you purchase any other snack items? Why or why not? The same is true for the typical respondent. Yet a brand manager for Mars, Incorporated wants to know what brand of candy you purchased last, what alternative brands you considered, and what factors led you to the brand selected. Because brand managers want answers to these questions, market researchers ask them. This, in turn, creates measurement error. Often respondents will give the name of a well-known brand, like Milky Way or Hershey. In other cases, respondents will mention a brand that they often purchase, but it may not be the last brand purchased.

To avoid the problem of a respondent's inability to recall, the researcher should keep the referenced time periods relatively short. For example, if the respondent says "Yes" to the question "Did you purchase a candy bar within the past 7 days?" then brand and purchase motivation questions can be asked. A poor question for Dish Network customers might be "How many movies have you rented in the past year to view at home on Dish Network?" might be replaced with the following:

a. How many movies have you rented in the past month to view on Dish Network?

b. Would you say that, in the last month, you rented more movies, fewer movies, or about the average number of movies you rent per month? (IF "MORE" or "LESS," ASK THE FOLLOWING QUESTION)

c. What would you say is the typical number of movies you rent per month?

Here are two questions from actual marketing research studies. The first is from a mail survey and the second from a telephone survey. Question one: In the past 3 months, how much have you spent on movies you saw advertised in the newspaper? Most people haven't a clue as to how much they have spent on movies in the last 3 months unless it is "nothing." And they certainly don't recall which of the movies were advertised where. Also, what if the respondent bought tickets for the whole family? Question two: Of your last 10 drinks of scotch, how many were at home? At a friend's? At a restaurant? At a bar or tavern? A light scotch drinker may have consumed 10 drinks over a period of not less than 2 years! Maybe he carries around a scotch intake logbook, but it's doubtful.

The above questions are bad, but the questions below, from a real mail panel survey, were written by either a careless questionnaire designer or one who lives quite differently from most of us. Question: How many times in an average day do you apply your usual underarm product? One to two times per day? Three to four times per day? Five to six times per day? More than six times per day? Question: How many times in an average day do you shower/bathe? One time per day? Two times per day? Three times per day? Four times per day? Five or more times per day? Good grooming is important, but perhaps these questions are over the line.

Consider the Respondent's Willingness to Answer the Question

A respondent may have a very good memory, yet not be willing to give a truthful reply. If an event is perceived as embarrassing, sensitive in nature, threatening, or divergent from the respondent's self-image, it is likely either not to be reported at all or to be distorted in a socially desirable direction.

> **respondent's willingness to answer**
> Embarrassing, sensitive, or threatening questions or questions divergent from respondent's self-image may cause them to refuse to answer.

Embarrassing questions that deal with topics such as borrowing money, personal hygiene, sexual activities, and criminal records must be phrased carefully to minimize measurement error. One technique is to ask the question in the third person—for example, "Do you think that most people charge more on their credit cards than they should? Why?" By generalizing the question to "most people," the researcher may be able to learn more about individual respondents' attitudes toward credit and debt.

Another method for soliciting embarrassing information is for the interviewer to state, prior to asking the question, that the behavior or attitude is not unusual—for example, "Millions of Americans suffer from hemorrhoids; do you or any member of your family suffer from this problem?" This technique, called *using counterbiasing statements*, makes embarrassing topics less intimidating for respondents to discuss.

Step Five: Establish Questionnaire Flow and Layout

After the questions have been properly formulated, the next step is to sequence them and develop a layout for the questionnaire. Questionnaires are not constructed haphazardly; there is a logic to the positioning of each section (see Exhibit 12.8). Experienced marketing researchers are well aware that good questionnaire development is the key to obtaining a completed interview. A well-organized questionnaire usually elicits answers that are more carefully thought out and detailed. Researcher wisdom has led to the following general guidelines concerning questionnaire flow.

Use Screening Questions to Identify Qualified Respondents

Most marketing research employs some type of quota sampling. Only qualified respondents are interviewed, and specific minimum numbers (quotas) of various types of qualified respondents may be sought. For example, a food products study generally has quotas of users of specific brands, a magazine study screens for readers, and a cosmetic study screens for brand awareness.

EXHIBIT 12.8	**How a Questionnaire Should Be Organized**		
Location	**Type**	**Examples**	**Rationale**
Screeners	Qualifying questions	"Have you been snow skiing in the past 12 months?" "Do you own a pair of skis?"	The goal is to identify target respondents.
First few questions	Warm-ups	"What brand of skis do you own?" "How many years have you owned them?"	Easy-to-answer questions show the respondent that the survey is simple.
First third of questions	Transitions	"What features do you like best about the skis?"	Questions related to research objectives require slightly more effort.
Second third	Difficult and complicated questions	"Following are 10 characteristics of snow skis. Please rate your skis on each characteristic, using the scale below."	The respondent has committed to completing the questionnaire.
Last third	Classifying and demographic questions	"What is the highest level of education you have attained?"	The respondent may leave some "personal" questions blank, but they are at the end of the survey.

→ screeners
Questions used to identify appropriate respondents.

Screeners (screening questions) may appear on the questionnaire, or a screening questionnaire may be filled out for everyone who is interviewed. Any demographics obtained provide a basis against which to compare persons who qualify for the full study. A long screening questionnaire can significantly increase the cost of the study, as more information must be obtained from every contact with a respondent. But it may provide important data on the nature of nonusers, nontriers, and persons unaware of the product or service being researched. Short screening questionnaires, such as the one presented in Exhibit 12.9, quickly eliminate unqualified persons and enable the interviewer to move immediately to the next potential respondent.

Most importantly, screeners provide a basis for estimating the costs of a survey. A survey in which all persons are qualified to be interviewed is going to be much cheaper to conduct than one with a 5 percent incidence rate. Many surveys are placed with field services mall surveys at a flat rate per completed questionnaire. The rate is based on a stated average interview time and incidence rate. Screeners are used to determine whether, in fact, the incidence rate holds true in a particular city. If it does not, the flat rate is adjusted accordingly.

Begin with a Question That Gets the Respondent's Interest
After introductory comments and screens to find a qualified respondent, the initial questions should be simple, interesting, and nonthreatening. To open a questionnaire with an income or age question could be disastrous. These are often considered threatening and immediately put the respondent on the defensive. The initial question should be easy to answer without much forethought.

Ask General Questions First
Once the interview progresses beyond the opening warm-up questions, the questionnaire should proceed in a logical fashion. First, general questions are asked to get the person thinking about a concept, company, or type of product; then the questionnaire moves to the specifics. For example, a questionnaire on shampoo might begin with "Have you purchased a hair spray, hair conditioner, or hair shampoo within the past 6 weeks?" Then it would ask about the frequency of shampooing, brands purchased in the past 3 months, satisfaction and dissatisfaction with brands purchased, repurchase intent, characteristics of an "ideal" shampoo, respondent's hair characteristics, and finally demographics.

Hello. I'm from Data Facts Research. We are conducting a survey among men, and I'd like to ask you a few questions.

1. Do you or does any member of your family work for an advertising agency, a marketing research firm, or a company that manufactures or sells shaving products?
   (TERMINATE)   Yes ( )
   (CONTINUE WITH Q. 2)   No ( )

2. How old are you? Are you . . . (READ LIST)
   (TERMINATE)   Under 15 yrs. old? ( )
   (CHECK QUOTA CONTROL FORM—IF QUOTA GROUP FOR
   WHICH THE RESPONDENT QUALIFIES IS NOT FILLED,   15 to 34 yrs. old? ( )
   CONTINUE, IF QUOTA GROUP IS FILLED, THEN TERMINATE.)   Over 34 yrs. old? ( )

3. The last time you shaved, did you use an electric razor or a razor that uses blades?
   (TERMINATE)   Electric Razor ( )
   (CONTINUE WITH Q. 4)   Blade Razor ( )

4. How many times have you shaved in the past 7 days?
   (IF LESS THAN THREE TIMES, TERMINATE. IF THREE OR MORE
   TIMES, CONTINUE WITH THE MAIN QUESTIONNAIRE.)

Exhibit 12.9

Screening Questionnaire That Seeks Men 15 Years of Age and Older Who Shave at Least Three Times a Week with a Blade Razor

Ask Questions That Require "Work" in the Middle   Initially, the respondent will be only vaguely interested in and understanding of the nature of the survey. As the interest-building questions appear, momentum and commitment to the interview will build. When the interview shifts to questions with scaled-response formats, the respondent must be motivated to understand the response categories and options. Alternatively, questions might necessitate some recall or opinion formation on the part of the respondent. Established interest and commitment must sustain the respondent in this part of the interview.

Insert "Prompters" at Strategic Points   Good interviewers can sense when a respondent's interest and motivation sag and will attempt to build them back up. However, it is always worthwhile for the questionnaire designer to insert short encouragements at strategic locations in the questionnaire. These may be simple statements such as "There are only a few more questions to go" or "This next section will be easier." Encouraging words may also be inserted as part of an introduction to a section: "Now that you have helped us with those comments, we would like to ask a few more questions."

prompters
Short encouraging statements to rebuild respondent interest.

Position Sensitive, Threatening, and Demographic Questions at the End   As mentioned earlier, the objectives of a study sometimes necessitate questions on topics about which respondents may feel uneasy. These topics should be covered near the end of the questionnaire to ensure that most of the questions are answered before the respondent becomes defensive or breaks off the interview. Another argument for placing sensitive questions toward the end is that by the time these questions are asked, interviewees have been conditioned to respond. In other words, the respondent has settled into a pattern of seeing or hearing a question and giving an answer.

Put Instructions in Capital Letters   To avoid confusion and to clarify what is a question and what is an instruction, all instructions for self-administered questionnaires should be in capital letters—for example, "IF 'YES' TO QUESTION 13, SKIP TO QUESTION 17." Capitalizing helps bring the instructions to the interviewer's or respondent's attention. Of course, this is done automatically on computer-based surveys.

Use a Proper Introduction and Closing   Every questionnaire must have an introduction and closing. The Council for Marketing and Opinion Research (CMOR) has developed a model survey introduction and closing based on research findings from a number of different studies. CMOR recommends the following:[11]

Model Introduction/Opening

- In order to gain the trust of the respondent, the interviewer should provide his or her first name or agreed upon contact name. Providing a last name is optional but is recommended for business-to-business studies or surveys involving professionals such as those in the medical field.
- Provide the name of the company that the interviewer represents and the name of the client/sponsor of the research whenever possible.
- Explain the nature of the study topic/subject matter in general terms.
- State, as early in the interview as possible, that no selling will be involved as a result of the call.
- The respondent should be told in the introduction the approximate length of the survey.
- It is recommended as standard practice to obtain two-party consent to monitoring/recording; that is, both the respondent and the interviewer should be informed that the call might be monitored/recorded for quality control purposes.
- Reinforce the fact that the respondent's time is appreciated/valued.
- Invite the respondent to participate in the survey, determine if the interview time is convenient, and, if not, offer an alternative callback time and date to complete the survey.

Hello, my name is _____ and I'm calling from (company). Today/Tonight we are calling to gather opinions regarding (general subject), and are not selling anything. This study will take approximately (length) and may be monitored (and recorded) for quality purposes. We would appreciate your time. May I include your opinions?

Model Closing

- At the conclusion of the survey, thank the respondent for his or her time.
- Express the desired intention that the respondent had a positive survey experience and will be willing to participate in future market research projects.
- Remind the respondent that his or her opinions do count.

Thank you for your time and cooperation. I hope this experience was a pleasant one and you will participate in other marketing research projects in the future. Please remember that your opinion counts! Have a good day/evening.

Alternative: Participate in collecting respondent satisfaction data to improve survey quality.

Thank you very much for taking part in this survey. Because consumers like you are such a valued part of what we do, I'd like you to think about the survey you just participated in. On a scale from 1 to 10 where 10 means "it was a good use of my time," and 1 means "it was not a good use of my time," which number between 1 and 10 best describes how you feel about your experience today? That's all the questions I have. Please remember that your opinion counts! Have a good day/evening!

Step Six: Evaluate the Questionnaire

Once a rough draft of the questionnaire has been designed, the marketing researcher is obligated to take a step back and critically evaluate it. This phase may seem redundant, given the careful thought that went into each question. But recall the crucial role played by the questionnaire. At this point in the questionnaire development, the following issues should be considered: (1) Is the question necessary? (2) Is the questionnaire too long? (3) Will the questions provide the information needed to accomplish the research objectives?

Is the Question Necessary?   Perhaps the most important criterion for this phase of questionnaire development is the necessity for a given question. Sometimes researchers and brand managers want to ask questions because "they were on the last survey we did like this" or because "it would be nice to know." Excessive numbers of demographic questions are very common. Asking for education data, numbers of children in multiple age categories, and extensive demographics on the spouse simply is not warranted by the nature of many studies.

> **necessary questions**
> Pertain directly to the stated survey objectives or are screeners, interest generators, or required transitions.

Each question must serve a purpose. Unless it is a screener, an interest generator, or a required transition, it must be directly and explicitly related to the stated objectives of the particular survey. Any question that fails to satisfy at least one of these criteria should be omitted.

Is the Questionnaire Too Long?   At this point, the researcher should role-play the survey, with volunteers acting as respondents. Although there is no magic number of interactions, the length of time it takes to complete the questionnaire should be averaged over a minimum of five trials. Any questionnaire to be administered in a mall or over the telephone should be a candidate for cutting if it averages longer than 20 minutes. Sometimes mall-intercept interviews can run slightly longer if an incentive is provided to the respondent. Most Internet surveys should take less than 15 minutes to complete.

Common incentives are movie tickets, pen and pencil sets, and cash or checks. The use of incentives often actually lowers survey costs because response rates increase and terminations during the interview decrease. If checks are given out instead of cash, the canceled checks can be used to create a list of survey participants for follow-up purposes.

A technique that can reduce the length of questionnaires is called a split-questionnaire design. It can be used when the questionnaire is long and the sample size is large. The questionnaire is split into one core component (such as demographics, usage patterns, and psychographics) and a number of subcomponents. Respondents complete the core component plus a randomly assigned subcomponent.

Will the Questions Provide the Information Needed to Accomplish the Research Objectives?   The researcher must make certain that the questionnaire contains sufficient numbers and types of questions to meet the decision-making needs of management. A suggested procedure is to carefully review the written objectives for the research project and then write each question number next to the objective that the particular question will address. For example, question 1 applies to objective 3, question 2 to objective 2, and so forth. If a question cannot be tied to an objective, the researcher should determine whether the list of objectives is complete. If the list is complete, the question should be omitted. If the researcher finds an objective with no questions listed beside it, appropriate questions should be added. Tips for writing a good questionnaire are provided in the Practicing Marketing Research feature on page 360.

> **approval by managers**
> Managerial review approval after questionnaire drafting to prevent false starts and expensive later redrafts.

Step Seven: Obtain Approval of All Relevant Parties

After the first draft of the questionnaire has been completed, copies should be distributed to all parties who have direct authority over the project. Practically speaking, managers may step in at any time in the design process with new information, requests, or concerns. When this happens, revisions are often necessary. It is still important to get final approval of the first draft even if managers have already intervened in the development process.

Managerial approval commits management to obtaining a body of information via a specific instrument (questionnaire). If the question is not asked, the data will not be gathered. Thus, questionnaire approval tacitly reaffirms what decision-making information is needed and how it will be obtained. For example, assume that a new product questionnaire asks about shape, material, end use, and packaging. By approving the form, the new-product development manager is implying, "I know what color the product will be" or "It is not important to determine color at this time."

Step Eight: Pretest and Revise

pretest
Trial run of a
questionnaire.

When final managerial approval has been obtained, the questionnaire must be pretested. No survey should be conducted without a pretest. Moreover, a pretest does not mean that one researcher is administering the questionnaire to another researcher. Ideally, a pretest is administered to target respondents for the study. In a **pretest**, researchers look for misinterpretations by respondents, lack of continuity, poor skip patterns, additional alternatives for precoded and closed-ended questions, and general respondent reaction to the interview. The pretest should be conducted in the same mode as the final interview—that is, if the study is to be an Internet survey, then the pretest should be too.

Step Nine: Prepare Final Questionnaire Copy

Even the final copy phase does not allow the researcher to relax. Precise instructions must be created when an interviewer is involved—for example, where to interview, target

PRACTICING MARKETING RESEARCH

Tips for Writing a Good Questionnaire

If you have ever sent what you thought was a "final" questionnaire to a marketing research supplier, only to have it returned to you full of wording changes, deletions, and other editorial comments, you're not alone. Writing a questionnaire does not, at first glance, appear to be a very difficult task: just figure out what you want to know, and write questions to obtain that information. But although writing questions is easy, writing good questions is not. Here are some do's and don'ts when writing questions.

1. *Avoid abbreviations, slang, or uncommon words that your audience might not understand.* For example: What is your opinion of

PPOs? It is quite possible that not everyone knows that PPO stands for Preferred Provider Organization. If the question targets the general public, the researcher might run into problems. On the other hand, if the question is for physicians or hospital administrators, then the acronym PPO is probably acceptable.

2. *Be specific.* The problem with vague questions is that they generate vague answers. For example: What is your household income? As respondents come up with numerous interpretations to this question, they will give all kinds of answers—income before taxes, income after taxes, and so on. Another example: How often did you attend sporting events during the past year? (1) Never, (2) Rarely, (3) Occasionally, (4)

Regularly. Again, this question is open for interpretation. People will interpret "sporting event" and the answer list differently—does "regularly" mean weekly, monthly, or what?

3. *On the other hand, don't overdo it.* When questions are too precise, people cannot answer them. They will either refuse or guess. For example: How many books did you read [last year]? You need to give them some ranges: (1) None, (2) 1–10, (3) 11–25, (4) 26–50, (5) More than 50.

4. *Make sure your questions are easy to answer.* Questions that are too demanding will also lead to refusals or guesses. For example: Please rank the following 20 items in order of importance to you when you are shopping for a new car. You're asking respondents to do a fair amount of calculating. Don't ask people to rank 20 items; have them pick the top 5.

4. *Don't assume too much.* This is a fairly common error, in which the question writer infers something about people's knowledge, attitudes, or behavior. For example: Do you tend to agree or disagree with the president's position on gun control? This question assumes that the respondent is aware that the president has a position on gun control and knows what that position is. To avoid this error, the writer must be prepared to do some educating. For example: "The president has recently stated his position on gun control. Are you aware that he has taken a stand on this issue?" If the answer is yes, then continue with: "Please describe in your own words what you understand his position on gun control to be." And, finally, "Do you tend to agree or disagree with his stand?"

6. *Watch out for double questions and questions with double negatives.* Combining questions or using a double negative leads to ambiguous questions and answers. For example: "Do you favor the legalization of marijuana for use in private homes but not in public places?" If this question precisely describes the respondent's position, then a "yes" answer is easily interpreted. But a "no" could mean the respondent favors use in public places but not in private homes, or opposes both, or favors both. Similarly, here is an example of a question with a double negative: "Should the police chief not be directly responsible to the mayor?" The question is ambiguous; almost any answer will be even more so.

7. *Check for bias.* A biased question can influence people to respond in a manner that does not accurately reflect their positions. There are several ways in which questions can be prejudiced. One is to imply that respondents should have engaged in a certain behavior. For example: "The movie, *XYZ*, was seen by more people than any other movie this year. Have you seen this movie?" So as not to appear "different," respondents may say yes even though they haven't seen the movie. The question should be: "Have you seen the movie, *XYZ*?" Another way to bias a question is to have unbalanced answer choices. For example: "Currently our country spends XX billion dollars a year on foreign aid. Do you feel this amount should be (1) increased, (2) stay the same, (3) decreased a little, (4) decreased somewhat, (5) decreased a great deal?" This set of responses encourages respondents to select a "decrease" option, since there are three of these and only one increase option.

Pretesting: The Survey before the Survey

All the rewriting and editing in the world won't guarantee success. However, pretesting is the least expensive way to make sure your questionnaire research project is a success. The primary purpose of a pretest is to make certain that the questionnaire gives the respondent clear, understandable questions that will evoke clear, understandable answers.[12]

After completion of the pretest, any necessary changes should be made. Managerial approval should then be re-obtained before going forward. If the original pretest results in extensive design and question alterations, a second pretest is in order. Effects of national differences are discussed in the feature on page 369.

respondents, and when to show respondents test items like alternative product designs. In a mail survey, compliance and subsequent response rates may be affected positively by a professional-looking questionnaire. For telephone interviews, the copy is typically read from a computer screen. Survey software for online interviews often lets the designer choose backgrounds, formats, and so forth.

Step Ten: Implement the Survey

Completion of the questionnaire establishes the basis for obtaining the desired decision-making information from the marketplace. As discussed in Chapter 2, most mall and telephone research interviewing is conducted by field service firms. It is the firm's job to complete the interviews and send them back to the researcher. In essence, field services are the in-person interviewers, the production line of the marketing research industry. A series of forms and procedures must be issued with the questionnaire to make certain that the field service firm gathers the data correctly, efficiently, and at a reasonable cost. Depending on the data-collection method, these may include supervisor's instructions, interviewer's instructions, screeners, call record sheets, and visual aids.

Supervisor's Instructions As mentioned earlier, mall, focus group, and some other types of research are handled by field services. This necessitates supervisor's instructions. **Supervisor's instructions** inform the field services firm of the nature of the study, start and completion dates, quotas, reporting times, equipment and facility requirements, sampling instructions, number of interviewers required, and validation procedures. In addition, detailed instructions are required for any taste test that involves food preparation. Quantities typically are measured and cooked using rigorous measurement techniques and devices.

> **supervisor's instructions**
> Written directions to the field service firm on how to conduct the survey.

A vital part of any study handled by a field service, supervisor's instructions establish the parameters for conducting the research. Without clear instructions, the interview may be conducted 10 different ways in 10 different cities. A sample page from a set of supervisor's instructions is shown in Exhibit 12.10.

Field Management Companies

Conducting fieldwork is much easier today than it was in years past. The stereotypical "kitchen table" field service firm is passing into history. In its place are companies that specialize in field management. **Field management companies**, such as QFact, On-Line Communications, and Direct Resource, generally provide questionnaire formatting, screener writing, development of instructional and peripheral materials, shipping services, field auditing, and all coordination of data collection, coding, and tab services required for the project. On completion of a study, they typically submit a single, comprehensive invoice for the project. Generally lean on staff, these companies provide the services clients need without attempting to compete with the design and analytical capabilities of full-service companies and ad agency research staffs.

> **field management companies**
> Firms that provide such support services as questionnaire formatting, screener writing, and coordination of data collection.

A number of full-service companies and qualitative professionals have discovered that using field management companies can be cost-effective; it can increase productivity by allowing them to take on more projects while using fewer of their internal resources. Several qualitative researchers have developed ongoing relationships with field management companies, whose personnel function as extensions of the consultant's staff, setting up projects and freeing up the researcher to conduct groups, write reports, and consult with clients.

Purpose	To determine from diet soft-drink users their ability to discriminate among three samples of Diet Dr Pepper and give opinions and preferences between two of the samples
Staff	3–4 experienced interviewers per shift
Location	One busy shopping center in a middle to upper-middle socioeconomic area. The center's busiest hours are to be worked by a double shift of interviewers.
	In the center, 3–4 private interviewing stations are to be set up, and a refrigerator and good counterspace made available for product storage and preparation.
Quota	192 completed interviews broken down as follows:
	A minimum of 70 Diet Dr Pepper users
	A maximum of 122 other diet brand users
Project materials	For this study, you are supplied the following:
	250 Screening Questionnaires
	192 Study Questionnaires
	4 Card A's
Product/preparation	For this study, our client shipped to your refrigerated facility 26 cases of soft-drink product. Each case contains 24 10-oz. bottles—312 coded with an *F* on the cap, 312 with an *S*.
	Each day, you are to obtain from the refrigerated facility approximately 2–4 cases of product—1–2 of each code. Product must be transported in coolers and kept refrigerated at the location. It should remain at approximately 42°F.
	In the center, you are to take one-half of the product coded *F* and place the #23 stickers on the bottles. The other half of the *F* product should receive #46 stickers.
	The same should be done for product *S*—one-half should be coded #34, the other half #68. A supervisor should do this task before interviewing begins. Interviewers will select product by *code number*. Code number stickers are enclosed for this effort.
	Each respondent will be initially testing three product samples as designated on the questionnaire. Interviewers will come to the kitchen, select the three designated bottles, open and pour 4 oz. of each product into its corresponding coded cup. The interviewer should cap and *refrigerate* leftover product when finished pouring and take only the 3 *cups* of product on a tray to respondent.

Exhibit 12.10

Sample Page of Supervisor's Instructions for a Diet Soft Drink Taste Test

Of course, like any other segment of the research industry, field management has its limitations. By definition, field management companies generally do not have design and analytical capabilities. This means that their clients may, on occasion, need to seek other providers to meet their full-service needs. In addition, because this is a relatively new segment of the industry, experience, services, and standards vary tremendously from firm to firm. It's advisable to carefully screen prospective companies and check references. These limitations notwithstanding, field management companies provide a way for researchers to increase their productivity in a cost-effective manner, while maintaining the quality of the information on which their company's decisions and commitments are based.

Impact of the Internet on Questionnaire Development

As with most other aspects of marketing research, the Internet has affected questionnaire development and use in several ways. For example, a marketing research company can now create a questionnaire and send it as an e-mail attachment to management for comments and approval; once approved, it can be placed on the client's server to be used as an Internet survey. Or researchers can simply use an Internet company like Vovici, Inquisite, Web Surveyor, SSI Web, or many others to create a survey on the Internet.

Perseus, for example, is a leading Internet self-service questionnaire-building site. It allows marketing researchers to create online surveys quickly and then view real-time results anytime and anywhere, using remote access. The advantage is that the marketing research client has no questionnaire software to install, and no programming or administration is required. All operations are automated and performed through the Vovici Web site. This includes survey design, respondent invitation, data collection, analysis, and results reporting.

Software for Questionnaire Development

Sawtooth Software offers some of the most widely used analytical and questionnaire development software in the world. The systems are both powerful and easy to use. SSI's online interviewing product is called SSI Web. Exhibit 12.11 illustrates the kinds of questions that can be used with SSI Web. Some of the capabilities of SSI Web are:

- **Easy-to-use, template-based authoring on the researcher's own PC**
- **Randomization of pages, questions, and response options**
- **Data piping**
- **Constructed (dynamic) lists:**

  One of the most powerful aspects of SSI Web is the ability to create custom lists of response options. These lists are defined by rules you specify and are customized to each respondent, based on the respondent's answers. The following example demonstrates how a constructed list might be used.

Which cities have you visited?	**Out of all the cities that you visited, which is your favorite?**
☒ Seattle	○ Seattle
☐ Portland →	○ San Diego
☒ San Diego	○ Denver
☒ Denver	
☐ Dallas	

- **Automatic question response verification.**
  Questions must be answered before moving to the next question.

- **Powerful skip logic**
  SSI Web makes it easy to add skip logic (branching) within your survey. Skips can be executed with the page loads (pre-skips) or after it has been submitted (post-skips).

FROM THE FRONT LINE

Practices That Simplify and Speed Up Design of a Good Questionnaire

Suzanne Wagner, Project Manager, DSS Research

I began my career in market research 20 years ago as a telephone interviewer for DSS Research, a national, full service market research firm in North Texas. It was this experience" on the front lines", I believe, that has helped me immensely in designing a good questionnaire. The key to successful questionnaire design, in my opinion, lies in thinking about how both the respondent and the interviewer will react to the survey instrument. Technical aspect aside, it is of the utmost importance that a survey instrument be logical and easy to understand for both interviewer and respondent. If your interviewers can not easily understand and relay the questionnaire to respondents, bad data will result. The same holds true if respondents can not readily comprehend and react to the questions being asked of them.

- **Refer back to the study objectives** as a guide to for the information you need to get from respondents to meet your objectives which leads you right into the next point.
- **Use index cards – real ones or virtual ones (there's an iPad app) to begin to lay out the survey.** When designing a survey from scratch, write out one question per index card, then you can shuffle questions around into the order that makes the most sense. This approach helps organize your thoughts and gets you thinking about skip patterns. I learned this tip from an account executive who had been in the business for many years and I still use it to this day.
- **Use language appropriate to the population surveyed.** It's fine to use technical jargon if you are interviewing doctors, lawyers or engineers, but not with the general public. Keep concepts and language as simple and as specific as possible and avoid slang, acronyms.
- **Size does matter.** We're in the lightning-fast 21st century now and attention spans are getting shorter. Respondent fatigue is a real issue and surveys need to be as short as possible to prevent this problem. Avoid redundancy and group similar questions into a logical order to help your questionnaire flow. Use headings to be read by interviewers in telephone or in-person surveys before a question series so respondents know what's coming and stay interested (e.g., "Now I'd like to ask you a few questions about XYZ."). Have clear interviewer instructions as to when and how often to read scales – for example: if a respondent is clearly grasping a scale that is going to stay the same for a long series of attribute ratings, the interviewer should stop reading that scale for that series. Rereading a scale over and over to a respondent who clearly already gets it only serves to lengthen the interview and aggravate the respondent.
- **Pre-test and monitor, monitor, monitor.** For telephone interviews, running a pre-test and monitoring (listening to actual interviews in real time) heavily during the first few days of interviewing will give you information about how the survey instrument flows and if interviewers or respondents are struggling with any questions. It will also give you information about timing and other technical aspects of the survey that you cannot get firsthand any other way. Procedures involving going through the survey with typical respondents or discussing the survey with them after they have completed it can be used for mail and online surveys.
- **Know your interviewers. Interviewers can and will** tell you what's working and what's not in your survey and give you some ideas on how to improve it. This is easy to do if you have in-house telephone data collection. If

you use outsource vendors instead of an in-house call center, start with an in-depth briefing by phone or Internet with them and later keep them interested and informed about the project. The more the interviewers know and understand about the background of a project, the client's intentions and the research objectives behind the study, the better your research project will go. An engaged interviewer is your best ally and having a rapport with your data collection team will help them feel a part of the process and keep them doing the best research possible for you.

- **Keep it simple.** Survey design can be challenging, and it is the key to a successful research project, but it's an art as much as it is a science. Use simple language, logical question grouping and flow, concise wording, and keep respondents interested (your interviewers are critical here)—these are the keys to creating a solid, useful survey instrument.

That means respondents can receive pages that only include the subset of questions that apply to them, and respondents can skip pages that are not relevant.

- **Quota control**
- **Foreign language character support**
- **Questionnaire preview and testing on local PC**
- **Ability to create your own custom questions with HTML and "Free Format" question type**
- **Power users may insert HTML, JavaScript, or Perl**
- **Respondent restart (without cookies)**
- **Similar look across different browsers, including Mac and legacy browsers**
- **Automatic respondent password generation, or import from text file**

In the global market of today, a product may be tested in many countries at the same time. The need for questionnaires in several different languages has grown considerably in the last decade.

Exhibit 12.11

Types of Questions That Can Be Used with SSI Web

Single Select Response (radio) question type

If you had the opportunity to visit one of the following cities, which one would you choose?
○ Seattle
○ Hong Kong
○ Miami
○ Paris

Multiple Select Response (checkbox)—question

Please select all of the activities you enjoy:

☐ Shopping   ☐ Walking
☐ Bowling   ☐ Skiing
☐ Swimming   ☐ Golfing
☐ Kayaking   ☐ Other (please specify)
☐ Bird Watching ☐ None of these

Single Select Response (combo box) question type

Which is your favorite holiday?

[↓]

(Holidays are listed in drop-down box.)

The Numeric question type. A response from 0 to 100 is required.

How old are you?   ☐

Open-end (multiple-line) question type

In the box below tell us about where you grew up.

Grid question type. This grid has select questions (radio buttons)
specified for the rows.

Please tell us how likely you are to participate in each activity over the next 3 months.

	Not Likely		Somewhat Likely		Very Likely
Shopping	○	○	○	○	○
Bowling	○	○	○	○	○
Swimming	○	○	○	○	○
Kayaking	○	○	○	○	○
Bird Watching	○	○	○	○	○

Grid question type. This example shows the flexibility in grids by
demonstrating how different question types can be
set for each row.

Please answer the following questions about the electronic products displayed below.

Which items do you own?	☐	☐	☐	☐
Which is your favorite?	○	○	○	○
How much would you pay for each?	$	$	$	$

Exhibit 12.11

Types of Questions That Can Be Used with SSI Web (*Continued*)

Ranking question type

Please rank the top three activities that you enjoy.
☐ Shopping
☐ Bowling
☐ Swimming
☐ Kayaking
☐ Bird Watching

Constant Sum question type

Given a budget of $3,000, please specify how much you would spend for each holiday.
☐ Easter
☐ 4th of July
☐ Halloween
☐ Thanksgiving
☐ Christmas
☐ New Years
☐ Total (Total is automatically computed each time numbers are entered into a holiday box.)

Free Format question type. The Free Format question type
allows researchers to specify their own HTML
to create custom questions.

Personal Information

First Name: _____

Last Name: _____

Street Address: _____

_____

City: _____ **State:** _____ **Zip:** _____ - _____

Gender: ○ **Male**   ○ **Female**

Interests: ☐ **Walking**

☐ **Running**

☐ **Hiking**

☐ **Swimming**

☐ **Eating**

Source: Sawtooth Software, Inc.

- ■ **Link to/from other online interviewing systems and Web sites**
- ■ **Online administrative module for real-time reports, download, and data management**
- ■ **Exports to common formats (including Excel, SPSS), with label**[13]

Facebook As a Survey Research Platform   In late 2010, Facebook launched Facebook Questions. It allows users to post surveys and questions about subjects of their choice, soliciting their friends—or the entire Facebook population—for information and opinions. As this text went to print, the service had gone through beta testing and will be further developed with the test group's feedback in mind.

Whether Facebook Questions will serve as a casual form of research or a more recreational "What song is it that goes X?" or "Which shoes look better with this belt?" remains to be seen, but company and brand Facebook pages will also have the ability to gauge how consumers feel about new products or potential launches and also establish a forum where users and brand fans can be heard right from the comfort of their own Facebook profiles.

Facebook Questions will appear on the user's profile and will also appear in the user's friends' News Feed, so answers are anticipated to be personalized and especially relevant to the poster. Photos can also be added if the user is trying to identify something, such as a type of flower in their garden.

The "social" aspect of Facebook Questions comes in the form of question suggestions and the helpful/unhelpful checkbox. Whenever polls or questions have been answered, users can post them to their own or their friends' profiles, and if a user sees a question for which a friend might have an answer, the user can "suggest" that question for a friend. Facebook Questions will also have a feature similar to ones seen on Digg, Amazon.com and Yahoo! Answers, where the users' viewing or responding to the question can (anonymously) mark whether they found a respondent's answer helpful or unhelpful. The most helpful answers will rise to the top. Users are also able to "follow" questions, so that a notification will be sent when another user responds to the question.[14]

GLOBAL RESEARCH

Survey Contamination from National Differences in Response Styles

Do people in different countries have characteristic and different styles of responding to questions? They do, report Hans Baumgartner, marketing professor at Pennsylvania State University, and Jan-Benedict E. M. Steenkamp, professor of international marketing research at Tilburg University in the Netherlands. Response styles, or non–content-based ways or responding, or simply, response biases, can contaminate questionnaire ratings and threaten the validity of research conclusions.

The researchers used a sample of 10,477 people drawn from 11 European Union countries and presented them a questionnaire with queries about their consumer behavior, response to media, demographics, and 60 attitudinal statements. These questions, using a 5-point Likert scale from "strongly agree" to "strongly disagree," focused on respondent attitudes about product choice, advertising response, new-product openness, health awareness, susceptibility to deal offers, and more.

The researchers identified five response styles: (1) agreement tendency, regardless of content; (2) disagreement tendency or habitual negativity; (3) tendency to endorse extreme responses; (4) tendency to respond either wide or narrow compared to the mean; and (5) tendency to use the middle-scale category due to presumed indecision, evasiveness, or indifference.

The results showed that across the 11 countries variance in scale scores due to response style ranged from 0 percent to 29 percent, with an average of 8 percent. A few categories were especially susceptible to distortion from response style; these included health consciousness (average of 22 percent variance), consumer ethnocentrism (16 percent), quality consciousness (14 percent), and environmental consciousness (12 percent). Response styles are thus "a source of systematic measurement error" that can threaten the validity of conclusions drawn from the data and produce "seriously biased conclusions."[15]

Questions

1. How would you screen potential respondents who exhibit the disagreement tendency or habitual negativity?

2. Come up with a series of survey questions that compensate for response bias where the respondent is clearly indecisive or evasive.

Today's global marketers offer a variety of products to their customers throughout the world. Many times, a new-product concept is tested simultaneously in a number of different countries, requiring questionnaires in a variety of languages.

Costs, Profitability, and Questionnaires

→ questionnaire costs and profitability
Factors affecting costs and profits include overestimating, overbidding, incidence rate, roadblocks to completed interviews, and premature interview terminations.

A discussion of questionnaires would not be complete without mentioning their impact on costs and profitability. Marketing research suppliers typically bid against one another for a client's project. A supplier who overestimates costs will usually lose the job to a lower-cost competitor. In all survey research, the questionnaire and incidence rate (see Chapter 6) are the core determinants of a project's estimated costs. When one of America's largest research suppliers examined costs and bids for all of its projects conducted by central-location telephone interviewing, it found that it had overestimated project costs 44 percent of the time during a recent 18-month period. The resulting overbidding had translated into millions of dollars of lost sales opportunities.

To avoid overbidding, managers must have a better understanding of questionnaire costs. In one central-location telephone study with a 50 percent incidence rate and calls lasting an average of 15 minutes, MARC, a large international marketing research firm, found that only 30 percent of the data-collection costs involved asking the questions. Seventy percent of the data-collection costs were incurred trying to reach a qualified respondent.[16]

Exhibit 12.12 depicts the numerous roadblocks an interviewer can encounter trying to get a completed interview. Each roadblock adds to the costs. MARC, for example, has found that simply adding a security screener to a questionnaire can increase the cost of interviewing by as much as 7 percent.

Another major source of extra cost in survey research is premature termination of interviews. People terminate interviews for four major reasons: the subject matter,

EXHIBIT 12.12	**Difficulties in Finding a Qualified Respondent in a Central-Location Telephone Interview**

1. Failed Attempts
    - Busy
    - No answer
    - Answering machine
    - Business number
    - Phone/language problem
    - Discontinued line

2. Cooperation Problems
    - Respondent not at home
    - Respondent refused to be interviewed

3. Screener Determines Respondent Not Eligible
    - Failed security test (works for marketing research firm, advertising agency, or the client)
    - Doesn't use the product
    - Demographic disqualification (wrong gender, age, etc.)
    - Quota filled (For example, survey has a quota of 500 users of Tide and 500 users of other clothes washing powders. Interviewer already has 500 Tide users; the current respondent uses Tide.)

4. Respondent Terminated during Interview

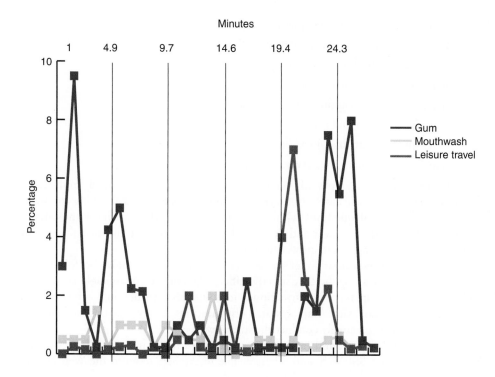

Exhibit 12.13

Actual Respondent
Termination Patterns
for Interviews in
Three Different
Product Categories

redundant or difficult-to-understand questions, questionnaire length, and changing the subject during an interview. People like to talk about some subjects and not others. For example, the subject of gum is no problem, but bringing up mouthwash results in many terminations. Exhibit 12.13 reveals that a 203-minute interview on gum results in few terminations (actual data). However, many people terminate a mouthwash interview within 3 minutes or in the 19- to 22-minute range. Terminations of a leisure travel interview don't become a serious problem until the interview reaches 20 minutes in length. Terminations usually mean that the interview must be redone and all the time spent interviewing the respondent was wasted. However, preliminary research has found that callbacks on terminated interviews can sometimes result in a completed interview.[17] (The same research on callbacks to persons who originally refused to be surveyed was not productive.)

Once managers understand the actual costs of data collection, they should be in a better position to bid on jobs with a high degree of cost accuracy. Better information should result in less overbidding and therefore more contracts.

SUMMARY

The questionnaire plays a critical role in the data-collection process. The criteria for a good questionnaire may be categorized as follows: (1) providing the necessary decision-making information, (2) fitting the respondent, and (3) meeting editing, coding, and data processing requirements.

The process of developing a questionnaire is a sequential one:

Step One. Determine survey objectives, resources, and constraints.

Step Two. Determine the data-collection method.

Step Three. Determine the question response format.

Step Four. Decide on the question wording.

Step Five. Establish questionnaire flow and layout.

Step Six. Evaluate the questionnaire.

Step Seven. Obtain approval of all relevant parties.

Step Eight. Pretest and revise.

Step Nine. Prepare final questionnaire copy.

Step Ten. Implement the survey.

The three different types of questions—open-ended, closed-ended, and scaled-response questions—each have advantages and disadvantages. In establishing the wording and positioning of questions within the questionnaire, the researcher must try to ensure that the wording is clear and does not bias the respondent and that the respondent will be able and willing to answer the questions.

During the implementation of survey research, procedures must be followed to ensure that the data are gathered correctly, efficiently, and at a reasonable cost. These include preparing supervisor's instructions, interviewer's instructions, screeners, call record sheets, and visual aids. Many research organizations are now turning to field management companies to actually conduct the interviews.

Questionnaire software and the Internet are having a major impact on survey design. Vovici Web surveyor, SSI Web, and others enable researchers to go to the Web site and create online surveys.

The role of the questionnaire in survey research costs can be a decisive one. If a research firm overestimates data-collection costs, chances are that it will lose the project to another supplier. Most data-collection costs are associated not with conducting the actual interview, but with finding a qualified respondent. A respondent's propensity to terminate an interview, which can be costly, is often based on the nature of the topic discussed.

KEY TERMS & DEFINITIONS

questionnaire Set of questions designed to generate the data necessary to accomplish the objectives of the research project; also called an *interview schedule* or *survey instrument*.

coding Process of grouping and assigning numeric codes to the various responses to a question.

survey objectives Outline of the decision-making information sought through the questionnaire.

open-ended questions Questions to which the respondent replies in her or his own words.

closed-ended questions Questions that require the respondent to choose from a list of answers.

dichotomous questions Closed-ended questions that ask the respondent to choose between two answers.

multiple-choice questions Closed-ended questions that ask the respondent to choose among several answers; also called *multichotomous questions*.

scaled-response questions Closed-ended questions in which the response choices are designed to capture the intensity of the respondent's feeling.

clarity in wording Achieved by avoiding ambiguous terminology, using reasonable, vernacular language adjusted to the target group, and asking only one question at a time.

respondent biasing Leading questions that give away the research goal or sponsor identity.

respondent's question-answering ability Factors affecting this ability include lack of required information, forgetfulness, or incomplete recall ability.

respondent's willingness to answer Embarrassing, sensitive, or threatening questions or questions divergent from respondent's self-image may cause them to refuse to answer.

screeners Questions used to identify appropriate respondents.

prompters Short encouraging statements to rebuild respondent interest.

necessary questions Pertain directly to the stated survey objectives or are screeners, interest generators, or required transitions.

approval by managers Managerial review and approval after questionnaire drafting to prevent false starts and expensive later redrafts.

pretest Trial run of a questionnaire.

supervisor's instructions Written directions to the field service firm on how to conduct the survey.

field management companies Firms that provide such support services as questionnaire formatting, screener writing, and coordination of data collection.

questionnaire costs and profitability Factors affecting costs and profits include overestimating, overbidding, incidence rate, roadblocks to completed interviews, and premature interview terminations.

QUESTIONS FOR REVIEW & CRITICAL THINKING

1. Explain the role of the questionnaire in the research process.
2. How do respondents influence the design of a questionnaire? Give some examples (e.g., questionnaires designed for engineers, baseball players, army generals, migrant farmworkers).
3. Discuss the advantages and disadvantages of open-ended questions and closed-ended questions.
4. Assume that you are developing a questionnaire about a new sandwich for McDonald's. Use this situation to outline the procedure for designing a questionnaire.
5. Give examples of poor questionnaire wording, and explain what is wrong with each question.
6. Once a questionnaire has been developed, what other factors need to be considered before the questionnaire is put into the hands of interviewers?
7. Why is pretesting a questionnaire important? Are there some situations in which pretesting is not necessary?
8. Design three open-ended and three closed-ended questions to measure consumers' attitudes toward BMW automobiles.

9. What's wrong with the following questions?
   a. How do you like the flavor of this high-quality Maxwell House coffee?
   b. What do you think of the taste and texture of this Sara Lee coffee cake?
   c. We are conducting a study for Bulova watches. What do you think of the quality of Bulova watches?

10. What do you see as the major advantages of using a field management company? What are the drawbacks?

11. Discuss the advantages and disadvantages of Web-based questionnaires.

12. Divide the class into groups of four or five. Next, match the groups evenly into supplier and client teams. The instructor will then pair a client team with a supplier team. Each client team should pick some aspect of the university such as student housing, student transportation, sports, sororities, fraternities, food on campus, or some other aspect of student life. Next, the client team should create four management objectives for their topic and construct a questionnaire to meet the management objectives. In addition, the questionnaire should include the following demographics: age, gender, major, and others determined by your instructor. Once the client team approves the questionnaire, both the client and supplier team members should complete 10 interviews each. The results should then be presented to the class. *Note:* This data can be formatted into SPSS for more detailed analysis later in the text.

(Team Activity)

WORKING THE NET

1. Visit *www.vovici.com* and take a series of free online surveys and evaluate the programs, questions, approach, assumptions, and results. *Note:* Vovici was formerly known as Perseus.

2. Log on to *www.surveymonkey.com* and *www.inquisite.com* and consider how suitable, or not, their online polling software would be for conducting market research for new customers for iPhone.

3. See what it's like to be at the receiving end of an online survey; take one or two surveys at *www.greenfield.com* and click on "Take a Survey."

REAL-LIFE RESEARCH • 12.1

Understanding Buyer Behavior

Yes, what you see below is an actual questionnaire (with very minimal modifications). It was a student-designed questionnaire (not from a business school) intended to understand shopping behavior in a midwestern city. It violates numerous principles of questionnaire design. See how many you can find as you read through the instrument.

Survey Instrument

1. How old are you? _____
2. How old is your husband/wife? _____
3. How long have you been married? _____
4. What is the highest level of education you or your husband/wife have achieved?
    a. No formal education
    b. Primary education
    c. Secondary education
    d. College
    e. Two-year college
    f. Four-year college
    g. Graduate college
5. What is the highest level of education your partner has achieved?
    a. No formal education
    b. Primary education
    c. Secondary education
    d. College
    e. Two-year college
    f. Four-year college
    g. Graduate college
6. Are you currently employed or engaged in an income-generating business?
    a. Yes
    b. No
7. (IF ANSWER IS YES, PROCEED WITH QUESTION #8. OTHERWISE, SKIP TO QUESTION #9.) How much do you make per month from your employment and/or business?
    a. _____ Enter amount in dollars.
8. Is your husband/wife currently employed or engaged in an income-generating business?
    a. Yes
    b. No
9. (IF ANSWER IS YES, PROCEED WITH QUESTION #10. OTHERWISE, SKIP TO QUESTION #11.) How much does your husband/wife make per month from his employment and/or business?
    a. _____ Enter amount in dollars.
10. Do you and your husband have any children?
    a. Yes
    b. No
11. (IF ANSWER IS YES, PROCEED WITH QUESTION #12. OTHERWISE, SKIP TO QUESTION #14.) How many children do you have?
    a. _____ Enter exact number.
12. What are the ages of your children? _____

13. Do they go to school? Where? _____

14. Between you and your husband, who is the dominant decision maker concerning general family issues such as where to live, when to go on vacations, what furniture to buy, etc.? a. I am b. My husband c. Neither or both

15. Are there any other adult family members living with you and your husband?

    a. Yes

    b. No

    c. Sometimes. Who? _____

16. Where do you shop? _____

17. Why there and not at another place? _____

    _____

    _____

18. How would you describe what they sell?

    a. Very good

    b. Quite good

    c. Not very good

    d. Poor

19. How did you learn about this store?

    a. On TV

    b. On the Internet

    c. Through friends

    d. Advertisement

    e. Newspaper

    f. I just happened to be passing by

20. I think my friends would enjoy shopping at this store.

    a. Very strongly agree

    b. Somewhat agree

    c. Agree

    d. Don't really agree

    e. Strongly disagree

21. What do you like best? _____

    _____

    _____

22. What could be improved? _____

    _____

    _____

Questions

1. Critique each question and explain how it could be improved.

2. Suggest some questions that could be used to understand shopping behavior, for both goods and services, in a midwestern city.

3. How should the revised questionnaire be reordered?

REAL-LIFE RESEARCH • 12.2

Enticing Americans to Buy New Products

In conjunction with the Better Homes and Gardens Best New Product Awards, Toronto-based BrandSpark International surveyed more than 50,000 U.S. consumers on topics such as "recessionary shopping behavior, healthy eating, future spending priorities, private labels versus premium brands, organic and natural foods, environmental accountability, and money-saving strategies.

"We can see the impact of the recent recession on attitudes towards the environment and health—with both losing ground in terms of importance," said Robert Levy, president and CEO of BrandSpark International and founder of the Best New Products Awards, in the press release. "People have made a big shift to eat at home more and as a result are spending more time and money in the grocery store. Finding new products that really deliver is more important than ever, especially with shoppers demanding greater value for money."

The BrandSpark American Shopper Study included questions about individual product appeal, intent to repurchase, consumer confidence level, and expected future spending habits, among other topics.

A few of the winning best new products were: Health and Beauty: Olay Professional Pro-X Wrinkle Protocol. Best in food and beverage category: Yoplaits Smoothie. Best in household care category: Cascade Complete All-in-1 Action Pacs. A complete list can be found at *www.bestnewproductawards.biz.*)

What are the top five purchase drivers for consumers?

In the food and beverage category

1. Taste
2. Price
3. Fresh
4. Looks appetizing
5. Smells Good

In health and beauty

1. Price
2. Proven effective
3. Simple to use
4. Trusted brand
5. Allergy-tested

In household products

1. Cleans thoroughly
2. Price
3. Effective
4. Delivers as promised
5. Works the first time

The survey also gathered opinions on two other much-discussed topics: green marketing and organic foods. "Over the past number of years, we have seen environmental accountability grow to be a major concern for American consumers," said Levy. Seventy-seven percent of Americans still feel that companies are exploiting green claims for marketing purposes. Packaging remains a top environmental concern for consumers, with 75 percent believing that manufacturers still have a long way to go to reduce the amount of packaging. Fifty-two percent of Americans feel it's important that a new product is better for the environment.

While interest in organic foods continues, consumers also place a value on foods that are free of artificial flavors or colors. Half of the consumers surveyed believe "It is important that a new product is made from all-natural ingredients" and 37 percent believe "It is more important to me that a product is natural than organic."

Levy attributed part of this to consumer skepticism. Among the consumers who didn't purchase organic products, 39 percent said they "don't trust that all products labeled as organic are actually organic" and "are confused by what the term organic actually guarantees." "It appears that further consumer education is required in the natural versus organic debate," said Levy.[18]

Questions

1. What types of survey research could have been used to gather this data? Which one would you have recommended? Why?

2. Carefully ready through the case and then list the various types of questions that may have been used to gather the data.

3. Create a questionnaire that could provide the information discussed in the case.

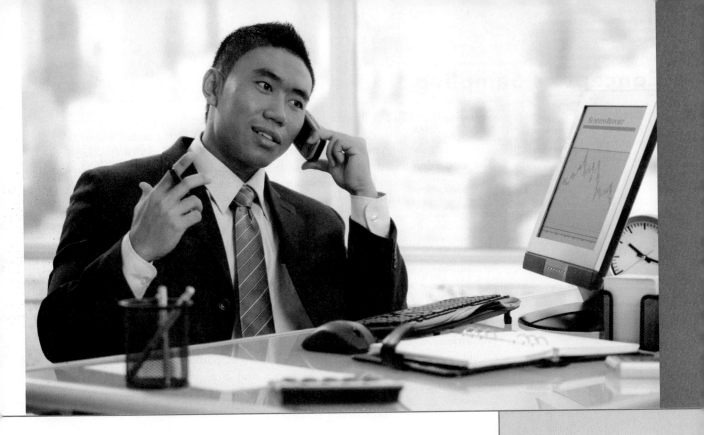

Basic Sampling Issues

CHAPTER 13

LEARNING OBJECTIVES

1. To understand the concept of sampling.

2. To learn the steps in developing a sampling plan.

3. To understand the concepts of sampling error and nonsampling error.

4. To understand the differences between probability samples and nonprobability samples.

5. To understand sampling implications of surveying over the Internet.

Concept of Sampling

→ sampling
Process of obtaining information from a subset of a larger group.

Sampling refers to the process of obtaining information from a subset (a sample) of a larger group (the universe or population). A user of marketing research then takes the results from the sample and makes estimates of the characteristics of the larger group. The motivation for sampling is to be able to make these estimates more quickly and at a lower cost than would be possible by any other means. It has been shown time and again that sampling a small percentage of a population can result in very accurate estimates. An example that you are probably familiar with is polling in connection with a presidential election. Most major polls use samples of 1,000 to 1,500 people to make predictions regarding the voting behavior of tens of millions of people and their predictions have proven to be remarkably accurate.

The key to making accurate predictions about the characteristics or behavior of a large population on the basis of a relatively small sample lies in the way in which individuals are selected for the sample. It is critical that they be selected in a scientific manner, which ensures that the sample is representative—that it is a true miniature of the population. All of the major types of people who make up the population of interest should be represented in the sample in the same proportions in which they are found in the larger population. This sounds simple, and as a concept, it is simple. However, achieving this goal in sampling from a human population is not easy.

Population

→ population
Entire group of people about whom information is needed; also called *universe* or *population of interest*.

In discussions of sampling, the terms *population* and *universe* are often used interchangeably.[1] In this textbook, we will use the term *population*. The **population**, or *population of interest*, is the entire group of people about whom the researcher needs to obtain information. One of the first steps in the sampling process is defining the population of interest. This often involves defining the target market for the product or service in question.

Consider a product concept test for a new nonprescription cold symptom-relief product, such as Contac. You might take the position that the population of interest includes everyone, because everyone suffers from colds from time to time. Although this is true, not everyone buys a nonprescription cold symptom-relief product when he or she gets a cold. In this case, the first task in the screening process would be to determine whether people have purchased or used one or more of a number of competing brands during some time period. Only those who had purchased or used one of these brands would be included in the population of interest.

Defining the population of interest is a key step in the sampling process. There are no specific rules to follow in defining the population of interest. What the researcher must do is apply logic and judgment in addressing the basic issue: Whose opinions are needed in order to satisfy the objectives of the research? Often, the definition of the population is based on the characteristics of current or target customers.

Sample versus Census

→ census
Collection of data obtained from or about every member of the population of interest.

In a **census**, data are obtained from or about every member of the population of interest. Censuses are seldom employed in marketing research, as populations of interest to marketers normally include many thousands or even millions of individuals. The cost and time required to collect data from a population of this magnitude are so great that censuses are usually out of the question. It has been demonstrated repeatedly that a relatively small but carefully chosen sample can very accurately reflect the characteristics of the population from which it is drawn. A **sample** is a subset of all the members of a

→ sample
Subset of all the members of a population of interest.

population. Information is obtained from or about a sample and used to make estimates about various characteristics of the total population. Ideally, the sample from or about which information is obtained is a representative cross section of the total population.

Note that the popular belief that a census provides more accurate results than a sample is not necessarily true. In a census of a human population, there are many impediments to actually obtaining information from every member of the population. The researcher may not be able to obtain a complete and accurate list of the entire population, or certain members of the population may refuse to provide information. Because of these barriers, the ideal census is seldom attainable, even with very small populations. You may have read or heard about these types of problems in connection with the 1990 and 2000 U.S. Census.[2]

Developing a Sampling Plan

The process of developing an operational sampling plan can be summarized by the seven steps shown in Exhibit 13.1. These steps are defining the population, choosing a data-collection method, identifying a sampling frame, selecting a sampling method, determining sample size, developing operational procedures, and executing the sampling plan.

Step One: Define the Population of Interest

The basic issue in developing a sampling plan is to specify the characteristics of those individuals or things (for example, customers, companies, stores) from whom or about whom information is needed to meet the research objectives. The population of interest is often specified in terms of geographic area, demographic characteristics, product or service usage characteristics, and/or awareness measures (see Exhibit 13.2). In surveys, the question of whether a particular individual does or does not belong to the population of interest is often dealt with by means of screening questions. Even with a list of the population and a sample from that list, researchers still need screening questions to qualify potential respondents. Exhibit 13.3 provides a sample sequence of screening questions.

Exhibit 13.1

Developing a Sampling Plan

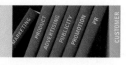

PRACTICING MARKETING RESEARCH

Driver's Licenses and Voter Registration Lists as Sampling Frames

Medical researchers at the University of North Carolina at Chapel Hill wanted to provide the most representative sampling frame for a population-based study of the spread of HIV among heterosexual African Americans living in eight rural North Carolina counties. They found that the list of driver's licenses for men and women aged 18 to 59 gave them the "best coverage" and a "more nearly complete sampling frame" for this population, one that permitted "efficient sampling," followed by voter registration lists. It far exceeded all census lists and at least four other available population lists.

Telephone directories, for example, are inadequate because they do not publish unlisted numbers, thereby eliminating those people from the study. Medicare lists only tally the elderly, disabled, or those with diagnosed diseases. Motor vehicle registries only cover people who own cars, and random-digit dialing does not tell a researcher whether or not the person called belongs to the targeted demographic subset. Census lists are not good enough either, the researchers found, because

driver's license files often exceeded in number the projected population based on the census, highlighting its inaccuracy. Furthermore, the list of registered drivers was superior to voter registration lists in identifying men in the desired population, inasmuch as fewer men were registered to vote than women.

In 1992, other medical researchers had employed driver's license lists as a sampling frame for their studies of bladder and breast cancer among adult blacks. But in 1994, a congressional act restricted the release of driver's license lists to applications for statistical analysis but not direct contact of license holders. Unfortunately for market researchers, subsequent congressional, judicial review, and legislation at the state level in selected states have kept this sampling frame methodology in a state of uncertainty and flux.[3]

Questions

1. What kinds of usable data could a statistical analysis of driver's license lists generate and how would you go about the study?

2. Identify two other market research categories in which driver's license lists would excel in providing accurate data.

In addition to defining who will be included in the population of interest, researchers should also define the characteristics of individuals who should be excluded. For example, most commercial marketing research surveys exclude some individuals for so-called security reasons. Very frequently, one of the first questions on a survey asks whether the respondent or anyone in the respondent's immediate family works in marketing research, advertising, or the product or service area at issue in the survey (see, for example, question 5 in Exhibit 13.3). If the individual answers "Yes" to this question, the interview is terminated. This type of question is called a *security question* because those who work in the industries in question are viewed as security risks. They may be competitors or work for competitors, and managers do not want to give them any indication of what their company may be planning to do.

There may be other reasons to exclude individuals. For example, the Dr Pepper Company might wish to do a survey among individuals who drink five or more cans, bottles, or glasses of soft drink in a typical week but do not drink Dr Pepper, because the

EXHIBIT 13.2	Some Bases for Defining the Population of Interest
Geographic Area	What geographic area is to be sampled? This is usually a question of the client's scope of operation. The area could be a city, a county, a metropolitan area, a state, a group of states, the entire United States, or a number of countries.
Demographics	Given the objectives of the research and the target market for the product, whose opinions, reactions, and so on are relevant? For example, does the sampling plan require information from women over 18, women 18–34, or women 18–34 with household incomes over $35,000 per year who work and who have preschool children?
Usage	In addition to geographic area and/or demographics, the population of interest frequently is defined in terms of some product or service use requirement. This is usually stated in terms of use versus nonuse or use of some quantity of the product or service over a specified period of time. The following examples of use screening questions illustrate the point: ■ Do you drink five or more cans, bottles, or glasses of diet soft drinks in a typical week? ■ Have you traveled to Europe for vacation or business purposes in the past two years? ■ Have you or has anyone in your immediate family been in a hospital for an overnight or extended stay in the past two years?
Awareness	The researcher may be interested in surveying those individuals who are aware of the company's advertising, to explore what the advertising communicated about the characteristics of the product or service.

Hello. I'm _____ with _____ Research. We're conducting a survey about products used in the home. May I ask you a few questions?

1. Have you been interviewed about any products or advertising in the past 3 months?

Yes	(TERMINATE AND TALLY)
No	(CONTINUE)

2. Which of the following hair care products, if any, have you used in the past month? (HAND PRODUCT CARD TO RESPONDENT; CIRCLE ALL MENTIONS)

1 Regular shampoo

2 Dandruff shampoo

3 Creme rinse/instant conditioner

4 "Intensive" conditioner

(INSTRUCTIONS: IF "4" IS CIRCLED—SKIP TO Q. 4 AND CONTINUE FOR "INTENSIVE" QUOTA; IF "3" IS CIRCLED BUT NOT "4"—ASK Q. 3 AND CONTINUE FOR "INSTANT" QUOTA)

3. You said that you have used a creme rinse/instant conditioner in the past month. Have you used either a creme rinse or an instant conditioner in the past week?

Yes (used in the past week)	(CONTINUE FOR "INSTANT" QUOTA)
No (not used in past week)	(TERMINATE AND TALLY)

4. Into which of the following groups does your age fall? (READ LIST, CIRCLE AGE)

X	Under 18	(CHECK AGE QUOTAS)
1	18–24	
2	25–34	
3	35–44	
X	45 or over	

5. Previous surveys have shown that people who work in certain jobs may have different reactions to certain products. Now, do you or does any member of your immediate family work for an advertising agency, a marketing research firm, a public relations firm, or a company that manufactures or sells personal care products?

Yes	(TERMINATE AND TALLY)
No	(CONTINUE)

(IF RESPONDENT QUALIFIES, INVITE HIM OR HER TO PARTICIPATE AND COMPLETE NAME GRID BELOW)

Exhibit 13.3

Example of Screening Question Sequence to Determine Population Membership

company is interested in developing a better understanding of heavy soft-drink users who do not drink its product. Therefore, researchers would exclude those who drank one or more cans, bottles, or glasses of Dr Pepper in the past week.

Step Two: Choose a Data-Collection Method

The selection of a data-collection method has implications for the sampling process.

- Mail surveys suffer from biases associated with low response rates (which are discussed in greater detail later in this chapter).

- Telephone surveys have a less significant problem with nonresponse, but suffer from call screening technologies used by potential respondents and the fact that some people have mobile phones only.

- Internet surveys have problems with professional respondents (discussed in Chapter 7) and the fact that the panel or e-mail lists used often do not provide appropriate representation of the population of interest.

Step Three: Identify a Sampling Frame

> **sampling frame**
> List of population elements from which units to be sampled can be selected or a specified procedure for generating such a list.

The third step in the process is to identify the **sampling frame**, which is a list of the members or elements of the population from which units to be sampled are to be selected. Identifying the sampling frame may simply mean specifying a procedure for generating such a list. In the ideal situation, the list of population members is complete and accurate. Unfortunately, there usually is no such list. For example, the population for a study may be defined as those individuals who have spent 2 or more hours on the Internet in the past week; there can be no complete listing of these individuals. In such instances, the sampling frame specifies a procedure that will produce a representative sample with the desired characteristics. Thus, there seldom is a perfect correspondence between the sampling frame and the population of interest.

For example, a telephone book might be used as the sample frame for a telephone survey sample in which the population of interest was all households in a particular city. However, the telephone book does not include households that do not have telephones and those with unlisted numbers. It is well established that those with listed telephone numbers are significantly different from those with unlisted numbers in regard to a number of important characteristics. Subscribers who voluntarily unlist their phone numbers are more likely to be renters, live in the central city, have recently moved, have larger families, have younger children, and have lower incomes than their counterparts with listed numbers.[4] There are also significant differences between the two groups in terms of purchase, ownership, and use of certain products. Sample frame issues are discussed in the Practicing Marketing Research feature on page 387.

Unlisted numbers are more prevalent in the western United States, in metropolitan areas, among nonwhites, and among those in the 18 to 34 age group. These findings have been confirmed in a number of studies.[5] The implications are clear: if representative samples are to be obtained in telephone surveys, researchers should use procedures that will produce samples including appropriate proportions of households with unlisted numbers. Address-based sampling discussed in the Practicing Marketing Research feature on page 385 offers a new approach to the problems of getting a proper sample frame.

> **random-digit dialing**
> Method of generating lists of telephone numbers at random.

One possibility is **random-digit dialing**, which generates lists of telephone numbers at random. This procedure can become fairly complex. Fortunately, companies such as Survey Sampling offer random-digit samples at a very attractive price. Details on the way such companies draw their samples can be found at *www.surveysampling.com/products_*

samples.php. Developing an appropriate sampling frame is often one of the most challenging problems facing the researcher.[7]

Step Four: Select a Sampling Method

The fourth step in developing a sampling plan is selection of a sampling method, which will depend on the objectives of the study, the financial resources available, time limitations, and the nature of the problem under investigation. The major alternative sampling methods can be grouped under two headings: probability sampling methods and non-probability sampling methods.

PRACTICING MARKETING RESEARCH

How to Achieve Near Full Coverage for Your Sample Using Address-Based Sampling[6]

Address-Based Sampling (ABS) offers potential benefits in comparison to a strictly telephone-based method of contact. Landlines offer access to only about 75 percent of U.S. households, and contacting people via wireless devices can be a complicated process. Market research firm Survey Sampling International (SSI), however, has found that using an ABS approach can almost completely fill that access gap.

SSI combines a telephone database with a mailing list—entries with a telephone number are contacted normally, while entries possessing only the address are sent a survey in the mail. Using the U.S. Postal Service's (USPS) Delivery Sequence File (DSF) combined with other commercial databases offering more complete information on individual households, SSI has been able to achieve coverage of 95 percent of postal households and 85 percent of those addresses matched to a name. Between 55 and 65 percent are matched to a telephone number, and demographic data can be accessed as well when creating a sample.

The trend toward mobile is making telephone surveys more difficult. Twenty percent of U.S. households have no landline. This is especially true of people in their 20s. ABS, however, still offers access to households that use a cell phone as the primary or only mode of communication, but it also provides greater geodemographic information and selection options than would an approach based strictly on a wireless database.

While ABS does face certain challenges—mail surveys are generally more expensive and multimode designs can lead to variable response rates—there are methods that can be used to compensate. Selection criteria can be modified to maximize the delivery efficiency of mailers. Appended telephone numbers can be screened as well to improve accuracy and response rates. On the whole, ABS helps research achieve a more complete sample with greater response rates and also allows respondents an option of exercising their preferred response channel.

Questions

1. Can you think of any demographic segments that might still be difficult to reach via ABS?

2. What are some ways researchers could use to mitigate the increased costs of mail surveys?

➡ **probability samples**
Samples in which every element of the population has a known, nonzero likelihood of selection.

➡ **nonprobability samples**
Samples in which specific elements from the population have been selected in a nonrandom manner.

The population for a study must be defined. For example, a population for a study may be defined as those individuals who have spent 2 or more hours on the Internet in the past week.

➡ **sample size**
The identified and selected population subset for the survey, chosen because it represents the entire group.

Probability samples are selected in such a way that every element of the population has a known, nonzero likelihood of selection.[8] Simple random sampling is the best known and most widely used probability sampling method. With probability sampling, the researcher must closely adhere to precise selection procedures that avoid arbitrary or biased selection of sample elements. When these procedures are followed strictly, the laws of probability hold, allowing calculation of the extent to which a sample value can be expected to differ from a population value. This difference is referred to as *sampling error*. The debate continues regarding whether online panels produce probability samples. These issues are discussed in the feature on page 387.

Nonprobability samples are those in which specific elements from the population have been selected in a nonrandom manner. *Nonrandomness* results when population elements are selected on the basis of convenience—because they are easy or inexpensive to reach. *Purposeful nonrandomness* occurs when a sampling plan systematically excludes or overrepresents certain subsets of the population. For example, if a sample designed to solicit the opinions of all women over the age of 18 were based on a telephone survey conducted during the day on weekdays, it would systematically exclude working women.

Probability samples offer several advantages over nonprobability samples, including the following:

■ The researcher can be sure of obtaining information from a representative cross section of the population of interest.

■ Sampling error can be computed.

■ The survey results can be projected to the total population. For example, if 5 percent of the individuals in a probability sample give a particular response, the researcher can project this percentage, plus or minus the sampling error, to the total population.

On the other hand, probability samples have a number of disadvantages, the most important of which is that they are usually more expensive than nonprobability samples of the same size. The rules for selection increase interviewing costs and professional time spent in designing and executing the sample design.[9]

Step Five: Determine Sample Size

Once a sampling method has been chosen, the next step is to determine the appropriate **sample size**. (The issue of sample size determination is covered in detail in Chapter 14.) In the case of nonprobability samples, researchers tend to rely on such factors as available budget, rules of thumb, and number of subgroups to be analyzed in their determination of sample size. However, with probability samples, researchers use formulas to calculate the sample size required, given target levels of *acceptable error* (the difference between sample result and population value) and *levels of confidence* (the likelihood that the confidence interval—sample result plus or minus the acceptable error—will take in the true population value). As noted earlier, the ability to make statistical inferences about population values based on sample results is the major advantage of probability samples.

Step Six: Develop Operational Procedures for Selecting Sample Elements

The operational procedures to be used in selecting sample elements in the data-collection phase of a project should be developed and specified, whether a probability or a nonprobability sample is being used.[11] However, the procedures are much more critical to the successful execution of a probability sample, in which case they should be detailed,

PRACTICING
MARKETING RESEARCH

Can a Single Online Respondent Pool Offer a Truly Representative Sample?[10]

Online research programs can often benefit by building samples from multiple respondent pools. Achieving a truly representative sample is a difficult process for many reasons. When drawing from a single source, even if researchers were to use various verification methods, demographic quotas, and other strategies to create a presumably representative sample, the selection methods themselves create qualitative differences—or allow them to develop over time. The same is true of the parameters under which the online community or respondent pool was formed (subject matter mix, activities, interaction opportunities, etc.). Each online community content site is unique, and members and visitors choose to participate because of the individual experience their preferred site provides. As such, the differences between each site start to solidify as site members share more and more similar experiences and differences within the site's community decrease. (Think, birds of a feather flock together.)

As such, researchers cannot safely assume that any given online respondent pool offers an accurate probability sample of the adult U.S. or Internet population. Consequently, both intrinsic (personality traits, values, locus of control, etc.) and extrinsic (panel tenure, survey participation rates, etc.) differences will contribute variations to response-measure distribution across respondent pools. To control distribution of intrinsic characteristics in the sample while randomizing extrinsic characteristics as much as possible, researchers may need to use random selection from multiple respondent pools.

The GfK Research Center for Excellence in New York performed a study to see how the distribution of intrinsic and extrinsic individual differences varied between respondent pools. Respondents were drawn from five different online resource pools, each using a different method to obtain survey respondents. A latent class regression method separated the respondents into five underlying consumer classes according to their Internet-usage driver profiles.

Researchers then tested which of the intrinsic characteristics tended to appear within the different classes. No variable appeared in more than three classes. Furthermore, the concentration of each class varied considerably across the five respondent pools from which samples were drawn.

Within the classes themselves, variations appeared in their demographic distributions. One of the five experienced a significant skew based on gender, and two other classes exhibited variable age concentrations, with one skewed toward younger respondents and the other toward older ones.

Overall, GfK's study revealed numerous variations across different respondent resource pools. As their research continues, current findings suggest that researchers must be aware of these trends, especially in choosing their member acquisition and retention strategies and in determining which and how many respondent pools to draw from.

Questions

1. If one respondent pool is not sufficient, how many do you think you would have to draw from to get a truly representative sample? Why do you think that?

2. When creating a sample, how would you propose accounting for the types of extrinsic characteristics mentioned?

Exhibit 13.4

**Classification of
Sampling Methods**

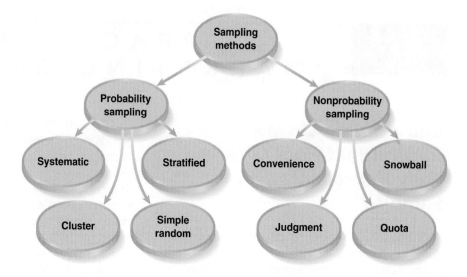

clear, and unambiguous and should eliminate any interviewer discretion regarding the selection of specific sample elements. Failure to develop a proper operational plan for selecting sample elements can jeopardize the entire sampling process. Exhibit 13.5 provides an example of an operational sampling plan.

Step Seven: Execute the Operational Sampling Plan

The final step in the sampling process is execution of the operational sampling plan. This step requires adequate checking to ensure that specified procedures are followed.

Sampling and Nonsampling Errors

> **population parameter**
> A value that accurately portrays or typifies a factor of a complete population, such as average age or income.

Consider a situation in which the goal is to determine the average gross income of the members of a particular population.[12] If the researcher could obtain accurate information about all members of the population, he or she could simply compute the population parameter average gross income. A **population parameter** is a value that defines a true characteristic of a total population. Assume that μ (the population parameter, average gross income) is $42,300. As already noted, it is almost always impossible to measure an entire population (take a census). Instead, the researcher selects a sample and makes inferences about population parameters from sample results. In this case, the researcher might take a sample of 400 from a population of 250,000. An estimate of the average age of the members of the population $(\bar{X})$ would be calculated from the sample values. Assume that the average gross income of the sample members is $41,100. A second random sample of 400 might be drawn from the same population, and the average again computed. In the second case, the average might be $43,400. Additional samples might be chosen, and a mean calculated for each sample. The researcher would find that the means computed for the various samples would be fairly close but not identical to the true population value in most cases.

Exhibit 13.5

Example of Operational Sampling Plan

In the instructions that follow, reference is made to follow your route around a block. In cities, this will be a city block. In rural areas, a block is a segment of land surrounded by roads.

1. If you come to a dead end along your route, proceed down the opposite side of the street, road, or alley, traveling in the other direction. Continue making right turns, where possible, calling at every third occupied dwelling.

2. If you go all the way around a block and return to the starting address without completing four interviews in listed telephone homes, attempt an interview at the starting address. (This should seldom be necessary.)

3. If you work an entire block and do not complete the required interviews, proceed to the dwelling on the opposite side of the street (or rural route) that is *nearest* the starting address. Treat it as the next address on your Area Location Sheet and interview that house only if the address appears next to an "X" on your sheet. If it does not, continue your interviewing to the left of that address. Always follow the right turn rule.

4. If there are no dwellings on the street or road opposite the starting address for an area, circle the block opposite the starting address, following the right turn rule. (This means that you will circle the block following a clockwise direction.) Attempt interviews at every third dwelling along this route.

5. If, after circling the adjacent block opposite the starting address, you do not complete the necessary interviews, take the next block found, *following a clockwise direction*.

6. If the third block does not yield the dwellings necessary to complete your assignment, proceed to as many blocks as necessary to find the required dwellings; follow a clockwise path around the primary block.

Source: From "Belden Associates Interviewer Guide," reprinted by permission. The complete guide is over 30 pages long and contains maps and other aids for the interviewer.

The accuracy of sample results is affected by two general types of error: sampling error and nonsampling (measurement) error. The following formula represents the effects of these two types of error on estimating a population mean:

$$\overline{X} = \mu \pm \epsilon_s \pm \epsilon_{ns}$$

where
$\overline{X}$ = Sample mean
μ = true population mean
ϵ_s = sampling error
ϵ_{ns} = nonsampling, or measurement, error

Sampling error results when the sample selected is not perfectly representative of the population. There are two types of sampling error: administrative and random. *Administrative error* relates to the problems in the execution of the sample—that is, flaws in the design or execution of the sample that cause it to be nonrepresentative of the population. These types of error can be avoided or minimized by careful attention to the design and execution of the sample. *Random sampling error* is due to chance and cannot be avoided. This type of error can be reduced, but never totally eliminated, by increasing the sample size. **Nonsampling**, or measurement **error**, includes all factors other than sampling error that may cause inaccuracy and bias in the survey results.

sampling error
Error that occurs because the sample selected is not perfectly representative of the population.

nonsampling error
All errors other than sampling error; also called *measurement error*.

Probability Sampling Methods

As discussed earlier, every element of the population has a known and equal likelihood of being selected for a probability sample. There are four types of probability sampling methods: simple random sampling, systematic sampling, stratified sampling, and cluster sampling.

FROM THE FRONT LINE

Sampling and Data Collection with Internet Panels

Michelle Dodd, Director of Project Management, DSS Research

Going once, going twice....sold to the lowest bidder!

Is it really that simple to select an Internet panel partner? The short answer is no. Selecting which Internet panel(s) to work with on a given project has many factors that must be taken into consideration.

First you start with getting bids. As usual, you need the bid "ASAP" since it is then incorporated into your proposal. You need to know the feasibility and cost since they ultimately impact your recommendation on data collection methodology. Some Internet panels are very responsive and quick to turn around their bids while others seem to need 2-3 days. The basic facts you must provide to the panels are the geography of interest, the estimated survey length and the qualifying incidence they can expect. If you must collect the data in a very short time frame (less than one week), that will be factored in as well.

The next item to consider is your previous experience with each panel. Do their bids tend to be pretty accurate? Are they consistently able to meet (or even exceed) their estimated feasibility? Do they over promise, leaving you in a lurch to finish collecting data in another way? Do you tend to find more speeders, duplicate respondents or fraudulent respondents in their population? Does the project manager respond to your questions in a timely manner and keep you updated as often as you like during the project?

So now you have bids from several different panels. How do you select one? One of the first criteria to consider is whether or not any one panel can fulfill all of your quota requirements on its own. It is preferable to field a study using just one panel than having to use two or more panels. This is primarily due to managing quotas and the reduced possibility of having duplicate respondents in your sample. If you are dealing with a limited geography and/or low incidence, it is likely that you will need to use multiple panels in order to meet your target quotas.

If you are fortunate enough to have more than one panel that can meet your quota requirements on its own, then cost and customer service come to the forefront of consideration. If you feel confident that each panel can successfully fill your quota requirements, you will likely select the one with the lower cost per interview (CPI). But customer service should not be overlooked. Most panels have good project managers that will work with you to get your study tested, launched and completed within the needed time frame. But if you are sweating bullets the whole time your project is in the field, wondering if you will meet quotas and meet your timeline, then a lower cost may not be worth it in the long run.

At the completion of the data collection phase, you may need to get data from a third party (such as Acxiom or Knowledge Based Marketing) appended to supplement or enhance your analysis. Not all Internet panels can or will help with this task. Some Internet panels do not capture name and physical address information on their panelists. Others may have this information but are not willing to share it. So if this is a possible requirement on your project, it is important to flesh it out up front to make sure that your panel partner(s) can and will provide this information for panelists who complete a survey on your project.

Simple Random Sampling

Simple random sampling is the purest form of probability sampling. For a simple random sample, the known and equal probability is computed as follows:

$$\text{Probability of selection} = \frac{\text{Sample size}}{\text{Population size}}$$

For example, if the population size is 10,000 and the sample size is 400, the probability of selection is 4 percent:

$$.04 = \frac{400}{10,000}$$

If a sampling frame (listing of all the elements of the population) is available, the researcher can select a **simple random sample** as follows:

1. Assign a number to each element of the population. A population of 10,000 elements would be numbered from 1 to 10,000.

2. Using a table of random numbers (such as Exhibit 1 in Appendix Three, "Statistical Tables"), begin at some arbitrary point and move up, down, or across until 400 (sample size) five-digit numbers between 1 and 10,000 have been chosen. The numbers selected from the table identify specific population elements to be included in the sample.

Simple random sampling is appealing because it seems easy and meets all the necessary requirements of a probability sample. It guarantees that every member of the population has a known and equal chance of being selected for the sample. Simple random sampling begins with a current and complete listing of the population. Such listings, however, are extremely difficult, if not impossible, to obtain. Simple random samples can be obtained in telephone surveys through the use of random digit dialing. They can also be generated from computer files such as customer lists; software programs are available or can be readily written to select random samples that meet all necessary requirements.

simple random sample Probability sample selected by assigning a number to every element of the population and then using a table of random numbers to select specific elements for inclusion in the sample.

Systematic Sampling

Because of its simplicity, **systematic sampling** is often used as a substitute for simple random sampling. It produces samples that are almost identical to those generated via simple random sampling.

To obtain a systematic sample, the researcher first numbers the entire population, as in simple random sampling. Then the researcher determines a *skip interval* and selects names based on this interval. The skip interval can be computed very simply through use of the following formula:

$$\text{Skip interval} = \frac{\text{Population size}}{\text{Sample size}}$$

systematic sampling Probability sampling in which the entire population is numbered and elements are selected using a skip interval.

For example, if you were using a local telephone directory and had computed a skip interval of 100, every 100th name would be selected for the sample. The use of this formula would ensure that the entire list was covered.

A random starting point should be used in systematic sampling. For example, if you were using a telephone directory, you would need to draw a random number to determine the page on which to start—say, page 53. You would draw another random number to determine the column to use on that page—for example, the third column. You would draw a final random number to determine the actual starting element in that column—say, the 17th name. From that beginning point, you would employ the skip interval until the desired sample size had been reached.

The main advantage of systematic sampling over simple random sampling is economy. Systematic sampling is often simpler, less time-consuming, and less expensive to use than simple random sampling. The greatest danger lies in the possibility that hidden patterns within the population list may inadvertently be pulled into the sample. However, this danger is remote when alphabetical listings are used.

Stratified Sampling

stratified sample
Probability sample that is forced to be more representative through simple random sampling of mutually exclusive and exhaustive subsets.

Stratified samples are probability samples that are distinguished by the following procedural steps:

1. The original, or parent, population is divided into two or more mutually exclusive and exhaustive subsets (for example, male and female).

2. Simple random samples of elements from the two or more subsets are chosen independently of each other.

Although the requirements for a stratified sample do not specify the basis on which the original or parent population should be separated into subsets, common sense dictates that the population be divided on the basis of factors related to the characteristic of interest in the population. For example, if you are conducting a political poll to predict the outcome of an election and can show that there is a significant difference in the way men and women are likely to vote, then gender is an appropriate basis for stratification. If you do not do stratified sampling in this manner, then you do not get the benefits of stratification, and you have expended additional time, effort, and resources for no benefit. With gender as the basis for stratification, one stratum, then, would be made up of men and one of women. These strata are mutually exclusive and exhaustive in that every population element can be assigned to one and only one (male or female) and no population elements are unassignable. The second stage in the selection of a stratified sample involves drawing simple random samples independently from each stratum.

Researchers prefer stratified samples to simple random samples because of their potential for greater statistical efficiency.[13] That is, if two samples are drawn from the same population—one a properly stratified sample and the other a simple random sample—the stratified sample will have a smaller sampling error. Also, reduction of a sampling error to a certain target level can be achieved with a smaller stratified sample. Stratified samples are statistically more efficient because one source of variation has been eliminated.

If stratified samples are statistically more efficient, why are they not used all the time? There are two reasons. First, the information necessary to properly stratify the sample frequently may not be available. For example, little may be known about the demographic characteristics of consumers of a particular product. To properly stratify the sample and to get the benefits of stratification, the researcher must choose bases for stratification that yield significant differences between the strata in regard to the measurement of interest. When such differences are not identifiable, the sample cannot be properly stratified. Second, even if the necessary information is available, the potential value of the information may not warrant the time and costs associated with stratification.

In the case of a simple random sample, the researcher depends entirely on the laws of probability to generate a representative sample of the population. With stratified sampling, the researcher, to some degree, forces the sample to be representative by making sure that important dimensions of the population are represented in the sample in their true population proportions. For example, the researcher may know that although men and women are equally likely to be users of a particular product, women are much more likely to be heavy users. In a study designed to analyze consumption patterns of the product, failure to properly represent women in the sample would result in a biased view of consumption patterns. Assume that women make up 60 percent of the population of interest and men account for 40 percent. Because of sampling fluctuations, a properly executed simple random sampling procedure might produce a sample made up of 55 percent women and 45 percent men. This is the same kind of error you would obtain if you flipped a coin 10 times. The ideal result of 10 coin tosses would be five heads and five tails, but more than half the time you would get a different result. In similar fashion, a properly drawn and executed simple random sample from a population made up of 60 percent women and 40 percent men is not likely to consist of exactly 60 percent women and 40 percent men. However, the researcher can force a stratified sample to have 60 percent women and 40 percent men.

Three steps are involved in implementing a properly stratified sample:

1. *Identify salient (important) demographic or classification factors*—Factors that are correlated with the behavior of interest. For example, there may be reason to believe that men and women have different average consumption rates of a particular product. To use gender as a basis for meaningful stratification, the researcher must be able to show with actual data that there are significant differences in the consumption levels of men and women. In this manner, various salient factors are identified. Research indicates that, as a general rule, after the six most important factors have been identified, the identification of additional salient factors adds little in the way of increased sampling efficiency.[14]

2. *Determine what proportions of the population fall into the various subgroups under each stratum* (for example, if gender has been determined to be a salient factor, determine what proportion of the population is male and what proportion is female). Using these proportions, the researcher can determine how many respondents are required from each subgroup. However, before a final determination is made, a decision must be made as to whether to use proportional allocation or disproportional, or optimal, allocation.

Under **proportional allocation**, the number of elements selected from a stratum is directly proportional to the size of the stratum in relation to the size of the population. With proportional allocation, the proportion of elements to be taken from each stratum is given by the formula n/N, where n = the size of the stratum and N = the size of the population.

Disproportional, or **optimal**, **allocation** produces the most efficient samples and provides the most precise or reliable estimates for a given sample size. This approach requires a double weighting scheme. Under this scheme, the number of sample elements to be taken from a given stratum is proportional to the relative size of the stratum and the standard deviation of the distribution of the characteristic under consideration for all elements in the stratum. This scheme is used for two reasons. First, the size of a stratum is important because those strata with greater numbers of elements are more important in determining the population mean. Therefore, such strata should have more weight in

→ **proportional allocation**
Sampling in which the number of elements selected from a stratum is directly proportional to the size of the stratum relative to the size of the population.

→ **disproportional, or optimal, allocation**
Sampling in which the number of elements taken from a given stratum is proportional to the relative size of the stratum and the standard deviation of the characteristic under consideration.

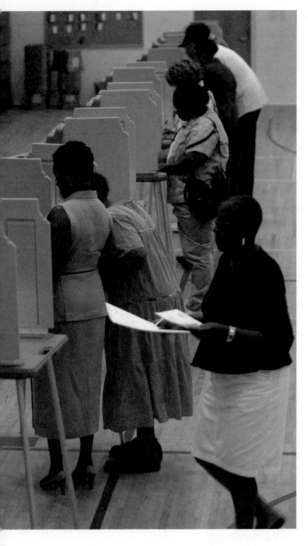

deriving estimates of population parameters. Second, it makes sense that relatively more elements should be drawn from those strata having larger standard deviations (more variation) and relatively fewer elements should be drawn from those strata having smaller standard deviations. Allocating relatively more of the sample to those strata where the potential for sampling error is greatest (largest standard deviation) is cost-effective and improves the overall accuracy of the estimates. There is no difference between proportional allocation and disproportional allocation if the distributions of the characteristic under consideration have the same standard deviation from stratum to stratum.[15]

3. *Select separate simple random samples from each stratum.* This process is implemented somewhat differently than traditional simple random sampling. Assume that the stratified sampling plan requires that 240 women and 160 men be interviewed. The researcher will sample from the total population and keep track of the number of men and women interviewed. At some point in the process, when 240 women and 127 men have been interviewed, the researcher will interview only men until the target of 160 men is reached. In this manner, the process generates a sample in which the proportion of men and women conforms to the allocation scheme derived in step 2.

Stratified samples are not used as often as one might expect in marketing research. The reason is that the information necessary to properly stratify the sample is usually not available in advance. Stratification cannot be based on guesses or hunches but must be based on hard data regarding the characteristics of the population and the relationship between these characteristics and the behavior under investigation. Stratified samples are frequently used in political polling and media audience research. In those areas, the researcher is more likely to have the information necessary to implement the stratification process.

A stratified sample may be appropriate in certain cases. For example, if a political poll is being conducted to predict who will win an election, a difference in the way men and women are likely to vote would make gender an appropriate basis for stratification.

cluster sample
Probability sample in which the sampling units are selected from a number of small geographic areas to reduce data collection costs.

Cluster Sampling

The types of samples discussed so far have all been single unit samples, in which each sampling unit is selected separately. In the case of **cluster samples**, the sampling units are selected in groups.[16] There are two basic steps in cluster sampling:

1. The population of interest is divided into mutually exclusive and exhaustive subsets.
2. A random sample of the subsets is selected.

If the sample consists of all the elements in the selected subsets, it is called a *one-stage cluster sample.* However, if the sample of elements is chosen in some probabilistic manner from the selected subsets, the sample is a *two-stage cluster sample.*

Both stratified and cluster sampling involve dividing the population into mutually exclusive and exhaustive subgroups. However, in stratified samples the researcher selects a sample of elements from each subgroup, while in cluster samples, the researcher selects a sample of subgroups and then collects data either from all the elements in the subgroup (one-stage cluster sample) or from a sample of the elements (two-stage cluster sample).

All the probability sampling methods discussed to this point require sampling frames that list or provide some organized breakdown of all the elements in the target population. Under cluster sampling, the researcher develops sampling frames that specify groups or clusters of elements of the population without actually listing individual elements. Sampling is then executed by taking a sample of the clusters in the frame and generating lists or other breakdowns for only those clusters that have been selected for the sample. Finally, a sample is chosen from the elements of the selected clusters.

The most popular type of cluster sample is the area sample in which the clusters are units of geography (for example, city blocks). Cluster sampling is considered to be a probability sampling technique because of the random selection of clusters and the random selection of elements within the selected clusters.

Cluster sampling assumes that the elements in a cluster are as heterogeneous as those in the total population. If the characteristics of the elements in a cluster are very similar, then that assumption is violated and the researcher has a problem. In the city-block sampling just described, there may be little heterogeneity within clusters because the residents of a cluster are very similar to each other and different from those of other clusters. Typically, this potential problem is dealt with in the sample design by selecting a large number of clusters and sampling a relatively small number of elements from each cluster.

Another possibility is **multistage area sampling**, or **multistage area probability sampling**, which involves three or more steps. Samples of this type are used for national surveys or surveys that cover large regional areas. Here, the researcher randomly selects geographic areas in progressively smaller units.

From the standpoint of statistical efficiency, cluster samples are generally less efficient than other types of probability samples. In other words, a cluster sample of a certain size will have a larger sampling error than a simple random sample or a stratified sample of the same size. To see the greater cost efficiency and lower statistical efficiency of a cluster sample, consider the following example. A researcher needs to select

> **multistage area sampling** Geographic areas selected for national or regional surveys in progressively smaller population units, such as counties, then residential blocks, then homes.

The most popular type of cluster sample is the area sample, in which the clusters are units of geography (for example, city blocks). A researcher, conducting a door-to-door survey in a particular metropolitan area, might randomly choose a sample of city blocks from the metropolitan area, select a sample of clusters, and then interview a sample of consumers from each cluster. All interviews would be conducted in the clusters selected, dramatically reducing interviewers' travel time and expenses. Cluster sampling is considered to be a probability sampling technique because of the random selection of clusters and the random selection of elements within the selected clusters.

a sample of 200 households in a particular city for in-home interviews. If she selects these 200 households via simple random sampling, they will be scattered across the city. Cluster sampling might be implemented in this situation by selecting 20 residential blocks in the city and randomly choosing 10 households on each block to interview. It is easy to see that interviewing costs will be dramatically reduced under the cluster sampling approach. Interviewers do not have to spend as much time traveling, and their mileage is dramatically reduced. In regard to sampling error, however, you can see that simple random sampling has the advantage. Interviewing 200 households scattered across the city increases the chance of getting a representative cross section of respondents. If all interviewing is conducted in 20 randomly selected blocks within the city, certain ethnic, social, or economic groups might be missed or over- or underrepresented.

As noted previously, cluster samples are, in nearly all cases, statistically less efficient than simple random samples. It is possible to view a simple random sample as a special type of cluster sample, in which the number of clusters is equal to the total sample size, with one sample element selected per cluster. At this point, the statistical efficiency of the cluster sample and that of the simple random sample are equal. From this point on, as the researcher decreases the number of clusters and increases the number of sample elements per cluster, the statistical efficiency of the cluster sample declines. At the other extreme, the researcher might choose a single cluster and select all the sample elements from that cluster. For example, he or she might select one relatively small geographic area in the city where you live and interview 200 people from that area. How comfortable would you be that a sample selected in this manner would be representative of the entire metropolitan area where you live?

Nonprobability Sampling Methods

In a general sense, any sample that does not meet the requirements of a probability sample is, by definition, a nonprobability sample. We have already noted that a major disadvantage of nonprobability samples is the inability to calculate sampling error for them. This suggests the even greater difficulty of evaluating the overall quality of nonprobability samples. How far do they deviate from the standard required of probability samples? The user of data from a nonprobability sample must make this assessment, which should be based on a careful evaluation of the methodology used to generate the nonprobability sample. Is it likely that the methodology employed will generate a cross section of individuals from the target population? Or is the sample hopelessly biased in some particular direction? These are the questions that must be answered. Four types of nonprobability samples are frequently used: convenience, judgment, quota, and snowball samples.

Convenience Samples

convenience samples
Nonprobability samples based on using people who are easily accessible.

Convenience samples are primarily used, as their name implies, for reasons of convenience. Companies such as Frito-Lay often use their own employees for preliminary tests of new product formulations developed by their R&D departments. At first, this may seem to be a highly biased approach. However, these companies are not asking employees to evaluate existing products or to compare their products with a competitor's products. They are asking employees only to provide gross sensory evaluations of new product formulations (for example, saltiness, crispness, greasiness). In such situations, convenience sampling may represent an efficient and effective means of obtaining the required information. This is particularly true in an exploratory situation, where there is a pressing need to get an inexpensive approximation of true value.

Some believe that the use of convenience sampling is growing at a faster rate than the growth in the use of probability sampling.[17] The reason, as suggested is the growing availability of databases of consumers in low-incidence and hard-to-find categories. For example, suppose a company has developed a new athlete's foot remedy and needs to conduct a survey among those who suffer from the malady. Because these individuals make up only 4 percent of the population, researchers conducting a telephone survey would have to talk with 25 people to find 1 individual who suffered from the problem. Purchasing a list of individuals known to suffer from the problem can dramatically reduce the cost of the survey and the time necessary to complete it. Although such a list might be made up of individuals who used coupons when purchasing the product or sent in for manufacturers' rebates, companies are increasingly willing to make the trade-off of lower cost and faster turnaround for a lower-quality sample.

Judgment Samples

The term **judgment sample** is applied to any sample in which the selection criteria are based on the researcher's judgment about what constitutes a representative sample. Most test markets and many product tests conducted in shopping malls are essentially judgment sampling. In the case of test markets, one or a few markets are selected based on the judgment that they are representative of the population as a whole. Malls are selected for product taste tests based on the researcher's judgment that the particular malls attract a reasonable cross section of consumers who fall into the target group for the product being tested.

> **judgment samples**
> Nonprobability samples in which the selection criteria are based on the researcher's judgment about representativeness of the population under study.

Quota Samples

Quota samples are typically selected in such a way that demographic characteristics of interest to the researcher are represented in the sample in target proportions. Thus, many people confuse quota samples and stratified samples. There are, however, two key differences between a quota sample and a stratified sample. First, respondents for a quota sample are not selected randomly, as they must be for a stratified sample. Second, the classification factors used for a stratified sample are selected based on the existence of a correlation between the factor and the behavior of interest. There is no such requirement in the case of a quota sample. The demographic or classification factors of interest in a quota sample are selected on the basis of researcher judgment.

> **quota samples**
> Nonprobability samples in which quotas, based on demographic or classification factors selected by the researcher, are established for population subgroups.

Snowball Samples

In **snowball samples**, sampling procedures are used to select additional respondents on the basis of referrals from initial respondents. This procedure is used to sample from low-incidence or rare populations—that is, populations that make up a very small percentage of the total population.[18] The costs of finding members of these rare populations may be so great that the researcher is forced to use a technique such as snowball sampling. For example, suppose an insurance company needed to obtain a national sample of individuals who have switched from the indemnity form of healthcare coverage to a health maintenance organization in the past 6 months. It would be necessary to sample a very large number of consumers to identify 1,000 that fall into this population. It would be far

> **snowball samples**
> Nonprobability samples in which additional respondents are selected based on referrals from initial respondents.

PRACTICING MARKETING RESEARCH

E-Mail Surveys of Web Site Usage—When Snowballing Fails to Snowball

Elaine Peterson, librarian and professor at Montana State University Libraries at Bozeman, Montana, wanted to evaluate user response and opinion regarding the school's popular digital library called the Montana Natural Resource Information System (NRIS). This highly visited Web site (1 million hits per month) presents information about plants, animals, and water status, as well as maps for the area. She used the snowball sampling approach in two stages: in-person interviews followed up a year later by e-mail surveys of the same respondents. In particular, Peterson wanted to see if snowball sampling would be successful if the survey were based exclusively on e-mail.

In the first round, Peterson interviewed 47 people representing 37 relevant organizations, either in person or on the telephone, expending about 45 minutes per interview. She found the respondents willing to provide references for colleagues. But a year later, after the NRIS Web site had been improved, Peterson got a surprise. Of the same respondents, only 32 percent answered the e-mail survey and all were reluctant to provide the names of colleagues for the snowball sample given in that format.

"The solicitation of names for potential participants, a key component of snowball sampling, proved to be more difficult with the e-mail survey," she observed. Using e-mails to get more names through snowball sampling was the most time-consuming activity in the e-mail survey, so that even though telephone interviews might seem to take longer, they produced better results in terms of usable new names. "The e-mail survey," Peterson said, "is not the best option for digital library evaluations."[19]

Questions

1. Come up with some plausible inducements or assurances for people receiving the e-mail survey to provide snowball references of friends.

2. What is the inherent difference between a telephone interview and an e-mail survey as regards an interviewee feeling comfortable giving names?

---

more economical to obtain an initial sample of 200 people from the population of interest and have each of them provide the names of an average of four other people to complete the sample of 1,000.

The main advantage of snowball sampling is a dramatic reduction in search costs. However, this advantage comes at the expense of sample quality. The total sample is likely to be biased because the individuals whose names were obtained from those sampled in the initial phase are likely to be very similar to those initially sampled. As a result, the sample may not be a good cross section of the total population. There is general agreement that some limits should be placed on the number of respondents obtained through referrals, although there are no specific rules regarding what these limits should be. This approach may also be hampered by the fact that respondents may be reluctant to give referrals. An approach used when snowballing did not work is described in the Practicing Marketing Research feature on page 398.

Internet Sampling

The advantages of Internet interviewing are compelling:

- *Target respondents can complete the survey at their convenience.* It can be completed late at night, over the weekend, and at any other convenient time.
- *Data collection is relatively inexpensive.* Once basic overhead and other fixed costs are covered, interviewing is essentially volume-insensitive. Thousands of interviews can be conducted at an actual data-collection cost of less than $1 per survey. This low cost may, to some extent, be offset by the need to use incentives to encourage responses. By comparison, a 10-minute telephone interview targeting people who make up 50 percent of the population may cost $15 or more per survey. Data entry and data processing costs are dramatically reduced because respondents essentially do the data entry for the researcher.
- *The interview can be administered under software control.* This allows the survey to follow skip patterns and do other "smart" things.
- *The survey can be completed quickly.* Hundreds or thousands of surveys can be completed in a day or less.[20]

Unfortunately, there is no large body of scientific research regarding the representativeness of Internet samples, as there is for other data-collection approaches. Those who have carefully evaluated Internet surveying are most concerned that the pool of people available in cyberspace does not correctly represent the general population. The group of Internet respondents tend to be richer, whiter, more male, and more tech-savvy.[21] The biases are becoming less pronounced over time as the percentage of the population connected to the Internet increases.[22] However, the nonrepresentativeness of Internet respondents will exist for some time into the future. This general problem is compounded by the fact that no comprehensive and reliable source of e-mail addresses exists.

Finally, research firms such as survey sampling and research now and tout the fact that they have developed large panels of individuals who have responded to their solicitations and have agreed to accept and complete online surveys.[23]

There are cases where Internet surveys, with all their other inherent advantages, may produce excellent samples. Those cases involve situations in which the client organization or the researcher has e-mail addresses for all members of a particular population. For example, high-technology firms such as Texas Instruments may have lists of essentially all individuals who make decisions regarding the purchase of their products for incorporation in other products. These industrial buyers are probably fairly heavy users of the Internet, both at home and at work. Selecting a true random sample of all members of such a population is relatively easy. At minimal cost, all the individuals can be sent invitations to participate and reminders to complete the survey. Response rates in excess of 70 percent are not uncommon for surveys of this type, especially if incentives are offered to encourage responses. Internet surveys are an emerging form of data collection that will probably become dominant at some point in the future. Their advantages are numerous and compelling. However, until the sampling issues discussed in this chapter can be resolved, the results of Internet surveys will be suspect because of lack of survey representativeness. Increasingly, researchers are blending data from online panels with data generated from telephone, mail, and other data-collection techniques to deal with the limitations of online panels. Issues in this type of sample blending are covered in the Practicing Marketing Research feature on page 400.

PRACTICING MARKETING RESEARCH

How Building a Blended Sample Can Help Improve Research Results[24]

Most researchers prefer building a sample from a single source. In many cases, however, getting a truly representative sample from a single source is becoming more difficult. Survey Sampling International (SSI) has used a blended sample approach of panels, Web traffic, and aligned interest groups, and has found the resulting quality of the data is higher than with a single source sample.

Using a blended sample source creates two benefits: (1) It helps capture the opinions of people who would not otherwise join panels, and (2) it increases heterogeneity. As the breadth of sources increases, however, it is important to identify the unique biases of each of those sources and control for it in order to ensure high sample quality. The only way to achieve this balance is to understand where the bias is coming from. By using a panel exclusively, for example, you might eliminate individuals with valuable opinions who just aren't willing to commit to joining the panel.

Researchers should also make sure their samples are consistent and predictable. Studies indicate that controlling just for demographics and other traditional balancing factors does not always account for the variations created by the distinct characteristics of different sample sources. Demographic quotas may work, but only if the selected stratification relates directly to the questionnaire topic. Comparing sources to external benchmarks can improve consistency as well, but often those benchmarks are not readily available.

SSI's research on variance between data sources indicates that psychographic and neurographic variables have a greater capacity to influence variance between diverse sources than traditional demographic variables have. Even still, these variables do not account for all the possible variance, so researchers must continue testing in order to ensure consistency within the blended sampling method.

SSI offers the following suggestions for creating a blended sample:

- Consider including calibration questions—Look for existing external benchmarks for your survey topic.

- Understand the sample blending techniques used to create your sample—Tell your sample provider what kind of source smoothing and quality control methods are being used.

- Know your sources—Ask your sample provider how source quality is being maintained.

- Plan ahead—Incorporate blending into the sample plan from the start.

- Ensure that respondents are satisfied with the research experience—Be aware that significantly high nonresponse and noncompletion rates can introduce bias as well.

Questions

1. Beyond the variables discussed, can you think of any others that might be relevant when creating a blended sample?

2. Do you think a blended sample would be useful, and if so would you be inclined to try it? Are there any situations in which you would think a single-source sample would be more effective? Why?

SUMMARY

The population, or universe, is the total group of people in whose opinions one is interested. A census involves collecting desired information from every member of the population of interest. A sample is simply a subset of a population. The steps in developing a sampling plan are as follows: define the population of interest, choose the data-collection method, identify the sampling frame, select the sampling method, determine sample size, develop and specify an operational plan for selecting sampling elements, and execute the operational sampling plan. The sampling frame is a list of the elements of the population from which the sample will be drawn or a specified procedure for generating the list.

In probability sampling methods, samples are selected in such a way that every element of the population has a known, nonzero likelihood of selection. Nonprobability sampling methods select specific elements from the population in a nonrandom manner. Probability samples have several advantages over nonprobability samples, including reasonable certainty that information will be obtained from a representative cross section of the population, a sampling error that can be computed, and survey results that can be projected to the total population. However, probability samples are more expensive than nonprobability samples and usually take more time to design and execute.

The accuracy of sample results is determined by both sampling and nonsampling error. Sampling error occurs because the sample selected is not perfectly representative of the population. There are two types of sampling error: random sampling error and administrative error. Random sampling error is due to chance and cannot be avoided; it can only be reduced by increasing sample size.

Probability samples include simple random samples, systematic samples, stratified samples, and cluster samples. Nonprobability samples include convenience samples, judgment samples, quota samples, and snowball samples. At the present time, Internet samples tend to be convenience samples. That may change in the future as better e-mail sampling frames become available.

KEY TERMS & DEFINITIONS

sampling Process of obtaining information from a subset of a larger group.

population Entire group of people about whom information is needed; also called *universe* or *population of interest*.

census Collection of data obtained from or about every member of the population of interest.

sample Subset of all the members of a population of interest.

sampling frame List of population elements from which units to be sampled can be selected or a specified procedure for generating such a list.

random-digit dialing Method of generating lists of telephone numbers at random.

probability samples Samples in which every element of the population has a known, nonzero likelihood of selection.

nonprobability samples Samples in which specific elements from the population have been selected in a nonrandom manner.

sample size The identified and selected population subset for the survey, chosen because it represents the entire group.

population parameter A value that accurately portrays or typifies a factor of a complete population, such as average age or income.

sampling error Error that occurs because the sample selected is not perfectly representative of the population.

nonsampling error All error other than sampling error; also called *measurement error*.

simple random sample Probability sample selected by assigning a number to every element of the population and then using a table of random numbers to select specific elements for inclusion in the sample.

systematic sampling Probability sampling in which the entire population is numbered and elements are selected using a skip interval.

stratified sample Probability sample that is forced to be more representative though simple random sampling of mutually exclusive and exhaustive subsets.

proportional allocation Sampling in which the number of elements selected from a stratum is directly proportional to the size of the stratum relative to the size of the population.

disproportional, or optimal, allocation Sampling in which the number of elements taken from a given stratum is proportional to the relative size of the stratum and the stan-

dard deviation of the characteristic under consideration.

cluster sample Probability sample in which the sampling units are selected from a number of small geographic areas to reduce data-collection costs.

multistage area sampling Geographic areas selected for national or regional surveys in progressively smaller population units, such as counties, then residential blocks, then homes.

convenience samples Nonprobability samples based on using people who are easily accessible.

judgment samples Nonprobability samples in which the selection criteria are based on the researcher's personal judgment about representativeness of the population under study.

quota samples Nonprobability samples in which quotas, based on demographic or classification factors selected by the researcher, are established for population subgroups.

snowball samples Nonprobability samples in which additional respondents are selected based on referrals from initial respondents.

QUESTIONS FOR REVIEW & CRITICAL THINKING

1. What are some situations in which a census would be better than a sample? Why are samples usually employed rather than censuses?

2. Develop a sampling plan for examining undergraduate business students' attitudes toward Internet advertising.

3. Give an example of a perfect sampling frame. Why is a telephone directory usually not an acceptable sampling frame?

4. Distinguish between probability and nonprobability samples. What are the advantages and disadvantages of each? Why are nonprobability samples so popular in marketing research?

5. Distinguish among a systematic sample, a cluster sample, and a stratified sample. Give examples of each.

6. What is the difference between a stratified sample and a quota sample?

7. American National Bank has 1,000 customers. The manager wishes to draw a sample of 100 customers. How could this be done using systematic sampling? What would be the impact on the technique, if any, if the list were ordered by average size of deposit?

8. Do you see any problem with drawing a systematic sample from a telephone book, assuming that the telephone book is an acceptable sample frame for the study in question?

9. Describe snowball sampling. Give an example of a situation in which you might use this type of sample. What are the dangers associated with this type of sample?

10. Name some possible sampling frames for the following:

    a. Patrons of sushi bars

    b. Smokers of high-priced cigars

    c. Snowboarders

    d. Owners of DVD players

    e. People who have visited one or more countries in Europe in the last year

    f. People who emigrated to the United States within the last 2 years

    g. People with allergies

11. Identify the following sample designs:

    a. The names of 200 patrons of a casino are drawn from a list of visitors for the last month, and a questionnaire is administered to them.

    b. A radio talk show host invites listeners to call in and vote yes or no on whether handguns should be banned.

    c. A dog food manufacturer wants to test a new dog food. It decides to select 100 dog owners who feed their dogs canned food, 100 who feed their dogs dry food, and 100 who feed their dogs semimoist food.

    d. A poll surveys men who play golf to predict the outcome of a presidential election.

WORKING THE NET

1. Toluna offers *QuickSurveys*, a self-service tool that enables you to conduct market research quickly, easily and cost effectively. You can:

   - Create a survey of up to 5 questions.

   - Select up-to 2,000 nationally representative respondents.

   - Pay online using a credit card or PayPal.

   - Immediately follow the results live online and complete within 24 hours (speed of completion may vary by country).

   With this system, once your survey has been created it will automatically appear live on targeted specific areas of Toluna.com—a global community site that provides a forum where over 4 million members interact and poll each other on a broad range of topics. Visit *www.toluna-group.com* to view a *QuickSurveys* flash demo.

2. Throughout 2008, Knowledge Networks worked in conjunction with the Associated Press and Yahoo! to repeatedly poll 2,230 people (from random telephone sampling) about likely election results and political preferences. Visit *www.knowledgenetworks.com* and evaluate their methodology and ultimate accuracy (or inaccuracy) on this topic.

REAL-LIFE RESEARCH • 13.1

The Research Group

The Research Group has been hired by the National Internet Service Providers Association to determine the following:

- What specific factors motivate people to choose a particular Internet service provider (ISP)?
- How do these factors differ between choosing an ISP for home use and choosing an ISP for business use?
- Why do people choose one ISP over the others? How many have switched ISPs in the past year? Why did they switch ISPs?
- How satisfied are they with their current ISP?
- Do consumers know or care whether an ISP is a member of the National Internet Service Providers Association?
- What value-added services do consumers want from ISPs (for example, telephone support for questions and problems)?

The Research Group underbid three other research companies to get the contract. In fact, its bid was more than 25 percent lower than the next lowest bid. The primary way in which The Research Group was able to provide the lowest bid related to its sampling methodology. In its proposal, The Research Group specified that college students would be used to gather the survey data. Its plan called for randomly selecting 20 colleges from across the country, contacting the chairperson of the marketing department, and asking her or him to submit a list of 10 students who would be interested in earning extra money. Finally, The Research Group would contact the students individually with the goal of identifying five students at each school who would ultimately be asked to get 10 completed interviews. Students would be paid $10 for each completed survey. The only requirement imposed in regard to selecting potential respondents was that they had to be ISP subscribers at the time of the survey. The Research Group proposal suggested that the easiest way to do this would be for the student interviewers to go to the student union or student center during the lunch hour and ask those at each table whether they might be interested in participating in the survey.

Questions

1. How would you describe this sampling methodology?
2. What problems do you see arising from this technique?
3. Suggest an alternative sampling method that might give the National Internet Service Providers Association a better picture of the information it desired.

REAL-LIFE RESEARCH • 13.2

New Mexico National Bank

New Mexico National Bank (NMNB) operates branches in 23 cities and towns throughout the state of New Mexico. The bank offers a complete range of financial services, including Visa and MasterCard credit cards. New Mexico National Bank (NMNB) has 53,400 people in the state using its credit cards. Based on their original applications, the bank has certain information about these individuals, including name, address, zip code, telephone number, income, education, and assets. NMNB is interesting in determining whether a relationship exists between the volume of purchases charged on credit cards and the demographic characteristics of the individual cardholders. For example, are individuals in certain parts of the state more or less likely to be heavy users of the card? Is there a relationship between a person's income and his or her level of card usage? Is there a relationship between the person's level of education and card usage? The data can be used to more effectively target offering sent through the mail if significant relationships are found. Paul Bruney, research director for NMNB, is in the process of developing a design for the research. If you were Paul Bruney, how would you answer the following questions?

Questions

1. How would you define the population of interest for the study?
2. What sampling frame(s) might you use for the project?
3. What procedure would you use to select a simple random sample from the sampling frame you chose above?
4. Would it make sense to use a stratified sample in the situation? Why or why not? How would you approach the process of developing a stratified sample from the sampling frame you chose?
5. Could you use the sampling frame to draw a cluster sample? How would you go about it? Would it make any sense to do this?
6. Which of the three probability sampling methods just mentioned would you choose for this study? Why would you choose that option?

CHAPTER **14**

Sample Size Determination

LEARNING OBJECTIVES

→ **1.** To learn the financial and statistical issues in the determination of sample size.

→ **2.** To discover methods for determining sample size.

→ **3.** To gain an appreciation of a normal distribution.

→ **4.** To understand population, sample, and sampling distributions.

→ **5.** To distinguish between point and interval estimates.

→ **6.** To recognize problems involving sampling means and proportions.

Determining Sample Size for Probability Samples

The process of determining sample size for probability samples involves financial, statistical, and managerial issues. As a general rule, the larger the sample is, the smaller the sampling error. However, larger samples cost more money, and the resources available for a project are always limited. Although the cost of increasing sample size tends to rise on a linear basis (double the sample size, almost double the cost), sampling error decreases at a rate equal to the square root of the relative increase in sample size. If sample size is quadrupled, data collection cost is almost quadrupled, but the level of sampling error is reduced by only 50 percent.

Managerial issues must be reflected in sample size calculations. How accurate do estimates need to be, and how confident must managers be that true population values are included in the chosen confidence interval? Some cases require high levels of precision (small sampling error) and confidence that population values fall in the small range of sampling error (the confidence interval). Other cases may not require the same level of precision or confidence.

Budget Available

The sample size for a project is often determined, at least indirectly, by the budget available. Thus, it is frequently the last project factor determined. A brand manager may have $50,000 available in the budget for a new product test. After deduction of other project costs (e.g., research design, questionnaire development, data processing), the amount remaining determines the size of the sample that can be surveyed. Of course, if the dollars available will not produce an adequate sample size, then management must make a decision: either additional funds must be found, or the project should be canceled.

Although this approach may seem highly unscientific and arbitrary, it is a fact of life in a corporate environment. Financial constraints challenge the researcher to develop research designs that will generate data of adequate quality for decision-making purposes at low cost. This "budget available" approach forces the researcher to explore alternative data-collection approaches and to carefully consider the value of information in relation to its cost.

Rule of Thumb

Potential clients may specify in the RFP (request for proposal) that they want a sample of 200, 400, 500, or some other size. Sometimes, this number is based on desired sampling error. In other cases, it is based on nothing more than past experience. The justification for the specified sample size may boil down to a "gut feeling" that a particular sample size is necessary or appropriate.

If the researcher determines that the sample size requested is not adequate to support the objectives of the proposed research, then she or he has a professional responsibility to present arguments for a larger sample size to the client and let the client make the final decision. If the client rejects arguments for a larger sample size, then the researcher may decline to submit a proposal based on the belief that an inadequate sample size will produce results with so much error that they may be misleading.[1]

Number of Subgroups Analyzed

In any sample size determination problem, consideration must be given to the number and anticipated size of various subgroups of the total sample that must be analyzed and about which statistical inferences must be made. For example, a researcher might decide that a sample of 400 is quite adequate overall. However, if male and female respondents must be analyzed separately and the sample is expected to be 50 percent male and 50 percent female, then the expected sample size for each subgroup is only 200. Is this number adequate for making the desired statistical inferences about the characteristics of the two groups? If the results are to be analyzed by both sex and age, then the problem gets even more complicated.

Assume that it is important to analyze four subgroups of the total sample: men under 35, men 35 and over, women under 35, and women 35 and over. If each group is expected to make up about 25 percent of the total sample, a sample of 400 will include only 100 respondents in each subgroup. The problem is that as sample size gets smaller, sampling error gets larger, and it becomes more difficult to tell whether an observed difference between two groups is a real difference or simply a reflection of sampling error.

Other things being equal, the larger the number of subgroups to be analyzed, the larger the required total sample size. It has been suggested that a sample should provide, at a minimum, 100 or more respondents in each major subgroup and 20 to 50 respondents in each of the less important subgroups.[2]

Traditional Statistical Methods

You probably have been exposed in other classes to traditional approaches for determining sample size for simple random samples. These approaches are reviewed in this chapter. Three pieces of information are required to make the necessary calculations for a sample result:

■ An estimate of the population standard deviation

■ The acceptable level of sampling error

■ The desired level of confidence that the sample result will fall within a certain range (result ± sampling error) of true population values

With these three pieces of information, the researcher can calculate the size of the simple random sample required.[3]

Normal Distribution

General Properties

The normal distribution is crucial to classical statistical inference. There are several reasons for its importance. First, many variables encountered by marketers have probability distributions that are close to the normal distribution. Examples include the number of cans, bottles, or glasses of soft drink consumed by soft drink users, the number of times that people who eat at fast-food restaurants go to such restaurants in an average month, and the average hours per week spent viewing television. Second, the normal distribution is useful for a number of theoretical reasons; one of the more important of these relates to the central limit theorem. According to the **central limit theorem**, for any population, regardless of its distribution, the distribution of sample means or sample proportions approaches a normal distribution as sample size increases. The importance of this tendency will become clear later in the chapter. Third, the normal distribution is a useful approximation of many other discrete probability distributions. If, for example, a researcher measured the heights of a large sample of men in the United States and plotted those values on a graph, a distribution similar to the one shown in Exhibit 14.1 would

➤ **central limit theorem**
Idea that a distribution of a large number of sample means or sample proportions will approximate a normal distribution, regardless of the distribution of the population from which they were drawn.

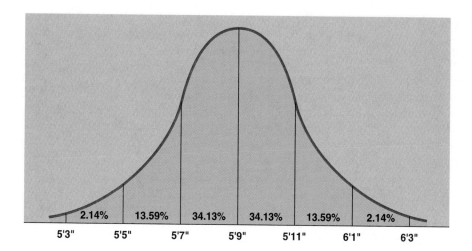

Exhibit 14.1

Normal Distribution for Heights of Men

result. This distribution is a **normal distribution**, and it has a number of important characteristics, including the following:

1. The normal distribution is bell-shaped and has only one mode. The mode is a measure of central tendency and is the particular value that occurs most frequently. (A bimodal, or two-mode, distribution would have two peaks or humps.)

2. The normal distribution is symmetric about its mean. This is another way of saying that it is not skewed and that the three measures of central tendency (mean, median, and mode) are all equal.

3. A particular normal distribution is uniquely defined by its mean and standard deviation.

4. The total area under a normal curve is equal to one, meaning that it takes in all observations.

5. The area of a region under the normal distribution curve between any two values of a variable equals the probability of observing a value in that range when an observation is randomly selected from the distribution. For example, on a single draw, there is a 34.13 percent chance of selecting from the distribution shown in Exhibit 14.1 a man between 5'7" and 5'9" in height.

6. The area between the mean and a given number of standard deviations from the mean is the same for all normal distributions. The area between the mean and plus or minus one standard deviation takes in 68.26 percent of the area under the curve, or 68.26 percent of the observations. This **proportional property of the normal distribution** provides the basis for the statistical inferences we will discuss in this chapter.

> **normal distribution**
> Continuous distribution that is bell-shaped and symmetric about the mean; the mean, median, and mode are equal.

> **proportional property of the normal distribution**
> Feature that the number of observations falling between the mean and a given number of standard deviations from the mean is the same for all normal distributions.

EXHIBIT 14.2	Area under Standard Normal Curve for Z Values (Standard Deviations) of 1, 2, and 3
Z Values (Standard Deviation)	**Area under Standard Normal Curve(%)**
1	68.26
2	95.44
3	99.74

Standard Normal Distribution

> **→ standard normal distribution**
> Normal distribution with a mean of zero and a standard deviation of one.

Any normal distribution can be transformed into what is known as a standard normal distribution. The **standard normal distribution** has the same features as any normal distribution. However, the mean of the standard normal distribution is always equal to zero, and the standard deviation is always equal to one. The probabilities provided in Table 2 in Appendix 2 are based on a standard normal distribution. A simple transformation formula, based on the proportional property of the normal distribution, is used to transform any value X from any normal distribution to its equivalent value Z from a standard normal distribution:

$$Z = \frac{\text{Value of the variable} - \text{Mean of the variable}}{\text{Standard deviation of the variable}}$$

Symbolically, the formula can be stated as follows:

> **→ standard deviation**
> Measure of dispersion calculated by subtracting the mean of the series from each value in a series, squaring each result, summing the results, dividing the sum by the number of items minus 1, and taking the square root of this value.

$$Z = \frac{X - \mu}{\sigma}$$

where
X = value of the variable
μ = mean of the variable
σ = standard deviation of the variable

The areas under a standard normal distribution (reflecting the percent of all observations) for various Z values (**standard deviations**) are shown in Exhibit 14.2. The standard normal distribution is shown in Exhibit 14.3.

Population and Sample Distributions

The purpose of conducting a survey based on a sample is to make inferences about the population, not to describe the sample. The population, as defined earlier, includes all possible individuals or objects from whom or about which information is needed to meet the objectives of the research. A sample is a subset of the total population.

Exhibit 14.3

Standard Normal Distribution

Note: The term Pr(Z) is read "the probability of Z."

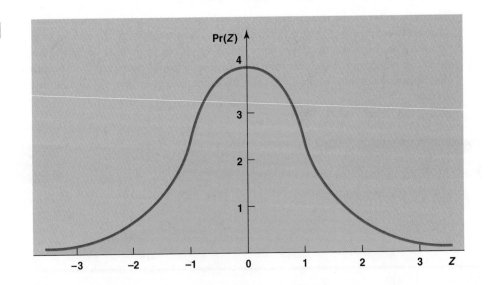

A **population distribution** is a frequency distribution of all the elements of the population. It has a mean, usually represented by the Greek letter μ; and a standard deviation, usually represented by the Greek letter σ.

A **sample distribution** is a frequency distribution of all the elements of an individual (single) sample. In a sample distribution, the mean is usually represented by X and the standard deviation is usually represented by S.

Sampling Distribution of the Mean

At this point, it is necessary to introduce a third distribution, the sampling distribution of the sample mean. Understanding this distribution is crucial to understanding the basis for our ability to compute sampling error for simple random samples. The **sampling distribution of the mean** is a conceptual and theoretical probability distribution of the means of all possible samples of a given size drawn from a given population. Although this distribution is seldom calculated, its known properties have tremendous practical significance. Actually, deriving a distribution of sample means involves drawing a large number of simple random samples (for example, 25,000) of a certain size from a particular population. Then, the means for the samples are computed and arranged in a frequency distribution. Because each sample is composed of a different subset of sample elements, all the sample means will not be exactly the same. If the samples are sufficiently large and random, then the resulting distribution of sample means will approximate a normal distribution. This assertion is based on the central limit theorem, which states that as sample size increases, the distribution of the means of a large number of random samples taken from virtually any population approaches a normal distribution with a mean equal to μ and a standard deviation (referred to as *standard error*) $S_{\bar{x}}$, where $n =$ sample size and

$$S_{\bar{x}} = \frac{\sigma}{\sqrt{n}}$$

The **standard error of the mean** ($S\bar{x}$) is computed in this way because the variance, or dispersion, within a particular distribution of sample means will be smaller if it is based on larger samples. Common sense tells us that with larger samples individual sample means will, on the average, be closer to the population mean.

It is important to note that the central limit theorem holds regardless of the shape of the population distribution from which the samples are selected. This means that, regardless of the population distribution, the sample means selected from the population distribution will tend to be normally distributed.

The notation ordinarily used to refer to the means and standard deviations of population and sample distributions and sampling distribution of the mean is summarized in Exhibit 14.4. The relationships among the population distribution, sample distribution, and sampling distribution of the mean are shown graphically in Exhibit 14.5.

population distribution
Frequency distribution of all the elements of a population.

sample distribution
Frequency distribution of all the elements of an individual sample.

sampling distribution of the mean
Theoretical frequency distribution of the means of all possible samples of a given size drawn from a particular population; it is normally distributed.

standard error of the mean
Standard deviation of a distribution of sample means.

EXHIBIT 14.4	Notation for Means and Standard Deviations of Various Distributions	
Distribution	Mean	Standard Deviation
Population	μ	σ
Sample	X	S
Sampling	$\mu_{\bar{x}} = \mu$	$S_{\bar{x}}$

The results of a simple random sample of fast-food restaurant patrons could be used to compute the mean number of visits for the period of one month for of the 1,000 samples.

Basic Concepts

Consider a case in which a researcher takes 1,000 simple random samples of size 200 from the population of all consumers who have eaten at a fast-food restaurant at least once in the past 30 days. The purpose is to estimate the average number of times these individuals eat at a fast-food restaurant in an average month.

If the researcher computes the mean number of visits for each of the 1,000 samples and sorts them into intervals based on their relative values, the frequency distribution shown in Exhibit 14.6 might result. Exhibit 14.7 graphically illustrates these frequencies in a histogram, on which a normal curve has been superimposed. As you can see, the histogram closely approximates the shape of a normal curve. If the researcher draws a large enough number of samples of size 200, computes the mean of each sample, and plots these means, the resulting distribution will be a normal distribution. The normal curve shown in Exhibit 14.7 is the sampling distribution of the mean for this particular problem. The sampling distribution of the mean for simple random samples that are large (30 or more observations) has the following characteristics:

- The distribution is a normal distribution.
- The distribution has a mean equal to the population mean.

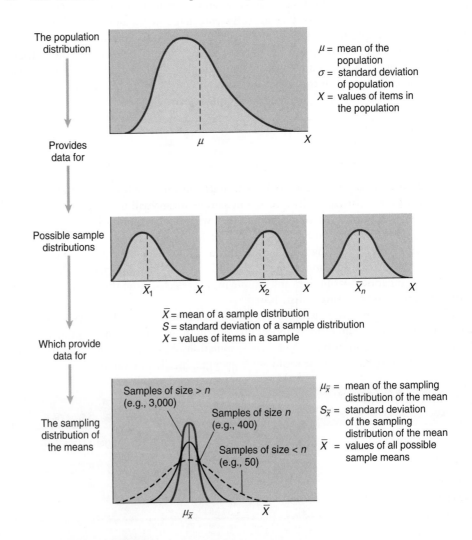

Exhibit 14.5

Relationships of the Three Basic Types of Distribution

Source: Adapted from *Statistics, A Fresh Approach*, 4th ed., by D. H. Sanders et al. © 1990 McGraw-Hill, Inc. Reprinted with permission of the McGraw-Hill Companies.

EXHIBIT 14.6	Frequency Distribution of 1,000 Sample Means: Average Number of Times Respondent Ate at a Fast-Food Restaurant in the Past 30 Days	
Number of Times	**Frequency of Occurrence**	
2.6–3.5	8	
3.6–4.5	15	
4.6–5.5	29	
5.6–6.5	44	
6.6–7.5	64	
7.6–8.5	79	
8.6–9.5	89	
9.6–10.5	108	
10.6–11.5	115	
11.6–12.5	110	
12.6–13.5	90	
13.6–14.5	81	
14.6–15.5	66	
15.6–16.5	45	
16.6–17.5	32	
17.6–18.5	16	
18.6–19.5	9	
Total	1,000	

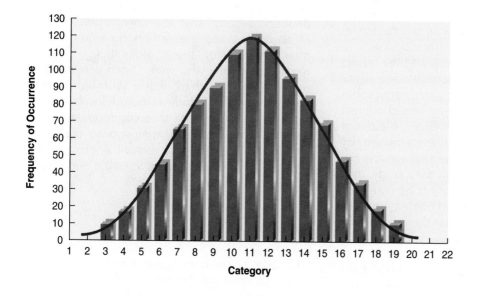

Exhibit 14.7

Actual Sampling Distribution of Means for Number of Times Respondent Ate at Fast-Food Restaurant in Past 30 Days

■ The distribution has a standard deviation (the standard error of the mean) equal to the population standard deviation divided by the square root of the sample size:

$$\sigma_{\bar{x}} = \frac{\sigma}{\sqrt{n}}$$

This statistic is referred to as the standard error of the mean (instead of the standard deviation) to indicate that it applies to a distribution of sample means rather than to the standard deviation of a sample or a population. Keep in mind that this calculation applies

GLOBAL RESEARCH

Nonresponse Bias in a Dutch Alcohol Consumption Study

The fact that some people fail to respond to a poll or respond only selectively to certain questions, ignoring others, can distort the accuracy of a survey. Market researchers call this nonresponse bias, and researchers at the Addiction Research Institute in Rotterdam, The Netherlands, concluded it can be a serious problem. In fact, response rates to surveys in The Netherlands had dropped from 80 percent in the 1980s to 60 percent at the end of the 1990s, and were still continuing to decline, all leading to a smaller sample size and accuracy loss in population estimates. People who don't respond to polls may have relevant characteristics different from responders.

In 2002, the researchers reviewed the results of a study done in 1999 on alcohol usage. Their research assumption was that abstainers probably didn't respond because they lacked interest in the subject and excessive drinkers did not respond because they were embarrassed by their usage. This hypothesis was borne out in the subsequent study. In designing their study, they knew that nonresponse bias cannot be corrected simply by weighting data based on demographic variables. They needed to poll the nonrespondents and evaluate if their answers differed from responders.

Originally, a random sample of 1,000 people, aged 16 to 69 years, was taken from the city registry of Rotterdam. Everyone received a mailed questionnaire about their alcohol consumption. After two reminders were sent, the response rate was 44 percent. For the follow-up study, the researchers chose 25 postal areas in Rotterdam and a secondary sample of 310 people. Of these, 133 had already responded to the first survey, and 177 did not, so these two groups were called primary respondents and primary nonrespondents, respectively. Members of the latter group were approached in person by the researchers in a series of five in-person attempts to conduct the interview at their homes. In the end, 48 primary nonrespondents could not be reached, leaving a final sample size for primary nonrespondents of 129.

Both groups were asked the same two questions: (1) do you ever drink alcohol?; and (2) do you ever drink six or more alcoholic beverages in the same day? The net response rate from the nonrespondents to both questions was 52 percent—in other words, even more nonresponse (48 percent) was encountered in the follow-up study.

More importantly the Dutch researchers discovered, first, that alcohol abstainers were underrepresented, but not frequent, excessive drinkers; second, that the underrepresentation of abstainers was greater among women than men, greater for those older than 35, and greater for those who were Dutch versus other nationalities; and third, that a thorough nonresponse follow-up study is called for (as mentioned, weighting data to accommodate this is insufficient) to evaluate nonresponse biases in any future studies. The potential answers of those who don't answer are valuable and statistically necessary for any study.[4]

Questions

1. The nonresponse bias came in with the extremes (abstainers and heavy drinkers) regarding alcohol use. Is there any weighting approach that might compensate for these two important groups of nonresponders so that a follow-up study would not be needed?

2. For the 48 percent who failed to respond to the second study, would a mailed questionnaire, insuring privacy, be worth the expense in terms of the improvement in statistical accuracy it might generate?

only to a simple random sample. Other types of probability samples (for example, stratified samples and cluster samples) require more complex formulas for computing standard error. Note that this formula does not account for any type of bias, including nonresponse bias discussed in the feature on page 414.

Making Inferences on the Basis of a Single Sample

In practice, there is no call for taking all possible random samples from a particular population and generating a frequency distribution and histogram like those shown in Exhibits 14.6 and 14.7. Instead, the researcher wants to take one simple random sample and make statistical inferences about the population from which it was drawn. The question is, what is the probability that any one simple random sample of a particular size will produce an estimate of the population mean that is within one standard error (plus or minus) of the true population mean? The answer, based on the information provided in Exhibit 14.2, is that there is a 68.26 percent probability that any one sample from a particular population will produce an estimate of the population mean that is within plus or minus one standard error of the true value, because 68.26 percent of all sample means fall in this range. There is a 95.44 percent probability that any one simple random sample of a particular size from a given population will produce a value that is within plus or minus two standard errors of the true population mean, and a 99.74 percent probability that such a sample will produce an estimate of the mean that is within plus or minus three standard errors of the population mean.

Point and Interval Estimates

The results of a sample can be used to generate two kinds of estimates of a population mean: point and interval estimates. The sample mean is the best **point estimate** of the population mean. Inspection of the sampling distribution of the mean shown in Exhibit 14.7 suggests that a particular sample result is likely to produce a mean that is relatively close to the population mean. However, the mean of a particular sample could be any

→ **point estimate**
Particular estimate of a population value.

The sampling distribution of the proportion is used to estimate the percentage of the population that watches a particular television program.

one of the sample means shown in the distribution. A small percentage of these sample means are a considerable distance from the true population mean. The distance between the sample mean and the true population mean is the sampling error.

Given that point estimates based on sample results are exactly correct in only a small percentage of all possible cases, interval estimates generally are preferred. An **interval estimate** is a particular interval or range of values within which the true population value is estimated to fall. In addition to stating the size of the interval, the researcher usually states the probability that the interval will include the true value of the population mean. This probability is referred to as the **confidence level**, and the interval is called the **confidence interval**.

Interval estimates of the mean are derived by first drawing a random sample of a given size from the population of interest and calculating the mean of that sample. This sample mean is known to lie somewhere within the sampling distribution of all possible sample means, but exactly where this particular mean falls in that distribution is not known. There is a 68.26 percent probability that this particular sample mean lies within one standard error (plus or minus) of the true population mean. Based on this information, the researcher states that he or she is 68.26 percent confident that the true population value is equal to the sample value plus or minus one standard error. This statement can be shown symbolically, as follows:

> **interval estimate**
> Interval or range of values within which the true population value is estimated to fall.

> **confidence level**
> Probability that a particular interval will include true population value; also called *confidence coefficient*.

> **confidence interval**
> Interval that, at the specified confidence level, includes the true population value.

$$\overline{X} - 1\sigma_{\overline{x}} \leq \mu \leq \overline{X} + 1\sigma_{\overline{x}}$$

By the same logic, the researcher can be 95.44 percent confident that the true population value is equal to the sample estimate ± 2 (technically 1.96) standard errors, and 99.74 percent confident that the true population value falls within the interval defined by the sample value ± 3 standard errors.

These statements assume that the standard deviation of the population is known. However, in most situations, this is not the case. If the standard deviation of the population were known, by definition the mean of the population would also be known, and there would be no need to take a sample in the first place. Because information on the standard deviation of the population is lacking, its value is estimated based on the standard deviation of the sample.

Sampling Distribution of the Proportion

Marketing researchers frequently are interested in estimating proportions or percentages rather than or in addition to estimating means. Common examples include estimating the following:

■ The percentage of the population that is aware of a particular ad.

■ The percentage of the population that accesses the Internet one or more times in an average week.

■ The percentage of the population that has visited a fast-food restaurant four or more times in the past 30 days.

■ The percentage of the population that watches a particular television program.

> **sampling distribution of the proportion**
> Relative frequency distribution of the sample proportions of many random samples of a given size drawn from a particular population; it is normally distributed.

In situations in which a population proportion or percentage is of interest, the sampling distribution of the proportion is used.

The **sampling distribution of the proportion** is a relative frequency distribution of the sample proportions of a large number of random samples of a given size drawn from a particular population. The sampling distribution of a proportion has the following characteristics:

■ It approximates a normal distribution.

■ The mean proportion for all possible samples is equal to the population proportion.

■ The standard error of a sampling distribution of the proportion can be computed with the following formula:

$$S_p = \sqrt{\frac{P(1 - P)}{n}}$$

where S_p = standard error of sampling distribution of proportion

P = estimate of population proportion

n = sample size

Consider the task of estimating the percentage of all adults who have purchased something over the Internet in the past 90 days. As in generating a sampling distribution of the mean, the researcher might select 1,000 random samples of size 200 from the population of all adults and compute the proportion of all adults who have purchased something over the Internet in the past 90 days for all 1,000 samples. These values could then be plotted in a frequency distribution and this frequency distribution would approximate a normal distribution. The estimated standard error of the proportion for this distribution can be computed using the formula provided earlier.

For reasons that will be clear to you after you read the next section, marketing researchers have a tendency to prefer dealing with sample size problems as problems of estimating proportions rather than means.

Determining Sample Size

Problems Involving Means

Consider once again the task of estimating how many times the average fast-food restaurant user visits a fast-food restaurant in an average month. Management needs an estimate of the average number of visits to make a decision regarding a new promotional campaign that is being developed. To make this estimate, the marketing research manager for the organization intends to survey a simple random sample of all fast-food users. The question is, what information is necessary to determine the appropriate sample size for the project? The formula for calculating the required sample size for problems that involve the estimation of a mean is as follows:[5]

$$n = \frac{Z^2 \sigma^2}{E^2}$$

where Z = level of confidence expressed in standard errors

σ = population standard deviation

E = acceptable amount of sampling error

Three pieces of information are needed to compute the sample size required:

1. The acceptable or allowable level of sampling error E.
2. The acceptable level of confidence Z. In other words, how confident does the researcher want to be that the specified confidence interval includes the population mean?
3. An estimate of the population standard deviation σ.

→ allowable sampling error
Amount of sampling error the researcher is willing to accept.

The level of confidence Z and **allowable sampling error** E for this calculation must be set by the researcher in consultation with his or her client. As noted earlier, the level of confidence and the amount of error are based not only on statistical criteria but also on financial and managerial criteria. In an ideal world, the level of confidence would always be very high and the amount of error very low. However, because this is a business decision, cost must be considered. An acceptable trade-off among accuracy, level of confidence, and cost must be developed. High levels of precision and confidence may be less important in some situations than in others. For example, in an exploratory study, you may be interested in developing a basic sense of whether attitudes toward your product are generally positive or negative. Precision may not be critical. However, in a product concept test, you would need a much more precise estimate of sales for a new product before making the potentially costly and risky decision to introduce that product in the marketplace.

→ population standard deviation
Standard deviation of a variable for the entire population.

Making an estimate of the **population standard deviation** presents a more serious problem. As noted earlier, if the population standard deviation were known, the population mean also would be known (the population mean is needed to compute the population standard deviation), and there would be no need to draw a sample. How can the researcher estimate the population standard deviation before selecting the sample? One or some combination of the following four methods might be used to deal with this problem:

1. *Use results from a prior survey.* In many cases, the firm may have conducted a prior survey dealing with the same or a similar issue. In this situation, a possible solution to the problem is to use the results of the prior survey as an estimate of the population standard deviation.

2. *Conduct a pilot survey.* If this is to be a large-scale project, it may be possible to devote some time and some resources to a small-scale pilot survey of the population. The results of this pilot survey can be used to develop an estimate of the population standard deviation that can be used in the sample size determination formula.

3. *Use secondary data.* In some cases, secondary data can be used to develop an estimate of the population standard deviation.

4. *Use judgment.* If all else fails, an estimate of the population standard deviation can be developed based solely on judgment. Judgments might be sought from a variety of managers in a position to make educated guesses about the required population parameters.

It should be noted that after the survey has been conducted and the sample mean and sample standard deviation have been calculated, the researcher can assess the accuracy of the estimate of the population standard deviation used to calculate the required sample size. At this time, if appropriate, adjustments can be made in the initial estimates of sampling error.[6]

Let's return to the problem of estimating the average number of fast-food visits made in an average month by users of fast-food restaurants:

■ After consultation with managers in the company, the marketing research manager determines that an estimate is needed of the average number of times that fast-food consumers visit fast-food restaurants. She further determines that managers believe that a high degree of accuracy is needed, which she takes to mean that the estimate should be within .10 (one-tenth) of a visit of the true population value. This value (.10) should be substituted into the formula for the value of E.

■ In addition, the marketing research manager decides that, all things considered, she needs to be 95.44 percent confident that the true population mean falls in the interval defined by the sample mean plus or minus E (as just defined). Two (technically, 1.96) standard errors are required to take in 95.44 percent of the area under a normal curve. Therefore, a value of 2 should be substituted into the equation for Z.

■ Finally, there is the question of what value to insert into the formula for σ. Fortunately, the company conducted a similar study one year ago. The standard deviation in that study for the variable—the average number of times a fast-food restaurant was visited in the past 30 days—was 1.39. This is the best estimate of σ available. Therefore, a value of 1.39 should be substituted into the formula for the value of σ. The calculation follows:

$$n = \frac{Z^2 \sigma^2}{E^2}$$
$$= \frac{2^2 (1.39)^2}{(.10)^2}$$
$$= \frac{4(1.93)}{.01}$$
$$= \frac{7.72}{.01}$$
$$= 772$$

Based on this calculation, a simple random sample of 772 is necessary to meet the requirements outlined.

Problems Involving Proportions

Now let's consider the problem of estimating the proportion or percentage of all adults who have purchased something via the Internet in the past 90 days. The goal is to take a simple random sample from the population of all adults to estimate this proportion.[7]

■ As in the problem involving fast-food users, the first task in estimating the population mean on the basis of sample results is to decide on an acceptable value for E. If, for example, an error level of 34 percent is acceptable, a value of .04 should be substituted into the formula for E.

■ Next, assume that the researcher has determined a need to be 95.44 percent confident that the sample estimate is within 34 percent of the true population proportion. As in the previous example, a value of 2 should be substituted into the equation for Z.

■ Finally, in a study of the same issue conducted one year ago, 5 percent of all respondents indicated they had purchased something over the Internet in the past 90 days. Thus, a value of .05 should be substituted into the equation for P.

The resulting calculations are as follows:

$$n = \frac{Z^2 [P(1 - P)]}{E^2}$$
$$= \frac{2^2 [.05(1 - .05)]}{.04^2}$$
$$= \frac{4(.0475)}{.0016}$$
$$= \frac{.19}{.0016}$$
$$= 119$$

Given the requirements, a random sample of 119 respondents is required. It should be noted that, in one respect, the process of determining the sample size necessary to estimate a proportion is easier than the process of determining the sample size necessary to estimate a mean: If there is no basis for estimating P, the researcher can make what is sometimes referred to as the most pessimistic, or worst-case, assumption regarding the value of P. Given the values of Z and E, what value of P will require the largest possible sample? A value of .50 will make the value of the expression $P(1 - P)$ larger than any possible value of P. There is no corresponding most pessimistic assumption that the researcher can make regarding the value of σ in problems that involve determining the sample size necessary to estimate a mean with given levels of Z and E.

Determining Sample Size for Stratified and Cluster Samples

The formulas for sample size determination presented in this chapter apply only to simple random samples. There also are formulas for determining required sample size and sampling error for other types of probability samples such as stratified and cluster samples. Although many of the general concepts presented in this chapter apply to these other types of probability samples, the specific formulas are much more complicated.[8] In addition, these formulas require information that frequently is not available or is difficult to obtain. For these reasons, sample size determination for other types of probability samples is beyond the scope of this introductory text.

Sample Size for Qualitative Research

The issue of sample size for qualitative research often comes up when making decisions about the number of traditional focus groups, individual depth interviews or online bulletin board focus groups to conduct. Given the relatively small sample sizes we intentionally use in qualitative research, the types of sample size calculation discussed in this chapter are never going to help us answer this question. Experts have discussed a rule based on experience and some analysis suggests that after we have talked to 20–30 people in a qualitative setting the general pattern of responses begins to stabilize. This issue is discussed in greater detail in the Practicing Marketing Research feature on page 421.

Population Size and Sample Size

You may have noticed that none of the formulas for determining sample size takes into account the size of the population in any way. Students (and managers) frequently find this troubling. It seems to make sense that one should take a larger sample from a larger population. But this is not the case. Normally, there is no direct relationship between the size of the population and the size of the sample required to estimate a particular population parameter with a particular level of error and a particular level of confidence. In fact, the size of the population may have an effect only in those situations where the size of the sample is large in relation to the size of the population. One rule of thumb is that an adjustment should be made in the sample size if the sample size is more than 5 percent of the size of the total population. The normal presumption is that sample elements are drawn independently of one another (**independence assumption**). This assumption is justified when the sample is small relative to the population. However, it is not appropriate when the sample is a relatively large (5 percent or more) proportion of the population. As a result, the researcher must adjust the results obtained with the standard formulas. For example, the formula for the standard error of the mean, presented earlier, is as follows:

independence assumption
Assumption that sample elements are drawn independently.

$$\sigma_{\bar{x}} = \frac{\sigma}{\sqrt{n}}$$

PRACTICING
MARKETING RESEARCH

In a qualitative research project, how large should the sample be? How many focus groups, individual depth interviews (IDIs), or online bulletin board focus groups are needed? One suggested rule is to make sure you do more than one group on a topic because any one group may be idiosyncratic. Another guideline is to continue doing groups or IDIs until we have reached a saturation point and are no longer hearing anything new. These rules are intuitive and reasonable, but they are not solidly grounded and do not really give us an optimal qualitative sample size. The approach proposed here gives some specific answers.

First, the importance of sample size in qualitative research must be understood.

Size Does Matter, Even for a Qualitative Sample

In qualitative work, we are trying to discover something. We may be seeking to uncover the reasons why consumers are or are not satisfied with a product; the product attributes that are important to users; possible consumer perceptions of celebrity spokespersons; the various problems that consumers experience with our brand; or other kinds of insights. It is up to a subsequent quantitative study to estimate, with statistical precision, the importance or prevalence of each perception.

The key point is this: Our qualitative sample must be big enough to ensure that we are likely to hear most or all of the perceptions that might be important.

Discovery Failure Can Be Serious

What might go wrong if a qualitative project fails to uncover an actionable perception (or attribute, opinion, need, experience, etc.)? Here are some possibilities:

A source of dissatisfaction is not discovered—and not corrected. In highly competitive industries, even a small incidence of dissatisfaction could dent the bottom line.

In the qualitative testing of an advertisement, a copy point that offends a small but vocal subgroup of the market is not discovered until a public relations fiasco erupts.

When qualitative procedures are used to pretest a quantitative questionnaire, an undiscovered ambiguity in the wording of a question may mean that some of the subsequent quantitative respondents give invalid responses. Thus, qualitative discovery failure eventually can result in quantitative estimation error due to respondent miscomprehension.

Therefore, size does matter in a qualitative sample, though for a different reason than in a quantitative sample. The following example shows how the risk of discovery failure may be easy to overlook even when it is formidable.

Basing the Decision on Calculated Probabilities

So, how can we figure the sample size needed to reduce the risk as much as we want? I am proposing two ways. One would be based on calculated probabilities similar to what we do for quantitative sample size estimation, but different.

The other way of figuring an appropriate sample size would be to consider the findings of some actual studies. Based on various studies, a sample size of 30 seems to be the point at which we will find out all the unique things that occur with any frequency.

Until someone comes up with a more definitive answer, an N of 30 respondents is a reasonable starting point for deciding the qualitative sample size that can reveal the full range (or nearly the full range) of potentially important customer perceptions. An N of 30 reduces the probability of missing a perception with a 10 percent incidence to less than 5 percent (assuming random sampling) and is at the upper end of the range found in the studies. If focus groups are desired, and we want to count each respondent separately toward the N we choose (e.g., getting an N of 30 from three groups with 10 respondents in each), then it is important for every respondent to have sufficient air time on the key issues. Also, it is critical for the moderator to control dominators and bring out the shy people, lest the distinctive perceptions of less-talkative customers are missed.[9]

Questions

1. Is sample size important in qualitative research? Why do you say that?

2. What is a reasonable target sample size for qualitative studies? What is that sample size based on?

For a sample that is 5 percent or more of the population, the independence assumption is dropped, producing the following formula:

$$\sigma_{\bar{x}} = \frac{\sigma}{\sqrt{n}} \sqrt{\frac{N-n}{N-1}}$$

→ finite population correction factor (FPC)
An adjustment to the required sample size that is made in cases where the sample is expected to be equal to 5 percent or more of the total population.

The factor $(N - n)/(N - 1)$ is referred to as the **finite population correction factor (FPC)**.

In those situations in which the sample is large (5 percent or more) in relation to the population, the researcher can appropriately reduce the required sample size using the FPC. This calculation is made using the following formula:

$$n' = \frac{nN}{N+n-1}$$

where n' = revised sample size
n = original sample size
N = population size

If the population has 2,000 elements and the original sample size is 400, then

$$n' = \frac{400(2000)}{2000 + 400 - 1} = \frac{800,000}{2399}$$
$$= 333$$

With the FPC adjustment, a sample of only 333 is needed, rather than the original 400.

The key is not the size of the sample in relation to the size of the population, but whether the sample selected is truly representative of the population. Empirical evidence shows that relatively small but carefully chosen samples can quite accurately reflect characteristics of the population. Many well-known national surveys and opinion polls, such as the Gallup Poll and the Harris Poll, are based on samples of fewer than 2,000. These polls have shown that the behavior of tens of millions of people can be predicted quite accurately using samples that are minuscule in relation to the size of the population.

PRACTICING MARKETING RESEARCH

Estimating with Precision How Many Phone Numbers Are Needed

Calculating how many phone numbers are needed for a project may seem like a difficult task, but following a few basic rules can make it simple. The formula used by Survey Sampling, Inc. (SSI) to calculate sample size involves four factors: (1) the number of completed interviews needed, (2) the working phone (or "reachable") rate, (3) the incidence rate, and (4) the contact / completion rate.

Completed Interviews

The number of completed interviews is based on the sample size calculation formula for simple random samples. It is the final sample size you want to achieve.

Working Phone Rate

The working phone rate varies with the sampling methodology used. An SSI RDD sample yields a 60 percent working phone rate. That is a good number to use in the formula for estimation purposes.

Incidence Rate

The incidence rate is the percentage of contacts that will qualify for the interview. Or put another way, what percentage of people who answer the phone (or reply to your mail questionnaire) will pass your screening questions? Accurate incidence data are critical to determining proper sample size. An incidence figure that is too high will leave you short of sample once your study is in the field.

Contact/Completion Rate

The last factor is the contact/completion rate. SSI defines this rate as the percentage of people who, once they qualify for your study, will agree to cooperate by completing the interview. There are several important elements you should consider when trying to reasonably estimate the completion rate:

- Contact rate
- Length of interview
- Sensitivity of topic
- Time of year
- Number of attempts/callbacks
- Length of time in the field

Provided that the interview is short (less than 10 minutes) and nonsensitive in nature, sufficient callbacks are scheduled, and the study will be in the field for an adequate period of time, SSI estimates a 30 percent completion rate. The completion rate should be adjusted according to the specifications of each study. If the subject matter is sensitive or the interview is long, the completion rate should be reduced. If the length of time in the field is less than one week, SSI recommends increasing the sample size by at least 20 percent.

An Example

Suppose you wish to complete 300 interviews in the United Kingdom. Using a random-digit sample, you can expect a working phone rate of 60 percent. Start by dividing the number of completed interviews you need (300) by the working phone rate (.60), to yield 500. You need to reach heavy soft drink users (17 percent of adults), and you estimate that 30 percent of the people contacted will complete the interview. Divide 500 by the incidence rate for the group under study (.17) and then by the completion rate (.30). This calculation shows you need 9,804 phone numbers to complete this survey.[10]

If you wish to complete 300 interviews in the United Kingdom, you need to determine the contact/completion rate in order to figure out how many calls will actually have to be made to complete the survey.

Determining How Many Sample Units Are Needed

Regardless of how the target sample size is determined, the researcher is confronted with the practical problem of figuring out how many sampling units (telephone numbers, addresses, and so on) will be required to complete the assignment. For example, if the target final sample size is 400, then obviously more than 400 telephone numbers will be needed to complete a telephone survey.

Some of the numbers on the list will be disconnected, some people will not qualify for the survey because they do not meet the requirements for inclusion in the population, and some will refuse to complete the survey. These factors affect the final estimate of the number of phone numbers, which may be used to place an order with a sample provider, such as Survey Sampling, Incorporated, or to ask the client for customer names and phone numbers for a satisfaction survey. This estimate must be reasonably accurate because the researcher wants to avoid paying for more numbers than are needed; on the other hand, the researcher doesn't want to run out of numbers during the survey and have to wait for more.

Estimating the number of sample units needed for a telephone sample is covered in the feature on page 423.

Statistical Power

Although it is standard practice in marketing research to use the formulas presented in this chapter to calculate sample size, these formulas all focus on *type I error*, or the error of concluding that there is a difference when there is not a difference. They do not explicitly deal with *type II error*, or the error of saying that there is no difference when there is a difference. The probability of not making a type II error is called **statistical power**.[11] The standard formulas for calculating sample size implicitly assume a power of 50 percent. For example, suppose a researcher is trying to determine which of two product concepts

→ **statistical power**
Probability of not making a type II error.

EXHIBIT 14.8	Sample Size Required to Detect Differences between Proportions from Independent Samples at Different Levels of Power and an Alpha of 0.25					
Difference to Detect	Power					
	50%	60%	70%	75%	80%	90%
0.01	19,205	24,491	30,857	34,697	39,239	52,530
0.05	766	977	1,231	1,384	1,568	2,094
0.10	190	242	305	343	389	518
0.15	83	106	133	150	169	226

has stronger appeal to target customers and wants to be able to detect a 5 percent difference in the percentages of target customers who say that they are very likely to buy the products. The standard sample size formulas indicate that a sample size of approximately 400 is needed for each product test. By using this calculation, the researcher implicitly accepts the fact that there is a 50 percent chance of incorrectly concluding that the two products have equal appeal.

Exhibit 14.8 shows the sample sizes required, at an alpha (probability of incorrectly rejecting the null hypothesis) of 0.25, for specific levels of power and specific levels of differences between two independent proportions. Formulas are available to permit power calculations for any level of confidence; however, they are somewhat complex and will not help you understand the basic concept of power. Programs available on the Internet can be used to make these calculations. To reproduce the numbers in Exhibit 14.8, go to *www. dssresearch. com/SampleSize/default.asp* and do the following:

- Click on the Two-Sample Using Percentage Values option under Sample Size.
- Enter the Sample 1 Percentage and the Sample 2 Percentage in the boxes so that the figures entered reflect the differences you want to be able to detect and the values are in the expected range. These figures are set at the 50 percent level (value of p in the standard sample size formula).
- Below those boxes, enter the Alpha and Beta Error Levels. Alpha is the value you would use for E in the standard sample size formula, and beta is the probability of incorrectly failing to reject the null hypothesis of no difference when a real difference exists. Power is equal to 1 – beta.
- Click on the Calculate Sample Size button at the bottom of the screen for the answer.

SUMMARY

Determining sample size for probability samples involves financial, statistical, and managerial considerations. Other things being equal, the larger the sample is, the smaller the sampling error. In turn, the cost of the research grows with the size of the sample.

There are several methods for determining sample size. One is to base the decision on the funds available. In essence, sample size is determined by the budget. Although seemingly unscientific, this approach is often a very realistic one in the world of corporate marketing research. The second technique is the so-called rule of thumb approach, which essentially involves determining the sample size based on a gut feeling or common practice. Samples of 300, 400, or 500 are often listed by the client in a request for proposal. A third technique for determining sample size is based on the number of subgroups to be analyzed. Generally speaking, the more subgroups that need to be analyzed, the larger is the required total sample size.

In addition to these methods, there are a number of traditional statistical techniques for determining sample size. Three pieces of data are required to make sample size calculations: an estimate of the population standard deviation, the level of sampling error that the researcher or client is willing to accept, and the desired level of confidence that the sample result will fall within a certain range of the true population value.

Crucial to statistical sampling theory is the concept of the normal distribution. The normal distribution is bell-shaped and has only one mode. It also is symmetric about its mean. The standard normal distribution has the features of a normal distribution; however, the mean of the standard normal distribution is always equal to zero, and the standard deviation is always equal to one. The transformation formula is used to transform any value X from any normal distribution to its equivalent value Z from a standard normal distribution. The central limit theorem states that the distribution of the means of a large number of random samples taken from virtually any population approaches a normal distribution with a mean equal to μ and a standard deviation equal to $S_{\bar{x}}$, where

$$S_{\bar{x}} = \frac{\sigma}{\sqrt{n}}$$

The standard deviation of a distribution of sample means is called the standard error of the mean.

When the results of a sample are used to estimate a population mean, two kinds of estimates can be generated: point and interval estimates. The sample mean is the best point estimate of the population mean. An interval estimate is a certain interval or range of values within which the true population value is estimated to fall. Along with the magnitude of the interval, the researcher usually states the probability that the interval will include the true value of the population mean—that is, the confidence level. The interval is called the confidence interval.

The researcher who is interested in estimating proportions or percentages rather than or in addition to means uses the sampling distribution of the proportion. The sampling distribution of the proportion is a relative frequency distribution of the sample proportions of a large number of random samples of a given size drawn from a particular population. The standard error of a sampling distribution of proportion is computed as follows:

$$S_p = \sqrt{\frac{P(1 - P)}{n}}$$

The following are required to calculate sample size: the acceptable level of sampling error E, the acceptable level of confidence Z, and an estimate of the population standard deviation 3. The formula for calculating the required sample size for situations that involve the estimation of a mean is as follows:

$$n = \frac{Z^2 \sigma^2}{E^2}$$

The following formula is used to calculate the required sample size for problems involving proportions:

$$n = \frac{Z^2[P(1-P)]}{E^2}$$

Finally, statistical power is the probability of not making a type II error. A type II error is the mistake of saying that there is not a difference when there is a difference. The standard sample size formula implicitly assumes a power of 50 percent. It may be important to use different levels of power depending on the nature of the decision in question.

KEY TERMS & DEFINITIONS

central limit theorem Idea that a distribution of a large number of sample means or sample proportions will approximate a normal distribution, regardless of the distribution of the population from which they were drawn.

normal distribution Continuous distribution that is bell-shaped and symmetric about the mean; the mean, median, and mode are equal.

proportional property of the normal distribution Feature that the number of observations falling between the mean and a given number of standard deviations from the mean is the same for all normal distributions.

standard normal distribution Normal distribution with a mean of zero and a standard deviation of one.

standard deviation Measure of dispersion calculated by subtracting the mean of the series from each value in a series, squaring each result, summing the results, dividing the sum by the number of items minus 1, and taking the square root of this value.

population distribution Frequency distribution of all the elements of a population.

sample distribution Frequency distribution of all the elements of an individual sample.

sampling distribution of the mean Theoretical frequency distribution of the means of all possible samples of a given size drawn from a particular population; it is normally distributed.

standard error of the mean Standard deviation of a distribution of sample means.

point estimate Particular estimate of a population value.

interval estimate Interval or range of values within which the true population value is estimated to fall.

confidence level Probability that a particular interval will include the true population value; also called *confidence coefficient*.

confidence interval Interval that, at the specified confidence level, includes the true population value.

sampling distribution of the proportion Relative frequency distribution of the sample proportions of many random samples of a given size drawn from a particular population; it is normally distributed.

allowable sampling error Amount of sampling error the researcher is willing to accept.

population standard deviation Standard deviation of a variable for the entire population.

independence assumption Assumption that sample elements are dream independently.

finite population correction factor (FPC) Adjustment to the required sample size that is made in cases where the sample is expected to be equal to 5 percent or more of the total population.

statistical power Probability of not making a type II error.

QUESTIONS FOR REVIEW & CRITICAL THINKING

1. Explain how the determination of sample size is a financial, statistical, and managerial issue.

2. Discuss and give examples of three methods that are used in marketing research for determining sample size.

3. A marketing researcher analyzing the fast-food industry noticed the following: The average amount spent at a fast-food restaurant in California was $3.30, with a standard deviation of $0.40. Yet in Georgia, the average amount spent at a fast-food restaurant was $3.25, with a standard deviation of $0.10. What do these statistics tell you about fast-food consumption patterns in these two states?

4. Distinguish among population, sample, and sampling distributions. Why is it important to distinguish among these concepts?

5. What is the finite population correction factor? Why is it used? When should it be used?

6. Assume that previous fast-food research has shown that 80 percent of the consumers like curly french fries. The researcher wishes to have a standard error of 6 percent or less and be 95 percent confident of an estimate to be made about curly french fry consumption from a survey. What sample size should be used for a simple random sample?

7. You are in charge of planning a chili cook-off. You must make sure that there are plenty of samples for the patrons of the cook-off. The following standards have been set: a confidence level of 99 percent and an error of less than 4 ounces per cooking team. Last year's cook-off had a standard deviation in amount of chili cooked of 3 ounces. What is the necessary sample size?

8. Based on a client's requirements of a confidence interval of 99.74 percent and acceptable sampling error of 2 percent, a sample size of 500 is calculated. The cost is estimated at $20,000. The client replies that the budget for this project is $17,000. What are the alternatives?

9. A marketing researcher must determine how many telephone numbers she needs order from a sample provider to complete a survey of ATM users. The goal is to complete 400 interviews with ATM users. From past experience, she estimates that 60 percent of the phone numbers provided will be working phone numbers. The estimated incidence rate (percentage of people contacted who are ATM users) is 43 percent. Finally, she estimates from previous surveys that 35 percent of the people contacted will agree to complete the survey. How many telephone numbers should she order?

WORKING THE NET

1. Log on to **http://research-advisors.com/documents/SampleSize-web.xls** to get a download of an Excel spreadsheet for a sample size table. The spreadsheet enables users to change the margin of error, confidence level, and population size. Experiment with different combinations.

2. For an online statistical power calculator, go to: **www.dssresearch.com/toolkit/spcalc/power.asp** Estimate the statistical power (type II error or beta error) for existing survey projects.

3. Use the sample size calculator online at **www.dssresearch.com/toolkit/sscalc/size.asp** to work out these problems. What size samples are needed for a statistical power of 70 percent in detecting a difference of 5 percent between the estimated percentages of recent CD buyers in two independent samples? Assume an expected percentage in the range of 50 percent and an alpha error of 5 percent.

REAL-LIFE RESEARCH • 14.1

Concomm

Concomm Telecom is a major provider of comprehensive communications services for residential users. It offers a package including local and long-distance telephone, digital cable, Internet, and monitored home security service. Concomm is in the process of building awareness of its brand in selected areas of the Southwestern United States. Now in its second year, the company plans to spend $22 million to promote awareness and brand image of its comprehensive package of services in the target area. Brand image and awareness are important to Concomm because it is competing with a number of much larger and better financed competitors, including AT&T, Verizon, and Comcast.

In the first year of the brand image campaign, Concomm spent $12 million pursuing the same goals of increasing awareness and brand image. In order to see if the campaign was successful, the company conducted tracking research by telephone. It conducted a pretest before the campaign began and a posttest at the end of the year. The surveys were designed to measure awareness and image of Concomm. Changes in either measure from the pretest to the posttest were to be attributed to the effects of the ad campaign. No other elements of the marketing strategy were changed during the course of the campaign.

Unaided, or top-of-mind, awareness ("What companies come to mind when you think of companies that provide residential communication services?") increased from 21 percent in the pretest to 25 percent in the posttest. In the pretest, 42 percent reported having a positive image of Concomm. This figure increased to 44 percent in the posttest. Though both key measures increased, the same sizes for the two tests were relatively small. Random samples of 100 consumers were used for both tests. Sampling error for the measure of awareness at 95.44 percent confidence is ± 8.7 percent. The comparable figure for the image measure is ± 9.9 percent. The value used for P in the formula is the posttest result. With these relatively large sampling errors and the relatively small changes in awareness and image, Concomm could only say with 95.44 percent confidence that awareness in the posttest was 25 percent ± 8.7 percent, or in the range of 16.3 percent to 33.7 percent. In regard to the image measure, it could only say with 95.44 percent confidence that the percentage of consumers with a positive image of Concomm in the posttest was 44 percent ± 9.9 percent, or in the range of 34.1 percent to 53.9 percent. Based on the relatively small changes in awareness and image and the relatively large errors associated with these measures, Concomm could not conclude with any confidence that either measure had actually changed.

The CEO of Concomm is concerned about the amount of money being spent on advertising and wants to know whether the advertising is actually achieving what it is supposed to achieve. She wants a more sensitive test so that a definitive conclusion can be reached regarding the effect of the advertising.

Questions

1. Show how the sampling errors for the posttest measures were calculated.
2. If the CEO wants to have 95.44 percent confidence that the estimates of awareness and positive image are within ± 2 percent of the true value, what is the required sample size?
3. What is the required sample size if the CEO wants to be 99.74 percent confident?
4. If the current budget for conducting telephone interviews is $20,000 and the cost per interview is $19, can Concomm reach the goal specified in question 3? With the $20,000 budget, what error levels can it reach for both measures? What is the budget required to reach the goal set in question 3?

REAL-LIFE RESEARCH • 14.2

HealthLife

HealthLife is a leading provider of employee wellness programs to Fortune 500 companies. Its programs are designed to improve employee health and wellness with the goal of developing a healthier, happier, more productive workforce. In addition, it has shown that its programs reduce medical claims for its clients. This is an important consideration given that nearly all of its clients are self-insured in regard to medical benefits. The company offers an array of programs and can tailor programs to the needs of individual clients. HealthLife is about to start the second year of a brand image campaign.

The company is planning to spend $3.5 million to promote awareness and a positive image of its services among Fortune 500 companies and their employees. It is pursuing this strategy because the market for its services is becoming more competitive as interest in employee wellness has grown and as more competitors have entered the market in recent years.

In the first year of the brand image campaign, HealthLife spent $3 million pursuing the same goals of increasing awareness and building its image. In order to see if the campaign was successful, the company conducted tracking research by telephone. It conducted a pretest before the campaign began and a posttest on its conclusion. The surveys were designed to measure awareness of HealthLife and the image of HealthLife among decision makers in Fortune 500 companies. Healthlife estimates an average of 20 executives were involved in the decision-making process for the purchase of its services per company, or a total target audience of around 10,000. Changes in either measure from the pretest to the posttest were to be attributed to the effects of the ad campaign. No other elements of this marketing strategy were changed during the course of the campaign.

Unaided or top-of-mind awareness (what companies come to mind when you think of companies that provide group health care coverage?) increased from 21 percent in the pretest to 25 percent in the posttest. In the pretest, 42 percent reported having a positive image of HealthLife. This figure increased to 44 percent in the posttest. Though both key measures increased, the sample sizes for the two tests were relatively small. Random samples of 100 decision makers were used for both tests. Sampling error for the measure of awareness at 95 percent confidence is ± 8.7 percent. The comparable figure for the image measure is ± 9.9 percent. The value used for p in the formula is the posttest result. With these relatively large sampling errors and the relatively small changes in awareness and image, HealthLife could only say with 95 percent confidence that awareness in the posttest was 25 percent ± 8.7 percent, or in the range of 16.3 percent to 33.7 percent. In regard to the image measure, it could only say with 95 percent confidence that the percent of targeted decision makers with a positive image of HealthLife in the posttest was 44 percent ± 9.9 percent, or in the range of 34.1 percent to 53.9 percent. Based on the relatively small changes in awareness and positive image and the relatively large errors associated with these measures, HealthLife could not conclude with any confidence that either measure had actually changed.

The CEO of HealthLife is concerned about the amount of money being spent on advertising and wants to know whether the advertising is achieving what it is supposed to achieve. She wants a more sensitive test so that a definitive conclusion regarding the effect of the advertising can be reached.

surveysolutions XP

SPSS JUMP START FOR CHI-SQUARE TEST

Questions

1. Show how the sampling error calculations for the posttest measures were calculated.
2. If the CEO wanted to be sure that the estimates of awareness and positive image are within ± 2 percent of the true value at 95 percent confidence, what is the required sample size?
3. Using all the same information used in question 2, what is the required sample size if the CEO wants to be 99.5 percent confident?
4. If the current budget for conducting the telephone interviews is $20,000 and the cost per interview is $19, can HealthLife reach the goal specified in question 3?

What error levels can it reach for both measures with the $20,000 budget? What is the required budget to reach the goal set in question 3?

Exercise 1: Sample Size Determination Using the Sample Means Method SPSS-H1

1. Go to the Wiley Web site at **www.wiley.com/college/mcdaniel** and download the *Segmenting the College Student Market for Movie Attendance* database to SPSS windows. Using the *Segmenting the College Student Market for Movie Attendance* database, assume that the most important items in the survey are in question 5, which has nine movie items in which respondents rate their relative importance (download a copy of the *Segmenting the College Student Market for Movie Attendance* questionnaire). Notice the computer coding for each of the variables, which is the same as that in the *variable view* option on the SPSS Data Editor.

2. The Sample Means method of sample size determination consists of:
   i.   required confidence level (z)
   ii. level of tolerable error (e)
   iii. estimated population variance (σ)
   iv. estimated sample size (n)
   v.   *Formula:* $n = (z^2 * \sigma^2)/e^2$

3. Of the various methods of deriving sample size, estimated population standard deviation can be estimated based on prior studies, expert judgment, or by conducting a pilot sample. For this problem, we are going to estimate population standard deviation using a ***pilot sample***. To do this you will use only the first 200 cases in the *Segmenting the College Student Market for Movie Attendance* database. Invoke the *data/select cases* sequence to select the first 200 cases in the database. We are assuming that these are responses to a pilot sample and we will use them to estimate the needed sample size.

4. Use the *analyze/descriptive statistics/descriptive* sequence to compute the standard deviation for variables Q5a–Q5i. We are assuming that each of the nine variables is equally important with respect to the research objective.

5. From your knowledge of sample size determination, you should know that the variable to select for sample size determination is the one with the largest standard deviation. Select that variable.

Answer the following questions:

1. Which of the nine movie theater items had the largest standard deviation?

   _____

2. Invoke the sample means method of sample size determination to make the necessary computations for each of the following:
   a. Compute sample size given the following:
      i.   Required confidence level (Z) is 95.44%.
      ii. Tolerable error (e) is .1 or 1/10 of a response point.
      iii. Standard deviation (σ) = _____
      iv. Sample size (n) = _____

b. Compute sample size given the following:

    i.   Required confidence level (Z) is 99.72%.

    ii.   Tolerable level (e) is .1 or 1/10 of a response point.

    iii. Standard deviation (σ) = _____

    iv. Sample size (n) = _____

3.   How do your computed sample sizes in the problems above compare to the total number of cases in the *Segmenting the College Student Market for Movie Attendance* database?

    _____

4.   We are going to assume that the objective of our research concerning students' attendance at movies can be expressed as a dichotomy (greater or lesser, etc.); for example, it doesn't matter how much one group attends movies over another group, but just *who* attends the most. To accomplish this we can use the much less complicated *sample proportions* formula. We are going to assume that we have no prior studies, hence, in the sample proportions formula $P = .5$ and $(1 - P) = .5$. ***You will not need SPSS to assist you with this computation.***

a. Compute sample size given the following:

    i.   Required confidence level (Z) is 95.44%.

    ii.   Tolerable error (e) is .05 or accuracy within 5% of the true population mean.

    iii. Standard deviation $P = .5$ and $(1 - P) = .5$

    iv. Sample size (n) = _____

c. Compute sample size given the following:

    i.   Required confidence level (Z) is 99.72%.

    ii.   Tolerable error (e) is .03 or accuracy within 3% of the true population mean.

    iii. Standard deviation $P = .5$ and $(1 - P) = .5$

    iv. Sample size (n) = _____

Exercise 2: Determining the Reliability/Confidence of Sample Results

1.   In the subsequent exercise, the objective will not be to determine the needed sample size, but to evaluate the confidence level of results derived from the entire *Segmenting the College Student Market for Movie Attendance* database. To evaluate this type of confidence, using the sample means formula, solve for Z instead of n. Hence, use the formula $Z^2 = n * e^2/\sigma^2$. Then take the square root of Z^2. Go to the normal distribution table in the appendix of your text to determine the confidence level associated with the database. For the sample proportions formula, solve for Z using the formula $Z^2 = (n * e^2)/[P(1 - P)]$, then take the square root of Z^2.

2.   For this problem again assume that question #5 has the most important questions in the questionnaire, with respect to the research objectives. Using the *analyze/ descriptive statistics/descriptives* sequence, compute the standard deviation for variables Q5a–Q5i. We are assuming that each of the nine variables are equally important with respect to the research objective. <u>Again, choose the variable with the largest standard deviation</u> to input into the analysis.

3. Given the preceding, compute the confidence level associated with the *Segmenting the College Student Market for Movie Attendance* database, given the following:

 1. a. Tolerable error is .1 or 1/10 of a response point

    b. Sample size = 500

    c. Standard deviation _____

 2. Confidence Level = _____ %

 3. How do the results in 2, above compare to the results in 2 of the sample size determination problem?

    _____

4. <u>Sample Proportions Formula</u>: Given the following information, compute the confidence level associated with the *Segmenting the College Student Marketing for Movie Attendance* database. ***You will not need SPSS to make this computation.***

 a. Tolerable error is .05 or 5%.

 b. Sample size = 500

 c. Standard deviation $P = .5$ and $(1 - P) = .5$

 Confidence Level = _____ %

 How do the results in this problem compare to the confidence level in #2 of (3)?

 _____

Data Processing And Fundamental Data Analysis

CHAPTER 15

LEARNING OBJECTIVES

→ **1.** To get an overview of the data analysis procedure.

→ **2.** To develop an understanding of the importance and nature of quality control checks.

→ **3.** To understand the data entry process and data entry alternatives.

→ **4.** To learn how surveys are tabulated.

→ **5.** To learn how to set up and interpret cross tabulations.

→ **6.** To comprehend the basic techniques of statistical analysis.

Okay, now we have reached the point where the survey is in the field (data collection is under way). At this point, we need to begin a number of processes that will, upon their completion, prepare the data being produced for the analysis phase. Although some of the elements are clerical in nature, these processes are critical in making sure that the data have integrity and are free of errors related to the process of taking down what respondents said in answering our questions and moving those answers to tabular and statistical displays. The steps in this process are covered in this chapter.

Overview of the Data Analysis Procedure

Once data collection has been completed and questionnaires have been returned, the researcher may be facing anywhere from a few hundred to several thousand interviews, each ranging from a few pages to 20 or more. DSS Research recently completed a mail study involving 1,300 questionnaires of 10 pages each. The 13,000 pages amounted to a stack of paper more than 3 feet high. How should a researcher transform all the information contained on 13,000 pages of completed questionnaires into a format that will permit the summarization necessary for detailed analysis? At one extreme, the researcher could read all the interviews, make notes while reading them, and draw some conclusions from this review of the questionnaires. The limitations of this approach are fairly obvious. Instead of this haphazard and inefficient approach, professional researchers follow a five-step procedure for data analysis:

Step One.	Validation and editing (quality control)
Step Two.	Coding
Step Three.	Data entry
Step Four.	Logical cleaning of data
Step Five.	Tabulation and statistical analysis

Step One: Validation and Editing

The purpose of the first step is twofold. The researcher wants to make sure that all the interviews actually were conducted as specified (validation) and that the questionnaires have been filled out properly and completely (editing).

Validation

First, the researcher must determine, to the extent possible, that each of the questionnaires to be processed represents a valid interview. Here, we are using the term *valid* in a different sense than in Chapter 10. In Chapter 10, validity was defined as the extent to which the item being measured was actually measured. In this chapter, **validation** is defined as the process of ascertaining that interviews were conducted as specified. In this context, no assessment is made regarding the validity of the measurement. The goal of validation is solely to detect interviewer fraud or failure to follow key instructions. You may have noticed that questionnaires presented throughout the text almost always have a place to record the respondent's name, address, and telephone number. This information is seldom used in any way in the analysis of the data; it is collected only to provide a basis for validation.

Professional researchers know that interviewer cheating does happen. Various studies have documented the existence and prevalence of interviewer falsification of several types.

➤ **validation**
Process of ascertaining that interviews actually were conducted as specified.

For this reason, validation is an integral and necessary step in the data processing stage of a marketing research project.

After all the interviews have been completed, the research firm recontacts a certain percentage of the respondents surveyed by each interviewer. Typically, this percentage ranges from 10 to 20 percent. If a particular interviewer surveyed 50 people and the research firm normally validates at a 10 percent rate, 5 respondents surveyed by that interviewer would be recontacted to determine:

1. Was the person actually interviewed?

2. Did the person who was interviewed qualify to be interviewed according to the screening questions on the survey? For example, the interview may have required that the person being interviewed come from a family with an annual household income of $25,000 or more. On validation, the respondent would again be asked whether the annual household income for his or her family was $25,000 or more per year.

3. Was the interview conducted in the required manner? For example, a mall survey should have been conducted in the designated mall. Was this particular respondent interviewed in the mall or was she or he interviewed at some other place, such as a restaurant or someone's home?

4. Did the interviewer cover the entire survey? Sometimes interviewers recognize that a potential respondent is in a hurry and may not have time to complete the entire survey. If respondents for that particular survey are difficult to find, the interviewer may be motivated to ask the respondent a few questions at the beginning and a few questions at the end and then fill out the rest of the survey without the respondent's input. Validation for this particular problem would involve asking respondents whether they were asked various questions from different points in the interview.

> "A Mall Survey Should be conducted in the designated mall. An important part of data analysis is validating that the data were gathered as specified."

Validation also usually involves checking for other problems. For example: Was the interviewer courteous? Did the interviewer speculate about the client's identity or the purpose of the survey? Does the respondent have any other comments about the interviewer or the interview experience?.

The purpose of the validation process, as noted earlier, is to ensure that interviews were administered properly and completely. Researchers must be sure that the research results on which they are basing their recommendations reflect the legitimate responses of target individuals.

Editing

Whereas validation involves checking for interviewer cheating and failure to follow instructions, **editing** involves checking for interviewer and respondent mistakes. Paper questionnaires usually are edited at least twice before being submitted for data entry. First, they may be edited by the field service firm that conducted the interviews, and then they are edited by the marketing research firm that hired the field service firm to do the interviewing. CATI, Internet, and other software-driven surveys have built-in logical checking. The editing process for paper surveys involves manual checking for a number of problems, including the following:

> ➤ **editing**
> Process of ascertaining that questionnaires were filled out properly and completely.

1. ***Whether the interviewer failed to ask certain questions or record answers for certain questions.*** In the questionnaire shown in Exhibit 15.1, no answer was recorded for question 19. According to the structure of the questionnaire, this question should have been asked of all respondents. Also, the respondent's name does not give a clear indication of gender. The purpose of the first edit—the field edit—is to

EXHIBIT 15.1 | Sample Questionnaire

Consumer Survey
Mobile Telephone Survey Questionnaire

Long Branch—Asbury, N.J.
(01-03) _001_

Date _1-05-01_

Respondent Telephone Number _____ _201-555-2322_ _____

Hello. My name is Sally with POST Research. May I please speak with the male or female head of the household?

(IF INDIVIDUAL NOT AVAILABLE, RECORD NAME AND CALLBACK INFORMATION ON SAMPLING FORM.)

(WHEN MALE/FEMALE HEAD OF HOUSEHOLD COMES TO PHONE): Hello, my name is _____, with POST Research. Your number was randomly selected, and I am not trying to sell you anything. I simply want to ask you a few questions about a new type of telephone service.

1. First, how many telephone calls do you make during a typical day?

(04)
0–2 1
3–5 2
6–10 . . . . ③
11–15 4
16–20 5
More than 20 6
Don't know 7

Now, let me tell you about a new service called cellular mobile telephone service, which is completely wireless. You can get either a portable model that may be carried in your coat pocket or a model mounted in any vehicle. You will be able to receive calls and make calls, no matter where you are. Although cellular phones are wireless, the voice quality is similar to your present phone service. This is expected to be a time-saving convenience for household use.

This new cellular mobile phone service may soon be widely available in your area.

2. Now, let me explain to you the cost of this wireless service. Calls will cost 26 cents a minute plus normal toll charges. In addition, the monthly minimum charge for using the service will be $7.50 and rental of a cellular phone will be about $40. Of course, you can buy the equipment instead of leasing it. At this price, do you think you would be very likely, somewhat likely, somewhat unlikely, or very unlikely to subscribe to the new phone service?

(05)
Very likely. 1
Somewhat likely . . . . ②
Somewhat unlikely 3
Very unlikely. . . . .(GO TO QUESTION 16) 4
Don't know . . . .(GO TO QUESTION 16) 5

INTERVIEWER—IF "VERY UNLIKELY" OR "DON'T KNOW," GO TO QUESTION 16.

3. Do you think it is likely that your employer would furnish you with one of these phones for your job?

(06)
No . . . .(GO TO QUESTION 5) 1
Don't know . . . .(GO TO QUESTION 5) 2
Yes. . . . .(CONTINUE). . . . . ③

INTERVIEWER—IF "NO" OR "DON'T KNOW," GO TO QUESTION 5; OTHERWISE CONTINUE.

4. If your employer did furnish you with a wireless phone, would you also purchase one for household use?

(07)
Yes. . . . .(CONTINUE). . . . . ①
No . . . .(GO TO QUESTION 16) 2
Don't know . . . .(GO TO QUESTION 16) 3

5. Please give me your best estimate of the number of mobile phones your household would use (write in "DK" for "Don't know").

Number of Units _____ _01_ _____ (08–09)

EXHIBIT 15.1 | *(Continued)*

6. Given that cellular calls made or received will cost 26 cents a minute plus normal toll charges during weekdays, how many calls on the average would you expect to make in a typical weekday?

RECORD NUMBER _____ *06* _____ (10–11)

7. About how many minutes would your average cellular call last during the week?

RECORD NUMBER _____ *05* _____ (12–13)

8. Weekend cellular calls made or received will cost 8 cents per minute plus normal toll charges. Given this, about how many cellular calls on the average would you expect to make in a typical Saturday or Sunday?

RECORD NUMBER _____ *00* _____ (14–15)

9. About how many minutes would your average cellular call last on Saturday or Sunday?

RECORD NUMBER _____ (16–17)

10. You may recall from my previous description that two types of cellular phone units will be available. The vehicle phone may be installed in any vehicle. The portable phone will be totally portable—it can be carried in a briefcase, purse, or coat pocket. The totally portable phones may cost about 25 percent more and may have a more limited transmitting range in some areas than the vehicle phone. Do you think you would prefer portable or vehicle phones if you were able to subscribe to this service?

	(18)
Portable	1
Vehicle	②
Both	3
Don't know	4

11. Would you please tell me whether you, on the average, would use a mobile phone about once a week, less than once a week, or more than once a week from the following geographic locations.

	Less Than Once a Week	Once a Week	More Than Once a Week	Never	
Monmouth County	1	2	③	4	(19)
(IF "NEVER," SKIP TO QUESTION 16)					
Sandy Hook	1	2	3	④	(20)
Keansburg	1	2	3	④	(21)
Atlantic Highlands	1	2	③	4	(22)
Matawan-Middletown	①	2	3	4	(23)
Red Bank	①	2	3	4	(24)
Holmdel	1	2	③	4	(25)
Eatontown	1	②	3	4	(26)
Long Branch	1	2	3	④	(27)
Freehold	1	2	3	④	(28)
Manalapan	1	2	3	④	(29)
Cream Ridge	1	2	3	④	(30)
Belmar	1	2	3	④	(31)
Point Pleasant	1	2	③	4	(32)

I'm going to describe to you a list of possible extra features of the proposed cellular service. Each option I'm going to describe will cost not more than $3.00 a month per phone. Would you please tell me if you would be very interested, interested, or uninterested in each feature:

	Very Interested	Interested	Uninterested
12. Call forwarding (the ability to transfer any call coming in to your mobile phone to any other phone).	①	2	3 (33)
13. No answer transfer (service that redirects calls to another number if your phone is unanswered).	1	2	③ (34)

EXHIBIT 15.1	Sample Questionnaire *(Continued)*

	Very Interested	Interested	Uninterested
14. Call waiting (a signal that another person is trying to call you while you are using your phone).	1	②	3 (35)
15. Voice mailbox (a recording machine that will take the caller's message and relay it to you at a later time. This service will be provided at $5.00 per month).	1	2	③ (36)

16. What is your age group? (READ BELOW)

(37)
Under 25 1
25–44 . . . . ②
45–64 3
65 and over 4
Refused, no answer, or don't know 5

17. What is your occupation?

(38)
Manager, official, or proprietor . . . . ①
Professional (doctors, lawyers, etc.) 2
Technical (engineers, computer programmers, draftsmen, etc.) 3
Office worker/clerical 4
Sales 5
Skilled worker or foreman 6
Unskilled worker 7
Teacher 8
Homemaker, student, retired 9
Not now employed X
Refused . . . . Y

18. Into which category did your total family income fall in 2002? (READ BELOW)

(39)
Under $15,000 1
$15,000–$24,999 2
$25,000–$49,999 3
$50,000–$74,999 4
$75,000 and over . . . . ⑤
Refused, no answer, don't know 6

19. (INTERVIEWER—RECORD SEX OF RESPONDENT):

(40)
Male 1
Female 2

20. May I have your name? My office calls about 10 percent of the people I talk with to verify that I have conducted the interview.
Gave name . . . . ①
Refused 2

_____*Jordan Beasley*_____
Name

Thank you for your time. Have a good day.

→ skip pattern
Sequence in which later questions are asked, based on a respondent's answer to an earlier question or questions.

identify these types of problems when there is still time to recontact the respondent and determine the appropriate answer to questions that were not asked. This may also be done at the second edit (by the marketing research firm), but in many instances there is not time to recontact the respondent and the interview has to be discarded.

2. **Whether skip patterns were followed.** According to the **skip pattern** in question 2 in Exhibit 15.1, if the answer to this question is "Very unlikely" or "Don't know," the interviewer should skip to question 16. The editor needs to make sure that the

Exhibit 15.2

Recording of Open-Ended Questions

A. Example of Improper Interviewer Recording of Response to an Open-Ended Question

Question: Why do you go to Burger King most often among fast food/quick service restaurants? (PROBE)

Response recorded:
The consumer seemed to think Burger King had better tasting food and better quality ingredients.

B. Example of Interviewer Failure to Probe a Response

Question: Same as Part A.

Only response recorded:
Because I like it.

C. Example of Proper Recording and Probing

Question: Same as Part A.

Response recorded:
Because I like it. (P)* I like it, and I go there most often because it is the closest place to where I work. (AE)** No.

*(P) is an interviewer mark indicating he or she has probed a response.

**(AE) is interviewer shorthand for "Anything else?" This gives the respondent an opportunity to expand on the original answer.

---

interviewer followed instructions. Sometimes, particularly during the first few interviews in a particular study, interviewers get mixed up and skip when they should not or fail to skip when they should.

3. ***Whether the interviewer paraphrased respondents' answers to open-ended questions.*** Marketing researchers and their clients usually are very interested in the responses to open-ended questions. The quality of the responses, or at least what was recorded, is an excellent indicator of the competence of the interviewer who recorded them. Interviewers are trained to record responses verbatim and not to paraphrase or insert their own language. They also are instructed to probe the initial response. The first part of Exhibit 15.2 shows an example of an interviewer's paraphrasing and interpretation of a response to an open-ended question. The second part of Exhibit 15.2 shows the result of interviewer failure to probe a response. The response is useless from a decision-making perspective. It comes as no surprise that the respondent goes to Burger King most often because he likes it. The third part of Exhibit 15.2 shows how an initial meaningless response can be expanded to a useful response by means of proper probing. A proper probe to the answer "Because I like it" would be "Why do you like it?" or "What do you like about it?" The respondent then indicates that he goes there most often because it is the fast-food restaurant most convenient to his place of work.

The person doing the editing must make judgment calls in regard to substandard responses to open-ended questions. She or he must decide at what point particular answers are so limited as to be useless and whether respondents should be recontacted.

The editing process is extremely tedious and time-consuming. However, it is a very important step in the processing of survey responses.

Step Two: Coding

As discussed in Chapter 12, **coding** refers to the process of grouping and assigning numeric codes to the various responses to a particular question. Most questions on surveys are closed-ended and precoded, meaning that numeric codes have been assigned to the various

> **coding** Process of grouping and assigning numeric codes to the various responses to a question.

responses on the questionnaire. All answers to closed-ended questions should be precoded, as they are in question 1 on the questionnaire in Exhibit 15.1. Note that each answer has a numeric code to its right; the answer "0–2" has the code 1, the answer "3–5" has the code 2, and so on. The interviewer can record the response by circling the numeric code next to the answer given by the respondent. In this case, the respondent's answer was seven calls per day. The code 3 next to the category "6–10" (calls per day) is circled.

Open-ended questions create a coding dilemma. They were phrased in an open-ended manner because the researcher either had no idea what answers to expect or wanted a richer response than is possible with a closed-ended question. As with editing, the process of coding responses to open-ended questions is tedious and time-consuming. In addition, the procedure is to some degree subjective.[1] For these reasons, researchers tend to avoid open-ended questions unless they are absolutely necessary.

Coding Process

The process of coding responses to open-ended questions includes the following steps:

1. *List responses.* Coders at the research firm prepare lists of the actual responses given to each open-ended question on a particular survey. In studies of a few hundred respondents, all responses may be listed. With larger samples, responses given by a sample of respondents are listed. The listing of responses may be done as part of the editing process or as a separate step, often by the same individuals who edited the questionnaires.

2. *Consolidate responses.* A sample list of responses to an open-ended question is provided in Exhibit 15.3. Examination of this list indicates that a number of the responses can be interpreted to mean essentially the same thing; therefore, they can be appropriately consolidated into a single category. This process of consolidation might yield the list shown in Exhibit 15.4. Consolidating requires a number of subjective decisions—for example, does response number 4 in Exhibit 15.3 belong in category 1, or should it have its own category? These decisions typically are made by a qualified research analyst and may involve client input.

EXHIBIT 15.3	Sample of Responses to Open-Ended Question

Question: Why do you drink that brand of beer? (BRAND MENTIONED IN ANSWER TO PREVIOUS QUESTION)

Sample responses:
1. Because it tastes better.
2. It has the best taste.
3. I like the way it tastes.
4. I don't like the heavy taste of other beers.
5. It is the cheapest.
6. I buy whatever beer is on sale. It is on sale most of the time.
7. It doesn't upset my stomach the way other brands do.
8. Other brands give me headaches. This one doesn't.
9. It has always been my brand.
10. I have been drinking it for over 20 years.
11. It is the brand that most of the guys at work drink.
12. All my friends drink it.
13. It is the brand my wife buys at the grocery store.
14. It is my wife's/husband's favorite brand.
15. I have no idea.
16. Don't know.
17. No particular reason.

EXHIBIT 15.4	Consolidated Response Categories and Codes for Open-Ended Responses from Beer Study		
Response Category Descriptor	Response Items from Exhibit 14.1 Included	Assigned Numeric Code	
Tastes better/like taste/tastes better than others	1, 2, 3, 4	1	
Low/lower price	5, 6	2	
Does not cause headache, stomach problems	7, 8	3	
Long-term use, habit	9, 10	4	
Friends drink it/influence of friends	11, 12	5	
Wife/husband drinks/buys it	13, 14	6	

EXHIBIT 15.5	Example Questionnaire Setup for Open-Ended Questions

37. Why do you drink that brand of beer? (BRAND MENTIONED IN PREVIOUS QUESTION)?

(48) _____ 2

Because it's cheaper. (P) Nothing. (AE) Nothing.

3. *Set codes.* A numeric code is assigned to each of the categories on the final consolidated list of responses. Code assignments for the sample beer study question are shown in Exhibit 15.4.

4. *Enter codes.* After responses have been listed and consolidated and codes set, the last step is the actual entry of codes. This involves several substeps:

   a. Read responses to individual open-ended questions on questionnaires.

   b. Match individual responses with the consolidated list of response categories and determine the appropriate numeric code for each response.

   c. Write the numeric code in the appropriate place on the questionnaire for the response to the particular question (see Exhibit 15.5) or enter the appropriate code in the database electronically.[2]

Here's an example of the process, using the listing of responses shown in Exhibit 15.3 and the consolidation and setting of codes shown in Exhibit 15.4.

■ You turn to the first questionnaire and read this response to the question "Why do you drink that brand of beer?": "Because it's cheaper."

■ You compare this response with the consolidated response categories and decide that it best fits into the "Low/lower price" category. The numeric code associated with this category is 2 (see Exhibit 15.4).

■ You enter the code in the appropriate place on the questionnaire (see Exhibit 15.5).

Automated Coding Systems

With CATI and Internet surveys, data entry and coding are completely eliminated for closed-ended questions. However, when the text of open-ended questions is electronically captured, a coding process is still required. A number of developments are making it likely that the tedious coding process for open-ended questions will soon be replaced with computer-based systems requiring limited high-level human intervention and decision making.

The TextSmart module of SPSS is one example of the new breed of automated coding systems. Algorithms based on semiotics[3] are at the heart of these systems and show great promise for speeding up the coding process, reducing its cost, and increasing its objectivity. Basically, these algorithms use the power of computers to search for patterns in open-ended responses and in group responses, based on certain keywords and phrases.

Step Three: Data Entry

→ data entry
Process of converting information to an electronic format.

Once the questionnaires have been validated, edited, and coded, it's time for the next step in the process—data entry. We use the term **data entry** here to refer to the process of converting information to a form that can be read by a computer. This process requires a data entry device, such as a computer terminal or a personal computer, and a storage medium, such as magnetic tape, a floppy disk, or a hard (magnetic) disk.

Intelligent Entry Systems

→ intelligent data entry
Form of data entry in which the information being entered into the data entry device is checked for internal logic.

Most data entry is done by means of intelligent entry systems. With **intelligent data entry**, the information entered is checked for internal logic. Intelligent entry systems can be programmed to avoid certain types of errors at the point of data entry, such as invalid or wild codes and violation of skip patterns.

Consider question 2 on the questionnaire in Exhibit 15.1. The five valid answers have the associated numeric codes 1 through 5. An intelligent data entry system programmed for valid codes would permit the data entry operator to enter only one of these codes in the field reserved for the response to this question. If the operator attempts to enter a code other than those defined as valid, the device will inform the data entry operator in some manner that there is a problem. The data entry device, for example, might beep and display a message on the screen that the entered code is invalid. It will not advance to the next appropriate field until the code has been corrected. Of course, it is still possible to incorrectly enter a 3 rather than the correct answer 2. Referring again to question 2, note that if the answer to the question is "Very unlikely" or "Don't know," then the data entry operator should skip to question 16. An intelligent data entry device will make this skip automatically.

The Data Entry Process

The validated, edited, and coded questionnaires have been given to a data entry operator seated in front of a personal computer. The data entry software system has been programmed for intelligent entry. The actual data entry process is ready to begin. Usually, the data are entered directly from the questionnaires, because experience has shown that a large number of errors are introduced when questionnaire data are transposed manually to coding sheets. Going directly from the questionnaire to the data entry device and associated storage medium is much more accurate and efficient. To better understand the mechanics of the process, look again at Exhibit 15.1.

■ In the upper right-hand corner of the questionnaire, the number 001 is written. This number uniquely identifies the particular questionnaire, which should be the first questionnaire in the stack that the data entry operator is preparing to enter. This number is an important point of reference because it permits the data entry staff to refer back to the original document if any errors are identified in connection with the data input.

■ To the left of the handwritten number 001 is (01–03). This tells the data entry operator that 001 should be entered into fields 01–03 of the data record. Throughout the questionnaire, the numbers in parentheses indicate the proper location on the data record for the circled code for the answer to each question. Question 1 has (04) associated with the codes for the answers to the question. Thus, the answer to this question would be entered in field 04 of the data record. Now, take a look at the open-ended question in Exhibit 15.5. As with closed-ended questions, the number in parentheses refers to the field on the data record where the code or codes for the response to this question should be entered. Note the number 2 written in to the right of (48); a 2 should be entered in field 48 of the data record associated with this questionnaire.

Exhibit 15.1 clearly illustrates the relationship between the layout of the questionnaire, in terms of codes (numbers associated with different answers to questions) and fields (places on the data record where the code is entered) and the layout of the data record.

Scanning

As all students know, the scanning of documents (test scoring sheets) has been around for decades. It has been widely used in schools and universities as an efficient way to capture and score responses to multiple-choice questions. However, until more recently, its use in marketing research has been limited. This limited use can be attributed to two factors: setup costs and the need to record all responses with a No. 2 pencil. Setup costs include the cost of special paper, special ink in the printing process, and very precise placement of the bubbles for recording responses. The break-even point, at which the savings in data entry costs exceeded the setup costs is in the 10,000 to 12,000 survey range. Therefore, for most surveys, scanning was not feasible.

However, changes in **scanning technology** and the advent of personal computers have changed this equation. Today, questionnaires prepared with any one of a number of Windows word-processing software packages and printed on a laser printer or by a standard printing process can be readily scanned, using the appropriate software and a scanner attached to a personal computer. In addition, the latest technology permits respondents to fill out the survey using almost any type of writing implement (any type of pencil, ballpoint pen, or ink pen). This eliminates the need to provide respondents with a No. 2 pencil and greatly simplifies the process of mailing surveys. Finally, the latest technology does not require respondents to carefully shade the entire circle or square next to their response choices; they can put shading, a check mark, an X, or any other type of mark in the circle or square provided for the response choice.[4]

As a result of these developments, the use of scannable surveys is growing dramatically. An analyst who expects more than 400 to 500 surveys to be completed will find scannable surveys to be cost-effective.

Though no reliable volume figures are available, it is an accepted fact that the amount of survey data being captured electronically is increasing. For example, electronic data capture is used in computer-assisted telephone interviewing, Internet surveys, disks-by-mail surveys, and TouchScreen kiosk surveys.

scanning technology
Form of data entry in which responses on questionnaires are read in automatically by the data entry device.

Step Four: Logical Cleaning of Data

At this point, the data from all questionnaires have been entered and stored in the computer that will be used to process them. It is time to do final error checking before proceeding to the tabulation and statistical analysis of the survey results. Many colleges have one or more statistical software packages available for the tabulation and statistical analysis of data, including SAS (Statistical Analysis System) and SPSS (Statistical Package for the Social Sciences), which have proven to be the most popular mainframe computer statistical packages. Most colleges have personal computer versions of SPSS and SAS, in addition to other PC statistical packages. The number of other PC packages is large and growing.

Regardless of which computer package is used, it is important to do a final computerized error check of the data, or what is sometimes referred to as **logical or machine cleaning of data.** This may be done through error checking routines and/or marginal reports.

Some computer programs permit the user to write **error checking routines.** These routines include a number of statements to check for various conditions. For example, if a particular field on the data records for a study should be coded with only a 1 or a 2, a logical statement can be written to check for the presence of any other code in that field. Some of the more sophisticated packages generate reports indicating how many times a particular condition was violated and the data records on which it was violated. With this list, the user can refer to the original questionnaires and determine the appropriate values.

> **logical or machine cleaning of data**
> Final computerized error check of data.

> **error checking routines**
> Computer programs that accept instructions from the user to check for logical errors in the data.

Step Five: Tabulation and Statistical Analysis

The survey results have been stored in a computer file and are free of logical data entry and interviewer recording errors. The next step is to tabulate the survey results.

One-Way Frequency Tables

The most basic tabulation is the **one-way frequency table**, which shows the number of respondents who gave each possible answer to each question. An example of this type of table appears in Exhibit 15.6. This table shows that 144 consumers (48 percent) said they would choose a hospital in Saint Paul, 146 (48.7 percent) said they would choose a hospital in Minneapolis, and 10 (3.3 percent) said they didn't know which location they would choose. A printout is generated with a one-way frequency table for every question on the survey. In most instances, a one-way frequency table is the first summary of survey results seen by the research analyst. In addition to frequencies, these tables typically indicate the percentage of those responding who gave each possible response to a question.

An issue that must be dealt with when one-way frequency tables are generated is what base to use for the percentages for each table. There are three options for a base:

> **one-way frequency table**
> Table showing the number of respondents choosing each answer to a survey question.

1. **Total respondents.** If 300 people are interviewed in a particular study and the decision is to use total respondents as the base for calculating percentages, then the percentages in each one-way frequency table will be based on 300 respondents.

2. **Number of people asked the particular question.** Because most questionnaires have skip patterns, not all respondents are asked all questions. For example, suppose question 4 on a particular survey asked whether the person owned any dogs and 200 respondents indicated they were dog owners. Since questions 5 and 6 on the same survey were to be asked only of those individuals who owned a dog, questions 5 and 6 should have been asked of only 200 respondents. In most instances, it would be appropriate to use 200 as the base for percentages associated with the one-way frequency tables for questions 5 and 6.

3. **Number of people answering the question.** Another alternative base for computing percentages in one-way frequency tables is the number of people who actually answered a particular question. Under this approach, if 300 people were asked a particular question but 28 indicated "Don't know" or gave no response, then the base for the percentages would be 272.

EXHIBIT 15.6	One-Way Frequency Table

Q.30 If you or a member of your family were to require hospitalization in the future, and the procedure could be performed in Minneapolis or Saint Paul, where would you choose to go?

	Total
Total	300
	100 %
To a hospital in Saint Paul	144
	48.0 %
To a hospital in Minneapolis	146
	48.7 %
Don't know/no response	10
	3.3%

EXHIBIT 15.7	One-Way Frequency Table Using Three Different Bases for Calculating Percentages

Q.35 Why would you not consider going to Saint Paul for hospitalization?

	Total* Respondents	Total Asked	Total Answering
Total	300	64	56
	100 %	100 %	100 %
They aren't good/service poor	18	18	18
	6 %	28 %	32 %
Saint Paul doesn't have the services/equipment that Minneapolis does	17	17	17
	6 %	27 %	30 %
Saint Paul is too small	6	6	6
	2 %	9 %	11 %
Bad publicity	4	4	4
	1 %	6 %	7 %
Other	11	11	11
	4 %	17 %	20 %
Don't know/no response	8	8	
	3 %	13 %	

*A total of 300 respondents were surveyed. Only 64 were asked this question because in the previous question those respondents said they would not consider going to Saint Paul for hospitalization. Only 56 respondents gave an answer other than "Don't know."

Ordinarily, the number of people who were asked a particular question is used as the base for all percentages throughout the tabulations, but there may be special cases in which other bases are judged appropriate. Exhibit 15.7 is a one-way frequency table in which three different bases are used for calculating percentages.

Some questions, by their nature, solicit more than one response from respondents. For example, consumers might be asked to name all brands of vacuum cleaners that come to mind. Most people will be able to name more than one brand. Therefore, when these answers are tabulated, there will be more responses than respondents. If 200 consumers are surveyed and the average consumer names three brands, then there will be 200 respondents and 600 answers. The question is, should percentages in frequency tables showing the results for these questions be based on the number of respondents or the

The base for each percentage must be determined before one-way frequency tables are run. If a survey question asks whether the person has a dog and 200 respondents indicate that they do, further questions designated for dog owners should have only 200 respondents.

EXHIBIT 15.8	Percentages for a Multiple-Response Question Calculated on the Bases of Total Respondents and Total Responses

Q.34 To which of the following towns and cities would you consider going for hospitalization?

	Total Respondents	Total Responses
Total	300	818
	100 %	100 %
Minneapolis	265	265
	88.3 %	32.4 %
Saint Paul	240	240
	80.0 %	29.3 %
Bloomington	112	112
	37.3 %	13.7 %
Rochester	92	92
	30.7 %	11.2 %
Minnetonka	63	63
	21.0 %	7.7 %
Eagan	46	46
	15.3 %	5.6 %

number of responses? Exhibit 15.8 shows percentages calculated using both bases. Most commonly, marketing researchers compute percentages for multiple-response questions on the basis of the number of respondents, reasoning that the client is primarily interested in the proportion of people who gave a particular answer.

Cross Tabulations

cross tabulation Examination of the responses to one question relative to the responses to one or more other questions.

Cross tabulations are likely to be the next step in analysis. They represent a simple-to-understand, yet powerful, analytical tool. Many marketing research studies go no further than cross tabulations in terms of analysis. The idea is to look at the responses to one question in relation to the responses to one or more other questions. Exhibit 15.9 shows

EXHIBIT 15.9	Sample Cross Tabulation

Q.30 If you or a member of your family were to require hospitalization in the future, and the procedure could be performed in Minneapolis or Saint Paul, where would you choose to go?

		Age			
	Total	18–34	35–54	55–64	65 or Over
Total	300	65	83	51	100
	100%	100%	100%	100%	100%
To a hospital in Saint Paul	144	21	40	25	57
	48.0	32.3%	48.2%	49.0%	57.0%
To a hospital in Minneapolis	146	43	40	23	40
	48.7%	66.2%	48.2%	45.1%	40.0%
Don't know/no response	10	1	3	3	3
	3.3%	1.5%	3.6%	5.9%	3.0%

a simple cross tabulation that examines the relationship between cities consumers are willing to consider for hospitalization and their age. This cross tabulation includes frequencies and percentages, with the percentages based on column totals. This table shows an interesting relationship between age and likelihood of choosing Minneapolis or Saint Paul for hospitalization. Consumers in successively older age groups are increasingly likely to choose Saint Paul and increasingly less likely to choose Minneapolis. Following are a number of considerations regarding the setup of cross-tabulation tables and the determination of percentages within them:

- The previous discussion regarding the selection of the appropriate base for percentages applies to cross-tabulation tables as well.
- Three different percentages may be calculated for each cell in a cross-tabulation table: column, row, and total percentages. Column percentages are based on the column total, row percentages are based on the row total, and total percentages are based on the table total. Exhibit 15.10 shows a cross-tabulation table in which the frequency and all three of the percentages are shown for each cell in the table.

EXHIBIT 15.10	Cross-tabulation Table with Column, Row, and Total Percentages*

Q.34 To which of the following towns and cities would you consider going for hospitalization?

	Total	Male	Female
Total	300	67	233
	100.0%	100.0%	100.0%
	100.0%	22.3%	77.7%
	100.0%	22.3%	77.7%
Saint Paul	265	63	202
	88.3%	94.0%	86.7%
	100.0%	23.6%	76.2%
	88.3%	21.0%	67.3%
Minneapolis	240	53	187
	80.0%	79.1%	80.3%
	100.0%	22.1%	77.9%
	80.0%	17.7%	62.3%
Bloomington	112	22	90
	37.3%	32.8%	38.6%
	100.0%	19.6%	80.4%
	37.3%	7.3%	30.0%

*Percentages listed are column, row, and total percentages, respectively.

PRACTICING MARKETING RESEARCH

Q Data Analysis Software a Very Functional Choice[5]

The Australian software design firm Numbers International recently released a new data analysis program called Q. Q offers researchers a wide range of advanced statistical testing and modeling tools, packaged in a way that allows even those not specializing in statistical analysis to get meaningful results when studying survey data of almost any question format.

Although some of its features may require some familiarization to fully grasp, Q is supported by numerous tools to help researchers get started. A 60-page quick-start guide provides an overview of tables, functions, and modeling tools, and an instant-start guide summarizes them into a one-page reference sheet. The software also comes with help functions, tutorials, and online training tools.

Unlike many analytical software packages, Q provides researchers with easy and direct access to the basic data, and it keeps them engaged with the data throughout the analytical process. Erik Heller, general manager of the Sydney office for market research firm Sweeney Research, has adopted Q with great success. He comments, "Where Q differentiates itself from other tools like SPSS is the extent to which it is intuitive and easy for people to immerse themselves in the data."

Most analytical functions are accessible through drop-down menus and toolbars and allow users to manipulate the data from the main view. Q's tools also allow for significant analytical depth. For those who just need basic reports of the data, Q offers straight crosstabs but also provides advance multivariate analysis to help identify deeper, more complex trends. When venturing into these more involved multivariate methods, however, Q always starts the researcher at the same level of the basic data and builds the analytical process up from there. The research stays grounded in progressively verifiable results. As the researcher proceeds, Q helps organize tables and data sets and can package them for delivery once the analysis is done. As Heller adds, "It is very easy for someone who is not that involved in the data analysis to go into the data and run some additional crosstabs." Q offers free Reader software, which allows recipients to easily view and access these reports even if its analytical functions are limited.

One slight weakness in the software is its limited range of output functions. With no support for Excel or PowerPoint and limited chart and graph options, the final reports that Q is able to produce may be less dynamic than those of some other data analysis programs. The current version of Q is also not the ideal choice for time-series analysis and multiwave research projects. Ultimately, its biggest weaknesses may be attributed to merely an overemphasis of function over style.

Question

1. Are you at all familiar with any other analytical software packages that can be used to study market research? If so, how does Q compare?

■ A common way of setting up cross-tabulation tables is to use columns to represent factors such as demographics and lifestyle characteristics, which are expected to be predictors of the state of mind, behavior, or intentions data, shown as rows of the table. In such tables, percentages usually are calculated on the basis of column totals. This approach permits easy comparisons of the relationship between, say, lifestyle characteristics and expected predictors such as sex or age. For example, in Exhibit 15.9, this approach facilitates examination of how people in different age groups

PRACTICING
MARKETING RESEARCH

Six Practical Tips for Easier Cross Tabulations

Cross tabulation is a valuable method of mining further data and significance and teasing out unsuspected relationships from your basic survey data. Here are six practical tips to improve your cross-tabulation gleanings from Custom Insight, a provider of Web-based survey software located in Carson City, Nevada (www.custominsight.com).

1. **Make Hypotheses.** You probably already have one or two hunches about what the data might yield in cross tabulation. Articulate your initial hypotheses and use them as a starting point for cross tabulation.

2. **Look for What Is Not There.** After you observe what the data manifestly shows, examine it for what it doesn't show, that is, relationships that you may have assumed to be real or substantive. For example, if your hypothesis postulates that people with higher incomes plan to make more purchases, the data may actually refute that and thus reveal a new set of data—that affluent people are not planning to spend.

3. **Scrutinize for the Obvious.** Some relationships among the data may be obvious (e.g., age and student status). Finding these evident connections early on will validate your results and inspire greater confidence that your survey interviewers did a competent job.

4. **Keep Your Mind Open.** Don't be tied to your hypotheses and assumptions. You may see data relationships that you hadn't expected and that are not congruent with your hypotheses. Think about the data from this new angle and formulate new hypotheses to account for them.

5. **Trust the Data.** If your results don't match your initial expectations, maybe they're wrong, not the data. Study the data for new relationships even if they contradict your starting hypotheses.

6. **Watch the "n."** Small totals should raise suspicions. If you have few respondents in a given category, do not trust the data or look for stronger trends first before drawing final conclusions. For example, your study shows that 38 percent of people under age 15 want a particular product, except that only 8 people comprise that 38 percent. Better is the fact that 88 percent of people under 15 are students. Even though the number of respondents is minimal, the relationship exhibited by the data (88 percent) is much stronger and can be trusted.[6]

differ in regard to the particular factor under examination. Exhibit 15.11 shows a cross-tabulation with the results to multiple questions shown as columns.

Cross tabulations provide a powerful and easily understood approach to the summarization and analysis of survey research results. However, it is easy to become swamped by the sheer volume of computer printouts if a careful tabulation plan has not been developed. The cross-tabulation plan should be created with the research objectives and hypotheses in mind. Some tips for developing and using cross tabulations are provided above. Because the results of a particular survey might be cross tabulated in an almost endless number of ways, it is important for the analyst to exercise judgment and select from all the possibilities only those cross tabulations that are truly responsive to the research objectives of the project. Spreadsheet programs such as Excel and nearly all statistics packages (SAS, SPSS, STATISTICA) can generate cross tabulations. Chapter 16 discusses the chi-square test, which can be used to determine whether the results in a particular cross-tabulation table are significantly different from what would be expected based on chance. In other words, confronted with the question of whether the response patterns of men differ significantly from those of women, the analyst can use this statistical procedure to determine whether the differences between the two groups likely occurred because of chance or likely reflect real differences. A software offering by an Australian firm is discussed in the Practicing Marketing Research feature on page 450.

Graphic Representations of Data

You have probably heard the saying "One picture is worth a thousand words." Graphic representations of data use pictures rather than tables to present research results. Results—particularly key results—can be presented most powerfully and efficiently through graphs. Things to avoid in the display of statistical data are provided in the Practicing Marketing Research feature on page 451.

Marketing researchers have always known that important findings identified by cross tabulation and statistical analysis could be best presented graphically. However, in the early years of marketing research, the preparation of graphs was tedious, difficult, and time-consuming. The advent of personal computers, coupled with graphics software and laser printers, has changed all of this. Spreadsheet programs such as Excel have extensive graphics capabilities, particularly in their Windows versions. In addition, programs designed for creating presentations, such as PowerPoint, permit the user to generate a

FROM THE FRONT LINE

Solid Set of Cross-Tabulations Critical

Suzanne Simpson, Director of Data Processing, DSS Research

A comprehensive, insightful, error free set of cross tabulations is the foundation for the analysis and reporting phases of any project. Error free is essential because tables can typically be checked against each other in certain ways and errors that slip through, though small, are rightfully very upsetting to clients and cast a shadow of doubt over the accuracy of all aspects of the project. In some cases, where tables with errors have been passed along to analysis and reporting, the errors may, when corrected, actually change the conclusions that were drawn. In all cases, where errors were passed along and

not caught, you've got to redo the analysis and the report. In many cases, the changes may be small, but in others, as noted above, they may be very large.

Developing an error free set of tables requires a keen eye for problems in the tables (e.g., tables that don't add up, skip patterns that have inconsistent numbers, incorrect labeling), a strong desire for consistency, and curiosity are critical.

Tables are only as good as the data used to create them. Clean data are the result of careful planning and meticulous checking processes. Familiarity with the data is a natural outcome of the cleaning process. A skilled programmer uses this familiarity to hunt for and find any inconsistencies that result from data entry or programming (CATI or Internet) errors. Inconsistencies to look for include:

• Were all the responses to rating scale questions entered to ascending order (lowest rating is lowest number, highest rating is highest number) with the exception of two or three questions?

- Did an unusual number of respondents fail to answer only one particular open-end question?
- Any discrepancies or errors in data processing are easily indentifiable and will be addressed at this stage.

In a clean set of tables, everything adds up, everything makes sense, you know it's right.

In addition to checking for inconsistencies and errors, you need to make sure that the data cuts you specify (the column in your tables) address all of the research objectives and related issues clearly. For example, if one objective is to quantify the relationship between income and likelihood to buy a new product then you need to make sure that you have a table showing income by likelihood to buy the new product. You might want to add another cut to the banner or columns in certain tables (see discussion of banner in this chapter) or perhaps filter some of the tables down to a smaller sub-set, and keep looking. The answers are there waiting to be discovered.

wide variety of high-quality graphics with ease. With these programs, it is possible to do the following:

- Quickly produce graphs.
- Display those graphs on the computer screen.
- Make desired changes and redisplay.
- Print final copies on a laser, inkjet, or dot matrix printer.

All of the graphs shown in the next several pages were produced using a personal computer, a laser printer, and a graphics software package.

Line Charts

Line charts are perhaps the simplest form of graphs. They are particularly useful for presenting a given measurement taken at several points over time. The results reveal similar sales patterns for 2001 and 2002, with peaks in June and generally low sales in January through March and September through December. Just Add Water is evaluating the sales data to identify product lines that it might add to improve sales during those periods.

EXHIBIT 15.11	A Stub and Banner Table

North Community College—Anywhere, U.S.A.
Q.1c. Are you single, married, or formerly married?

		Zones			Gender		Age		
	Total	1	2	3	M	F	18–34	35–54	55 and over
Total	300	142	103	55	169	131	48	122	130
	100%	100%	100%	100%	100%	100%	100%	100%	100%
Married	228	105	87	36	131	97	36	97	95
	76%	74%	84%	65%	78%	74%	75%	80%	73%
Single	5	1	2	2	4	1	2	1	2
	2%	1%	2%	4%	2%	1%	4%	1%	2%
Formerly married	24	11	10	3	12	12	3	9	12
	8%	8%	10%	5%	7%	9%	6%	7%	9%
Refused to answer	43	25	4	14	22	21	7	15	21
	14%	18 %	4%	25%	13%	16%	15%	12%	16%

EXHIBIT 15.12

Race			Family Profile		Vote History		Registered Voter	
White	Black	Other	Child < 18 Years	Child > 18 Years	2–3 Times	4 Times or More	Yes	No
268	28	4	101	53	104	196	72	228
100%	100%	100%	100%	100%	100%	100%	100%	100%
207	18	3	82	39	80	148	58	170
77%	64%	75%	81%	74%	77%	76%	81%	75%
5	—	—	—	—	2	3	1	4
2%	—	—	—	—	2%	2%	1%	2%
18	6	—	5	6	10	14	3	21
7%	21%	—	5%	11%	10%	7%	4%	9%
38	4	1	14	8	12	31	10	33
14%	14%	25%	14%	15%	12%	16%	14%	14%

Pie Charts

Pie charts are another type of graph that is frequently used. They are appropriate for displaying marketing research results in a wide range of situations. Exhibit 15.12 shows radio music preferences gleaned from a survey of residents of several Gulf Coast metropolitan areas in Louisiana, Mississippi, and Alabama. Note the three-dimensional effect produced by the software for this example.

Bar Charts

Bar charts may be the most flexible of the three types of graphs discussed in this section. Anything that can be shown in a line graph or a pie chart also can be shown in a bar chart. In addition, many things that cannot be shown—or effectively shown—in other types of graphs can be readily illustrated in bar charts. Four types of bar charts are discussed here.

1. *Plain bar chart.* As the name suggests, plain bar charts are the simplest form of bar chart. The same information displayed in the pie chart in Exhibit 15.13 is shown in the bar chart in Exhibit 15.14. Draw your own conclusions regarding whether the pie chart or the bar chart is the more effective way to present this information. Exhibit 15.14 is a traditional two-dimensional chart. Most of the software packages available today can take the same information and present it with a three-dimensional effect, as shown in Exhibit 15.15. Again, decide for yourself which approach is visually more appealing and interesting.

2. ***Clustered bar chart.*** The clustered bar chart is one of three types of bar charts useful for showing the results of cross tabulations. The radio music preference results are cross tabulated by age in

Exhibit 15.13

Three-Dimensional Pie Chart for Types of Music Listened to Most Often

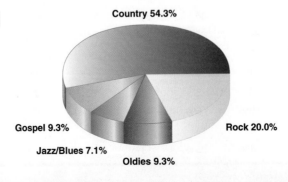

Country 54.3%
Gospel 9.3%
Jazz/Blues 7.1%
Oldies 9.3%
Rock 20.0%

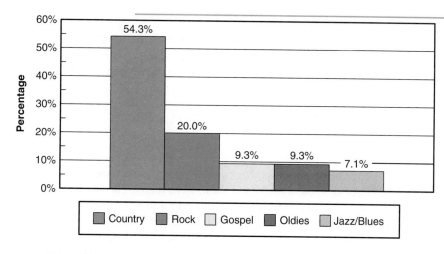

Exhibit 15.14

Simple Two Dimensional Bar Chart for Types of Music Listened to Most Often

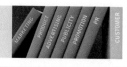

PRACTICING MARKETING RESEARCH

Expert Tips on Making Bad Graphics Every Time

He may sound tongue-in-cheek, but information visualization expert Juan C. Dürsteler thinks the funny approach to teaching data graphic design can be effective. Ideally, a reader's reaction to an excellent graphic should be an exclamation as to how interesting the data are. But often data graphics fail to work that way. Dürsteler, who earned his Ph.D. from the Universidad Politécnica de Catalunya in Spain in computer-assisted design systems, adapts and comments on the design specifications of Howard Wainer laid down in his book, *Visual Revelations* (Lawrence Erlbaum, 1997). Dürsteler assigns them to two primary categories of misapproach: (1) occultation and (2) inconsistency. Follow these approaches, and your data graphics, he assures us, will be terrible.

Occultation: This means, simply, hide everything important and avoid showing the relevant data. Specifically, Dürsteler offers six recommendations under this topic to ensure your design is terrible:

- Reduce to a minimum the data density (put miniscule data on a large chart).
- Minimize the data/ink ratio (use a little ink for the data but lots for the axis, reference grid, and labels).
- Hide the key differences (use a scale that makes them hard to see).
- Display the data out of proper context (omit previous supporting data).
- Put a lot of attention on the trivial (ensure that what catches one's attention is not the key conclusion).
- Make sure your labels are hard to read, incomplete, and unclear (there are lots of ways to achieve this: be original).

Inconsistency: Employ inconsistent techniques in your data codification and graphic presentation, change tactics and emphases in midstream, Dürsteler notes, and you'll be on your way to achieving this technique for bad graphics:

- Ignore the codification (make the lengths or data areas nonproportional to its values).
- Focus your codes in one dimension, next represent them in many dimensions (codify the lengths and then show areas or volumes).
- Shift your regularity in the middle of the axis (for example, start with steps of 8 years, then end up with 1-year steps).
- Contrast the values between curves or alter the situation regarding the origin of the data so this you cannot compare in the same conditions (stacked bar charts are good for this).[7]

Questions

1. Come up with two more ways to hide data and two more ways to be inconsistent in presenting data graphics.

2. Find three examples of inept data graphics from either academic or mainstream published sources and analyze how they fail.

Exhibit 15.18. The graph shows that country music is mentioned most often as the preferred format by those over 35 and those 35 or under. The graph also shows that rock music is a close second for those 35 or under and is least frequently mentioned by those over 35. The results suggest that if the target audience is those in the 35 or under age group, then a mix of country and rock music is appropriate. A focus on country music probably would be the most efficient approach for those over 35.

3. **Stacked bar chart.** Like clustered bar charts, stacked bar charts are helpful in graphically representing cross-tabulation results. The same music preference data shown in Exhibit 15.15 are presented as a stacked bar chart in Exhibit 15.17.

Exhibit 15.15

Simple Three-Dimensional Bar Chart for Types of Music Listened to Most Often

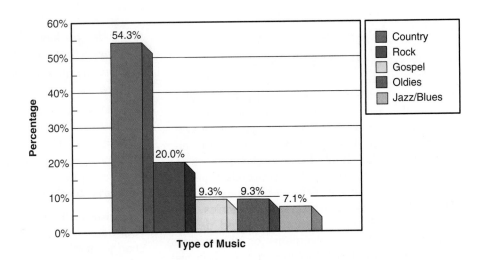

Exhibit 15.16

Clustered Bar Chart for Types of Music Listened to Most Often by Age

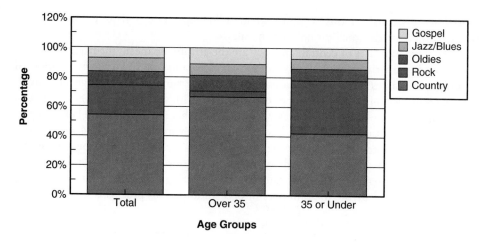

Exhibit 15.17

Stacked Bar Chart for Types of Music Listened to Most Often by Age

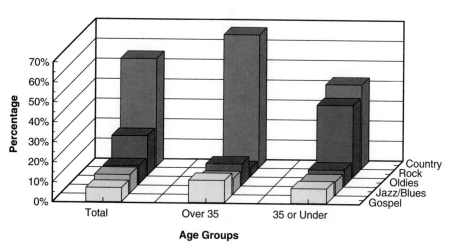

Exhibit 15.18

Multiple-Row, Three-Dimensional Bar Chart for Types of Music Listened to *Most* Often by Age

4. ***Multiple-row, three-dimensional bar chart.*** This type of bar chart provides what we believe to be the most visually appealing way of presenting cross-tabulation information. The same music preference data displayed in Exhibits 15.16 and 15.17 are presented in a multiple-row, three-dimensional bar chart in Exhibit 15.18.

Descriptive Statistics

Descriptive statistics are the most efficient means of summarizing the characteristics of large sets of data. In a statistical analysis, the analyst calculates one number or a few numbers that reveal something about the characteristics of large sets of data.

Measures of Central Tendency

Before beginning this section, you should review the types of data scales presented in Chapter 10. Recall that there are four basic types of measurement scales: nominal, ordinal, interval, and ratio. Nominal and ordinal scales are sometimes referred to as nonmetric scales, whereas interval and ratio scales are called metric scales. Many of the statistical procedures discussed in this section and in following sections require metric scales, whereas others are designed for nonmetric scales.

The three measures of central tendency are the arithmetic mean, median, and mode. The **mean** is properly computed only from interval or ratio (metric) data. It is computed by adding the values for all observations for a particular variable, such as age, and dividing the resulting sum by the number of observations. With survey data, the exact value of the variable may not be known; it may be known only that a particular case falls in a particular category. For example, an age category on a survey might be 18 to 34 years of age. If a person falls into this category, the person's exact age is known to be somewhere between 18 and 34. With grouped data, the midpoint of each category is multiplied by the number of observations in that category, the resulting totals are summed, and the total is then divided by the total number of observations. This process is summarized in the following formula:

> **mean**
> Sum of the values for all observations of a variable divided by the number of observations.

$$\overline{X} = \frac{\sum_{i=1}^{h} f_i X_i}{n}$$

where f_i = frequency of the *i*th class
            X_i = midpoint of that class
            h = number of classes
            n = total number of observations

> **median**
> Value below which 50 percent of the observations fall.

The **median** can be computed for all types of data except nominal data. It is calculated by finding the value below which 50 percent of the observations fall. If all the values for a particular variable were put in an array in either ascending or descending order, the median would be the middle value in that array. The median is often used to summarize variables such as income when the researcher is concerned that the arithmetic mean will be affected by a small number of extreme values and, therefore, will not accurately reflect the predominant central tendency of that variable for that group.

> **mode**
> Value that occurs most frequently.

The **mode** can be computed for any type of data (nominal, ordinal, interval, or ratio). It is determined by finding the value that occurs most frequently. In a frequency distribution, the mode is the value that has the highest frequency. One problem with using the mode is that a particular data set may have more than one mode. If three different values occur with the same level of frequency and that frequency is higher than the frequency for any other value, then the data set has three modes. The mean, median, and mode for sample data on beer consumption are shown in Exhibit 15.19.

Measures of Dispersion

Frequently used measures of dispersion include standard deviation, variance, and range. Whereas measures of central tendency indicate typical values for a particular variable, measures of dispersion indicate how spread out the data are. The dangers associated with relying only on measures of central tendency are suggested by the example shown in Exhibit 15.19. Note that average beer consumption is the same in both markets—3 cans/bottles/glasses. However, the standard deviation is greater in market two, indicating more dispersion in the data. Whereas the mean suggests that the two markets are the same, the added information provided by the standard deviation indicates that they are different.

EXHIBIT 15.19	Mean, Median, and Mode for Beer Consumption Data

A total of 10 beer drinkers (drink one or more cans, bottles, or glasses of beer per day on the average) were interviewed in a mall-intercept study. They were asked how many cans, bottles, or glasses of beer they drink in an average day.

Respondent	Number of Cans/ Bottles/Glasses Per Respondent Day
1	2
2	2
3	3
4	2
5	5
6	1
7	2
8	2
9	10
10	1

Mode = 2 cans/bottles/glasses

Median = 2 cans/bottles/glasses

Mean = 3 cans/bottles/glasses

EXHIBIT 15.20	Measures of Dispersion and Measures of Central Tendency

Consider the beer consumption data presented below for two markets.

Respondent	Number of Cans/ Bottles/Glasses Market One	Number of Cans/ Bottles/Glasses Market Two
1	2	1
2	2	1
3	3	1
4	2	1
5	5	1
6	1	1
7	2	1
8	2	3
9	10	10
10	1	10
Mean	3	3
Standard deviation	2.7	3.7

Though mean consumption is the same in both markets the standard deviation shows there is much more dispersion in consumption in Market Two.

The formula for computing the standard deviation for a sample of observations is as follows:

$$S = \sqrt{\frac{\sum_{i=1}^{n} (X_i - \bar{X})^2}{n - 1}}$$

where S = sample standard deviation
X_i = value of the ith observation
$\bar{X}$ = sample mean
n = sample size

Occupation is an example of a categorical variable. The only results that can be reported for a variable of this type are the frequency and the relative percentage with which each category was encountered.

The variance is calculated by using the formula for standard deviation with the square root sign removed. That is, the sum of the squared deviations from the mean is divided by the number of observations minus 1. Finally, the range is equal to the maximum value for a particular variable minus the minimum value for that variable.

Percentages and Statistical Tests

In performing basic data analysis, the research analyst is faced with the decision of whether to use measures of central tendency (mean, median, mode) or percentages (one-way frequency tables, cross tabulations). Responses to questions either are categorical or take the form of continuous variables. Categorical variables such as "Occupation" (coded 1 for professional/managerial, 2 for clerical, etc.) limit the analyst to reporting the frequency and relative percentage with which each category was encountered. Variables such as age can be continuous or categorical, depending on how the information was obtained. For example, an interviewer can ask people their actual age or ask them which category (under 35, 35 or older) includes their age. If actual age data are available, mean age can be readily computed. If categories are used, one-way frequency tables and cross tabulations are the most obvious choices for analysis. However, continuous data can be put into categories, and means can be estimated for categorical data by using the formula for computing a mean for grouped data (presented earlier).

Finally, statistical tests are available that can indicate whether two means—for example, average expenditures by men and average expenditures by women at fast-food restaurants—or two percentages differ to a greater extent than would be expected by chance (sampling error) or whether there is a significant relationship between two variables in a cross-tabulation table. These tests are discussed in Chapter 16.

SUMMARY

Once the questionnaires have been returned from the field, a five-step process takes place. These steps are (1) validation and editing, which are quality control checks, (2) coding, (3) data entry, (4) logical cleaning of data, and (5) tabulation and statistical analysis. The first step in the process, making sure that the data have integrity, is critical. Otherwise, the age-old adage is true: "Garbage in, garbage out." Validation involves determining with as much certainty as possible that each questionnaire is, in fact, a valid interview. A valid interview in this sense is one that was conducted in an appropriate manner. The objective of validation is to detect interviewer fraud or failure to follow key instructions. Validation is accomplished by recontacting a certain percentage of the respondents surveyed by each interviewer. Any surveys found to be fraudulent are eliminated from the database. After the validation process is completed, editing begins. Editing involves checking for interviewer and respondent mistakes—making certain that all required questions were answered, that skip patterns were followed properly, and that responses to open-ended questions were accurately recorded.

Upon completion of the editing, the next step is to code the data. Most questions on surveys are closed-ended and precoded, which means that numeric codes already have been assigned to the various responses on the questionnaire. With open-ended questions, the researcher has no idea in advance what the responses will be. Therefore, the coder must establish numeric codes for response categories by listing actual responses to open-ended questions and then consolidating those responses and assigning numeric codes to the consolidated categories. Once a coding sheet has been created, all questionnaires are coded using the coding sheet categories.

The next step is data entry. Today, most data entry is done by means of intelligent entry systems that check the internal logic of the data. The data typically are entered directly from the questionnaires. New developments in scanning technology have made a more automated approach to data entry cost-effective for smaller projects.

Machine cleaning of data is a final, computerized error check of the data, performed through the use of error checking routines and/or marginal reports. Error checking routines indicate whether or not certain conditions have been met. A marginal report is a type of frequency table that helps the user determine whether inappropriate codes were entered and whether skip patterns were properly followed.

The final step in the data analysis process is tabulation of the data. The most basic tabulation involves a one-way frequency table, which indicates the number of respondents who gave each possible answer to each question. Generating one-way frequency tables requires the analyst to determine a basis for percentages. For example, are the percentages to be calculated based on total respondents, number of people asked a particular question, or number answering a particular question? Tabulation of data is often followed by cross tabulation—examination of the responses to one question in relation to the responses to one or more other questions. Cross tabulation is a powerful and easily understood approach to the analysis of survey research results.

Statistical measures provide an even more powerful way to analyze data sets. The most commonly used statistical measures are those of central tendency: the arithmetic mean, median, and mode. The arithmetic mean is computed only from interval or ratio data by adding the values for all observations of a particular variable and dividing the resulting sum by the number of observations. The median can be computed for all types of data except nominal data by finding the value below which 50 percent of the observations fall. The mode can be computed for any type of data by simply finding the value that occurs most frequently. The arithmetic mean is, by far, the most commonly used measure of central tendency.

In addition to central tendency, researchers often want to have an indication of the dispersion of the data. Measures of dispersion include standard deviation, variance, and range.

KEY TERMS & DEFINITIONS

validation Process of ascertaining that interviews actually were conducted as specified.

editing Process of ascertaining that questionnaires were filled out properly and completely.

skip pattern Sequence in which later questions are asked, based on a respondent's answer to an earlier question or questions.

coding Process of grouping and assigning numeric codes to the various responses to a question.

data entry Process of converting information to an electronic format.

intelligent data entry Form of data entry in which the information being entered into the data entry device is checked for internal logic.

scanning technology Form of data entry in which responses on questionnaires are read in automatically by the data entry device.

logical or machine cleaning of data Final computerized error check of data.

error checking routines Computer programs that accept instructions from the user to check for logical errors in the data.

marginal report Computer-generated table of the frequencies of the responses to each question, used to monitor entry of valid codes and correct use of skip patterns.

one-way frequency table Table showing the number of respondents choosing each answer to a survey question.

cross tabulation Examination of the responses to one question relative to the responses to one or more other questions.

mean Sum of the values for all observations of a variable divided by the number of observations.

median Value below which 50 percent of the observations fall.

mode Value that occurs most frequently.

QUESTIONS FOR REVIEW & CRITICAL THINKING

1. What is the difference between measurement validity and interview validation?

2. Assume that Sally Smith, an interviewer, completed 50 questionnaires. Ten of the questionnaires were validated by calling the respondents and asking them one opinion question and two demographic questions over again. One respondent claimed that his age category was 30–40, when the age category marked on the questionnaire was 20–30. On another questionnaire, in response to the question "What is the most important problem facing our city government?" the interviewer had written, "The city council is too eager to raise taxes." When the interview was validated, the respondent said, "The city tax rate is too high." As a validator, would you assume that these were honest mistakes and accept the entire lot of 50 interviews as valid? If not, what would you do?

3. What is meant by the editing process? Should editors be allowed to fill in what they think a respondent meant in response to open-ended questions if the information seems incomplete? Why or why not?

4. Give an example of a skip pattern on a questionnaire. Why is it important to always follow the skip patterns correctly?

5. It has been said that, to some degree, coding of open-ended questions is an art. Would you agree or disagree? Why? Suppose that, after coding a large number of questionnaires, the researcher notices that many responses have ended up in the "Other" category. What might this imply? What could be done to correct this problem?

6. Describe an intelligent data entry system. Why are data typically entered directly from the questionnaire into the data entry device?

7. What is the purpose of machine cleaning data? Give some examples of how data can be machine cleaned. Do you think that machine cleaning is an expensive and unnecessary step in the data tabulation process? Why or why not?

8. It has been said that a cross tabulation of two variables offers the researcher more insightful information than does a one-way frequency table. Why might this be true? Give an example.

9. Illustrate the various alternatives for using percentages in one-way frequency tables. Explain the logic of choosing one alternative method over another.

10. Explain the differences among the mean, median, and mode. Give an example in which the researcher might be interested in each of these measures of central tendency.

11. Calculate the mean, median, mode, and standard deviation for the following data set:

Respondent	Times Visited Whitehall Mall in Past 6 Months	Times Visited Northpark Mall	Times Visited Sampson Mall in Past 6 Months
A	4	7	2
B	5	11	16
C	13	21	3
D	6	0	1
E	9	18	14
F	3	6	8
G	2	0	1
H	21	3	7
I	4	11	9
J	14	13	5
K	7	7	12
L	8	3	25
M	8	3	9

12. Enter the following data into an Excel spreadsheet. Include the column headings (Q1, Q2, and Q3), as well as the numeric values. The definitions of the numeric values are provided at the bottom of the table. Use the Pivot Table feature in Excel (found under the Data option) to cross tabulate the likelihood of purchase (row) by gender (column) and income level (column). What conclusions can you draw about the relationship between gender and likelihood of purchase and that between income and likelihood of purchase?

Respondent	Likelihood of Purchase	Gender	Income
A	5	2	3
B	4	2	3
C	4	2	2
D	3	1	2

Respondent	Likelihood of Purchase	Gender	Income
E	1	1	2
F	5	2	3
G	5	2	3
H	4	1	3
I	1	1	2
J	1	1	2
K	2	1	1
L	5	2	3
M	5	2	3
N	4	1	3
O	3	1	2
P	3	1	2
Q	4	2	3
R	5	2	3
S	2	1	1
T	2	1	1

Likelihood of purchase: very likely = 5, likely = 4, undecided = 3, unlikely = 2, very unlikely = 1
Gender: male = 1, female = 2
Income: under $30,000 = 1, $30,000 to $75,000 = 2, over $75,000 = 3

13. Using data from a newspaper or magazine article, create the following types of graphs:

a. Line graph

b. Pie chart

c. Bar chart

WORKING THE NET

1. Microsoft Office Online offers data graphics software called Microsoft Office Visio 2007 enabling users to construct their own data graphics, adjust color shapes to fit the data, and customize data format; try out the downloadable demonstration offered at: *http://office.microsoft.com/en-us/visio/HA101829791033.aspx*.

2. To stay updated on the newest software and algorithms for statistical uses, visit the Web site of the *Journal of Statistical Software* at: *www.jstatsoft.org*.

REAL-LIFE RESEARCH • 15.1

PrimeCare

PrimeCare is a group of 12 emergency medical treatment clinics in the Columbus and Toledo, Ohio, markets. The management group for PrimeCare is considering a communications campaign that will rely mainly on radio ads to boost its awareness and quality image in the market. The ad agency of Dodd and Beck has been chosen to develop the campaign. Currently, the plan is to focus on PrimeCare's experienced, front-line health professionals.

Two themes for the ad campaign are now being considered. One theme ("We are ready!") focuses primarily on the special training given to PrimeCare's staff, and the second theme ("All the experts—all the time") focuses primarily on PrimeCare's commitment to having the best, trained professionals available at each PrimeCare facility 24/7. Dodd and Beck's research team has conducted a survey of consumers to gauge the appeal of the two campaigns. Overall results and results broken down by gender and by location are shown in the table.

		Gender		Location	
	Total	Male	Female	Columbus	Toledo
Total	400	198	202	256	144
	100%	100.0%	100.0%	100.0%	100.0%
Prefer "Ready"	150	93	57	124	26
Campaign	37.5%	47.0%	28.2%	48.4%	18.1%
Prefer "All the	250	105	145	132	118
Time" campaign	62.5%	53.0%	71.8%	51.6%	81.9%

Questions

1. Which theme appears to have more appeal overall? Justify your answer.
2. How does the appeal of the campaigns differ between men and women? What is your basis for that conclusion?
3. Are the campaign themes equally attractive to residents of Columbus and Toledo? Why do you say that?

REAL-LIFE RESEARCH • 15.2

Tico Taco

Tico Taco has recently opened its 17th store in Wyoming. Currently, the chain offers tacos, fajitas, and burritos. Management is considering offering a super taco that would be two times as large as their regular taco and would contain 6 ounces of ground beef. The basic taco has spiced ground beef, lettuce, and cheese. Management feels that the super taco should offer more options.

A marketing research study was undertaken to determine what those other options should be. A key question on the survey was, "What, if anything, do you normally add to a taco that you have prepared at home besides meat?" The question is open-ended, and the coding categories that have been established for the question are shown in the table.

Responses	Code
Avocado	1
Cheese (Monterey Jack/cheddar)	2
Guacamole	3
Lettuce	4
Mexican hot sauce	5
Olive (black/green)	6

Responses	Code
Onion (red/white)	7
Peppers (red/green)	8
Pimiento	9
Sour cream	0
Other	X

Questions

1. How would you code the following responses?
   a. I usually add a green, avocado-tasting hot sauce.
   b. I cut up a mixture of lettuce and spinach.
   c. I'm a vegetarian; I don't use meat at all. My taco is filled only with guacamole.
   d. Every now and then I use a little lettuce, but normally I like cilantro.

2. Is there anything wrong with having a great number of responses in the "Other" category? What problem does this present for the researcher?

SPSS EXERCISES FOR CHAPTER 15

Exercise 1: Machine Cleaning Data

1. Go to the Wiley Web site at **www.wiley.com/college/mcdaniel** and download the Segmenting the College Student Market for Movie Attendance database to SPSS Windows. This database will have several errors for you to correct. In the SPSS Data Editor, go the variable view option and notice the **computer coding** for each variable.

2. Also from the Wiley Web site, download a copy of the Segmenting the College Student Market for Movie Attendance questionnaire. Notice the computer coding for each of the variables which is the same as that in the variable view option on the SPSS Data Editor. This information will be important in finding errors in the database.

3. In the SPSS Data Editor, invoke the analyze/descriptive statistics/frequencies sequence to obtain frequencies for all of the variables in the database.

4. From the SPSS Viewer output screen, determine which variables have input errors Summarize the errors using the followings template as a guide.

Questionnaire Number	Variable Containing error	Incorrect Value	Correct Value

Go back to the data view screen of the SPSS Data Editor.

5. Another possible source of errors is in question 8. Notice that in this question the sum of the answers should be 100 percent. Create a summated variable for question 8 (Q8a 3 Q8b 3 Q8c 3 Q8d) to check for errors by invoking the transform/compute sequence. Now, compute a frequency distribution for Q8sum. The values that are not "100" indicate an input error. (Such an error could be the result of the respondent not totaling percentages to 100, but for this machine cleaning exercise, the assumption is that it is an input error.) Summarize the errors using the template above.

6. Once you have completed summarizing the variables containing errors, go back to the data view screen of the SPSS Data Editor. Position the cursor on each of the variables containing errors. Use the ctrl-f function to find the questionnaire numbers where the errors occurred. At this point, you will need the corrected database, or the database with no errors. Your professor has access to this database with no errors. After getting the corrected database, finish filling in the table in part (4) above with the correct values. Then make the changes in your database, so that you have a database with no errors. Be sure to resave your database after correcting it for errors.

7. After machine cleaning your data, rerun the analyze/descriptive statistics/frequencies sequence to obtain frequencies for your corrected database.

8. You will use the results of this exercise to answer the questions in Exercises 2 and 4.

Exercise 2: Analysis of Data with Frequency Distributions

If you did not complete Exercise 1, you will need the corrected database from your professor. After getting the corrected database, use the analyze/descriptive statistics/frequencies sequence to obtain frequency distributions for all of the variables in your database except the questionnaire number (Q No).

If you completed Exercise 1, you will have a corrected database, which consists of frequency distributions for each of the variables in the database.

Answer the following questions.

1. What percentage of all respondents attended at least 1 movie in the past year? _____%

2. What percentage of all respondents never buy food items at a movie? _____%

3. Produce a table indicating the percentage of all respondents who consider each of the movie theater items in question 5 of the questionnaire very important. List the top 5 movie items in descending order (start with the movie items that have the highest percentage of very important responses).

For example:

Movie Item	Percentage of Respondents
Movie item with the highest percentage	75.0%
Movie item with the 2nd highest percentage, etc.	39.2%

4. What percentage of respondents consider the "newspaper" a very important source of information about movies playing at movie theaters? _____%

5. What percentage of respondents consider the "Internet" a very unimportant source of information about movies playing at movie theaters? _____%

6. By observing the distribution of responses for Q8a, Q8b, Q8c, and Q8d, which is the most popular purchase option for movie theater tickets? _____

7. Produce a table listing in descending order the percentage of respondents that consider each of the movie theater information sources (Q7) very important.

For example:

Movie Theater Information Sources	Percentage of Respondents Indicating Very Important
Internet	55%
Newspaper	31%

Exercise 3: Analysis of Data with Descriptive Statistics

If you did not complete Exercise 1 or 2, you will need the corrected database from your professor. The objective of this exercise is to analyze data using measures of central tendency and measures of dispersion. To analyze means and standard deviations, use the analyze/descriptive statistics/descriptives sequences. To analyze medians and modes, use the analyze/descriptive statistics/frequencies sequence, and select statistics. You will see the box with all three measures of central tendency (mean, median, and mode).

On the questionnaire, question 5 utilizes a 4-point Itemized Rating scale (illustrated below). This scale is balanced and can be assumed to yield interval scale/metric data. Given the preceding, invoke SPSS to calculate the mean and standard deviation for all of the variables in question 5 (Q5a–Q5i).

Very unimportant	Somewhat unimportant	Somewhat important	Very important
1	2	3	4

Answer the following questions.

1. Using only the **mean** for each of the variables, which of the movie theater items was considered "most important"? _____

2. Using only the **standard deviation** for each of the variables, for which question was there the greatest amount of agreement? _____ *Hint:* Least amount of dispersion regarding the response to the movie item

3. Questions 4 and 6 utilize multiple-choice questions that yield nonmetric data, but that are ordinal scale. The appropriate measures of central tendency for nonmetric data are the median and the mode.

a. What is the median response for question 4, concerning the amount a person spends on food/drink items at a movie? _____

Never buy food items at movies	Up to $7.49	$7.50 to $14.99	$15.00 or more
(0)	(1)	(2)	(3)

b. Concerning question 6, the distance a person would drive to see a movie on a "big screen," what is the mode of that distribution of responses?

Zero	1 to 9 miles	11 to 24 miles	25 to 49 miles	503 miles
(0)	(1)	(2)	(3)	(4)

4. In this question the objective will be to compare the results of median and mean responses for Q3.

   a. Mean response: _____

   b. Median response: _____

   c. Standard deviation: _____

   d. Minimum response: _____

   e. Maximum response: _____

5. When the responses to a question contain extreme values, the mean response can lie in the upper or lower quartile of the response distribution. In such a case, the median value would be a better indicator of an average response than the mean value. Given the information you obtained from answering question 4 above, is the mean or median a better representative of the "average" response to Q3?

_____

_____

_____

Exercise 4: Analysis of Demographic Characteristics Using Charts

If you completed Exercise 1 and/or Exercise 2, you will have the information to complete this exercise.

   If you did not complete either Exercise 1 or 2, you will need to get a corrected soft-drink database from your professor. After getting the database, use the **analyze–descriptive statistics/frequencies** sequence to obtain frequency distributions for the demographic questions (questions 11–14).

   Complete the following.

1. Display the demographic data for each of the four demographic variables in tables.

2. For each demographic variable, illustrate the table results using some type of graphic representation of the data (pie charts, line charts, or bar charts).

Note: Some students who are proficient in Excel may want to paste their databases into an Excel spreadsheet for the geographical depiction of the demographic variables.

CHAPTER **16**

Statistical Testing Of Differences And Relationships

LEARNING OBJECTIVES

→ **1.** To become aware of the nature of statistical significance.

→ **2.** To understand the concept of hypothesis development and how to test hypotheses.

→ **3.** To understand the difference between type I and type II errors.

→ **4.** To be familiar with several of the more common statistical tests of goodness of fit, hypotheses about one mean, hypotheses about two means, and hypotheses about proportions.

→ **5.** To learn about analysis of variance.

This chapter addresses statistical techniques that can be used to determine whether observed differences are likely to be real differences or whether they are likely attributable to sampling error.

Evaluating Differences and Changes

The issue of whether certain measurements are different from one another is central to many questions of critical interest to marketing managers. Some specific examples of managers' questions follow:

■ Our posttest measure of top-of-mind awareness (first brand mentioned unaided) is slightly higher than the level recorded in the pretest. Did top-of-mind awareness really increase or is there some other explanation for the increase? Should we fire or commend our agency?

■ Our overall customer satisfaction score increased from 92 percent 3 months ago to 93.5 percent today. Did customer satisfaction really increase? Should we celebrate?

■ Satisfaction with the customer service provided by our cable TV system in Dallas is, on average, 1.2 points higher on a 10-point scale than is satisfaction with the customer service provided by our cable TV system in Cincinnati. Are customers in Dallas really more satisfied? Should the customer service manager in Cincinnati be replaced? Should the Dallas manager be rewarded?

■ In a recent product concept test, 19.8 percent of those surveyed said they were very likely to buy the new product they evaluated. Is this good? Is it better than the results we got last year for a similar product? What do these results suggest in terms of whether to introduce the new product?

■ A segmentation study shows that those with incomes of more than $30,000 per year frequent fast-food restaurants 6.2 times per month on average. Those with incomes of $30,000 or less go an average of 6.7 times. Is this difference real—is it meaningful?

■ In an awareness test, 28.3 percent of those surveyed have heard of our product on an unaided basis. Is this a good result?

These are the common questions in marketing and marketing research. Although considered boring by some, statistical hypothesis testing is important because it helps researchers get closer to the answers to these questions. We say "closer" because certainty is never achieved in answering these questions in marketing research.

Statistical Significance

The basic motive for making statistical inferences is to generalize from sample results to population characteristics. A fundamental tenet of statistical inference is that it is possible for numbers to be different in a mathematical sense but not significantly different in a statistical sense. For example, suppose cola drinkers are asked to try two cola drinks in a blind taste test and indicate which they prefer; the results show that 51 percent prefer one test product and 49 percent prefer the other. There is a mathematical difference in the results but the difference would appear to be minor and unimportant. The difference probably is well within the range of accuracy of researchers' ability to measure taste preference and thus probably is not significant in a statistical sense. Three different concepts can be applied to the notion of differences when we are talking about results from samples:

■ *Mathematical differences.* By definition, if numbers are not exactly the same, they are different. This does not, however, mean that the difference is either important or statistically significant.

statistical significance
A difference that is large enough that it is not likely to have occurred because of chance or sampling error.

■ *Statistical significance.* If a particular difference is large enough to be unlikely to have occurred because of chance or sampling error, then the difference is **statistically significant.**

■ *Managerially important differences.* One can argue that a difference is important from a managerial perspective only if results or numbers are sufficiently different. For example, the difference in consumer responses to two different packages in a test market might be statistically significant but yet so small as to have little practical or managerial significance.[1]

This chapter covers different approaches to testing whether results are statistically significant.

Hypothesis Testing

hypothesis
Assumption or theory that a researcher or manager makes about some characteristic of the population under study.

A **hypothesis** is an assumption or theory guess that a researcher or manager makes about some characteristic of the population being investigated. The marketing researcher is often faced with the question of whether research results are different enough from the norm that some element of the firm's marketing strategy should be changed. Consider the following situations.

■ The results of a tracking survey show that awareness of a product is lower than it was in a similar survey conducted 6 months ago. Are the results significantly lower? Are the results sufficiently lower to call for a change in advertising strategy?

■ A product manager believes that the average purchaser of his product is 35 years of age. A survey is conducted to test this hypothesis and the survey shows that the average purchaser of the product is 38.5 years of age. Is the survey result different enough from the product manager's belief to cause him to conclude that his belief is incorrect?

■ The marketing director of a fast-food chain believes that 60 percent of her customers are female and 40 percent are male. She does a survey to test this hypothesis and finds that, according to the survey, 55 percent are female and 45 percent are male. Is this result different enough from her original theory to permit her to conclude that her original theory was incorrect?

All of these questions can be evaluated with some kind of statistical test. In hypothesis testing, the researcher determines whether a hypothesis concerning some characteristic of the population is likely to be true, given the evidence. A statistical hypothesis test allows us to calculate the probability of observing a particular result if the stated hypothesis is actually true.[2]

There are two basic explanations for an observed difference between a hypothesized value and a particular research result. Either the hypothesis is true and the observed difference is likely due to sampling error or the hypothesis is false and the true value is some other value.

Steps in Hypothesis Testing

Five steps are involved in testing a hypothesis. First, the hypothesis is specified. Second, an appropriate statistical technique is selected to test the hypothesis. Third, a decision rule is specified as the basis for determining whether to reject or fail to reject (FTR) the null hypothesis H_0. Please note that we did not say "reject H_0 or accept H_0." Although a seemingly small distinction, it is an important one. The distinction will be discussed in greater detail later on. Fourth, the value of the test statistic is calculated and the test is performed. Fifth, the conclusion is stated from the perspective of the original research problem or question.

Step One: Stating the Hypothesis Hypotheses are stated using two basic forms: the null hypothesis H_0 and the alternative hypothesis H_a. The **null hypothesis** H_0 (sometimes called the *hypothesis of the status quo*) is the hypothesis that is tested against its complement, the alternative hypothesis H_a (sometimes called the *research hypothesis of interest*). Suppose the manager of Burger City believes that his operational procedures will guarantee that the average customer will wait 2 minutes in the drive-in window line. He conducts research, based on the observation of 1,000 customers at randomly selected stores at randomly selected times. The average customer observed in this study spends 2.4 minutes in the drive-in window line. The null hypothesis and the alternative hypothesis might be stated as follows:

> **null hypothesis**
> The hypothesis of status quo, no difference, no effect.

- Null hypothesis H_0: Mean waiting time 2 minutes.
- Alternative hypothesis H_a: Mean waiting time 2 minutes.

It should be noted that the null hypothesis and the alternative hypothesis must be stated in such a way that both cannot be true. The idea is to use the available evidence to ascertain which hypothesis is more likely to be true.

Step Two: Choosing the Appropriate Statistical Test As you will see in the following sections of this chapter, the analyst must choose the appropriate statistical test, given the characteristics of the situation under investigation. A number of different statistical tests, along with the situations where they are appropriate, are discussed in this chapter. Exhibit 16.1 provides a guide to selecting the appropriate test for various situations. All the tests in this table are covered in detail later in this chapter. The Practicing Marketing Research feature below further addresses this issue.

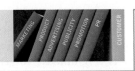

PRACTICING MARKETING RESEARCH

Choosing the Right Test for the Right Situation

How's a researcher to know which kind of statistical testing procedure software to use to generate marketing research data tables? Three basic rules can help marketers determine which testing procedure should be employed in a given situation:

- There is a difference between "two groups" and "three or more groups."
- There is a difference between percentages and means.
- There is a difference between matched samples and independent samples.

When testing percentages with dependent groups, chi-squares should be used for three or more groups, and Z tests should be used for two groups. When testing means, ANOVAs (Analysis of Variance) are used in the case of three or more group, and t tests are used for the two-group case. (See the accompanying table.)

Which Test Should I Use?		
When measuring...	2 Groups	3+ Groups
Percentages	Z test	chi-square
Means	t test	ANOVA

Although analytic software can be very useful for quickly processing survey data, researchers must be careful how they use it. Default settings in many analytic software packages will run the same test automatically, frequently violating the first rule above when testing three or more groups. Thus, in the case of percentages, many software tools will often apply multiple Z tests instead of a chi-square and, in the case of means, multiple t tests instead of an ANOVA.

Statistically, using the wrong test in these instances will result in a confidence level below what you think you are using. For example, when comparing the percentages in three different groups, the chi-square method will determine whether they vary statistically by running a single test comparing percentages for all three groups simultaneously. In contrast, the Z test will run three separate tests, comparing group A to group B, B to C, and C to A individually. Ultimately it is possible that the tests could produce different outcomes, where one test would suggest a statistically significant difference exists across the three groups while others would suggest no statistically significant difference.

Essentially, the chi-square test is taking all the information into account at once, whereas the Z test is running multiple tests on selected portions of the data. In most cases, the results of using the wrong test will probably not lead marketing managers to any critical mistakes based on the research; however, using the wrong testing method can seriously undermine credibility. As a matter of quality control, this error can be easily avoided if researchers are careful to use the right tests and settings when performing their analysis.[3]

Questions

1. Aside from the automatic settings in analytic software mentioned above, can you think of any other procedural factors that might cause a researcher to misapply certain tests?

2. If you have access to analytic software, run a Z test and a chi-square test on the same set of data (you might try pulling one from earlier in the chapter) and compare the results. Were they significantly different? If they did not produce the same results, can you see why?

Step Three: Developing a Decision Rule   Based on our previous discussions of distributions of sample means, you may recognize that one is very unlikely to get a sample result that is exactly equal to the value of the population parameter. The problem is determining whether the difference, or deviation, between the actual value of the sample mean and its expected value based on the hypothesis could have occurred by chance (5 times out of 100, for example) if the statistical hypothesis is true. A **decision rule**, or standard, is needed to determine whether to reject or fail to reject the null hypothesis. Statisticians state such decision rules in terms of significance levels.

> ➤ **decision rule**
> Rule or standard used to determine whether to reject or fail to reject the null hypothesis.

The significance level (α) is critical in the process of choosing between the null and alternative hypotheses. The level of significance—.10, .05, or .01, for example—is the probability that is considered too low to justify acceptance of the null hypothesis.

Consider a situation in which the researcher has decided that she wants to test a hypothesis at the .05 level of significance. This means that she will reject the null hypothesis if the test indicates that the probability of occurrence of the observed result (for example, the difference between the sample mean and its expected value) because the chance or sampling error is less than 5 percent. Rejection of the null hypothesis is equivalent to supporting the alternative hypothesis.

Step Four: Calculating the Value of the Test Statistic   In this step, the researcher does the following:

■ Uses the appropriate formula to calculate the value of the statistic for the test chosen.

■ Compares the value just calculated to the critical value of the statistic (from the appropriate table), based on the decision rule chosen.

■ Based on the comparison, determines to either reject or fail to reject the null hypothesis H_0.

EXHIBIT 16.1	Statistical Tests and Their Uses				
Area of Application	Subgroups or Samples	Level Scaling	Test	Special Requirements	Example
Hypotheses about frequency distribution	One	Nominal	χ^2	Random sample	Are observed differences in the number of people responding to three different promotions likely/not likely due to chance?
	Two or more	Nominal	χ^2	Random sample, independent samples	Are differences in the number of men and women responding to a promotion likely/not likely due to chance?
Hypotheses about means	One (large sample)	Metric (interval or ratio)	Z test for one mean	Random sample, $n \geq 30$	Is the observed difference between a sample estimate of the mean and some set standard or expected value of the mean likely/not likely due to chance?
	One (small sample) Two (large sample)	Metric (interval or ratio) Metric (interval or ratio)	t test for one mean Z test for one mean	Random sample, $n < 30$ Random sample, $n \geq 30$	Same as for small sample above Is the observed difference between the means for two subgroups (mean income for men and women) likely/not likely due to chance?
	Three or more	Metric (interval or ratio)	One-way ANOVA	Random sample	Is the observed variation between means for three or more subgroups (mean expenditures on entertainment for high-, moderate-, and low-income people) likely/not likely due to chance?
Hypotheses about proportions	One (large sample)	Metric (interval or ratio)	Z test for one proportion	Random sample, $n \geq 30$	Is the observed difference between a sample estimate of proportion (percentage who say they will buy) and some set standard or expected value likely/not likely due to chance?
	Two (large sample)	Metric (interval or ratio)	Z test for two proportions	Random sample, $n \geq 30$	Is the observed difference between estimated percentages for two subgroups (percentage of men and women who have college degrees) likely/not likely due to chance?

Step Five: Stating the Conclusion The conclusion summarizes the results of the test. It should be stated from the perspective of the original research question.

Types of Errors in Hypothesis Testing

Hypothesis tests are subject to two general types of errors, typically referred to as type I error and type II error. A **type I error** involves rejecting the null hypothesis when it is, in fact, true. The researcher may reach this incorrect conclusion because the observed difference between the sample and population values is due to sampling error. The researcher must decide how willing she or he is to commit a type I error. The probability of committing a type I error is referred to as the *alpha* (α) *level*. Conversely, $1 - \alpha$ is the probability of making a correct decision by not rejecting the null hypothesis when, in fact, it is true.

A **type II error** involves failing to reject the null hypothesis when it actually is false. A type II error is referred to as a *beta* (β) *error*. The value $1 - \beta$ reflects the probability of making a correct decision in rejecting the null hypothesis when, in fact, it is false. The four possibilities are summarized in Exhibit 16.2.

As we consider the various types of hypothesis tests, keep in mind that when a researcher rejects or fails to reject the null hypothesis, this decision is never made with

type I error (α error) Rejection of the null hypothesis when, in fact, it is true.

type II error (β error) Failure to reject the null hypothesis when, in fact, it is false.

EXHIBIT 16.2	Type I and Type II Errors	
Actual State of the Null Hypothesis	**Fail to Reject H_0**	**Reject H_0**
H_0 is true	Correct $(1 - \alpha)$	Type I error (α)
H_0 is false	Type II error (β)	Correct $(1 - \beta)$

100 percent certainty. There is a probability that the decision is correct, and there is a probability that the decision is not correct. The level of α is set by the researcher, after consulting with his or her client, considering the resources available for the project, and considering the implications of making type I and type II errors. However, the estimation of β is more complicated and is beyond the scope of our discussion. Note that type I and type II errors are not complementary; that is, $\alpha + \beta \neq 1$.

It would be ideal to have control over n (the sample size), α (the probability of a type I error), and β (the probability of a type II error) for any hypothesis test. Unfortunately, only two of the three can be controlled. For a given problem with a fixed sample size, n is fixed, or controlled. Therefore, only one of α and β can be controlled.

Assume that for a given problem you have decided to set $\alpha = .05$. As a result, the procedure you use to test H_0 versus H_a will reject H_0 when it is true (type I error) 5 percent of the time. You could set $\alpha = 0$ so that you would never have a type I error. The idea of never rejecting a correct H_0 sounds good. However, the downside is that β (the probability of a type II error) is equal to 1 in this situation. As a result, you will always fail to reject H_0 when it is false. For example, if $\alpha = 0$ in the fast-food service time example, where H_0 is mean waiting time = 2 minutes, then the resulting test of H_0 versus H_a will automatically fail to reject H_0 (mean waiting time = 2 minutes) whenever the estimated waiting time is any value other than 2 minutes. If, for example, we did a survey and determined that the mean waiting time for the people surveyed was 8.5 minutes, we would still fail to reject (FTR) H_0. As you can see, this is not a good compromise. We need a value of α that offers a more reasonable compromise between the probabilities of the two types of errors. Note that in the situation in which $\alpha = 0$ and $\beta = 1$, $\alpha + \beta = 1$. As you will see later on, this is not true as a general rule.

The value of α selected should be a function of the relative importance of the two types of errors. Suppose you have just had a diagnostic test. The purpose of the test is to determine whether you have a particular medical condition that is fatal in most cases. If you have the disease, a treatment that is painless, inexpensive, and totally without risk will cure the condition 100 percent of the time. Here are the hypotheses to be tested:

> H_0: Test indicates that you do not have the disease.
> H_a: Test indicates that you do have the disease.

Thus,

> $\alpha = P$ (rejecting H_0 when it is true)
> $= $ (test indicates that you have the disease when you do not have it)
> $\beta = P$ (FTR H_0 when in fact it is false)
> $= P$ (test indicates that you do not have the disease when you do have it)

Clearly, a type I error (measured by α) is not nearly as serious as a type II error (measured by β). A type I error is not serious because the test will not harm you if you are well. However, a type II error means that you will not receive the treatment you need even though you are ill.

The value of β is never set in advance. When α is made smaller, β becomes larger. If you want to minimize type II error, then you choose a larger value for α in order to make β smaller. In most situations, the range of acceptable values for α is .01 to .1.

PRACTICING MARKETING RESEARCH

Why in Medicine a Two-Tailed Test Is Preferable to a One-Tailed Test

The one-tailed hypothesis test in clinical research can seem very attractive, efficient, low-cost, and productive, yet it has some hidden problems. Lemuel A. Loye, MD, and Alan T. N. Tita, MD, physicians at the University of Texas and Baylor College of Medicine, respectively, argue that ethical researchers should studiously avoid one-tailed or one-sided testing in medical research for both ethical and cost-efficiency reasons. Why? Because a one-tailed test of a drug, for example, assumes that the drug will be safe and so the test produces no surprises and only demonstrates an unknown level of efficacy—and it will do so with a lower cost and smaller sample size.

In fact, however, that's simply not the case, as the doctors explain. In the 1990s, Dr. Loye was part of a research effort called the Cardiac Arrhythmia Suppression Trial (CAST), which used one-tailed testing of a prescription drug that was supposed to stop irregular heartbeats. CAST researchers assumed unquestioningly that this was the likely result; as it turned out, it wasn't. A lot of people died from the drug, far more than any statistical projection expected.

This incident highlights the shortcomings of one-tailed testing in medicine, say Loye and Tita: It excludes the possibility of harmful effect or negative result because the test cannot distinguish a harmful effect from a null effect (that no action or change happened). The one-tailed test does not allow researchers to draw the correct conclusions if they are proved wrong by the actual results, if the drug is harmful.

The medical community needs assurance that an injury or a negative result is not due to sampling error, and normally this assurance would come from measuring type I error. The trouble here is that one cannot tell what type I error is associated with a harmful finding in a one-tailed test exclusively designed to show only one result—that of benefit. The one-tailed test yields less "strength of evidence" for a positive result than a two-tailed test, and that may jeopardize patient health and lead to patient harm.

One-tailed testing has other limitations in medical research, too. One advantage often proposed in its favor is the reduced sample size required. This is a fallacy, Loye and Tita point out, because 79 percent of the observations needed in a two-tailed test are also needed in a one-tailed test that treats the same subject or drug. Thus any reduction in sample size that is achieved is modest at best.

Furthermore, if the one-tailed test produces a negative result, unanticipated by the test design, retesting is required. A two-tailed study in the first place needs only 63 percent of the total sample size for two separate one-tailed tests and of course avoids the necessity of test repetition. Finally, the two-sided test is "ultimately more informative" when faced with an unexpected outcome and can prevent subsequent patient exposure to or harm from interventions otherwise (wrongly) greenlighted by a one-tailed test.[4]

Questions

1. Are there any circumstances in clinical research where a one-tailed test would be ethically justified?

2. Are there any situations in market research where a one-tailed test might yield data that could lead to harmful effects or conclusions?

In the case of the diagnostic test situation, you might choose a value of α at or near .1 because of the seriousness of a type II error. Conversely, if you are more concerned about type I errors in a given situation, then a small value of α is appropriate. For example, suppose you are testing commercials that were very expensive to produce, and you are concerned about the possibility of rejecting a commercial that is really effective. If there is no real difference between the effects of type I and type II errors, as is often the case, an α value of .05 is commonly used.

Accepting H₀ versus Failing to Reject (FTR) H₀

Researchers often fail to make a distinction between accepting H_0 and failing to reject H_0. However, as noted earlier, there is an important distinction between these two decisions. When a hypothesis is tested, H_0 is presumed to be true until it is demonstrated as likely to be false. In any hypothesis testing situation, the only other hypothesis that can be accepted is the alternative hypothesis H_a. Either there is sufficient evidence to support H_a (reject H_0) or there is not (fail to reject H_0). The real question is whether there is enough evidence in the data to conclude that H_a is correct. If we fail to reject H_0, we are saying that the data do not provide sufficient support of the claim made in H_a—not that we accept the statement made in H_0.

One-Tailed versus Two-Tailed Test

Tests are either one-tailed or two-tailed. The decision as to which to use depends on the nature of the situation and what the researcher is trying to demonstrate. For example, when the quality control department of a fast-food organization receives a shipment of chicken breasts from one of its vendors and needs to determine whether the product meets specifications in regard to fat content, a one-tailed test is appropriate. The shipment will be rejected if it does not meet minimum specifications. On the other hand, the managers of the meat company that supplies the product should run two-tailed tests to determine two factors. First, they must make sure that the product meets the minimum specifications of their customer before they ship it. Second, they want to determine whether the product exceeds specifications because this can be costly to them. If they are consistently providing a product that exceeds the level of quality they have contracted to provide, their costs may be unnecessarily high.

The classic example of a situation requiring a two-tailed test is the testing of electric fuses. A fuse must trip, or break contact, when it reaches a preset temperature or a fire may result. On the other hand, you do not want the fuse to break contact before it reaches the specified temperature or it will shut off the electricity unnecessarily. The test used in the quality control process for testing fuses must, therefore, be two-tailed. The issue of one-tailed versus two-tailed tests is discussed in the feature on page 477.

Example of Performing a Statistical Test

Income is an important determinant of the sales of luxury cars. Lexus North America (LNA) is in the process of developing sales estimates for the Southern California market, one of its key markets. According to the U.S. Census, the average annual family income in the market is $55,347. LNA has just completed a survey of 250 randomly selected households in the market to obtain other measures needed for its sales forecasting model. The recently completed survey indicates that the average annual family income in the market is $54,323. The actual value of the population mean (μ) is unknown. This gives us two estimates of μ: the census result and the survey result. The difference between these two estimates could make a substantial difference in the estimates of Lexus sales produced by LNA's forecasting model. In the calculations, the U.S. Census Bureau estimate is treated as the best estimate of μ.

FROM THE FRONT LINE

More Tips on Significance Testing

Paul Schmiege, Marketing Science, DSS Research

On the quantitative side of the marketing research industry, you spend a great deal of time measuring and comparing. But unlike grabbing a yardstick and measuring a physical quantity, your measurements have sampling error. ('Sampling error' is a technical term and does not connate a mistake.) Then when you compare two measurements, both of which have sampling error, you can not be 100% confident that a difference even exists. That's where statistics comes in and says, "Though you can't be 100% confident, you can test to see if we are 95% or 90% confident that a difference exists."

The point of making comparisons is to help lead you as interpreters of data to evaluations. "Is this difference important, is it something that we should act on, should we continue with the same advertising strategy to increase unaided awareness?" Unfortunately, statistics can not answer those questions for you.

The distinction between testing a difference with a statistical test and evaluating the meaning or importance of said difference is important to remember. The former, The single most common test in marketing research is the two-sample *t* test. You use it to answer questions like this: "Last year, the percentage of respondents aware of our brand on an unaided basis was 43.2%. This year the corresponding percentage was 47.5%. Is this difference significant?" This type of question is so common you might not ever see any other test in your entire career. Because the two-sample t test is so important, it is good to keep at least two points in mind about it:

- The two-sample *t* test is a two-tail test. It asks, "Does a significant difference exist?" It does not ask, "Is the first significantly greater than the second?" or "Is the first significantly less than the second?" Consequently, if a significant difference exists you should say, "A statistically significant difference exists, and that observed difference is higher (or lower)."
- The two-sample *t* test is run with the assumption of equal variances. The true standard deviation for the combined populations is unknown, so you "pool" the two sample standard deviations together to calculate something similar to a weighted average. In academic research, you would first test whether to assume equal or unequal variance, but you will probably never have to do that in the business world.

For any given observed difference, there are sample sizes large enough that the difference will be significant in a two-sample *t* test (sample sizes go in the denominator of the equation). Or to think of it from another perspective, when you start testing with larger and larger sample sizes, smaller and smaller differences become statistically significant, but practical significance remains the same. Is a 0.5% increase worth telling management about even if it should happen to be statistically significant? Probably not.

In the end always remember that the technical term "statistical significance" is not the same as the more intuitive terms like "practical significance" or "importance." At the heart of its technical meaning, significance in the field of statistics means the difference is likely greater than we would expect due to sampling error. Don't mistake a statistical test, a useful tool in the evaluation, for the evaluation itself.

The quality control department of a fast-food organization would probably do a one-tailed test to determine whether a shipment of chicken breasts met product specifications. However, the managers of the meat company that supplied the chicken breasts would probably do a two-tailed test.

LNA decides to statistically compare the census and survey estimates. The statistics for the sample are

$$\overline{X} = \$54,323$$
$$S = \$4,323$$
$$n = 250$$

The following hypotheses are produced:

$$H_0: \mu = \$55,347$$
$$H_a: \mu \neq \$55,347$$

The decision makers at LNA are willing to use a test that will reject H_0 when it is correct only 5 percent of the time ($\alpha = .05$). This is the significance level of the test. LNA will reject H_0 if $|\overline{X} - \$55,347|$ is larger than can be explained by sampling error at $\alpha = .05$

Standardizing the data so that the result can be directly related to Z values in Exhibit 2 in Appendix 3, we have the following criterion:

Reject H_0 if $|(\overline{X} - \$55,347)/(S/\sqrt{n})|$ is larger than can be explained by sampling error at $\alpha = .05$. This expression can be rewritten as

$$\left| \frac{\overline{X} - \$55,347}{S/\sqrt{n}} \right| > k$$

What is the value of k? If H_0 is true and the sample size is large (≥ 30), then (based on the central limit theorem) X approximates a normal random variable with a mean equal to 0 and a standard deviation equal to 1.

Exhibit 16.3

Shaded Area Is
Significance Level α

$$\text{Mean} = \mu = \$55{,}347$$
$$\text{Standard deviation} = \frac{S}{\sqrt{n}}$$

That is, if H_0 is true, $(\overline{X} - \$55{,}347)/(S/\sqrt{n})$ approximates a standard normal variable Z for samples of 30 or larger with a mean equal to 0 and a standard deviation equal to 1.

We will reject H_0 if $|Z| > k$. When $|Z| > k$, either $Z > k$ or $Z < -k$, as shown in Exhibit 16.3. Given that

$$P(|Z| > k) = .05$$

the total shaded area is .05, with .025 in each tail (two-tailed test). The area between 0 and k is .475. Referring to Exhibit 2 in Appendix 3, we find that $k = 1.96$. Therefore, the test is

$$\text{Reject } H_0 \text{ if } \left| \frac{\overline{X} - \$55{,}347}{S/\sqrt{n}} \right| > 1.96$$

and FTR H_0 otherwise. In other words,

$$\text{Reject } H_0 \text{ if } \left| \frac{\overline{X} - \$55{,}347}{S/\sqrt{n}} \right| > 1.96 \text{ or if } \left| \frac{\overline{X} - \$55{,}347}{S/\sqrt{n}} \right| < 1.96$$

The question is, is $\overline{X} = \$54{,}323$ far enough away from $\$55{,}347$ for LNA to reject H_0? The results show that

$$Z = \frac{\overline{X} - \$55{,}347}{S/\sqrt{n}}$$
$$= \frac{\$54{,}323 - \$55{,}347}{\$4{,}322/\sqrt{250}} = -3.75$$

Because $-3.75 < -1.96$, we reject H_0. On the basis of the sample results and $\alpha = .05$, the conclusion is that the average household income in the market is not equal to \$55,347. If H_0 is true ($\mu = \$55,347$), then the value of X obtained from the sample (\$54,323) is 3.75 standard deviations to the left of the mean on the normal curve for X. A value of X this far away from the mean is very unlikely (probability is less than .05). As a result, we conclude that H_0 is not likely to be true, and we reject it.

Having said all this, we caution against an overreliance on statistical tests and significance/nonsignificance. The Practicing Marketing Research feature below covers this point in greater detail.

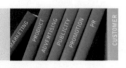

PRACTICING MARKETING RESEARCH

Does Statistical Precision Validate Results?[5]

The presence of statistical significance in marketing research analysis can be deceptive. *Statistical* significance does not necessarily mean that the difference has any *practical* significance. In addition to large sample sizes, there are many potential sources of error that can create problems for researchers when identifying statistically significant differences.

Generally, two kinds of error affect the validity of statistical measurements. *Random error* introduces error variance, but as it occurs randomly across respondents, it does not add statistical bias to the data. *Systematic error* is consistent across respondents, creating a bias within the data that may or may not be known. Typically, the causes for these kinds of error fall into two categories: sampling error, arising in the process of building a respondent pool; and measurement error, arising from the way the questionnaire is constructed.

Sampling Error

Three major sources of sampling error include under coverage, nonresponse, and self-selection.

1. *Under coverage*—Under coverage occurs when a certain segment of the population is not adequately represented.

2. *Nonresponse*—Nonresponse error is a result of portions of the population being unwilling to participate in research projects.

3. *Self-selection*—Self-selection can result from respondents having control over survey completion. For instance, participants in an online survey panel might get bored and opt out before the survey is over.

Measurement Error

The following six types of measurement error can result in random or systematic error.

1. *Question interpretation*—Respondents may interpret vague or ambiguously worded questions differently.

2. *Respondent assumptions*—Regardless of the way a question is worded, respondents still bring personal assumptions to the table, including any number of varying external factors influencing their understanding of the question.

3. *Question order*—Respondents might answer a question differently depending on where it falls in the survey, as their opinions might be influenced by their thoughts on surrounding questions.

4. *Method variance*—Researchers must be aware of potential errors introduced by the method used to deliver the survey.

5. *Attribute wording*—The way in which survey attributes are described may elicit different answers from respondents.

6. *Omitting important questions*—Systematic error most commonly results from inadequate coverage of critical variables within the question battery. Absent variables can significantly affect the results of data analysis.

Managerial Significance

Researchers must be careful to differentiate between resultant random and systematic errors. Furthermore, they must also realize that statistical precision does not necessarily validate results. Rather than focusing on statistical significance in and of itself, researchers need to identify results that have managerial significance—results that are relevant to the decision-making process. Given a large enough sample, any null hypothesis can be discounted, and any two means can be shown to be statistically different. An absence of statistical significance may be just as relevant as any demonstrated statistical significance. As

such, statistical testing should be used as a tool to discover practical insights, not to define them.

Questions

1. Of the potential causes for error described above, which do you think would be easiest to identify? Hardest? Explain your reasoning.

2. Can you think of any ways that could help researchers determine whether occurrences of statistical significance in their results have managerial significance?

Commonly Used Statistical Hypothesis Tests

A number of commonly used statistical hypothesis tests of differences are presented in the following sections. Many other statistical tests have been developed and are used, but a full discussion of all of them is beyond the scope of this text.

The distributions used in the following sections for comparing the computed and tabular values of the statistics are the Z distribution, the t distribution, the F distribution, and the chi-square (χ^2) distribution. The tabular values for these distributions appear in Exhibits 2, 3, 4, and 5 of Appendix 3.

Independent versus Related Samples

In some cases, one needs to test the hypothesis that the value of a variable in one population is equal to the value of that same variable in another population. Selection of the appropriate test statistic requires the researcher to consider whether the samples are independent or related. **Independent samples** are those in which measurement of the variable of interest in one sample has no effect on measurement of the variable in the other sample. It is not necessary that there be two different surveys, only that the measurement of the variable in one population has no effect on the measurement of the variable in the other population. In the case of **related samples**, measurement of the variable of interest in one sample may influence measurement of the variable in another sample.

If, for example, men and women were interviewed in a particular survey regarding their frequency of eating out, there is no way that a man's response could affect or change the way a woman would respond to a question in the survey. Thus, this would be an example of independent samples. On the other hand, consider a situation in which the researcher needed to determine the effect of a new advertising campaign on consumer awareness of a particular brand. To do this, the researcher might survey a random sample of consumers before introducing the new campaign and then survey the same sample of consumers 90 days after the new campaign was introduced. These samples are not independent. The measurement of awareness 90 days after the start of the campaign may be affected by the first measurement.

➤ **independent samples**
Samples in which measurement of a variable in one population has no effect on measurement of the variable in the other.

➤ **related samples**
Samples in which measurement of a variable in one population may influence measurement of the variable in the other.

Degrees of Freedom

➤ **degrees of freedom**
Number of observations in a statistical problem that are free to vary.

Many of the statistical tests discussed in this chapter require the researcher to specify degrees of freedom in order to find the critical value of the test statistic from the table for that statistic. The number of **degrees of freedom** is the number of observations in a statistical problem that are not restricted or are free to vary.

The number of degrees of freedom (d.f.) is equal to the number of observations minus the number of assumptions or constraints necessary to calculate a statistic. Consider the problem of adding five numbers when the mean of the five numbers is known to be 20. In this situation, only four of the five numbers are free to vary. Once four of the numbers are known, the last value is also known (can be calculated) because the mean value must be 20. If four of the five numbers were 14, 23, 24, and 18, then the fifth number would have to be 21 to produce a mean of 20. We would say that the sample has $n - 1$ or 4 degrees of freedom. It is as if the sample had one less observation—the inclusion of degrees of freedom in the calculation adjusts for this fact.

Goodness of Fit

Chi-Square Test

As noted earlier in the text, data collected in surveys are often analyzed by means of one-way frequency counts and cross tabulations.[6] The purpose of a cross tabulation is to study relationships among variables. The question is, do the numbers of responses that fall into the various categories differ from what one would expect? For example, a study might involve partitioning users into groups by gender (male, female), age (under 18, 18 to 35, over 35), or income level (low, middle, high) and cross tabulating on the basis of answers to questions about preferred brand or level of use. The **chi-square** (χ^2) **test** enables the research analyst to determine whether an observed pattern of frequencies corresponds to, or fits, an "expected" pattern.[7] It tests the "goodness of fit" of the observed distribution to an expected distribution. We will look at the application of this technique to test distributions of cross-tabulated categorical data for a single sample and for two independent samples.

➤ **chi-square test**
Test of the goodness of fit between the observed distribution and the expected distribution of a variable.

Chi-Square Test of a Single Sample   Suppose the marketing manager of a retail electronics chain needs to test the effectiveness of three special deals (deal 1, deal 2, and deal 3). Each deal will be offered for a month. The manager wants to measure the effect of each deal on the number of customers visiting a test store during the time the deal is on. The number of customers visiting the store under each deal is as follows:

Deal	Month	Customers per Month
1	April	11,700
2	May	12,100
3	June	11,780
Total		35,580

The marketing manager needs to know whether there is a significant difference between the numbers of customers visiting the store during the time periods covered by the three deals. The chi-square (χ^2) one-sample test is the appropriate test to use to answer this question. This test is applied as follows:

1. Specify the null and alternative hypotheses.

   ■ Null hypothesis H_0: The numbers of customers visiting the store under the various deals are equal.

■ Alternative hypothesis H_a: There is a significant difference in the numbers of customers visiting the store under the various deals.

2. Determine the number of visitors who would be expected in each category if the null hypothesis were correct (E_i). In this example, the null hypothesis is that there is no difference in the numbers of customers attracted by the different deals. Therefore, an equal number of customers would be expected under each deal. Of course, this assumes that no other factors influenced the number of visits to the store. Under the null (no difference) hypothesis, the expected number of customers visiting the store in each deal period would be computed as follows:

$$E_i = \frac{TV}{N}$$

where TV = total number of visits

N = number of months

Thus,

$$\chi^2 = \frac{35,580}{3} = 11,860$$

The researcher should always check for cells in which small expected frequencies occur because they can distort χ^2 results. No more than 20 percent of the categories should have an expected frequency of less than 5, and none should have an expected frequency of less than 1. This is not a problem in this case.

3. Calculate the χ^2 value, using the formula

$$\chi^2 = \sum_{i=1}^{k} \frac{(O_i - E_i)^2}{E_i}$$

where O_i = observed number in ith category

E_i = expected number in ith category

k = number of categories

For this example,

$$\chi^2 = \frac{(11,700 - 11,860)^2}{11,860} + \frac{(12,100 - 11.860)^2}{11,860}$$

$$+ \frac{(11,780 - 11,860)^2}{11,860}$$

$$= 7.6$$

4. Select the level of significance α. If the .05 level of significance (α) is selected, the tabular χ^2 value with 2 degrees of freedom ($k - 1$) is 5.99. (See Exhibit 4 in Appendix 3 for $k - 1 = 2$ d.f., $\alpha = .05$.)

5. State the result. Because the calculated χ^2 value (7.6) is higher than the table value (5.99), we *reject the null hypothesis*. Therefore, we conclude with 95 percent confidence that customer response to the deals was significantly different. Unfortunately, this test tells us only that the overall variation among the cell frequencies is greater

than would be expected by chance. It does not tell us whether any individual cell is significantly different from the others.

Chi-Square Test of Two Independent Samples   Marketing researchers often need to determine whether there is any association between two or more variables. Before formulation of a marketing strategy, questions such as the following may need to be answered: Are men and women equally divided into heavy-, medium-, and light-user categories? Are purchasers and nonpurchasers equally divided into low-, middle-, and high-income groups? The chi-square (χ^2) test for two independent samples is the appropriate test in such situations.

The technique will be illustrated using the data from Exhibit 16.4. A convenience store chain wants to determine the nature of the relationship, if any, between gender of customer and frequency of visits to stores in the chain. Frequency of visits has been divided into three categories: 1 to 5 visits per month (light user), 6 to 14 visits per month (medium user), and 16 and above visits per month (heavy user). The steps in conducting this test follow.

1. State the null and alternative hypotheses.

   ■ Null hypothesis H_0: There is no relationship between gender and frequency of visits.

   ■ Alternative hypothesis H_a: There is a significant relationship between gender and frequency of visits.

2. Place the observed (sample) frequencies in a $k \times r$ table (cross tabulation or contingency table), using the k columns for the sample groups and the r rows for the conditions or treatments. Calculate the sum of each row and each column. Record

EXHIBIT 16.4	Data for 32 Test of Two Independent Samples						
Visits to Convenience Store by Males				**Visits to Convenience Stores by Females**			
Number X_m	Frequency f_m	Percent	Cumulative Percent	Number X_f	Frequency f_f	Percent	Cumulative Percent
2	2	4.4	4.4	2	5	7.0	7.0
3	5	11.1	15.6	3	4	5.6	12.7
5	7	15.6	31.1	4	7	9.9	22.5
6	2	4.4	35.6	5	10	14.1	36.6
7	1	2.2	37.8	6	6	8.5	45.1
8	2	4.4	42.2	7	3	4.2	49.3
9	1	2.2	44.4	8	6	8.5	57.7
10	7	15.6	60.0	9	2	2.8	60.6
12	3	6.7	66.7	10	13	18.3	78.9
15	5	11.1	77.8	12	4	5.6	84.5
20	6	13.3	91.1	15	3	4.2	88.7
23	1	2.2	93.3	16	2	2.8	91.5
25	1	2.2	95.6	20	4	5.6	97.2
30	1	2.2	97.8	21	1	1.4	98.6
40	1	2.2	100.0	25	1	1.4	100.0

$n_m = 45$ $n_f = 71$

Mean number of visits by males, $\bar{X}_m = \dfrac{\sum X_m f_m}{45} = 11.5$ Mean number of visits by females, $\bar{X}_f = \dfrac{\sum X_f f_f}{71} = 8.5$

those totals at the margins of the table (they are called *marginal totals*). Also, calculate the total for the entire table (*N*).

	Male	Female	Totals
1–5 visits	14	26	40
6–14 visits	16	34	50
15 and above visits	15	11	26
Totals	45	71	116

SPSS JUMP START FOR CHI-SQUARE TEST

Steps that you need to go through to do the chi-square test problem shown in the book are provided below along with the output produced. Use the data set **Chisqex**, which you can download from the Web site for the text.

Steps in SPSS

1. Select *Analyze → Descriptive Statistics → Crosstabs*.
2. Move **bin** to Rows.
3. Move **gender** to Columns.
4. Click Statistics.
5. Check box for Chi-square.
6. Click Continue.
7. Click OK.

SPSS Output for Chi-Square Test

Crosstabs

Case Processing Summary

	Cases					
	Valid		Missing		Total	
	N	Percent	N	Percent	N	Percent
Bin * Gender	116	100.0%	0	.0%	116	100.0%

Bin * Gender Crosstabulation

Count

		Gender		Total
		Male	Female	
Bin	1-5 visits	14	26	40
	6-14 visits	16	34	50
	15 and above visits	15	11	26
Total		45	71	116

Chi-Square Tests

	Value	df	Asymp. Sig. (2-sided)
Pearson Chi-Square	5.125[a]	2	.077
Likelihood Ratio	5.024	2	.081
Linear-by-Linear Association	2.685	1	.101
N of Valid Cases	116		

a. 0 cells (.0%) have expected count less than 5. The minimum expected count is 10.09.

3. Determine the expected frequency for each cell in the contingency table by calculating the product of the two marginal totals common to that cell and dividing that value by *N*.

	Male	Female
1–5 visits	$\frac{45 \times 40}{116} = 15.5$	$\frac{71 \times 40}{116} = 24.5$
6–14 visits	$\frac{45 \times 50}{116} = 19.4$	$\frac{71 \times 50}{116} = 30.6$
15 and above visits	$\frac{45 \times 26}{116} = 10.1$	$\frac{71 \times 26}{116} = 15.9$

The x^2 value will be distorted if more than 20 percent of the cells have an expected frequency of less than 5 or if any cell has an expected frequency of less than 1. The test should not be used under these conditions.

4. Calculate the value of χ^2 using

$$\chi^2 = \sum_{i=1}^{r} \sum_{j=1}^{k} \frac{(O_{ij} - E_{ij})^2}{E_{ij}}$$

where O_{ij} 5 observed number in the ith row of the jth column
E_{ij} 5 expected number in the ith row of the jth column

For this example,

$$\chi^2 = \frac{(14 - 15.52)^2}{15.52} + \frac{(26 - 24.48)^2}{24.48} + \frac{(16 - 19.4)^2}{19.4}$$
$$+ \frac{(34 - 30.6)^2}{30.6} + \frac{(15 - 10.09)^2}{10.09} + \frac{(11 - 15.91)^2}{15.91}$$
$$= 5.1$$

5. State the result. The tabular χ^2 value at a .05 level of significance and $(r - 1) \times (k - 1) = 2$ degrees of freedom is 5.99 (see Exhibit 4 of Appendix 3). Because the calculated $\chi^2 = 5.1$ is less than the tabular value, we *fail to reject (FTR) the null hypothesis* and conclude that there is no significant difference between males and females in terms of frequency of visits.

Hypotheses about One Mean

Z Test

→ **Z test**
Hypothesis test used for a single mean if the sample is large enough and drawn at random.

One of the most common goals of marketing research studies is to make some inference about the population mean. If the sample size is large enough ($n \geq 30$), the appropriate test statistic for testing a hypothesis about a single mean is the **Z test**. For small samples ($n < 30$) the t test with $n - 1$ degrees of freedom (where $n =$ sample size) should be used.

Video Connection, a Dallas video store chain, recently completed a survey of 200 consumers in its market area. One of the questions was "Compared to other video stores in the area, would you say Video Connection is much better than average, somewhat better than average, average, somewhat worse than average, or much worse than average?" Responses were coded as follows:

Response	Code
Much better	5
Somewhat better	4
Average	3
Somewhat worse	2
Much worse	1

The mean rating of Video Connection is 3.4. The sample standard deviation is 1.9. How can the management of Video Connection be confident that its video stores' mean rating is significantly higher than 3 (average in the rating scale)? The Z test for hypotheses about one mean is the appropriate test in this situation. The steps in the procedure follow.

1. Specify the null and alternative hypotheses.
   - Null hypothesis $H_0:M \leq 3$ (M = response on rating scale)
   - Alternative hypothesis $H_a:M > 3$

2. Specify the level of sampling error (α) allowed. For $\alpha = .05$ the table value of Z(critical) = 1.64. (See Exhibit 3 in Appendix 2 for d.f. = ∞, .05 significance, one-tail. The table for t is used because $t = Z$ for samples greater than 30.) Management's need to be very confident that the mean rating is significantly higher than 3 is interpreted to mean that the chance of being wrong because of sampling error should be no more than .05 (an $\alpha = .05$).

PRACTICING MARKETING RESEARCH

Taking the Z Test into the Classroom and Courtroom— Two Practical Uses

Statisticians customarily use the Z test to test a hypothesis about a single mean when the sample size is sufficiently large—typically, greater than 30 elements. Here are two practical applications of the Z test as used by the California State Personnel Board to assess differences in populations and by lawyers to analyze juror challenges.

Testing Teacher Population Statistics

Hazelwood School District v. United States (1977) involved the issue of whether appropriate numbers of black teachers had been hired for a school in Saint Louis County, Missouri, proportional to the black population of the county and state. Legal researchers used a one-sample Z test to determine whether a random population sample matched the total population—in this case, pertaining to the number of qualified black teachers in a population versus how many had actually been hired in a specific school district.

The hypothesis presumed that the two populations matched; the Z test showed they did not. Specifically, the researchers used the Z test to examine the null hypothesis that any variation in gender, age, or ethnic background between the

two groups was due to random variation. The Z test enabled researchers to reject the null hypothesis. It also set a research precedent and established a viable protocol for other school districts, including the California State Personnel Board (CSPB), provided the ratio between population and sample size is at least 5:1 and preferably 10:1.

The CSPB uses the one-sample Z test to study disparities in sample populations drawn from specially indicated populations. According to Mel Majesty, PhD, who wrote a paper on the issue for the CSPB, the Board uses the Z test "to compare applications accepted for a particular California State classification (population) with class composition (sample) for that classification." In actual terms, this might involve the number of women in the classification (the sample) contrasted with the number of women in the California labor force (total population). Majesty explained that the Board uses the Z test to see whether p–P is a big enough difference that its occurrence cannot be ascribed to chance—in other words, it is significant in real-world terms. Generally, majesty states, significance is accepted if the Z value is equal to or greater than 1.65 and if a one-tailed test at a .05 level of significance is used.[8]

Lawyer Advocacy or Verbal Discrimination?

Suppose you are involved in equitable juror selection for an important case and you want to assess unintentional discrimination. Marvin L. Longabaugh, a practicing attorney and president of Magellan Research, an opinion research firm in Las Vegas, Nevada, says that the Z test is well suited for this assessment. It provides a means for both parties (prosecution and defense) to see if a question presented to jurors that seems "plausibly neutral" is discriminatory.

Longabaugh conducted a survey of 408 potential jurors for a trial in Clark County, Nevada. For his Z test he used a 98 percent significance threshold. Participants were polled on demographic questions pertaining to gender, ethnic background, educational level, and other factors; then they were given a list of "indicator statements" and were asked whether they agreed with the statements; finally, they were asked personal background questions, such as about previous jury duty.

The results were cross tabulated to show that answers correlated with demographic traits. Then the researchers applied the Z test to identify demographic traits that significantly deviated from the mean. These traits fell into three categories: (1) protected classes (gender and race); (2) suspect classes (income, marital status, age, education, and religion); and (3) other classes (number of children living at home, job type, industry, and length of residence in the county). In this way, the Z test highlighted any question that, if presented to a prospective juror with that specific demographic trait, could potentially result in discrimination if the opposing lawyer used the answer as a basis for a peremptory challenge during jury selection.

If a lawyer wants to eliminate a "facially neutral" but suspect question from the jury selection protocol, Longabaugh explains, he can use the Z test to show with minutely focused precision that, for example, it discriminates against people whose income is less than $20,000 a year, who are married, or who are junior college graduates. The Z test, he concludes, is a "meaningful and nondiscriminatory method" for the courts to honor important legal precedents and guidelines (such as Supreme Court rulings) on the parameters for advocacy versus discrimination in peremptory challenges to potential jurors.[9]

Questions

1. Identify two other job areas where the Z test would be helpful in distinguishing sample size and total population matches or disparities.

2. Should the Z test be used routinely in jury selection?

3. Determine the sample standard deviation (S), which is given as $S = 1.90$.

4. Calculate the estimated standard error of the mean, using the formula

$$S_{\bar{X}} = \frac{S}{\sqrt{n}}$$

where $S_{\bar{X}}$ = estimated standard error of the mean

In this case,

$$S_{\bar{X}} = \frac{1.9}{\sqrt{200}} = 0.13$$

5. Calculate the test statistic:

$$Z = \frac{(\text{Sample mean}) - \left(\begin{array}{c}\text{Population mean specified} \\ \text{under the null hypothesis}\end{array}\right)}{\text{Estimated standard error of the mean}}$$

$$= \frac{3.4 - 3}{0.13} = 3.07$$

6. State the result. *The null hypothesis can be rejected* because the calculated Z value (3.07) is larger than the critical Z value (1.64). Management of Video Connection can infer with 95 percent confidence that its video stores' mean rating is significantly higher than 3. Further discussion of Z test application is provided in the feature above.

t Test

→ **t test**
Hypothesis test used for a single mean if the sample is too small to use the *Z* test.

As noted earlier, for small samples ($n < 30$), the ***t* test** with $n - 1$ degrees of freedom is the appropriate test for making statistical inferences. The t distribution also is theoretically correct for large samples ($n \geq 30$). However, it approaches and becomes indistinguishable from the normal distribution for samples of 30 or more observations. Although the Z test is generally used for large samples, nearly all statistical packages use the t test for all sample sizes.

To see the application of the t test, consider a soft-drink manufacturer that test markets a new soft drink in Denver. Twelve supermarkets in that city are selected at random and the new soft drink is offered for sale in these stores for a limited period. The company estimates that it must sell more than 1,000 cases per week in each store for the brand to be profitable enough to warrant large-scale introduction. Actual average sales per store per week for the test are shown in the accompanying table.

Here is the procedure for testing whether sales per store per week are more than 1,000 cases:

1. Specify the null and alternative hypotheses.
   - Null hypothesis H_0: $\bar{X} \leq 1,000$ cases per store per week ($\bar{X} =$ average sales per store per week).
   - Alternative hypothesis H_a: $X > 1,000$ cases per store per week.

Store	Average Sales per Week (X_i)
1	870
2	910
3	1,050
4	1,200
5	860
6	1,400
7	1,305
8	890
9	1,250
10	1,100
11	950
12	1,260

Mean sales per week, $\bar{X} = \dfrac{\sum\limits_{i=1}^{n} X_i}{n} = 1087.1$

2. Specify the level of sampling error (α) allowed. For $\alpha = .05$, the table value of t(critical) $= 1.796$. (See Exhibit 3 in Appendix 3 for $12 - 1 = 11$ d.f., $\alpha = .05$, one-tail test. A one-tailed t test is appropriate because the new soft drink will be introduced on a large scale only if sales per week are more than 1,000 cases.)

3. Determine the sample standard deviation (*S*) as follows:

$$S = \sqrt{\dfrac{\displaystyle\sum_{i=1}^{n}(X_i - \overline{X})^2}{n-1}}$$

where X_i = observed sales per week in *i*th store

$\overline{X}$ = average sales per week

n = number of stores

For the sample data,

$$S = \sqrt{\dfrac{403,822.9}{(12-1)}} = 191.6$$

Further discussion of the *t* test is provided in the SPSS feature on page 000.

surveysolutions XP

SPSS JUMP START FOR *t* TEST

Steps that you need to go through to do the *t*-test problem shown in the book are provided below along with the output produced. Use the data set **TTestex**, which you can download from the Web site for the text.

1. Select *Analyze → Compare Means → One-Sample T Test*.
2. Move **sales** to Test Variable(s).
3. Input 1000 after Test Value.
4. Click OK.

SPSS Output for T Test

T-Test

One-Sample Statistics

	N	Mean	Std. Deviation	Std. Error Mean
Average Sales per Week	12	1087.08	191.602	55.311

One-Sample Test

	Test Value = 1000					
				Mean Difference	95% Confidence Interval of the Difference	
	t	df	Sig. (2-tailed)		Lower	Upper
Average Sales per Week	1.574	11	.144	87.083	-34.65	208.82

Note:

SPSS here only lists the significance for a two-tailed test. We need the significance of a one-tailed test, which is half this. .072 is greater than = .05 so fail to reject the null hypothesis.

4. Calculate the estimated standard error of the mean $(S_{\bar{X}})$, using the following formula:

$$S_{\bar{X}} = \frac{S}{\sqrt{n}}$$

$$= \frac{191.6}{\sqrt{12}} = 55.3$$

5. Calculate the *t*-test statistic:

$$Z = \frac{(\text{Sample mean}) - \left(\begin{array}{c}\text{Population mean}\\\text{under the null hypothesis}\end{array}\right)}{\text{Estimated standard error of the mean}}$$

$$= \frac{1{,}087.1 - 1000}{55.31} = 1.6$$

6. State the result. *The null hypothesis cannot be rejected* because the calculated value of *t* is less than the critical value of *t*. Although mean sales per store per week ($\overline{X} = 1087.1$) are higher than 1,000 units, the difference is not statistically significant, based on the 12 stores sampled. On the basis of this test and the decision criterion specified, the large-scale introduction of the new soft drink is not warranted.

Hypotheses about Two Means

Marketers are frequently interested in testing differences between groups. In the following example of testing the differences between two means, the samples are independent.

The management of a convenience store chain is interested in differences between the store visit rates of men and women. Believing that men visit convenience stores more often than women, management collected data on convenience store visits from 1,000 randomly selected consumers. Testing this hypothesis involves the following steps:

1. Specify the null and alternative hypotheses.
   - ■ Null hypothesis H_0: $M_m - M_f \leq 0$; the mean visit rate of men (M_m) is the same as or less than the mean visit rate of women (M_f).
   - ■ Alternative hypothesis H_a: $M_m - M_f > 0$; the mean visit rate of men (M_m) is higher than the mean visit rate of women (M_f).

   The observed difference in the two means (Exhibit 16.4) is $11.49 - 8.51 = 2.98$.

2. Set the level of sampling error (α). The managers decided that the acceptable level of sampling error for this test is $\alpha = .05$. For $\alpha = .05$ the table value of Z(critical) $= 1.64$. (See Exhibit 3 in Appendix 3 for d.f. $= \infty$, .05 significance, one-tail. The table for *t* is used because $t = Z$ for samples greater than 30.)

3. Calculate the estimated standard error of the differences between the two means as follows:

$$S_{X_{m-f}} = \sqrt{\frac{S_m^2}{n_m} + \frac{S_f^2}{n_f}}$$

where

S_m = estimated standard deviation of population *m* (men)
S_f = estimated standard deviation of population *f* (women)
n_m = sample size for sample *m*
n_f = sample size for sample *f*

Therefore,

$$S_{\bar{X}_{m-f}} = \sqrt{\frac{(8.16)^2}{45} + \frac{(5.23)^2}{71}} = 1.37$$

Note that this formula is for those cases in which the two samples have unequal variances. A separate formula is used when the two samples have equal variances. When this test is run in SAS and many other statistical packages, two *t* values are provided—one for each variance assumption.

4. Calculate the test statistic *Z* as follows:

$$Z = \frac{\left(\begin{array}{c}\text{Difference between means}\\\text{of first and second sample}\end{array}\right) - \left(\begin{array}{c}\text{Difference between means}\\\text{under the null hypothesis}\end{array}\right)}{\text{Standard error of the differences between the two means}}$$

$$= \frac{(11.49 - 8.51) - 0}{1.37} = 2.18$$

5. State the result. The calculated value of *Z* (2.18) is larger than the critical value (1.64), so *the null hypothesis is rejected.* Management can conclude with 95 percent confidence $(1 - \alpha = .95)$ that, on average, men visit convenience stores more often than do women.

Before launching new services designed for families with an annual income of more than $50,000, the bank needs to be certain about the percentage of its customers who meet or exceed this threshold income.

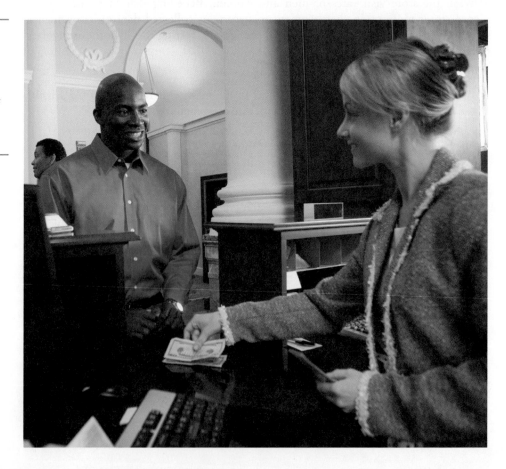

Hypotheses about Proportions

In many situations, researchers are concerned with phenomena that are expressed in terms of percentages.[10] For example, marketers might be interested in testing for the proportion of respondents who prefer brand A versus those who prefer brand B or those who are brand loyal versus those who are not.

Proportion in One Sample

A survey of 500 customers conducted by a major bank indicated that slightly more than 74 percent had family incomes of more than $50,000 per year. If this is true, the bank will develop a special package of services for this group. Before developing and introducing the new package of services, management wants to determine whether the true percentage is greater than 60 percent. The survey results show that 74.3 percent of the bank's customers surveyed reported family incomes of $50,000 or more per year. The procedure for the **hypothesis test of proportions** follows:

1. Specify the null and alternative hypotheses.
   - Null hypothesis H_0: $P \leq .60$.
   - Alternative hypothesis H_a: $P > .60$ (P = proportion of customers with family incomes of $50,000 or more per year).

2. Specify the level of sampling error (α) allowed. For $\alpha = .05$, the table value of Z(critical) = 1.64. (See Exhibit 3 in Appendix 3 for d.f. = ∞, .05 significance, one-tail. The table for t is used because $t = Z$ for samples greater than 30.)

3. Calculate the estimated standard error, using the value of P specified in the null hypothesis:

> **hypothesis test of proportions**
> Test to determine whether the difference between proportions is greater than would be expected because of sampling error.

$$S_p = \sqrt{\frac{P(1 - P)}{n - 1}}$$

where P = proportion specified in the null hypothesis
n = sample size

Therefore,

$$S_p = \sqrt{\frac{.6(1 - .6)}{35 - 1}} = .084$$

4. Calculate the test statistic as follows:

$$Z = \frac{(\text{Observed proportion} - \text{Proportion under null hypothesis})}{\text{Estimated standard error } (S_p)}$$

$$= \frac{0.7429 - 0.60}{.084} = 1.7$$

The *null hypothesis is rejected* because the calculated Z value is larger than the critical Z value. The bank can conclude with 95 percent confidence ($1 - \alpha = .95$) that more than

60 percent of its customers have family incomes of $50,000 or more. Management can introduce the new package of services targeted at this group.

Two Proportions in Independent Samples

In many instances, management is interested in the difference between the proportions of people in two different groups who engage in a certain activity or have a certain characteristic. For example, management of a convenience store chain had reason to believe, on the basis of a research study, that the percentage of men who visit convenience stores nine or more times per month (heavy users) is larger than the percentage of women who do so. The specifications required and the procedure for testing this hypothesis are as follows.

1. Specify the null and alternative hypotheses:

   ■ Null hypothesis H_0: $P_m - P_f \leq 0$; the proportion of men (P_m) reporting nine or more visits per month is the same as or less than the proportion of women (P_f) reporting nine or more visits per month.

   ■ Alternative hypothesis H_a: $P_m - P_f > 0$; the proportion of men (P_m) reporting nine or more visits per month is greater than the proportion of women (P_f) reporting nine or more visits per month.

   The sample proportions and the difference can be calculated from Exhibit 16.4 as follows:

$$P_m = \frac{26}{45} = .58$$

$$P_f = \frac{30}{71} = .42$$

$$P_m - P_f = .58 - .42 = .16$$

2. Set the level of sampling error α at .10 (management decision). For $\alpha = .10$, the table value of Z(critical) $= 1.28$. (See Exhibit 3 in Appendix 3 for d.f. $= \infty$, .10 significance, one-tail. The table for t is used because $t = Z$ for samples greater than 30.)

3. Calculate the estimated standard error of the differences between the two proportions as follows:

$$S_{P_{m-f}} = \sqrt{P(1 - P)\left(\frac{1}{n_m} + \frac{1}{n_f}\right)}$$

where $\quad P = \dfrac{n_m P_m + n_f P_f}{n_m + n_f}$

P_m = proportion in sample m (men)

P_f = proportion in sample f (women)

n_m = size of sample m

n_f = size of sample f

Therefore,

$$P = \frac{45(.58) + 71(.41)}{45 + 71} = .48$$

and $\quad S_{P_{m-f}} = \sqrt{.48(1 - .48)\left(\frac{1}{45} + \frac{1}{71}\right)} = .10$

4. Calculate the test statistic.

$$Z = \frac{\left(\begin{array}{c}\text{Difference between}\\\text{observed proportions}\end{array}\right) - \left(\begin{array}{c}\text{Difference between proportions}\\\text{under the null hypothesis}\end{array}\right)}{\begin{array}{c}\text{Estimated standard error of the differences}\\\text{between the two means}\end{array}}$$

$$= \frac{(.58 - .42) - 0}{.10} = 1.60$$

5. State the result. *The null hypothesis is rejected* because the calculated Z value (1.60) is larger than the critical Z value (1.28 for $\alpha = .10$). Management can conclude with 90 percent confidence ($1 - \alpha = .90$) that the proportion of men who visit convenience stores nine or more times per month is larger than the proportion of women who do so.

It should be noted that if the level of sampling error α had been set at .05, the critical Z value would equal 1.64. In this case, we would fail to reject (FTR) the null hypothesis because Z(calculated) would be smaller than Z(critical).

Analysis of Variance (ANOVA)

When the goal is to test the differences among the means of two or more independent samples, **analysis of variance (ANOVA)** is an appropriate statistical tool. Although it can be used to test differences between two means, ANOVA is more commonly used for hypothesis tests regarding the differences among the means of several (C) independent groups (where $C \geqslant 3$). It is a statistical technique that permits the researcher to determine whether the variability among or across the C sample means is greater than expected because of sampling error.

The Z and t tests described earlier normally are used to test the null hypothesis when only two sample means are involved. However, in situations in which there are three or more samples, it would be inefficient to test differences between the means two at a time. With five samples and associated means, 10 t tests would be required to test all pairs of means. More important, the use of Z or t tests in situations involving three or more means increases the probability of a type I error. Because these tests must be performed for all possible pairs of means, the more pairs, the more tests that must be performed. And the more tests performed, the more likely it is that one or more tests will show significant differences that are really due to sampling error. At an α of .05, this could be expected to occur in 1 of 20 tests on average.

One-way ANOVA is often used to analyze experimental results. Suppose the marketing manager for a chain of brake shops was considering three different services for a possible in-store promotion: wheel alignment, oil change, and tune-up. She was interested in knowing whether there were significant differences in potential sales of the three services.

Sixty similar stores (20 in each of three cities) were selected at random from among those operated by the chain. One of the services was introduced in each of three cities. Other variables under the firm's direct control, such as price and advertising, were kept at the same level during the course of the experiment. The experiment was conducted for a 30-day period, and sales of the new services were recorded for the period.

Average sales for each shop are shown below. The question is, are the differences among the means larger than would be expected due to chance?

> **analysis of variance (ANOVA)**
> Test for the differences among the means of two or more independent samples.

A brake shop might use analysis of variance to analyze experimental results with respect to several new services before deciding on a particular new service to offer.

Chicago (Wheel Alignment)		Cleveland (Oil Change)		Detroit (Tune-Up)	
310	318	314	321	337	310
315	322	315	340	325	312
305	333	350	318	330	340
310	315	305	315	345	318
315	3 85	299	322	320	322
345	310	309	295	325	335
340	312	299	302	328	341
330	308	312	316	330	340
320	312	331	294	342	320
315	340	335	308	330	310
$\overline{X} = 323$		$\overline{X} = 315$		$\overline{X} = 328$	

1. Specify the null and alternative hypotheses.
    - Null hypothesis H_0: $M_1 = M_2 = M_3$; mean sales of the three items are equal.
    - Alternative hypothesis H_a: The variability in group means is greater than would be expected because of sampling error.

2. Sum the squared differences between each subsample mean ($\overline{X}_j$) and the overall sample mean ($\overline{X}_t$) weighted by sample size (n_j). This is called the *sum of squares among groups* or *among group variation* (SSA). SSA is calculated as follows:

$$SSA = \sum_{j=1}^{C} n_j(\overline{X}_j - \overline{X}_t)^2$$

In this example, the overall sample mean is

$$\overline{X}_t = \frac{20(323) + 20(315) + 20(328)}{60} = 322$$

Thus,

$$SSA = 20(323 - 322)^2 + 20(315 - 322)^2 + 20(328 - 322)^2 = 1720$$

The greater the differences among the sample means, the larger the SSA will be.

3. Calculate the variation among group means as measured by the *mean sum of squares among groups* (MSA). The MSA is calculated as follows:

$$MSA = \frac{\text{Sum of squares among groups (SSA)}}{\text{Degrees of freedom (d.f.)}}$$

where   Degrees of freedom = number of groups (C) − 1

In this example,

$$\text{d.f.} = 3 - 1 = 2$$

Thus,

$$MSA = \frac{1720}{2} = 860$$

4. Sum the squared differences between each observation (X_{ij}) and its associated sample mean ($\overline{X}_j$) accumulated over all C levels (groups). Also called the *sum of squares within groups* or *within group variation*, it is generally referred to as the *sum of squared error* (SSE). For this example, the SSE is calculated as follows:

$$SSE = \sum_{j=1}^{C} \sum_{i=1}^{n_j} (X_{ij} - \overline{X}_j)^2$$
$$= (6644) + (4318) + (2270) = 13,232$$

5. Calculate the variation within the sample groups as measured by the mean sum of squares within groups. Referred to as *mean square error* (MSE), it represents an estimate of the random error in the data. The MSE is calculated as follows:

$$MSE = \frac{\text{Sum of squares within groups (SSE)}}{\text{Degrees of freedom (d.f.)}}$$

The number of degrees of freedom is equal to the sum of the sample sizes for all groups minus the number of groups (C):

$$d.f. = \left(\sum_{j=1}^{K} n_j \right) - C$$
$$= (20 + 20 + 20) - 3 = 57$$

Thus,

$$MSE = \frac{13,232}{57} = 232.14$$

As with the Z distribution and t distribution, a sampling distribution known as the *F distribution* permits the researcher to determine the probability that a particular calculated value of F could have occurred by chance rather than as a result of the treatment effect. The F distribution, like the t distribution, is really a set of distributions whose shape changes slightly depending on the number and size of the samples involved. To use the **F test**, it is necessary to calculate the degrees of freedom for the numerator and the denominator.

➤ *F* test
Test of the probability that a particular calculated value could have been due to chance.

6. Calculate the F statistic as follows:

$$F = \frac{MSA}{MSE}$$
$$= \frac{860}{232.14} = 3.70$$

The numerator is the MSA, and the number of degrees of freedom associated with it is 2 (step 3). The denominator is the MSE, and the number of degrees of freedom associated with it is 57 (step 5).

7. State the results. For an alpha of .05, the table value of F (critical) with 2 (numerator) and 57 (denominator) degrees of freedom is approximately 3.15. (See Table 5 in Appendix 3 for d.f. for denominator = 5, d.f. for numerator = 2, .05 significance.) The calculated F value (3.70) is greater than the table value (3.15), and so *the null hypothesis is rejected*. By rejecting the null hypothesis, we conclude that the variability observed in the three means is greater than expected due to chance.

The results of an ANOVA generally are displayed as follows:

Source of Variation	Sum of Squares	Degrees of Freedom	Mean Square	F Statistic
Treatments	1,720 (SSA)	2 (C − 1)	860 (MSA)	3.70 calculated
Error	13,232 (SSE)	57 (n − C)	232.14 (MSE)	
Total	14,592 (SST)	59 (n − 1)		

An example of an ANOVA application is provided in the Practicing Marketing Research feature below.

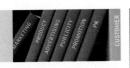

PRACTICING MARKETING RESEARCH

12 Coins, 3 Shops, 2 Microbiologists, and 1 Test—ANOVA

ANOVA, or the analysis of variance, is a statistical test devised in the 1920s by the English statistician, Ronald A. Fisher. British microbiologists Richard Armstrong and Anthony Hilton, both at Aston University in Birmingham, England, recently found it to be the "most appropriate method" for statistical analysis of complex data sets—in this case coins collected from a butcher's shop, news agent's office, and a sandwich shop.

The researchers took four coins randomly from each premise and analyzed them for bacterial populations. Armstrong and Hilton described their procedure as a one-way ANOVA with four replications performed in a randomized test design. The procedure took into account the variation between the various observations and partitioned these variations into portions correlated with the differences they found between the three shops and even

the variation among the four coins collected in each shop. Even so, this was a single-factor ANOVA experiment, the only variable being the shop.

They next performed a factorial experiment, studying several factors at once, namely, the influence of the type of dishcloth (cloth or sponge) and the prior rinsing of the material on the quantity of bacteria transferred to a food preparation surface as well as interactions between the two variables. Then they performed an even more factorially complex ANOVA study to determine how well two strains of bacteria survived on inoculated pound notes measured at 10 time intervals. The ANOVA method enabled them to discern a subtle pattern of three-factor interactions among the variables (such as the slight interaction between surface type and bacterial strain), the decline of bacterial numbers over time in variance with the type of surface, and the decline of one bacterial strain in numbers faster than the other in the same circumstance.

Each of these investigations yielded a datarich ANOVA table, information that health inspectors surely would find practical and immediately useful. The researchers had high praise for the ANOVA technique, calling it a "powerful method of investigation" for applied microbiology because it could highlight the effect of single factors as well as their interaction. Even better, combining different factors in one study is efficient and often reduces the number of replications needed.[11]

Questions

1. Can you devise a four-factor ANOVA test for the microbiologists?

2. The microbiologists applied their different ANOVA tests to food-service-related shops. How might it be applied to a dentist's office?

P Values and Significance Testing

For the various tests discussed in this chapter, a standard—a level of significance and associated critical value of the statistics—is established, and then the value of the statistic is calculated to see whether it beats that standard. If the calculated value of the statistic exceeds the critical value, then the result being tested is said to be statistically significant at that level.

However, this approach does not give the exact probability of getting a computed test statistic that is largely due to chance. The calculations to compute this probability, commonly referred to as the *p* value, are tedious to perform by hand. Fortunately, they are easy for computers. The ***p* value** is the most demanding level of statistical (not managerial) significance that can be met, based on the calculated value of the statistic. Computer statistical packages usually use one of the following labels to identify the probability that the distance between the hypothesized population parameter and the observed test statistic could have occurred due to chance:

→ **P value**
Exact probability of getting a computed test statistic that is due to chance. The smaller the *p* value, the smaller the probability that the observed result occurred by chance.

- *p* value
- ≤ PROB
- PROB =

The smaller the *p* value, the smaller the probability that the observed result occurred by chance (sampling error).

An example of computer output showing a *p* value calculation appears in Exhibit 16.5. This analysis shows the results of a *t* test of the differences between means for two independent samples. In this case, the null hypothesis H_0 is that there is no difference between what men and women would be willing to pay for a new communications service. (The variable name is GENDER, with the numeric codes of 0 for males and 1 for females. Subjects were asked how much they would be willing to pay per month for a new wireless communications service that was described to them via a videotape. Variable ADDEDPAY

EXHIBIT 16.5	Sample *t*-Test Output

```
Stat.   Grouping: GENDER (pcs. sta)
Basic   Group 1: G_1:1
Stats   Group 2: G_2:0
```

Variable	Mean G_1:1	Mean G_2:0	t value	df	P	Valid N G_1:1	Valid N G_2:0
ADDED PAY	16.82292	20.04717	−1.32878	200	.185434	96	106

is their response to the question.) The results show that women are willing to pay an average of $16.82 for the new service and men are willing to pay $20.04. Is this a significant difference? The calculated value for t of -1.328 indicates, via the associated p value of .185, that there is an 18.5 percent chance that the difference is due to sampling error. If, for example, the standard for the test were set at .10 (willing to accept a 10 percent chance of incorrectly rejecting H_0), then the analyst would *fail to reject* H_0 in this case.

SUMMARY

The purpose of making statistical inferences is to generalize from sample results to population characteristics. Three important concepts applied to the notion of differences are mathematical differences, managerially important differences, and statistical significance.

A hypothesis is an assumption or theory that a researcher or manager makes about some characteristic of the population being investigated. By testing, the researcher determines whether a hypothesis concerning some characteristic of the population is valid. A statistical hypothesis test permits the researcher to calculate the probability of observing the particular result if the stated hypothesis actually were true. In hypothesis testing, the first step is to specify the hypothesis. Next, an appropriate statistical technique should be selected to test the hypothesis. Then, a decision rule must be specified as the basis for determining whether to reject or fail to reject the hypothesis. Hypothesis tests are subject to two types of errors called type I (α error) and type II (β error). A type I error involves rejecting the null hypothesis when it is, in fact, true. A type II error involves failing to reject the null hypothesis when the alternative hypothesis actually is true. Finally, the value of the test statistic is calculated, and a conclusion is stated that summarizes the results of the test.

Marketing researchers often develop cross tabulations, whose purpose usually is to uncover interrelationships among the variables. Usually the researcher needs to determine whether the numbers of subjects, objects, or responses that fall into some set of categories differ from those expected by chance. Thus, a test of goodness of fit of the observed distribution in relation to an expected distribution is appropriate. One common test of goodness of fit is chi square.

Often marketing researchers need to make inferences about a population mean. If the sample size is equal to or greater than 30 and the sample comes from a normal population, the appropriate test statistic for testing hypotheses about means is the Z test. For small samples, researchers use the t test with $n-1$ degrees of freedom when making inferences (n is the size of the sample).

When researchers are interested in testing differences between responses to the same variable, such as advertising, by groups with different characteristics, they test for differences between two means. A Z value is calculated and compared to the critical value of Z. Based on the result of the comparison, they either reject or fail to reject the null hypothesis. The Z test also can be used to examine hypotheses about proportions from one sample or independent samples.

When researchers need to test for differences among the means of three or more independent samples, analysis of variance is an appropriate statistical tool. It is often used for hypothesis tests regarding the differences among the means of several independent groups. It permits the researcher to test the null hypothesis that there are no significant differences among the population group means.

KEY TERMS & DEFINITIONS

statistical significance A difference that is large enough that it is not likely to have occurred because of chance or sampling error.

hypothesis Assumption or theory that a researcher or manager makes about some characteristic of the population under study.

null hypothesis The hypothesis of status quo, no difference, no effect.

decision rule Rule or standard used to determine whether to reject or fail to reject the null hypothesis.

type I error (α error) Rejection of the null hypothesis when, in fact, it is true.

type II error (β error) Failure to reject the null hypothesis when, in fact, it is false.

independent samples Samples in which measurement of a variable in one population has no effect on measurement of the variable in the other.

related samples Samples in which measurement of a variable in one population may influence measurement of the variable in the other.

degrees of freedom Number of observations in a statistical problem that are free to vary.

chi-square test Test of the goodness of fit between the observed distribution and the expected distribution of a variable.

Z test Hypothesis test used for a single mean if the sample is large enough and drawn at random.

t test Hypothesis test used for a single mean if the sample is too small to use the Z test.

hypothesis test of proportions Test to determine whether the difference between proportions is greater than would be expected because of sampling error.

analysis of variance (ANOVA) Test for the differences among the means of two or more independent samples.

F test Test of the probability that a particular calculated value could have been due to chance.

p value Exact probability of getting a computed test statistic that is due to chance. The smaller the p value, the smaller the probability that the observed result occurred by chance.

QUESTIONS FOR REVIEW & CRITICAL THINKING

1. Explain the notions of mathematical differences, managerially important differences, and statistical significance. Can results be statistically significant and yet lack managerial importance? Explain your answer.

2. Describe the steps in the procedure for testing hypotheses. Discuss the difference between a null hypothesis and an alternative hypothesis.

3. Distinguish between a type I error and a type II error. What is the relationship between the two?

4. What is meant by the terms *independent samples* and *related samples*? Why is it important for a researcher to determine whether a sample is independent?

5. Your university library is concerned about student desires for library hours on Sunday morning (9:00 A.M.–12:00 P.M.). It has undertaken to survey a random sample of 1,600 undergraduate students (one-half men, one-half women) in each of four status levels (i.e., 400 freshmen, 400 sophomores, 400 juniors, 400 seniors). If the percentages of students preferring Sunday morning hours are those shown below, what conclusions can the library reach?

	Seniors	Juniors	Sophomores	Freshmen
Women	70	53	39	26
Men	30	48	31	27

6. A local car dealer was attempting to determine which premium would draw the most visitors to its showroom. An individual who visits the showroom and takes a test drive is given a premium with no obligation. The dealer chose four premiums and offered each for one week. The results are as follows.

Week	Premium	Total Given Out
1	Four-foot metal stepladder	425
2	$50 savings bond	610
3	Dinner for four at a local steak house	510
4	Six pink flamingos plus an outdoor thermometer	705

Using a chi-square test, what conclusions can you draw regarding the premiums?

7. A market researcher has completed a study of pain relievers. The following table depicts the brands purchased most often, broken down by men versus women. Perform a chi-square test on the data and determine what can be said regarding the cross tabulation.

Pain Relievers	Men	Women
Anacin	40	55
Bayer	60	28
Bufferin	70	97
Cope	14	21
Empirin	82	107
Excedrin	72	84
Excedrin PM	15	11
Vanquish	20	26

8. A child psychologist observed 8-year-old children behind a one-way mirror to determine how long they would play with a toy medical kit. The company that designed the toy was attempting to determine whether to give the kit a masculine or a feminine orientation. The lengths of time (in minutes) the children played with the kits are shown below. Calculate the value of t and recommend to management whether the kit should have a male or a female orientation.

Boys	Girls	Boys	Girls
31	26	67	9
12	38	67	9
41	20	25	16
34	32	73	26
63	16	36	81
7	45	41	20
		15	5

9. American Airlines is trying to determine which baggage handling system to put in its new hub terminal in San Juan, Puerto Rico. One system is made by Jano Systems, and the second is manufactured by Dynamic Enterprises. American has installed a small Jano system and a small Dynamic Enterprises system in two of its low-volume terminals. Both terminals handle approximately the same quantity of baggage each month. American has decided to select the system that provides the minimum number of instances in which passengers disembarking must wait 20 minutes or longer for baggage. Analyze the data that follow and determine whether there is a significant difference at the .95 level of confidence between the two systems. If there is a difference, which system should American select?

Minutes of Waiting	Jano Systems (Frequency)	Dynamic Enterprises (Frequency)
10–11	4	10
12–13	10	8
14–15	14	14
16–17	4	20
18–19	2	12
20–21	4	6
22–23	2	12
24–25	14	4
26–27	6	13
28–29	10	8
30–31	12	6
32–33	2	8
34–35	2	8
36 or more	2	2

10. Menu space is always limited in fast-food restaurants. However, McDonald's has decided that it needs to add one more salad dressing to its menu for its garden salad and chef salad. It has decided to test market four flavors: Caesar, Ranch-Style, Green Goddess, and Russian. Fifty restaurants were selected in the North-Central region to sell each new dressing. Thus, a total of 200 stores were used in the research project. The study was conducted for 2 weeks; the units of each dressing sold are shown in the following table. As a researcher, you want to know if the differences among the average daily sales of the dressings are larger than can be reasonably expected by chance. If so, which dressing would you recommend be added to the inventory throughout the United States?

Day	Caesar	Ranch-Style	Green Goddess	Russian
1	155	143	149	135
2	157	146	152	136
3	151	141	146	131
4	146	136	141	126
5	181	180	173	115
6	160	152	170	150
7	168	157	174	147
8	157	167	141	130
9	139	159	129	119
10	144	154	167	134
11	158	169	145	144
12	172	183	190	161
13	184	195	178	177
14	161	177	201	151

WORKING THE NET

1. Calculating the *p* value and performing a *Z* or *t* test are much easier when done by computers. For a *p* value calculator, usable without fee, visit: ***www.graphpad.com/quickcalcs/PValue1.cfm.***

   For a *Z* test calculator, also free to use, visit: ***www.changbioscience.com/stat/ztest.html***

   For a *t* test online calculator, available also with no charge, visit: ***www.graphpad.com/quickcalcs/ttest1.cfm.***

2. Educators at Tufts University offer a helpful tutorial on reading the output from a one-way analysis of variance, an ANOVA table. Study this at: ***http://www.JerryDallal.com/LHSP/aov1out.htm.***

REAL-LIFE RESEARCH • 16.1

Nala Chan is an advertising executive with Stewart Bakin Advertising. She is responsible for the Global Bazaar account and has just finished reviewing the results of a recent customer study in the top 40 U.S. markets. The study was conducted by Internet panel in 2011 and included people who shopped at Global Bazaar in the 30 days prior to the date of the survey. The accompanying table shows selected survey results broken down by market segments (columns) identified in research previously conducted by Global. The first two rows are based on actual sales data; the rest of the table shows results from the most recent survey with statistical testing of differences. The first six rows show key metrics used by Global to guide its marketing strategy. Some of the key metrics come from actual sales data, whereas others come from the recent survey. All results, except those for the first two rows, are for the segments or based on segment column totals.

	Market Segments				
	Single	Single	Married	Married	Married
Variable	18–25	26–40	18–25	26–40	over 40
Percent of current customer base[a]	15%	20%	27%	29%	9%
Percent of sales[a]	10%	13%	29%	34%	14%
Top of mind awareness of Global Bazaar[a]	34%*	29%*	45%	51%**	53%**
Image index (100-point scale)[b]	69%*	70%*	85%	92%**	93%**
Likely to shop at Global Bazaar in next 30 days	21%*	19%*	33%	39%**	42%**
Likely to shop at a competitive store in next 30 days	38%**	40%**	28%	23%*	25%*
Number of children under 23 years Average number	2.38	2.10	0	0	0.29
Income Median income	$28,000*	$39,500	$44,430	$56.580**	$69,170**
% HH income over $75,000	29%	28%	15.3%*	28%	36%

	Market Segments				
Variable	Single 18–25	Single 26–40	Married 18–25	Married 26–40	Married over 40
Education					
% College degree or more	9%*	29%**	26%**	21%	21%
Ethnic makeup					
% white	94%	92%	91%	95%	95%
% black	3%	4%	6%	2%	4%
% Hispanic	2%	2%	2%	2%	1%
% Other	4%	4%	3%	4%	2%

[a]Based on actual customer data. Significance testing not appropriate.

[b]Index developed by Global Bazaar based on multiple measures from survey—higher is better.

*Significantly lower than average for all customers surveyed.

**Significantly higher than average for all customers surveyed.

Questions

1. Which segment provides the largest percentage of sales?
2. In which segment does Global have the highest top of mind awareness?
3. Which two segments account for over 60 percent of sales?
4. In what segment does Global perform most poorly? Explain all the dimensions of their poor performance in this segment.
5. Based on these results, what advice would you give to Global?

REAL-LIFE RESEARCH • 16.2

New Mexico Power

Marc Guerraz is the new marketing research director for New Mexico Power, an investor-owned, vertically integrated electric utility involved in the generation, transmission, distribution, and energy service domains of the electricity industry. Marc was hired to help New Mexico Power transition to a competitive environment for energy services, which will occur in one year. In this environment, customers will be allowed to select their provider of electricity, much as customers now select long-distance telecommunications service from providers such as Sprint, Verizon, and SBC.

One of the crucial questions for New Mexico Power is that of current customer retention. How many current customers will switch to another provider of electric services during the first 6 months of competition? To address this question, Marc and his team designed and fielded a survey in the current service territory of New Mexico Power. They had 500 customers give complete answers to all questions. Initial results indicate that 22 percent of customers would switch. The margin of error is 4 percent, which means that (at the 95 percent confidence level) the actual percentage of customers switching could be as low as 18 percent or as high as 26 percent. New Mexico Power senior management is concerned about this error range of 4 percent, which means that error spans a total of 8 percentage points. Further customer retention efforts must be budgeted now, and New Mexico Power senior management wants firmer numbers on which to base strategies and budgets.

Questions

1. How could the error range be reduced without collecting more data? Would you recommend taking this approach? Why/Why not?

2. Do you think New Mexico Power senior management would find this approach to reducing the error range satisfactory?

3. If 500 more respondents were surveyed and 30 percent of them indicated that they would switch, what would the error range become?

SPSS EXERCISES FOR CHAPTER 16

Exercise 1: Analyzing Data Using Cross-Tabulation Analysis

Note: Go to the Wiley Web site at *www.wiley.com/college/mcdaniel* and download the *Segmenting the College Student Market for Movie Attendance* database to SPSS windows.

Use the *analyze/descriptive statistics/crosstab* sequence to obtain cross-tabulated results. In addition, click on the "cell" icon and make sure the *observed, expected, total, row,* and *column* boxes are checked. Then, click on the "statistics" icon and check the *chi-square* box. Once you run the analysis, on the output for the chi-square analysis, you will only need the *Pearson chi-square statistic* to assess whether or not the results of the crosstab are statistically significant.

In this exercise we are assessing whether or not persons who attend movies at movie theaters are demographically different from those who do not. Invoke the crosstab analysis for the following pairs of variables:

 a. Q1 & Q11
 b. Q1 & Q12
 c. Q1 & Q13
 d. Q1 & Q14

Answer questions 1–6 using only the sample data. Do not consider the results of the *chi-square test.*

1. What % of males do not attend movies at movie theaters? _____%

2. What % of all respondents are African American and do not attend movies at movie theaters? _____%

3. What % of respondents not attending movies at movie theaters are in the 19–20 age category? _____%

4. Which classification group is most likely to attend movies   _____
   at movie theaters?

5. Which age category is least likely to attend movies at a   _____
   movie theater?

6. Are Caucasians less likely to attend movie theaters   _____
   than African Americans?

For question 7, the objective is to determine statistically whether, in the population from which the sample data was drawn, there were demographic differences in persons who attend and do not attend movies at movie theaters. We do this by using the results of the *chi-square test for independent samples*.

7. Evaluate the chi-square statistic in each of your crosstab tables. Construct a table to summarize the results. For example:

Variables	Pearson Chi-Square	Degrees of Freedom	Asymp sig.	Explanation
Q1 (attend or not attend movies at movie theaters & Q12 (gender)	2.71	1	.10	We can be 90% confident that based on our sample results, males differ significantly from females in their tendency to attend or not attend movies at movie theaters.

Exercise 2: t/Z Test for Independent Samples

Use the *analyze/compare means/independent samples t-test* sequence to complete this exercise. This exercise compares males and females regarding the information sources they utilize to search for information about movies at movie theaters. SPSS calls the variable in which the means are being computed the *test variable,* and the variable in which we are grouping responses the *grouping variable*.

Note: In statistics, if a sample has fewer than 30 observations or cases, then we invoke a *t* test. If there are 30 or more cases, we invoke a *z* test, as *the t test values and z test values are virtually the same; hence SPSS refers only to a t test.*

Answer the following questions.

The result of the *t* test generates a table of **group statistics**, which is based only on the **sample** data. The other output table generated by the *t* test has statistical data from which we can determine whether or not the sample results can be generalized to the population from which the sample data was drawn. If the *t* test is significant, then we can use the group statistics to determine the specifics of the computed results. For example, a significant *t* test may tell us that males differ from females regarding the importance they place on the newspaper as an information source, but the group statistics tell us "who" considers it most important.

From our *sample data*, can we generalize our results to the population by saying that males differ from females regarding the importance they place on various information sources to get information about movies at movie theaters by:

1. the newspaper (Q7a)?
2. the Internet (Q7b)?
3. phoning in to the movie theater for information (Q7c)?
4. the television (Q7d)?
5. friends or family (Q7e)?

You may want to use the template below to summarize your *t* test results. For example:

Variables	Variance Prob of Sig Diff	Means Prob of Sig Diff	Interpretation of Results
Q12 (gender) & Q7a (newspaper)	.000	.035	96.5% confident that based on our sample results, males differ significantly from females concerning the importance they place on the newspaper as an information source about movies at movie theaters **(means test).** 100% confident that males and females were significantly different regarding the variance of response within each gender **(variance test).**

Exercise 3: ANOVA Test for Independent Samples

Invoke the *analyze/compare means/One-Way ANOVA* sequence to invoke the ANOVA test to complete this exercise. This exercise compares the responses of freshmen, sophomores, juniors, seniors, and graduate students to test for significant differences in the importance placed on several movie theater items. For the ANOVA test, SPSS calls the variable in which means are being computed the *independent variable* and the variable in which we are grouping responses the *factor variable*. Be sure to click the *options* icon and check *descriptives* so that the output will produce the mean responses by student classification for the sample data. As with the *t* test, the ANOVA test produces a table of *descriptives* based on sample data. If our ANOVA test is significant, the *descriptives* can be used to determine, for example, which student classification places the most importance on comfortable seats.

Answer the following questions:

From our sample data, can we generalize our results to the population by saying that there are significant differences across the classification of students by the importance they place on the following movie theater items?

1. Video arcade at the movie theater (Q5a)?
2. Soft drinks and food items (Q5b)
3. Plentiful restrooms (Q5c)
4. Comfortable chairs (Q5d)
5. Auditorium-type seating (Q5e)
6. Size of the movie theater screens (Q5f)
7. Quality of the sound system (Q5g)
8. Number of screens at a movie theater (Q5h)
9. Clean restroom (Q5i)
10. Using only the *descriptive statistics,* which classification group (Q13) places the least amount of importance on clean restrooms (Q5i)? _____
11. Using only the *descriptive statistics,* which classification group (Q13) places the greatest amount of importance on quality of sound system (Q5i)? _____

Summarize the results of your ANOVA analysis using a table similar to the one below.

Variables	Degrees of Freedom	F-Value	Probability of Insignificance	Interpretation of Results
Q5a (importance of a video arcade) & Q13 (student classification)	4,461	12.43	.001	99.9% confident that based on the sample results, students differ significantly by classification concerning the importance placed on there being a video arcade at the movie theater.

surveysolutions XP

CHAPTER 17

Bivariate Correlation And Regression

LEARNING OBJECTIVES

→ **1.** To comprehend the nature of correlation analysis.

→ **2.** To understand bivariate regression analysis.

→ **3.** To become aware of the coefficient of determination R^2.

In this chapter, we will cover techniques that will permit you to evaluate the relationships between two variables.

Bivariate Analysis of Association

In many marketing research studies, the interests of the researcher and manager go beyond issues that can be addressed by the statistical testing of differences discussed in Chapter 16. They may be interested in the degree of association between two variables. Statistical techniques appropriate for this type of analysis are referred to as **bivariate techniques**. When more than two variables are involved, the techniques employed are known as *multivariate techniques*. Multivariate techniques are discussed in Chapter 18.

When the degree of association between two variables is analyzed, the variables are classified as the **independent** (predictor) **variable** and the **dependent** (criterion) **variable**. Independent variables are those that are believed to affect the value of the dependent variable. Independent variables such as price, advertising expenditures, or number of retail outlets may, for example, be used to predict and explain sales or market share of a brand—the dependent variable. Bivariate analysis can help provide answers to questions such as the following: How does the price of our product affect its sales? What is the relationship between household income and expenditures on entertainment?

It must be noted that none of the techniques presented in this chapter can be used to prove that one variable caused an observed change in another variable. They can be used only to describe the nature of statistical relationships between variables.

The analyst has a large number of bivariate techniques from which to choose. This chapter discusses two procedures that are appropriate for metric (ratio or internal) data—bivariate regression and Pearson's product–moment correlation—and one that is appropriate for ordinal (ranking) data—Spearman rank-order correlation. Other statistical procedures that can be used for analyzing the statistical relationship between two variables include the two-group t test, chi-square analysis of crosstabs or contingency tables, and ANOVA (analysis of variance) for two groups. All of these procedures were introduced and discussed in Chapter 16.

> **bivariate techniques**
> Statistical methods of analyzing the relationship between two variables.

> **independent variable**
> Variable believed to affect the value of the dependent variable.

> **dependent variable**
> Variable expected to be explained or caused by the independent variable.

Bivariate Regression

Bivariate regression analysis is a statistical procedure appropriate for analyzing the relationship between two variables when one is considered the dependent variable and the other the independent variable. For example, a researcher might be interested in analyzing the relationship between sales (dependent variable) and advertising (independent variable). If the relationship between advertising expenditures and sales can be accurately captured by regression analysis, the researcher can use the resulting model to predict sales for different levels of advertising. When the problem involves using two or more independent variables (for example, advertising and price) to predict the dependent variable of interest, multiple regression analysis (discussed in Chapter 18) is appropriate.

Nature of the Relationship

One way to study the nature of the relationship between the dependent and the independent variable is to plot the data in a **scatter diagram**. The dependent variable Y is plotted on the vertical axis, whereas the independent variable X is plotted on the horizontal axis. By examining the scatter diagram, one can determine whether the relationship between the two variables, if any, is linear or curvilinear. If the relationship appears to be

> **bivariate regression analysis**
> Analysis of the strength of the linear relationship between two variables when one is considered the independent variable and the other the dependent variable.

> **scatter diagram**
> Graphic plot of the data with dependent variable on the Y (vertical) axis and the independent variable on the X (horizontal) axis. Shows the nature of the relationship between the two variables, linear or nonlinear.

Exhibit 17.1

**Types of
Relationships Found
in Scatter Diagrams**

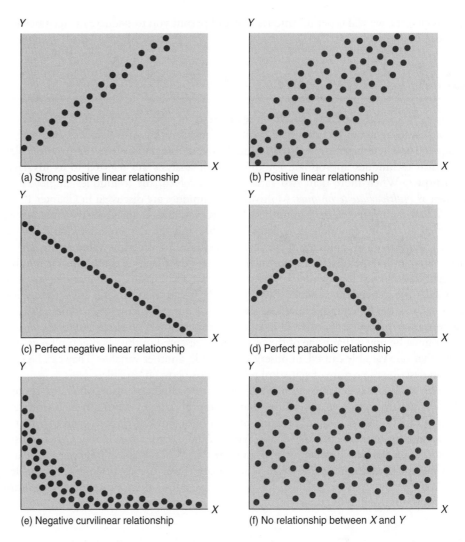

(a) Strong positive linear relationship

(b) Positive linear relationship

(c) Perfect negative linear relationship

(d) Perfect parabolic relationship

(e) Negative curvilinear relationship

(f) No relationship between X and Y

linear or close to linear, linear regression is appropriate. If a nonlinear relationship is shown in the scatter diagram, curve-fitting nonlinear regression techniques are appropriate. These techniques are beyond the scope of this discussion.

Exhibit 17.1 depicts several kinds of underlying relationships between the X (independent) and Y (dependent) variables. Scatter diagrams (a) and (b) suggest a positive linear relationship between X and Y. However, the linear relationship shown in (b) is not as strong as that portrayed in (a); there is more scatter in the data shown in (b). Diagram (c) shows a perfect negative, or inverse, relationship between variables X and Y. An example might be the relationship between price and sales. As price goes up, sales go down. As price goes down, sales go up. Diagrams (d) and (e) show nonlinear relationships between the variables; appropriate curve-fitting techniques should be used to mathematically describe these relationships. The scatter diagram in (f) shows no relationship between X and Y.

Example of Bivariate Regression

Stop 'N Go recently conducted a research effort designed to measure the effect of vehicular traffic past a particular store location on annual sales at that location. To control for other factors, researchers identified 20 stores that were virtually identical on all other variables known to have a significant effect on store sales (for example, square footage, amount of parking, demographics of the surrounding neighborhood). This particular analysis is part of an overall effort by Stop 'N Go to identify and quantify the effects of various factors that affect store sales. The ultimate goal is to develop a model that can be used to screen potential sites for store locations and select, for actual purchase and store construction, the ones that will produce the highest level of sales.

After identifying the 20 sites, Stop 'N Go took a daily traffic count for each site over a 30-day period. In addition, from internal records, the company obtained total sales data for each of the 20 test stores for the preceding 12 months (see Exhibit 17.2).

EXHIBIT 17.2	Annual Sales and Average Daily Vehicular Traffic	
Store Number (i)	Average Daily Vehicular Count in Thousands (X_i)	Annual Sales in Thousands of Dollars (Y_i)
1	62	1121
2	35	766
3	36	701
4	72	1304
5	41	832
6	39	782
7	49	977
8	25	503
9	41	773
10	39	839
11	35	893
12	27	588
13	55	957
14	38	703
15	24	497
16	28	657
17	53	1209
18	55	997
19	33	844
20	29	883

A scatterplot of the resulting data is shown in Exhibit 17.3. Visual inspection of the scatterplot suggests that total sales increase as average daily vehicular traffic increases. The question now is how to characterize this relationship in a more explicit, quantitative manner.

Least-Squares Estimation Procedure The least-squares procedure is a fairly simple mathematical technique that can be used to fit data for X and Y to a line that best represents the relationship between the two variables. No straight line will perfectly represent every observation in the scatterplot. This is reflected in discrepancies between the actual values (dots on the scatter diagram) and predicted values (values indicated by the line). Any straight line fitted to the data in a scatterplot is subject to error. A number of lines could be drawn that would seem to fit the observations in Exhibit 17.3.

The least-squares procedure results in a straight line that fits the actual observations (dots) better than any other line that could be fitted to the observations. Put another way, the sum of the squared deviations from the line (squared differences between dots and the line) will be lower for this line than for any other line that can be fitted to the observations.

The general equation for the line is $Y = a + bX$. The estimating equation for regression analysis is

$$Y = \hat{a} + \hat{b}X + e$$

where
- Y = dependent variable, annual sales in thousands of dollars
- $\hat{a}$ = estimated Y intercept for regression line
- $\hat{b}$ = estimated slope of regression line, regression coefficient
- X = independent variable, average daily vehicular traffic in thousands of vehicles
- e = error, difference between actual value and value predicted by regression line

Exhibit 17.3

Scatterplot of Annual Sales by Traffic

Values for $\hat{a}$ and $\hat{b}$ can be calculated from the following equations:

$$\hat{b} = \frac{\sum X_i Y_i - n\bar{X}\bar{Y}}{\sum X_i^2 - n(\bar{X})^2}$$

$$\hat{a} = \bar{Y} - \hat{b}\bar{X}$$

where $\bar{X}$ = mean value of X
$\bar{Y}$ = mean value of Y
n = sample size (number of units in the sample)

With the data from Exhibit 17.4, $\hat{b}$ is calculated as follows:

$$\hat{b} = \frac{734,083 - 20(40.8)(841.3)}{36,526 - 20(40.8)^2} = 14.7$$

The value of $\hat{a}$ is calculated as follows:

$$\hat{a} = \bar{Y} - \hat{b}\bar{X}$$
$$= 841.3 - 14.72(40.8) = 240.9$$

Thus, the estimated regression function is given by

$$\hat{Y} = \hat{a} + \hat{b}X$$
$$= 240.9 + 14.7(X)$$

where $\hat{Y}$ (Y-hat) is the value of the estimated regression function for a given value of X.

EXHIBIT 17.4	Least-Squares Computation				
Store	X	Y	X^2	Y^2	XY
1	62	1,121	3,844	1,256,641	69,502
2	35	766	1,225	586,756	26,810
3	36	701	1,296	491,401	25,236
4	72	1,304	5,184	1,700,416	93,888
5	41	832	1,681	692,224	34,112
6	39	782	1,521	611,524	30,498
7	49	977	2,401	954,529	47,873
8	25	503	625	253,009	12,575
9	41	773	1,681	597,529	31,693
10	39	839	1,521	703,921	32,721
11	35	893	1,225	797,449	31,255
12	27	588	729	345,744	15,876
13	55	957	3,025	915,849	52,635
14	38	703	1,444	494,209	26,714
15	24	497	576	247,009	11,928
16	28	657	784	431,649	18,396
17	53	1,209	2,809	1,461,681	64,077
18	55	997	3,025	994,009	54,835
19	33	844	1,089	712,336	27,852
20	29	883	841	779,689	25,607
Sum	816	16,826	36,526	15,027,574	734,083
Mean	40.8	841.3			

According to the estimated regression function, for every additional 1,000 vehicles per day in traffic (X), total annual sales will increase by \$14,720 (estimated value of b). The value of $\hat{a}$ is 240.9. Technically, $\hat{a}$ is the estimated value of the dependent variable (Y, or annual sales) when the value of the independent variable (X, or average daily vehicular traffic) is zero.

SPSS JUMP START FOR REGRESSION

Steps that you need to go through to do the bivariate regression problem shown in the book are provided below along with the output produced. Use the data set **Bivregex**, which you can download from the Web site for the text.

Steps in SPSS

1. Select *Analyze →Regression →Linear*.
2. Move **y** to Dependent.

3. Move **x** to Independent(s).
4. Click OK.

SPSS Output for Regression

Regression

Variables Entered/Removed[b]

Model	Variables Entered	Variables Removed	Method
1	Traffic[a]	.	Enter

a. All requested variables entered.

b. Dependent Variable: Sales

Model Summary

Model	R	R Square	Adjusted R Square	Std. Error of the Estimate
1	.896[a]	.803	.792	97.640

a. Predictors: (Constant). Traffic

ANOVA[b]

Model		Sum of Squares	df	Mean Square	F	Sig.
1	Regression	700255.40	1	700255.399	73.451	.000[a]
	Residual	171604.80	18	9533.600		
	Total	871860.20	19			

a. Predictors: (Constant). Traffic

b. Dependent Variable: Sales

Coefficients[a]

Model		Unstandardized Coefficients		Standardized Coefficients	t	Sig.
		B	Std. Error	Beta		
1	(Constant)	240.857	73.383		3.282	.004
	Traffic	14.717	1.717	.896	8.570	.000

a. Dependent Variable: Sales

Regression Line Predicted values for Y, based on calculated values for $\hat{a}$ and $\hat{b}$ are shown in Exhibit 17.5. In addition, errors for each observation $(Y - \hat{Y})$ are shown. The regression line resulting from the $\hat{Y}$ values is plotted in Exhibit 17.6.

Strength of Association: R^2 The estimated regression function describes the nature of the relationship between X and Y. Another important factor is the strength of the relationship between the variables. How widely do the actual values of Y differ from the values predicted by the model?

EXHIBIT 17.5			Predicted Values and Errors for Each Observation			
Store	**X**	**Y**	**$\hat{Y}$**	**$Y - \hat{Y}$**	**$(Y - \hat{Y})^2$**	**$(Y - \overline{Y})^2$**
1	62	1,121	1,153.3	−32.2951	1,043	78,232
2	35	766	755.9	10.05716	101	5,670
3	36	701	770.7	−69.6596	4,852	19,684
4	72	1,304	1,300.5	3.537362	13	214,091
5	41	832	844.2	−12.2434	150	86
6	39	782	814.8	−32.8098	1,076	3,516
7	49	977	962.0	15.02264	226	18,414
8	25	503	608.8	−105.775	11,188	114,447
9	41	773	844.2	−71.2434	5,076	4,665
10	39	839	814.8	24.19015	585	5
11	35	893	755.9	137.0572	18,785	2,673
12	27	588	638.2	−50.2088	2,521	64,161
13	55	957	1,050.3	−93.2779	8,701	13,386
14	38	703	800.1	−97.0931	9,427	19,127
15	24	497	594.1	−97.0586	9,420	118,542
16	28	657	652.9	4.074415	17	33,966
17	53	1,209	1,020.8	188.1556	35,403	135,203
18	55	997	1,050.3	−53.2779	2,839	24,242
19	33	844	726.5	117.4907	13,804	7
20	29	883	667.6	215.3577	46,379	1,739
Sum	816	16,826	16,826		171,605	871,860
Mean	40.8	841				

→ **coefficient of determination**
Percentage of the total variation in the dependent variable explained by the independent variable.

The **coefficient of determination**, denoted by R^2, is the measure of the strength of the linear relationship between X and Y. The coefficient of determination measures the percentage of the total variation in Y that is "explained" by the variation in X. The R^2 statistic ranges from 0 to 1. If there is a perfect linear relationship between X and Y (all the variation in Y is explained by the variation in X), then R^2 equals 1. At the other

Exhibit 17.6

Least-Squares Regression Line Fitted to Sample Data

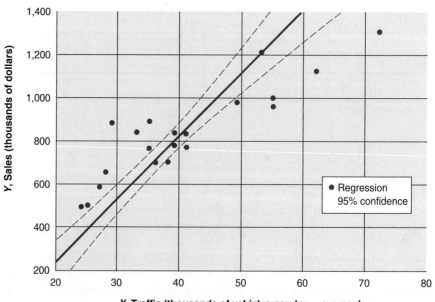

extreme, if there is no relationship between X and Y, then none of the variation in Y is explained by the variation in X, and R^2 equals 0.

$$R^2 = \frac{\text{Explained variation}}{\text{Total variation}}$$

where

Explained variation = Total variation − Unexplained variation

The coefficient of determination for the Stop 'N Go data example is computed as follows. [See Exhibit 17.5 for calculation of $(Y - \hat{Y})^2$ and $(Y - \overline{Y})^2$.]

$$
\begin{aligned}
R^2 &= \frac{\text{Total variation} - \text{Unexplained variation}}{\text{Total variation}} \\
&= 1 - \frac{\text{Unexplained variation}}{\text{Total variation}} \\
&= 1 - \frac{\sum_{i=1}^{n} (Y_i - \hat{Y}_i)^2}{\sum_{i=1}^{n} (Y_i - \overline{Y})^2} \\
&= 1 - \frac{171,605}{871,860} = .803
\end{aligned}
$$

Of the variation in Y (annual sales), 80 percent is explained by the variation in X (average daily vehicular traffic). There is a very strong linear relationship between X and Y.

Statistical Significance of Regression Results In computing R^2, the total variation in Y was partitioned into two component sums of squares:

Total variation = Explained variation + Unexplained variation

The total variation is a measure of variation of the observed Y values around their mean $\overline{Y}$. It measures the variation of the Y values without any consideration of the X values.

Total variation, known as the *total sum of squares* (SST), is given by

$$\text{SST} = \sum_{i=1}^{n} (Y_i - \overline{Y})^2 = \sum_{i=1}^{n} Y_i^2 - \left(\frac{\sum_{i=1}^{n} Y_i^2}{n} \right)$$

The explained variation, or the **sum of squares due to regression** (SSR), is given by

> **sum of squares due to regression**
> Variation explained by the regression.

$$\text{SSR} = \sum_{i=1}^{n} (\hat{Y}_i - \overline{Y})^2 = a \sum_{i=1}^{n} Y_i + b \sum_{i=1}^{n} X_i Y_i - \left(\frac{\sum_{i=1}^{n} Y_i}{n} \right)^2$$

Exhibit 17.7 depicts the various measures of variation (that is, sum of squares) in a regression. SSR represents the differences between Y_i (the values of Y predicted by the estimated regression equation) and $\overline{Y}$ (the average value of Y). In a well-fitting regression

Exhibit 17.7

Measures of Variation in a Regression

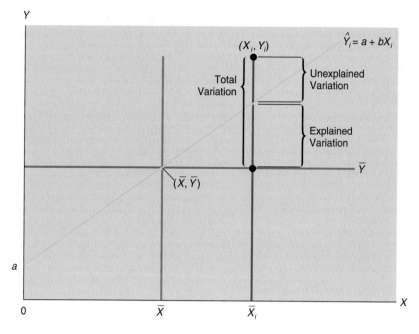

equation, the variation explained by regression (SSR) will represent a large portion of the total variation (SST). If $Y_i = \hat{Y}_i$ at each value of X, then a perfect fit has been achieved. All the observed values of Y are then on the computed regression line. Of course, in that case, SSR ≠ SST.

The unexplained variation, or **error sum of squares** (SSE), is obtained from

> **error sum of squares**
> Variation not explained by the regression.

$$SSE = \sum_{i=1}^{n} (Y_i - \hat{Y}_i)^2 = \sum_{i=1}^{n} Y_i^2 - a\sum_{i=1}^{n} Y_i - b\sum_{i=1}^{n} X_iY_i$$

In Exhibit 17.7, note that SSE represents the residual differences (error) between the observed and predicted Y values. Therefore, the unexplained variation is a measure of scatter around the regression line. If the fit were perfect, there would be no scatter around the regression line and SSE would be zero.

In studying the relationship between vehicular traffic and sales, the coefficient of determination may be used to measure the percent of the total variation.

Hypotheses Concerning Overall Regression   Here we, as the researchers, are interested in hypotheses regarding the computed R^2 value for the problem. Is the amount of variance explained in the result (by our model) significantly greater than we would expect due to chance? Or, as with the various statistical tests discussed in Chapter 16, to what extent can we rule out sampling error as an explanation of the results? Analysis of variance (an F test) is used to test the significance of the results.

An analysis of variance table is set up as shown in Exhibit 17.8. The computer output for our example appears in Exhibit 17.9. The breakdowns of the total sum of squares and associated degrees of freedom are displayed in the form of an analysis of variance (ANOVA) table. We use the information in this table to test the significance of the linear relationship between Y and X. As noted previously, an F test will be used for this purpose. Our hypotheses are as follows:

■ Null hypothesis H_0: There is no linear relationship between X (average daily vehicular traffic) and Y (annual sales).

■ Alternative hypothesis H_a: There is a linear relationship between X and Y.

As in other statistical tests, we must choose α. This is the likelihood that the observed result occurred by chance, or the probability of incorrectly rejecting the null hypothesis. In this case, we decide on a standard level of significance: $\alpha = .05$. In other words, if the calculated value of F exceeds the tabular value, we are willing to accept a 5 percent chance of incorrectly rejecting the null hypothesis. The value of F, or the F ratio, is computed as follows (see Exhibit 17.9):

$$F = \frac{MSR}{MSE}$$
$$= \frac{700{,}255}{9{,}534} = 73.5$$

EXHIBIT 17.8	Analysis of Variance				
Source of Variation	Degrees of Freedom	Sum of Squares	Mean Square		F Statistic
Regression (explained)	1	SSR	$MSR = \dfrac{SSR}{1}$		$F = \dfrac{MSR}{MSE}$
Residual (unexplained)	$n - 2$	SSE	$MSE = \dfrac{SSE}{n-2}$		
Total	$n - 1$	SST			

EXHIBIT 17.9	Regression Analysis Output

STAT. MULTIPLE REGRESS.	Regression Summary for Dependent Variable: $R = .89619973$ $R^2 = .80317395$ Adjusted $R^2 = .79223917$ $F(1,18) = 73.451$ $p < .00000$ Std. Error of estimate: 97.640					
N = 20	BETA	St. Err. of BETA	B	St. Err. of B	t(18)	p-level
Intercpt			240.8566	73.38347	3.282164	.004141
X	.896200	.104570	14.7168	1.71717	8.570374	.000000

We will reject the null hypothesis if the calculated F statistic is greater than or equal to the table, or critical, F value. The numerator and denominator degrees of freedom for this F ratio are 1 and 18, respectively. As noted earlier, it was decided that an alpha level of .05 ($\alpha = .05$) should be used.

The table, or critical, value of F with 1 (numerator) and 18 (denominator) degrees of freedom at $\alpha = .05$ is 4.49 (see Exhibit 5 in Appendix 2). Because the calculated value of F is greater than the critical value, we reject the null hypothesis and conclude that there is a significant linear relationship between the average daily vehicular traffic (X) and annual sales (Y). This result is consistent with the high coefficient of determination R^2 discussed earlier.

Hypotheses about the Regression Coefficient b   Finally, we may be interested in making hypotheses about b, the regression coefficient. As you may recall, b is the estimate of the effect of a one-unit change in X on Y. The hypotheses are as follows:

- Null hypothesis H_0: $b = O$.
- Alternative hypothesis H_a: $b \neq O$.

The appropriate test is a t test, and, as you can see from the last line of Exhibit 17.9, the computer program calculates the t value (8.57) and the p value (probability of incorrectly rejecting the null hypothesis of .0000). See Chapter 16 for a more detailed discussion of p values. Given the α criterion of .05, we would reject the null hypothesis in this case.

Correlation Analysis

Correlation for Metric Data: Pearson's Product–Moment Correlation

correlation analysis
Analysis of the degree to which changes in one variable are associated with changes in another.

Correlation is the degree to which changes in one variable (the dependent variable) are associated with changes in another. When the relationship is between two variables, the analysis is called simple, or bivariate, **correlation analysis**. With metric data, **Pearson's product–moment correlation** may be used. Additional discussion of issues around this type of analysis is provided in the Global Research features on page 527 and page 530.

In our example of bivariate regression, we used the coefficient of determination R^2 as a measure of the strength of the linear relationship between X and Y. Another descriptive measure, called the *coefficient of correlation R*, describes the degree of association between X and Y. It is the square root of the coefficient of determination with the appropriate sign (+ or –):

Pearson's product–moment correlation
Correlation analysis technique for use with metric data.

$$R = \pm\sqrt{R^2}$$

The value of R can range from –1 (perfect negative correlation) to +1 (perfect positive correlation). The closer R is to ± 1, the stronger the degree of association between X and Y. If R is equal to zero, then there is no association between X and Y.

If we had not been interested in estimating the regression function, we could have computed R directly from the data for the convenience store example, using this formula:

$$R = \frac{n\Sigma XY - (\Sigma X)(\Sigma Y)}{\sqrt{[n\Sigma X^2 - (\Sigma X)^2][n\Sigma Y^2 - (\Sigma Y)^2]}}$$

$$= \frac{20(734,083) - (816)(16,826)}{\sqrt{[20(36,526) - (816)^2][20(15,027,574) - (16,826)^2]}}$$

$$= .896$$

GLOBAL RESEARCH

Rethinking the Applicability of Pearson's Product–Moment Correlation

Is Pearson's product–moment correlation the best way to test reliability between a test and its retest scores? Maybe not, say Miaofen Yen, PhD, RN, and Li-Hua Lo, PhD, RN, both professors at National Cheng Jung University in Tainan, Taiwan. In statistics, the authors explain, the reliability of a measure means "the proportion of the observed score variance due to the true scores, that is, the ratio of true score variance to total score variance." Typically, statisticians use the Pearson correlation to calculate the reliability of results from test to retest, especially in nursing research, which is the domain of the authors. But research shows that this method has three limitations.

First, Pearson's calculation is designed to show the relationship between two variables, but it is inappropriate to apply this correlation to two data sets from the same variable. Second, when multiple tests are employed, it's hard to discern variations from test to test; when one concept is measured three times, generating three scores, one cannot create correlation coefficients for all three scores at the same time. Third, Pearson's is unable to detect systematic errors even though test and retest scores may be "perfectly correlated," as Miaofen and Li-Hua say.

An alternative approach called intraclass correlation, or ICC, and also known as generalizing coefficient, addresses these three limitations. Three issues need to be borne in mind when using ICC: First, the study design should focus on reliability, not correlation; second, the correct statistical model must be selected—either a one-way or a two-way random model depending on study conditions; and third, the number of measures in the study must be carefully considered.

Miaofen Yen and Li-Hua Lo demonstrated the strength of ICC on a study of competence for breast self-examination. The study looked at perceived competence and perceived barriers to the self-exam. The doctors engaged 10 nurses to complete the research study twice over a two-week period, polling them on 20 questions, each with a 5-point scale. Then they used ICC to run the test–retest reliability gauge. The calculations produced two ICC coefficients: The first was a single measure ICC (0.640), and the second was an average measure ICC (0.781). But it was the first result that the researchers found most applicable because in practical terms they would only give the test once.

The ICC value of 0.640 was close to the Pearson's value of 0.643, but ICC showed its merit in the area of discerning systematic error. When a systematic error of 12 points was introduced, the two resulting coefficients were found to be different. Pearson's was 0.643 and ICC was 0.554, demonstrating ICC's greater sensitivity to systematic error and its suitability for test–retest reliability.[1]

Questions

1. Find several published examples of test–retest reliability studies done with Pearson's product–moment correlation and evaluate whether ICC would have given better results.

2. Why is Pearson's correlation unable to accurately reflect systematic errors, and how does ICC better accommodate this function?

In this case, the value of *R* indicates a positive correlation between the average daily vehicular traffic and annual sales. In other words, successively higher levels of sales are associated with successively higher levels of traffic. Issues related to using both bivariate and multivariate correlation to get a more complete picture are discussed in the Practicing Marketing Research feature on page 531.

Another way to summarize and present correlation results is provided in the Practicing Marketing Research feature on page 529.

SPSS JUMP START FOR CORRELATION

Steps that you need to go through to do the correlation problem shown in the book are provided below along with the output produced. Use the data set **Correx**, which you can download from the Web site for the text.

Steps in SPSS

1. Select *Analyze → Correlate →Bivariate*.
2. Move **x** to Variables.
3. Move **y** to Variables.
4. Click OK.

SPSS Output for Correlation

Correlations

Correlations

		Traffic	Sales
Traffic	Pearson Correlation	1	.896**
	Sig. (2-tailed)	.	.000
	N	20	20
Sales	Pearson Correlation	.896**	1
	Sig. (2-tailed)	.000	.
	N	20	20

**. Correlation is significant at the 0.01 level

PRACTICING MARKETING RESEARCH

Do Your "BESD" When Explaining Correlation Results[2]

A correlation coefficient ranges from -1 to 1, with higher numbers (in either the positive or negative direction) indicating a stronger association between variables.

Two often used methods of explaining correlation often fall short of providing clients with a clear understanding of what the results mean.

One way is by computing the "percent of variance accounted for," which is done by squaring the correlation coefficient. Thus, if the correlation between two variables, say education and income, is .5, we can say that 25 percent of the variance in income is accounted for by variation in education.

The second way has sometimes been called the "soft-drink description." This is the process of dividing correlations into the categories of small, medium, and large. Many researchers consider correlations below .3 small, those from .3 to .5 medium, and those greater than .5 large.

This way of explaining the importance of correlations is easily grasped and provides some direction for clients.

A third technique developed by social scientists in the 1980s—the binomial effect size display (BESD)—helps to bring to life the importance (or unimportance) of your results. For example, say your goal was to predict repeat purchase behavior among a group of customers—half of whom have made a repeat purchase, half of whom have not—using a customer attitudes index and the correlation is .50 and that "25 percent of the variance in repeat purchase behavior is explained by variation in scores on the index." Your client might think the result is not very important ("Only 25 percent?!"). He or she would be wrong, and the BESD can show why.

We begin by constructing a 2 x 2 matrix as shown in Table 1, with two levels for the customer attitudes index (scorers in the top half and scorers in the bottom half) and two levels for purchase behavior (repeat purchase/no repeat purchase). Computing the cell entries begins with the assumption that there is no correlation between the measures. If this were the case, we would expect that 50 percent of the customers who scored in the top half of the index made repeat purchases and 50 percent who scored in the bottom half of the index made repeat purchases. This would give us 50 percent in each cell, since all rows and columns must add to 100 percent.

Table 1	Example of binomial effect size display for a correlation of Q		
		REPEAT PURCHASE?	
		Yes	No
CUSTOMER ATTITUDES INDEX SCORE	Top Half	50%	50%
	Bottom Half	50%	50%

To represent the correlation in the matrix, remove the decimal point from the correlation, divide this number by two and add the result (25) to the top left cell. Now adjust all cells so that all rows and columns add to 100 (see Table 2).

The BESD tells us that 75 percent of those who scored in the top half on the customer attitudes index made a repeat purchase and only 25 percent of those scoring in the bottom half did so. The meaning of this result is easily grasped, and the implications are fairly clear. Moving from bottom to top on the customer

attitudes index increases the probability of a repeat purchase by three times—an important result.

Table 2	Example of binomial effect size display for a correlation of .5		
		REPEAT PURCHASE?	
		Yes	No
CUSTOMER ATTITUDES INDEX SCORE	Top Half	75%	25%
	Bottom Half	25%	75%

The BESD is a flexible technique because it can be used with any kind of data that can be meaningfully dichotomized. So, the next time you want to communicate the importance of your correlation results in a way that is meaningful to your client (and in a way that will keep him or her awake during your presentation) remember to do your BESD.

Questions

1. What are two traditional ways to explain correlation results to a client? Describe each.
2. What is the BESD approach? Does it make results easier to digest by clients? Why/why not?

GLOBAL RESEARCH

Pearson's Product–Moment Correlation Fine-Tunes Medical Statistics

Pearson's product–moment correlation is an appropriate statistical tool for cases involving a comparison between two variables, X and Y, with metric data. It produces a coefficient, called r,

which results from dividing the covariance of two variables by the product of their standard deviations. It measures the degree of a linear relationship between two variables, indicating this as a range of +1 to -1.

Statisticians may thank an English professor named Karl Pearson (1857–1936) for this calculation. In 1911, Pearson founded the Department of Applied Statistics at University College in London,

England, the first academic statistics department in the world. Since then, researchers in many fields, especially medicine, have relied on Pearson's to fine-tune their data, as the following medical example vividly shows.

Chronic Fatigue Syndrome Studies

Researchers at the Human Performance Laboratory and Department of Internal Medicine at Vrije Universiteit Brussel in Brussels, Belgium, assembled a test group of 427 women with clinically diagnosed Chronic Fatigue Syndrome (CFS) and a control group of 204 age-matched women with sedentary lifestyles to participate in an exercise program to test heart rate. The women used a stationary ergometric bicycle and pedaled for 8 to 12 minutes as their oxygen levels, heart rate, and other physical parameters were monitored.

The researchers used the Pearson's calculation to study variations in the associations between variables within each group (test and control). They also employed Pearson's to discern any differences in the exercise parameters between the two groups. The purpose was to yield a better understanding of how exercise capacity varied between both groups. As the data show, Pearson's provided clear-cut correlations.

The calculation showed, for example, the correlation differences in terms of workload at anaerobic threshold (WAT, reduced oxygen intake) for maximum heart rate was 0.37 for CFS women compared to 0.70 for control-group sedentary women. It also showed that the maximum respiratory quotient for CFS women was positively associated with WAT ($r = 0.26$; $P < .001$ [P = difference]) and negatively associated with HRAT (heart rate at anaerobic threshold: $r = 0.15$; $P < .01$). Among women in the control group, the maximum respiratory quotient was positively correlated with the resting heart rate, ($r = 0.17$; $P < .02$) and negatively correlated with WAT ($r = 0.24$; $P < .002$).

Overall, Pearson's showed that "variation in heart rate was strongly related to changes in exercise capacity in patients with CFS." The researchers state that theirs was the first large-scale study to assess exercise capacity in a large population of CFS sufferers; the report, aided by Pearson's correlation, validated the belief that people with CFS have significantly reduced exercise capacity, sometimes up to 50 percent.[3]

Questions

1. Explain the statistical operating principle that accounts for Pearson's ability to clearly show differences between the two groups as reflected in the r values.

2. Is there an r value, possibly on the high side, that would seem suspect if reported for this study?

PRACTICING MARKETING RESEARCH

When Bivariate and Multivariate Correlation Combined Give the Best Picture

Social researchers Douglas Kirby, Karin Coyle, and Jeffrey B. Gould wanted to assess the relationships between conditions of poverty and birthrates among young teenagers in California. They collected data from 1,811 zip codes in which any teenage births had been recorded between 1991 and 1996. They excluded all zip code areas that did not have at least 200 young women aged 15–17 (which they called "young-teenage birthrates") to get a sample of 1,192 zip codes.

Their dependent variable was the mean of the yearly birthrates for women in this group. Their independent variables included 19 demographic features, which they culled from a list of 177 social indicators. Of these 19 independent measures, 3 dealt with ethnicity and 16 represented other factors such as education, employment, marital status, income level, and housing status.

Using these data, the researchers calculated the simple bivariate correlation and regression coefficients between young teenage birthrate and the 19 social measures, one at a time. Their bivariate analysis results showed that the number of families living in conditions of poverty in a given zip code was "highly related" to the birthrate among teenagers 15–17. The bivariate correlations, they concluded, "show that a single variable, the proportion of households living below the poverty line, is highly related to the young-teenage birthrate." Bivariate analysis also demonstrated that median household income and the number of homes receiving public assistance are also highly related and that three of the four poverty measures have the largest regression coefficients.

But the researchers wanted to look at a bigger picture of relationships and control for the "correlates" of family poverty level. So they shifted to multivariate correlation to make connections among multiple manifestations of poverty, low educational levels and employment status, and high levels of employment. They found that these factors also have a "large impact" on teenage birthrates. Multivariate correlation showed that the number of families living at or below poverty levels "remained by far the most important predictor" of teenage birthrate.[4]

Similarly, researcher and author Clayton E. Cramer found that the sequential application of bivariate and then multivariate correlation produced the best results in his study of the effectiveness of the Brady Handgun Violence Prevention Act of 1993. Bivariate analysis is easy to perform, Cramer says, and works well for certain types of research problems, such as comparing brands of gun ammunition or suggesting that factor A did not cause factor B or that factor A affected factor B.

But when you tackle "hard social problems" such as those associated with crime and gun control, using only two variables is insufficient for figuring out true causality. "Unlike bivariate correlation analysis, multivariate correlation analysis can help identify some truly subtle relationships—where a 3 percent increase in A may cause a 1 percent increase in B." Multivariate analysis is "a devilishly complex technique," and scientists using it can make legitimate mistakes hard to detect except by other scientists, Cramer says, but application of it produced strong data that the Brady Law had no effect on homicide rates.[5]

SUMMARY

The techniques used to analyze the relationship between variables taken two at a time are called bivariate analyses. Bivariate regression analysis allows a single dependent variable to be predicted from knowledge about a single independent variable. One way to examine the underlying relationship between a dependent and an independent variable is to plot them on a scatter diagram. If the relationship appears to be linear, then linear regression analysis may be used. If it is curvilinear, then curve-fitting techniques should be applied. The general equation for a straight line fitted to two variables is given by

$$Y = a + bX$$

where Y = dependent variable

X = independent variable

a = Y intercept

b = amount Y increases with each unit increase in X

Both *a* and *b* are unknown and must be estimated. This process is known as simple linear regression analysis. Bivariate least-squares regression analysis is a mathematical technique for fitting a line to measurements of the two variables *X* and *Y*. The line is fitted so that the algebraic sum of deviations of the actual observations from the line is zero and the sum of the squared deviations is less than it would be for any other line that might be fitted to the data.

The estimated regression function describes the nature of the relationship between *X* and *Y*. In addition, researchers want to know the strength of the relationship between the variables. This is measured by the coefficient of determination, denoted by R^2. The coefficient of determination measures the percent of the total variation in *Y* that is "explained" by the variation in *X*. The R^2 statistic ranges from 0 to 1. An analysis of variance (ANOVA) approach also can be used for regression analysis. The total variation is known as the total sum of squares (SST). The explained variation, or the sum of squares due to regression (SSR), represents the variability explained by the regression. The unexplained variation is called the error sum of squares (SSE).

Correlation analysis is the measurement of the degree to which changes in one variable are associated with changes in another. Correlation analysis will tell the researcher whether the variables are positively correlated, negatively correlated, or independent.

KEY TERMS & DEFINITIONS

bivariate techniques Statistical methods of analyzing the relationship between two variables.

scatter diagram Graphic plot of the data with dependent variable on the *Y* (vertical) axis and the independent variable on the *X* (horizontal) axis. Shows the nature of the relationship between the two variables, linear or nonlinear.

independent variable Variable believed to affect the value of the dependent variable.

dependent variable Variable expected to be explained or caused by the independent variable.

bivariate regression analysis Analysis of the strength of the linear relationship between two variables when one is considered the independent variable and the other the dependent variable.

coefficient of determination Percentage of the total variation in the dependent variable explained by the independent variable.

sum of squares due to regression Variation explained by the regression.

error sum of squares Variation not explained by the regression.

correlation analysis Analysis of the degree to which changes in one variable are associated with changes in another.

Pearson's product–moment correlation Correlation analysis technique for use with metric data.

QUESTIONS FOR REVIEW & CRITICAL THINKING

1. Give examples of three marketing problems for which correlation analysis would be appropriate.

2. A sales manager of a life insurance firm administered a standard multiple-item job satisfaction scale to all the members of the firm's salesforce. The manager then

correlated (Pearson's product–moment correlation) job satisfaction score with years of school completed for each salesperson. The resulting correlation was .11. On the basis of this analysis, the sales manager concluded: "A salesperson's level of education has little to do with his or her job satisfaction." Would you agree or disagree with this conclusion? Explain the basis for your position.

3. What purpose does a scatter diagram serve?

4. Explain the meaning of the coefficient of determination. What does this coefficient tell the researcher about the nature of the relationship between the dependent and independent variables?

5. It has been observed in the past that when an AFC team wins the Super Bowl, the stock market rises in the first quarter of the year in almost every case. When an NFC team wins the Super Bowl, the stock market falls in the first quarter in most cases. Does this mean that the direction of movement of the stock market is caused by which conference wins the Super Bowl? What does this example illustrate?

6. The following table gives data collected by a convenience store chain for 20 of its stores.

Column 1: ID number for each store

Column 2: Annual sales for the store for the previous year in thousands of dollars

Column 3: Average number of vehicles that pass the store each day, based on actual traffic counts for one month

Column 4: Total population that lives within a 2-mile radius of the store, based on 1990 census data

Column 5: Median family income for households within a 2-mile radius of the store, based on 2000 census data

Store ID No.	Annual Sales (thousands of dollars)	Average Daily Traffic	Population in 2-Mile Radius	Average Income in Area
1	$1,121	61,655	17,880	$28,991
2	$ 766	35,236	13,742	$14,731
3	$ 595	35,403	19,741	$ 8,114
4	$ 899	52,832	23,246	$15,324
5	$ 915	40,809	24,485	$11,438
6	$ 782	40,820	20,410	$11,730
7	$ 833	49,147	28,997	$10,589
8	$ 571	24,953	9,981	$10,706
9	$ 692	40,828	8,982	$23,591
10	$1,005	39,195	18,814	$15,703
11	$ 589	34,574	16,941	$ 9,015
12	$ 671	26,639	13,319	$10,065
13	$ 903	55,083	21,482	$17,365
14	$ 703	37,892	26,524	$ 7,532
15	$ 556	24,019	14,412	$ 6,950
16	$ 657	27,791	13,896	$ 9,855
17	$1,209	53,438	22,444	$21,589
18	$ 997	54,835	18,096	$22,659
19	$ 844	32,916	16,458	$12,660
20	$ 883	29,139	16,609	$11,618

Answer the following:

a. Which of the other three variables is the best predictor of sales? Compute correlation coefficients to answer the question.

b. Do the following regressions:

   (1). Sales as a function of average daily traffic

   (2). Sales as a function of population in a 2-mile radius

c. Interpret the results of the two regressions.

7. Interpret the following:

   a. $Y = .11 + .009X$, where Y is the likelihood of sending children to college and X is family income in thousands of dollars. Remember: It is family income in *thousands*.

   (1). According to our model, how likely is a family with an income of $100,000 to send their children to college?

   (2). What is the likelihood for a family with an income of $50,000?

   (3). What is the likelihood for a family with an income of $17,500?

   (4). Is there some logic to the estimates? Explain.

   b. $Y = .25 - .0039X$, where Y is the likelihood of going to a skateboard park and X is age.

   (1). According to our model, how likely is a 10-year-old to go to a skateboard park?

   (2). What is the likelihood for a 60-year-old?

   (3). What is the likelihood for a 40-year-old?

   (4). Is there some logic to the estimates? Explain.

8. The following ANOVA summary data are the result of a regression with sales per year (dependent variable) as a function of promotion expenditures per year (independent variable) for a toy company.

$$F = \frac{MSR}{MSE} = \frac{34,276}{4,721}$$

The degrees of freedom are 1 for the numerator and 19 for the denominator. Is the relationship statistically significant at $\alpha = .05$? Comment.

WORKING THE NET

1. For an informative and practical tutorial with examples and graphs on different regression models with count data (including Poisson, negative binomial, zero-inflated count models, and others), visit: *www.ats.ucla.edu/stat/stata/seminars/count_presentation/count.htm*.

2. For a free online statistical calculator to work with the Pearson's product–moment correlation, see: *www.wessa.net*.

3. Take a look at the video on correlation at *http://www.youtube.com/watch?v=Fd-V9W7dK04*.

REAL-LIFE RESEARCH • 17.1

Axcis Athletic Shoes

Fred Luttrell is the new product development manager for Axcis Athletic Shoe Company. He recently completed consumer testing of 12 new shoe concepts. As part of this test, a panel of consumers was asked to rate the 12 shoe concepts on two attributes, overall quality and style. A 10-point scale was used with anchors at 10 = best possible and 1 = worst possible.

The panel of 20 consumers met as a group and came up with the ratings as a group. Fred believes that there is a relationship between the style ratings and the overall quality ratings. He believes that shoes receiving higher ratings on style also will tend to receive higher ratings on overall quality. The ratings results for the 12 shoe concepts are as follows.

Shoe Model	Style Rating	Quality Rating	Shoe Model	Style Rating	Quality Rating
1	9	8	7	9	7
2	7	7	8	7	9
3	6	8	9	8	6
4	9	9	10	10	9
5	8	7	11	6	5
6	5	5	12	9	10

Questions

1. Which of the statistical procedures covered in this chapter is appropriate for addressing Fred's theory? Why would you choose that technique over the other?

2. Use the technique that you chose to determine whether Fred's theory is supported by the statistical evidence. State the appropriate null and alternative hypotheses. Is Fred's theory supported by the statistical evidence? Why or why not?

REAL-LIFE RESEARCH • 17.2

The Carter Regional Blood Center

In the past, many small communities had their own blood programs and patients received whole blood. It usually was organized by local hospital and civic leaders to meet the needs of the community. Based on advances in medical knowledge, patients today are rarely given whole blood but receive only those components necessary for their well-being.

However, testing, processing, and separating blood into its components requires a specialized staff and equipment that are extremely costly for every community to duplicate. As a result, the nation's blood collection system is now regionalized. Blood is collected in small communities and transported to regional blood centers where it is processed. The blood is stored at these centers, with the quantities and types of blood needed returned to the small communities for their use. As a result of this centralized process, many small town blood programs are now part of larger regional programs.

Research has greatly improved our understanding of how disease is and is not transmitted through blood transfusions. Because of this, many individuals who were once rejected as blood donors can now donate. At one time, the average rejection rate for people willing to give blood was about 14 percent. Now it is less than 5 percent. Typically a person can donate blood six times a year, but those who do donate in the United States usually do so less than once a year.

The Carter Regional Blood Center in Fort Worth, Texas is a regional center for six counties, including Tarrant (Fort Worth), Parker, Ellis, Collin, Erath, and Johnson. The center had an increased need for blood and blood components primarily because of the growing number of open heart and kidney transplant procedures performed in the region. Also, regular transfusions of blood platelets are demanded by a growing number of patients undergoing chemotherapy for cancer or on the AIDS drug, AZT. To meet the demand for blood and blood components, the administrators of the center decided that a marketing orientation was needed. The first step in this process was to gain some understanding of the target market. In particular, they were interested in the relationship between donations and age and donations and income. They did a pilot study that involved collecting data form a random sample of 20 donors. The data are shown in the following table.

- Column 1 – ID number assigned to each donor.
- Column 2 – Number of pints donated in past 2 years.
- Column 3 – Age of donor in years.
- Column 4 – Years of education for donor.

Questions

1. Which of the other two variables is most closely associated with Pints Donated? Compute correlation coefficients to answer the question.
2. Do the following regressions.
   a. Amount donated as a function of Age.
   b. Amount donated as a function of Education.
3. Interpret the results of the two regressions.

Results of Carter Donor Survey

RESPONDENT #	PINTS DONATED	AGE	EDUCATION IN YEARS
1	10	42	19
2	1	21	16
3	2	24	12
4	2	27	14
5	1	23	10
6	7	39	16
7	5	35	16
8	4	38	14
9	3	33	12
10	2	30	13
11	5	36	16
12	6	37	17
13	2	22	12
14	8	40	16
15	1	24	16
16	7	36	18
17	1	22	11
18	2	25	12
19	2	26	13
20	3	29	16

surveysolutions XP ●

SPSS EXERCISES FOR CHAPTER 17

Exercise 1: Bivariate Regression

Use the *analyze/regression/linear* sequence to invoke bivariate regression analysis. This exercise attempts to explain the variation in the *number of movies the respondent attends in an average month* (*Q3*). Hence, **Q3** is the **dependent variable**. Invoke the bivariate regression procedure for the following pairs of variables:

1. Q3 and Q5d (movie theater item—importance of comfortable chairs)
2. Q3 and Q5e (movie theater item—auditorium type seating)
3. Q3 and Q7a (movie theater information source—newspaper)
4. Q3 and Q7b (movie theater information source—Internet)
5. Q3 and Q7c (movie theater information source—phone in for information)
6. Q3 and Q9 (self-perception of how physically active)
7. and Q10 (self-perception of how socially active)

Summarize the results of the bivariate regression analysis by filling in tables similar to the following ones.

Model	Regression coefficient	t	Sig.
Constant			
Q5d			
Q5e, etc.			

Variables	Model R^2	Model F-value	Sig.
Q5d			
Q5e, etc.			

1. At the 95 percent level of confidence, which of the regression models (list the pairs of variables) are significant (list the dependent variables)?

    _____

    _____

2. ***Interpretation of the regression coefficients:*** Use the following table to summarize the regression coefficient, *b*, in each of the seven regression models.

Model	Regression Coefficient b	t	Sig. of b	Interpretation of the Regression Coefficient b
Example Q3 & Q5b	.244	4.147	.000	A one-unit increase in Q5b is associated with a .244 increase in monthly movie attendance

3. Using the regression results, compute Y(Q3) if Q5d = 4. _____

4. Using the regression results, compute Y(Q3) if Q7c = 2. _____

5. Using the regression results, compute Y(Q3) if Q9 = 3. _____

6. Which of the seven models in the bivariate regression analysis _____
   explained the most variation in Q3 (*Hint: R^2*)?

7. In which of the seven models does the independent variable's _____
   regression coefficient cause the largest change in Q3 for a one-unit change in the
   independent variable?

Exercise 2: Pearson's Product–Moment Correlation

Use the *analyze/correlate/bivariate* sequence to invoke bivariate correlation analysis. This exercise utilizes the metric correlation technique (Pearson's), which requires that both variables in the bivariate analysis be of at least interval measurement scale. The objective of this exercise is to examine the association between various pairs of variables.

Invoke the bivariate correlation procedure utilizing the Pearson coefficient to evaluate the association between the following pairs of variables:

a. Q3 and Q8a (purchase option for movie tickets—Internet)

b. Q9 (self-perception of how physically active) and Q10 (self-perception of how socially active)

c. Q8a (purchase option for movie tickets—Internet) and Q7b (importance of the Internet as a source of information about movies at movie theaters)

d. Q5b (movie theater item—importance of soft drinks and food items) and Q9 (self-perception of how physically active)

e. Q5h (movie theater item—number of screens at a movie theater) and Q10 (self-perception of how socially active)

With the results of the bivariate correlation using the Pearson coefficient, fill in a table similar to the following.

Variables	Pearson Coefficient (include 3)	Probability of an insignificant correlation in the population (based on the sample results)	Interpretation of the results

Questions to Answer: (Assume a significant relationship requires at least a **95 percent** level of confidence.)

1. Of the five correlations computed, which pair of variables had the strongest association? _____

2. Of the three correlations computed, which pair of variables had the weakest association? _____

3. Do people who perceive themselves as more physically active have a greater or lesser need for food and drink at a movie theater? _____

4. Are people who use the Internet to purchase movie tickets more or less likely to use the Internet to get information about movies at movie theaters? _____

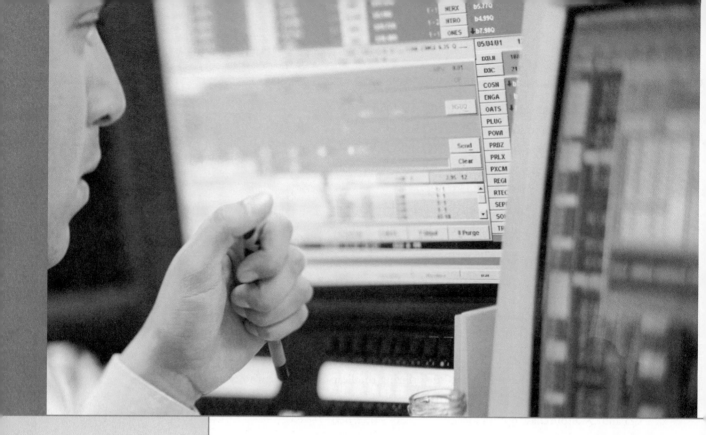

CHAPTER 18

Multivariate Data Analysis

LEARNING OBJECTIVES

1. To define multivariate data analysis.

2. To describe multiple regression analysis and multiple discriminant analysis.

3. To learn about cluster analysis and factor analysis.

4. To develop an understanding of conjoint analysis.

5. To gain an understanding of data mining.

Multivariate Analysis Procedures

Advances in computer hardware and software have provided the basis for remarkable developments in the use of powerful statistical procedures for the analysis of marketing research data. These developments have made it possible to analyze large amounts of complex data with relative ease. In particular, multivariate analysis procedures have been extremely significant in this data analysis revolution. The hot job market for people with skills in this area is discussed in the accompanying Practicing Marketing Research feature.

PRACTICING MARKETING RESEARCH

Statistician: The Hot Job of the Future[1]

With the dramatic proliferation of digital data over the last several years, professionals in the fields of statistics and data analysis are becoming hot commodities. At top companies like Google and IBM, new recruits holding a PhD in a statistics field can land jobs with starting salaries as high as $125,000. In a world where almost anything can be monitored or measured, the applications created through advanced data analysis are opening up a wealth of opportunities.

The key is the statisticians. All the raw data in the world, in and of itself, is not very useful until its significance can be determined. That's why companies are calling on the statisticians to turn these treasure troves of raw data into applicable and actionable information. Google, for example, employs statisticians to continuously find new ways to improve its search algorithms. Statistical analysts have been upgrading Google's crawler software, which is used to update its search index. Analytical improvements are helping the software better identify Web sites that are more frequently updated over Web sites that have gone dormant. Because of the scale of Google's operations (running the same operations billions and trillions of times), even incremental improvements can have a dramatic effect.

IBM is looking to take advantage of opportunities in the field as well, with the introduction of its Business Analytics and Optimization Services Department, by providing data mining and analysis services to other firms. The unit originally comprised 200 of IBM's top mathematicians, statisticians, and researchers, but the company plans to expand through training and new hiring to tap the expertise of over 4,000 staff members.

As many statisticians point out, however, the use of statistics is not without its challenges. If not carefully analyzed, the massive amount of data available can overwhelm statistical models, and even strong statistical correlations in the data do not necessarily indicate a causal relationship. Still, as the explosion of available data continues, the ability to identify mathematically abnormal relationships in the data creates a wealth of opportunities. Organizations need to be able to properly explain these abnormalities though, and that's why they need the best analysts and statisticians. These skill sets are quickly becoming the kind you can take to the bank!

Questions

1. Where have you recently seen the use of statistics and data analysis where you might not have expected it? How was it being used?

2. Top companies are finding that many talented analysts and statisticians actually have backgrounds in other disciplines such as economics, mathematics, and computer sciences. How do you think these disciplines relate to and inform the approach to data analysis?

→ **multivariate analysis**
A general term for statistical procedures that simultaneously analyze multiple measurements on each individual or object under study.

The term **multivariate analysis** refers to the simultaneous analysis of multiple measurements on each individual or object being studied.[2] Some experts consider any simultaneous statistical analysis of more than two variables to be multivariate analysis. Multivariate analysis procedures are extensions of the univariate and bivariate statistical procedures discussed in Chapters 16 and 17.

A number of techniques fall under the heading of multivariate analysis procedures. In this chapter, we will consider five of these techniques:

- ◼ Multiple regression analysis
- ◼ Multiple discriminant analysis
- ◼ Cluster analysis
- ◼ Factor analysis
- ◼ Conjoint analysis

You may have been exposed to multiple regression analysis in introductory statistics courses. The remaining procedures are newer, less widely studied, or both. Summary descriptions of the techniques are provided in Exhibit 18.1.

Although awareness of multivariate techniques is far from universal, they have been around for decades and have been widely used for a variety of commercial purposes. Fair Isaac & Co. has built a 600 million business around the commercial use of multivariate techniques.[3] The firm and its clients have found that they can predict with surprising accuracy who will pay their bills on time, who will pay late, and who will not pay at all. The federal government uses secret formulas, based on the firm's analyses, to identify tax evaders. Fair Isaac has also shown that results from its multivariate analyses help in identifying the best sales prospects. A range of multivariate procedures are covered in the Practicing Marketing Research feature on page 543.

Multivariate Software

The computational requirements for the various multivariate procedures discussed in this chapter are substantial. As a practical matter, running the various types of analyses presented requires a computer and appropriate software. Until the late 1980s, most types of multivariate analyses discussed in this chapter were done on mainframe or minicomputers because personal computers were limited in power, memory, storage capacity, and

EXHIBIT 18.1	**Brief Descriptions of Multivariate Analysis Procedures**
Multiple regression analysis	Enables the researcher to predict the level of magnitude of a dependent variable based on the levels of more than one independent variable.
Multiple discriminant analysis	Enables the researcher to predict group membership on the basis of two or more independent variables.
Cluster analysis	Is a procedure for identifying subgroups of individuals or items that are homogeneous within subgroups and different from other subgroups.
Factor analysis	Permits the analyst to reduce a set of variables to a smaller set of factors or composite variables by identifying underlying dimensions in the data.
Conjoint analysis	Provides a basis for estimating the utility that consumers associate with different product features or attributes.

PRACTICING
MARKETING RESEARCH

Eleven Techniques for Analyzing Data[4]

The astute marketing researcher knows that different marketing questions often require different types of analytical tools. With the wide array of tools at their disposal, researchers need to understand the strengths and weaknesses of each. Here are 11 techniques that researchers may consider—and when.

1. **Multiple Regression Analysis**—analyzes one metric dependent variable in relation to multiple metric independent variables. Normality, linearity, and equal variance assumptions must be carefully observed. Often used in forecasting.

2. **Logistic Regression Analysis**—consists of a variation of multiple regression designed to create a probabilistic assessment of a binary choice, comparing predicted and observed events. Predicts consumer behavior in the presence of alternate choices.

3. **Discriminant Analysis**—organizes people and observations into homogeneous groups. Requires metric independent variables with high normality. Used for classifying people according to specific characteristic, for instance, buyer and nonbuyer.

4. **Multivariate Analysis of Variance (MANOVA)**—compares categorical independent variables with multiple metric dependent variables, determining dependence relationships across various groups. Used in experiment design. If sample sizes are too large, the model becomes impractical.

5. **Factor Analysis**—reduces a wide range of variables into a smaller set of factors, generally of three to five variables each. No dependent variables. Major analysis methods include common factor analysis and principal component analysis.

6. **Cluster Analysis**—creates subgroups out of similar individuals or objects within a large data set. Not all individuals or objects may fit within the defined subgroups. Major clustering methods include hierarchical, non-hierarchical, and a combination of the two.

7. **Multidimensional Scaling (MDS)**—uses perceptual mapping to convert consumer judgments into multidimensional distances. An exploratory technique, useful when dealing with unknown comparison bases. Typically requires four times as many objects as dimensions.

8. **Correspondence Analysis**—creates a perceptual map of object attribute ratings through dimensional reduction. Useful when assessing a wide range of attributes. Often used to examine an advertising campaign's effectiveness. A combination of independent and dependent variables can result in difficulties in interpretation.

9. **Conjoint Analysis**—evaluates both objects and attribute levels. Combines functions of compositional and dependence techniques. Produces models indicating ideal product attribute combinations.

10. **Canonical Correlation**—correlates independent and dependent variables simultaneously, using metric independent variables or nonmetric categorical variables. Has fewest restrictions of any multivariate technique, but also fewest assumptions.

11. **Structural Equation Modeling (SEM)**—employs a variety of techniques (e.g., LISREL, latent variable analysis, confirmatory factor analysis) to simultaneously examine numerous relationships between variable sets. Used to evaluate multiple scaled attributes or build summated scales.

Questions

1. What questions do you think you should be asking when choosing a multivariate analysis technique?

2. Have you ever done a project in which the analytical technique chosen was not the best fit? What difficulties did you encounter as a result?

range of software available. Those limitations are in the past. Personal computers have the power to handle just about any problem that a marketing researcher might encounter. Most problems can be solved in a matter of seconds, and a wide variety of outstanding Windows software is available for multivariate analysis. SPSS for Windows is the most widely used by professional marketing researchers.

SPSS includes a full range of software modules for integrated database creation and management, data transformation and manipulation, graphing, descriptive statistics, and multivariate procedures. It has an easy-to-use, graphical interface. Additional information on the SPSS product line can be found at *http://www.spss.com/software/statistics* and *http://www.spss.com/software/modeler*. A number of other useful resources are available at the SPSS site:

- Technical support, product information, FAQs (frequently asked questions), various downloads, and product reviews
- Examples of successful applications of multivariate analysis to solve real business problems
- Discussions of data mining and data warehousing applications

Multiple Regression Analysis

Researchers use multiple regression analysis when their goal is to examine the relationship between two or more metric predictor (independent) variables and one metric dependent (criterion) variable.[5] Under certain circumstances, described later in this section, nominal predictor variables can be used if they are recoded as binary variables.

multiple regression analysis
Procedure for predicting the level or magnitude of a (metric) dependent variable based on the levels of multiple independent variables.

Multiple regression analysis is an extension of bivariate regression, discussed in Chapter 17. Instead of fitting a straight line to observations in a two-dimensional space, multiple regression analysis fits a plane to observations in a multidimensional space. The output obtained and the interpretation are essentially the same as for bivariate regression. The general equation for multiple regression is as follows:

$$Y = a + b_1 X_1 + b_2 X_2 + b_3 X_3 + \cdots + b_n X_n$$

where
Y = dependent or criterion variable
a = estimated constant
$b_1 - b_n$ = coefficients associated with the predictor variables so that a change of one unit in X will cause a change of b_1 units in Y; values for the coefficients are estimated from the regression analysis
$X_1 - X_n$ = predictor (independent) variables that influence the dependent variable

For example, consider the following regression equation (in which values for a, b_1, and b_2 have been estimated by means of regression analysis):

$$\hat{Y} = 200 + 17X_1 + 22X_2$$

where
$\hat{Y}$ = estimated sales in units
X_1 = advertising expenditures
X_2 = number of salespersons

This equation indicates that sales increase by 17 units for every $1 increase in advertising and 22 units for every one-unit increase in number of salespersons.

Applications of Multiple Regression Analysis

There are many possible applications of multiple regression analysis in marketing research:

- Estimating the effects of various marketing mix variables on sales or market share
- Estimating the relationship between various demographic or psychographic factors and the frequency with which certain service businesses are visited
- Determining the relative influence of individual satisfaction elements on overall satisfaction
- Quantifying the relationship between various classification variables, such as age and income, and overall attitude toward a product or service
- Determining which variables are predictive of sales of a particular product or service

Multiple regression analysis can serve one or a combination of two basic purposes: (1) predicting the level of the dependent variable, based on given levels of the independent variables, and (2) understanding the relationship between the independent variables and the dependent variable.

Multiple Regression Analysis Measures

In the discussion of bivariate regression in Chapter 17, a statistic referred to as the **coefficient of determination**, or R^2, was identified as one of the outputs of regression analysis. This statistic can assume values from 0 to 1 and provides a measure of the percentage of the variation in the dependent variable that is explained by variation in the independent variables. For example, if R^2 in a given regression analysis is calculated to be .75, this means that 75 percent of the variation in the dependent variable is explained by variation in the independent variables. The analyst would always like to have a calculated R^2 close to 1. Frequently, variables are added to a regression model to see what effect they have on the R^2 value.

The b values, or **regression coefficients**, are estimates of the effect of individual independent variables on the dependent variable. It is appropriate to determine the likelihood that each individual b value is the result of chance. This calculation is part of the output provided by virtually all statistical software packages. Typically, these packages compute the probability of incorrectly rejecting the null hypothesis of $b_n = 0$.

> **coefficient of determination**
> Measure of the percentage of the variation in the dependent variable explained by variations in the independent variables.

> **regression coefficients**
> Estimates of the effect of individual independent variables on the dependent variable.

Dummy Variables

In some situations, the analyst needs to include nominally scaled independent variables such as gender, marital status, occupation, and race in a multiple regression analysis. **Dummy variables** can be created for this purpose. Dichotomous nominally scaled independent variables can be transformed into dummy variables by coding one value (for example, female) as 0 and the other (for example, male) as 1. For nominally scaled independent variables that can assume more than two values, a slightly different approach is required. Consider a question regarding racial group with three possible answers: African American, Hispanic, or Caucasian. Binary or dummy variable coding of responses requires the use of two dummy variables, X_1 and X_2, which might be coded as follows:

> **dummy variables**
> In regression analysis, a way of representing two-group or dichotomous, nominally scaled independent variables by coding one group as 0 and the other as 1.

	X_1	X_2
If person is African American	1	0
If person is Hispanic	0	1
If person is Caucasian	0	0

Multiple regression analysis can be used to estimate the relationship between various demographic or psychographic factors and the frequency with which a service business is hired.

Potential Use and Interpretation Problems

The analyst must be sensitive to certain problems that may be encountered in the use and interpretation of multiple regression analysis results. These problems are summarized in the following sections.

Collinearity   One of the key assumptions of multiple regression analysis is that the independent variables are not correlated (collinear) with each other.[6] If they are correlated, the predicted Y value is unbiased, and the estimated B values (regression coefficients) will have inflated standard errors and will be inaccurate and unstable. Larger than expected coefficients for some b values are compensated for by smaller than expected coefficients for others. This is why you still produce reliable estimates of Y and why you can get sign reversals and wide variations in b values with **collinearity**, but still produce reliable estimates of Y.

> **collinearity**
> Correlation of independent variables with each other, which can bias estimates of regression coefficients.

The simplest way to check for collinearity is to examine the matrix showing the correlations between each variable in the analysis. One rule of thumb is to look for correlations between independent variables of .30 or greater. If correlations of this magnitude exist, then the analyst should check for distortions of the b values. One way to do this is to run regressions with the two or more collinear variables included and then run regressions again with the individual variables. The b values in the regression with all variables in the equation should be similar to the b values computed for the variables run separately.

A number of strategies can be used to deal with collinearity. Two of the most commonly used strategies are (1) to drop one of the variables from the analysis if two variables are heavily correlated with each other and (2) to combine the correlated variables in some fashion (for example, an index) to form a new composite independent variable, which can be used in subsequent regression analyses.

Causation   Although regression analysis can show that variables are associated or correlated with each other, it cannot prove **causation**. Causal relationships can be confirmed only by other means (see Chapter 9). A strong logical or theoretical basis must be developed to support the idea that a causal relationship exists between the independent variables and the dependent variable. However, even a strong logical base and supporting statistical results demonstrating correlation are only *indicators* of causation.

Scaling of Coefficients   The magnitudes of the regression coefficients associated with the various independent variables can be compared directly only if they are scaled in the same units or if the data have been standardized. Consider the following example:

$$\hat{Y} = 50 + 20X_1 + 20X_2$$

where $\hat{Y}$ = estimated sales volume

X_1 = advertising expenditures in thousands of dollars

X_2 = number of salespersons

At first glance, it appears that an additional dollar spent on advertising and another salesperson added to the salesforce have equal effects on sales. However, this is not true because X_1 and X_2 are measured in different kinds of units. Direct comparison of regression coefficients requires that all independent variables be measured in the same units (for example, dollars or thousands of dollars) or that the data be standardized. *Standardization* is achieved by taking each number in a series, subtracting the mean of the series from the number, and dividing the result by the standard deviation of the series. This process converts any set of numbers to a new set with a mean of 0 and a standard deviation of 1. The formula for the standardization process is as follows:

$$\frac{X_i - \overline{X}}{\sigma}$$

where X_i = individual number from a series of numbers

$\overline{X}$ = mean of the series

σ = standard deviation of the series

Sample Size   The value of R^2 is influenced by the number of predictor variables relative to sample size.[7] Several different rules of thumb have been proposed; they suggest that the number of observations should be equal to at least 10 to 15 times the number of predictor variables. For the preceding example (sales volume as a function of advertising expenditures and number of salespersons) with two predictor variables, a minimum of 20 to 30 observations would be required.

Example of Multiple Regression Analysis

This sample problem and others in this chapter use data from the research described in the appendix to this chapter. United Wireless Communications believes that five variables are important in determining how much target customers are willing to pay each month to have wireless service. The five items are consumer importance ratings of the following service features: range of coverage, mobility, sound quality, ability to place and receive calls when away from home, and average monthly bill. This hypothesis is based on the results of focus groups and other research conducted by United

Wireless Communications. All six variables (the dependent variable and five predictor variables) were measured in the survey. The five predictor variables were all measured on a nine-point scale, where 9 means the attribute is "very important" and 1 means the attribute is "very unimportant." The five predictors can be found under question 3 in the survey in the appendix to this chapter (United Wireless Communications Data Set).

To test English's hypothesis, the following model was estimated, using multiple regression analysis:

$$\hat{Y} = a + b_1X_1 + b_2X_2 + b_3X_3 + b_4X_4 + b_5X_5$$

where $\hat{Y}$ = dependent variable, amount willing to pay each month to have wireless service (ADDED)

a = constant term, or Y-axis intercept

$b_1 - b_5$ = regression coefficients to be estimated

X_1 = first independent variable, importance rating of range of coverage (RANGE)

X_2 = second independent variable, importance rating of mobility (MOBILITY)

X_3 = third independent variable, importance rating of sound quality (SOUND)

X_4 = fourth independent variable, importance rating of ability to place and receive calls when away from home (PRECEIV)

X_5 = fifth independent variable, importance rating of average monthly bill (AVGBILL)

The estimated regression equation is

$$\hat{Y} = .82 + .44X_1 + .69X_2 + .21X_3 + .45X_4 + 1.44X_5$$

Complete regression results generated with the SPSS software package are shown in Exhibit 18.2. These results provide the following information:

■ All the regression coefficients (b_1, b_2, and so on) have positive signs. This indicates that higher importance ratings on each of the five independent variables are associated with the willingness to pay more for wireless service, as expected.

■ The regression coefficient (b) shows the estimated effect of a one-unit increase in each of the associated independent variables on the dependent variable. The estimated unstandardized coefficients are shown under the column labeled "B." The results show, for example, that a one-unit increase in the importance rating of RANGE is associated with a $0.44 increase in the amount an individual is willing to pay per month for wireless service. The column labeled BETA shows the regression coefficient computed with standardized data. According to these estimates, MOBILITY has a greater effect on the amount prospective customers are willing to pay for the service than does any of the other four independent variables. AVGBILL is second in importance, and RANGE and PRECEIV are tied for third place. Interestingly, according to the model, SOUND has the smallest relative effect on the amount prospective customers are willing to pay.

SPSS JUMP START FOR MULTIPLE REGRESSION ANALYSIS

Steps that you need to go through to do the multiple regression analysis example shown in this chapter are provided below along with the output produced. Use the data set **Mulregex**, which you can download from the Web site for the text.

Steps in SPSS

1. Select *Analyze → Regression → Linear*.
2. Move **added** to Dependent.
3. Move **range, mobility, sound, preceiv**, and **avgbill** to Independent(s).
4. Click OK.

SPSS Output for Multiple Regression Analysis

Regression

Variables Entered/Removed[b]

Model	Variables Entered	Variables Removed	Method
1	avgbill, preceiv, sound, mobility, range	.	Enter

a. All requested variables entered.

b. Dependent Variable: added

Model Summary

Model	R	R Square	Adjusted R Square	Std. Error of the Estimate
1	.866[a]	.749	.743	1.486

a. Predictors: (Constant), avgbill, preceiv, sound, mobility, range

ANOVA[b]

Model		Sum of Squares	df	Mean Square	F	Sig.
1	Regression	1282.226	5	256.445	116.085	.000[a]
	Residual	428.569	194	2.209		
	Total	1710.795	199			

a. Predictors: (Constant), avgbill, preceiv, sound, mobility, range

b. Dependent Variable: added

Coefficients[a]

Model		Unstandardized Coefficients		Standardized Coefficients	t	Sig.
		B	Std. Error	Beta		
1	(Constant)	.819	1.667		.491	.624
	range	.441	.104	.211	4.249	.000
	mobility	.687	.065	.522	10.541	.000
	sound	.209	.125	.067	1.667	.097
	preceiv	.449	.123	.206	3.645	.000
	avgbill	1.444	.173	.321	8.329	.000

a. Dependent Variable: added

- The adjusted R^2 value is .743, indicating that 74.3 percent of the variation in the amount consumers are willing to pay for wireless service is explained by the variation in the five independent, or predictor, variables.

EXHIBIT 18.2	Regression Summary for Dependent Variable: ADDED					

$R = .86573182$ $R = 3.74949158$ Adjusted $R^2 = .74303518$
$F(95,194) = 116.09$ $P = 0.0000$ Std. error of estimate: 1.4863

	Beta	St. Err of BETA	B	St. Err of B	t(194)	p level
INTERCEPT			0.82	1.67	0.49	0.62
RANGE	0.21	0.05	0.44	0.10	4.25	0.00
MOBILITY	0.52	0.05	0.69	0.07	10.54	0.00
SOUND	0.07	0.04	0.21	0.13	1.67	0.10
PRECEIV	0.21	0.06	0.45	0.12	3.65	0.00
AVGBILL	0.32	0.04	1.44	0.17	8.33	0.00

Multiple Discriminant Analysis

Although **multiple discriminant analysis** is similar to multiple regression analysis,[8] there are important differences. In the case of multiple regression analysis, the dependent variable must be **metric**; in multiple discriminant analysis, the dependent variable is **nominal or categorical** in nature. For example, the dependent variable might be usage status for a particular product or service. A particular respondent who uses the product or service might be assigned a code of 1 for the dependent variable, and a respondent who does not use it might be assigned a code of 2. Independent variables might include various metric measures, such as age, income, and number of years of education. The goals of multiple discriminant analysis are as follows:

■ Determine if there are statistically significant differences between the average discriminant score profiles of two (or more) groups (in this case, users and nonusers).

■ Establish a model for classifying individuals or objects into groups on the basis of their values on the independent variables.

■ Determine how much of the difference in the average score profiles of the groups is accounted for by each independent variable.

The general discriminant analysis equation follows:

$$Z = b_1X_1 + b_2X_2 + \cdots + b_nX_n$$

where Z = discriminant score
$b_1 - b_n$ = discriminant weights
$X_1 - X_n$ = independent variables

The **discriminant score**, usually referred to as the *Z score*, is the score derived for each individual or object by means of the equation. This score is the basis for predicting the group to which the particular object or individual belongs. *Discriminant weights*, often referred to as **discriminant coefficients**, are computed by means of the discriminant analysis program. The size of the discriminant weight (or coefficient) associated with a particular independent variable is determined by the variance structure of the variables in the equation. Independent variables with large discriminatory power (large differences between groups) have large weights and those with little discriminatory power have small weights.

The goal of discriminant analysis is the prediction of a categorical variable. The analyst must decide which variables would be expected to be associated with the probability of a person or object falling into one of two or more groups or categories. In a statistical

→ **multiple discriminant analysis**
Procedure for predicting group membership for a (nominal or categorical) dependent variable on the basis of two or more independent variables.

→ **metric scale**
A type of quantitative that provides the most precise measurement.

→ **nominal or categorical**
A type of nonmetric qualitative data scale that only uses numbers to indicate membership in a group (e.g., 1 = male, 2 = female). Most mathematical and statistical procedures cannot be applied to nominal data.

→ **discriminant score**
Score that is the basis for predicting to which group a particular object or individual belongs; also called *Z score*.

→ **discriminant coefficient**
Estimate of the discriminatory power of a particular independent variable; also called *discriminant weight*.

sense, the problem of analyzing the nature of group differences involves finding a linear combination of independent variables (the discriminant function) that shows large differences in group means. Multiple discriminant analysis outperforms multiple regression analysis in some applications where they are both appropriate.

Applications of Multiple Discriminant Analysis

Discriminant analysis can be used to answer many questions in marketing research:

- How are consumers who purchase various brands different from those who do not purchase those brands?
- How do consumers who show high purchase probabilities for a new product differ in demographic and lifestyle characteristics from those with low purchase probabilities?
- How do consumers who frequent one fast-food restaurant differ in demographic and lifestyle characteristics from those who frequent another fast-food restaurant?
- How do consumers who have chosen either indemnity insurance, HMO coverage, or PPO coverage differ from one another in regard to healthcare use, perceptions, and attitudes?

Example of Multiple Discriminant Analysis

United Wireless Communications' marketing director wants to know if the five importance ratings used in the regression analysis predict whether an individual currently has a wireless telephone. Wireless telephone ownership is captured by question 7 on the survey in the appendix to this chapter. Those who currently have wireless telephones were assigned the code of 1, and those who do not currently have wireless telephones were assigned the code of 0. Previous research conducted by United suggested that the five independent variables (RANGE, MOBILITY, SOUND, PRECEIV, and AVGBILL) should be good predictors of wireless telephone ownership. The following discriminant model was designed to test this hypothesis:

$$Z = b_1X_1 + b_2X_2 + b_3X_3 + b_4X_4 + b_5X_5$$

where Z = discriminant score

b_1-b_5 = discriminant coefficients or weights

X_1 = first independent variable, importance rating of range of coverage (RANGE)

X_2 = second independent variable, importance rating of mobility (MOBILITY)

X_3 = third independent variable, importance rating of sound quality (SOUND)

X_4 = fourth independent variable, importance rating of ability to place and receive calls when away from home (PRECEIV)

X_5 = fifth independent variable, importance rating of average monthly bill (AVGBILL)

The discriminant analysis results are

$$Z = -.02X_1 + .22X_2 - .36X_3 + .55X_4 - .07X_5$$

These results show that the ability to place and receive calls when away from home (PRECEIV) is the most important variable in discriminating between current users and nonusers of wireless telephone service, and range of coverage (RANGE) is the least important variable.

Another important role of discriminant analysis is to classify objects or people. In this example, the goal was to correctly classify consumers into two groups—those that currently have wireless telephone service and those that do not have wireless telephone service. To determine whether the estimated discriminant model is a good predictor, a **classification matrix** (sometimes called a *confusion matrix*) is used. The classification matrix produced for this problem is shown in Exhibit 18.3. This table shows that the model correctly predicted 73.8 percent of current wireless nonusers as nonusers. However, it incorrectly predicted that 33, or 26.2 percent, of the nonusers were users. The model also predicted that 71.6 percent of current wireless users were users but that 28.4 percent were nonusers. Overall, the model correctly classified 73 percent of all respondents as wireless users or nonusers. This is far better than an analyst would expect to do on a chance basis. Thus, the conclusion is that the five independent variables are significant predictors of whether or not a particular individual is a current wireless user.

Statistical tests are available to indicate whether the resulting classification is better than could be expected by chance. When group sizes are unequal and the goal is to correctly predict membership in the two groups, one simple approach is to use the proportional chance criterion. The formula is as follows:

> **classification matrix**
> A matrix or table that shows the percentages of people or things correctly and incorrectly classified by the discriminant model.

$$C_{PRO} = p^2 - (1 - p)^2$$

where p = proportion of individuals in group 1
$1 - p$ = proportion of individuals in group 2

In this case, group 1 (nonusers) includes 126 people or 63 percent of the total (126/200). Calculation of the proportional chance criterion follows:

$$C_{PRO} = .63^2 - (1 - .63)^2$$
$$= 5.397 - .137$$
$$= 5.534, \text{ or } 53.4\%$$

The classification matrix model correctly classified 93 of the nonusers and 53 of the users, for a total of 146 out of 200, or 73 percent, correctly classified. This exceeds the proportional chance criterion of 53.4 percent by a wide margin and shows that the model did a better job than could be expected by chance.

EXHIBIT 18.3 | **Classification Matrix (pcstext.sta)**

Rows: Observed classifications
Columns: Predicted classifications

	Percent Correct	G_1:0 p = .63000	G_2:1 p = .37000
G_1:0	73.8	93	33
G_2:1	71.6	21	53
Total	73.0	114	86

SPSS JUMP START FOR MULTIPLE DISCRIMINANT ANALYSIS

Steps that you need to go through to do the multiple discriminant analysis shown in the book are provided below along with the output produced. Use the data set **Muldiscrimex**, which you can download from the Web site for the text.

Steps in SPSS

1. Select *Analyze → Classify → Discriminant*.
2. Move **cell** to Grouping Variable.
3. Click Define Range.
4. Set Minimum to 0 and Maximum to 1.
5. Click Continue.
6. Move **range, mobility, sound, preceiv**, and **avgbill** to Independents.
7. Click Classify.
8. Check box for Summary table.

9. Click Continue.
10. Click OK.

Selected SPSS Output for Multiple Discrimination Analysis

Discriminant

Standardized Canonical Discriminant Function Coefficients

	Function 1
range	-.031
mobility	.456
sound	-.338
preceiv	.668
avgbill	.047

Structure Matrix

	Function 1
preceiv	.893
mobility	.768
range	.446
sound	-.202
avgbill	-.029

Pooled within-groups correlations between discriminating variables and standardized canonical discriminant functions

Variables ordered by absolute size of correlation within function.

Classification Statistics

Classification Results[a]

		cell	Predicted Group Membership 0	Predicted Group Membership 1	Total
Original	Count	0	77	49	126
		1	11	63	74
	%	0	61.1	38.9	100.0
		1	14.9	85.1	100.0

a. 70.0% of original grouped cases correctly classified.

Cluster Analysis

The term **cluster analysis** generally refers to statistical procedures used to identify objects or people that are similar in regard to certain variables or measurements. The purpose of cluster analysis is to classify objects or people into some number of mutually exclusive and exhaustive groups so that those within a group are as similar as possible to one another.[9] In other words, clusters should be homogeneous internally (within cluster) and heterogeneous externally (between clusters).

→ **cluster analysis**
General term for statistical procedures that classify objects or people into some number of mutually exclusive and exhaustive groups on the basis of two or more classification variables.

Procedures for Clustering

A number of different procedures (based on somewhat different mathematical and computer routines) are available for clustering people or objects. However, the general approach underlying all of these procedures involves measuring the similarities among people or objects in regard to their values on the variables used for clustering.[10] Similarities among the people or objects being clustered are normally determined on the basis of some type of distance measure. This approach is best illustrated graphically. Suppose an analyst wants to group, or cluster, consumers on the basis of two variables: monthly frequency of eating out and monthly frequency of eating at fast-food restaurants. Observations on the two variables are plotted in a two-dimensional graph in Exhibit 18.4. Each dot indicates the position of one consumer in regard to the two variables. The distance between any pair of points is positively related to how similar the corresponding individuals are when the two variables are considered together (the closer the dots, the more similar the individuals). In Exhibit 18.4, consumer *X* is more like consumer *Y* than like either *Z* or *W*.

Inspection of Exhibit 18.4 suggests that three distinct clusters emerge on the basis of simultaneously considering frequency of eating out and frequency of eating at fast-food restaurants:

- Cluster 1 includes those people who do not frequently eat out or frequently eat at fast-food restaurants.
- Cluster 2 includes consumers who frequently eat out but seldom eat at fast-food restaurants.
- Cluster 3 includes people who frequently eat out and also frequently eat at fast-food restaurants.

The fast-food company can see that its customers are to be found among those who, in general, eat out frequently. To provide more insight for the client, the analyst should develop demographic, psychographic, and behavioral profiles of consumers in cluster 3.

As shown in Exhibit 18.4, clusters can be developed from scatterplots. However, this time-consuming, trial-and-error procedure becomes more tedious as the number of variables used to develop the clusters or the number of objects or persons being clustered

Exhibit 18.4
Cluster Analysis Based on Two Variables

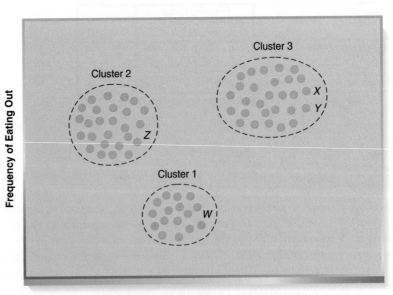

Frequency of Going to Fast-Food Restaurants

Clustering people according to how frequently and where they eat out is a way of identifying a particular consumer base. An upscale restaurant can see that its customers fall into cluster 2 and possibly cluster 3 in Exhibit 18.4.

increases. You can readily visualize a problem with two variables and fewer than 100 objects. Once the number of variables increases to three and the number of observations increases to 500 or more, visualization becomes impossible. Fortunately, computer algorithms are available to perform this more complex type of cluster analysis. The mechanics of these algorithms are complicated and beyond the scope of this discussion. The basic idea behind most of them is to start with some arbitrary cluster boundaries and modify the boundaries until a point is reached where the average interpoint distances within clusters are as small as possible relative to average distances between clusters.

Example of Cluster Analysis

United Wireless Communications wants to explore the issue of market segmentation using the data from the consumer survey. It believes that the market can be segmented on the basis of the eight attribute importance responses (question 3 in the Appendix) and that the resulting clusters might be further described on the basis of demographic and usage data.

EXHIBIT 18.5	Cluster Sizes and Average Ratings on Attribute Importance Variables		
Variable	Cluster 1 ($n = 62$)	Cluster 2 ($n = 55$)	Cluster 3 ($n = 83$)
RANGE	6.8	8.1	8.2
MOBILITY	4.5	8.1	8.2
SOUND	8.1	8.5	8.5
PLACE	6.7	8.3	8.7
PRECEIV	6.8	8.5	8.6
AVGBILL	8.6	8.4	8.8
TELEPHON	8.1	6.3	8.7
INSTALL	7.2	5.1	8.5

→ **K-means cluster analysis**
Multivariate procedure that groups people or objects into clusters based on their closeness to each other on a number of variables.

In order to address this issue, cluster analysis was performed using the **K-means cluster analysis** procedure. Because cluster analysis does not produce a "best" solution, United Wireless Communications experimented with a number of different solutions before choosing a three-cluster solution on the basis of the distinctness of the clusters. The sizes of the three clusters and their average ratings on the eight attribute importance questions are summarized in Exhibit 18.5. Average attribute ratings are also summarized in a line graph in Exhibit 18.6. This solution has the following characteristics:

■ Cluster 3 is the largest, with 83 respondents, and cluster 2 is the smallest, with 55 respondents.

■ In regard to attribute importance ratings, clusters 2 and 3 are the most similar. They have almost identical average importance ratings on six of the eight attributes. They do differ significantly in regard to price sensitivity (TELEPHON and INSTALL). Members of cluster 3 assign a much higher importance to the price of the required equipment and installation/activation charges.

■ Cluster 1 differs markedly from clusters 2 and 3. In particular, members of this cluster view RANGE, MOBILITY, PLACE, and PRECEIV to be significantly less important than do the members of the other two clusters.

■ Members of clusters 2 and 3 are the best targets for the new wireless service, based on the importance they place on the RANGE, MOBILITY, PRECEIV, and PLACE variables. In the early stages of product introduction, cluster 3 members represent the most attractive target because of their relative insensitivity to price. Cluster 2 members might be targeted later, assuming that prices fall over time, which is the projected scenario.

The clusters also differ in regard to demographic and usage data. This issue was addressed by cross tabulating cluster membership with the various demographic and usage measures available in the survey.

■ Cluster 1 individuals are the lightest users of all telephone services. They are about equally likely to be male or female, are least likely (by a narrow margin) to be married, are younger than members of the other groups, and come from households with the largest number of adults.

■ Cluster 2 individuals are the heaviest users of most telephone services. They are much more likely to be female and are very similar to the members of cluster 3 on most other demographic measures.

Exhibit 18.6

Average Attribute Importance Ratings for Three Clusters

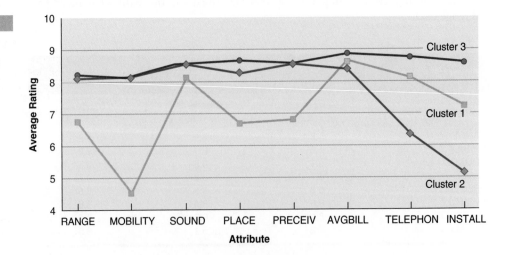

■ Cluster 3 members are between the other two groups in regard to usage of most telephone services. They are more likely to be male than female, are most likely to be married, are older than members of the other groups, and are willing to pay the highest amount, on average, for wireless service.

United Wireless Communications' management is, as always, left with the question of what to do based on these findings. Preliminary analysis suggests that the company's initial target should be members of cluster 3, for the reasons just mentioned. Later, as prices fall, an appropriate strategy might be to expand the target to include the members of cluster 2. Members of cluster 1 should be targeted only after United Wireless Communications has achieved saturation penetration levels among members of clusters 2 and 3. This plan can be operationalized by more careful analysis of the demographic characteristics of the members of the three clusters and the implementation of a sales and media plan to maximize communication with the most likely prospects.

Additional discussion of using cluster analysis for market segmentation in provided in the accompanying From the Front Lines feature.

FROM THE FRONT LINE

How to Segment a Market Using Cluster Analysis

Mike Foytik, Chief Technical Officer, DSS Research

Although many alternative statistical techniques have come and gone over the years, traditional K-means cluster analysis has proven to be a reliable and efficient way of segmenting any market. Cluster analysis is the one approach that is readily available in all statistical packages and provides satisfactory results in all but the most extreme circumstances.

Before running cluster analysis, or any other form of segmentation, you must first determine what "basis" variables should be chosen to define the segments. Your segmentation solution can only be as good as the variables you choose to build that solution. In order to select the right basis variables, review the overall objectives of the segmentation. Whatever insights you hope to uncover in the marketplace or characteristics you are trying to reveal must be present in your basis variables. If the objective is to identify the best customers for a new product you are offering, product preference must be included as a basis variable along with attitudes or demographic characteristics that might be correlated with their product preference.

Research objectives, past experience, knowledge of the market, qualitative research and analysis of the available data may all be used to identify the best basis variable candidates. Unless you have a very specific, narrowly defined objective for segmenting your market, it is generally better to start with a wide array of basis variables and narrow the selection through analyses and testing.

Once your basis variables are selected, various data manipulation and transformations are needed to prepare your dataset for cluster analysis. If using basis variables with different rating scales, standardization is in order to prevent a larger scale from dominating the clusters. Dummy variables, log and non-linear transformations and composite variables may need to be created to accentuate patterns in the data or rescale items with large magnitude. You should look at the response distribution of potential basis variables to insure there is enough variation on each item to effectively differentiate respondents. The more items included as basis variables related to a common theme, the more the resulting solution will be focused on that theme. To avoid including too many related items as basis variables, factor analysis or correlation analysis can be used to select a representative subset from a large array of potential basis variables. We have found it more beneficial to select a subset of raw variables from a factor solution rather than using the factor scores themselves as basis variables.

Once your basis variables are determined, running a cluster analysis is very easy. Just input the basis variables, select the number of clusters you wish to identify in your data and you are on your way. However, evaluating the results and identifying the best solution is a skill that can only be developed through trial and error. The better you understand what you are looking for, the more likely you are to arrive at a solution that meets your needs. There are different metrics that can help you determine how many clusters / segments should be in your final solution, but there is no single criterion that gives the absolute best results every time.

You can narrow your set of potential solutions by using heuristics such as requiring a minimum segment size that is at least 10% of your overall sample and opting for the solution with the fewest segments when there does not appear to be a clear cut advantage between two or more options. If an extremely small segment (usually less than 1% of your sample) keeps appearing in your output, consider treating that segment as outliers and removing them from the analysis. To modify an existing solution that does not quite meet your objectives, try swapping some basis variables with other correlated measures, simply remove some items that do not appear to be contributing to the overall results, add related items to strengthen the impact of a particular characteristic you believe is underrepresented in the solution or search for new basis variables to realign the segments along a dimension not showing up in the current solutions.

Analysis of variance (ANOVA) is an excellent tool for evaluating the results of any segmentation solution being considered. First, use ANOVA to insure you have sufficient variation amongst all your basis variables. Then apply ANOVA to all relevant survey questions and external data points to determine how well the solution differentiates respondents on all items of interest. By highlighting the highest and lowest items on each survey question that product significant variation across segments (high F-value on ANOVA test), you can quickly focus your attention on the items that best differentiate and define each segment. Once you can attach a meaningful name or persona to each segment and those segments address the your overall objectives, you have a solution worth considering.

Don't give up too quickly if a meaningful solution is not immediately identified. Try lots of data runs, rethink your basis variables and look for ways to pull parts of one solution you like together with segments from another solution that has positive traits.

Factor Analysis

→ **factor analysis**
Procedure for simplifying data by reducing a large set of variables to a smaller set of factors or composite variables by identifying underlying dimensions of the data.

The purpose of **factor analysis** is data simplification.[11] The objective is to summarize the information contained in a large number of metric measures (for example, rating scales) with a smaller number of summary measures, called *factors*. As with cluster analysis, there is no dependent variable.

Many phenomena of interest to marketing researchers are actually composites, or combinations, of a number of measures. These concepts are often measured by means of rating questions. For instance, in assessing consumer response to a new automobile, a general concept such as "luxury" might be measured by asking respondents to rate different cars on attributes such as "quiet ride," "smooth ride," or "plush carpeting." The product designer wants to produce an automobile that is perceived as luxurious but knows that a variety of features probably contribute to this general perception. Each attribute rated should measure a slightly different facet of luxury. The set of measures should provide a better representation of the concept than a single global rating of "luxury."

EXHIBIT 18.7	Importance Ratings of Luxury Automobile Features			
Respondent	Smooth Ride	Quiet Ride	Acceleration	Handling
Bob	5	4	2	1
Roy	4	3	2	1
Hank	4	3	3	2
Janet	5	5	2	2
Jane	4	3	2	1
Ann	5	5	3	2
Average	4.50	3.83	2.33	1.50

Several measures of a concept can be added together to develop a composite score or to compute an average score on the concept. Exhibit 18.7 shows data on six consumers who each rated an automobile on four characteristics. You can see that those respondents who gave higher ratings on "smooth ride" also tended to give higher ratings on "quiet ride." A similar pattern is evident in the ratings of "acceleration" and "handling." These four measures can be combined into two summary measures by averaging the pairs of ratings. The resulting summary measures might be called "luxury" and "performance" (see Exhibit 18.8).

Factor Scores

Factor analysis produces one or more factors, or composite variables, when applied to a number of variables. A **factor**, technically defined, is a linear combination of variables. It is a weighted summary score of a set of related variables, similar to the composite derived by averaging the measures. However, in factor analysis, each measure is first weighted according to how much it contributes to the variation of each factor.

In factor analysis, a factor score is calculated on each factor for each subject in the data set. For example, in a factor analysis with two factors, the following equations might be used to determine factor scores:

> **factor**
> A linear combination of variables that are correlated with each other.

$$F_1 = .40A_1 + .30A_2 + .02A_3 + .05A_4$$
$$F_2 = .01A_1 + .04A_2 + .45A_3 + .37A_4$$
$$\text{where} \quad F_1 - F_n = \text{factor scores}$$
$$A_1 - A_n = \text{attribute ratings}$$

With these formulas, two factor scores can be calculated for each respondent by substituting the ratings she or he gave on variables A_1 through A_4 into each equation. The coefficients in the equations are the factor scoring coefficients to be applied to each respondent's ratings. For example, Bob's factor scores (see Exhibit 18.8) are computed as follows:

$$F_1 = .40(5) + .30(4) + .02(2) + .05(1) = 3.29$$
$$F_2 = .01(5) + .04(4) + .45(2) + .37(1) = 2.38$$

In the first equation, the factor scoring coefficients, or weights, for A_1 and A_2 (.40 and .30) are large, whereas the weights for A_3 and A_4 are small. The small weights on A_3 and A_4 indicate that these variables contribute little to score variations on factor 1 (F_1). Regardless of the ratings a respondent gives to A_3 and A_4, they have little effect on his or

EXHIBIT 18.8	Average Ratings of Two Factors	
Respondent	**Luxury**	**Performance**
Bob	4.5	1.5
Roy	3.5	1.5
Hank	3.5	2.5
Janet	5.0	2.0
Jane	3.5	1.5
Ann	5.0	2.5
Average	4.25	1.92

her score on F_1. However, variables A_3 and A_4 make a large contribution to the second factor score (F_2), whereas A_1 and A_2 have little effect. These two equations show that variables A_1 and A_2 are relatively independent of A_3 and A_4 because each variable takes on large values in only one scoring equation.

The relative sizes of the scoring coefficients are also of interest. Variable A_1 (with a weight of .40) is a more important contributor to factor 1 variation than is A_2 (with a smaller weight of .30). This finding may be very important to the product designer when evaluating the implications of various design changes. For example, the product manager might want to improve the perceived luxury of the car through product redesign or advertising. The product manager may know, based on other research, that a certain expenditure on redesign will result in an improvement of the average rating on "smooth ride" from 4.3 to 4.8. This research may also show that the same expenditure will produce a half-point improvement in ratings on "quiet ride." The factor analysis shows that perceived luxury will be enhanced to a greater extent by increasing ratings on "smooth ride" than by increasing ratings on "quiet ride" by the same amount.

Factor Loadings

➤ **factor loading**
Correlation between factor scores and the original variables.

The nature of the factors derived can be determined by examining the **factor loadings**. Using the scoring equations presented earlier, a pair of factor scores (F_1 and F_2) are calculated for each respondent. Factor loadings are determined by calculating the correlation (from 31 to 31) between each factor (F_1 and F_2) score and each of the original ratings variables. Each correlation coefficient represents the loading of the associated variable on the particular factor. If A_1 is closely associated with factor 1, the loading or correlation will be high, as shown for the sample problem in Exhibit 18.9. Because the loadings are correlation coefficients, values near 31 or 31 indicate a close positive or negative association. Variables A_1 and A_2 are closely associated (highly correlated) with scores on factor 1, and variables A_3 and A_4 are closely associated with scores on factor 2.

Stated another way, variables A_1 and A_2 have high loadings on factor 1 and serve to define the factor; variables A_3 and A_4 have high loadings on and define factor 2.

EXHIBIT 18.9	Factor Loadings for Two Factors	
	Correlation with	
Variable	**Factor 1**	**Factor 2**
A_1	.85	.10
A_2	.76	.06
A_3	.06	.89
A_4	.04	.79

Naming Factors

Once each factor's defining variables have been identified, the next step is to name the factors. This is a somewhat subjective step, combining intuition and knowledge of the variables with an inspection of the variables that have high loadings on each factor. Usually, a certain consistency exists among the variables that load highly on a given factor. For instance, it is not surprising to see that the ratings on "smooth ride" and "quiet ride" both load on the same factor. Although we have chosen to name this factor "luxury," another analyst, looking at the same result, might decide to name the factor "prestige."

Number of Factors to Retain

In factor analysis, the analyst is confronted with a decision regarding how many factors to retain. The final result can include from one factor to as many factors as there are variables. The decision is often made by looking at the percentage of the variation in the original data that is explained by each factor. In this case, the first and second factors explain a total of 92.5 percent of the variability in the four measures (see Exhibit 18.10). The last two factors explain only 7.5 percent of the variation and contribute little to the objective of data simplification.

There are many different decision rules for choosing the number of factors to retain. Probably the most appropriate decision rule is to stop factoring when additional factors no longer make sense. The first factors extracted are likely to exhibit logical consistency; later factors are usually harder to interpret, for they are more likely to contain a large amount of random variation.

Example of Factor Analysis

Once again, we refer to the United Wireless Communications survey results for an example of factor analysis. In this instance, United Wireless Communications is interested in determining or identifying attributes that go together. As suggested earlier, this will permit United Wireless Communications to identify clusters of benefits that are associated in the minds of target customers and to design market communications that speak to these related benefits. As you may recall, factors identified via factor analysis represent underlying supervariables constructed from pieces of the original input variables.

After experimenting with several different solutions, we settled on the three-factor solution as the "best" solution, based on statistical and interpretability criteria. Factor analysis procedures produce a number of different types of output. One key type of output is the matrix of factor loadings. Factor loadings, as noted earlier, are the simple correlations between each of the original input variables and each factor, or supervariable, identified in the analysis. The factor loadings for the three-factor solution to this problem are shown in Exhibit 18.11. Information on the proportion of the total variance in the original eight input variables explained by each factor is provided at the bottom of the table. These data show that the three factors explain 72 percent of the variance in the eight original input variables. An interpretation of the factors follows:

- Factor 1 loads heavily or correlates on the following input variables: RANGE, MOBILITY, PLACE, and PRECEIV. We conclude that "staying in touch" is an appropriate name for this factor; different analysts might look at these results and come up with somewhat different names for the factor. However, given the four variables on which this factor loads, it clearly has something to do with the ability to reach and be reached by other people at all times.

- Factor 2 correlates or loads on the variables AVGBILL, TELEPHON, and INSTALL. A quick review indicates that all of these variables have something to do with cost; therefore, we simply call this the "cost" factor.

EXHIBIT 18.10	Percentage of Variation in Original Data Explained by Each Factor
Factor	**Percent of Variation Explained**
1	55.0
2	37.5
3	4.8
4	2.7

EXHIBIT 18.11	Factor Loadings (Varimax raw) (pcstext.sta) Extraction: Principal Components		
	Factor 1	**Factor 2**	**Factor 3**
RANGE	0.70	−0.10	0.39
MOBILITY	0.83	−0.09	0.07
SOUND	0.03	0.03	0.96
PLACE	0.85	0.19	−0.12
PRECEIV	0.91	−0.02	0.02
AVGBILL	−0.04	0.69	0.29
TELEPHON	−0.01	0.83	−0.11
INSTALL	0.06	0.77	0.02
Proportion of total variance	0.34	0.23	0.15

■ Factor 3 correlates strongly with only one of the original input variables—SOUND. Therefore, we call it the "sound quality" factor.

This analysis suggests, for example, that it would be logical to send consumers information about RANGE, MOBILITY, PLACE, and PRECEIV issues in the same mailing. The analysis might also provide useful direction for the design of initial market communications.

Conjoint Analysis

> **→ conjoint analysis**
> Multivariate procedure used to quantify the value that consumers associate with different levels of product/service attributes or features.

Conjoint analysis is a popular multivariate procedure used by marketers to help determine what features a new product or service should have and how it should be priced. It can be argued that conjoint analysis has become popular because it is a more powerful, more flexible, and often less expensive way to address these important issues than is the traditional concept testing approach.[12]

Conjoint analysis is not a completely standardized procedure.[13] A typical conjoint analysis application involves a series of steps covering a variety of procedures; it is not a single procedure as is, for example, regression analysis. Fortunately, conjoint analysis is not difficult to understand, as we demonstrate in the following example concerning the attributes of golf balls.

Example of Conjoint Analysis

Put yourself in the position of a product manager for Titleist, a major manufacturer of golf balls. From focus groups recently conducted, past research studies of various types, and your own personal experience as a golfer, you know that golfers tend to evaluate golf balls in terms of three important features or attributes: average driving distance, average ball life, and price.

You also recognize a range of feasible possibilities for each of these features or attributes, as follows:

1. Average driving distance
   - 10 yards more than the golfer's average
   - Same as the golfer's average
   - 10 yards less than the golfer's average
2. Average ball life
   - 54 holes
   - 36 holes
   - 18 holes
3. Price per ball
   - $2.00
   - $2.50
   - $3.00

From the perspective of potential purchasers, the ideal golf ball would have the following characteristics:

- Average driving distance—10 yards above average
- Average ball life—54 holes
- Price—$2.00

From the manufacturer's perspective, which is based on manufacturing cost, the ideal golf ball would probably have these characteristics:

- Average driving distance—10 yards below average
- Average ball life—18 holes
- Price—$3.00

This golf ball profile is based on the fact that it costs less to produce a ball that travels a shorter distance and has a shorter life. The company confronts the eternal marketing dilemma: the company would sell a lot of golf balls but would go broke if it produced and sold the ideal ball from the golfer's perspective. However, the company would sell very few balls if it produced and sold the ideal ball from the manufacturer's perspective. As always, the "best" golf ball from a business perspective lies somewhere between the two extremes.

A traditional approach to this problem might produce information of the type displayed in Exhibit 18.12. As you can see, this information does not provide new insights regarding which ball should be produced. The preferred driving distance is 10 yards above average and the preferred average ball life is 54 holes. These results are obvious without any additional research.

Considering Features Conjointly In conjoint analysis, rather than having respondents evaluate features individually, the analyst asks them to evaluate features conjointly or in combination. The results of asking two different golfers to rank different combinations of "average driving distance" and "average ball life" conjointly are shown in Exhibits 18.13 and 18.14.

As expected, both golfers agree on the most and least preferred balls. However, analysis of their second through eighth rankings

Conjoint analysis could be used by a manufacturer of golf balls to determine the three most important features of a golf ball and to see which ball meets the most needs of both consumer and manufacturer.

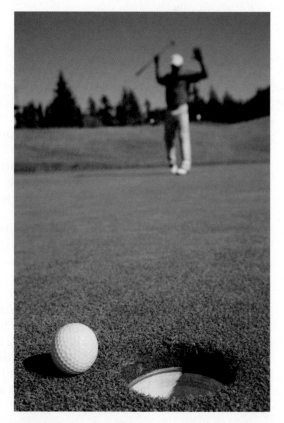

EXHIBIT 18.12	Traditional Nonconjoint Rankings of Distance and Ball Life Attributes			
	Average Driving Distance		**Average Ball Life**	
	Rank	Level	Rank	Level
	1	275 yards	1	54 holes
	2	250 yards	2	36 holes
	3	225 yards	3	18 holes

EXHIBIT 18.13	Conjoint Rankings of Combinations of Distance and Ball Life for Golfer 1		
	Ball Life		
Distance	54 holes	36 holes	18 holes
275 yards	1	2	4
250 yards	3	5	7
225 yards	6	8	9

EXHIBIT 18.14	Conjoint Rankings of Combinations of Distance and Ball Life for Golfer 2		
	Ball Life		
Distance	54 holes	36 holes	18 holes
275 yards	1	3	6
250 yards	3	5	8
225 yards	4	7	9

makes it clear that the first golfer is willing to trade off ball life for distance (accept a shorter ball life for longer distance), while the second golfer is willing to trade off distance for longer ball life (accept shorter distance for a longer ball life).

This type of information is the essence of the special insight offered by conjoint analysis. The technique permits marketers to see which product attribute or feature potential customers are willing to trade off (accept less of) to obtain more of another attribute or feature. People make these kinds of purchasing decisions every day (for example, they may choose to pay a higher price for a product at a local market for the convenience of shopping there).

utilities
The relative value of attribute levels determined through conjoint analysis.

Estimating Utilities   The next step is to calculate a set of values, or **utilities**, for the three levels of price, the three levels of driving distance, and the three levels of ball life in such a way that, when they are combined in a particular mix of price, ball life, and driving distance, they predict a particular golfer's rank order for that particular combination. Estimated utilities for golfer 1 are shown in Exhibit 18.15. As you can readily see, this set of numbers perfectly predicts the original rankings. The relationship among these numbers or utilities is fixed, though there is some arbitrariness in their magnitude. In other words, the utilities shown in Exhibit 18.15 can be multiplied or divided by any constant and the same relative results will be obtained. The exact procedures for estimating these utilities are beyond the scope of this discussion. They are normally calculated by using procedures related to regression, analysis of variance, or linear programming.

The trade-offs that golfer 1 is willing to make between "ball life" and "price" are shown in Exhibit 18.16. This information can be used to estimate a set of utilities for "price" that can be added to those for "ball life" to predict the rankings for golfer 1, as shown in Exhibit 18.17.

This step produces a complete set of utilities for all levels of the three features or attributes that successfully capture golfer 1's trade-offs. These utilities are shown in Exhibit 18.18.

Simulating Buyer Choice For various reasons, the firm might be in a position to produce only 2 of the 27 golf balls that are possible with each of the three levels of the three attributes. The possibilities are shown in Exhibit 18.19. If the calculated utilities for golfer 1 are applied to the 2 golf balls the firm is able to make, then the results are the total utilities shown in Exhibit 18.20. These results indicate that golfer 1 will prefer the ball with the longer life over the one with the greater distance because it has a higher

EXHIBIT 18.15	Ranks (in parentheses) and Combined Metric Utilities for Golfer 1—Distance and Ball Life		
	Ball Life		
Distance	54 holes 50	36 holes 25	18 holes 0
275 yards	(1) 150	(2) 125	(4) 100
250 yards	(3) 110	(5) 85	(7) 60
225 yards	(6) 50	(8) 25	(9) 0

EXHIBIT 18.16	Conjoint Rankings of Combinations of Price and Ball Life for Golfer 1		
	Ball Life		
Price	54 holes	36 holes	18 holes
$2.00	1	2	4
$2.50	3	5	7
$3.00	6	8	9

EXHIBIT 18.17	Ranks (in parentheses) and Combined Metric Utilities for Golfer 1—Price and Ball Life		
	Ball Life		
Price	54 holes 50	36 holes 25	18 holes 0
$2.00	(1) 70	(2) 45	(4) 20
$2.50	(3) 55	(5) 30	(7) 5
$3.00	(6) 50	(8) 25	(9) 0

EXHIBIT 18.18	Complete Set of Estimated Utilities for Golfer 1				
Distance		**Ball Life**		**Price**	
Level	Utility	Level	Utility	Level	Utility
275 yards	100	54 holes	50	$1.25	20
250 yards	60	36 holes	25	$1.50	5
225 yards	0	18 holes	0	$1.75	0

EXHIBIT 18.19	Ball Profiles for Simulation	
Attribute	Distance Ball	Long-Life Ball
Distance	275	250
Life	18	54
Price	$2.50	$3.00

EXHIBIT 18.20	Estimated Total Utilities for the Two Sample Profiles			
	Distance Ball		**Price**	
Attribute	Level	Utility	Level	Utility
Distance	275	100	250	60
Life	18	0	54	50
Price	$2.50	5	$3.00	0
Total utility	105	110		

total utility. The analyst need only repeat this process for a representative sample of golfers to estimate potential market shares for the 2 balls. In addition, the analysis can be extended to cover other golf ball combinations.

The three steps discussed here—collecting trade-off data, using the data to estimate buyer preference structures, and predicting choice—are the basis of any conjoint analysis application. Although the trade-off matrix approach is simple, useful for explaining conjoint analysis, and effective for problems with small numbers of attributes, it is currently not widely used. An easier and less time-consuming way to collect conjoint data is to have respondents rank or rate product descriptions on a paper questionnaire or to use computer-based interviewing software that applies certain rules to determine what questions and product profiles to present to each respondent based on his or her previous answers.

As suggested earlier, there is much more to conjoint analysis than has been discussed in this section. However, if you understand this simple example, then you understand the basic concepts that underlie conjoint analysis.

Limitations of Conjoint Analysis

Like many research techniques, conjoint analysis suffers from a certain degree of artificiality. Respondents may be more deliberate in their choice processes in this context than in a real situation. The survey may provide more product information than respondents would get in a real market situation. Finally, it is important to remember that the advertising and promotion of any new product or service can lead to consumer perceptions that are very different from those created via descriptions used in a survey.

Data Mining[14]

Data mining is a relatively new field that draws upon statistics (including all of the tools discussed in this chapter), artificial intelligence, database management, and computer science to identify patterns in market data sets. It is an increasingly important tool for business to transform the exponentially growing quantities of digital data into business intelligence as firms seek informational advantages to improve efficiency and effectiveness. It is applied in a wide range of areas, but we are particularly interested in its applications to marketing problems. Extending our earlier comments, the primary reason for using data mining in marketing is to analyze large collections of observational, survey or, experimental data regarding buyer behavior.

Data Mining Process

Pre-processing Before we can apply data mining tools, we must assemble a target data set relevant to the problem of interest. Data mining can only uncover patterns and relationships in the data we feed into them. Typically, the data set we are using must be large enough to include all the patterns that exist in the real world, though not so large as to make the assembly too costly or too time-consuming. Once assembled, the data set must be cleaned in a process where we remove those observations that contain excessive noise or error and missing data.

The actual data mining process typically involves four classes of tasks:[15]

- **Clustering.** This is a task of discovering groups and structures in the data that are similar on certain, selected sets of variables. These are groupings that are not obvious and are not based on a single set of variables or just a few of them. We normally evaluate a number of solutions to decide which one to use. Cluster analysis, one of the techniques discussed in Chapter 18, is commonly used to address as the analytical tool for this analysis.

- **Classification.** Here, we apply the structure we identified with cluster analysis or some other technique to another subset of the same data. For example, we might apply customer segments identified in the clustering process using a subset of data or data from a survey to an entire customer database. If the results are similar to what we achieved in the first step then we move ahead. Otherwise, we need to go back and reanalyze.

- **Modeling.** Here we use regression or a similar technique to model the relationship or predict subgroup membership when we mask the membership identified as described above. We are looking for high predictive accuracy, and if we don't get it then we need to repeat the previous steps.

- **Application.** If we have successfully completed the first three steps, then we are ready to put what we have learned to work to improve the efficiency and effectiveness of our marketing efforts. For example, if we get a sales inquiry, we might get enough information from the inquirer to classify them into a market segment and then provide information on the version of our product or service known to be most preferred by members of that segment, stress the sales points known to be most likely to resonate with members of that segment, and so on.

Results Validation

A final step of knowledge discovery from the target data and modeling is to attempt to verify the patterns produced by the data mining algorithms in the wider data set. Not every pattern and relationship we identify in the previous steps turns out to be valid in the real world. In the evaluation process, we use a test data set that was not used to develop the data mining algorithm. The patterns that we identified or learned are applied to the test data, and the resulting output is compared to the desired output. For example, a data mining algorithm developed to predict those most likely to respond to a mail offer would be developed or trained on certain past mail offers. Once developed or trained, the algorithm developed from the test mailings would be applied to either other mailings not used in the development of the algorithm or to actual results from a mailing recently completed. If the data mining algorithm does not meet the desired accuracy standards, then it is necessary to go through the previous steps again in order to develop an algorithm or model with the desired level of accuracy.

Privacy Concerns and Ethics

Most believe that data mining itself is ethically neutral. However, the ways in which data mining can be used raise ethical questions regarding privacy, legality, and ethics. For example, data mining data sets for national security or law enforcement purposes has raised privacy concerns.

Commercial Data Mining Software and Applications

There are an increasing number of highly integrated packages for data mining, including:

- SAS Enterprise Miner
- SPSS Modeler
- *STATISTICA* Data Miner

SUMMARY

Multivariate analysis refers to the simultaneous analysis of multiple measurements on each individual or object being studied. Some of the more popular multivariate techniques include multiple regression analysis, multiple discriminant analysis, cluster analysis, factor analysis, and conjoint analysis.

Multiple regression analysis enables the researcher to predict the magnitude of a dependent variable based on the levels of more than one independent variable. Multiple regression fits a plane to observations in a multidimensional space. One statistic that results from multiple regression analysis is called the coefficient of determination, or R^2. The value of this statistic ranges from 0 to 1. It provides a measure of the percentage of the variation in the dependent variable that is explained by variation in the independent variables. The b values, or regression coefficients, indicate the effect of the individual independent variables on the dependent variable.

Whereas multiple regression analysis requires that the dependent variable be metric, multiple discriminant analysis uses a dependent variable that is nominal or categorical in nature. Discriminant analysis can be used to determine if statistically significant differences exist between the average discriminant score profiles of two (or more) groups. The technique can also be used to establish a model for classifying individuals or objects into groups on the basis of their scores on the independent variables. Finally, discriminant analysis can be used to determine how much of the difference in the average score profiles of the groups is accounted for by each independent variable. The discriminant score, called a Z score, is derived for each individual or object by means of the discriminant equation.

Cluster analysis enables a researcher to identify subgroups of individuals or objects that are homogeneous within the subgroup, yet different from other subgroups. Cluster analysis requires that all independent variables be metric, but there is no specification of a dependent variable. Cluster analysis is an excellent means for operationalizing the concept of market segmentation.

The purpose of factor analysis is to simplify massive amounts of data. The objective is to summarize the information contained in a large number of metric measures such as rating scales with a smaller number of summary measures called factors. As in cluster analysis, there is no dependent variable in factor analysis. Factor analysis produces factors, each of which is a weighted composite of a set of related variables. Each measure is weighted according to how much it contributes to the variation of each factor. Factor loadings are determined by calculating the correlation coefficient between factor scores and the original input variables. By examining which variables load heavily on a given factor, the researcher can subjectively name that factor.

Perceptual maps can be produced by means of factor analysis, multidimensional scaling, discriminant analysis, or correspondence analysis. The maps provide a visual representation of how brands, products, companies, and other objects are perceived relative to each other on key features such as quality and value. All the approaches require, as input, consumer evaluations or ratings of the objects in question on some set of key characteristics.

Conjoint analysis is a technique that can be used to measure the trade-offs potential buyers make on the basis of the features of each product or service available to them. The technique permits the researcher to determine the relative value of each level of each feature. These estimated values are called utilities and can be used as a basis for simulating consumer choice.

Data mining draws upon statistics, artificial intelligence and computer science to identify patterns in market data sets. It is becoming increasingly important as the available data grows exponentially

KEY TERMS & DEFINITIONS

multivariate analysis General term for statistical procedures that simultaneously analyze multiple measurements on each individual or object under study.

multiple regression analysis Procedure for predicting the level or magnitude of a (metric) dependent variable based on the levels of multiple independent variables.

coefficient of determination Measure of the percentage of the variation in the dependent variable explained by variations in the independent variables.

regression coefficients Estimates of the effect of individual independent variables on the dependent variable.

dummy variables In regression analysis, a way of representing two-group or dichotomous, nominally scaled independent variables by coding one group as 0 and the other as 1.

collinearity Correlation of independent variables with each other, which can bias estimates of regression coefficients.

causation Inference that a change in one variable is responsible for (caused) an observed change in another variable.

scaling of coefficients A method of directly comparing the magnitudes of the regression coefficients of independent variables by scaling them in the same units or by standardizing the data.

multiple discriminant analysis Procedure for predicting group membership for a (nominal or categorical) dependent variable on the basis of two or more independent variables.

metric scale A type of quantitative that provides the most precise measurement.

nominal or categorical A type of nonmetric, qualitative data scale that only uses numbers to indicate membership in a group (e.g., 1 = male, 2 = female). Most mathematical and statistical procedures cannot be applied to nominal data.

discriminant score Score that is the basis for predicting to which group a particular object or individual belongs; also called *Z score*.

discriminant coefficient Estimate of the discriminatory power of a particular independent variable; also called *discriminant weight*.

classification matrix A matrix or table that shows the percentages of people or things correctly and incorrectly classified by the discriminant model.

cluster analysis General term for statistical procedures that classify objects or people into some number of mutually exclusive and exhaustive groups on the basis of two or more classification variables.

K-means cluster analysis Multivariate procedure that groups people or objects into clusters based on their closeness to each other on a number of variables.

factor analysis Procedure for simplifying data by reducing a large set of variables to a smaller set of factors or composite variables by identifying underlying dimensions of the data.

factor A linear combination of variables that are correlated with each other.

factor loading Correlation between factor scores and the original variables.

conjoint analysis Multivariate procedure used to quantify the value that consumers associate with different levels of product/service attributes or features.

utilities The relative value of attribute levels determined through conjoint analysis.

QUESTIONS FOR REVIEW & CRITICAL THINKING

1. Distinguish between multiple discriminant analysis and cluster analysis. Give several examples of situations in which each might be used.

2. What purpose does multiple regression analysis serve? Give an example of how it might be used in marketing research. How is the strength of multiple regression measures of association determined?

3. What is a dummy variable? Give an example using a dummy variable.

4. Describe the potential problem of collinearity in multiple regression. How might a researcher test for collinearity? If collinearity is a problem, what should the researcher do?

5. A sales manager examined age data, education level, a personality factor that indicated level of introvertedness/extrovertedness, and level of sales attained by the company's 120-person salesforce. The technique used was multiple regression analysis. After analyzing the data, the sales manager said, "It is apparent to me that the higher the level of education and the greater the degree of extrovertedness a salesperson has, the higher will be an individual's level of sales. In other words, a good education and being extroverted cause a person to sell more." Would you agree or disagree with the sales manager's conclusions? Why?

6. The factors produced and the results of the factor loadings from factor analysis are mathematical constructs. It is the task of the researcher to make sense out of these factors. The following table lists four factors produced from a study of cable TV viewers. What label would you put on each of these four factors? Why?

		Factor Loading
Factor 1	I don't like the way cable TV movie channels repeat the movies over and over.	.79
	The movie channels on cable need to spread their movies out (longer times between repeats).	.75
	I think the cable movie channels just run the same things over and over and over.	.73
	After a while, you've seen all the pay movies, so why keep cable service.	.53
Factor 2	I love to watch love stories.	.76
	I like a TV show that is sensitive and emotional.	.73
	Sometimes I cry when I watch movies on TV.	.65
	I like to watch "made for TV" movies.	.54
Factor 3	I like the religious programs on TV (negative correlation).	−.76
	I don't think TV evangelism is good.	.75
	I do not like religious programs.	.61
Factor 4	I would rather watch movies at home than go to the movies.	.63
	I like cable because you don't have to go out to see the movies.	.55
	I prefer cable TV movies because movie theaters are too expensive.	.46

7. The following table is a discriminant analysis that examines responses to various attitudinal questions from cable TV users, former cable TV users, and people who have never used cable TV. Looking at the various discriminant weights, what can you say about each of the three groups?

		Discriminant Weights		
		Users	**Formers**	**Nevers**
Users				
A19	Easygoing on repairs	−.40		
A18	No repair service	−.34		
A7	Breakdown complainers	+.30		
A5	Too many choices	−.27		
A13	Antisports	−.24		
A10	Antireligious	+.17		
Formers				
A4	Burned out on repeats		+.22	
A18	No repair service		+.19	
H12	Card/board game player		+.18	
H1	High-brow		−.18	
H3	Party hog		+.15	
A9	DVD preference		+.16	

	Discriminant Weights		
	Users	Formers	Nevers
Nevers			
A7	Breakdown complainer		−.29
A19	Easygoing on repairs		+.26
A5	Too many choices		+.23
A13	Antisports		+.21
A10	Antireligious		−.19

8. The following table shows regression coefficients for two dependent variables. The first dependent variable is willingness to spend money for cable TV. The independent variables are responses to attitudinal statements. The second dependent variable is stated desire never to allow cable TV in their homes. By examining the regression coefficients, what can you say about persons willing to spend money for cable TV and those who will not allow cable TV in their homes?

	Regression Coefficients
Willing to Spend Money for Cable TV	
Easygoing on cable repairs	−3.04
Cable movie watcher	2.81
Comedy watcher	2.73
Early to bed	−2.62
Breakdown complainer	2.25
Lovelorn	2.18
Burned out on repeats	−2.06
Never Allow Cable TV in Home	
Antisports	0.37
Object to sex	0.47
Too many choices	0.88

WORKING THE NET

1. For a demonstration of TwoStep cluster analysis using a scalable cluster analysis algorithm, visit: *www.spss.com/spss/data_analysis.htm*

2. For some easy to digest and comprehensive information on multivariate analysis, visit *http://core.ecu.edu/psyc/wuenschk/spss/SPSS-MV.htm*

REAL-LIFE RESEARCH • 18.1

Satisfaction Research for Pizza Quik

The Problem: Pizza Quik is a regional chain of pizza restaurants operating in seven states in the Midwest. Pizza Quik has adopted a Total Quality Management (or TQM) orientation.[17] As part of this orientation, the firm is committed to the idea of market-driven quality. That is, it intends to conduct a research project to address the issue of how its customers define quality and to learn from the customers themselves what they expect in regard to quality.

Research Objectives: The objectives of the proposed research are:

- To identify the key determinants of customer satisfaction
- To measure current customer satisfaction levels on those key satisfaction determinants
- To determine the relative importance of each key satisfaction determinant in deriving overall satisfaction
- To provide recommendations to management regarding where to direct the company's efforts

Methodology: The first objective was met by means of qualitative research. A series of focus groups were conducted with customers to determine which attributes of Pizza Quik's product and service are most important to them. Based on this analysis, the following attributes were identified.

- Overall quality of food
- Variety of menu items
- Friendliness of Pizza Quik's employees
- Provision of good value for the money
- Speed of service

In the second stage of the research, central-location telephone interviews were conducted with 1,200 randomly selected individuals who had purchased or eaten at a Pizza Quik restaurant (in the restaurant or take-out) in the past 30 days. Key information garnered in the survey included:

- Overall rating of satisfaction with Pizza Quik on a 10-point scale (1 = poor and 10 = excellent)
- Rating of Pizza Quik on the five key satisfaction attributes identified in the qualitative research, using the same 10-point scale as for overall satisfaction
- Demographic characteristics

Results and Analysis: Extensive cross tabulations and other traditional statistical analyses were conducted. A key part of the analysis was to estimate a regression model with overall satisfaction as the dependent variable and satisfaction with key product and service attributes as the predictors. The results of this analysis were:

$$S = .48X_1 + .13X_2 + .27X_3 + .42X_4 + .57X_5$$

where

$$
\begin{aligned}
S &= \text{overall satisfaction rating} \\
X_1 &= \text{rating of food quality} \\
X_2 &= \text{rating of variety of menu} \\
X_3 &= \text{rating of friendliness of employees} \\
X_4 &= \text{rating of value} \\
X_5 &= \text{rating of speed of service}
\end{aligned}
$$

Average ratings on the 10-point scale for overall satisfaction and the five key attributes were:

$$S = 7.3$$
$$X_1 = 6.8$$
$$X_2 = 7.7$$
$$X_3 = 8.4$$
$$X_4 = 6.9$$
$$X_5 = 8.2$$

The regression coefficients provide estimates of the relative importance of the different attributes in determining overall satisfaction. The results show that X_5 (rating of speed of service) is the most important driver of overall satisfaction. The results also indicate that a one-unit increase in average rating on speed of service will produce an increase of .57 in average satisfaction rating. For example, the current average rating on speed of service is 8.2. If, by providing faster service, Pizza Quik could increase this rating to 9.2, then it would expect the average satisfaction rating to increase to 7.87. X_1 (rating of food quality) and X_4 (rating of value) are not far behind speed of service in their effect on overall satisfaction according to the regression estimates. At the other extreme, X_2 (rating of variety of menu) is least important in determining overall satisfaction, and X_3 (rating of friendliness of employees) is in between in importance.

The performance ratings provide a different picture. According to the average ratings, customers believe Pizza Quik is doing the best job on X_3 (friendliness of employees) and the worst job on X_1 (food quality).

Questions

1. Plot the importance and performance scores in a matrix. One axis would be importance from low to high and the other would be performance from low to high.
2. Which quadrant should you pay the most attention to? Why?
3. Which quadrant or quadrants should you pay the least attention to? Why?
4. Based on your analysis, where would you advise the company to focus its effort? What is the rationale behind this advice?

REAL-LIFE RESEARCH • 18.2

Custom Car Wash Systems

Custom Car Wash Systems offers car wash franchises throughout the United States. Currently, 872 car washes franchised by Custom are in operation. As part of its service to franchisees, Custom runs a national marketing and advertising program.

Carl Bahn is the senior vice president in charge of marketing for Custom. He is currently in the process of designing the marketing and advertising campaigns for the upcoming year. Bahn believes that it is time for Custom to take a more careful look at user segments in the market. Based on other analyses, he and his associates at Custom have decided that the upcoming campaign should target the heavy user market. Through other research, Custom has defined "heavy car wash users" as those individuals who have their cars washed at a car wash facility three or more times per month on average. "Light users" are defined as those who use such a facility less than three times a month but at least four times a year. "Nonusers" are defined as those who use such a facility less than four times per year.

Bahn and his associates are currently in the process of attempting to identify those factors that discriminate between heavy and light users. In the first stage of this analysis, Custom conducted interviews with 50 customers at 100 of its locations for a total of 5,000 interviews. Cross tabulation of the classification variables with frequency of use suggests that four variables may be predictive of usage heaviness: vehicle owner age, annual income of vehicle owner, age of vehicle, and socioeconomic status of vehicle owner (based on an index of socioeconomic variables).

Custom retained a marketing research firm called Marketing Metrics to do further analysis for the company. Marketing Metrics evaluated the situation and decided to use multiple discriminant analysis to further analyze the survey results and identify the relative importance of each of the four variables in determining whether a particular individual is a heavy or light user. The firm obtained the following results:

$$Z = .18X_1 + .53X_2 - .49X_3 + .93X_4$$

where X_1 = age of vehicle owner
X_2 = annual income of vehicle owner
X_3 = age of vehicle
X_4 = socioeconomic status of owner (as measured by an index in which a higher score means higher status)

Questions

1. What would you tell Bahn about the importance of each predictor variable?
2. What recommendations would you make to him about the type of people Custom should target, based on its interest in communicating with heavy users?

Appendix: United Wireless Communications Data Set

This appendix includes a description of a data set obtained from an actual survey done for a client in the wireless communications business. Here, you will also find descriptions of the research objectives, the methodology used, and the physical layout of the data set.

Research Objectives

The objectives of the research were as follows:

To determine the likelihood of purchasing the new wireless communications service at various monthly service charges and equipment costs.

■ To measure the importance of various wireless communications service attributes.

■ To determine expected usage patterns and usage heaviness for the new wireless service.

- To determine usage heaviness of existing residential and long-distance telephone services.
- To measure current expenditures on local and long-distance services.
- To determine, for purposes of market segmentation, the demographic characteristics of likely purchasers and nonpurchasers.

Methodology

A summary description of the methodology employed for this research follows:

- *Sample size.* 200 consumers.
- *Qualified respondents.* Individuals 18 years of age or older from households with annual incomes of $30,000 or more.
- *Sample area.* National probability sample.
- *Sample type.* Random sample based on random digit dialing.
- *Sampling error.* ±7.1 percent with 95 percent confidence.
- *Data-collection method.* All surveying was done by means of central-location telephone interviewing, using a computer-assisted approach. Interviewing was supervised and unobtrusively monitored. All interviewing was conducted from a central-location telephone interviewing facility.
- *Interview length.* Surveys averaged 10 minutes in length.
- *Survey timing.* All interviewing was conducted during February 2000.
- *Questionnaire.* A copy of the questionnaire employed for the study follows this methodology summary.

Description of the Data Set

The description of the data set is keyed to the questionnaire. The data are available on the CD-ROM in the back of this textbook in two formats: ASCII and .dbf. The ASCII file has the name unitedwireless.TXT, and the other file has the name unitedwireless.dbf. The unitedwireless.dbf file can be directly imported into most statistical packages by using the import feature.

The locations of the numerical representations of the responses to each question for the ASCII file are shown in parentheses throughout the questionnaire. The variable names for the .dbf file are shown in the left margin in capital letters. If you employ the import feature of the statistical package you are using, these names should be correctly imported with the data and will appear at the top of the column containing the data for the particular question.

Wireless Survey

ADDED

1. Before we begin the next exercise, how much more would you be willing to pay each month to receive wireless service? This is in addition to what you are currently paying for basic telephone service to your home. **ENTER THE AMOUNT. TYPE "0" FOR NOTHING, "5" FOR $5, ETC.**

   _____Additional amount willing to pay to receive wireless service (4–6)

2. Considering the phone service that you currently have, please indicate the probability that you will purchase one of the new wireless services presented as an **addition** to your existing service.

   Indicate your likelihood to purchase each wireless service on a 0 to 100 scale, where 0 means you are not at all likely to purchase that telephone service and 100 means you are extremely likely to purchase that telephone service for your home.

W25100   a. How likely would you be to purchase the new wireless service if your monthly service charge was $25 and the cost of the telephone was $100?

_____Likelihood to purchase (7–9)

W500   b. How likely would you be to purchase the new wireless service if your monthly service charge was $50 and the cost of the telephone was $0?

_____Likelihood to purchase (10–12)

3. Now I would like for you to rate several attributes on their level of importance to you when selecting telephone service. For each factor, use a 9-point scale, where 9 means the attribute is "**very important**" (VI) and 1 means the attribute is "**very unimportant**" (VU) to you when selecting local telephone service. How important is . . . **READ LIST AND ROTATE**

	Attributes	VI								VU	
RANGE	Range of coverage	9	8	7	6	5	4	3	2	1	(13)
MOBILITY	Mobility	9	8	7	6	5	4	3	2	1	(14)
SOUND	Sound quality (sound and static)	9	8	7	6	5	4	3	2	1	(15)
PLACE	Ability to place calls when away from home	9	8	7	6	5	4	3	2	1	(16)
PRECEIV	Ability to place and receive calls when away from home	9	8	7	6	5	4	3	2	1	(17)
AVGBILL	Average monthly telephone bill	9	8	7	6	5	4	3	2	1	(18)
TELEPHON	Price of telephone equipment	9	8	7	6	5	4	3	2	1	(19)
INSTALL	Installation/activation charges	9	8	7	6	5	4	3	2	1	(20)

CAR   4. If you purchased wireless service, what percentage of your calls (made and received) on the wireless service would be from your car? **ENTER A PERCENTAGE FROM 0 TO 100**

_____ Percentage of wireless calls from your car (21–23)

MET   5. What percentage of calls using wireless service would be within the Orlando metropolitan area?

_____ Percentage of wireless calls within metropolitan area (24–26)

HOME   6. And what percentage of your wireless calls would be made in and around your home or neighborhood?

_____ Percentage of wireless calls in and around the home (27–29)

And now, I have just a few questions concerning telephone usage in your household.

CELL   7. Do you own or use a wireless phone?

(30)
1   YES
2   NO

MAKES   8. Considering the local telephone calls of all members of your household for a **typical day**, how many calls would you say your household MAKES in a typical day?

_____ Number of calls MADE by household per day (31–32)

RECV   9. How many calls would you say your household receives in a typical day?

_____ Number of calls RECEIVED by household per day (33–34)

LMAKE   10. Now considering the number of long-distance calls of all members of your household for a **typical week**, how many long-distance calls would you say your household MAKES in a typical week?

_____ Number of long-distance calls MADE by household per week (35–36) LRECV

11. How many long-distance calls would you say your household receives in a typical week?

_____ Number of long-distance calls RECEIVED by household per week (37–38)

MONTHLY   12. How much is your average monthly telephone bill, including **local and long-distance charges**?

_____ Average monthly telephone bill (39–41)

PAYCALL   13. How often do you use a pay telephone for personal calls in a typical month?

_____ Number of pay telephone calls per mo. (42–43) GENDER

14. INDICATE GENDER BY OBSERVATION

(44)

   1   MALE
   2   FEMALE

MARRIED 15. Are you married?

(45)

   1   YES
   2   NO
   3   Refused

AGE 16. Which of the following categories includes your age?

(46)

   1   18–24
   2   25–34
   3   35–44
   4   45–54
   5   55–64
   6   65 and older
   7   Refused

ADULTS 17. How many adults age 18 and over are currently living in your household including yourself?

_____ Number of adults (47)

CHILDREN 18. Do you have any children age 18 and under currently living in your household?

(48)

   1   YES
   2   NO
   3   RF

INCOME 19. Which of the following categories includes the total annual income of all members of your household before taxes?

(49)

   1   Less than $35,000
   2      $35,000–$49,999
   3      $50,000–$74,999
   4      $75,000 or more
   5   DK/RF

Thanks for participating.

Name _____ Telephone _____

Address _____

Interviewer # _____ Length of interview _____

Source: Courtesy of DSS Research.

Role of Marketing Research in the Organization and Ethical Issues

Marketing Research across the Organization

1. The question of data interpretation is not fully resolved in business today. Someone must still look at the data and decide what they really mean. Often this is done by the people in marketing research. Defend the proposition that persons in engineering, finance, and production should interpret all marketing research data

when the survey results affect their operations. What are the arguments against this position?

2. Marketing research data analysis for a large electric utility found that confidence in the abilities of the repairperson is the customers' primary determinant of their satisfaction or dissatisfaction with the electric utility. Armed with these findings, the utility embarked on a major advertising campaign extolling the heroic characteristics of the electric utility repairperson. The repairpeople hated the campaign. They knew that they couldn't live up to the customer expectations created by the advertising. What should have been done differently?

3. When marketing research is used in strategic planning, it often plays a role in determining long-term opportunities and threats in the external environment. Threats, for example, may come from competitors' perceived future actions, new competitors, governmental policies, changing consumer tastes, or a variety of other sources. Management's strategic decisions will determine the long-term profitability, and perhaps even the survival, of the firm. Most top managers are not marketing researchers or statisticians; therefore, they need to know how much confidence they can put into the data. Stated differently, when marketing researchers present statistical results, conclusions, and recommendations, they must understand top management's tolerance for ambiguity and imprecision. Why? How might this understanding affect what marketing researchers present to management? Under what circumstances might the level of top management's tolerance for ambiguity and imprecision shift?

Ethical Dilemma

Branding the Black Box in Marketing Research

Marketing research discovered branding in the mid-1980s and it experienced phenomenal growth in the 1990s, which continues today. Go to virtually any large marketing research firm's Web site, and you'll see a vast array of branded research products for everything from market segmentation to customer value analysis—all topped off with a diminutive ^{SM}, ^{TM}, or $^{®}$. Here's just a sample: MARC's Designor^{SM}, Market Facts' Brand Vision$^{®}$, Maritz Research's 80/203$^{®}$ Relationship Manager, and Total Research's TRBC^{TM}, a scale bias correction algorithm.

A common denominator across some of these products is that they are proprietary, which means the firms won't disclose exactly how they work. That's why they're also known pejoratively as black boxes. A black box method is proprietary—a company is able to protect its product development investment. And if customers perceive added value in the approach, suppliers can charge a premium price to boot. (Black boxes and brand names are not synonymous. Almost all proprietary methods have a clever brand name, but there are also brand names attached to research methods that are not proprietary.)

At least two factors have given rise to this branding frenzy. First, competitive pressures force organizations to seek new ways to differentiate their product offerings from those of their competitors. Second, many large research companies are publicly held, and publicly held companies are under constant pressure to increase sales and profits each quarter. One way to do this is to charge a premium price for services. If a company has a proprietary method for doing a marketing segmentation study, presumably it can charge more for this approach than another firm using publicly available software such as SPSS or SAS. Ironically, it is possible that some black boxes are perfectly standard software such as SPSS and SAS; but if their proponents won't say how they work, or which techniques are used, these methods are still black boxes.

Questions

1. Is the use of branded black box models unethical?

2. Should marketing research suppliers be forced to explain to clients how their proprietary models work?

3. Should firms be required by law to conduct validity and reliability tests on their models to demonstrate that they are better than nonproprietary models?

Source: Terry Grapentine, "You Can't Take Human Nature Out of Black Boxes," *Marketing Research* (Winter 2001), p. 21.

	SPSS EXERCISES FOR CHAPTER 18

Exercise 1: Multivariate Regression

This exercise uses multivariate regression to explain and predict how many movies a respondent attends in a month.

1. Go to the Web site for the text and download the Movie database.

2. Open the database in SPSS and view the variables under Variable View. We will be using the independent variables Q2 Q4 Q6 Q8a Q8b Q8c Q8d Q9 Q10 Q12 and Q13 to predict the dependent variable Q3.
    We are including the variables Q4 and Q6 as is. Strictly speaking, is this proper? What might you want to do instead and why? Why might you decide to leave a variable in bins instead? Would it ever be proper to use a variable like Q11 as is?

3. Go to Analyze → Descriptive Statistics → Descriptives and move Q3 Q2 Q4 Q6 Q8a Q8b Q8c Q8d Q9 Q10 Q12 and Q13 to the Variable(s) box and click OK. Multivariate techniques require that every variable have a legitimate value. If a respondent did not answer every question, then the analyst must either ignore the observation entirely or impute estimates for the missing values. The default for statistical software is to ignore those observations automatically. We will not do imputation for this exercise.

    a. What will the sample size be for later multivariate techniques?
    b. Is this sample size large enough for multivariate regression?
    c. What would some possible problems be if the sample size were not large enough?
    d. Are the minimum and maximum values for each variable within the proper range? A value that is out of range would indicate either a data input error or a user-defined missing value like "Refused" or "Don't Know." Data input errors should be corrected or deleted. User-defined missing values should be declared in SPSS.
    e. Are all the variables within the proper range?

4. Go to Analyze → Regression → Linear.
    Move Q3 to Dependent.
    Move Q2 Q4 Q6 Q8a Q8b Q8c Q8d Q9 Q10 Q12 Q13 to Independent(s).
    Change Method to Stepwise.
    Click OK.

   a.   Which independent variables did the stepwise regression select? Why not the rest?
   b.   Is each variable chosen significant?
   c.   Are the variables that have not been chosen necessarily insignificant?
   d.   Is the model significant?
   e.   Does this method guarantee that you get the "best" model?

5.   Go to Analyze → Descriptive Statistics → Descriptives and remove Q6 Q8a Q8b Q8c Q8d Q9 Q10 and Q12 from the Variable(s) box, so that only Q3 Q2 Q4 and Q13 remain in the box and then click OK.
     What is the sample size now?

6.   Go to Analyze → Regression → Linear.
     Move Q3 to Dependent.
     Remove Q6 Q8a Q8b Q8c Q8d Q9 Q10 and Q12 from Independent(s) so that only Q2 Q4 and Q13 remain.
     Change Method to Enter.
     Click OK.

   a.   How and why does this model differ from the model based on stepwise regression?
   b.   Which model is better?

Interpretation

1.   How does stated importance affect the number of times one attends movies?

2.   How does spending money on snacks affect the number of times one attends movies?

3.   How does student classification affect the number of times one attends movies?

4.   If a sophomore thought that going to the movies was somewhat important and typically spent $12 on snacks, how many times per month would he or she attend movies based on this model?

5.   Do any of the variables, according to the results, appear to have an effect on the number of times one attends movies, or does it seem that other factors not covered in this survey are driving movie attendance?

Exercise 2: Factor Analysis

This exercise uses factor analysis to explore how survey respondents consider various aspects of a theater visit.

1.   Go to the Web site for the text and download the Movie database.

2.   Open the database in SPSS and view the variables under Variable View. Notice that question 5 has 9 importance rating items.

3.   Go to Analyze → Descriptive Statistics → Descriptives and move Q5a through Q5i to the Variable(s) box and click OK.

   a.   Which item is the most important?
   b.   Which item is the least important?

Multivariate techniques require that every variable have a legitimate value. If a respondent did not answer every question, then the analyst must either ignore the observation entirely or impute estimates for the missing values. The default for statistical software is to ignore those observations automatically. We will not get involved with imputation for this exercise.

a.   What will the sample size be for later multivariate techniques?

b.   Is this sample size large enough for factor analysis?

c.   What would some possible problems be if the sample size were not large enough?

d.   It is a good idea to check that the minimum and maximum values for each variable are within the proper range. A value that is out of range indicates either a data input error or a user-defined missing value such as "Refused" or "Don't Know." Data input errors should be corrected or deleted. User-defined missing values should be declared in SPSS.

e.   Are all the variables within the proper range?

4.   Go to Analyze → Descriptive Statistics → Descriptives and move Q5a through Q5i to the Variables box and click OK.

Examine the resulting correlations matrix.

a.   Other than the 1's down the main diagonal of the matrix, what is the highest correlation in absolute value?

b.   Does any variable "just not fit" with the others?

c.   Does multicollinearity appear to exist among some of the items?

5.   Go to Analyze → Data Reduction → Factor.

Move Q5a through Q5i to the Variables box.
Click the Rotation button, place a check in front of "Varimax," and click Continue.
Click the Options button.
Place a check in front of "Sorted by size."
Place a check in front of "Suppress absolute values less than" and set the value after it to .25.
Click Continue.
Click OK.
SPSS produces a lot of output Factor Analysis. It is possible to create much more output than we have generated here by setting various subcommands and options.

a.   How many factors did SPSS create?

b.   Why did it stop at that number?

c.   How could you change the defaults to create a different number of factors?

d.   Go to the output entitled Total Variance Explained. How much variance was explained in this Factor Analysis?

e.   Go to the output entitled Rotated Component Matrix. Why are some elements in this matrix blank?

f.   Do the components or factors make sense?

g.   Can you identify a common theme for each component or factor?

Interpretation

1.   Is this a good factor solution? Why do you say that?

2.   How might you create a better factor solution?

3.   What understanding has this analysis helped you gain about how moviegoers perceive their movie-going experience?

4.   What recommendations would you give a manager of a movie house based on this analysis?

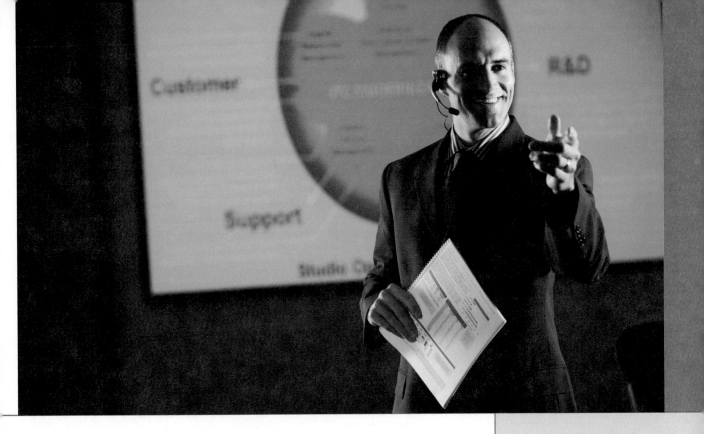

Communicating The Research Results

LEARNING OBJECTIVES

→ **1.** To become aware of the primary purposes of a research report.

→ **2.** To learn how to organize and prepare a research report.

→ **3.** To gain insight into how to interpret and present marketing research results.

→ **4.** To understand the appropriate style and format for marketing research reports.

→ **5.** To learn how to make a personal presentation.

→ **6.** To understand the effective use and communication of marketing research information.

The research report is the culmination of all of our efforts. It is critical that it clearly conveys key findings and their implications. This chapter addresses this important issue.

The Research Report

The research objectives, the decisions to be made based on the research, and a vision of the analysis and the report to be written should have guided the researcher through the design and execution of the research. For a survey-based project, the development of the questionnaire, in particular, should have been based on continuous reference to the research objectives. Now, we have the data, it has been cross tabulated, statistical testing has been performed, extensive statistical analysis has been conducted, and the researcher and her team have spent time sifting through all of this information and relating it back to the original objectives and the decisions associated with those objectives. This process could go on and on, but deadlines in the schedule push the process to a conclusion, often faster than we would like. The importance of the research objectives in this process is illustrated in the Practicing Marketing Research feature below.

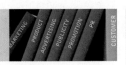

PRACTICING
MARKETING RESEARCH

The Relationship between Clarity and Project Success[1]

The first step in any successful research project is knowing the objectives. Before taking on any other tasks, market researchers and clients should clearly identify specific objectives for the project. Well-defined research objectives will serve as basic guideposts for making decisions over the course of the project.

Research objectives should address several different issues. First, they indicate whether the project calls for exploration or measurement of an issue. If the former, the project will employ qualitative methodologies, and if the latter then quantitative methodologies. Generally, exploratory research should precede measurement. Next, the objectives should identify the categories of data you wish to examine.

Research objectives should also clearly define the target population, based on the data and methodologies chosen. As a researcher, you'll need to make sure that respondents are properly qualified to offer valid opinions of or feedback to your questions. Finally, identify any comparisons that you might want to make. In performing comparisons,

make sure different data sets are collected in a consistent manner.

Another key to creating research objectives is knowing how the research will ultimately be used. Will it be used to inform product development? Will the research help the client create more productive marketing messages? Is the goal of the research to find out more about the existing customer base? Understanding how the research will be used increases the clarity of the objectives.

Marketers must also identify how many objectives to have. Time limitations on focus groups and surveys will often dictate how many objectives you are able to address in a given project. If you cannot narrow down your objectives to fit time constraints, you might split your survey or project in two.

Survey questions should reflect the research objectives. During the writing process, organize each question according to the research objective it addresses. Ultimately if questions are aligned with research objectives, it will be much easier to organize the resulting data when it comes time to create the final report.

The analysis plan and the final report should focus on the research objectives as well. The analysis plan can help researchers identify ahead of time how best to analyze and tabulate the data. By determining the analysis plan before writing the questionnaire, the researcher can design questions to elicit specific types of information. Framing the final report around the research objectives enables clients to clearly see how the results of the study inform or fulfill the questions and goals they had at the outset.

By clearly defining research objectives upfront and incorporating them in every phase of the research project, you will produce better results that can then be used as the basis for subsequent projects.

Questions

1. If fulfilling research objectives is so important, wouldn't it make sense to create just one objective per research project as the best means of keeping the project on track? Why or why not?

2. Have you ever seen a research project or performed one yourself in which the objectives were not well defined? How did that affect the results?

The researcher has a tremendous amount of information—piles of crosstabs, reams of statistical analyses, tons of notes, and an assortment of other pieces of information. The challenge is: How to package all of this in a coherent report that efficiently and effectively communicates the key findings and the decision implications of those findings? We like to think of this process as one of trying to figure out how to tell a story. Before you can tell a story, you have to have a pretty good idea of where the story is going to end up. All the analysis brings one to that conclusion. Once you know or have ascertained the key points that you want to make, it becomes much easier to map out what you need to get across to your readers to bring them to that same conclusion.

It is important that a research firm have a consistent style for reporting. This puts all analysts on the same page so that even a glance at a report will tell clients it was produced by a certain research firm. Having said all this, we must admit that when a client has a different internal standard for reporting, it is sometimes necessary to follow a different approach than the one recommended above. In some cases, the client may even dictate that the research supplier produce the report on the client's PowerPoint template according to the client's style rules.

Organizing the Report

The traditional research report follows an outline like the following one:

1. **Title Page.** The title page should be dominated by the name of the project. Other elements that should be included are the name of the client organization, name of the research firm, and date of the report.

2. **Table of Contents.** This should not exceed one page and should list the major sections of the report along with the page numbers on which they start. It is a convenience for the reader and, often, the researcher in that it permits quick reference for finding specific information in the report.

3. **Executive Summary.** This is perhaps the most difficult part of the report to write because it must succinctly cover the key findings and any recommendations that flow from those findings. Not all reports include recommendations. Whether they include recommendations depends on the nature of the research, what is expected from the research firm, and what the research found. However, all research reports should include key findings. What makes it tough to do the executive summary is that it should be short (two to four pages at a maximum), and many researchers

find it very difficult to summarize the massive amount of information available to them in just two to four pages. It is easy to be long winded, but it is difficult to be compact in your summarization. The executive summary should not summarize every single finding but should focus on those findings that are important and relevant to the goals of the research.

4. **Background.** The background sets the context for the research and addresses such things as the overall goal of the research, the decisions that need to be made, the company's strength and weaknesses regarding the issue in question, and other similar information. It should not be more than one or two pages. Again, it is often difficult to compress a lot of information down to its essentials.

5. **Methodology.** Here we should discuss how the research was done and why it was done that way. Issues that need to be addressed include who was interviewed, why did we interview those people, how were they interviewed (for example, telephone survey, mail survey, Internet survey, or some hybrid of these methods), why were they interviewed in that manner, how were people selected, what type of sampling methodology did we use, whether the sample is a representative sample, how many people did we interview, how were the completed surveys processed, what special statistical procedures were used and why did we use those procedures, and so forth. It is not necessary that this section be long—one to two pages is appropriate. If it is necessary to address some technical elements of the methodology in a more extensive manner, then more detailed information on, for example, statistical procedures used should be provided in an appendix.

6. **Findings.** This is typically the longest section of the report and should summarize results for almost every question on the survey.

7. **Appendices.** This final section of the report provides a number of supporting items such as a copy of the questionnaire, a set of cross tabulations for every question on the survey (client can look up specific issues not addressed in the findings), and other supporting material such as detailed technical information on special research procedures and techniques.

Interpreting the Findings

executive summary
Portion of a research report that explains why the research was done, what was found, what those findings mean, and what action, if any, management should undertake.

conclusions
Generalizations that answer the questions raised by the research objectives or otherwise satisfy the objectives.

The most difficult task for individuals who are writing a research report for the first time is interpreting the findings to arrive at conclusions and then using these conclusions to formulate recommendations. The **executive summary** is the portion of the report that explains what the research found, what the data mean, and what action, if any, should be taken, based on the research. The difficulties of this process are completely understandable, given that the marketing researcher is often inundated with piles of computer printouts, stacks of questionnaires, hundreds of pages of cross tabulations, the results of hundreds of statistical tests, pages and pages of statistical analysis printouts, and a scratch pad full of notes on the project. There is, however, a systematic method that the researcher can follow to draw conclusions.

The research objectives and background stated early in the marketing research process should serve as the primary guide for interpreting findings and drawing conclusions.

Conclusions are generalizations that answer the questions raised by the research objectives or otherwise satisfy the objectives. These conclusions are derived through the process of *induction,* or generalizing from small pieces of information. The researcher should try to merge the information and then paraphrase it in a few descriptive

FROM THE FRONT LINE

Preparing an Effective and Insightful Report

Kevin Weseman II, Director of Analytics, DSS Research

There is no "secret" to writing a good report. Most people think that it takes slick charts and flowery prose with polysyllabic words to make a report worthy of its intended audience, particularly when there are executives involved. In truth, the best reports are those which address the objectives of the research using the most simple, straight-forward approach possible. Think about it, if you were an executive and you only had five minutes to review the results of a study would you want to wade through someone's dissertation or would you want the results laid out in an easily digestible manner?

A good report ties together all of the pertinent details into a nice, neat package, but it begins and ends with the executive summary. The executive summary should provide a narrative for the research – it should tell the story of the data without being too verbose. We have found that a bulleted outline approach works best to achieve this goal. This means that the main statement of each bullet should directly address an objective and supporting statements should be brief and pointed. Remember, an executive summary is a high level synopsis and the reader should not feel mired down in details, so do not mindlessly regurgitate figures. That said, anyone who reads the executive summary should immediately have answers to the objectives of the research without the need to see any of the charts or graphs that follow.

The body of the report is where the "supporting evidence" resides. Survey and modeling results are presented in greater detail in this section. This does not mean that every detail and nuance in the data should be charted and scrutinized - it is best to only chart results which have a direct bearing on the findings discussed in the executive summary. Also, any charts or graphs which are used should be intuitive and not required a long explanation for the reader to understand – if this is necessary then the data was not presented properly. At DSS, we typically provide a slide summary, or takeaway, for each slide. This helps focus the reader on the important findings for each slide and it assists the analyst in formulating the story that will be told in the executive summary.

In addition to the executive summary and detailed findings, a good report also contains a brief discussion of the methodology for the research – the who, what, why, when and where. Again, this should only take as much space as necessary to give the reader the peace of mind that the research design is solid.

There is no "secret" to writing a good report. Sure, you should utilize a formula for creating a report which incorporates rules and style guidelines, but the art of actually reading between the data points and trying the findings together in a coherent and concise story is something that can only be accomplished through trial and error. This can take years to master, so anyone who starts practicing while they are still in school will have a distinct advantage over their competition.

statements that generalize the results. In short, the conclusion of a research report should be a statement or series of statements that communicate the results of the study to the reader but would not necessarily include any of the data derived from the statistical analysis. The real process of developing the report requires the art of the story teller, as described in the Practicing Marketing Research feature on page 591.

Format of the Report

The format and preparation of marketing research reports have changed dramatically over the last 15 years. The pressure to find more efficient and effective ways to communicate research results has pushed researchers toward a heavy reliance on presentation software to tell their stories. Microsoft's PowerPoint totally dominates the market today.

A typical marketing research report tells its story with pictures or graphics. This is what clients expect and what the researcher is expected to deliver. It is not unusual for clients to specify that they want graphics-based reports in their RFPs. Research reports that might have included 50 or more pages of text and a handful of graphs in the past are now presented in a limited amount of text, perhaps just a few pages if it were all strung together, and 20 or 30 pages of graphs and tables. This approach enables time-pressed executives to quickly grasp the story and the key findings and move ahead to conclusions and recommendations. Most clients today just want a copy of the PowerPoint presentation instead of a long, detailed traditional report.

Graphics, text boxes, bulleted lists, and the like are used to interpret the meaning of various graphs. Examples of pages from a report prepared using presentation software are provided in Exhibits 19.1 through 19.9.

Formulating Recommendations

→ recommendations
Conclusions applied to marketing strategies or tactics that focus on a client's achievement of differential advantage.

Recommendations are gained from the process of deduction. The marketing researcher applies the conclusions to specific areas in order to make suggestions for marketing strategies or tactics. A recommendation usually focuses on how the client can gain a differential advantage. A *differential advantage* is a true benefit offered by a potential marketing mix that the target market cannot obtain anywhere else (for example, American Airlines having exclusive U.S. carrier landing rights at a foreign airport).

In some cases, a marketing researcher must refrain from making specific recommendations and must instead fall back on more general ones. For example, the marketing researcher might not have sufficient information about the resources and experience base of the company or about the decision maker to whom the report is being directed. Or the researcher may have been notified that the recommendations will be determined by the decision maker. Under these circumstances, the researcher offers conclusions and stops at that point.

The final report represents the culmination of the research effort. The quality of the report and its recommendations often determine whether a client will return to a supplier. Within a corporation, an internal report prepared by a research department may have less impact, but a history of preparing excellent reports may lead to merit salary increases and, ultimately, promotion for a research staff member.

Challenges in communicating marketing research findings are covered in the Practicing Marketing Research feature on page 592.

The Presentation

Clients may expect a presentation of the research results. A presentation serves many purposes. It requires that the interested parties assemble and become reacquainted with the research objectives and methodology. It also brings to light any unexpected events or findings and highlights the research conclusions. In fact, for some decision makers in the company, the presentation will be their *only* exposure to the findings; they will never read the report. Other managers may only skim the written report, using it as a memory-recall trigger for points made in the presentation. In short, effective communication in the presentation is absolutely critical.

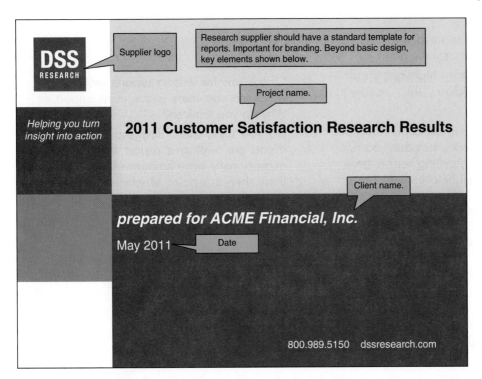

Exhibit 19.1

Sample Title Slide

PRACTICING
MARKETING RESEARCH

Getting to the Heart of Preparing Quantitative Research Reports[2]

Data is certainly at the core of any research report, but reams of data tables alone do not show the complete picture. When creating a quantitative research report, your job as the researcher is to present the data in a way that tells a meaningful and compelling story. Of course the data from your study is important. Your clients, however, ultimately will be using the report to make critical business decisions and will have a much more difficult time doing so if they have to sift through mountains of data themselves. There are several strategies that you, the researcher, can take to ensure that a report communicates the most important results of the study and presents the client with the most useful information from which they can make their decisions.

First, by staying current on the client's market, including macro- and micro-level trends and competitor activities, you can better understand the significance of the resulting data from your study. Second, you should address each study objective by using your data to frame a concrete answer to the question raised by each objective. Third, by adding a one- or two-page summary to the report, you can help the client step away from the details and see the big picture.

When you sit down to actually write the report, the following tips can help you keep your presentation on track:

- Lay out a road map for your report before you start writing it. Your executive summary can help you organize your writing.

- Keep the insights in your executive summary clear, concise, and to the point.

- Create slides that support each insight from the summary.

- Include only the data in each slide that is essential for communicating the point.
- Use graphics and color to highlight important ideas and guide the reader's attention.

Remember: Numbers may be at the heart of a quantitative research report, but they do not tell the whole story. A compelling report presents only the data that will help a client better understand the material. Your job is to sort through the data to write a report that most effectively and efficiently communicates the information your client needs.

Questions

1. Of the tips for writing reports listed above, which do you think is the most important? Why do you think so?

2. Do you think these suggestions still apply if you are writing a report that covers an exceptionally large amount of data? Do you think there's a point at which you have no choice but to lay all the data out there, or do you think there are ways of managing large amounts of data in your presentation? Explain your reasoning.

PRACTICING
MARKETING RESEARCH

Lost in Translation: Challenges Researchers Face in Communicating Their Results to Clients[3]

For anyone in a specialized field like market research, there comes a point at which the specialist must figure out how to communicate this expertise to those who do not have that kind of expertise. For market researchers, even long-standing clients at some point will want an explanation of the researcher's methodology—but these methodologies are often complex. Communicating this information accurately, however, can be critical for clients as they make strategic decisions.

Market researchers generally face two major challenges to producing compelling research for clients. First, they must use their research to convey a practical view of the world. Second, they must apply the appropriate level of analytics.

Researchers often make mistakes facing the first challenge when they view their analysis

in a vacuum or reduce it to a one- or two-dimensional view. Researchers must discipline themselves to analyze research data based on multiple dimensions. Because of the great diversity of the market, researchers who view trends from a single dimension are likely to miss particular opportunities. A segmentation approach can help researchers produce a more complete picture of the groups of people the client wishes to identify.

The primary difficulty in confronting the second challenge—determining the appropriate level of analytics to apply—is that the necessary level of analytics varies directly with the ease of understanding the data. So as the analytics uncover more granular details, it becomes increasingly more difficult to see the broader picture. Researchers may be tempted to oversimplify things in an effort to make them more accessible to their clients, but this only results in thin, unreliable analysis. And complex and jargon-filled reports ultimately offer clients no insight at all. It is not easy to balance these extremes, so understanding the client's needs and what they are willing to pay for is a solid place to start. Once the client's expectations are known, the strategies for making deeper analysis more accessible will become more apparent.

Researchers should not hesitate to exercise their capabilities. By addressing the challenges of producing research that reflects real-life situations and analysis that is both clear and sufficiently deep, researchers can greatly help clients improve their profitability.

Questions

1. Which of these two challenges do you think is the more difficult to address? Why?

2. How would you go about clarifying the client's needs and expectations? What kinds of issues would you look for, and what kinds of questions would you ask?

Table of Contents

Background and Objectives	2
Executive Summary	3
Methodology	5
Research Findings	6
Overall Satisfaction	7
Plan Loyalty	8
Network, Policies, and Other Plan Items	10
Quality and Compensation Issues	14
ACME Staff	21
ACME Processes	26
Communications	32
Demographics	34
Appendices	
Appendix A: Key Driver Statistical Model	38
Appendix B: Questionnaire	48
Appendix C: Crosstabulations	49

Not more than a page. Helps user refer to specific areas of interest. List major sections.

2011 Customer Satisfaction Research | ACME Financial | May 2011   1   DSS Research

Exhibit 19.2

Sample Table of Contents

Making a Presentation

An effective presentation is tailored to the audience. It takes into account the receivers' frame of reference, attitudes, prejudices, educational background, and time constraints. The speaker must select words, concepts, and illustrative figures to which the audience can relate. A good presentation allows time for questions and discussion.

One reason presentations are sometimes inadequate is that the speaker lacks an understanding of the barriers to effective communication. A second factor is that the speaker fails to recognize or admit that the purpose of many research reports is persuasion. *Persuasion* does not imply stretching or bending the truth, but rather using research

Exhibit 19.3

Sample Background and Objectives

Keep it concise. Put key objectives in bulleted list.

Background and Objectives

Background. ACME, like other progressive organizations, wants to develop a program to assess customer satisfaction with the services they receive from the organization. This information will be used in ACME's quality improvement efforts. The goal is to provide rational direction for those efforts.

Objectives. This type of research is designed to achieve the following objectives:

- Measure overall satisfaction with ACME compared to the competition.

- Measure customer satisfaction with ACME's new Web site where all transactions with ACME can be handled.

- Measure satisfaction with specific elements of all other programs and services provided to customers by ACME.

- Identify major reasons for satisfaction/dissatisfaction.

- Evaluate and classify program and service elements on the basis of their importance to customers and ACME's perceived performance of ACME (i.e., identify areas of strength and opportunities for improvement).

Exhibit 19.4

Sample First Page of Executive Summary

Focus on key findings, not just reiteration of detailed results.	**Executive Summary**

The majority are loyal, but satisfaction declined.

- Four out of five customers see their relationship with ACME continuing on a long-term basis. Over half are categorized as secure or favorable and can be considered loyal to ACME.
- Two-thirds report they are satisfied with ACME in 2008. However, this is a significant decline from 80.1% in 2010.
- ACME overall satisfaction and loyalty measures are significantly lower than the National Average.

Heavy Users are highly satisfied; Light Users less so.

- Heavy users report significantly higher satisfaction than light users and are more likely to see their relationship with ACME continuing on a long-term basis.
- Although only a small percentage of customers is categorized as alienated, Light Users make up a higher proportion of this group.

ACME processes are primary areas of strength.

- Both the customer service and application processes are identified through key driver analysis as areas of strength for ACME.
- Satisfaction with the billing process continues an upward trend. Ratings are on par with the National Average and significantly higher than 2010.

Staff ratings remain strong, with knowledge a key asset.

- The majority of customers are satisfied with all aspects related to ACME staff. About four out of five are satisfied with staff knowledge, the area of highest satisfaction across all staff levels.
- Although still high, relatively lower staff ratings are associated with accessibility related measures. Key driver analysis identifies ease of reaching staff as an opportunity for improvement.

2011 Customer Satisfaction Research | ACME Financial | May 2011   3   DSS Research

Exhibit 19.5

Sample Methodology Slide

Explain what was done in a simple, straightforward manner.	**Methodology**

Questionnaire. DSS was responsible for developing the survey instrument. ACME approved the final draft of the questionnaire. A copy of the mail survey instrument used is provided in Appendix B.

Methodology employed. Eligible respondents included a list of customers provided by ACME. The sample design is as follows:

	2011			2010			2009		
	Heavy Users	Light Users	Overall	Heavy Users	Light Users	Overall	Heavy Users	Light Users	Overall
Completed surveys	52	60	112	101	71	172	87	71	158
Mailed Surveys	200	200	400	200	200	400	200	200	400
Returned undeliverable surveys	NA	NA	4	NA	NA	8	NA	NA	14
Response rate	26.0%	30.0%	28.0%	50.5%	35.5%	43.0%	43.5%	35.5%	39.5%
Adjusted response rate**	NA	NA	28.3%	NA	NA	43.9%	NA	NA	40.9%
Sample error*	NA	NA	±7.9%	NA	NA	±5.6%	NA	NA	±6.1%
Initial survey mailed	February 28, 2011			March 7, 2010			February 28, 2009		
Second survey mailed	March 21, 2011			March 28, 2010			March 21, 2009		
Last day to accept surveys	April 27, 2011			May 2, 2010			April 25, 2009		

Data collection. All data were collected by DSS Research.

Data processing and analysis. DSS processed all completed surveys and analyzed the results. A complete set of survey tabulations is provided in Appendix C of this report.

* At 95% confidence, using the most pessimistic assumption regarding variance (p=0.5).
** Excludes undeliverables.

2011 Customer Satisfaction Research | ACME Financial | May 2011   4   DSS Research

findings to reinforce conclusions and recommendations. In preparing a presentation, the researcher should keep the following questions in mind:

- What do the data really mean?
- What impact do they have?

Exhibit 19.6

Graphics Make Communication More Efficient

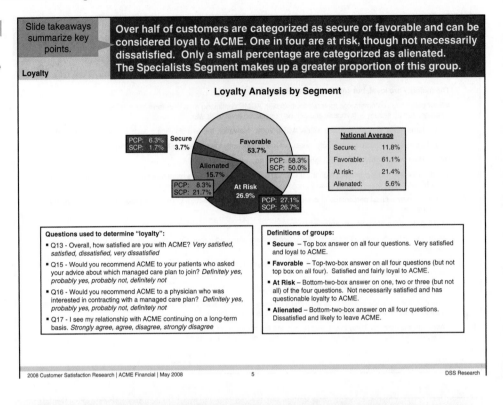

Exhibit 19.7

Multiple Graphics Provide Summary on a Topic

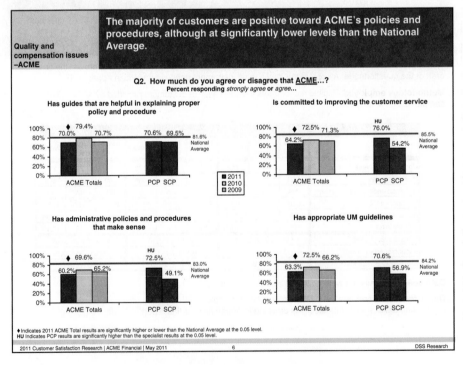

- What have we learned from the data?
- What do we need to do, given the information we now have?
- How can future studies of this nature be enhanced?
- What could make this information more useful?

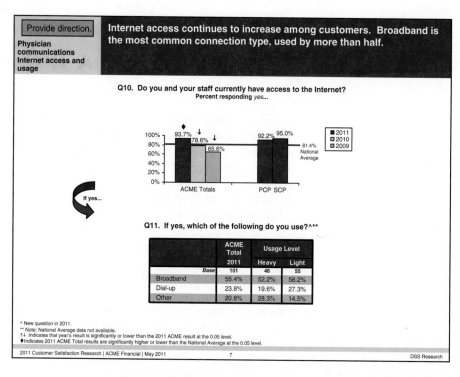

Exhibit 19.8

Graphic and Table Work Together

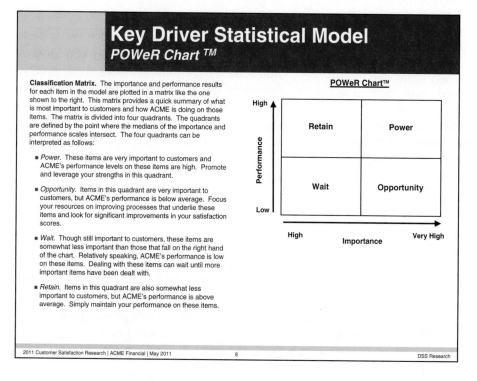

Exhibit 19.9

Graphics and Text Tell How to Interpret Statistical Results

Presentations on the Internet

With PowerPoint, publishing presentations to the Web is easier than ever. Publication to the Web enables individuals to access the presentation, regardless of where they are or when they need to access it. In addition, researchers can present results at multiple locations on the Internet. The steps are very simple:

PRACTICING MARKETING RESEARCH

The Market Researchers' Wish List[4]

It's not uncommon for market researchers to also participate in the technology development at their firm. Confirmit, a market research firm, polls those researchers in its Market Research Software Survey, to get feedback on emerging industry trends and the role technology is playing in companies across the industry. A recent survey identified some changes in reporting methods and how researchers were using software in these areas.

In a single year, Confirmit found significant shifts in the distribution methods being used for research reports. PowerPoint presentations remained the most popular over that period, but it fell from being used in 56 percent of all projects to 48 percent. MS Word documents, printed tabs, and Acrobat PDFs all declined as well. Online results delivery remained static, and interactive analysis—the only distribution method to increase in usage—rose slightly from 8 to 10 percent. And while it appears that many researchers are using multiformat delivery, even that modality appears to be on the decline. Even though 52 percent of companies considered crosstab report production capabilities as essential, only 14 percent of companies actually used them.

Concerning researchers' wishes for analysis and reporting tools, two main points seemed to emerge. First, 74 percent rated PowerPoint issues as one of their top three priorities, asking software developers to create some solution that would automate the process of having to manually manipulate imported data and charts into presentation quality material. Second, three-fifths of respondents assessed the state of online analysis tools to be unsatisfactory, and they were actively looking for alternate solutions to what was available. A smaller proportion, 38 percent, expressed a desire for better desktop analytical tools as a top three priority as well.

Questions

1. Which distribution methods do you think would be most useful for research reports? Are some better suited for particular situations? Would you use multiformat delivery?

2. Have you used any software for generating research reports? How well did it work? What would be at the top of your wish list based on your experience?

---

1. Open your presentation in PowerPoint. To see what your slides will look like on the Web, choose "Web Page Preview" from the "File" menu. After you have made any edits, choose "Save as Web Page" from the same menu.

2. The "Save As" dialog box allows you to change the title of your presentation to whatever you want displayed in the title bar of your visitor's browser.

3. The "Publish" button takes you to the "Publish as Web Page" dialog box, where you can customize your presentation.

4. The "Web Options" dialog box lets you specify the way your published file will be stored on the Web server and whether to update internal links to these files automatically.

See the Practicing Marketing Research Feature above for information on trends in report delivery.

SUMMARY

The six primary sections of a contemporary marketing research report are, in order: the table of contents, background and objectives, executive summary, methodology, findings, and appendixes with supporting information.

The primary objectives of the marketing research report are to state the specific research objectives, explain why and how the research was done, present the findings of the research, and provide conclusions and recommendations. Most of these elements are contained in the executive summary. The conclusions do not necessarily contain statistical numbers derived from the research but rather generalize the results in relation to the stated objectives. Nor do conclusions suggest a course of action. This is left to the recommendations, which direct the conclusions to specific marketing strategies or tactics that would place the client in the most positive position in the market.

The marketing research report of today makes heavy use of graphics to present key findings. For most researchers, PowerPoint is the software of choice for creating research reports. In terms of mechanics, reports minimize the use of words, feed information to clients in "minibites," and make extensive use of bulleted charts and graphics. In addition to the written report, which is often nothing more than a copy of the PowerPoint presentation, a presentation of research results is often required. It is common for research reports to be published on the Internet by the client or by the researcher at the client's request. This has the advantage of making the results available to individuals worldwide in the client's organization. The Internet can also be used to support simultaneous presentation of the research results in multiple locations.

KEY TERMS & DEFINITIONS

executive summary Portion of a research report that explains why the research was done, what was found, what those findings mean, and what action, if any, management should undertake.

conclusions Generalizations that answer the questions raised by the research objectives or otherwise satisfy the objectives.

recommendations Conclusions applied to marketing strategies or tactics that focus on a client's achievement of differential advantage.

QUESTIONS FOR REVIEW & CRITICAL THINKING

1. What are the roles of the research report? Give examples.
2. Distinguish among findings, conclusions, and recommendations in a research report.
3. Why should research reports contain executive summaries? What should be contained in an executive summary?

WORKING THE NET

1. Go to *http://www.gallup.com* and examine some of the special reports on American opinions, such as those found under "Social Issues and Policy." Do these reports meet the criteria discussed in the text for good marketing research reports? Why or why not?

2. Go to *http://www.presentations.com.* Describe the different ways this organization can help an individual become a more effective speaker.

REAL-LIFE RESEARCH • 19.1

The United Way

The United Way was concerned about the attitudes of nondonors toward the organization with the theory that their reasons for not donating are tied to their perceptions of United Way. They are also interested in getting a sense of what factors might convert nondonors to donors. The executive summary from the research report is provided below. Each heading and the text that follows were provided on PowerPoint slides in the report, and the presentation was provided by the research firm that conducted the study of these issues.

Executive Summary Objectives and Methodology

- The general purposes of this study were to determine the attitudes of nondonors toward the United Way, to assess the reasons for not donating, and to ascertain factors that may influence nondonors to contribute in the future.
- The study relied on primary data gathered through online surveys.
- The study employed a probability sample.
- Responses were obtained from 726 respondents.

Findings

- The percentage with positive perceptions of the United Way was greater than the percentage having negative perceptions. However, the majority had no opinions about United Way.
- Only 5.2 percent rated United Way fair or poor in providing benefits to those in need.
- United Way actually spends 9 to 10 percent of contributions on administrative costs, although 80.6 percent believed that the United Way used more than 10 percent of its contributions on administrative costs.
- Primary reasons for not contributing were contribution to other charities or religious organizations, personal financial circumstances, lack of knowledge of how donated funds are used, personal beliefs, absence of favorite charities, pressure to contribute, and preference to donate time rather than money.

- Of those who were asked to contribute, pressure seemed somewhat important in influencing their decision not to contribute.

- Of those who indicated that personal financial reasons influenced their decision not to give, 35.6 percent indicated they would give to United Way if asked.

- Other charities and religious denominations are clearly in competition with United Way for donations.

- Many respondents indicated that they would contribute if they could specify the charity to receive their contributions, had more knowledge about the United Way and the charities it supports, were asked to give, had less pressure to give, could use payroll deduction, and had the option of spreading contributions over time.

- Of those whose place of employment participated in the United Way campaign, 49.6 percent had been asked to give but did not.

- Workplace campaigns reach a large number of executives and professional and administrative personnel in the higher-income brackets but do not reach a significant number of service personnel or lower-income households.

Conclusions

- Negative perceptions do not appear to be a major factor affecting reasons for not contributing. However, a positive perception does not necessarily translate into a contribution.

- Noncontributors lack sufficient information regarding the United Way to form an accurate perception of the organization.

- There is a lack of knowledge concerning the United Way and the organizations to which it allocates contributions.

- Respondents believe that the United Way uses more for administrative costs than it actually does.

- The United Way is in competition for a limited number of charity dollars.

Recommendations

- Conduct additional research to determine noncontributor's level of knowledge of the United Way and the purpose that the United Way serves.

- Increase education for potential contributors regarding the United Way's purpose, the organizations it supports, and the United Way's reasonable administrative costs.

- Expand the frequency of campaigns in the workplace and develop ways to increase awareness of the methods of contributing.

- Develop appropriate competitive marketing strategy to address the United Way's competitors.

Questions

1. Do you think that the executive summary provides guidance for decision-making information?

2. Are all of the elements present that should be included in an executive summary as discussed in this chapter?

3. Do the findings, conclusions, and recommendations logically follow from the objectives? Why or why not?

REAL-LIFE RESEARCH • 19.2

TouchWell Tracking Research

TouchWell is a large health plan in a major metropolitan area in the western United States. TouchWell has been buffeted by all of the problems experienced by managed care organizations, including the following:

1. Fierce competition from other plans.

2. Financial concerns associated with rising medical costs on the one hand and pressure to keep premiums low on the other hand.

3. The stream of negative publicity about HMOs and managed care plans.

However, TouchWell has managed to continue to grow during this period through aggressive marketing to both business decision makers, who make choices among group health insurance plans for their employees, and consumers. Its marketing programs have been guided by an equally aggressive marketing research program. Senior managers at TouchWell are convinced that they could make better decisions if they had the information necessary to make those decisions. Their research program has included a mix of qualitative and quantitative research covering market segmentation, product testing, communications testing, and tracking research (sometimes referred to as attitude, awareness, and usage—AA&U—research).

A high-level presentation to TouchWell's senior management by Alpha Research, covering four waves of tracking research, follows. The presentation includes key measurements from the tracking research, such as unaided plan awareness, general impressions of HMOs, reasons for negative impressions, and impressions of TouchWell and key competitors.

TouchWell believes that maintaining high plan awareness is an important part of the process of selling to both business decision makers and consumers. Impressions of HMOs in general provide management with some idea of the context in which they are selling their product, and specific impressions of TouchWell and its major competitors provide measures of image.

TouchWell Tracking Research

**Summary of Findings from
2005 and 2007**

prepared by Alpha Research

Background

- The information summarized in this report is based on telephone surveys conducted by Alpha Research in 2005 and 2007
- Two waves of research were conducted in each year:
  - ➤ 2005—March and October.
  - ➤ 2007—January and November.
- In all the waves of research, separate samples and survey instruments were used for:
  - ➤ Consumers with group health coverage through an employer who were the decision makers for group health coverage for the household.
  - ➤ Individuals from companies that offer group health coverage to their employees who make decisions regarding coverage for their companies.
- Random samples were used for all surveys. Sample sizes were as follows:
  - ➤ 2005 Pretest—Business (400), Consumer (500).
  - ➤ 2005 Posttest—Business (400), Consumer (400).
  - ➤ 2007 Pretest—Business (400), Consumer (400).
  - ➤ 2007 Posttest—Business (400), Consumer (400).

Consumers: Unaided Plan Awareness

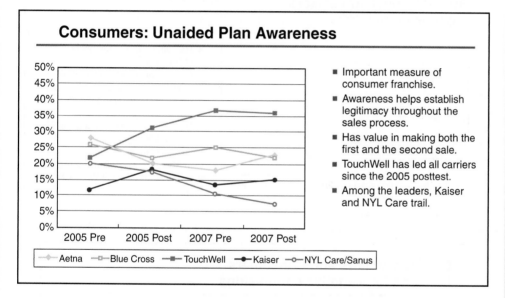

- Important measure of consumer franchise.
- Awareness helps establish legitimacy throughout the sales process.
- Has value in making both the first and the second sale.
- TouchWell has led all carriers since the 2005 posttest.
- Among the leaders, Kaiser and NYL Care trail.

Business Decision Makers: Unaided Plan Awareness

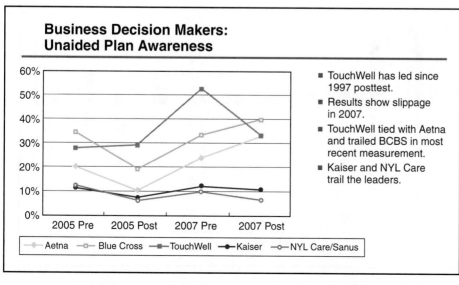

- TouchWell has led since 1997 posttest.
- Results show slippage in 2007.
- TouchWell tied with Aetna and trailed BCBS in most recent measurement.
- Kaiser and NYL Care trail the leaders.

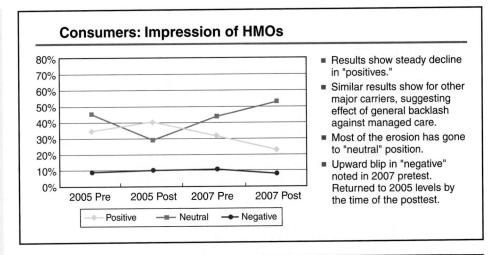

Consumers: Impression of HMOs

- Results show steady decline in "positives."
- Similar results show for other major carriers, suggesting effect of general backlash against managed care.
- Most of the erosion has gone to "neutral" position.
- Upward blip in "negative" noted in 2007 pretest. Returned to 2005 levels by the time of the posttest.

Business Decision Makers: Impression of HMOs

- Results show steady decline in "positives."
- Similar results show for other major carriers, suggesting effect of general backlash against managed care.
- Most of the erosion has gone to "neutral" position.
- Upward blip in "negative" noted in 2007 pretest. Returned to 2005 levels by the time of the posttest.

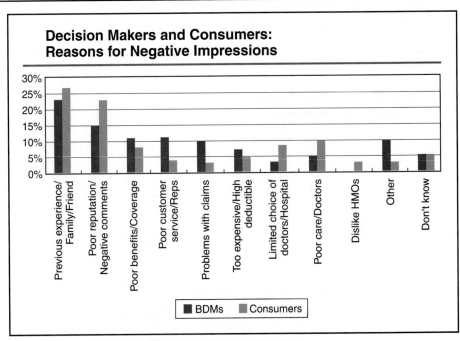

Decision Makers and Consumers: Reasons for Negative Impressions

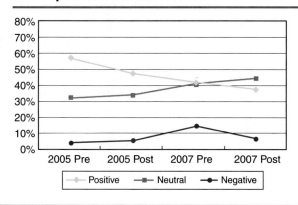

Business Decision Makers: Impression of TouchWell

- Results show steady decline in "positives."
- Similar results show for other major carriers, suggesting effect of general backlash against managed care.
- Most of the erosion has gone to "neutral" position.
- Upward blip in "negative" noted in 2007 pretest. Returned to 2005 levels by the time of the posttest.

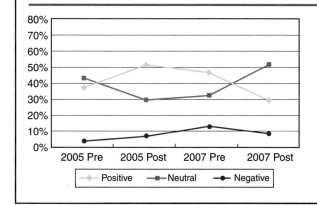

Consumers: Impression of TouchWell

- Steady downward trend in "positive" ratings from consumers since the 2005 posttest.
- Among major carriers, only BCBS has shown a slight increase.
- Managed care backlash evident in the results.

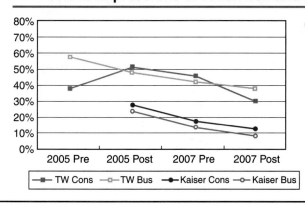

Consumers and Business Decision Makers: Positive Impressions of TouchWell and Kaiser

- Though both show a declining trend, TouchWell leads Kaiser by a wide margin among both consumers and business decision makers.

Questions

1. Comment on the general quality of the presentation. Are the slides easy to understand? Do they effectively convey key information? What suggestions would you have for improving this presentation?

2. Comment on the content of the slides regarding unaided plan awareness for both consumers and business decision makers. What are the implications for TouchWell?

3. What do the slides show with respect to the image or impressions that consumers and business decision makers have regarding HMOs? How have these impressions changed over time? What are the major reasons for negative impressions of HMOs among business decision makers and consumers?

4. What has happened to TouchWell's image over the four waves of research? How do these changes differ for business decision makers and consumers?

Managing Marketing Research

LEARNING OBJECTIVES

→ **1.** To understand what clients want from a marketing research supplier or department.

→ **2.** To learn about managing a marketing research supplier organization.

→ **3.** To become familiar with marketing research outsourcing.

→ **4.** To gain insights into the unique management issues of managing a corporate marketing research department.

→ **5.** To see what marketing research departments are doing to gain a more strategic role in the corporation.

→ **6.** To examine how corporations are measuring the contribution of marketing research to the organization.

The marketing research industry is going through interesting times. Large multinational research firms are growing by acquisition and organic growth, marketers are challenging their research partners to provide more value, the Internet and digital innovations continue to transform the marketplace, and new research technologies are being developed and commercialized. A study of 249 marketing research professionals found respondents claiming that these are exciting times but also challenging times.[1] They predict that the future of the marketing research profession will be driven more by a combination of creativity and technical capability. This means that the industry must attract managers with unique skill sets to survive and grow in this environment.

A second survey of 512 research professionals conducted by Rockhopper Research of Summit, New Jersey, identified a number of problems faced by the industry today:

- 73 percent felt that research is becoming commoditized and clients are less willing to pay for quality.
- 70 percent said clients are demanding shorter time lines for projects and faster delivery of findings.
- 63 percent agreed that nonresearcher management are conducting their own surveys on the Web.
- 45 percent foresaw less demand for primary research, thanks to managers who think they can learn anything they need by going online.[2]

We will examine how research managers on both the supplier side and in the corporate research departments are meeting the challenges and opportunities in today's business environment.

Consolidating the Number of Acceptable Suppliers

Beginning in 2010, and continuing today, research clients are reducing their supplier lists, constantly reviewing contracts to see which ones can be eliminated, amended, or terminated. The key to staying on the acceptable vendor lists, according to research buyers, is in the contribution a supplier makes to the company. This means understanding the clients' industry, tracking industry trends, and customizing their offerings to meet the clients' unique needs.[3]

Marketing Research Supplier Management

What Do Clients Want?

Managing a marketing research supplier organization involves understanding what clients want and expect, maintaining good communications with the client, effectively managing the research process, good time management, cost management, and client profitability management. If a marketing research department in a large organization is conducting its own research, then it will also face these same managerial issues. If it farms out its research, then good management requires selecting the right vendor. A research department must also try to become less of an "order-taker" and play a greater role in the marketing decision-making process within the organization.

Market Directions, a marketing research firm in Kansas City, Missouri, asked marketing research clients across the United States to rate the importance of several statements about research companies and research departments. Replies from a wide range of industries are summarized in the following top-10 list:

1. Maintains client confidentiality.
2. Is honest.

3. Is punctual.

4. Is flexible.

5. Delivers against project specifications.

6. Provides high-quality output.

7. Is responsive to the client's needs.

8. Has high quality-control standards.

9. Is customer-oriented in interactions with client.

10. Keeps the client informed throughout a project.[4]

The two most important factors, confidentiality and honesty, are ethical issues, which were covered earlier in the text. The remaining issues relate to managing the research function and maintaining good communication.

FROM THE FRONT LINE

Making Difficult Clients Happy

Tammy Austin, VP Marketing, DSS Research

It is a gratifying process to work with clients, most of them. Dealing with difficult clients is stressful, but rewarding when handled properly. The practices I follow have worked for me and can work for you in turning potentially disastrous projects into successful ones.

- **Listen.** Listen carefully to your client about the project. This allows you to identify client needs and understand their objectives. If necessary, ask questions calmly and pay attention to their answer. Recognizing different viewpoints will often prevent any aggressive conduct from a client.

- **Keep detailed notes.** Document all specifications and milestones for both parties, so everything is detailed in writing and can be used later as a reference. Keep detailed records of all communication with difficult clients and steps taken to address their concerns. Write an action plan to prevent any future issues or misunderstandings. Maintain a log of items to be addressed (based on the schedule and ad hoc client requests) and who should deal with them and by when. Competent record keeping is critical in keeping the client focused, and it helps you address any unanticipated issues. Depending on the project, hold weekly or monthly review meetings of the issues log (these can be conference calls) to keep the communication lines open and the project on track.

- **Be flexible** You may have to compromise to work out satisfying outcomes for your client.

- **Take the client's point of view.** Be proactive and focus on client needs. Try to see things from their point of view and speak their language. Using procedural/methodological terminology can be confusing to clients and can interfere with good communication.

- **Solve problems.** Don't blame the client; look for solutions. The ultimate priority is to agree on a mutually beneficial solution rather than win an argument.

Follow up. Follow up on problem resolution to make sure the client is content. Even if you do not want repeat business from this client, you don't want them to have negative feelings toward your company. The marketing research industry is small and problems left unsolved or solved unprofessionally can damage your company's reputation.

A survey of client firms found a generally high level of satisfaction with research suppliers (4.08 on a 5-point scale).[5] Clients were most satisfied with data quality and on-time delivery. Relative cost had the lowest average score. Three suppliers consistently score well in this annual survey. They are the Cincinnati-based firms, Directions Research and Burke, Inc., as well as Syracuse, New York-based KS&R.

Communication

The key to good supplier–client relations is excellent communication. Every project should have a liaison who serves as a communication link between the supplier and the client. In large firms, this individual may be an account executive or a project manager, while in small firms, he or she may be an owner or a partner. But whatever the job title, the liaison must communicate accurately, honestly, and frequently with the client.

Before a project begins, the communication liaison should go over the project objectives, methodology, and timing with the client to make certain that there are no misunderstandings. The client should then sign off on the questionnaire, thereby agreeing that the questionnaire is sufficient to gather the raw data needed to accomplish the research objectives.

John Colias, vice president of MARC Research, says the following about communication between a research supplier and its client:

When a company hires a market research firm to design a study, the supplier must operate as part of the team of researchers and marketers. To be an effective member of the team, the supplier must also intimately understand the marketing questions. This understanding results from interactive dialogue among the researcher, marketer, and the supplier about the marketing questions and business decisions. Such a dialogue crystallizes the research objectives into concrete deliverables that directly influence business decisions.[6]

The liaison must ascertain how often the client wants progress reports. At a minimum, these reports should be issued weekly. The report should cover the status of the project, unusual problems encountered, and, if it is a cost-plus project, expenses incurred to date. *Cost-plus* refers to actual costs plus an additional markup to cover overhead. Cost-plus projects are typically found in situations where a research department of a large corporation, such as Ford Motors, conducts a project for another department.

The Key Role of the Project Manager. Because a majority of all research projects are conducted by relatively large research supplier firms, most research clients interact with a project manager and not a company owner. Thus, to the research client, the project manager is the supplier. The best project director helps the client define the research objectives and research design, executes the project flawlessly, monitors the project closely, delivers beyond expectations, and provides insights about the findings.

The project directors that a client wants to use over and over again are those whom the client doesn't have to worry about. This type of project director understands all aspects of the research process, is familiar with the project's objectives, and ensures that the outcome will be above expectations. The client may find out about problems that arise during the project but knows the project director will fix them. The project director provides a safety net; the client is assured that at the end of the project there will be excellence, not disaster. Project directors of this caliber raise the bar for other market research suppliers.[7]

On the other hand, a poor project director can result in a supplier being dropped from the acceptable vendor list. Actions that can destroy a supplier–client relationship are as follows:

■ The project director is never around to take calls; he or she delegates everything to a junior person who can't answer questions or solve problems.

■ The project director does not report problems that occur during the project, and the client is surprised when they finally erupt at the end.

■ Projects consistently come in late or over budget with no advance notice.[8]

Managing the Research Process

Research management has seven important goals beyond excellent communication: building an effective organization, assurance of data quality, adherence to time schedules, cost control, client profitability management, and staff management and development.

Organizing the Supplier Firm
Traditionally, most marketing research firms were organized around functions. Large suppliers, for example, may have separate departments for sampling, questionnaire programming, field, coding, tabulation, statistics, and sales. Even the client service staff may be separate from those who manage projects and write questionnaires and reports. Each of these departments has a head who is expert in the functions of that department and manages work assignments within the department. Projects flow from department to department.

A functional form of organization allows technical people to perform backroom tasks such as programming and data analysis and the "people people" to handle project management and client contact. It provides for knowledgeable supervision, so that, for example, beginners in sample design are working under the direction of veteran experts. It permits the development of good work processes and quality standards, so that tasks are performed consistently. It lets the difficulty of a given project be matched with the skill of the person doing it, so that routine work is given to junior staff and the most complex tasks are reserved for the expert. This matching of work and skill levels leads to happier staff and lower project costs.

Yet functional organizations are not without their problems. Department staff can become focused on the execution of their task, to the detriment of the whole process and the client. Departmental standards and scheduling policies may take on lives of their own, optimizing the efficiency and quality of a department's work but making timely completion of the whole project difficult. By becoming removed from client contact, departments can become inwardly oriented, viewing clients as problems rather than the source of their livelihood. Interdepartmental communication and scheduling can become time-consuming and flawed, as project managers or operations schedulers negotiate each project's schedule with a series of independent department heads. Each department may feel that it is performing perfectly, yet the whole process viewed from the outside can seem rigid, bureaucratic, and ineffective.

In response to problems like these, some companies are organizing by teams. They are breaking up functional departments and organizing their staff into units based around client groups or research types. These teams include people with all or most of the skills necessary to complete a study from beginning to end. A typical team might include several client service/ project management people, a field director, a questionnaire programmer, and a tab specwriter. Staff are frequently cross-trained in multiple functions. The team is almost always headed by a senior staff member with a client service or project management background.

There are many variations on this theme. Within the teams, work may remain specialized (the specwriter does the tables), or there can be extensive cross-training (everyone does tables). Highly specialized functions (such as statistical analysis) that are carried out by one or two experts may remain as functional departments, available to all. A hybrid approach is also possible, where some functions are moved within the teams, while others (such as field management) remain as separate departments.

Because each client group controls its own resources, scheduling and communication are easier. With no department heads or central scheduling to go through, the group head directly prioritizes the work of everyone working on his or her projects.

> ➤ **research management**
> Overseeing the development of excellent communication systems, data quality, time schedules, cost controls, client profitability, and staff development.

PRACTICING MARKETING RESEARCH

Doing High-Quality Work—On Time

Here are seven tips on time management for marketing management project research directors.

Manage expectations. Most job descriptions for project directors mention writing skills, facility with mathematics, organizational ability, and experience with presentations, but managing expectations may be the most critical skill to master. If you're pretty sure that the work will be done by Thursday, don't say you're "shooting for Wednesday." You're better off promising Friday and giving yourself a chance to be a hero.

Think about priorities. When the client has a crisis, sometimes you just have to drop everything and help out. Clients are, after all, the ones paying our salaries. Even without a crisis, however, it doesn't hurt to think about your priorities. The time-management books suggest concentrating on the most important tasks only and ignoring the others until they too join the "most important" list. If you don't mind a messy desk, this is pretty good advice.

Think about leverage. What if the client is not in crisis mode, but you still have 10 things to do? Concentrate first on the tasks that require contributions from others. If the interviewers are waiting for your briefing or the data processing people are waiting for your codes, then everyone's work is backing up.

Provide regular updates. It is amazing how many games of voice-mail tag can be avoided by filling out a simple form. Set up a form that you can fax or e-mail every day explaining how many interviews have been finished, where the incidence is coming out, how you are doing on interview length, and whatever other facts your client requires. If you are working with 10 field services on a study, get them to fill out update forms too—this saves you another 10 calls a day.

Be on the lookout for problems. A statistician I worked with used to say, "All lists are bad." Actually, he used a stronger term—"the trick is to find out why this particular list is bad."

Project directing is problem solving. Incidence estimates will be off, questionnaires will be too long, respondents will be uncooperative, and lists will be, uh, bad. Spending a little extra time on instructions, briefings, and safety checks today will save a lot of extra work tomorrow.

When you discover a problem, let the client know quickly. You can stick a problem in a folder for a day or two, but it's not likely to solve itself. The sooner the client hears about the problem, the sooner he or she can adjust schedules or budgets. In my experience, you can almost always go back to a client—once—to discuss changes in specifications, schedules, and budgets. But you need to bring these issues up early, when your client still has some flexibility. Surprises at the 11th hour are both painful and time-consuming for everyone.

If you need to bring up a problem, don't be afraid to suggest some solutions as well. Suggesting solutions will help to solve the issue quickly and efficiently. As a general rule, the range of possible solutions is not hard to come up with. The following should cover about 80 percent of all possible problems:

- Order more sample.
- Change the screening criteria.
- Raise the incentives.
- Rebrief the interviewers.
- Reschedule the focus groups.
- Reduce the number of interviews.
- Lengthen the interviewing schedule.
- Increase the budget.

The challenge is in getting beyond the issue of who is to blame and determining which solution will work best this time.[9]

Questions

1. Would you like to be a project manager? Why or why not?

2. What do you think are the most important characteristics of a good project manager?

Technical and operations personnel become closer to clients and more aligned with their needs. By reducing the organizational distance between the client and these staff members, it is easier for them to appreciate the client's situation and focus on serving his or her needs.

Staff may develop more flexibility and broader skills. Cross-training and cross-assignment of work are easier when all the people involved report to the same person.[10]

Effective time management is becoming increasingly important in all aspects of professional life. One requirement of research management is to keep a project on the schedule specified by the client.

Data Quality Management   Perhaps the most important objective of research management is to ensure the quality or integrity of the data produced by the research process. You have probably heard announcers on television say, "The poll had a margin of error of 3 percent." Some problems and implicit assumptions are associated with this statement. First, you learned in the discussion of sampling error in Chapter 13 that this statement is missing an associated level of confidence. In other words, how confident are the pollsters that the poll has a margin of error of 3 percent? Are they 68.26 percent confident, 95.44 percent confident, 99.74 percent confident, or confident at some other level? Second, this statement does not make clear that the margin of error applies only to *random sampling error*. The implicit, or unstated, assumption is that there are no other sources of error, that all other sources of error have been effectively dealt with by the research design and procedures, or that all other sources of error have been effectively randomized by taking summary measures across the entire sample. By definition, error is random when there are just as many errors in one direction as in the other direction, leaving overall measures, such as averages, unaffected. Marketing research managers can help assure high-quality data by having policies and procedures in place to minimize sources of error (see Chapter 6).

A recent Harris poll found that there are a lot of misperceptions about error out there. After surveying 1,052 U.S. adults, Harris reported the following:

- Fifty-two percent of all adults believe, wrongly, that statements about "the margin of error being plus or minus 3 percent" mean that "all of the results of the survey are accurate to within a maximum of 3 percent given all types of error."

- A 66 percent majority of adults believe, wrongly, that the phrase "margin of error" includes calculation of errors caused by "how the questions are worded."

- Large minorities believe, wrongly, that the calculation of the margin of error includes errors in developing a representative base or weighting errors (45 percent), mistakes made by interviewers (45 percent), and errors because of where the questions are placed in the survey (40 percent).

- Only 12 percent of the public agrees that the words "margin of error" should only address one specific source of error, sampling error—as they almost always do.

A 56 percent majority believes that statements about margin of error do not make it clear that this calculation excludes all sources of error except for sampling error for a pure random sample.[11]

Marketing researchers must not only attempt to minimize error, but also do a better job of explaining the term *margin of error*. Simply saying "a survey statistic has a margin of error of plus or minus 3 percent" gives the typical audience a false impression of accuracy. Readers should be informed of other possible sources of error, such as interviewer bias or question wording, even if it is not feasible or practical to calculate these errors.

Also, managers must have in place procedures to ensure the careful proofing of all text, charts, and graphs in written reports and other communications provided to the client. Mistakes may mislead a client into making the wrong decision. Suppose the data suggest purchase intent at 18 percent, but the report shows 81 percent; this typographical mistake could easily lead to an incorrect decision. If the client finds even small mistakes, the credibility of the researcher and all of the research findings may be brought into serious question. The rule of thumb is to never provide information to the client that has not been very carefully checked.

Time Management   A second goal of research management is to keep the project on schedule. Time management is important in marketing research because clients often have a specified time schedule that they must meet. For example, it may be absolutely imperative that the research results be available on March 1 so that they can be presented at the quarterly meeting of the new product committee. The findings will affect whether the test product will receive additional funding for development.

Two problems that can play havoc with time schedules are inaccuracies in estimates of the incidence rate and the interview length. A lower-than-expected incidence rate will require more interviewing resources than originally planned to get the job done on time. If the research manager does not have idle resources to devote to the project, then it will take longer to complete. The same is true for a longer-than-anticipated interview.

Recall that the *incidence rate* is the percentage of persons or households out of the general population that fit the qualifications to be interviewed in a particular study. Often, estimates of incidence rate are based not on hard-and-fast data but on data that are incomplete, relatively inaccurate, or dated. Incidence rate problems can not only increase the amount of time required to complete the sample for the project but also negatively affect the costs of the data-collection phase of the research.

The project manager must have early information regarding whether or not a project can be completed on time. If a problem exists, the manager must first determine whether anything can be done to speed up the process. Perhaps training additional interviewers would help expedite completion of the survey. A second option might be to increase the incentive to complete an online survey. The researcher must inform the client that the project is going to take longer than expected. The researcher can then explore with the client whether a time extension is possible or what changes the client might be willing to make to get the project completed on the original time schedule. For example, the client might be willing to reduce the total sample size or shorten the length of the interview by eliminating questions that are judged to be less critical. Thus, it is very important that the system be structured so that both the researcher and the client are alerted to potential problems within the first few days of the project.

Time management, like cost control, requires that systems be put in place to inform management as to whether or not the project is on schedule. Policies and procedures must be established to efficiently and quickly solve schedule problems and promptly notify the client about the problem and potential solutions. In the Practicing Marketing Research feature on page 612, Joshua Libresco, executive vice president of OSR Group, a marketing research firm in San Rafael, California, offers several tips on how overworked marketing research project directors can better manage their time and still provide high-quality work.

Cost Management   In comparison to data quality and time management, cost management is straightforward. All it requires is adherence to good business practices, such as procedures for cost tracking and control. In particular, good procedures for cost control include the following elements:

- Systems that accurately capture data collection and other costs associated with the project on a daily basis.
- Daily reporting of costs to the communication liaison. Ideally, reports should show actual costs in relation to budget.

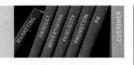

PRACTICING MARKETING RESEARCH

Managing a Marketing Research Firm for Profitability

Good financial systems are very helpful in managing for profitability, but they aren't sufficient. Even more important, is business focus. There are some very profitable businesses in this industry that have fairly basic financial information, and many companies with extensive financial data and even more extensive losses. The key is what you do with the information you have.

Owners of most profitable research companies manage them for profit. That doesn't mean they are bad researchers, or ruthless, or cheap. It does mean that the CEO or partners recognize that they are running a business first and foremost. How does this show?

■ They hold senior staff accountable for project or account profitability in a firm but fair way.

■ They accept unfavorable financial information and act on it, rather than trying to argue it away or change the metric so that unprofitable activity looks profitable.

■ They are willing to make the hard decisions to let people go who can't deliver acceptable sales or manage a study on budget. They will make the even harder decision to exit a client relationship that can't be made profitable rather than hanging on forever in hope.

■ They know what their findings and recommendations are worth to clients, and price to that value rather than looking solely at cost.

■ They believe in the value of their company's work and the fairness of its prices, and don't back down quickly when faced with price pressure.[12]

■ Policies and practices in the research organization that require the liaison to communicate the budget picture to clients and to senior managers at the research company.

■ Policies and practices that quickly identify overbudget situations and then find causes and seek solutions.

If the project is overbudget because the client provided information that proved to be erroneous (for example, incidence rate, interview length), then it is imperative that the client be offered options early in the process: a higher cost, smaller sample size, shorter interview, or some combination of these. If the firm waits until the project is complete to communicate this problem to the client, the client is likely to say, "You should have told me sooner—there is nothing I can do now." In this situation, the firm will probably have to swallow the cost overrun.

Michael Mitrano, a partner in Transition Strategies Corporation, a management consulting firm, discusses managing a marketing research firm for profitability in the Practicing Marketing Research feature above.

Outsourcing and Insourcing. From the early 2000s until 2009, the hot trend was outsourcing. By 2010, the tide had turned toward insourcing. The term **outsourcing** as used in this text is having personnel in another country perform some, or all, of the functions involved in a marketing research project. When a research firm sets up a wholly-owned foreign subsidiary, it is called **captive outsourcing**. Simple outsourcing is where a

> **outsourcing**
> Having personnel in another country perform some, or all, of the functions involved in a marketing research project.

> **captive outsourcing**
> When a research firm creates a wholly-owned foreign facility for outsourcing.

domestic research company enters into a relationship with a foreign company that provides a variety of marketing research functions. For example, Cross-Tab Services of Mumbai, India, offers online survey programming, data processing, data analysis, and other services. Other services that may be outsourced are data management and panel management. A number of issues need to be considered when one is outsourcing, as shown in Exhibit 20.1.

Recently, firms (mostly on the client side), have moved to insourcing as a way to cut costs. Rather than use suppliers, they are conducting online surveys themselves. It is a means of generating more research insights with a smaller budget. This is a boon for firms like ConfirmIT which offer a software platform that enables suppliers and research clients to create and deliver surveys, collect data, and prepare and share detailed analysis. MarketSight and Vovici offer much the same thing with slightly different twists. As insourcing accelerates, online research tool vendors should experience annual growth rates of 15 to 20 percent.[13] Insourcing began with routine studies of customers and some qualitative research. It is now shifting to online marketing research communities and enterprise customer satisfaction and loyalty feedback management.

Client Profitability Management

While marketing research departments in large companies may be able to focus on doing "on-demand" projects for internal clients, marketing research suppliers have to think about profitability. The old adage that 20 percent of the clients generate 80 percent of the profits is often true.

Custom Research Incorporated (CRI), of Minneapolis, realized that it had too many clients—or too few good ones.[14] The company divided its clients into four categories based on the client's perceived value to CRI's bottom line (see Exhibit 20.2). Only 10 of

EXHIBIT 20.1	Outsourcing Issues
Issues	**Management Strategies**
Confidentiality	Proper confidentiality and data security agreements need to be signed with third-party providers and senior personnel of captive centers. Frequent audits are also recommended to ensure compliance.
Infrastructure	It is important that the destination country and the city selected within the country have access to required infrastructure such as power, bandwidth, good connectivity through airports, hotel facilities for visits by customer's team, and of course talented workers.
Quality of deliverables	Careful documentation is important for processes executed in any location, but they are doubly important in the case of offshore outsourcing. Also, proper systems and protocols must be laid down for communication between teams in the client country and in the vendor country.
Domain knowledge	It is important to ensure that the senior members of the team in the offshore location have a strong domain understanding of market research and do not have just an IT or data processing background.
Cultural issues	It is necessary to understand the culture of the offshore location and the sensitivities of the people. Cultural misunderstandings can cause misgivings and can affect the quality of work.
Job losses in the client country and associated negative publicity for the agency	Good people can be retained and be provided jobs in other roles in the same agency in order to fuel the growth that will result from the cost savings realized. It is important to have a proper PR initiative to explain the benefits of offshoring to the economy of the client country. (Economic studies have shown that in the long term offshoring leads to greater benefits for the economy of the client country and actually creates more jobs.)
Employee liability	This risk is not an issue if one outsources to third-party providers. If one is going the captive route, then it is important to carefully study the employment laws of the destination country to ensure no legal conflicts.

Source: Ashwin Mittal and Kedar Sohoni, "A Brief Guide to Oursourcing," *Quirk's Marketing Research Review* (November 2005), p. 70.

Exhibit 20.2

CRI's Client Profitability Analysis

HIGH/LOW
About half of these customers were new ones that CRI figured would become more profitable over time. The other half were right on the line—on the verge of high/high.

HIGH/HIGH
At the top: These customers had pared down their suppliers and clearly valued an ongoing relationship with CRI. They accounted for 29% of sales.

HIGH VOLUME LOW MARGIN	HIGH VOLUME HIGH MARGIN
11 CUSTOMERS	**10** CUSTOMERS
101 CUSTOMERS LOW VOLUME LOW MARGIN	**35** CUSTOMERS LOW VOLUME HIGH MARGIN

LOW/LOW
CRI once believed it could make many of these customers more loyal, but time revealed that this group wanted to work with various suppliers.

LOW/HIGH
These were small customers who were very profitable. Was there more potential for sales in this group?

CRI's 157 customers fell into the most desirable category (generating a high dollar volume and a high profit margin). Another 101 customers contributed very little to the top or bottom line. In short, CRI was spending too much time and too many valuable employee resources on too many unprofitable customers.

In assessing which customers to keep, CRI calculated the profit for each one by subtracting all direct costs and selling expenses from the total revenues brought into CRI by that customer for the year. That is, CRI asked, "What costs would we not incur if this customer went away?" The cutoff points for high and low scores were purely subjective; they corresponded to CRI's goals for profit volume and profit margin. CRI management decided that it had to systematically drop a large number of old customers and carefully screen potential new customers. CRI's screening questions for new customers are shown in Exhibit 20.3.

Using the customer's analysis, CRI went from 157 customers and $11 million in revenue to 78 customers and $30 million in revenue. Most importantly, profits more than doubled. Managers had calculated they'd need to reap about 20 to 30 percent more business from some two dozen companies to help make up for the roughly 100 customers they planned to "let go" within 2 years. This was accomplished by building a close personal relationship with the clients that remained. The process involved CRI's researching the industry, the client company, and its research personnel to fully understand the client's needs. For each client, CRI created a Surprise and Delight plan to deliver a "value-added" bonus to the client. For example, Dow Brands received some complimentary software that CRI knew the company needed. This one-on-one relationship marketing has been the key to CRI's success.

Staff Management and Development

The primary asset of any marketing research firm is its people. Proprietary techniques and models can help differentiate a marketing research company, but eventually its success depends on the professional nature of its staff and their determination to deliver a

EXHIBIT 20.3	Screening Questions Used by CRI and the Rationale for Each Question
Question	**Rationale**
How did you hear about us?	A bad answer: "I found you in the Yellow Pages." Unlike many companies, CRI doesn't ask this question so that it can decide how to divvy up the marketing dollars. "If someone finds us in the Yellow Pages, they have no reason to use us over anyone else," CRI cofounder Judy Corson explains. A good answer: "A colleague of mine worked with you at another company."
What kind of work is it (in terms of industry or scope)?	More than anything, the answer reveals whether the caller is trying to price a quick, one-time project or one that's totally outside CRI's realm. If so, the caller is referred to an indirect competitor.
What's your budget?	That's akin to asking someone how much money he or she makes, but the prospect's response to a ballpark guess on the cost of the project helps CRI ascertain what the client has in mind.
What are your decision criteria?	CRI knows that it doesn't fare well in blind bidding or in drawn-out, committee-style decisions, so it's interested in dealing with callers who have some level of decision-making power—and assiduously avoids getting involved in anything that smells like a bidding war.
Whom are we competing against for your business?	CRI likes to hear the names of its chief rivals, a half-dozen large companies, including the M/A/R/C Group, Market Facts, and Burke Marketing Research.
Why are you thinking of switching?	"There's a two-edged sword here," explains cofounder Jeff Pope. "Clients that are hard to break into are better because they don't switch too easily. But you need a way to get in—so a legitimate need for a new supplier is OK." Each month only 2 or 3 of 20 to 30 callers answer enough questions correctly to warrant more attention. So why spend time with the rest? "Do unto others. . . . You never know where people will go."

Source: Susan Greco, "Choose or Lose," *INC.* (December 1998), pp. 57–59, 62–66.

quality product. Consequently, recruiting and retaining a competent, enthusiastic staff are crucial and constant management challenges.

Kathleen Knight is president and CEO of BAIGlobal, Incorporated, a Tarrytown, New York, marketing research firm. She offers several suggestions for staff development in a research firm:

1. *Create an environment that encourages risk taking, experimentation, and responsibility.* The benefits to the research firm, such as new service development, new techniques, and business growth, outweigh any potential risks. However, employees need to feel that they will be supported in taking risks. New ideas and different business approaches need to be treated with respect and given room to develop.

2. *Foster recognition and accountability.* Recognize good effort and reward it. One of the best forms of reward is visibility within the company. Make sure that everyone knows when an outstanding job was done and that excellence matters.

3. *Provide job autonomy within a certain structure.* Marketing research is a technical science, and the numbers have to add up. But it also is a business, and projects have to generate money to pay the bills. Within these boundaries, there are many different ways to get the job done. Let employees put their personal stamp on a project and they will feel like true partners in their work.

4. *Attract and support people with entrepreneurial attitudes.* Set business goals and management parameters; then let the staff determine the path to take to get the job done. This allows each person to leverage his or her own abilities and achieve the highest level of success.

5. *Connect rewards to a business result.* Providing open financial data to researchers seems to create a business consciousness that is exciting for all. Often, very talented researchers know little about the financial dynamics of the industry. They welcome the chance to learn and thus become more accountable for bottom-line results.

FROM THE FRONT LINE

10 Tips for a Winning Proposal

Emily Waters and Sarah Beck both Account Executives DSS Research

A well-crafted proposal will help you generate more business and win new clients. Keep these tips in mind when responding to Requests for Proposal (RFPs):

1. **Follow all instructions provided in the RFP.** This includes information requests, page length guidelines, formatting instructions and labeling. Closely following instructions demonstrates your attention to detail, while failure to comply with instructions can result in disqualification of your proposal.

2. **Fully answer all of the questions asked, but don't go overboard providing extraneous information.** Your responses should be clear and concise.

3. **Remember to "sell" your company.** Be sure to stress the key reasons why potential clients should choose you. What differentiates your company from the rest? Clients want to avoid making risky decisions, so take the opportunity to highlight why you're the right choice.

4. **Avoid submitting a "stock" proposal.** There will often be opportunities to borrow from your past proposals, but customize your content enough to avoid delivering a generic, "cookie cutter" proposal.

5. **Know your audience.** Proposals prepared for new clients are often more detailed than those for existing clients who are already familiar with your company. If you are given the evaluation criteria that will be most important to your audience, tailor your proposal toward those areas.

6. **Know how much contact is appropriate and allowed.** In some cases, you will be required to work through a designated contact and communication with others will be prohibited. However, if the RFP process is less structured, you may be allowed to have direct contact with decision makers. In this case, you have a valuable opportunity to influence the decision in your favor.

7. **Plan ahead!** Turnaround times for proposals are often short. Review the RFP early and compile a list of questions for your potential client. Most RFPs provide a deadline for submitting your questions, so you'll only get one shot at having them answered. If you will also require information from sub-contractors or colleagues to complete the response, request that information as early as possible to avoid a last minute rush.

8. **Clearly outline your assumptions about project specifications and pricing.** You will rarely be given every piece of information you need to price a project, so you'll need to make some assumptions. Use your experience and available data from similar projects to make reasonable assumptions. Don't be afraid to ask your colleagues for their opinions if you lack significant experience with the type of project on which you're bidding. Be sure to clearly state all assumptions in your proposal.

9. **Only propose an alternative solution when you are asked for one.** If you are asked to provide alternative solutions or suggestions, by all means, provide them. But if you're not specifically asked to change the RFP specifications, stick to what you're asked for.

10. **Submit your response on time!** Late proposals are generally not considered. Be sure to submit your response on time or all of your hard work will be wasted! If you are required to submit hard copies, plan ahead to be sure they arrive at their destination on time.

6. *Open your financial books.* Research firms can provide senior employees with full financial information to let them know how well they are doing across the months and years. The bottom line is the best aggregate measure of performance—individually, as a group, and as a firm. Opening the books establishes a common mission and goal across the organization.

7. *Offer diversity within your organization.* It's fun and exciting to learn new products, serve new clients, and work with a new research team. A chance at a new position is often the spark someone needs to really do well within a firm. And the possibility of this kind of job change seems to add to the satisfaction that employees feel. If you pay attention to individuals and create a career path across disciplines within your organization, it's more likely that talented researchers will stay.

8. *Provide clear promotional paths.* Employees like to know how they can advance and want to feel some control over their careers. Clear criteria and expectations go a long way toward helping researchers feel comfortable. In the marketing research business, the best training is as an apprentice, working with senior researchers doing interesting work. Talented people will grow and prosper where the expectations are that senior managers will be mentors, that junior staff will learn, and that excellent work produced together will lead to everyone's career advancement.[15]

Managing a Marketing Research Department

A manager of a marketing research department within a corporation faces a different set of issues from a research supplier. Among these issues are effective spending of the research budget, prioritizing projects for the corporation, retaining skilled staff, selecting the right research suppliers, moving the marketing research function to a more strategic role in the firm, and measuring return on investment for marketing research.

Allocating the Research Department Budget[16]

No matter who controls the research project budget, it's important to spend money and (most importantly) research staff time wisely. That is especially important when the clients (new-product development managers or brand managers) fund each project and cannot understand why the marketing research department doesn't have the staff time to do whatever they want. In that case, many research heads are learning how to prioritize projects. There are several effective ways to accomplish that.

A research study found that only about 20 percent of research projects are focused on strategically important issues. The other 80 percent of projects are focused on tactical issues, such as setting prices, advertising, distributing products, or adding new features to existing products. Researchers and clients agree that they would prefer to spend more time on the strategic issues, such as identifying promising new markets or developing new products and services.[17]

For example, one research group took it upon itself to improve its firm's new-product development process by bringing together experts from marketing research, marketing, research and development, manufacturing, and sales to design a new process.

Another research group head learned to facilitate strategic planning (an ad hoc effort in her firm), so that she could help her executive team plan when cross-functional action was needed.

Several research heads said that they try to meet with their clients annually before budgeting season begins to talk about what research issues will be most important to clients in the coming year. Both parties then agree on the vital projects for the coming year and on how much time or money to allocate to them. While everyone admits that unforeseen circumstances almost always force the plans to be altered, having an annual plan enables a manager to adapt quickly and be flexible.

Many department heads say that they believe it's important for the research group to have a discretionary budget for important projects. That is considered especially important if research projects are usually funded by the clients. One new director of research used the discretionary budget to study why demand for his organization's main product appeared to be dropping in the face of a changing industry. Another researcher paid for a project on store designs because he felt that the designs were probably holding back sales—and he was right. Still another group paid to learn scenario planning and used it to help clients pick options for new-product testing.

Prioritizing Projects Estimating the financial return from a research project is a great way to rationalize spending across projects because it provides a quantitative methodology that helps clients identify "must-have" versus "nice-to-have" projects. It is not only an effective way of turning away less important work; it also helps strengthen relations with clients because it shows that researchers are thinking about their bottom line, too. We will present a way to measure return on investment (ROI) for marketing research, created by research consultants Diane Schmalensee and A. Dawn Lesh, later in the chapter.

Estimating the ROI for a given project has several advantages. First, estimating the expected returns on research before beginning work may help: Focus the research on important research objectives and clarify client needs; differentiate projects that are likely to be implemented (and thus have a higher ROI) from those that may not lead to action; clarify how much money and time it is worth spending on a project given its expected financial payoff.

Second, measuring the payoff of research does not end during the planning stages. Ideally, researchers check back with their clients after the work is completed to validate the actual payoff. This permits researchers and clients to learn how accurate the original ROI estimate was as well as how to improve future estimates.

Finally, having ROI discussions with clients both before and after projects is a great way to show that the research function is a partner with its clients—sharing client objectives and spending research monies effectively. This process has the added benefit of allowing overworked research staff to shrink or delay less important research.

Retaining Skilled Staff When researchers are feeling overworked and finding it difficult to meet client needs without sacrificing their personal time needs, they begin to burn out and think about working elsewhere. Losing a skilled staff member can damage a research group. It means more work for the remaining staff members, and it can leave a hole in valuable client relationships. It is especially important to recognize and reward hard-working staff members. How can this be done? Research shows that staff members of marketing research departments value doing interesting and fulfilling work, getting recognition for a job well done, and earning adequate pay.[18] What is adequate pay? A 2010 client-side salary survey shows average compensation by job title in Exhibit 20.4.

A few techniques for retaining key research staff are as follows:

1. *Conduct regular performance reviews that give continuing feedback on a job well done*—or offer ways to improve. Many staff members think their bosses play favorites during performance reviews. So department heads try to use clear performance criteria for each position and offer objective appraisals for everyone.

EXHIBIT 20.4	Client-Side Researchers' Compensation		
Job Title	**Base**	**Bonus**	**Total**
Senior Vice President or Vice President	$152,841	$27,341	$180,182
Market Research Director/Senior Direction	$127,229	$20,187	$147,416
Market Research Manager	$92,612	$9,144	$101,756
Account Executive/Manager	$69,000	$4,500	$73,500
Customer Insights Manager	$93,612	$7,621	$101,241
Director of Marketing	$108,611	$6,889	$115,500
Brand Manager or Product Manager	$85,286	$3,857	$89,143
Project Manager	$76,520	$11,440	$87,960
Senior Research Analyst	$77,916	$5,133	$83,048
Research Analyst	$54,923	$3,631	$58,554
Statistician	$65,750	$3,750	$69,500
Research Assistant	$42,000	$667	$42,667
Sales/Account Representative	$67,500	$38,333	$105,833

Source: Joseph Rydholm, "Stable Earnings, Wandering Eye?" *Quirk's Marketing Research Review,* July 2010, p. 30.

2. *Offer public recognition for great work.* Some groups mention great work during staff meetings; post client comments on a "wall of fame" in the department; have bosses send personal letters to staff members at home, praising their work; hold pizza parties for teams that have performed "above and beyond"; or simply have the head of the department stop by a staff member's office to offer congratulations and thanks.

3. *Give differential pay raises that recognize superior performance.* While across-the-board, uniform pay increases are often used (because they are the easiest to administer), they do not recognize the high performers—and they allow the lower performers to believe they are doing adequate work.

4. *Vary the work.* In order to keep everyone interested, some research groups identify one-off projects and then allow staff members to volunteer for them. Examples of special projects could include a project that will feed into the firm's strategic plans, formation of a high-visibility cross-functional team, or a project that uses a new technique or addresses an unusually interesting topic.[19]

Bonnie Eisenfeld, an independent marketing research consultant, talks about some nonquantitative skill aspects of an ideal marketing research job seeker in the following Practicing Marketing Research box.

Selecting the Right Marketing Research Suppliers

Once the nature, scope, and objectives of the project have been determined, the next step is to assess the capabilities of alternative suppliers. Some research vendors have a particular area of specialization. Some firms specialize in advertising or customer satisfaction research, while others are devoted to a particular technique (for example, conjoint analysis or market segmentation) or data-collection method (for example, mall intercepts, mail surveys, or Internet panels).

PRACTICING MARKETING RESEARCH

Soft Skills of an Ideal Marketing Researcher

Ideal marketing researchers need good quantitative skills. More importantly in today's competitive and dynamic markets, new researchers need other skills and characteristics,

Lifelong Learners

The best researchers are avid readers, travelers, online searchers or news junkies—in short, lifelong learners. Their accumulated knowledge and skills are often applied in surprising ways. For example, analogies from evolutionary biology can help explain the competitive situation in a market.

Researchers are curious people. They want to know about human behavior, attitudes and opinions, and their underlying reasons and motivations. A curious person asks question, listens carefully to the answers, and probes for more information from respondents.

One test for curiosity in the hiring process is to observe how many questions the candidate asks in the interview, particularly questions on subjects other than compensation. However, watching a candidate conduct a research interview or focus group is the better test.

Adapted Easily

In addition to a solid academic background, successful hires must be able to adapt easily and understand that brevity is prized in the business world. New researchers have to get used to corporate deadlines and move faster, sometimes sacrificing methodological precision and sometimes arriving at conclusions with less-than-perfect data.

In addition to a broad educational background, I advise new entrants to get experience as an interviewer. There is no substitute for the learning you acquire from actually conducting an interview. It enhances your ability to write a real-life questionnaire that respondents will be willing to answer.

Act as a Partner

The in-house researcher is not just a messenger between corporate management and an outside vendor. Ideally, a researcher should act as a partner with the strategist or decision maker. He or she must understand the context and information needs of the business and, based on management's research objectives, help create questions and then collect data to answer the questions. Thus, every researcher should take advantage of opportunities for education and training offered by their organization to obtain the business knowledge necessary for context.[20]

Questions

1. What skills do you think are required to be a great marketing researcher?
2. Where would you rank communication skills on your list?

A research department manager should beware of firms committed to a particular technique and/or data-collection method, as they are more likely to "force" the department's research project into their particular model, rather than tailor the research to fit the specific needs of the research department's project.

Research department managers must consider the size of the firms in their decision. The size of the vendor is an extremely important decision criterion. It is important not to overwhelm a small firm with an enormous project, and, conversely, a small project may not get the proper attention at a large firm.

The general rule is to favor the smallest firm consistent with the scope of the project. However, any project that accounts for 30 percent or more of a marketing research supplier's annual revenues may be too large for that firm to handle effectively.

The research department manager should establish, upfront, the individual who will be managing the project. It should be determined in advance who would be responsible for the day-to-day management of the project. That is, will it be the person who "sold" the project or a project director hundreds of miles away? If the contact becomes unavailable, will competent support staff be available?

The research department manager needs to become acquainted with the backgrounds of the potential vendors. There are some general questions that every potential vendor should be asked to determine the stability of the company and its qualifications to complete the project in a satisfactory manner. These questions would include:

- How long has the vendor been in business?
- For what other companies has the vendor conducted research projects? Remember it is imperative to request references and check them for each firm.
- What are the academic backgrounds and experience of those persons who will be working on the project, that is, the project director, field director, data processing manager, and so forth? Does the composition of the project team strike the right balance between top-level management and technical researchers and analysts?
- Does the success of the project depend on the capabilities of a subcontractor? If the marketing research supplier will be subcontracting any elements of the project, it is important that the subcontractor and his or her qualifications be identified.

Also, the research manager should review the quality control standards of each potential vendor. The validity of the results of any research project is dependent on the quality control measures practiced by the vendor. For example, on telephone studies, what are the procedures with respect to callbacks, monitoring, and validation? It is prudent to avoid firms that do not follow generally accepted practices in their operations.

The reputations of the firms must be considered in the decision. Reputation is important, but a department should not pay a larger premium for it. However, some situations may require the services of a prestigious research firm because a company plans to publicize the results, or use them in advertisements, so having the best reputation available may actually be a good investment. For example, Dell touts its standings in J. D. Power Customer Satisfaction surveys.

Finally, a manager should avoid letting price be the sole determining factor in the selection. When reviewing proposals, price should be the last item to be considered.[21]

Today, many client companies are looking beyond traditional selection criteria and are seeking a partner as opposed to a research provider. "Suppliers should try to be better business consultants," partnering with buyers to get to know buyers' companies and industries thoroughly, says Beth Shriver, staff research manager at Akron, Ohio-based diversified energy company FirstEnergy Corporation. Through partnerships—rather than just supplier/buyer relationships—research vendors can help buyers make better use of the copious amounts of data that most companies already have in-house, Shriver says.[22]

Gala Amoroso, Marketing Research Director at McCormick & Company, the huge consumer packaged goods firm, claims she also wants closer relationships with her research suppliers. "A partner, to me, would be the difference between a company we call when we have a project . . . versus a company we talk to whether we have a project or not," she says. A partner-like supplier would move beyond filling McCormick's research needs to anticipate its needs, finding ways to mine insights from the company's existing data, and working with the company to unearth better and better insights, she says.[23]

Selecting the right supplier in the United States can be a difficult task. The problem expands exponentially in a developing country like Russia. The Russian market research industry is growing rapidly, driven both by domestic growth and the huge interest in the country by foreign inventors. In a country where market research was virtually nonexistent less than two decades ago, foreign and domestic research suppliers and clients are conducting large volumes of work aimed at helping new companies expand into Russia and established companies defend and extend their positions. Tatiana Klimenko, Manager of the Moscow research firm B2B Vector, and Matthew Harrison, Director of International Operations for B2B International, discuss selecting a research supplier in the following Global Research box.

GLOBAL RESEARCH

Picking a Russian Research Supplier

Business-to-business research represents a significant niche in the Russian research industry. It is developing quickly as domestic and international clients alike recognize the value of researching Russian markets. When considering commissioning a market research supplier in Russia, here are three recommendations:

Scoping. Russia is a vast country and it is impossible to research it all at once. Is it really the whole of Russia you are interested in? If you entered the Russian market, would you really be able to service Vladivostok on the Pacific coast as well as Moscow? Are your customers really spread equally throughout the country, or are they concentrated in one or two regions? Far better to focus on the region or regions that are important to you.

Professional rates for a professional job. Traveling around a country the size of Russia is expensive. In "European" Russia, particularly Moscow, travel, flights, rents, hotels, and most other overheads are comparatively expensive. This has a direct impact on all businesses' prices. Most importantly of all, professional and experienced business-to-business researchers are uncommon in Russia, and their fees tend to reflect that.

Trust the agency. Conducting market research in Russia is different from conducting research in North America or Western Europe. Face-to-face contact is key. Incentives, which are seen as an acknowledgment of a respondent's expertise, are more necessary than in western Europe. Telephone questionnaires are shorter than in the United States and Canada, whereas face-to-face interviews in Russia can take as long as an hour. The line of questioning tends to be more direct and less projective than may be the case on a Western questionnaire. The good-quality agencies that are now operating in Russia are well positioned to advise you on these issues and ensure that you get the most from your project.[24]

Questions

1. Do you think that conducting research in Russia is any different than, say, China? Why?

2. If you were a large American research supplier, would you want to establish are office in Moscow? Why?

Moving Marketing Research into a Decision-Making Role

A more strategic managerial question regarding the marketing research department is the role and importance of marketing research in the managerial decision-making process. The researchers' challenge is to shed their long-held traditional role as a support function—one that reacts to requests from project and new-product development managers and then focuses on producing the numbers but not on their meaning to the business.

Experts agree that, to earn the ear of senior management, researchers must move beyond the task of simply crunching numbers and churning out results; they need to understand the underlying business issues at stake and adjust the information they gather and how they analyze it. They also must reach out to other departments, building relationships and a better understanding of the issues companywide. "We need to evolve just from doing research to doing insights," says Peter Daboll, chief of insights for Sunnyvale, California-based Yahoo! Inc. "If you want to be at the table you have to be senior. [To be senior means to] go from collecting, collating and presenting to anticipating, reconciling and recommending. . . . [Executives] want the freaking answer, not the tool to give them the answer."[25]

"I strongly emphasize that while [the research managers and associates] may be in my official marketing research department—it's my insistence that they view themselves as members of the business team" first and foremost, says Daryl Papp, Lilly's director of U.S. market research. He adds that about half of his department comprises professionals who come from areas of marketing other than research for a several-year "broadening assignment" to learn about the company's businesses. Papp believes that having marketing researchers sit side by side with other colleagues who aspire to high-level management helps contribute to the business-oriented mentality in his department.[26]

The Market Research Executive Board (MREB) reports that 69 percent of senior executives want research to be a strategic partner, but only 29 percent of them currently view research as such. Furthermore, execs who view research as a strategic partner are much more likely to have changed decisions based on research than those who view research as an analytic resource (57 percent vs. 33 percent).[27]

Marketing research departments can take several specific actions to increase their internal standing and achieve strategic, consultative relevance. These are: Be driven by impact; bring leadership to strategic priorities; develop rich consumer and market insights; use creativity to innovate; and communicate for impact.[28]

Driven by Impact.   In some research departments, success is defined by a project that is well executed—a questionnaire that the client is happy with, fieldwork that's done on time and on budget, a report or presentation that often summarizes "all the news that's fit to print," Then the researcher moves on to his or her next project. Performance reviews focus on quality of project management skills.

Contrast this with what the company's senior management wants from research. The company is investing substantial dollars in research, so it wants to see marketplace impact as a result of its investment. And senior management's time is increasingly precious, so they just want to know the key insights and how the company should act on the insights. If there is little or no marketplace impact as a result of the research investment, why should they keep investing?

Marketplace impact doesn't happen automatically from identifying insights. Insights must be integrated with business economics and organizational strengths and weaknesses, then communicated and subsequently acted upon by the appropriate internal function.

Research departments need to provide an environment in which marketplace impact is integral to the department's vision and mission, an environment that makes provoking impact part of the research culture and that rewards impact.

Bring Leadership to Strategic Priorities.   Researchers often complain that they spend too much time and money researching tactical issues while major strategic issues struggle to get budget. When this happens, it speaks "opportunity" and is a clear indication that research programs and budgets are not reviewed at a high enough level in the organization. It may be that the research budget is controlled by a brand-level marketing person and that the rolled-up departmental research budget is never reviewed with senior management. Or it may be that senior management doesn't believe (or isn't aware) that research can help with the major strategic issues.

Research department managers must understand the major strategic issues facing the company. Then, it must determine what information is required to address these issues. Finally, a research strategic plan must be created and presented to senior management.

Develop Rich Consumer and Market Insights.   An **insight** includes discovery together with marketplace impact: "Insight is new knowledge that has the potential to create significant marketplace impact."

The toolkit for identifying insights has expanded in recent years. Online research capabilities have made segmentation and other quantitative techniques much more affordable, and enabled virtual-shopping capabilities. Ethnographic research has become mainstream. Neuroscience, eye-tracking and facial-coding methodologies are evolving. Hosted online panel communities provide an opportunity for dialogue with consumers, and among consumers, over time. Listening to social media has become extremely important.

The challenge today is in unearthing insights that lead to competitive advantage, that can be leveraged to trigger an emotional consumer response and that ultimately provides the opportunity for significant marketplace impact.

> **insight**
> Newer knowledge that has the potential to create significant marketing impact.

Use Creativity to Innovate.   Senior management loves innovation because it can lead to higher current and future earnings. **Innovation** is the successful implementation of creative ideas within an organization. **Creativity** is the ability to generate and recognize potentially useful ideas. Creativity then, is a necessary prerequisite for innovation. Marketing researchers can build innovation into presentations and research recommendations by following the creative problem-solving process (see Exhibit 20.5)

> **innovation**
> The successful implementation of creative ideas within an organization.

> **creativity**
> The ability to generate and recognize potentially useful ideas.

Communicate for Impact.   The richest insight in the world doesn't add value unless some action is taken. Research needs to take responsibility for making change happen as a result of insight development. Communicating for impact is critical. The job of the presentation is to create impact—period. Anything else is superfluous.

The following pointers will help create impact:

- Tell a story with your presentation, and tell it succinctly.
- Leverage visual storytelling, incorporating video where possible.
- Know your audience and their ingoing beliefs. Address potential problems before delivering the presentation.
- Your audience wants to know what they should do, not what you did.
- Your job doesn't end when the presentation is given. Take responsibility for making action happen.[29]

Measuring Marketing Research's Return on Investment (ROI)   The old view of marketing as an art form disappeared long ago. In its place is the notion of strict accountability. Marketing expenditures become investments, with performance measures coming from the world of finance. So it has become increasingly fashionable in large corporations to demand that marketing research prove its worth. The approach that is gaining in popularity is ROI. Recall that ROI is simply the after-tax income from an

Exhibit 20.5 **The Creative Problem-Solving Process**	Creative problem solving begins with an assessment of the situation. The process then follows three phases with two of the phases consisting of multiple steps. Each step has a convergence part and a divergence part. Divergence is when issues, wishes, ideas, or actions are elicited. Convergence is when they are winnowed down to one or a few for further exploration.

Phase one is problem exploration and consists of these three steps:

1. **Identify the challenge:** Here a vision is imagined in divergent mode, then identified in convergent mode.

2. **Facts and feelings exploration:** This is the classic research step. A divergent list of facts, feelings, and relevant data is made. In convergent mode salient data points are identified.

3. **Problem framing and reframing:** The original vision is reexamined in light of the salient data, and alternate problem frames are generated in divergent mode. One challenge statement is selected in convergence—and transformed into a question that inspires answers to solve the problem.

Phase two of the process is idea generation. It has one step:

4. **Idea generation:** As many ideas as possible are generated to answer the question converged upon in problem framing. The goal is a breakthrough option or idea. In convergence the ideas are clustered and combined, and ultimately one or a small subset is selected.

The last phase, phase three, is getting into action. It has two steps:

5. **Solution development:** The idea(s) selected in step 4 is (are) examined and improved using criteria developed/diverged upon for the challenge. Ideas are enhanced by building them up to better match key criteria using additional ideation.

6. **Action planning:** In this final step a process for implementing the idea is developed and mapped out. Divergent thinking takes place around assistors, resistors, and ways to make the plan exciting, and convergence creates a standard action/work plan.

Source: Greg Fraley, "Create or Perish," February 2009, p. 56.

investment divided by the dollar amount of the investment. Several arguments can be made against using ROI to measure the value of marketing research to an organization.

First, ROI is theoretically flawed because it divides the profit return by the expenditure instead of subtracting it. All reputable bottom-line metrics, such as profit, cash flow, payback, and shareholder value, subtract expenditure from income. Dividing one into the other distorts the result.

Second, ROI was invented to compare alternative uses of capital, based on their projected percentage return on that capital. Market research (MR), however, is usually a stream of costs that continue for the purposes of comparison in each and every year. Market research is rarely an investment in the true sense of the word.

Third, improving ROI tends to suboptimize expenditure. Most investments have diminishing profit returns. The early profits give the greatest ROI, but maximizing productivity (i.e., total profit return) requires more expenditure beyond that. Would you rather, at the same low level of risk, have a 100 percent return on $2 or an 80 percent return on $1,000? This objection arises directly from the division rather than subtraction anomaly.

Fourth, ROI usually focuses on the short term and does not consider the effects on the marketing asset (brand equity) or the dynamic development of marketing over longer time periods.

Fifth, the purpose of the ROI ratio is to compare alternative expenditures. Research is not really an alternative to the elements of the marketing mix it should control. Such a comparison does not contrast like with like. Internal information, such as the management accounts or budgets, is a closer comparison as it fights with marketing metrics for space on the dashboard used by top management to help drive the business. And yet when did anyone call for the ROI on the internal accounting function?[30]

Despite the negatives, the growing popularity of ROI deserves further examination into how it can be operationalized. Two approaches are ROI Lite and ROI Complete created by Dawn Lesh, president of New York-based A. Dawn Lesh International, and Diane Schmalensee, president of Schmalensee Partners in Chestnut Hill, Massachusetts.[31]

ROI Lite. To measure ROI Lite, MR asks the client for two estimates during pre-project planning:

1. The anticipated dollar value of the decision that will be based on the research.
2. The anticipated increase in confidence of making the "right" decision. For example, instead of saying a decision is worth $10 million, a client might say it's worth $8 million to $12 million. Or a client could say he or she expects his or her confidence to rise 40 to 60 percent.

With the answers to these questions, MR can calculate the expected ROI Lite using the following formula.

$$\text{ROI Lite} = \frac{\$ \text{ Value} \times \text{Increased Confidence}}{\text{Cost of Research}}$$

For example, assume a firm has to decide which of five creative approaches to use in a $2 million advertising campaign.

■ Since it is uncertain how the advertising will affect sales, the firm decides to use the $2 million campaign cost as the value estimate. No one knows which of the five approaches is best, so the confidence of randomly picking the best one is only 20 percent.

■ The firm believes that after the research it will be 80 percent confident of making the best decision (an increase of 60 percent).

■ The cost of the copy testing is $250,000.

$$\text{ROI Lite} = \frac{\$2M \times 60\%}{\$250K} = \frac{\$1.2M}{\$250K} = 480\%$$

This ROI Lite discussion can help determine how much to invest in the research. If the dollar value of a decision is small or the expected decrease in uncertainty is low, then the budget should be kept small. After the research is completed, MR meets again with the client to revise the ROI Lite estimate in light of what was learned.

ROI Complete. ROI Complete is similar to ROI Lite except that it adds the concept of the likelihood of taking action. MR and the client discuss the estimated likelihood of taking action with and without the research. If the firm usually acts without research, then MR may not be able to raise the likelihood of acting, and the firm should not spend much money on the research. However, if the firm seldom acts without research, then the research is more valuable.

The following equation is used:

$$\text{ROI Complete} = \frac{\$ \text{ Value} \times \text{Increased Confidence} \times \text{Increased Likelihood of Acting}}{\text{Cost of Research}}$$

For example, suppose the decision is whether or not to enter a new market.

■ Costs (including research, manufacturing, and marketing) are estimated to be $20 million, and potential revenue is estimated at $50 million in the first year. The client and MR agree to use the first year's net income of $30 million as the expected dollar value. (Note that a few sophisticated MR departments calculate the net present value of the continuing revenue stream, but we have kept the example simple.)

■ The executives know that entering a new market is risky. They are only 10 percent confident of making the right decision without research. With the research, they estimate that they will be 70 percent confident—an increase of 60 percent.

■ The executives often act without research. The estimated likelihood of acting without research (based on past history) is 50 percent. They expect this would rise to 80 percent after the research—an increase of 30 percent.

■ The cost of the research is $1 million. The firm decides to go forward with the research because there will be an anticipated positive 540 percent ROI by the end of the first year.

$$\text{ROI Complete} = \frac{\$30M \times 60\% \times 30\%}{\$1M} = \frac{\$5.4M}{\$1M} = 540\%$$

After the research is completed, MR and the client recalculate ROI.

What if the research says the firm should not enter the market? In that case, the research still has a positive ROI since it saves the firm from investing in a losing venture. Using the previous example, suppose that the research made the firm 80 percent certain it would lose its $20 million investment. Before the research, the firm was 50 percent likely to act and make a losing decision, which means the return on the research is 800 percent:

$$\text{Actual ROI} = \frac{\$20M \times 80\% \times 50\%}{\$1M} = \frac{\$8M}{\$1M} = 800\%$$

What if the research convinces the firm to avoid the market it originally preferred (as shown above) but to invest in an alternative market that would generate a new profit of $30 million in the first year? Assume the firm is 70 percent confident that the alternative is the best one (an increase of 60 percent since it had only 10 percent confidence in it before the research). Also assume that the research increases the likelihood of actually entering a new market by 30 percent. Then the ROI is even higher:

$$\text{Actual ROI} = \frac{(\$20M \times 80\% \times 50\%) + (\$30M \times 60\% \times 30\%)}{\$1M}$$
$$= \frac{\$8M + \$5.4M}{\$1M} = 1,340\%$$

What if the client decides not to act even though the research projects a positive outcome? This often happens when there are changes in leadership or other uses for the capital. In that case, ROI is 0 percent, but the post-research discussion makes clear that this is the client's choice and not MR's fault.

It's not always easy to ask clients how likely they are to take action. Sometimes firms commission research simply to bless a decision that has already been made. Or firms may expect the research to increase their knowledge without necessarily leading to action. Examples of this would be new segmentation research or customer satisfaction tracking. In these cases, the likelihood of acting and the dollar value would depend entirely on what was learned. One MR director said, "Just like estimating the return on IT investments, there are so many assumptions necessary that you can never be sure your estimate will be close. For some kinds of exploratory research, you don't know until you're done whether or not it will produce anything of financial value." Because these discussions are difficult, some MR groups prefer to use ROI Lite rather than ROI Complete.[32]

The benefits of quantifying the economic value of research include:

- Increased credibility with senior management and other functional areas
- Increased focus on the factors in the processes that drive the most economic value
- A greater probability that research will be viewed as an investment rather than an expense
- More ammunition in defending the research budget
- Better prioritization and allocation of research resources
- More incentive for the research department to stay involved through execution[33]

SUMMARY

Supplier research marketing management has six important goals beyond excellent communication: creation of an effective organization, assurance of data quality, adherence to time schedules, cost control, client profitability management, and staff management and development. Many research firms are transitioning to a team-based organization from the traditional functional organizational structure. Marketing research managers can help ensure high-quality data by attempting to minimize sources of error. Researchers should also strive for better client and audience understanding of the margin of error concept. Time management requires a system to notify management of potential problems and policies to solve behind-schedule situations both efficiently and quickly. Cost management demands good cost-tracking and cost control processes. Client profitability management requires that the marketing research supplier determine how much each client contributes to the researcher's overall profitability. Unprofitable clients should be dropped; marginally profitable clients should be developed into high-profit clients or dropped. The supplier should use relationship marketing to build a solid, increasingly profitable long-term relationship with clients identified as high-profit contributors. Finally, staff management and development requires that employees be encouraged to take risks and assume responsibility, be recognized for a job well done, and be offered job autonomy, financial rewards tied to business results, new challenges, and a clear career path.

While outsourcing has been popular for some time, many client-side firms have begun to insource as well. Outsourcing can often save time and money. Outsource firms offer programming, data processing, data analysis, data management, and panel management. Some important issues when considering outsourcing are confidentiality, infrastructure, quality of deliverables, domain, knowledge, culture considerations, potential negative publicity from job losses, and employee liability. Insourcing can also conserve resources and save time. The availability of sophisticated online research tools has resulted in many firms doing Internet surveys themselves. Insourcing has spread from basic online survey to research online communities, and enterprise customer satisfaction and loyalty feedback management.

A manager of a marketing research department within a corporation faces a different set of issues than from a research supplier. Among these are effective spending of the research budget, prioritizing projects for the corporation, retaining skilled staff, selecting the right research suppliers, moving the marketing research function to a more strategic role in the firm, and measuring return on investment for marketing research.

One technique for prioritizing projects is to focus first on strategic projects and then on the tactical. This is also true for allocating the corporate research budget. Also, projects should be funded that have the highest potential ROI. Ways to retain key staff are to offer interesting and fulfilling work, recognizing someone for a job well done, and offering competitive pay.

A manager of a corporate research department must develop methodologies and skills for selecting the right research suppliers. This includes assessing competing supplier capabilities and reviewing the quality controls of each supplier. Today, many client-side companies are moving beyond traditional selection criteria and are asking for a partner as opposed to simply a research supplier.

The objective of many research departments is to move from being simply data collectors to partners in the strategic decision process. The chapter makes a number of suggestions on how to make this a reality. Finally, a number of corporations are now measuring the ROI on marketing research. This tool, when applied to marketing research can lead to increased credibility with senior management and other advantages.

KEY TERMS & DEFINITIONS

research management Overseeing the development of excellent communication systems, data quality, time schedules, cost controls, client profitability, and staff development

outsourcing Having personnel in another country perform some, or all, of the functions involved in a marketing research project.

captive outsourcing When a research firm creates a wholly-owned foreign facility for outsourcing.

insight New knowledge that has the potential to create significant marketplace impact.

innovation Successful implementation of creative ideas within an organization.

creativity The ability to generate and recognize potentially useful ideas.

QUESTIONS FOR REVIEW & CRITICAL THINKING

1. Should a survey presentation say, "The margin of error is plus or minus 3 percent"? If not, what problem does it present?

2. Describe four different ways a manager can help ensure high data quality.

3. What policies need to be put in place to ensure that research projects are handled in a timely manner? What steps should be taken if a project falls behind schedule?

4. How can a research supplier develop its employees?

5. Should every firm conduct a client profitability study? Why?

6. Is outsourcing beneficial to the marketing research industry? Why or why not? What about insourcing?

7. Explain the relationship between insights, creativity, and innovation.

8. How should one allocate a corporate marketing research budget? Is this the only way?

9. What is an acceptable method of prioritizing research projects in a research department?

10. What should marketing research do in order to play a more strategic role in the organization?

11. Assume that a company is trying to determine whether to enter a new market. The estimated first year's revenue is $2.2 million. Because management knows a little about this market, they are 20 percent confident that they can make the right decision without research. With research, they will be 80 percent confident. The estimated likelihood of moving into the market without research is 40 percent. This figure would rise to 80 percent after the research. The cost of the research is $400,000. What is the ROI after the first year?

12. What steps and actions should a research supplier take to try to become a strategic partner with a research client?

WORKING THE NET

1. Go to *www.worldopinion.com* or *www.Quirks.com* and find an article on managing marketing research firms. Summarize this article for the class.

2. Go to Google, or another search engine, and look up "marketing research outsourcing." present your findings to the class.

REAL-LIFE RESEARCH • 20.1

Walther Research Deals with Managing Project Managers

Larry Walther started his research company in 1992 in Phoenix, Arizona. He began with a few local clients and two employees. Interviewers were hired as subcontractors and were paid only when his clients paid Larry. In order to make ends meet, he opened several mall locations and set up a focus group facility. By taking in work as a field service as well as a full-service research company he began to grow. In 1997, his sales reached $1 million, and he had 20 employees. Today the firm has 300 employees.

Larry's growth slowly led to the creation of a functional organization structure. This seemed to happen as much by chance as by design. For example, to get control over the 15 client service/salespeople, they were put into a separate department. The same thing happened with questionnaire design and programming, advanced analytics, database management, and so forth.

Larry's company has grown beyond his wildest dreams, yet all is not well in the organization. Recently, he lost a number of key people, and morale seems to be low throughout the company. Some clients have complained about late projects and unsatisfactory reports. In fact, he recently lost one of his oldest and best clients. Much of the problem, but certainly not all, seems to be his project managers and a lack of project control. An informal survey by Larry of his best clients found:

- The field service recruited unqualified respondents.
- Underqualified interviewers were used for executive interviews.

- The moderator could not keep up with changes that were made in the discussion guide.
- The report lacked depth, interpretation, or insight.
- The presentation or report was disorganized and confusing.

Larry also heard this story from one of his better clients: The client's project report was due to the client on a Friday. The project director was leaving for vacation that day and arranged for someone else in Larry's firm to send the report to the client. However, the project director neglected to tell the client that she was going on vacation and did not give the client the name and phone number of the alternate contact person. The day the report was due, the client called the project director and got a message that she was on vacation. Naturally, the client panicked and called one of Larry's senior assistants asking, "Where's my report?" The client got the report that day as expected, but the relationship with Walther Research has suffered severe damage.

Questions

1. Larry is considering reorganizing. What should he do?

2. What are the advantages of keeping a functional organizational structure? What are the disadvantages?

3. What might he gain from a team structure? Are there any risks in moving to this form of organization?

4. What should Larry do about directing and controlling his project managers?

REAL-LIFE RESEARCH • 20.2

Maxwell Research Considers Outsourcing to Cross-Tab in India

Maxwell Research, a full-service research firm located in Austin, Texas, specializes in custom research. The firm has grown dramatically in recent years, serving primarily the hospitality, travel, and consumer packaged goods industries. Mike Maxwell, CEO and founder, says that the firm's success is attributable to providing outstanding service to their clients. Maxwell doesn't have "black-box" copyrighted models or huge Internet panels; instead he has a razor-like focus on its clients. The firm has a unique key-account program for its 15 top accounts. Each key account manager must reside in the city where the key account is located in order to be available 24/7. Mike believes face-to-face contact the moment a key client calls or has a problem is the best method for having excellent customer relationship management.

While sales have increased a minimum of 20 percent annually since 2005, net profits have not. In fact, the net profit margin has fallen in each of the last 3 years. Last year it dropped 6 percent. Mike knew that his labor-intensive, customer-oriented approach was part of the problem. His attitude has been, "Let's overstaff if necessary to make sure that we can meet clients' deadlines during crunch times." Now, Mike is rethinking his strategy.

One possible approach to lowering labor costs is outsourcing. He has heard good things about a company located in India called Cross-Tab. The firm also has an office in Bellevue, Washington. An examination of Cross-Tab's Web site reveals the following:

Overview

Cross-Tab provides a full range of market research and analytics solutions to global clients. From managing end-to-end research operations to market research process outsourcing, secondary research, and sample procurement services, Cross-Tab is committed to delivering high-quality market research services at offshore prices.

Our experience spans:

- End-to-end management of multinational market research projects
- Online and CATI data collection in 65 countries and 25 languages
- Outsourcing services for major market research processes
- Sample procurement
- Building and managing respondent panels

Survey Programming

Cross-Tab's survey programming team has extensive experience in market research as well as in multiple programming packages, which are leveraged to support specific client requirements. Cross-Tab staff is proficient in the use of tools such as ConfirmIT, SPSS-Dimensions, mrinterview (mrStudio Interview Module), Net-MR, Illume, Perseus, and QuestionPro to deliver moderate to complex project requirements.

Cross-Tab programmers are certified by ConfirmIT, SPSS, and GMI. They are experienced in using Java script, APS, and programming surveys in Flash, and are adept at managing survey look and feel to ensure an engaged respondent. Our team can also add images, audio, and audiovisual stimuli to the survey. They can program multilingual studies and questionnaires with complex logic. Some features include:

- Save-and-return functionality
- Data pre-population from SPSS or other database
- Table of Contents organization of multiple survey sections or parts
- Highly customized error messaging
- Versioning (easy reuse of survey questions across business units but customized formatting per business unit)
- Rolling back of incomplete surveys
- Translation of survey into various languages (we have managed scripting in 25 languages)
- Scripting conjoint and discrete choice modeling researches, online advertising testing, and virtual shelf testing
- Online reporting of results and setting of reporters for real-time tabulations
- Advanced quota settings
- Pass-back linkage to allow clients to match respondents to their panel
- Ensuring proper data layouts at the back end to generate data files as required by the analysis team

If desired, we can also provide survey fielding, monitoring, and data-handling services along with the survey scripting service.

CASE STUDY

Client: A U.S. based marketing consultancy provider

Nature of the project

- Multilingual survey programming
- Three sets of questionnaire for three different profiles
- CATI interviewing was done in such a way that the respondents were viewing the questionnaire online—two sets of the questionnaire were programmed and inter-linked such that the same questions were seen by the interviewed and the respondent.

What we did

- We programmed this complex survey where a profile was generated for each respondent depending on his responses in the screener section.
- One of the three questionnaire sets was mailed to the respondent based on his profile.
- Each set had twelve conjoint screens.

How did it help the client?

- The client was able to achieve the desired functionality from this complex survey.
- The client was able to complete the project successfully within time line.
- The client was able to get substantial cost savings.[34]

Questions

1. What do you think about Mike's labor-intensive focus on customer service? What are the advantages and disadvantages?
2. What are the advantages and disadvantages for Maxwell Research to engage in outsourcing?
3. What are some key issues Maxwell needs to resolve before it signs an outsourcing agreement?
4. Will outsourcing solve Maxwell's ROI problem? What might happen to sales revenue?

PHOTO CREDITS

APPENDIX ONE

Comprehensive Cases

A
**Biff Targets an Online Dating Service
for College Students**

B
**Freddy Favors Fast Food and
Convenience for College Students**

C
**Superior Online Student Travel—
A Cut Above**

D
**Rockingham National
Bank Visa Card Survey**

Comprehensive Case A

Biff Targets an Online Dating Service for College Students

Biff Henderson, a distant cousin of Bif Henderson of the *David Letterman Show*, graduated from the California state system three years ago. Being a bit shy, Biff had decided that the best way to meet girls was through an online dating service. His hits and misses during his college days led him to think that there must be a better way for college students to hook up. The big, generic services like Match.com and Yahoo Personals didn't meet his needs. Also, speed dating at Starbucks and name swapping at the Apple Store were unsuccessful.

Biff decided that if the big online services weren't right for him they must not be right for thousands of other college students as well. A little secondary research indicated that there are about 2.5 million subscribers to online dating services nationwide and this number is expected to double in the next few years. By utilizing scientifically derived compatibility tests and demographic preferences, a person can quickly filter through numerous candidates to find the person or persons whom they would most like to contact. Biff liked the idea of targeting only college students in order to attract singles looking for a more defined dating pool.

Biff decided that to become a member of his new service the person had to be enrolled in a college or university. He didn't necessarily have to be a full-time student, but he did have to be currently enrolled. A single student will be able to search by region, specific university, and/or by major field of study. A unique feature that Biff is considering will be called "Biff's Bashes." These will be all-inclusive spring break and summer week-long vacations to places like Cancun or Daytona Beach. Biff will provide airfare, hotel, ground transportation, five dinners, three lunches, and nightly mixers with music. "Biff's Bashes" will be open only to members of his online service.

Biff wonders about the demand for his "bashes" as well as what college students would ideally like to see in an online dating service. For example, might they also be interested in single cycling or weekend hiking trips? While virtually all college students may be surfing the net for love, there are a tiny minority that may be predators or dangerous criminals. Biff is therefore thinking about offering background checks for an additional fee. Another service might be bodyguards or escorts for singles meeting for the first time. Biff felt that this service might be desirable for students living in large cities that aren't completely comfortable with dating online.

Biff decided that what was needed was some good marketing research.

ONLINE DATING SERVICE FOR COLLEGE STUDENTS

S1. Which of the following categories includes your age?
1 Under 18—THANK AND TERM
2 18–20
3 21–25
4 26–30
5 31 or older
6 Refused—THANK AND TERM

S2. Are you currently enrolled as a full-time or part-time student in any of the following types of institutions?
1 Community college
2 Junior college / two-year program
3 University / four-year program
4 None of the above—THANK AND TERM

Q1. How familiar are you with the concept of online dating services, where people pay a membership fee to post a profile and picture online and can then search through profiles/pictures of members of the opposite sex for the purpose of meeting people to date?

5 Extremely familiar
4 Very familiar
3 Somewhat familiar
2 Not too familiar
1 Not at all familiar

Q2. How interested are you in the general concept of an online dating service as a way of meeting members of the opposite sex? HOW ABOUT SAME SEX?

5 Extremely interested
4 Very interested
3 Somewhat interested
2 Not too interested
1 Not at all interested

Q3. Which of the following dating services are you aware of? Please select all that apply.
ROTATE LIST A–J.

A Match.com
B Yahoo! Personals
C PerfectMatch.com
D AmericanSingles.com
E eHarmony.com
F FriendFinder.com
G Date.com
H Speed dating
I Apple Store
J Great Expectations
K None of the above—SKIP TO Q7

(INCLUDE ALL MENTIONS FROM Q3)

Q4. Which of the following dating services have you ever tried?

A Match.com
B Yahoo! Personals
C PerfectMatch.com
D AmericanSingles.com
E eHarmony.com
F FriendFinder.com
G Date.com
H Speed dating
I Apple Store
J Great Expectations
K None of the above—SKIP TO Q7

(ASK Q5 FOR ALL MENTIONS IN Q4)

Q5. Overall, how satisfied are you with your experience with (ANSWER FROM Q4)?

5 Completely satisfied
4 Very satisfied
3 Somewhat satisfied
2 Not too satisfied
1 Not at all satisfied

(ASK FOR ALL Q4 MENTIONS RATED A "1" OR "2" IN Q5)

Q6. Why are you less than satisfied with your experience with (ANSWER FROM Q3)? Please select all answers that apply. ROTATE A–J.

A Small/limited selection of members of the opposite sex
B Too large/overwhelming selection of members of the opposite sex
C Poor quality selection of members of the opposite sex
D Cost/fees too high

E   Members not honest in their profile/picture
F   Bad experiences on dates
G   No personality/compatibility test included in membership
H   No organized social events included in membership
I   No criminal background check included in membership
J   Requires too much time
K   Other (please specify)_____

Q7. A new online dating service may be introduced in the near future. Membership in this service would be limited to those enrolled in a college or university (full or part time) and students would be able to search by region, specific university and/or by major field of study. Members would also be able to utilize a compatibility test and demographic preferences to filter through numerous candidates to find the person or persons who they would most like to contact.

How interested are you in this particular concept of an online dating services as a way of meeting members of the opposite sex?
5   Extremely interested
4   Very interested
3   Somewhat interested
2   Not too interested—SKIP TO Q14
1   Not at all interested—SKIP TO Q14

Q8. What would be an appropriate monthly fee for this basic service?
1   $1–$5
2   $6–$10
3   $11–$15
4   $16–$20
5   $21–$25
6   $26–$30
7   More than $30

Q9. How important is it that all members pass a criminal background check prior to being allowed to join the online service?
5   Extremely important
4   Very important
3   Somewhat important
2   Not too important
1   Not at all important

Q10. How interested would you be in having a bodyguard or escort accompany you on your first date with a member of the opposite sex?
5   Extremely interested
4   Very interested
3   Somewhat interested
2   Not too interested
1   Not at all interested

Q11. In addition to the services described earlier, this new online dating service may also include some organized social events, such as spring break and summer week-long vacations to places like Cancun or Daytona Beach. Members would be provided with airfare, hotel accommodations, ground transportation, five dinners, three lunches, and nightly mixers with music. These social events would be open only to members of the online dating service.

If you were a member of this online dating service, how likely would you be to participate in this type of organized social event?
5   Extremely likely
4   Very likely
3   Somewhat likely
2   Not too likely
1   Not at all likely

Q12. This new online dating service may also include some shorter organized social events, such as single cycling or weekend hiking trips. These social events would be open only to members of the online dating service.

If you were a member of this online dating service, how likely would you be to participate in this type of organized social event?

5   Extremely likely
4   Very likely
3   Somewhat likely
2   Not too likely
1   Not at all likely

Q13. What other organized social events would you be likely to participate in? Please mark all that apply.

A   Movie night
B   Game night
C   Happy hour
D   Dinner at a local restaurant
E   Volunteer work
F   Other (please specify)_____

SKIP TO END

Q14. Would you be more interested in this online dating service if it also included any of the following additional benefits?

	Much more interested	Somewhat more interested	No more interested
A All-inclusive week-long trips during spring break and summer to places like Cancun or Daytona Beach	3	2	1
B Single cycling or weekend hiking trips	3	2	1
C Happy hours, game nights, movie nights, etc.	3	2	1
D Mandatory criminal background check for members	3	2	1
E Bodyguard/escort service on first dates	3	2	1

Those are all of our questions. Thank you for your help!

Exercises

1.   Using secondary data from the Internet and the "Real People-Real Data" database, determine if Biff should move forward with his project.

2.   If the new service is a "go," prepare a detailed marketing plan (see Appendix Two) of what should be offered to give Biff a competitive advantage.

Comprehensive Case B

Freddy Favors Fast Food and Convenience for College Students

Freddy Bender shared a college dorm room with Jack Mendenhall throughout his four-year tenure at a large northeastern university. They were not only roommates but best friends as well. Freddy, having a solid quantitative background, helped Jack prepare for exams in statistics and marketing research. After graduation, Freddy put in eight years as a loan officer with CitiBank in New York, whereas Jack moved to California to work in his father's venture capital firm, Mendenhall Partners.

Freddy is a fast-food junkie, or as it is called in the business, a "heavy user." His love of fast food has always been coupled with a desire to be in the business. Freddy knows that college students often fall into the "heavy user" category. A little secondary research revealed that almost half of all college students (46 percent) say that they ate fast food one or two times in the prior week. Three in ten (28 percent) say they ate it three to five times in that same period, while 13 percent claim to have eaten it five or more times![1] College students spend $4.8 billion per year at fast-food restaurants.[2]

Freddy's dream is to open a chain of fast-food restaurants coupled with a convenience store on or near major college campuses. The notion is to carry a limited line of convenience goods and serve quality fast food in a Starbuck's-like atmosphere with comfy sofas, chairs, and WiFi. Freddy knows that price is paramount but that variety and quality are important to college students.

Further research showed that a limited version of Freddy's ideas had worked extremely well for Tedeschi Food Shops Inc., operator of Tedeschi Food Shops, Li'l Peach, and Store 24. Store 24 is the chain's primary store brand in college markets, such as Boston and the areas around the University of New Hampshire and the University of Connecticut. "In our stores, we seem to be students' destination for lunch, dinner and late-dinner/early-breakfast," said Joe Hamza, director of marketing. Fresh, quality foods have made these stores destinations for students, Hamza said. "Students also look at quick in-and-out and at variety—healthy, vegetarian, ethnic, ready-to-eat, or heat-and-eat meals—as big variables."[3]

Indeed, Store 24 was an early observer of the low-carb trend and offers vegetarian options and ethnic foods, such as sushi, Italian, and Middle Eastern dishes like tabouli and hummus. "These kids are diverse ethnically and look at these dishes as a vegetarian or healthy alternative to the steak and cheese," Hamza said. "Our growth comes from the innovative items, not from the turkey or roast beef sandwiches."[4]

A telephone call to Jack Mendenhall, Freddy's college roommate, resulted in a very receptive attitude to provide venture capital. Jack said, "Bring me a viable marketing plan, and we will provide the funds for the first 10 restaurants. If these prove successful, additional funding won't be a problem." Freddy was elated!

Freddy knew that marketing research would be necessary before he could build his marketing plan. He needed answers to a number of questions. These included: Is a Starbuck's-like atmosphere desirable? What type of fast food should be offered? Should the quality/price point be above, below, or at the level of the national chains? What is the best mix of convenience goods to carry for college students? Is there some other service or product that the stores can offer to build foot traffic and loyalty?

FAST FOOD AND CONVENIENCE FOR COLLEGE STUDENTS

S1. What is your current age?

1   Under 18—THANK AND TERM
2   18
3   19
4   20
5   21
6   22
7   23–25
8   26–30
9   31 or older

S2. Are you currently enrolled in any of the following types of institutions?
1　Junior college
2　Community college/two-year program
3　University/four-year program
4　None of the above—THANK AND TERM

Q1. How many times have you visited a **fast food** restaurant in the last seven days? Please do not include restaurants where you were served by a waiter or waitress.
1　None/zero—SKIP TO Q8
2　One time
3　Two times
4　Three times
5　Five times
6　Five or more times

Q2. For which of the following meal types did you eat fast food in the last seven days? Please mark all that apply.
A　Breakfast
B　Lunch
C　Afternoon snack
D　Dinner
E　Evening/late night snack
F　Other

Q3. Many fast food restaurants offer combo meals or value meals, which typically include a main dish, a side dish and a drink for a discounted price. How often do you buy combo or value meals, when they are available, versus purchasing single items a la carte?
1　Always
2　Often
3　Seldom
4　Never

Q4. How important are each of the following factors when deciding with fast food restaurant to visit? ROTATE FACTORS.
A　Taste
B　Convenience of location
C　Price
D　Healthy food choices available
E　Food quality
F　Cleanliness of restaurant
G　General atmosphere of restaurant
H　Ethnic food choices available
I　Vegetarian food choices available
J　Freshness of the food
　　5　Extremely important
　　4　Very important
　　3　Somewhat important
　　2　Not too important
　　1　Not at all important

Q5. When you visit fast food restaurants, how often do you stay and eat the food in the restaurant versus getting it to go or going through the drive-through window?
1　Always—SKIP TO Q8
2　Often
3　Seldom
4　Never

Q6. If a fast food restaurant had comfortable sofas and chairs, where you could socialize with friends, and wireless Internet connection, how likely would you be to stay and cat your food there rather than getting it go or going through the drive-through window?
5　Extremely likely
4　Very likely

    3   Somewhat likely
    2   Not too likely
    1   Not at all likely

Q7. Why do you say that? Please be as specific as possible.

_____

Q8. How many times have you purchased/consumed the following convenient foods in the last seven days?
  A Candy bar
  B Chips or pretzels
  C Microwavable frozen meal like Hungry Man or Lean Cuisine
  D Hot Pocket
  E Ramen Noodles
  F Microwavable popcorn
  G Ice cream
  H Soup
  I Bagel or donut
  J Cookie
  K Pre-packaged/ready-to-eat salad
  L Fruit
  M Pre-made, refrigerated sandwich
     1 None/zero
     2 One time
     3 Two times
     4 Three times
     5 Four times
     6 Four or more times

(IF Q1=1, CONTINUE, ALL OTHERS, SKIP TO END)

Q9. Why have you not visited any fast food restaurants in the last seven days? Please select all that apply. ROTATE FACTORS.
  A Don't like the taste of fast foods
  B Inconvenience of locations
  C Price
  D Healthy food choices not available
  E Poof food quality
  F Poor cleanliness of restaurants
  G Poor general atmosphere of restaurants
  H Ethnic food choices not available
  I Vegetarian food choices not available
  J Lack of freshness of the food
  K Atypical week—I usually do eat some fast food in a typical week
  L Other

Q10. If a fast food restaurant had comfortable sofas and chairs, wireless Internet connection, and a variety of fresh, healthy American and ethnic food choices and convenience items, how likely would you be to visit?
  5 Extremely likely
  4 Very likely
  3 Somewhat likely
  2 Not too likely
  1 Not at all likely

Q11. Why do you say that? Please be as specific as possible.

_____

Thank you. Those are all of our questions.

_____

Exercise

Using your "Real People-Real Data" database plus secondary information that you find on the Internet, build a marketing plan (see Appendix Two) for Freddy to take to Jack.

Notes

1. "Fast Fact" (Fast Food), *Youth Market Alert*, November 1, 2004.
2. Barbara Grondin Francella, "The College Try: Around the Clock Value and Variety are the Way to Students' Hearts and Stomachs," *Convenience Store News* (August 23, 2004).
3. Ibid.
4. Ibid.

Comprehensive Case C

Superior Online Student Travel—A Cut Above

Over 41 million people purchase travel online. Consumers are most satisfied with their ability to book airfares online. Consider the following percentages of online travel users:

Booking airfare online: 43 percent

Obtaining general destination information: 39 percent

Making lodging arrangements: 36 percent

Renting a car online: 33 percent

Making entertainment arrangements: 31 percent[1]

Mary Ann Johnson knew that, with limited funds and fairly high levels of customer satisfaction, such as shown above, she couldn't compete with the likes of Travelocity, Orbitz, or Expedia. Her only hope was to find a niche market from which to launch her online travel site. Previous experience with Sabre and Orbitz gave Mary Ann a good working knowledge of the online travel business.

Mary Ann found that several firms were already serving the college market such as Student City and Student Universe. Student City seemed to emphasize spring break and party time, whereas Student Universe focused on student airfares. While Mary Ann didn't want to ignore either of these offerings, she felt that a different approach might prove successful.

Mary Ann wondered if her partnering with several universities to offer educational trips to various international destinations, led by a professor, for credit would have an appeal. Her idea was to highlight 10 or more trips in the summer and 5 over the Christmas break. The trips would be offered by a major field of study. For example, an art major might sign up for a trip featuring the Picasso Museum, Rodin Museum, and the Louvre in Paris, the Uffizi in Florence, and the museums of the Vatican in Rome. The tour would be led by an art history professor and would result in three college credits.

Similarly, a marketing major would find a tour that visited Nestlé, the World Trade Organization, and Solomon Skis in Switzerland, Carrefour (the huge department store chain) in Paris, Airbus in Toulouse, and Volkswagen in Germany. At each business, the global marketing manager would discuss the firm's global marketing strategy. The tour would be led by a marketing professor.

All tours would be all inclusive, except lunches, and would feature a day of sightseeing and a half-day free time.

Mary Ann had the contracts and the know-how to set up the tours. Her concern was determining what tours should be offered and the demand for the tours. She knew that she would offer student airfares, student forums (but she was unsure of the topics), rail passes, discounts to college-oriented hotels and hostels, and travel insurance on her Web site. Beyond this, she wasn't sure. A big question was whether to offer spring break packages. Although very profitable, might these clash with her positioning as an education-oriented online travel service? If she did decide to feature spring break, what should the package include, and what destinations should be featured?

ONLINE STUDENT TRAVEL

S1. What is your current age?
  1 Under 18—THANK AND TERM
  2 18
  3 19
  4 20
  5 21
  6 22
  7 23–25
  8 26–30
  9 31 or older

S2. Are you currently enrolled in any of the following types of institutions?
  1 Junior college
  2 Community college/two-year program
  3 University/four-year program
  4 None of the above—THANK AND TERM

Q1. Which of the following online travel purchase sites are you aware of? Please mark all that apply.
  A Travelocity
  B Expedia
  C Orbitz
  D Sabre
  E Student City
  F Student Universe
  G Cheap Tickets
  H None of the above—SKIP TO Q8

  (INCLUDE MENTIONS FROM Q1)

Q2. Which online travel purchase sites have you **ever used**?
  A Travelocity
  B Expedia
  C Orbitz
  D Sabre
  E Student City
  F Student Universe
  G Cheap Tickets
  H None of the above—SKIP TO Q8

  (INCLUDE MENTIONS FROM Q2)

Q3. Which online travel purchase sites have you used in the **past year**?
  A Travelocity
  B Expedia
  C Orbitz
  D Sabre
  E Student City
  F Student Universe

G   Cheap Tickets
H   None of the above—SKIP TO Q8

(INCLUDE MENTIONS FROM Q3. ASK FOR EACH TRAVEL SITE.)

Q4. What did you use the online travel site for? Please select all that apply for each travel site used.
A   Travelocity
B   Expedia
C   Orbitz
D   Sabre
E   Student City
F   Student Universe
G   Cheap Tickets
   A   Obtain general destination information
   B   Book a <u>spring break</u> travel package (including two or more
       of airfare, lodging/cruise and car rental)
   C   Book a <u>non-spring break</u> travel package (including two or
       more of airfare, lodging/cruise and car rental)
   D   Book airfare
   E   Book lodging
   F   Book car rental
   G   Book a cruise
   H   Purchase entertainment tickets
   I   Other (please specify)_____

Q5. Did this travel site offer you a student discount on your purchase(s)?
A   Travelocity
B   Expedia
C   Orbitz
D   Sabre
E   Student City
F   Student Universe
G   Cheap Tickets
   1   Yes
   2   No
   3   Don't know

Q6. In general, do you prefer to purchase all-inclusive travel packages, that include your airfare,
lodging and meals or do you prefer to purchase each item separately?
1   Prefer all-inclusive packages
2   Prefer to purchase items separately

Q7. Why do you say that? Please be as specific as possible.

_____

Q8. Have you ever participated in a study-abroad program, where you obtain college credits by
taking a class at a university in a foreign country?
1   Yes
2   No

Q9. Please consider the following concept that could be offered through an online travel site:
Educational trips to various international destinations, led by a professor, offered for three class
credits at your college or university. All tours would be all-inclusive (except lunches) and feature
a day of sightseeing and a half-day of free time. Trips would be offered during the summer break
and/or Christmas break and would be organized by major fields of study (i.e. marketing, art,
etc.). The cost would be comparable to the price for a regular three-credit class and would be
approximately two weeks in length. ??? Two examples could be as follows:

1) A trip for art majors including the Picasso Museum, Rodin Museum, and the Louvre in Paris, the
Uffizi in Florence, and the museums of the Vatican in Rome, led by an art history professor.

2) A trip for marketing majors including a tour that visited Nestle, the World Trade Organization, and
Solomon Skis in Switzerland, Carrefour (the huge department store chain) in Paris, Airbus in

Toulouse, and Volkswagen in Germany to learn about each firm's global business strategy, led by a marketing professor.

How interested would you be in earning college credits through an educational trip abroad, such as those described above?
5 Extremely interested
4 Very interested
3 Somewhat interested
2 Not too interested
1 Not at all interested

Q10. Why do you say that? Please be as specific as possible.

_____

(IF Q9=2 OR 1, SKIP TO Q13)

Q11. Each package would include student airfare, student forums, rail passes (if applicable), discounts to college-oriented hotels and hostels, and travel insurance. What else, if anything, should these package include? Please be as specific as possible.

_____

Q12. How interested would you be in visiting each of the following destinations on an educational trip? Please mark all that apply.
A Africa
B Asia
C Australia
D Central America
E Europe
F Middle East
G South America
   5 Extremely interested
   4 Very interested
   3 Somewhat interested
   2 Not too interested
   1 Not at all interested

Q13. In your opinion, should this online travel site offer spring break packages in addition to these educational trips?
1 Yes
2 No—SKIP TO Q16

Q14. How interested would you be in each of the following spring break destinations? ROTATE A–P.
A Cancun, Mexico
B Cabo San Lucas, Mexico
C Cozumel, Mexico
D South Padre Island, TX
E Daytona Beach, FL
F Key West, FL
G Acapulco, Mexico
H Myrtle Beach, SC
I Bahamas
J Lake Havasu, AZ
K Mazatlan, Mexico
L Puerto Vallarta, Mexico
M Las Vegas, NV
N Panama City, FL
O South Beach, FL
P Jamaica
Q New York, NY
R Chicago, IL

S Telluride, CO
    5 Extremely interested
    4 Very interested
    3 Somewhat interested
    2 Not too interested
    1 Not at all interested

Q15. What should a spring break package include? Please mark all that apply.
  A Airfare
  B Lodging/hotel
  C Car rental
  D Some meals at your hotel (i.e. breakfast and lunch or breakfast and dinner each day)
  E All meals at your hotel (breakfast, lunch and dinner each day)
  F Alcoholic drink vouchers good at your hotel
  G Discounted club admission
  H Discounted entertainment tickets
  I Shuttle bus to and from the airport
  J Food vouchers good at any local restaurant
  K Other (please specify)_____

Q16. Which of the following best describes your major area of study?
   1 Architecture
   2 Business Administration
   3 Education
   4 Engineering
   5 Law/Public Safety
   6 Liberal Arts
   7 Nursing
   8 Science
   9 Social Work
 10 Urban and Public Affairs
 11 Other

Thank you. Those are all of our questions.

Exercise

Using secondary data from the Internet and the "Real People-Real Data" database, advise Mary Ann on constructing her website and marketing plan (see Appendix Two).

Note

1. "Consumers Going Online Before Going on the Road," *PR Newswire*, (June 28, 2005).

Comprehensive Case D

Rockingham National Bank Visa Card Survey

Company Background   Rockingham National Bank, located in Chicago, Illinois, is attempting to expand the market for its Visa card. It is examining certain target groups to determine its ability to penetrate the credit card market with special offers.

Purpose of the Study The purpose of this research study is to evaluate how teachers in Illinois will respond to specific credit card promotional offers. Specifically, the questionnaire was designed to achieve the following objectives:

☐ Develop a demographic, psychographic, credit card ownership, and credit card usage profile of teachers.

☐ Determine the likelihood that teachers would respond to several different concepts for a credit card offer.

☐ Determine which demographic, psychographic, attitudinal, credit card ownership, and credit card usage variables are the best predictors of likelihood to respond to the concept credit card offers.

☐ Make predictions regarding the likely level of response to a credit card offer to the teacher market.

☐ Identify those features most likely to induce teachers to respond to a credit card offer.

Research Approach All data were collected by means of central-location telephone interviewing from the Ameridata facility in Arlington, Texas, by experienced Ameridata interviewers.

The interviews were conducted with software-driven interfaces to virtually eliminate tabulation errors. All interviewing was supervised and monitored by Ameridata personnel.

The geographic area covered was the state of Illinois. The sample was selected following the criteria for a simple random sample; qualified respondents were individuals licensed to teach in Illinois. A total of 400 interviews were completed.

ROCKINGHAM BANK CREDIT CARD SURVEY OF TEACHERS

(ASK TO SPEAK TO RESPONDENT LISTED ON THE SAMPLE SHEET. IF ANOTHER MEMBER OF THE HOUSEHOLD IS WILLING TO DO THE SURVEY, THANK the person for his or her WILLINGNESS, BUT EXPLAIN THAT you NEED TO COMPLETE THE INTERVIEW WITH THE LISTED RESPONDENT.)

Hello, my name is _____ with Ameridata Research, an independent marketing research firm. I would like to ask you a few questions about credit card usage. First, let me assure you this is not a sales call, you will not be contacted again, and my questions will only take a few minutes of your time. (READ ONLY IF NEEDED) Let me assure you that this is not a sales call; we are only conducting research on credit card usage and are interested in your opinions about credit cards.

1. First of all, please tell me whether you strongly agree, agree, neither agree nor disagree, disagree, or strongly disagree with each of the following statements (READ LIST; ROTATE):

		SA	A	NAD	D	SD	DK
a.	Money may not be everything, but it's got a big lead over whatever is second	5	4	3	2	1	6
b.	Money can't buy happiness.	5	4	3	2	1	6
c.	It is important for me to be fashionable and chic.	5	4	3	2	1	6
d.	I buy things even though I can't afford them.	5	4	3	2	1	6
e.	I make only the minimum payments on my credit cards.	5	4	3	2	1	6
f.	I sometimes buy things to make myself feel better.	5	4	3	2	1	6
g.	Shopping is fun.	5	4	3	2	1	6
h.	During the last three years, my financial situation has gotten worse.	5	4	3	2	1	6

		SA	A	NAD	D	SD	DK
i.	I am satisfied with my present financial situation.	5	4	3	2	1	6
j.	Buying things gives me a lot of pleasure.	5	4	3	2	1	6
k.	You can tell a lot about people by the credit cards they use.	5	4	3	2	1	6
l.	I attach great importance to money.	5	4	3	2	1	6
m.	I attach great importance to credit cards.	5	4	3	2	1	6
n.	I attach great importance to material possessions.	5	4	3	2	1	6
o.	I generally read all offers that I receive through the mail just to know what they are about.	5	4	3	2	1	6

2. Please tell me which of the following credit cards you carry with you. Do you carry . . . (PROBE FOR VISA OR MASTERCARD)
   1. Visa? (ASK FOR NUMBER OF VISA CARDS) _____
   2. MasterCard? (ASK FOR NUMBER OF MASTERCARDS) _____
   3. Discover?
   4. American Express?
   5. Optima?
   6. AT&T Universal?
   7. GM?
   8. Ford?
   9. None (SKIP TO Q.11)

3. Which card do you use the most often? (PROBE FOR ONE ANSWER ONLY; IF RESPONDENT IS UNABLE TO GIVE ONLY ONE RESPONSE, TAKE THE FIRST RESPONSE GIVEN)
   1. Visa
   2. MasterCard
   3. Discover
   4. American Express
   5. Optima
   6. AT&T Universal
   7. GM
   8. Ford
   9. DON'T KNOW (SKIP TO Q.11)

(IF "VISA" OR "MASTERCARD" IS MENTIONED IN Q.3, ASK Q.4. OTHERWISE, SKIP TO Q.11)

4. Which bank issued this Visa/MasterCard?
   [MASTERCARD ISSUERS]
   1. Associates National Bank
   2. Chase Manhattan
   3. Citibank
   4. Credit union issued
   5. First Bank
   6. Household
   7. MBNA
   8. Other
   9. DK
   [VISA ISSUERS]
   1. Associates National Bank
   2. Bank of America
   3. Citibank
   4. Credit union issued
   5. First Bank
   6. Household
   7. MBNA
   8. Other
   9. DK

5. Why do you use [ANSWER FROM Q.3] most often?
   1   Convenience
   2   Only card owned/carried
   3   Interest rate
   4   Wide acceptance
   5   Cash back
   6   Cash rebate
   7   Billing cycle/grace period
   8   No annual fee
   9   Issued by a local bank
   10   Corporate/business card
   11   Credit limit
   12   Itemized bill
   13   It's a Gold Card.
   14   Rebate toward automobile purchase
   15   Relationship with organization sponsoring card (IF YES, "Which organization?")
   16   Other

6. What is the interest rate on the balances that you carry on the card you use most often?
   1   Less than 8 percent
   2   8–8.9 percent
   3   9–9.9 percent
   4   10–10.9 percent
   5   11–11.9 percent
   6   12–12.9 percent
   7   13–13.9 percent
   8   14–14.9 percent
   9   15–15.9 percent
   10   16–16.9 percent
   11   17–17.9 percent
   12   18–18.9 percent
   13   19–19.9 percent
   14   20 percent or more

7. What is your credit limit on the card you can use the most?
   _____ Credit limit

8. Is the card you use most often a Gold Card?
   1   Yes
   2   No
   3   DK

9. Does the card you use most often . . . (READ LIST)

	Yes	No	DK
Charge an annual fee?	1	2	3
Offer cash rebates/cash back on purchases?	1	2	3
Offer extended warranties on products you buy?	1	2	3
Offer buyer protection policies on products you buy (to replace the product if damaged, lost, or stolen)?	1	2	3
Offer a photo credit card?	1	2	3

10. Besides a lower interest rate, what feature or features would a new card need to have to convince you to obtain it?
   1   No annual fee
   2   Preapproved
   3   Rebate/cash back/free offers
   4   Business/corporate card
   5   Gold Card
   6   High credit limit

    7   Wide acceptance
    8   Other

11. Have you received any credit card offers in the past year?
    1   Yes   (CONTINUE)
    2   No   (SKIP TO Q.17)
    3   DK   (SKIP TO Q.17)

12. Approximately how many credit offers have you received in the past year?
    _____ Number of offers received

13. Have you responded to any of these offers?
    1   Yes   (CONTINUE)
    2   No   (SKIP TO Q.16)
    3   DK   (SKIP TO Q.17)

14. To which offer or offers did you respond?
    1   Visa
    2   MasterCard
    3   Discover
    4   American Express
    5   Optima
    6   AT&T Universal
    7   GM
    8   Ford
    9   Other

15. Why did you respond [to this offer/these offers]? (ASK FOR EACH RESPONSE IN Q.14)
    1   No annual fee
    2   Preapproved
    3   Interest rate
    4   Build credit rating
    5   Convenience/emergencies
    6   Rebate/cash back/free offers
    7   Business/corporate card
    8   Gold Card
    9   Credit limit
   10   Travel
   11   Grocery shopping
   12   Wide acceptance
   13   Other
    (SKIP TO Q.17)

16. Why didn't you respond to any of the offers? (PROBE)
    1   Interest rate too high
    2   Have too many credit cards
    3   Credit card balances too high
    4   Credit limit
    5   Interest rate confusing
    6   Do not use credit cards
    7   Do not need any more credit cards
    8   Not preapproved/fear of being turned down
    9   Other
   10   DK

17. Have you closed or stopped using any credit cards in the past year?
    1   Yes   (CONTINUE)
    2   No   (SKIP TO Q.20)
    3   DK   (SKIP TO Q.20)

18. Which card or cards have you stopped using?
    1   Visa
    2   MasterCard
    3   Discover

    4   American Express
    5   Optima
    6   AT&T Universal
    7   Other

19. Why have you stopped using this card? (ASK FOR EACH RESPONSE IN Q.18)
    1   Interest rate
    2   Annual fee
    3   Own too many credit cards
    4   Balance too high
    5   Billing problems
    6   Never used it
    7   Limited acceptance
    8   Consolidation of debt
    9   Other

20. Would you say that your attitudes toward the use of credit cards have changed in the past year?
    1   Yes   (CONTINUE)
    2   No   (SKIP TO Q.22)
    3   DK   (SKIP TO Q.22)

21. (IF "YES" IN RESPONSE TO Q.20, ASK) How have your attitudes changed? (PROBE)

22. In comparison with a year ago, would you say you are using your credit cards . . . (READ LIST)
    1   Less often?
    2   About the same?
    3   More often?
    4   DK

23. In comparison with a year ago, which of the following statements is true in regard to your total credit card balances? (READ LIST)
    1   They are less.
    2   They are about the same.
    3   They are greater.
    4   DK

24. Now, I would like to find out how you feel about a particular credit card offer. We are not making this offer to you today—we are only interested in how you feel about the offer. (READ LIST OF OFFER FEATURES. RESPONDENTS WILL BE ASKED about ONE OF THE FOLLOWING SCENARIOS—100 FOR EACH SCENARIO)

	Preapproved	Application
6.0% Intro APR		
9.9% Intro APR		

☐ You receive [an application/a preapproved application] for a Limited Edition Visa card.
☐ There is no annual fee.
☐ It has a [9.9 /6.0] percent initial APR through March 2004.
☐ After that, the APR will be 16.9 percent.
☐ You can immediately transfer balances from other cards up to your credit limit—you can do this through March 2004 with no cash advance fees.
☐ It has a credit limit of up to $5,000.

25. On a scale of 0 to 100, where 0 is not at all likely and 100 is extremely likely, how likely would you be to respond to this offer?
    _____ Likelihood

26. What, if anything, do you particularly LIKE about this offer? (PROBE: "Anything else?")
    1   No annual fee
    2   Good interest rate
    3   Good offer in general
    4   Features/benefits
    5   Ability to transfer balances

   6   Credit limit
   7   Appealing offer in general
   8   Advantages over other offers
   9   MasterCard/Visa brand
  10 Identifies you as a professional
  11 Prestige of Limited Edition's name
  12 Other

27. What, if anything, do you particularly DISLIKE about this offer? (PROBE: "Anything else?")
   1   Interest rate too high
   2   Don't use credit cards
   3   Interest rate confusing
   4   Not competitive with current card
   5   Interest rate change after March
   6   No reason
   7   Other
   8   DK

28. Is the interest rate in the Visa credit card offer clear and understandable?
   1   Yes
   2   No
   3   DK/NS

29. Using a scale of 1 to 10, where 1 is poor and 10 is excellent, please tell me how you would rate the following product features in the Visa credit card offer that was just described. (ROTATE TO REFLECT INTRODUCTORY PERCENTAGE RATE AND BEING PREAPPROVED/HAVING TO APPLY)
_____ No annual fee
_____ 9.9/6.0 percent introductory rate through March 2004
_____ 16.9 percent APR after March 2004
_____ Being preapproved/receiving an application
_____ Ability to transfer balances from other cards
_____ Credit limit of up to $5,000

30. Do you consider this Visa credit card offer to be better than, about the same as, or worse than . . .

	Better	Same	Worse	DK
Discover Card?	1	2	3	4
American Express Optima Card?	1	2	3	4
AT&T Universal Card?	1	2	3	4
GM or Ford Card?	1	2	3	4
Other MasterCard/Visa for teaching professionals?	1	2	3	4
Credit card you use most often?	1	2	3	4

31. (IF BETTER OR WORSE IN Q.30, ASK) Why do you feel that way? (PROBE)

32. In evaluating a credit card offer, how important are the following things to you? Please use a 1 to 10 scale, where 1 is very unimportant and 10 is very important. How important is . . . ? (READ LIST AND ROTATE)
_____ Being preapproved?
_____ Interest rate?
_____ Annual fee?
_____ Credit limit?
_____ Billing cycle/grace period?
_____ Reputation of issuer?
_____ Extended warranty/buyer protection?
_____ No charges if monthly balance is paid?
_____ Cash advance?
_____ Financing payment plan?
_____ 24-hour service for lost or stolen cards?
_____ Ability to transfer balances from other cards?
_____ Rebates?
Finally, just a few questions to help us classify your responses.

33. (INDICATE SEX OF RESPONDENT)
    1 Male
    2 Female

34. Are you currently married or not married?
    1 Married
    2 Not married
    3 RF

35. Which of the following categories includes your age? Are you . . .
    1 18–24?
    2 25–34?
    3 35–44?
    4 45–54?
    5 55–64?
    6 65 or over?
    7 RF

36. What is the highest level of education completed by the primary wage earner in your household?
    1 Less than high school graduate
    2 High school graduate
    3 Some college
    4 College graduate
    5 Any postgraduate work
    6 RF

37. What is your occupation? (PROBE FOR TYPE OF BUSINESS, ETC.)

38. (IF MARRIED) What is your spouse's occupation? (PROBE FOR TYPE OF BUSINESS, ETC.)

39. Which of the following categories includes the total annual income of all the working members of your household before taxes?
    1 Under $15,000
    2 $15,000–$24,999
    3 $25,000–$39,999
    4 $40,000–$54,999
    5 $55,000–$69,999
    6 $70,000 or more
    7 DK
    8 RF

That concludes our survey, and I would like to thank you for taking the time to assist us.

NAME _____

TELEPHONE (_____) _____

INTERVIEWER NUMBER _____

Exercises

1. Use the survey results to respond to each research objective specified at the beginning of the case.
2. How are those who use Visa or MasterCard most often different from those who use American Express most often?
3. Describe respondents' attitudes toward credit limits.
4. Discuss credit card offers and the teachers' responses. Also, discuss credit card closings.
5. How did respondents react to the new credit card proposals?
6. Use multivariate statistics to determine the strongest predictors of response to the new credit card offers.

APPENDIX TWO

Considerations in Creating a Marketing Plan

I. MARKETING OVERVIEW

- ☐ What is the mission of the firm?
- ☐ What business are we in?
- ☐ What are the strategic goals of the organization?
- ☐ What do we sell?
- ☐ What are our target markets?
- ☐ What are the basic assumptions implicit in this plan?

II. OBJECTIVES

- ☐ Sales goals
- ☐ Profit goals
- ☐ Customer-service goals

III. SITUATION ANALYSIS

- ☐ Is a strategic window opening or closing?
- ☐ What are our competitive advantages?
- ☐ Are these competitive advantages sustainable, and can we protect them?

A. Potential Internal Strengths and Weaknesses
- ☐ Managerial knowledge and capabilities
- ☐ Technology (internal)
- ☐ Employee attitudes
- ☐ Employee productivity
- ☐ Competitive intelligence
- ☐ Ability to produce quality products and services
- ☐ Marketing skills
- ☐ Quality control procedures
- ☐ Research and development skills
- ☐ Financial strength
- ☐ Management Information System

B. Potential External Opportunities and Threats
- ☐ Understanding of social/cultural values in the marketplace
- ☐ Understanding changing demographics
- ☐ Economic climate
- ☐ Understanding emerging technology
- ☐ Availability of natural resources
- ☐ Comprehension of the political and legal environment
- ☐ Understanding our competitors

C. Creation of Contingency Plans
- ☐ Take advantage of opportunities
- ☐ Mitigate threats

IV. MARKETING STRATEGY

A. Target Market Strategy
- ☐ Target market defined demographically and psychographically
- ☐ Forecasted change in size and growth rate of the target market
- ☐ Who is the decision maker?
- ☐ What is their decision process?
- ☐ Needs of the target market
- ☐ How do they view our products/services versus the competition?
- ☐ What does the target market want from us?
- ☐ Who are our best customers?

☐ Are some customers not profitable?

☐ How loyal are our customers?

B. Marketing Mix

☐ Is the marketing mix fully integrated in order to achieve the marketing objectives?

1. Product/Service

☐ What are our major product/service offerings?

☐ What benefits do they offer?

☐ Profitability of each item in our product/service mix

☐ What is our brand equity?

☐ Scope, quality, and gaps in the product line

☐ Perceptions of our warranty

☐ Quality of our packaging

☐ Effectiveness of our new product development

☐ Service quality?

2. Price

☐ How does target market view price versus value?

☐ Are we above/below or at the price level of our competition?

☐ How price sensitive is the target market?

☐ Discounts?

☐ Geographic price differences?

☐ Profitability per product/service

☐ Methods of payment

☐ Bundling considerations?

☐ Leasing options?

3. Distribution

☐ Do we have effective supply chain management?

☐ Where does the target market expect to buy our product?

☐ Are we using the most efficient modes of transportation?

☐ Are customers satisfied with our delivery time?

☐ Are our warehouses/distribution centers strategically located and cost effective?

☐ Quality of order fulfillment

☐ How are channels evolving and what does this mean for us?

4. Promotion

☐ Do we have an effective integrated marketing communications (IMC) plan?

☐ What is our positioning strategy and unique selling proposition and are they communicated properly in the IMC plan?

☐ Is our message resulting in increased sales?

☐ Advertising media used and effectiveness of the mix

☐ Advertising timing strategies

☐ Advertising agency functions and relationship with our organization

☐ Effectiveness of each sales promotion activity

☐ Objectives of each sales promotion activity

☐ Sales call effectiveness

☐ Frequency of sales calls on key accounts? Other accounts?

☐ How is salesforce organized and compensated?

☐ How are prospects identified and then forwarded to the sales force?

☐ Do we have adequate geographic sales coverage?

☐ Effectiveness of sales management

- ☐ Quality of our public relations program
- ☐ Components of our public relations program and their contribution to IMC.

V. IMPLEMENTATION, EVALUATION, AND CONTROL
- ☐ Resources necessary to implement the plan (budgets)
- ☐ Timing and order of activities
- ☐ Other required data to implement the plan
- ☐ Assigning authority and responsibility
- ☐ Projected outcomes in terms of sales and market share
- ☐ Criteria for determining the success of the plan
- ☐ Timing of evaluations

APPENDIX THREE

Statistical Tables

1
Random Digits

2
Standard Normal Distribution:
Z-values

3
***t*-Distribution**

4
Chi-Square Distribution

5
***F*-Distribution**

EXHIBIT 1 — Random Digits

63271	59986	71744	51102	15141	80714	58683	93108	13554	79945
88547	09896	95436	79115	08303	01041	20030	63754	08459	28364
55957	57243	83865	09911	19761	66535	40102	26646	60147	15702
46276	87453	44790	64122	45573	84358	21625	16999	13385	22782
55363	07449	34835	15290	76616	67191	12777	21861	68689	03263
69393	92785	49902	58447	42048	30378	87618	26933	40640	16281
13186	29431	88190	04588	38733	81290	89541	70290	40113	08243
17726	28652	56836	78351	47327	18518	92222	55201	27340	10493
36520	64465	05550	30157	82242	29520	69753	72602	23756	54935
81628	36100	39254	56835	37636	02421	98063	89641	64953	99337
84649	48968	75215	75498	49539	74240	03466	49292	36401	45525
63291	11618	12613	75055	43915	26488	41116	64531	56827	30825
70502	53225	03655	05915	37140	57051	48393	91322	25653	06543
06426	24771	59935	49801	11082	66762	94477	02494	88215	27191
20711	55609	29430	70165	45406	78484	31639	52009	18873	96927
41990	70538	77191	25860	55204	73417	83920	69468	74972	38712
72452	36618	76298	26678	89334	33938	95567	29380	75906	91807
37042	40318	57099	10528	09925	89773	41335	96244	29002	46453
53766	52875	15987	46962	67342	77592	57651	95508	80033	69828
90585	58955	53122	16025	84299	53310	67380	84249	25348	04332
32001	96293	37203	64516	51530	37069	40261	61374	05815	06714
62606	64324	46354	72157	67248	20135	49804	09226	64419	29457
10078	28073	85389	50324	14500	15562	64165	06125	71353	77669
91561	46145	24177	15294	10061	98124	75732	00815	83452	97355
13091	98112	53959	79607	52244	63303	10413	63839	74762	50289
73864	83014	72457	22682	03033	61714	88173	90835	00634	85169
66668	25467	48894	51043	02365	91726	09365	63167	95264	45643
84745	41042	29493	01836	09044	51926	43630	63470	76508	14194
48068	26805	94595	47907	13357	38412	33318	26098	82782	42851
54310	96175	97594	88616	42035	38093	36745	56702	40644	83514
14877	33095	10924	58013	61439	21882	42059	24177	58739	60170
78295	23179	02771	43464	59061	71411	05697	67194	30495	21157
67524	02865	39593	54278	04237	92441	26602	63835	38032	94770
58268	57219	68124	73455	83236	08710	04284	55005	84171	42596
97158	28672	50685	01181	24262	19427	52106	34308	73685	74246
04230	16831	69085	30802	65559	09205	71829	06489	85650	38707
94879	56606	30401	02602	57658	70091	54986	41394	60437	03195
71446	15232	66715	26385	91518	70566	02888	79941	39684	54315
32886	05644	79316	09819	00813	88407	17461	73925	53037	91904
62048	33711	25290	21526	02223	75947	66466	06332	10913	75336
84534	42351	21628	53669	81352	95152	08107	98814	72743	12849
84707	15885	84710	35866	06446	86311	32648	88141	73902	69981
19409	40868	64220	80861	13860	68493	52908	26374	63297	45052
57978	48015	25973	66777	45924	56144	24742	96702	88200	66162
57295	98298	11199	96510	75228	41600	47192	43267	35973	23152
94044	83785	93388	07833	38216	31413	70555	03023	54147	06647
30014	25879	71763	96679	90603	99396	74557	74224	18211	91637
07265	69563	64268	88802	72264	66540	01782	08396	19251	83613
84404	88642	30263	80310	11522	57810	27627	78376	36240	48952
21778	02085	27762	46097	43324	34354	09369	14966	10158	76089

EXHIBIT 2 | Standard Normal Distribution: *Z*-values

Entries in the table give the area under the curve between the mean and *Z* standard deviations above the mean. For example, for *Z* = 1.25, the area under the curve between the mean and *Z* is .3944.

Area or Probability

0   Z

Z	.00	.01	.02	.03	.04	.05	.06	.07	.08	.09
.0	.0000	.0040	.0080	.0120	.0160	.0199	.0239	.0279	.0319	.0359
.1	.0398	.0438	.0478	.0517	.0557	.0596	.0636	.0675	.0714	.0753
.2	.0793	.0832	.0871	.0910	.0948	.0987	.1026	.1064	.1103	.1141
.3	.1179	.1217	.1255	.1293	.1331	.1368	.1406	.1443	.1480	.1517
.4	.1554	.1591	.1628	.1664	.1700	.1736	.1772	.1808	.1844	.1879
.5	.1915	.1950	.1985	.2019	.2054	.2088	.2123	.2157	.2190	.2224
.6	.2257	.2291	.2324	.2357	.2389	.2422	.2454	.2486	.2518	.2549
.7	.2580	.2612	.2642	.2673	.2704	.2734	.2764	.2794	.2823	.2852
.8	.2881	.2910	.2939	.2967	.2995	.3023	.3051	.3078	.3106	.3133
.9	.3159	.3186	.3212	.3238	.3264	.3289	.3315	.3340	.3365	.3389
1.0	.3413	.3438	.3461	.3485	.3508	.3531	.3554	.3577	.3599	.3621
1.1	.3643	.3665	.3686	.3708	.3729	.3749	.3770	.3790	.3810	.3830
1.2	.3849	.3869	.3888	.3907	.3925	.3944	.3962	.3980	.3997	.4015
1.3	.4032	.4049	.4066	.4082	.4099	.4115	.4131	.4147	.4162	.4177
1.4	.4192	.4207	.4222	.4236	.4251	.4265	.4279	.4292	.4306	.4319
1.5	.4332	.4345	.4357	.4370	.4382	.4394	.4406	.4418	.4429	.4441
1.6	.4452	.4463	.4474	.4484	.4495	.4505	.4515	.4525	.4535	.4545
1.7	.4554	.4564	.4573	.4582	.4591	.4599	.4608	.4616	.4625	.4633
1.8	.4641	.4649	.4656	.4664	.4671	.4678	.4686	.4693	.4699	.4706
1.9	.4713	.4719	.4726	.4732	.4738	.4744	.4750	.4756	.4761	.4767
2.0	.4772	.4778	.4783	.4788	.4793	.4798	.4803	.4808	.4812	.4817
2.1	.4821	.4826	.4830	.4834	.4838	.4842	.4846	.4850	.4854	.4857
2.2	.4861	.4864	.4868	.4871	.4875	.4878	.4881	.4884	.4887	.4890
2.3	.4893	.4896	.4898	.4901	.4904	.4906	.4909	.4911	.4913	.4916
2.4	.4918	.4920	.4922	.4925	.4927	.4929	.4931	.4932	.4934	.4936
2.5	.4938	.4940	.4941	.4943	.4945	.4946	.4948	.4949	.4951	.4952
2.6	.4953	.4955	.4956	.4957	.4959	.4960	.4961	.4962	.4963	.4964
2.7	.4965	.4966	.4967	.4968	.4969	.4970	.4971	.4972	.4973	.4974
2.8	.4974	.4975	.4976	.4977	.4977	.4978	.4979	.4979	.4980	.4981
2.9	.4981	.4982	.4982	.4983	.4984	.4984	.4985	.4985	.4986	.4986
3.0	.4986	.4987	.4987	.4988	.4988	.4989	.4989	.4989	.4990	.4990

EXHIBIT 3 | *t*-Distribution

Entries in the table give *t*-values for an area or probability in the upper tail of the
t-distribution. For example, with 10 degrees of freedom and a .05 area
in the upper tail, $t_{.05} = 1.812$.

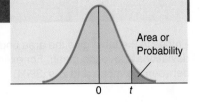

Area or
Probability

0   *t*

Degrees of Freedom	Area in Upper Tail				
	.10	.05	.025	.01	.005
1	3.078	6.314	12.706	31.821	63.657
2	1.886	2.920	4.303	6.965	9.925
3	1.638	2.353	3.182	4.541	5.841
4	1.533	2.132	2.776	3.747	4.604
5	1.476	2.015	2.571	3.365	4.032
6	1.440	1.943	2.447	3.143	3.707
7	1.415	1.895	2.365	2.998	3.499
8	1.397	1.860	2.306	2.896	3.355
9	1.383	1.833	2.262	2.821	3.250
10	1.372	1.812	2.228	2.764	3.169
11	1.363	1.796	2.201	2.718	3.106
12	1.356	1.782	2.179	2.681	3.055
13	1.350	1.771	2.160	2.650	3.012
14	1.345	1.761	2.145	2.624	2.977
15	1.341	1.753	2.131	2.602	2.947
16	1.337	1.746	2.120	2.583	2.921
17	1.333	1.740	2.110	2.567	2.898
18	1.330	1.734	2.101	2.552	2.878
19	1.328	1.729	2.093	2.539	2.861
20	1.325	1.725	2.086	2.528	2.845
21	1.323	1.721	2.080	2.518	2.831
22	1.321	1.717	2.074	2.508	2.819
23	1.319	1.714	2.069	2.500	2.807
24	1.318	1.711	2.064	2.492	2.797
25	1.316	1.708	2.060	2.485	2.787
26	1.315	1.706	2.056	2.479	2.779
27	1.314	1.703	2.052	2.473	2.771
28	1.313	1.701	2.048	2.467	2.763
29	1.311	1.699	2.045	2.462	2.756
30	1.310	1.697	2.042	2.457	2.750
40	1.303	1.684	2.021	2.423	2.704
60	1.296	1.671	2.000	2.390	2.660
120	1.289	1.658	1.980	2.358	2.617
∞	1.282	1.645	1.960	2.326	2.576

EXHIBIT 4 | Chi-Square Distribution

Entries in the table give χ^2_α values, where α is the area or probability in the upper tail of the chi-square distribution. For example, with 10 degrees of freedom and a .01 area in the upper tail, χ^2_α 23.2093.

Area or Probability

χ^2_α

Degrees of Freedom	Area in Upper Tail									
	.995	.99	.975	.95	.90	.10	.05	.025	.01	.005
1	.0000393	.000157	.000982	.000393	.015709	2.70554	3.84146	5.02389	6.63490	7.87944
2	.0100251	.0201007	.0506356	.102587	.210720	4.60517	5.99147	7.37776	9.21034	10.5966
3	.0717212	.114832	2.15795	.351846	.584375	6.25139	7.81473	9.34840	11.3449	12.8381
4	.206990	.297110	.484419	.710721	1.063623	7.77944	9.48773	11.1433	13.2767	14.8602
5	.411740	.554300	.831211	1.145476	1.61031	9.23635	11.0705	12.8325	15.0863	16.7496
6	.675727	.872085	1.237347	1.63539	2.20413	10.6446	12.5916	14.4494	16.8119	18.5476
7	.989265	1.239043	1.68987	2.16735	2.83311	12.0170	14.0671	16.0128	18.4753	20.2777
8	1.344419	1.646482	2.17973	2.73264	3.48954	13.3616	15.5073	17.5346	20.0902	21.9550
9	1.734926	2.087912	2.70039	3.32511	4.16816	14.6837	16.9190	19.0228	21.6660	23.5893
10	2.15585	2.55821	3.24697	3.94030	4.86518	15.9871	18.3070	20.4831	23.2093	25.1882
11	2.60321	3.05347	3.81575	4.57481	5.57779	17.2750	19.6751	21.9200	24.7250	26.7569
12	3.07382	3.57056	4.40379	5.22603	6.30380	18.5494	21.0261	23.3367	26.2170	28.2995
13	3.56503	4.10691	5.00874	5.89186	7.04150	19.8119	22.3621	24.7356	27.6883	29.8194
14	4.07468	4.66043	5.62872	6.57063	7.78953	21.0642	23.6848	26.1190	29.1413	31.3193
15	4.60094	5.22935	6.26214	7.26094	8.54675	22.3072	24.9958	27.4884	30.5779	32.8013
16	5.14224	5.81221	6.90766	7.96164	9.31223	23.5418	26.2962	28.8454	31.9999	34.2672
17	5.69724	6.40776	7.56418	8.67176	10.0852	24.7690	27.5871	30.1910	33.4087	35.7185
18	6.26481	7.01491	8.23075	9.39046	10.8649	25.9894	28.8693	31.5264	34.8053	37.1564
19	6.84398	7.63273	8.90655	10.1170	11.6509	27.2036	30.1435	32.8523	36.1908	38.5822
20	7.43386	8.26040	9.59083	10.8508	12.4426	28.4120	31.4104	34.1696	37.5662	39.9968
21	8.03366	8.89720	10.28293	11.5913	13.2396	29.6151	32.6705	35.4789	38.9321	41.4010
22	8.64272	9.54249	10.9823	12.3380	14.0415	30.8133	33.9244	36.7807	40.2894	42.7958
23	9.26042	10.19567	11.6885	13.0905	14.8479	32.0069	35.1725	38.0757	41.6384	44.1813
24	9.88623	10.8564	12.4011	13.8484	15.6587	33.1963	36.4151	39.3641	42.9798	45.5585
25	10.5197	11.5240	13.1197	14.6114	16.4734	34.3816	37.6525	40.6465	44.3141	46.9278
26	11.1603	12.1981	13.8439	15.3791	17.2919	35.5631	38.8852	41.9232	45.6417	48.2899
27	11.8076	12.8786	14.5733	16.1513	18.1138	36.7412	40.1133	43.1944	46.9630	49.6449
28	12.4613	13.5648	15.3079	16.9279	18.9392	37.9159	41.3372	44.4607	48.2782	50.9933
29	13.1211	14.2565	16.0471	17.7083	19.7677	39.0875	42.5569	45.7222	49.5879	52.3356
30	13.7867	14.9535	16.7908	18.4926	20.5992	40.2560	43.7729	46.9792	50.8922	53.6720
40	20.765	22.1643	24.4331	26.5093	29.0505	51.8050	55.7585	59.3417	63.6907	66.7659
50	27.9907	29.7067	32.3574	34.7642	37.6886	63.1671	67.5048	71.4202	76.1539	79.4900
60	35.5346	37.4848	40.4817	43.1879	46.4589	74.3970	79.0819	83.2976	88.3794	91.9517
70	43.2752	45.4418	48.7576	51.7393	55.3290	85.5271	90.5312	95.0231	100.425	104.215
80	51.1720	53.5400	57.1532	60.3915	64.2778	96.5782	101.879	106.629	112.329	116.321
90	59.1963	61.7541	65.6466	69.1260	73.2912	107.565	113.145	118.136	124.116	128.299
100	67.3276	70.0648	74.2219	77.9295	82.3581	118.498	124.342	129.561	135.807	140.169

EXHIBIT 5	*F*-Distribution

Entries in the table give F_α values, where is the area or probability in the upper tail of the *F*-distribution. For example, with 12 numerator degrees of freedom, 15 denominator degrees of freedom, and a .05 area in the upper tail, $F_{.05} = 2.48$.

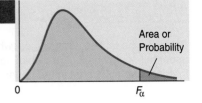

Area or Probability

0　　　　F_α

Table of $F_{.05}$ Values

Numerator Degrees of Freedom

	1	2	3	4	5	6	7	8	9	10	12	15	20	24	30	40	60	120	∞
1	161.4	199.5	215.7	224.6	230.2	234.0	236.8	238.9	240.5	241.9	243.9	245.9	248.0	249.1	250.1	251.1	252.2	253.3	254.30
2	18.51	19.00	19.16	19.25	19.30	19.33	19.35	19.37	19.38	19.40	19.41	19.43	19.45	19.45	19.46	19.47	19.48	19.49	19.50
3	10.13	9.55	9.28	9.12	9.01	8.94	8.89	8.85	8.81	8.79	8.74	8.70	8.66	8.64	8.62	8.59	8.57	8.55	8.53
4	7.71	6.94	6.59	6.39	6.26	6.16	6.09	6.04	6.00	5.96	5.91	5.86	5.80	5.77	5.75	5.72	5.69	5.66	5.63
5	6.61	5.79	5.41	5.19	5.05	4.95	4.88	4.82	4.77	4.74	4.68	4.62	4.56	4.53	4.50	4.46	4.43	4.40	4.36
6	5.99	5.14	4.76	4.53	4.39	4.28	4.21	4.15	4.10	4.06	4.00	3.94	3.87	3.84	3.81	3.77	3.74	3.70	3.67
7	5.59	4.74	4.35	4.12	3.97	3.87	3.79	3.73	3.68	3.64	3.57	3.51	3.44	3.41	3.38	3.34	3.30	3.27	3.23
8	5.32	4.46	4.07	3.84	3.69	3.58	3.50	3.44	3.39	3.35	3.28	3.22	3.15	3.12	3.08	3.04	3.01	2.97	2.93
9	5.12	4.26	3.86	3.63	3.48	3.37	3.29	3.23	3.18	3.14	3.07	3.01	2.94	2.90	2.86	2.83	2.79	2.75	2.71
10	4.96	4.10	3.71	3.48	3.33	3.22	3.14	3.07	3.02	2.98	2.91	2.85	2.77	2.74	2.70	2.66	2.62	2.58	2.54
11	4.84	3.98	3.59	3.36	3.20	3.09	3.01	2.95	2.90	2.85	2.79	2.72	2.65	2.61	2.57	2.53	2.49	2.45	2.40
12	4.75	3.89	3.49	3.26	3.11	3.00	2.91	2.85	2.80	2.75	2.69	2.62	2.54	2.51	2.47	2.43	2.38	2.34	2.30
13	4.67	3.81	3.41	3.18	3.03	2.92	2.83	2.77	2.71	2.67	2.60	2.53	2.46	2.42	2.38	2.34	2.30	2.25	2.21
14	4.60	3.74	3.34	3.11	2.96	2.85	2.76	2.70	2.65	2.60	2.53	2.46	2.39	2.35	2.31	2.27	2.22	2.18	2.13
15	4.54	3.68	3.29	3.06	2.90	2.79	2.71	2.64	2.59	2.54	2.48	2.40	2.33	2.29	2.25	2.20	2.16	2.11	2.07
16	4.49	3.63	3.24	3.01	2.85	2.74	2.66	2.59	2.54	2.49	2.42	2.35	2.28	2.24	2.19	2.15	2.11	2.06	2.01
17	4.45	3.59	3.20	2.96	2.81	2.70	2.61	2.55	2.49	2.45	2.38	2.31	2.23	2.19	2.15	2.10	2.06	2.01	1.96
18	4.41	3.55	3.16	2.93	2.77	2.66	2.58	2.51	2.46	2.41	2.34	2.27	2.19	2.15	2.11	2.06	2.02	1.97	1.92
19	4.38	3.52	3.13	2.90	2.74	2.63	2.54	2.48	2.42	2.38	2.31	2.23	2.16	2.11	2.07	2.03	1.98	1.93	1.88
20	4.35	3.49	3.10	2.87	2.71	2.60	2.51	2.45	2.39	2.35	2.28	2.20	2.12	2.08	2.04	1.99	1.95	1.90	1.84
21	4.32	3.47	3.07	2.84	2.68	2.57	2.49	2.42	2.37	2.32	2.25	2.18	2.10	2.05	2.01	1.96	1.92	1.87	1.81
22	4.30	3.44	3.05	2.82	2.66	2.55	2.46	2.40	2.34	2.30	2.23	2.15	2.07	2.03	1.98	1.94	1.89	1.84	1.78
23	4.28	3.42	3.03	2.80	2.64	2.53	2.44	2.37	2.32	2.27	2.20	2.13	2.05	2.01	1.96	1.91	1.86	1.81	1.76
24	4.26	3.40	3.01	2.78	2.62	2.51	2.42	2.36	2.30	2.25	2.18	2.11	2.03	1.98	1.94	1.89	1.84	1.79	1.73
25	4.24	3.39	2.99	2.76	2.60	2.49	2.40	2.34	2.28	2.24	2.16	2.09	2.01	1.96	1.92	1.87	1.82	1.77	1.71
26	4.23	3.37	2.98	2.74	2.59	2.47	2.39	2.32	2.27	2.22	2.15	2.07	1.99	1.95	1.90	1.85	1.80	1.75	1.69
27	4.21	3.35	2.96	2.73	2.57	2.46	2.37	2.31	2.25	2.20	2.13	2.06	1.97	1.93	1.88	1.84	1.79	1.73	1.67
28	4.20	3.34	2.95	2.71	2.56	2.45	2.36	2.29	2.24	2.19	2.12	2.04	1.96	1.91	1.87	1.82	1.77	1.71	1.65
29	4.18	3.33	2.93	2.70	2.55	2.43	2.35	2.28	2.22	2.18	2.10	2.03	1.94	1.90	1.85	1.81	1.75	1.70	1.64
30	4.17	3.32	2.92	2.69	2.53	2.42	2.33	2.27	2.21	2.16	2.09	2.01	1.93	1.89	1.84	1.79	1.74	1.68	1.62
40	4.08	3.23	2.84	2.61	2.45	2.34	2.25	2.18	2.12	2.08	2.00	1.92	1.84	1.79	1.74	1.69	1.64	1.58	1.51
60	4.00	3.15	2.76	2.53	2.37	2.25	2.17	2.10	2.04	1.99	1.92	1.84	1.75	1.70	1.65	1.59	1.53	1.47	1.39
120	3.92	3.07	2.68	2.45	2.29	2.17	2.09	2.02	1.96	1.91	1.83	1.75	1.66	1.61	1.55	1.50	1.43	1.35	1.25
∞	3.84	3.00	2.60	2.37	2.21	2.10	2.01	1.94	1.88	1.83	1.75	1.67	1.57	1.52	1.46	1.39	1.32	1.22	1.00

Table of $F_{.05}$ Values

Numerator Degrees of Freedom

	1	2	3	4	5	6	7	8	9	10	12	15	20	24	30	40	60	120	∞
1	4052	4999.5	5403	5625	5764	5859	5928	5982	6022	6056	6106	6157	6209	6235	6261	6287	6313	6339	6366
2	98.50	99.00	99.17	99.25	99.30	99.33	99.36	99.37	99.39	99.40	99.42	99.43	99.45	99.46	99.47	99.47	99.48	99.49	99.50
3	34.12	30.82	29.46	28.71	28.24	27.91	27.67	27.49	27.35	27.23	27.05	26.87	26.69	26.60	26.50	26.41	26.32	26.22	26.13
4	21.20	18.00	16.69	15.98	15.52	51.21	14.98	14.80	14.66	14.55	14.37	14.20	14.02	13.93	13.84	13.75	13.65	13.56	13.46
5	16.26	13.27	12.06	11.39	10.97	10.67	10.46	10.29	10.16	10.05	9.89	9.72	9.55	9.47	9.38	9.29	9.20	9.11	9.06
6	13.75	10.92	9.78	9.15	8.75	8.47	8.26	8.10	7.98	7.87	7.72	7.56	7.40	7.31	7.23	7.14	7.06	6.97	6.88
7	12.25	9.55	8.45	7.85	7.46	7.19	6.99	6.84	6.72	6.62	6.47	6.31	6.16	6.07	5.99	5.91	5.82	5.74	5.65
8	11.26	8.65	7.59	7.01	6.63	6.37	6.18	6.03	5.91	5.81	5.67	5.52	5.36	5.28	5.20	5.12	5.03	4.95	4.86
9	10.56	8.02	6.99	6.42	6.06	5.80	5.61	5.47	5.35	5.26	5.11	4.96	4.81	4.73	4.65	4.57	4.48	4.40	4.31
10	10.04	7.56	6.55	5.99	5.64	5.39	5.20	5.06	4.94	4.85	4.71	4.56	4.41	4.33	4.25	4.17	4.08	4.00	3.91
11	9.65	7.21	6.22	5.67	5.32	5.07	4.89	4.74	4.63	4.54	4.40	4.25	4.10	4.02	3.94	3.86	3.78	3.69	3.60
12	9.33	6.93	5.95	5.41	5.06	4.82	4.64	4.50	4.39	4.30	4.16	4.01	3.86	3.78	3.70	3.62	3.54	3.45	3.36
13	9.07	6.70	5.74	5.21	4.86	4.62	4.44	4.30	4.19	4.10	3.96	3.82	3.66	3.59	3.51	3.43	3.34	3.25	3.17
14	8.86	6.51	5.56	5.04	4.69	4.46	4.28	4.14	4.03	3.94	3.80	3.66	3.51	3.43	3.35	3.27	3.18	3.09	3.00
15	8.68	6.36	5.42	4.89	4.56	4.32	4.14	4.00	3.89	3.80	3.67	3.52	3.37	3.29	3.21	3.13	3.05	2.96	2.87
16	8.53	6.23	5.29	4.77	4.44	4.20	4.03	3.89	3.78	3.69	3.55	3.41	3.26	3.18	3.10	3.02	2.93	2.84	2.75
17	8.40	6.11	5.18	4.67	4.34	4.10	3.93	3.79	3.68	3.59	3.46	3.31	3.16	3.08	3.00	2.92	2.83	2.75	2.65
18	8.29	6.01	5.09	4.58	4.25	4.01	3.84	3.71	3.60	3.51	3.37	3.23	3.08	3.00	2.92	2.84	2.75	2.66	2.57
19	8.18	5.93	5.01	4.50	4.17	3.94	3.77	3.63	3.52	3.43	3.30	3.15	3.00	2.92	2.84	2.76	2.67	2.58	2.49
20	8.10	5.85	4.94	4.43	4.10	3.87	3.70	3.56	3.46	3.37	3.23	3.09	2.94	2.86	2.78	2.69	2.61	2.52	2.42
21	8.02	5.78	4.87	4.37	4.04	3.81	3.64	3.51	3.40	3.31	3.17	3.03	2.88	2.80	2.72	2.64	2.55	2.46	2.36
22	7.95	5.72	4.82	4.31	3.99	3.76	3.59	3.45	3.35	3.26	3.12	2.98	2.83	2.75	2.67	2.58	2.50	2.40	2.31
23	7.88	5.66	4.76	4.26	3.94	3.71	3.54	3.41	3.30	3.21	3.07	2.93	2.78	2.70	2.62	2.54	2.45	2.35	2.26
24	7.82	5.61	4.72	4.22	3.90	3.67	3.50	3.36	3.26	3.17	3.03	2.89	2.74	2.66	2.58	2.49	2.40	2.31	2.21
25	7.77	5.57	4.68	4.18	3.85	3.63	3.46	3.32	3.22	3.13	2.99	2.85	2.70	2.62	2.54	2.45	2.36	2.27	2.17
26	7.72	5.53	4.64	4.14	3.82	3.59	3.42	3.29	3.18	3.09	2.96	2.81	2.66	2.58	2.50	2.42	2.33	2.23	2.13
27	7.68	5.49	4.60	4.11	3.78	3.56	3.39	3.26	3.15	3.06	2.93	2.78	2.63	2.55	2.47	2.38	2.29	2.20	2.10
28	7.64	5.45	4.57	4.07	3.75	3.53	3.36	3.23	3.12	3.03	2.90	2.75	2.60	2.52	2.44	2.35	2.26	2.17	2.06
29	7.60	5.42	4.54	4.04	3.73	3.50	3.33	3.20	3.09	3.00	2.87	2.73	2.57	2.49	2.41	2.33	2.23	2.14	2.03
30	7.56	5.39	4.51	4.02	3.70	3.47	3.30	3.17	3.07	2.98	2.84	2.70	2.55	2.47	2.39	2.30	2.21	2.11	2.01
40	7.31	5.18	4.31	3.83	3.51	3.29	3.12	2.99	2.89	2.80	2.66	2.52	2.37	2.29	2.20	2.11	2.02	1.92	1.80
60	7.08	4.98	4.13	3.65	3.34	3.12	2.95	2.82	2.72	2.63	2.50	2.35	2.20	2.12	2.03	1.94	1.84	1.73	1.60
120	6.85	4.79	3.95	3.48	3.17	2.96	2.79	2.66	2.56	2.47	2.34	2.19	2.03	1.95	1.86	1.76	1.66	1.53	1.38
∞	6.63	4.61	3.78	3.32	3.02	2.80	2.64	2.51	2.41	2.32	2.18	2.04	1.88	1.79	1.70	1.59	1.47	1.32	1.00

ENDNOTES

Chapter 1

1. www.marketingpower.com accessed October 25,2010

2. "Women Take No-Muss, No Fuss, Approach to Beauty Products," *Quirk's Marketing Research Review*, July, 2010, p. 74.3.

3. "Understanding Discontinuous Opportunities," *Marketing Research,* Fall 1999, p.9.

4. Stephen E. Brown, Anders Gustafsson and Lars Witell, "Beyond Products," *Wall Street Journal*, June 22, 1009, p. R7.

5. "Satisfaction Not Guaranteed," *Business Week*, June 19, 2006, p. 33.

6. "Why Some Customers Are More Equal Than Others," *Fortune*, September 19, 1994, pp. 215–224; and William Wright, "Determinants of Customer Loyalty and Financial Performance," *Journal of Management Accounting Research,* January 2009, pp. 1-12.

7. Sunil Gupta, Donald Lehmann, and Jennifer Ames Stuart, "Valuing Customers," *Journal of Marketing Research*, February 2004, pp. 7–18.

8. "How Current Are your beliefs about Social Media?" *Marketing Research,* Fall 2010, p. 26.

9. "Compulsively Connected? Millennials Can't Not Social Network," *Quirk's Marketing Research Review,* July 2010, p.6.

10. "Basic Research Loses Some Allure," *Wall Street Journal,* October 7, 2009, p. A3.

11. Michael Fielding, "Resorts' email Alerts Revive Flat Business on Slopes," *Marketing News*, March 1, 2005, pp. 17–18.

12. Christine Wright-Isak and David Prensky, "Early Marketing Research: Science and Application," *Marketing Research,* Fall 1993, pp. 16–23.

13. Percival White, *Market Analysis: In Principles and Methods*, 2nd ed. (New York: McGraw-Hill 1925).

14. Much of this section is taken from David W. Steward, "From Methods and Projects to Systems and Process: The Evolution of Marketing Research Techniques," *Marketing Research,* September 1991, pp. 25–34.

15. William D. Neal, "Getting Serious about Marketing Research," *Marketing Research*, Summer 2002, pp. 24–28.

16. "Online Research Still Reigns Supreme," *Quirk's Marketing Research Review,* July 2010 pp. 50-59.

17. "Don't Call Me Wired," *Next,* July 12, 2010, p. 20.

18. "Digital Hot List," *Digital,* October 11, 2010, p. 20

19. "Retailers and Consumers Reach Symbiosis Through Couponing," *Quirk's Marketing Research Review,* October 2010, p. 8.

Chapter 2

1. Jack Honomichl, "Global Top 25," *Marketing News*, August 30, 2010, p. 10.

2. Ibid.

3. "Research 2010: More Work, More Data, Same Budgets," *Quirk's Marketing Research Review* February, 2010, pp. 96-97.

4. The Nielsen Company profile is from: Jack Homomichl, "Honomichl Top 50," *Marketing News* June 30, 2010, pp. 23-24.

5. "Kraft's Miracle Whip Targets Core Consumers with '97 Ads," *Advertising Age*, February 3, 1997, p. 12; also see "Ketchup, Mustard and Mayonnaise in the U.S.," www.packagedfacts.com, accessed October 28, 2010.

6. Presentation by Jerry Thomas at the University of Texas at Arlington MS in Marketing Research Spring Conference, 2009.

7. Honomichl, June 30, 2010, p. 18.

8. "Surviving in 2010: Research's Changes of Focus," *Marketing News*, February 28, 2010, pp. 30-33.

9. Ibid.

10. Ibid.

11. Ibid.

12. Ibid.

13. "Show Them and Tell Them," *Quirk's Marketing Research Review*, January 2010, pp. 36-39.

14. "Research 2010 . . . ," p. 97.

15. These ethical theories are from: Catherine Rainbow, "Descriptions of Ethical Theories and Principles," www.bio.davidson.edu/people/Kabernd/Indep/carainbow.htm, June 22, 2005.

16. "New York State Sues Survey Firm for Allegedly Tricking Students," *Wall Street Journal*, August 30, 2002.

17. Shelby Hunt, Lawrence Chonko, and James Wilcox, "Ethical Problems of Marketing Researchers," *Journal of Marketing Research*, August 1984, p. 314. Reprinted by permission of the American Marketing Association.

18. Terry Grapentine, "You Can't Take the Human Nature out of Black Boxes," *Marketing Research*, Winter 2004, pp. 20-22.

19. "Let Me Help You With That," *Quirk's Marketing Research Review*, October 2008, pp. 30-36.

20. Ibid.

21. "A Web Pioneer Profiles Users by Name, *Wall Street Journal*, October 25, 2010, pp. A1, A16.

22. The U.S.-E.U. & Swiss Safe Harbors Frameworks," www.export.gov, accessed October 27, 2010.

23. "Professional Researcher Certification," www.mra-net.org, accessed October 21, 2010

24. Mark Goodin, "Clean Up Your Act," *Quirk's Marketing Research Review*, December 2010, pp. 38-43.

25. Johann Feitner, "Driving the Message Home," *Quirk's Marketing Research Review*, October 2007, pp. 40-43.

Chapter 3

1. Terry H. Grapentine and Dianne Weaver, "Business Goals Are Key to Proper Marketing Research," *Marketing News*, September 15, 2006, pp. 28-31.

2. Ted Grenager, "A Revolution In A Box," *Brandweek*, October 25, 2010, p. 17.

3. Ibid.

4. Bonnie Eisenfeld, "Knowing What You Want," *Quirk's Marketing Research Review*, July 2010, pp. 66-70.

5. Terry H. Grapentine and Dianne Weaver, "Business Goals Are Key to Proper Marketing Research," *Marketing News*, September 15, 2006, pp. 28–31.

6. Diane Schmalensee and Dawn Lesh, "How to Make Research More Actionable," *Marketing Research*, Winter 1998/Spring 1999, pp. 23–26. Reprinted with permission from *Marketing Research,* published by the American Marketing Association.

7. Todd Wasserman, "K-C Tries Seeing Things From Consumer's POV," *Brandweek*, September 5, 2005, p. 6.

8. "Request for Proposal: Write It Well and You Will Be On Your Way," *Marketing News,* February 15, 2008, p. 8.

9. Joseph Rydholm, "What Do Clients Want from a Research Firm?" *Marketing Research Review*, October 1995, p. 82.

10. Fred Luthans and Janet K. Larsen, "How Managers Really Communicate," Human Relations 39 (1986), pp. 161–178; and Harry E. Penley and Brian Hawkins, "Studying Interpersonal Communication in Organizations: A Leadership Application," *Academy of Management Journal 28* (1985), pp. 309-326.

11. Rohit Deshpande and Scott Jeffries, "Attitude Affecting the Use of Marketing Research in Decision Making: An Empirical Investigation," in Educators' Conference Proceedings, Series 47, edited by Kenneth L. Bernhardt et al. (Chicago: American Marketing Association, 1981), pp. 1–4.

12. Rohit Deshpande and Gerald Zaltman, "Factors Affecting the Use of Market Information: A Path Analysis," *Journal of Marketing Research 19* (February 1982), pp. 14–31; Rohit Deshpande, "A Comparison of Factors Affecting Researcher and Manager Perceptions of Market Research Use," *Journal of Marketing Research 21* (February 1989), pp. 32–38; Hanjoon Lee, Frank Acito, and Ralph Day, "Evaluation and Use of Marketing Research by Decision Makers: A Behavioral Simulation," *Journal of Marketing Research 24* (May 1987), pp. 187–196; and Michael Hu, "An Experimental Study of Managers' and Researchers' Use of Consumer Market Research," *Journal of the Academy of Marketing Science 14* (Fall 1986), pp. 44–51; and Rohit Deshpande and Gerald Zaltman, "A Comparison of Factors Affecting Use of Marketing Information in Consumer and Industrial Firms," *Journal of Marketing Research 24* (February 1987), pp. 114–118.

13. Joe Cardador and Mark Hunter, "Back to Basics," *Quirk's Marketing Research Review*, March 2009, pp. 46-53.

Chapter 4

1. John Goodman and David Beinhacker. "By the Numbers," *Quirk's Marketing Research Review*, October 2003, pp. 18, 82.

2. "Survey Says: BtoB Database Marketers Are All Grown Up," *BtoB*, October 8, 2007, p. 26.

3. "A Potent New Tool for Selling Database Marketing," *BusinessWeek*, September 5, 1994, pp. 56–62.

4. Julie Schlosser, "Looking for Intelligence in Ice Cream," *Fortune*, March 17, 2003. pp. 114–120.

5. Joan Raymond, "Home Field Advantage," *American Demographics*, April 2001, pp. 34–36.

6. "Interview with Mike Foytik, DSS Research," conducted by Roger Gates, February 11, 2011. Reprinted by permission.

7. "What've You Done for Us Lately?" *BusinessWeek* (April 23, 1999), pp. 24–34.

8. "Looking for Patterns," *Wall Street Journal* (June 21, 1999), pp. R16, R20.

9. Gordon Plutsky, "Behavioral Targeting: Does It Make Sense For a Company?", www.cmo.com, accessed June 17, 2010.

10. "Exploring Ways to Build a Better Consumer Profile," *Wall Street Journal*, March 15, 2010, B4.

11. "Connect the Thoughts," *Adweek Media*, June 29, 2009, pp. 10-11.

12. Ibid.

13. "Behave," *Marketing News*, September 15, 2008, pp. 13-15.

14. "Sites Feed Personal Details to New Tracking Industry," http://online.wsj.com, July 31, 2010.

15. Ibid.

16. "Tracking Is An Assault On Liberty, With Real Dangers," *Wall Street Journal*, August 7-8, 2010, pp. W1-W2.

17. "Scrapers Dig Deep for Data on Web," *Wall Street Journal*, October 12, 2010, pp. A1, A18.

18. Ibid.

19. Ibid.

20. "To Stem Privacy Abuses, Industry Groups Will Track Web Trackers," *Wall Street Journal*, June 24, 2010, pp. B1-B2.

21. www.privacy.org., February 13, 2001.

22. "The Great Data Heist," *Fortune*, May 16, 2005. pp. 66–75.

23. "Choice Point to Exit Non-FCRA. Consumer-Sensitive Data Markets," (www.choicepoint.com), March 4, 2005.

24. "Hackers Aren't Only Threat to Privacy," *Wall Street Journal*, June 23, 2010, p. B5.

25. Ibid.

26. Ibid.

27. "On My Mind: The Privacy Hoax: Consumers Say They Care about Internet Privacy But Don't Act That Way. Let the Market Rule," *Forbes*, October 14, 2002, pp. 42–44.

28. Donna Gillin and Jane Sheppard, "The Fallacy of Gelling Paid for Your Opinions," *Marketing Research,* Fall 2003, p. 8.

29. The section on GIS has been updated by Joshua Been, The University of Texas at Arlington.

30. Case Study—Avon Products, November 2004 http://www.tactician.com/News/News_CS_AVON1104.asp

31. "Turning a Map into a Layer Cake of Information," *New York Times*, January 20, 2000, Thursday, Late Edition—Final, Section G; Page 1, Column 1, Circuits, 2132 words, by Catherine Greenman.

32. Amy Cortese, "Is Your Business in the Right Spot? *Business 2.0*, May 2004, pp. 76–77.

33. "Sanitized for Your Perfection," *Brandweek*, January 9, 2006, p. 17.

34. Ibid.

35. Joseph Rydholm, "Report shows the changing face of motherhood," *Quirk's Marketing Research Review*, June 2010, pp. 76-77.

Chapter 5

1. Projections by the authors. October 2010.

2. "Second Half of '09 Could Set Research in Motion," *Quirk's Marketing Research Review*, July, 2009, p. 80. Forecast updated by the authors.

3. "Motives Are as Important as Words When Group Describes a Product," *Marketing News*, August 28, 1987, p. 49.

4. John Houlahan, "In Defense of the Focus Group," *Quirk's Marketing Research Review*, October 2003, pp. 16, 84.

5. Alison Stein Wellner, "The New Science of Focus Groups," *American Demographics*, March 2003, pp. 29–33.

6. Ibid., p. 32.

7. Peter Tuckel, Elaine Leppo, and Barbara Kaplan, "Focus Groups under Scrutiny," *Marketing Research*, June 1992, pp. 12–17; see also "Break These Three Focus Group Rules," *Quirk's Marketing Research Review*, December 1999, pp. 50–53.

8. Marilyn Rausch, "Qualities of a Beginning Moderator," *Quirk's Marketing Research Review*, December 1996, p. 24. Reprinted by permission of *Quirk's Marketing Research Review*; also see: Tom Neveril, "Ten Qualities for Qualitative Researchers," *Quirk's Marketing Research Review*, June 2004, pp. 18–21.

9. Naomi Hendersen, "Strong Bonds Yield Solid Results," *Marketing Research,* Winter 2008, pp. 32-34.

10. Dennis Rook, "Out of Focus Groups," *Marketing Research,* Summer 2003, pp. 10–15.

11. "Selecting a Moderator," *Quirk's Marketing Research Review*, May 2010, p. 68

12. "How to Make Sure Your Moderator Does Great Groups," *Quirk's Marketing Research Review*, March 2009, pp. 16-18.

13. Jacob Brown, "For Best Results, Plan Ahead," *Quirk's Marketing Research Review*, November 2005, pp. 44–47.

14. "Qualitative Research Panels: A New Spin on Traditional Focus Groups," *Quirk's Marketing Research Review*, May 2010, pp. 18-20.

15. "In My Professional Opinion," *Quirk's Marketing Research Review*, May 2009, pp. 52-55.

16. Naomi Henderson, "Art and Science of Effective In-Depth Qualitative Interviews," *Quirk's Marketing Research Review*, December 1998, pp. 24–31; reprinted by permission; "Dangerous Intersections," *Marketing News*, February 28, 2000, p. 18; and "Go In-Depth with Depth Interviews," *Quirk's Marketing Research Review*, April 2000, pp. 36–40.

17. "Dealing With the Digresser," *Quirk's Marketing Research Review*, December 2008, pp. 32-35.

18. Henderson, "Art and Science of Effective In-Depth Qualitative Interviews," p. 26.

19. Gerald Berstell and Denise Nitterhouse, "Asking All the Right Questions," *Marketing Research*, Fall 2001, pp. 15–20.

20. "One-on-Ones Put the Quality in Qualitative," *Quirk's Marketing Research Review*, November 2006, pp. 16–18.

21. Jennifer Haid, "Understand the Mind of the Market," *Quirk's Marketing Research Review*, December 2004, pp. 26–31.

22. Carla Penel and Will Leskin, "Mixing Art and Science," *Quirk's Marketing Research Review*, May 2006, pp. 48–50.

23. "Toward a Broader Definition," *Quirk's Marketing Research Review*, May 2006, p. 64.

24. The material on analogies is from: Andrew Cutler, "What's the Real Story?" *Quirk's Marketing Research Review*, December 2006, pp. 38–45.

25. The material on personification is from Cutler, "What's the Real Story?" *Quirk's Marketing Research Review*, December 2006, pp. 38–45.

26. Ronald Lieber, "Storytelling: A New Way to Get Closer to Your Customer," *Fortune*, February 3, 1997, pp. 102–110; see also "Marketers Seek the Naked Truth in Consumers' Psyches," *Wall Street Journal*, May 30, 1997, pp. B1, B13; for details on Zaltman's technique, see Gwendolyn Catchings-Castello, "The ZMET Alternative," *Marketing Research*, Summer 2000, pp. 6–12.

27. Tom Neveril, "I'll Always Go Back to That Hotel," *Quirk's Marketing Research Review*, December 2009, p. 42.

28. Anna Lilleegen, "A Storied Destination," *Quirk's Marketing Research Review*, November 2005, pp. 24–29.

29. Joseph Rydholm, "Steering In the Right Direction," *Quirk's Marketing Research Review*, May 2010, pp. 26-32.

Chapter 6

1. "Research Department As Bellwether?" *Quirk's Marketing Research Review*, June 2005, p. 8; and "Industry Study Finds Researchers Struggling, Adapting," *Quirk's Marketing Research Review*, December 2009, pp. 160-161.

2. Reprinted with permission from the Respondent Cooperation and Industry Image Survey (New York: Council for Marketing and Opinion Research, 2003), p. 2; also see Joseph Rydholm, "A Cooperative Effort on Cooperation," *Quirk's Marketing Research Review*, November 2006, pp. 137–138; Chezy Ofir, Itamar Simonson, and Song-OH Yoon, "The Robustness of the Effects of Consumers' Participation in Marketing Research: The Case of Service Quality Evaluation," *Journal of Marketing Research*, November 2009, pp. 105-114; Bert Weijters, Niels Schillewaert, and Maggie Geuens, "Assessing Response Styles Across Modes of Data Collection," *Journal of The Academy of Marketing Science*, Fall 2008, pp. 409-422.

3. Matthew Harrison, "Learning the Language," *Marketing Research*, Winter 2006, pp. 11–16, updated by the authors. Also see: "Meeting Western Needs in an Eastern Setting," *Quirk's Marketing Research Review*, November 2008, pp. 30-35.

4. www.mrsi.com/instore.html, June 11, 2005.

5. "SPSS Debuts Advancement in Predictive Dealing," *Quirk's Marketing Research Review*, January 2009, p. 12.

6. S.J. Blumberg and J.V. Luke, "Wireless Substitution: Early Release of Estimates from the National Health Interview Survey, July-December 2009." National Center for Health Statistics, May 2010. Available online: www.cdc.gov/nchs/data/nhis/earlyrelease/wireless201005.htm.

7. "Cellphone Numbers Just Don't Add Much to Political Polling," *Wall Street Journal*, February 1, 2008, p. 131; and "Be Mindful of Cellphone Interviews," *Marketing Management*, Summer 2009, p. 4.

8. "Calling Cell Phones – the FCC Makes a Bad Regulation Worse," *Quirk's Marketing Research Review*, July 2010, pp. 18-20.

9. Amanda Durkee, "First Impressions Are Everything in B-to-B Telephone Surveys," *Quirk's Marketing Research Review*, March 2005, pp. 30–32.

10. For a high-tech variation of the self-administered questionnaire see John Weisberg, "The MCAPI Primer," *Quirk's Marketing Research Review*, February 2003, pp. 24–34; see also Karl Feld and Steven Wygant, "Einterviewers Add Human Touch to Web-based Research," *Quirk's Marketing Research Review*, July-August 2000, pp. 36–41.

11. "Mail Surveys—The Right Alternative," *Quirk's Marketing Research Review*, July–August 2005, p. 18.

12. SurveySpot Panel, April 2004.

13. Amanda Lenhart, Rich Ling, Scott Campbell, Kristen Purcell, "Teens and Mobile Phones," Pew Research Center, April 20, 2010.

14. "Pro Football Still Rules in the U.S.," *Quirk's Marketing Research Review*, March 2006, p. 10.

Chapter 7

1. *http://www.internetworldstats.com/stat.htm*, "Internet Usage Statistics: The Internet Big Picture—World Internet Users and Population Stats."

2. Kira Signer and Andy Korman, "One Billion and Growing," *Quirk's Marketing Research Review* (July/August 2006), pp. 62–67.

3. Ibid.

4. Conversation with Craig Stevens, EVP of Research Now Market Research, based on company research (November 2, 2007); also see "Market Research," *Marketing News* (September 15, 2007), p. 16.

5. Ibid.

6. Tim Macer and Sheila Wilson, "Online Makes More Inroads," *Quirk's Marketing Research Review* (February 2007), pp. 50–58.

7. *http://blog.vovici.com/blog/bid/21872/Blog-Analysis-as-Market-Research* "Blog Analysis as Market Research," by Jeffrey Henning, posted 9/23/2009.

8. This section is from *www.lib.berkeley.edu/TeachingLib/Guides/Internet/Strategies.html*.

9. This section is adapted from Nick Wingfield, "A Marketer's Dream," *Wall Street Journal* (December 7, 1998), p. R20.

10. This section is adapted from ibid.

11. Kate Maddox, "Virtual Panels Add Real Insight for Marketers," *Advertising Age* (June 29, 1998), pp. 34, 40; and "Turning the Focus Online," *Marketing News* (February 28, 2000), p. 15; see also "The Hows, Whys, Whens and Wheres of Online Focus Groups," *MRA Alert* (December 1999), p. 21, and "Online Group Messaging," Marketing News (September 1, 2007), p. 24.

12. *http://www.focusgrouptips.com/online-focus-groups.html*, "How to Use Online Focus Groups."

13. Hy Mariampolski and Pat Sabena, "Qualitative Research Develops in China," *Quirk's Marketing Research Review* (December 2002), pp. 44–49.

14. Matthew Harrison, "Why Online Focus Groups Can Work for B2B Research: Open for Business," *Quirk's Marketing Research Review* (March 2010), p. 42.

15. *www.channelM2.com* (November 5, 2007).

16. Vauhini Vara, "Researchers Mine Web for Focus Groups," *The Wall Street Journal* (November 17, 2007), p. B3E.

17. Gregory S. Heist, "Beyond Brand Building," *Quirk's Marketing Research Review* (July/August 2007), pp. 62–67.

18. Ibid.

19. Ibid.

20. Ibid.

21. *http://www.focusgrouproom.com/depth.php*, "Online Depth Interviews."

22. *http://www.decisionanalyst.com/Services/OnlineQualitative.dai*, "Internet-Adapted Qualitative Techniques: Time Extended Online Dept Interviews."

23. Amy Savin, "Liven Up Your Qualitative with These Online Solutions," *Quirk's Marketing Research Review* (December 2009), p. 24.

24. Chris Yalonis, "The Revolution in e-Research," *CASRO Marketing Research Journal* (1999), pp. 131–133; "The Power of On-line Research," *Quirk's Marketing Research Review* (April 2000), pp. 46–48; Bill MacElroy, "The Need for Speed," *Quirk's Marketing Research Review* (July–August 2002), pp. 22–27; Cristina Mititelu, "Internet Surveys: Limits and Beyond Limits," *Quirk's Marketing Research Review* (January 2003), pp. 30–33; Nina Ray, "Cybersurveys Come of Age," *Marketing Research* (Spring 2003), pp. 32–37; "Online Market Research Booming, According to Survey," *Quirk's Marketing Research Review* (January 2005); Roger Gates, "Internet Data Collection So Far," speech given to Kaiser Permanente (May 2005); and Gabe Gelb, "Online Options Change Biz a Little—And a Lot," *Marketing News* (November 1, 2006), pp. 23–24.

25. Misha Neverov and Robert Schieffer, "Tips on Conducting Research in Russia: From an Old Order, a New Frontier," *Quirk's Marketing Research Review* (November 2009), p. 42.

26. Gates, "Internet Data Collection So Far."

27. Lee Smith, "Online Research's Time Has Come as a Proven Methodology," *CASRO Journal* (2002), pp. 45–50.

28. Bill MacElroy, "International Growth of Web Survey Activity," *Quirk's Marketing Research Review* (November 2000), pp. 48–51.

29. Tim Macer and Sheila Wilson, "A Report on the 2009 Globalpark Market Research Software Survey: Online Research Still Reigns Supreme," *Quirk's Marketing Research Review* (July 2010), p. 50.

30. "Tips Offer Better Response Rates, Engaging Surveys," *Marketing News* (April 1, 2007), p. 28.

31. Jamin Brazil, Aaron Jue, Chandra Mulkins, and Jayme Plunkett, "Capture Their Interest," *Quirk's Marketing Research Review* (July/August 2006), pp. 46–54.

32. Ibid.

33. "Timing Appears to Be Everything with Survey Invitations," *Quirk's Marketing Research Review* (March 2007), p. 8.

34. *www.comscore.com/custom-research/sample.asp* Also referenced by Mary Beth Weber, Sigma Validation at AMA 2005 Marketing Research Conference, Boston (September 25–28, 2005), "Why Validate Internet Research?"

35. *http://techcrunch.com/2010/01/05quantcast-mobile-web-apple-android/* "US Mobile Web Usage Grew 110 Percent Last Year."

36. Tim Snaith, "Mobile Research—The Fifth Methodology? Like the Early Days of Online Research, Opportunities Exist as Questions Persist," *Quirk's Marketing Research Review* (August 2009), p. 26.

37. Birgi Martin, "Research-to-Go," *Quirk's Marketing Research Review* (November 2007), pp. 68–72.

38. Ibid.

39. "Good Things Come to Brands That Give," *Brandweek* (March 19, 2007), p. 6.

Chapter 8

1. "Loose Change, Lotion, and Expired Coupons," *Quirk's Marketing Research Review*, February 2008, p. 20.

2. Author's estimate.

3. "The Chocolate War," *Marketing Research*, Winter 2005, p. 4.

4. "Paying More to Get More," *Quirk's Marketing Research Review*, December 2008, p. 44.

5. "Business Ethnography and the Discipline of Anthropology," *Quirk's Marketing Research Review*, February 2009, pp. 20–27; also see: "Watch Me As I Buy," *Quirk's Marketing Research Review*, February 2010, pp. 32–35.

6. "The Science of Desire," *Business Week*, June 5, 2006, p. 104.

7. Ibid.

8. Ibid.

9. "Trendy Method or Essential Tool?" *Quirk's Marketing Research Review*, February 2009, pp. 34–37.

10. Martha C. Rivera, "An Enriching Process," *Quirk's Marketing Research Review*, November 2005, pp. 30–37.

11. Jerry Thomas, "Worth a Thousand Words," *Decision Analyst Flyer*, 2006.

12. "Mystery Shopper," *Smart Money*, December 2005, p. 98.

13. Randall Brandt, "Improve the Customer Experience," *Quirk's Marketing Research Review*, January 2006, p. 68.

14. "Get Your Restaurant's Data To-Go," *Quirk's Marketing Research Review*, January 2009, p. 66.

15. "Getting the Most Out of Every Shopper," *Business Week*, February 9, 2009, pp. 45–46; "Testing Positive," *Quirk's Marketing Research Review*, March 2009, pp. 20–24; and "A Research Plan You Can Take to the Bank," *Quirk's Marketing Research Review*, January 2010, pp. 50–53.

16. Newl Templin, republished with permission of the *Wall Street Journal* "Undercover with a Hotel Spy," *Wall Street Journal*, May 12, 1999, pp. B1, B12; permission conveyed through Copyright Clearance Center, Inc., and Celina Abernathy, Sonic Drive-In.

17. Rebecca Gardyn, "What's on Your Mind?" *American Demographics*, April 2000, pp. 31–33.

18. "Brain Scanning Surprises Researchers in Sunscreen Study," *Quirk's Marketing Research Review*, October 2010, p. 6; also see: "This Is Your Brain On Advertising," *Quirk's Marketing Research Review*, August 2009, pp. 32–35.

19. "Too Much Information," *Quirk's Marketing Research Review*, August 2010, pp. 58–62.

20. John Cacioppo and Richard Petty, "Physiological Responses and Advertising Effects," *Psychology and Marketing*, Summer 1985, pp. 115–126; and Jack Shimell, "Testing Ads Using Galvanic Skin Response Measurements," *Quirk's Marketing Research Review*, March 2002, pp. 46–55.

21. "Check Your Head," *Marketing News*, March 30, 2009, p. 22.

22. "Tobii Glasses Aim to Make Eye-Tracking More Mobile," *Quirk's Marketing Research Review*, October 2010, p. 14.

23. "The Proof Is In the Pupil," *Quirk's Marketing Research Review*, April 2009, pp. 38–42.

24. Andy Rasking, "A Face Any Business Can Trust," *Business 2.0*, December 2003, pp. 58–60.

25. Ibid; also see Dan Hill, "What Lies Beneath," *Quirk's Marketing Research Review*, October 2006, pp. 68–74.

26. "Billboards That Can See You," WSJ, September 3, 2010, p. B5; and "Ad Displays Track Age," *Wall Street Journal*, February 3, 2010, p. B5.

27. www.pretesting.com/print.html, November 8, 2010.

28. "Cracking the Code," *AdWeek Media*, August 17, 2009, pp. 1–4.

29. "Nielsen Lands Data Deal," *Wall Street Journal*, December 2, 2008, p. B7.

30. "Media Measurement On the Move," *Brandweek*, February 10, 2010, p. M4.

31. www.symphonyiri.com, accessed November 8, 2010.

32. "Cookies Cause Bitter Backlash," *Wall Street Journal*, September 20, 2010, pp. B1–B2.

33. "Target-Marketing Becomes More Communal," *Wall Street Journal*, November 5, 2009, p. B10

34. "The Web's New Gold Mine: Your Secrets," *Wall Street Journal*, July 31 – August 1, 2010, pp. W1–W2.

35. "A Web Pioneer Profiles Users by Name," *Wall Street Journal*, October 25, 2010, pp. A1, A16.

36. www.comscore.com, accessed November 8, 2010.

37. "Everyone Hates ComScore," *Fortune*, September 29, 2008, pp. 60–62.

38. "By the Numbers: Social Networks," *Fortune*, September 6, 2010, p. 34.

39. Ibid.

40. "Does UGC Make You Say Ugh," *Quirk's Marketing Research Review*, August 2010, pp. 24–28.

41. "Making Sense of the Chatter," *Quirk's Marketing Research Review*, August 2010, pp. 48–51.

42. "Does UGC Make . . ."

43. Raymond R. Burke, "Virtual Shopping: Breakthrough in Marketing Research," *Harvard Business Review*, March/April 1996, pp. 120–131.

44. Ellen Byron, "A Virtual View of the Store Aisle," *Wall Street Journal*, October 3, 2007, pp. B1, B12.

45. Ibid.

46. Ibid.; also see "Virtual Shopping, Real Results, *Brandweek*, April 16, 2009, pp. 16–18.

47. Constantine von Hoffman, "Masters of Funky Flex," *Brandweek*, September 25, 2006, pp. 23–24.

48. Maren Elwood, "Of Stoves and Laptops," *Quirk's Marketing Research Review*, May 2010, pp. 42–45.

Chapter 9

1. Thomas D. Cook and Donald T. Campbell, *Experimentation: Design Analysis Issues for Field Settings* (Chicago: Rand McNally, 1979).

2. See Claire Selltiz et al., *Research in Social Relations*, rev. ed. (New York: Holt, Rinehart & Winston, 1959), pp. 80–82.

3. A good example of a laboratory experiment is described in Caroll Mohn, "Simulated-Purchase 'Chip' Testing vs. Trade-Off Conjoint Analysis—Coca-Cola's Experience." *Marketing Research* (March 1990), pp. 49–54.

4. A. G. Sawyer, "Demand Artifacts in Laboratory: Experiments in Consumer Research," *Journal of Consumer Research 2* (March 1975), pp. 181–201; and N. Giges, "No Miracle in Small Miracle: Story Behind Failure," *Advertising Age* (August 1989), p. 76.

5. Natasha Singer, "The Fountain of Old Age," *The New York Times* (February 6, 2011). Available at http://www.nytimes.com/2011/02/06/business/06aging.html (accessed March 3, 2011).

6. John G. Lynch, "On the External Validity of Experiments in Consumer Research," *Journal of Consumer Research 9* (December 1982), pp. 225–239.

7. Richard C. Becherer, D.B.A, Lawrence M. Richard, Ph.D., and James B. Wiley, Ph.D., "Predicting Market Behavior: Are Psychographics Really Better?" *Journal of the Academy of Marketing Science 5*, no. 2 (Spring 1977) pp. 75–84.

8. For a more detailed discussion of this and other experimental issues, see Thomas D. Cook and Donald T. Campbell, "The Design and Conduct of Quasi-Experiments and True Experiments in Field Settings," in M. Dunnette, ed., *Handbook of Industrial and Organizational Psychology* (Skokie, IL: Rand McNally, 1978).

9. Ibid.

10. Bob Gertsley, "Data Use: The Insidious Top-Box and Its Effects on Measuring Line Share," *Quirk's Marketing Research Review* (August 2008), p. 20.

11. For further discussion of the characteristics of various types of experimental designs, see Donald T. Campbell and Julian C. Stanley, *Experimental and Quasi-Experimental Design for Research* (Chicago: Rand McNally, 1966); see also Richard Bagozzi and Youjar Ti, "On the Use of Structural Equation Models in Experimental Design," *Journal of Marketing Research 26* (August 1989), pp. 225–270.

12. Thomas D. Cook and Donald T. Campbell, *Quasi-Experimentation: Design and Analysis Issues for Field Settings* (Boston: Houghton Mifflin, 1979), p. 56.

13. Stefan Althoff, "Does the Survey Sender's Gender Matter?" *Quirk's Marketing Research Review 31*, no. 2 (February 2007), pp. 24, 26.

14. T. Karger, "Test Marketing as Dress Rehearsals," *Journal of Consumer Marketing 2* (Fall 1985), pp. 49–55; Tim Harris, "Marketing Research Passes Toy Marketer Test," *Advertising Age* (August 24, 1987), pp. 1, 8; John L. Carefoot, "Marketing and Experimental Designs in Marketing Research: Uses and Misuses," *Marketing News* (June 7, 1993), p. 21; and Jim Miller and Sheila Lundy, "Test Marketing Plugs into the Internet," *Consumer Insights* (Spring 2002), p. 23.

15. Norma Ramage, "Testing, Testing 1–2–3," *Marketing Magazine 110*, no. 25 (July 18, 2005).

16. "Annual Population Estimates and Demographic Factors of Growth by Census Metropolitan area, Canada, from July to June—Population Estimates and Factors of Growth." Statistics Canada. July 1, 2009. http://www.statcan.gc.ca/pub/91-214-x/20008000/t021-eng.htm. Retrieved January 31, 2011.

17. Jay Klompmaker, G. David Hughes, and Russell I. Haley, "Test Marketing in New Product Development," *Harvard Business Review* (May–June 1976), p. 129; and N. D. Cadbury, "When, Where and How to Test Market," *Harvard Business Review* (May–June 1985), pp. 97–98.

18. G. A. Churchill & Jr. *Basic Marketing Research*, 4th ed. (Fort Worth, TX: Dryden Press, 2001), pp. 144–145.

19. Melvin, P. "Choosing Simulated Test Marketing Systems." *Marketing Research, 4*, no. 3 (September 1992), pp. 14–16.

20. Ibid.

21. Joseph Rydholm, "To Test or Not to Test," *Quirk's Marketing Research Review* (February 1992), pp. 61–62.

22. "Test Marketing Is Valuable, but It's Often Abused," *Marketing News* (January 2, 1987), p. 40.

23. "Guide to Test Market Selection and Planning," *Creative Marketing* (2000).

24. "Denmark, the World's Best Test Market," *Copenhagen Capacity* (November 23, 2005) online at: *www.copcap .com/composite-9206.htm.*

25. "South Korea: Tech's Test Market," *BusinessWeek* (March 4, 2003) online edition: *www.businessweek .com/technology/content/mar2003/tc2003034 4357 tc105.htm.*

26. Deborah L. Vence, "Proper Message, Design in Global Markets Require Tests," *Marketing News* (September 1, 2006), pp. 18–25.

27. "Miller to Test Market Low-Cal Craft Beers in Minneapolis," *Minneapolis-St. Paul Business Journal* (December 14, 2007).

28. Roger Fillion, "Denver Test Market for Beer Ads," *Rocky Mountain News* (July 4, 2006).

29. Jeremiah McWilliams, "Anheuser-Busch Test Markets New Vodka Brand," *St. Louis Post-Dispatch* (November 27, 2007).

30. Dina Berta, "Utah City Turns Out to be Best Test Market for Brazilian Concept," *Nation's Restaurant News* (September 22, 2003).

31. Jim Miller, "Global Research: Evaluating New Products Globally; Using Consumer Research to Predict Success,"*PDMA Visions Magazine* (October 2002) online at: *www.pdma.org/visions/print. php?doc=oct02/research3.html.*

Chapter 10

1. Adapted from Brian Toyne and Peter G.P. Walters, *Global Marketing Management: A Strategic Perspective* (Boston: Allyn & Bacon, 1989), p. 201. Used with permission of Allyn & Bacon.

2. F. N. Kerlinger, *Foundations of Behavioral Research*, 3rd ed. (New York: Rinehart and Winston, 1986), p. 403; see also Mel Crask and R. J. Fox, "An Exploration of the Internal Properties of Three Commonly Used Research Scales," *Journal of Marketing Research Society*, October 1987, pp. 317–319.

3. Adapted from Claire Selltiz, Laurence Wrightsman, and Stuart Cook, *Research Methods in Social Relations*, 3rd ed. (New York: Holt Rinehart and Winston, 1976), pp. 164–168.

4. Martin Weinberger, "Seven Perspectives on Consumer Research," *Journal of Marketing Research*, December 1989, pp. 9–17. Reprinted by permission of the American Marketing Association.

5. Bill MacElroy, "The Anonymity Gradient," *Quirk's Marketing Research Review*, October 1997, pp. 34–35. Reprinted by permission.

6. See David Hardesty and William Bearden, "The Use of Expert Judges in Scale Development: Implications for Improving Face Validity of Measures of Unobservable Constructs," *Journal of Business Research*, February 2004, pp. 98–107.

7. See Edward McQuarrie, "Integration of Construct and External Validity by Means of Proximal Similarity: Implications for Laboratory Experiments in Marketing," *Journal of Business Research*, February 2004, pp. 142–153.

8. Adapted from: William Trochim, *Research Methods Knowledge Base, www.atomicdog.com/trochim*, October 20, 2006.

9. Craig Bailey, "Examine Ways to Maximize Surveys," *Marketing News*, October 28, 2002, p. 46.

10. "Commonality Found Among Shopping Styles Across the World," *Quirk's Marketing Research Review*, November 2010, p. 8.

11. Kathryn Kranhold, "Client-Satisfaction Tool Takes Root," *Wall Street Journal*, July 10, 2006, p. B3.

Chapter 11

1. See Brian Sternthal and C. Samuel Craig, *Consumer Behavior: An Information Processing Perspective* (Englewood Cliffs, NJ: Prentice Hall, 1982), pp. 157–162; see also Barbara Loken and Ronald Hoverstad, "Relationships between Information Recall and Subsequent Attitudes: Some Exploratory Findings," *Journal of Consumer Research 12* (September 1985), pp. 155–168.

2. Robert E. Smith and William Swinyard, "Attitude Behavior Consistency: The Impact of Product Trial versus Advertising," *Journal of Marketing Research 20* (August 1983), pp. 257–267.

3. See Richard Lutz, "The Rise of Attitude Theory in Marketing," in Harold Kassarjian and Thomas Robertson, eds., *Perspectives in Consumer Behavior*, 4th ed. (Upper Saddle River, NJ: Prentice Hall, 1991), pp. 317–339.

4. The first five factors are taken from John Mowen and Michael Minor, *Consumer Behavior*, 5th ed. (Upper Saddle River, NJ: Prentice Hall, 1998), p. 263.

5. Linda F. Alwitt and Ida E. Berger, "Understanding the Link between Environmental Attitudes and Consumer Product Usage: Measuring the Moderating Rise of Attitude Strength," in Leigh McAlister and Michael Rothschild, eds., *Advances in Consumer Research 20* (1992), pp. 194–198.

6. Pete Cape, "Slider Scales in Online Surveys," Paper originally presented at the CASRO Panel Conference in New Orleans, LA, February 2009. Available at *http://www.surveysampling.com/sites/all/files/SSI%20Sliders%20White%20Pape.pdf* (accessed March 8, 2011).

7. Gerald Albaum, Catherine Roster, Julie H. Yu, and Robert D. Rogers, "Simple Rating Scale Formats: Exploring Extreme Response," *International Journal of Market Research 49*, no. 5 (2007), pp. 633–649.

8. For an excellent discussion of the semantic differential, see Charles E. Osgood, George Suci, and Percy Tannenbaum, *The Measurement of Meaning* (Urbana: University of Illinois Press, 1957). Also see Karin Braunsberger and Roger Gates (2009), "Developing Inventories for Satisfaction and Likert Scales in a Service Environment," *Journal of Services Marketing, 23*, no. 4, pp. 219–225.

9. Ibid., pp. 140–153, 192, 193; see also William D. Barclay, "The Semantic Differential as an Index of Brand Attitude," *Journal of Advertising Research 4* (March 1964), pp. 30–33.

10. Theodore Clevenger, Jr., and Gilbert A. Lazier, "Measurement of Corporate Images by the Semantic Differential," *Journal of Marketing Research 2* (February 1965), pp. 80–82.

11. John V. Colias (2007). "Global Segmentation—Dealing with Cross-Cultural Differences in Survey Rating Scale Usage," [white paper] produced by Decision Analyst. Available at http://decisionanalyst.com/Downloads/GlobalSegmentation.pdf (accessed March 31, 2011).

12. Michael J. Etzel, Terrell G. Williams, John C. Rogers, and Douglas J. Lincoln, "The Comparability of Three Stapel Forms in a Marketing Setting," in Ronald F. Bush and Shelby D.

Hunt, eds., *Marketing Theory: Philosophy of Science Perspectives* (Chicago: American Marketing Association, 1982), pp. 303–306.

13. An excellent article on purchase intent is: Pierre Chandon, Vicki Morwitz, and Werner Reinartz, "Do Intentions Really Predict Behavior? Self Generated Validity Effects in Survey Research," *Journal of Marketing* (April 2005), pp. 1–14.

14. Rich Raquet, "Are Political Polls More Accurate Because They Force Choices?" *TRC Market Research* (April 16, 2010). Available at *http://trchome.com/trc-blogs/r-squared/403-are-political-polls-more-accurate-because-they-force-choices.html* (accessed March 2, 2011).

15. Albert Bemmaor, "Predicting Behavior from Intention-to-Buy Measures: The Parametric Case," *Journal of Marketing Research* (May 1995), pp. 176–191.

16. We use a more conservative set of weights than those recommended by Linda Jamieson and Frank Bass, "Adjusting Stated Intention Measures to Predict Trial Purchase of New Products: A Comparison of Models and Methods," *Journal of Marketing Research* (August 1989), pp. 336–345.

17. This section on scale conversions is from Rajan Sambandam, "Scale Conversions," *Quirk's Marketing Research Review* (December 2006), pp. 22–28.

18. William O. and Richard G. Netemeyer, *Handbook of Marketing Scales*, 2nd ed. (Newbury Park, CA: Sage Publications, 1999), pp. 1–9.

19. Brian Engelland, Bruce Alford, and Ron Taylor, "Cautions and Precautions on the Use of Borrowed Scales in Marketing Research," *Proceedings: Society for Marketing Advances* (November 2001).

20. J. A. Krosnick and L. R. Fabrigar, "Designing Rating Scales for Effective Measurement in Surveys," in L. Lybert, M. Collins, L. Decker, E. Deleeuw, C. Dippo, N. Schwarz, and D. Trewing, eds., *Survey Measurement and Process Quality* (New York: Wiley-Interscience, 1997). Also see Madhubalan Viswanathan, Seymore Sudman, and Michael Johnson, "Maximum Versus Meaningful Discrimination in Scale Response: Implications for Validity Measurement of Consumer Perceptions about Products," *Journal of Business Review* (February 2004), pp. 108–124.

21. Julia Lin, "Data Use: Does the Rating Scale Make a Difference in Factor Analysis?" *Quirk's Marketing Research Review* (April 2008), p. 22.

22. This section is based on James H. Myers and Mark I. Alpert, "Determinant Buying Attitudes: Meaning and Management," *Marketing Management* (Summer 1997), pp. 50–56.

23. William Wells and Leonard Lo Scruto, "Direct Observation of Purchasing Behavior," *Journal of Marketing Research* (August 1996), pp. 42–51.

24. Tim Jastrzembski and Barbara Leable, "Unearthing the Truth," *Quirks Marketing Research Review* (November 2002), pp. 20–21, 78–80.

Chapter 12

1. Keith Price, "Maximizing Respondent Cooperation," *Quirk's Marketing Research Review 19*, no. 7, July–August 2005, pp. 78–81.

2. Janet Westergaard, "Your Survey, Our Needs," *Quirk's Marketing Research Review 19*, no. 10, November 2005, pp. 64–66.

3. R. M. Groves, S. Presser, and S. Dipko, "The Role of Topic Interest in Survey Participation Decisions," *Public Opinion Quarterly 68*, no. 1, Spring 2004, pp. 2–31.

4. Neil Kalt, "Address Objectives Without Objections," *Quirk's Marketing Research Review*, May 2009, pp. 58-64.

5. Matt Schroder, "Laddering Showed Infiniti How Drivers Viewed Its Around-View Monitor Technology" *Quirk's Marketing Research Review*, October 2009, p. 26.

6. This section is adapted from Naomi Henderson, "The Power of Probing," *Marketing Research*, Winter 2007, pp. 38-39.

7. Ibid.

8. Alexa Smith, "Ask Overlooked Questions for Greater Insights," *Marketing News*, September 15, 2003, pp. 27–28.

9. "Intelligent Survey Design," *Quirk's Marketing Research Review*, July 2010, pp. 42-46.

10. "Ask and You Shall Receive," *Quirk's Marketing Research Review*, October 2010, pp. 66-68.

11. ww.CMOR.org, June 15, 2005; also see: "A Playbook for Creating Survey Introductions For Online Panels," *Quirk's Marketing Research Review*, March 24, 2009.

12. Lynn Newmann, "That's a Good Question," *American Demographics*, June 1995), pp. 10–15. Reprinted from *American Demographics* magazine with permission. Copyright © 1995, Cowles Business Media, Ithaca, New York.

13. www.sawtooth.com, November 15, 2010.

14. Hans Baumgartner and Jan-Benedict E. M. Steenkamp, "Response Styles in Marketing Research: A Cross-National Investigation," *Journal of Marketing Research 38*, no. 2, May 2001, pp. 143–156.

15. "Could Researchers Get Answers From Facebook Answers?" *Quirk's Marketing Research Review*, November 2010, p. 6.

16. Internal company documents supplied to the authors by M/A/R/C, Inc.

17. Internal company documents supplied to the authors by M/A/R/C, Inc.

18. Joseph Rydholm, "New Product Survey Plumbs Consumer Mind-Sets," *Quirk's Marketing Research Review*, March 2010, pp. 68-69.

Chapter 13

1. For excellent discussions of sampling, see Seymour Sudman, Applied Sampling (New York: Academic Press, 1976), and L. J. Kish, Survey Sampling (New York: John Wiley & Sons, 1965).

2. "Report of the President's Blue Ribbon Panel on the Census," *American Statistical Association* (2003); Brad Edmondson, "The Cliffhanger Census," *American Demographics* (January 1998), p. 2.

3. A. Adimora Adaora, Victor J. Schoenbach, et al., "Driver's License and Voter Registration Lists as Population-Based Sampling Frames for Rural African Americans," *Annals of Epidemiology 11*, no. 60 (August 2001), pp. 385–388.

4. S. Sudman, *Applied Sampling*, pp. 63–67.

5. G. J. Glasser and G. D. Metzger, "Random-Digit Dialing as a Method of Telephone Sampling," *Journal of Marketing Research 9* (February 1972), pp. 59–64; and S. Roslow and L. Roslow, "Unlisted Phone Subscribers Are Different," *Journal of Advertising 12* (August 1972), pp. 59–64.

6. Survey Sampling International.

7. Charles D. Cowan, "Using Multiple Sample Frames to Improve Survey Coverage, Quality, and Costs," *Marketing Research* (December 1991), pp. 66–69.

8. James McClove and P. George Benson, *Statistics for Business and Economics* (San Francisco: Dellen Publishing, 1988), pp. 184–185; and "Probability Sampling in the Real World," *CATI NEWS* (Summer 1993), pp. 1, 4–6; Susie Sangren, "Survey and Sampling in an Imperfect World," *Quirk's Marketing Research Review* (April 2000), pp. 16, 66–69.

9. R. J. Jaeger, *Sampling in Education and the Social Sciences* (New York: Longman, 1984), pp. 28–35.

10. Michael A. Fallig and Derek Allen, "An Examination of Strategies for Panel-Blending," *Quirk's Marketing Research Review* (July 2009), p. 50.

11. Lewis C. Winters, "What's New in Telephone Sampling Technology?" *Marketing Research* (March 1990), pp. 80–82; and "A Survey Researcher's Handbook of Industry Terminology and Definitions" (Fairfield, CT: Survey Sampling, 1992), pp. 3–20.

12. For discussions of related issues, see John E. Swan, Stephen J. O'Connor, and Seug Doug Lee, "A Framework for Testing Sampling Bias and Methods of Bias Reduction in a Telephone Survey," *Marketing Research* (December 1991), pp. 23–34; Charles D. Cowan, "Coverage Issues in Sample Surveys: A Component of Measurement Error," *Marketing Research* (June 1991), pp. 65–68; and Susie Sangren, "Survey and Sampling in an Imperfect World." pp. 16, 66–69.

13. For an excellent discussion of stratified sampling, see William G. Cochran, *Sampling Techniques*, 2nd ed. (New York: John Wiley & Sons, 1963); and Sangren, "Survey and Sampling in an Imperfect World." pp. 16, 66–69.

14. Sudman, "Applied Science," pp. 110–121.

15. Ibid.

16. Earl R. Babbie, *The Practice of Social Research*, 2nd ed. (Belmont, CA: Wadsworth Publishing, 1979), p. 167.

17. "Convenience Sampling Outpacing Probability Sampling" (Fairfield, CT: Survey Sampling, March 1994), p. 4.

18. Leo A. Goodman, "Snowball Sampling," *Annuals of Mathematical Statistics 32* (1961), pp. 148–170.

19. Elaine Peterson, "Evaluation of Digital Libraries Using Snowball Sampling," *First Monday—Peer-Reviewed Journal on the Internet 10*, no. 5 (May 2005); published at: *www.firstmonday.org/Issues/issue10_5/Peterson* Elaine Peterson and Vicky York, "User Evaluation of the Montana Natural Resource Information System (NRIS)," *D-Lib Magazine 9*, no. 7/8 (July/August 2003), published at: *www.dlib.org/dlib/july03/peterson/07peterson.html*

20. Douglas Rivers, "Fulfilling the Promise of the Web," *Quirk's Marketing Research Review* (February 2000), pp. 34–41.

21. Roger Gates and Michael Foytik, "Implementing an HRA on the Internet: Lessons Learned," *Society of Prospective Medicine* (October 1998).

22. Beth Clarkson, "Research and the Internet: A Winning Combination," *Quirk's Marketing Research Review* (July 1999), pp. 46–51.

23. Gates and Foytik, "Implementing an HRA on the Internet."

24. "New Research from Survey Sampling International Suggests Sample Blending Results in Better Data Quality," *Market Research Bulletin* (April 26, 2010). Available at http://marketresearchbulletin.com/?p5537 (accessed March 9, 2011).

Chapter 14

1. Tom McGoldrick, David Hyatt, and Lori Laffin., "How Big Is Big Enough?" *Marketing Tools* (May 1998), pp. 54–58.

2. McGoldrick et al., "How Big Is Big Enough?" pp. 54–58.

3. Lafayette Jones, "A Case for Ethnic Sampling," *Promo* (October 1, 2000), p. 12.

4. M. H. Vivienne, C. J. Lahaut, et al., "Non-Response Bias in a Sample Survey on Alcohol Consumption," *Alcohol & Alcoholism 37*, no. 3 (2002), pp. 256–260.

5. Gang Xu, "Estimating Sample Size for a Descriptive Study in Quantitative Research," *Quirk's Marketing Research Review* (June 1999), pp. 14, 52–53.

6. Susie Sangren, "A Simple Solution to Nagging Questions," pp. 18, 53.

7. Gang Xu, "Estimating Sample Size for a Descriptive Study in Quantitative Research."

8. For discussions of these techniques, see Bill Williams, *A Sampler on Sampling* (New York: John Wiley & Sons, 1978); and Richard Jaeger, *Sampling in Education and the Social Sciences* (New York: Longman, 1984).

9. Peter DePaulo, "Sample Size for Qualitative Research," *Quirks Marketing Research Review* (December 2000).

10. Survey Sampling, "Estimate Sample Size with Precision," *The Frame* (January 1999), p. 1.

11. David Anderson, Dennis Sweeney, and Thomas Williams, *Statistics for Business and Economics*, 4th ed. (St. Paul, MN: West Publishing, 1990), pp. 355–357.

Chapter 15

1. Joseph Rydholm, "Dealing with Those Pesky Open-Ended Responses," *Quirk's Marketing Research Review* (February 1994), pp. 70–79.

2. Raymond Raud and Michael A. Fallig, "Automating the Coding Process with Neural Networks," *Quirk's Marketing Research Review* (May 1993), pp. 14–16, 40–47.

3. For information on semiotics, see Paul Cobley, Litza Jansz, and Richard Appignanesi, *Introducing Semiotics* (Melborne, Australia: Totem Books, 1997); Marcel Danesi, *Of Cigarettes, High Heels and Other Interesting Things: An Introduction to Semiotics* (New York: St. Martin's Press, 1998); and Umberto Eco, *Semiotics and the Philosophy of Languages* (Bloomington: Indiana University Press, 1986).

4. Joseph Rydholm, "Scanning the Seas: Scannable Questionnaires Give Princess Cruises Accuracy and Quick Turnaround," *Quirk's Marketing Research Review* (May 1993), pp. 38–42.

5. Tim Macer, "Software Review: Q Data Analysis Software," *Quirk's Marketing Research Review* (August 2010), p. 20.

6. "Cross Tabulation," *Custom Insight* (2005), at: *www.custominsight.com/articles/crosstab-sample.asp*.

7. Juan C. Dürsteler, "Rules to Make a Bad Graphic Representation," *InfoVis, The Digital Magazine of InfoVis.net* (December 16, 2002), Message No. 109.

Chapter 16

1. Hank Zucker, "What Is Significance?" *Quirk's Marketing Research Review* (March 1994), pp. 12, 14; Gordon A. Wyner, "How High Is Up?" *Marketing Research* (Fall 1993), pp. 42–43; Gordon A. Wyner, "The 'Significance' of Marketing Research," *Marketing Research* (Fall 1993), pp. 43–45; and Patrick M. Baldasare and Vikas Mittel, "The Use, Misuse and Abuse of Significance," *Quirk's Marketing Research Review* (November 1994), pp. 16, 32.

2. Dr. Ali Khounsary, "What Is Statistically Significant?" *Ask a Scientist*, Mathematics Archives (1999), Argonne National Laboratory, Department of Energy, at: *www.newton.dep.anl.gov/askasci/math99/math99052.htm*.

3. Stephen J. Hellebusch, "One Chi Square Beats Two Z-tests," *Marketing News* (June 4, 2001), p. 11.

4. Lemuel A. Loye and Alan T. N. Tita "Defending the Rationale for the Two-Tailed Test in Clinical Research," *Circulation 105* (2002), pp. 3062–3065.

5. Terry H. Grapentine, "Statistical Significance Revisited," *Quirks Marketing Research Review* (April 2011). pp. 18–23.

6. Thomas Exter, "What's Behind the Numbers," *Quirk's Marketing Research Review* (March 1997), pp. 53–59.

7. Tony Babinec, "How to Think about Your Tables," *Quirk's Marketing Research Review* (January 1991), pp. 10–12. For a discussion of these issues, see Gopal K. Kanji, *100 Statistical Tests*, (London: Sage Publications, 1993), p. 75.

8. Mel Majesty, "Use of the One-Sample *Z* Test to Assess Population-Sample Disparities," California State Personnel Board [no publication date given], at: www.spb.ca.gov/WorkArea/downloadasset.aspx?id31314.

9. Marvin L. Longabaugh, "The Z-Test for Percentages: A Statistical Tool to Detect Pretextually Neutral Juror Challenges," *Richmond Journal of Law & Technology 13*, no. 2 (2006), pp. 1–31, available online at: *http://law. richmond.edu/jolt/v13i2/article6.pdf*.

10. Gary M. Mullet, "Correctly Estimating the Variances of Proportions," *Marketing Research* (June 1991), pp. 47–51.

11. Richard Armstrong and Anthony Hilton, "The Use of Analysis of Variance (ANOVA) in Applied Microbiology," *Microbiologist* (December 2004), pp. 18–21; available online at: *www.blackwell-publishing. com/Microbiology/pdfs/anova.pdf*.

Chapter 17

1. Miaofen Yen and Li-Hua Lo, "Examining Test–Retest Reliability: An Intra-Class Correlation Approach," *Nursing Research 51*, no. 1 (January–February 2002), pp. 59–62.

2. Adam DiPaula, "Do Your 'BESD' When Explaining Correlation Results," *Quirks Marketing Research Review* (November 2000).

3. Pascale de Becker, Johan Roeykens, et al., "Exercise Capacity in Chronic Fatigue Syndrome," *Archives of Internal Medicine 160* (November 27, 2000), pp. 3270–3277.

4. Douglas Kirby et al., "Manifestations of Poverty and Birthrates among Young Teenagers in California Zip Code Areas," *Family Planning Perspectives 33*, no. 2 (March–April 2001), reprinted by the Alan Guttmacher Institute at: *www.guttmacher.org/pubs/journals/3306301.html.*

5. Clayton E. Cramer, "Antigunners Admit Brady Failed," and "Is Gun Control Reducing Murder Rates?" (August 2000), at: *www.claytoncramer.com.*

Chapter 18

1. Steve Lohr, "For Today's Graduate, Just One Word—Statistics," *The New York Times* (August 5, 2009). Available at *http://www.nytimes.com/2009/08/06/technology/06stats.html?_r=2&scp=1&sq= for+today%27s+graduate%2C+just+one+word%3A+statistics&st=nyt* (accessed April 12, 2011).

2. For an excellent and highly understandable presentation of all the multivariate techniques presented in this chapter, see Joseph Hair, Rolph Anderson, Ron Tatham, and William Black, *Multivariate Data Analysis,* 5th ed. (New York: Prentice Hall, 1998); see also Charles J. Schwartz, "A Marketing Research's Guide to Multivariate Analysis," *Quirk's Marketing Research Review* (November 1994), pp. 12–14.

3. Joseph R. Garber, "Deadbeat Repellant," *Forbes* (February 14, 1994), p. 164.

4. Michael Richarme (2007). "Eleven Multivariate Analysis Techniques: Key Tools in Your Marketing Research Survival Kit," [white paper] produced by Decision Analyst. Available at *http://decisionanalyst.com/Downloads/MultivariateAnalysisTechniques.pdf* (accessed April 1, 2011).

5. For a thorough discussion of regression analysis, see Larry D. Schroeder, *Understanding Regression Analysis: An Introductory Guide (Quantitative Applications in the Social Sciences),* (SAGE Publications, 1986).

6. Charlotte H. Mason and William D. Perreault Jr., "Collinear Power and Interpretation of Multiple Regression Analysis," *Journal of Marketing Research* (August 1991), pp. 268–280; Doug Grisaffe, "Appropriate Use of Regression in Customer Satisfaction Analyses: A Response to William McLauchlan," *Quirk's Marketing Review* (February 1993), pp. 10–17; and Terry Clark, "Managing Outliers: Qualitative Issues in the Handling of Extreme Observations in Market Research," *Marketing Research* (June 1989), pp. 31–45.

7. See Hair et al., *Multivariate Data Analysis,* p. 46.

8. William D. Neal, "Using Discriminant Analysis in Marketing Research: Part 1," *Marketing Research* (September 1989), pp. 79–81; William D Neal, "Using Discriminant Analysis in Marketing Research: Part 2," *Marketing Research* (December 1989), pp. 55–60; and Steve Struhl, "Multivariate and Perceptual Mapping with Discriminant Analysis," *Quirk's Marketing Research Review* (March 1993), pp. 10–15, 43.

9. See Girish Punj and David Stewart, "Cluster Analysis in Marketing Research: Review and Suggestions for Application," *Journal of Market Research 20* (May 1983), pp. 134–138; and G. Ray Funkhouser, Anindya Chatterjee, and Richard Parker, "Segmenting Samples," *Marketing Research* (Winter 1994), pp. 40–46.

10. Susie Sangren, "A Survey of Multivariate Methods Useful for Market Research," *Quirk's Marketing Research Review* (May 1999), pp. 16, 63–69.

11. This section is based on material prepared by Glen Jarboe; see also Paul Green, Donald Tull, and Gerald Albaum, *Research for Marketing Decision,* 5th ed. (Englewood Cliffs, NJ: Prentice Hall, 1998), pp. 553–573.

12. Dick Wittink and Phillipe Cattin, "Commercial Use of Conjoint Analysis: An Update," *Journal of Marketing* (July 1989), pp. 91–96; see also Rajeev Kohli, "Assessing Attribute Significance in Conjoint Analysis: Nonparametric Tests and Empirical Validation," *Journal of Marketing Research* (May 1988), pp. 123–133.

13. Examples of current issues and applications are provided in Richard Smallwood, "Using Conjoint Analysis for Price Optimization," *Quirk's Marketing Research Review* (October 1991), pp. 10–13; Paul E. Green, Abba M. Krieger, and Manoj K. Agarwal, "Adaptive Conjoint Analysis: Some

Caveats and Suggestions," *Journal of Marketing Research* (May 1991), pp. 215–222; Paul E. Green and V. Srinivasan, "Conjoint Analysis in Marketing: New Developments with Implications for Research and Practice," *Journal of Marketing Research Review* (October 1990), pp. 3–19; Joseph Curry, "Determining Product Feature Price Sensitivities," *Quirk's Marketing Research Review* (November 1990), pp. 14–17; Gordon A. Wyner, "Customer-Based Pricing Research," *Marketing Research* (Spring 1993), pp. 50–52; Steven Struhl, "Discrete Choice Modeling Comes to the PC," *Quirk's Marketing Research Review* (May 1993), pp. 12–15, 36–41: Steven Struhl, "Discrete Choice: Understanding a Better Conjoint . . . ," *Quirk's Marketing Research Review* (June/July 1994), pp. 12–15, 36–39; Bashir A. Datoo, "Measuring Price Elasticity," *Marketing Research* (Spring 1994), pp. 30–34; Gordon A. Wyner, "Uses and Limitations of Conjoint Analysis—Part 1," *Marketing Research* (June 1992), pp. 12–44; and Gordon A. Wyner, "Uses and Limitations of Conjoint Analysis—Part II," *Marketing Research* (September 1992), pp. 46–47; Yilian Yuan and Gang Xu, "Conjoint Analysis in Pharmaceutical Marketing Research," *Quirk's Marketing Research Review* (June 2001), pp. 18, 54–61; and Bryan Orme, "Assessing the Monetary Value of Attribute Levels with Conjoint Analysis: Warnings and Suggestions," *Quirk's Marketing Research Review* (May 2001), pp. 16, 44–47.

14. Mehmed Kantardzic, *Data Mining: Concepts, Models, Methods, and Algorithms* John Wiley & Sons, IBSN 0471228524. OCLC 50055336 (*http://www.worldcat.org/oclc/50055336*); and Y. Peng, G. Kou, Y. Shi, and Z. Chen (2008). "A Descriptive Framework for the Field of Data Mining and Knowledge Discovery." *International Journal of Information Technology and Decision Making*, 7, No.47:639–682. Doi: 10.1142/S0219622008003204 (http://dx.doi.org/10.1142%2FS0219622008003204).

15. *Journal of Information Technology and Decision Making*, 7, No.47 7:639–682 *http://www.thearling.com/text/dmwhite/dmwhite.htm*.

Chapter 19

1. Bonnie W. Eisenfeld, "How Clear Research Objectives Can Lead a Project to Success," *Quirk's Marketing Research Review* (July 2010), p. 66.

2. Ron Weidemann II and Albert Fitzgerald, "By the Numbers: Mastering the Art of Writing Quantitative Research Reports," *Quirk's Marketing Research Review* (April 2008), p. 26.

3. Luke Williams and Timothy L. Keiningham, "How Deep Do You Go? When Presenting Research Results, Use Your Skill Set to Find the Right Mix of Detail and Perspective," *Quirk's Marketing Research Review* (May 2008), p. 76.

4. Tim Macer and Sheila Wilson, "Do Something about PowerPoint!" *Quirk's Marketing Research Review* (March 2008), p. 61.

Chapter 20

1. "Now and for the Future," *Quirk's Marketing Research Review*, August 2010, pp. 52–57.

2. "Industry Study Finds Researchers Struggling, Adapting," *Quirk's Marketing Research Review*, December 2009, pp. 160-161.

3. Joseph Rydholm, "Research 2010: More Work, More Data, Same Budget," *Quirk's Marketing Research Review*, February 2010, pp. 96–97.

4. Joseph Rydholm, "What Do Clients Want from a Research Firm?" *Quirk's Marketing Research Review*, October 1996, p. 80.

5. "Is Supplier Research Quality Improving?" *Marketing News*, September 30, 2009, pp. 38–39.

6. John Walters and John Colias, "The Simple Secret to Effective Market Research," *CASRO Journal*, 2002, pp. 65–66.

7. Bonnie Eisenfeld, "Managing the Satisfiers and Dissatisfiers," *Quirk's Marketing Research Review*, May 2008, pp. 70–75.

8. Ibid.

9. Joshua Libresco, reprinted with permission from *Marketing News*, published by the American Marketing Association, from "Advice for the Juggler", January 4, 1999, pp. 13, 23.

10. The material on organizing a supplier firm is from: Michael Mitrano, "Supplier Side: Organizing Your Company—Are Project Teams the Answer?" *Quirk's Marketing Research Review*, April 2002, pp. 20, 68.

11. Joseph Rydholm, "No Margin for Margin of Error," *Quirk's Marketing Research Review*, February 2008, pp. 117–118.

12. Michael Mitrano, "Managing for Profitability," *Quirk's Marketing Research Review*, March 2002, pp. 24, 76.

13. Rydholm, "Research 2010…"

14. Susan Greco, "Choose or Lose." Reprinted with permission from *Inc.* magazine, February 2001. Copyright 1998 by Gruner & Jahr USA Publishing.

15. Kathleen Knight, "Finding and Retaining Research Staff: A Perspective," *Quirk's Marketing Research Review*, February 1998, pp. 18, 54. Reprinted by permission.

16. The sections on allocating the research budget, prioritizing projects, and retaining skilled staff are from Diane Schmalensee and A. Dawn Lesh, "Creating Win-Win Relationships," *Marketing Research*, Winter 2007.

17. Ibid.

18. Ibid.

19. Ibid.

20. Bonnie Eisenfeld, "The Quest for the Ideal Marketing Researcher," *Quirk's Marketing Research Review*, August 2009, pp. 56–57.

21. Adapted from Richard Snyder, "Selecting the Right Research Vendor," *Quirk's Marketing Research Review*, November 2002, pp. 62–65.

22. "More for the Money," *Marketing News*, June 30, 2009, pp. 8–10.

23. Ibid.

24. Tatiana Klimenko and Matthew Harrison, "Gaining a Foothold," *Quirk's Marketing Research Review*, November 2010, pp. 58–62.

25. Allison Enright, "Give 'em What They Need," *Marketing News*, February 1, 2008, p. 30.

26. Ibid.; also see Natalie Jobity and Jeff Scott, "Practices Make Perfect—Improving Research and Consulting Through Collaboration," *CASRO Journal* (2002), pp. 19–24; and Diane Schmalensee and Dawn Lesh, "Show Them and Tell Them," *Quirk's Marketing Research Review*, January 2010, pp. 36–38.

27. Ian Lewis, "A Road Map to Increased Relevance," *Quirk's Marketing Research Review*, January 2010, pp. 28–34.

28. The material on "Achieving Strategic Consultative Relevance," is adapted from: Lewis, "A Road Map."

29. Ibid.

30. Tim Ambler, "Differing Dimensions," *Marketing Research*, Fall 2004, pp. 8–13; also see: "Measure Up," *Marketing News*, May 30, 2009, pp. 8–11

31. This section of ROI is from A. Dawn Lesh and Diane Schmalensee, "Measuring Returns of Research," *Marketing Research*, Fall 2004, pp. 22–27.

32. Ibid.

33. Brett Hagins, "The ROI On Calculating Researcher's ROI," *Quirk's Marketing Research Review*, May 2010, p. 52.

34. www.cross-tab.com, February 13, 2010.

GLOSSARY

ad hoc mail surveys Questionnaires sent to selected names and addresses without prior contact by the researcher; sometimes called one-shot mail surveys.

after-only with control group design True experimental design that involves random assignment of subjects or test units to experimental and control groups, but no premeasurement of the dependent variable.

allowable sampling error Amount of sampling error the researcher is willing to accept.

analogy Comparison of two items based on similarities.

analysis of variance (ANOVA) Test for the differences among the means of two or more independent samples.

applied research Research aimed at solving a specific, pragmatic problem— better understanding of the marketplace, determination of why a strategy or tactic failed, or reduction of uncertainty in management decision making.

appropriate time order of occurrence Change in an independent variable occurring before an observed change in the dependent variable.

approval by managers Managerial review and approval after questionnaire drafting to prevent false starts and expensive later redrafts.

attitude Enduring organization of motivational, emotional, perceptual, and cognitive processes with respect to some aspect of a person's environment.

balanced scales Measurement scales that have the same number of positive and negative categories.

basic, or pure, research Research aimed at expanding the frontiers of knowledge rather than solving a specific, pragmatic problem.

before and after with control group design True experimental design that involves random assignment of subjects or test units to experimental and control groups and pre- and postmeasurements of both groups.

behavioral targeting The use of online and offline data to understand a consumerís habits, demographics, and social networks in order to increase the effectiveness of online advertising.

bivariate regression analysis Analysis of the strength of the linear relationship between two variables when one is considered the independent variable and the other the dependent variable.

bivariate techniques Statistical methods of analyzing the relationship between two variables.

call center telephone interviews Interviews conducted by calling respondents from a centrally located marketing research facility.

captive outsourcing When a research firm creates a wholly-owned foreign facility for outsourcing.

cartoon test Projective test in which the respondent fills in the dialogue of one of two characters in a cartoon.

case analysis Reviewing information from situations that are similar to the current one.

causal research Research designed to determine whether a change in one variable likely caused an observed change in another.

causal studies Research studies that examine whether the value of one variable causes or determines the value of another variable.

causation Inference that a change in one variable is responsible for (caused) an observed change in another variable.

census Collection of data obtained from or about every member of the population of interest.

central limit theorem Idea that a distribution of a large number of sample means or sample proportions will approximate a normal distribution, regardless of the distribution of the population from which they were drawn.

chance variation Difference between the sample value and the true value of the population mean.

chi-square test Test of the goodness of fit between the observed distribution and the expected distribution of a variable.

clarity in wording Achieved by avoiding ambiguous terminology, using reasonable, vernacular language adjusted to the target group, and asking only one question at a time.

classification matrix A matrix or table that shows the percentages of people or things correctly and incorrectly classified by the discriminant model.

closed online panel recruitment Inviting only prevalidated individuals or those with shared known characteristics to enroll in a research panel.

closed-ended questions Questions that require the respondent to choose from a list of answers.

cluster analysis General term for statistical procedures that classify objects or people into some number of mutually exclusive and exhaustive groups on the basis of two or more classification variables.

cluster sample Probability sample in which the sampling units are selected from a number of small geographic areas to reduce data-collection costs.

coding Process of grouping and assigning numeric codes to the various responses to a question.

coding Process of grouping and assigning numeric codes to the various responses to a question.

coefficient of determination Measure of the percentage of the variation in the dependent variable explained by variations in the independent variables.

coefficient of determination Percentage of the total variation in the dependent variable explained by the independent variable.

collinearity Correlation of independent variables with each other, which can bias estimates of regression coefficients.

commercial online panel Group of individuals who have agreed to receive invitations to do online surveys from a particular panel company such as eRewards or SSI. The panel company charges organizations doing surveys for access to the panel. Charges are usually so much per survey depending on survey length and the type of people being sought for the survey. The panel company controls all access to the members of its panel.

comparative scales Measurement scales in which one object, concept, or person is compared with another on a scale.

computer-assisted telephone interviews (CATI) Call center telephone interviews in which interviewers enter respondents' answers directly into a computer.

conclusions Generalizations that answer the questions raised by the research objectives or otherwise satisfy the objectives.

concomitant variation Statistical relationship between two variables.

concomitant variation The degree to which a presumed cause and a presumed effect occur or vary together.

concurrent validity Degree to which another variable, measured at the same point in time as the variable of interest, can be predicted by the measurement instrument.

confidence interval Interval that, at the specified confidence level, includes the true population value.

confidence level Probability that a particular interval will include the true population value; also called *confidence coefficient*.

conjoint analysis Multivariate procedure used to quantify the value that consumers associate with different levels of product/service attributes or features.

constant sum scales Measurement scales that ask the respondent to divide a given number of points, typically 100, among two or more attributes, based on their importance to him or her.

constitutive definition Statement of the meaning of the central idea or concept under study, establishing its boundaries; also known as *theoretical*, or *conceptual*, *definition*.

construct validity Degree to which a measurement instrument represents and logically connects, via the underlying theory, the observed phenomenon to the construct.

constructs Specific types of concepts that exist at higher levels of abstraction.

consumer drawings Projective technique in which respondents draw what they are feeling or how they perceive an object.

consumer orientation The identification of and focus on the people or firms most likely to buy a product and the production of a good or service that will meet their needs most effectively.

contamination Inclusion in a test of a group of respondents who are not normally there—for example, buyers from outside the test market who see an advertisement intended only for those in the test area and who enter the area to purchase the product being tested.

content validity Representativeness, or sampling adequacy, of the content of the measurement instrument.

convenience samples Nonprobability samples based on using people who are easily accessible.

convergent validity Degree of correlation among different measurement instruments that purport to measure the same construct.

cookie A text file placed on a user's computer in order to identify the user when she or he revisits the Web site.

correlation analysis Analysis of the degree to which changes in one variable are associated with changes in another.

creativity The ability to generate and recognize potentially useful ideas.

criterion-related validity Degree to which a measurement instrument can predict a variable that is designated a criterion.

cross tabulation Examination of the responses to one question relative to the responses to one or more other questions.

custom research firms Companies that carry out customized marketing research to address specific projects for corporate clients.

data entry Process of converting information to an electronic format.

data mining The use of statistical and other advanced software to discover nonobvious patterns hidden in a database.

database marketing Marketing that relies on the creation of a large computerized file of customers' and potential customers' profiles and purchase patterns to create a targeted marketing mix.

decision rule Rule or standard used to determine whether to reject or fail to reject the null hypothesis.

decision support system (DSS) An interactive, personalized information management system, designed to be initiated and controlled by individual decision makers.

degrees of freedom Number of observations in a statistical problem that are free to vary.

Delphi Method Rounds of individual data collection from knowledgeable people. Results are summarized and returned to the participants for further refinement.

dependent variable A symbol or concept expected to be explained or influenced by the independent variable.

dependent variable Variable expected to be explained or caused by the independent variable.

descriptive function The gathering and presentation of statements of fact.

descriptive studies Research studies that answer the questions who, what, when, where, and how.

design control Use of the experimental design to control extraneous causal factors.

determinant attitudes Those consumer attitudes most closely related to preferences or to actual purchase decisions.

diagnostic function The explanation of data or actions.

dichotomous questions Closed-ended questions that ask the respondent to choose between two answers.

discriminant coefficient Estimate of the discriminatory power of a particular independent variable; also called *discriminant weight*.

discriminant score Score that is the basis for predicting to which group a particular object or individual belongs; also called *Z score*.

discriminant validity Measure of the lack of association among constructs that are supposed to be different.

discussion guide Written outline of topics to be covered during a focus group discussion.

disguised observation Process of monitoring people who do not know they are being watched.

disproportional, or optimal, allocation Sampling in which the number of elements taken from a given stratum is proportional to the relative size of the stratum and the standard deviation of the characteristic under consideration.

door-to-door interviews Interviews conducted face-to-face with consumers in their homes.

dummy variables In regression analysis, a way of representing two-group or dichotomous, nominally scaled independent variables by coding one group as 0 and the other as 1.

editing Process of ascertaining that questionnaires were filled out properly and completely.

electroencephalograph (EEG) Machine that measures electrical pulses on the scalp and generates a record of electrical activity in the brain.

elimination of other possible causal factors Hard to prove that something else did not cause change in *B*.

equivalent form reliability Ability of two very similar forms of an instrument to produce closely correlated results.

error checking routines Computer programs that accept instructions from the user to check for logical errors in the data.

error sum of squares Variation not explained by the regression.

ethics Moral principles or values, generally governing the conduct of an individual or group.

ethnographic research Study of human behavior in its natural context, involving observation of behavior and physical setting.

executive interviews Industrial equivalent of door-to-door interviewing.

executive summary Portion of a research report that explains why the research was done, what was found, what those findings mean, and what action, if any, management should undertake.

experience surveys Discussions with knowledgeable individuals, both inside and outside the organization, who may provide insights into the problem.

experiment Research approach in which one variable is manipulated and the effect on another variable is observed.

experimental design Test in which the researcher has control over and manipulates one or more independent variables.

experimental effect Effect of the treatment variable on the dependent variable.

experiments Research to measure causality, in which the researcher changes one or more independent variables and observes the effect of the changes on the dependent variable.

exploratory research Preliminary research conducted to increase understanding of a concept, to clarify the exact nature of the problem to be solved, or to identify important variables to be studied.

external validity Extent to which causal relationships measured in an experiment can be generalized to outside persons, settings, and times.

F-test Test of the probability that a particular calculated value could have been due to chance.

face validity Degree to which a measurement seems to measure what it is supposed to measure.

factor analysis Procedure for simplifying data by reducing a large set of variables to a smaller set of factors or composite variables by identifying underlying dimensions of the data.

factor loading Correlation between factor scores and the original variables.

factor A linear combination of variables that are correlated with each other.

field experiments Tests conducted outside the laboratory in an actual environment, such as a marketplace.

field management companies Firms that provide such support services as questionnaire formatting, screener writing, and coordination of data collection.

field service firms Companies that only collect survey data for corporate clients or research firms.

finite population correction factor (FPC) Adjustment to the required sample size that is made in cases where the sample is expected to be equal to 5 percent or more of the total population.

focus group facility Research facility consisting of a conference room or living room setting and a separate observation room with a one-way mirror or live audio-visual feed.

focus group moderator Person hired by the client to lead the focus group; this person should have a background in psychology or sociology or, at least, marketing.

focus group Group of 8 to 12 participants who are led by a moderator in an in-depth discussion on one particular topic or concept.

frame error Error resulting from an inaccurate or incomplete sampling frame.

galvanic skin response (GSR) Change in the electric resistance of the skin associated with activation responses; also called *electrodermal response*.

garbologists Researchers who sort through people's garbage to analyze household consumption patterns.

geographic information system (GIS) A system that provides both a means of maintaining geographic databases and a tool capable of complex spatial analysis to provide information for a decision support system.

goal orientation A focus on the accomplishment of corporate goals; a limit set on consumer orientation.

graphic rating scales Measurement scales that include a graphic continuum, anchored by two extremes.

group dynamics Interaction among people in a group.

hermeneutic research Research that focuses on interpretation through conversations.

history Intervention, between the beginning and end of an experiment, of outside variables or events that might change the dependent variable.

hypothesis test of proportions Test to determine whether the difference between proportions is greater than would be expected because of sampling error.

hypothesis A conjectural statement about a relationship between two or more variables that can be tested with empirical data.

hypothesis Assumption or theory that a researcher or manager makes about some characteristic of the population under study.

independence assumption Assumption that sample elements are dream independently.

independent samples Samples in which measurement of a variable in one population has no effect on measurement of the variable in the other.

independent variable A symbol or concept over which the researcher has some control and that is hypothesized to cause or influence the dependent variable.

independent variable Variable believed to affect the value of the dependent variable.

individual depth interviews One-on-one interviews that probe and elicit detailed answers to questions, often using nondirective techniques to uncover hidden motivations.

innovation Successful implementation of creative ideas within an organization.

insight New knowledge that has the potential to create significant marketplace impact.

instant analysis Moderator debriefing, offering a forum for brainstorming by the moderator and client observers.

instrument variation Changes in measurement instruments (e.g., interviewers or observers) that might affect measurements.

intelligent data entry Form of data entry in which the information being entered into the data entry device is checked for internal logic.

internal consistency reliability Ability of an instrument to produce similar results when used on different samples during the same time period to measure a phenomenon.

internal database A collection of related information developed from data within the organization.

internal validity Extent to which competing explanations for the experimental results observed can be ruled out.

interrupted time-series design Research in which repeated measurements of an effect interrupts previous data patterns.

interval estimate Interval or range of values within which the true population value is estimated to fall.

interval scales Scales that have the characteristics of ordinal scales, plus equal intervals between points to show relative amounts; they may include an arbitrary zero point.

interviewer error, or interviewer bias Error that results from the interviewer's influencing—consciously or unconsciously—the respondent.

itemized rating scales Measurement scales in which the respondent selects an answer from a limited number of ordered categories.

judgment samples Nonprobability samples in which the selection criteria are based on the researcher's personal judgment about representativeness of the population under study.

K-means cluster analysis Multivariate procedure that groups people or objects into clusters based on their closeness to each other on a number of variables.

laboratory experiments Experiments conducted in a controlled setting.

Likert scales Measurement scales in which the respondent specifies a level of agreement or disagreement with statements expressing either a favorable or an unfavorable attitude toward the concept under study.

logical or machine cleaning of data Final computerized error check of data.

longitudinal study Study in which the same respondents are resampled over time.

low-ball pricing Quoting an unrealistically low price to secure a firm's business and then using some means to substantially raise the price.

mail panels Precontacted and prescreened participants who are periodically sent questionnaires.

mall-intercept interviews Interviews conducted by intercepting mall shoppers (or shoppers in other high-traffic locations) and interviewing them face-to-face.

management decision problem A statement specifying the type of managerial action required to solve the problem.

marginal report Computer-generated table of the frequencies of the responses to each question, used to monitor entry of valid codes and correct use of skip patterns.

marketing concept A business philosophy based on consumer orientation, goal orientation, and systems orientation.

marketing mix The unique blend of product/service, pricing, promotion, and distribution strategies designed to meet the needs of a specific target market.

marketing research aggregator A company that acquires, catalogs, reformats, segments, and resells reports already published by large and small marketing research firms.

marketing research objective A goal statement, defining the specific information needed to solve the marketing research problem.

marketing research problem A statement specifying the type of information needed by the decision maker to help solve the management decision problem and how that information can be obtained efficiently and effectively.

marketing research The planning, collection, and analysis of data relevant to marketing decision making and the communication of the results of this analysis to management.

marketing strategy A plan to guide the long-term use of a firm's resources based on its existing and projected internal capabilities and on projected changes in the external environment.

marketing An organizational function and a set of processes for creating, communicating, and delivering value to customers and for managing customer relationships in ways that benefit the organization and its shareholders.

maturation Changes in subjects occurring during the experiment that are not related to the experiment but that may affect subjects' response to the treatment factor.

mean Sum of the values for all observations of a variable divided by the number of observations.

measurement error Systematic error that results from a variation between the information being sought and what is actually obtained by the measurement process.

measurement instrument bias Error that results from the design of the questionnaire or measurement instrument; also known as questionnaire bias.

measurement Process of assigning numbers or labels to persons, objects, or events in accordance with specific rules for representing quantities or qualities of attributes.

median Value below which 50 percent of the observations fall.

metric scale A type of quantitative that provides the most precise measurement.

mode Value that occurs most frequently.

mortality Loss of test units or subjects during the course of an experiment, which may result in nonrepresentativeness.

multidimensional scales Scales designed to measure several dimensions of a concept, respondent, or object.

multiple discriminant analysis Procedure for predicting group membership for a (nominal or categorical) dependent variable on the basis of two or more independent variables.

multiple regression analysis Procedure for predicting the level or magnitude of a (metric) dependent variable based on the levels of multiple independent variables.

multiple time-series design An interrupted time-series design with a control group.

multiple-choice questions Closed-ended questions that ask the respondent to choose among several answers; also called *multichotomous questions*.

multistage area sampling Geographic areas selected for national or regional surveys in progressively smaller population units, such as counties, then residential blocks, then homes.

multivariate analysis General term for statistical procedures that simultaneously analyze multiple measurements on each individual or object under study.

mystery shoppers People who pose as consumers and shop at a company's own stores or those of its competitors to collect data about customer–employee interactions and to gather observational data; they may also compare prices, displays, and the like.

necessary questions Pertain directly to the stated survey objectives or are screeners, interest generators, or required transitions.

neural network A computer program that mimics the processes of the human brain and thus is capable of learning from examples to find patterns in data.

newsgroup An Internet site where people can read and post messages devoted to a specific topic.

nominal or categorical A type of nonmetric, qualitative data scale that only uses numbers to indicate membership in a group (e.g., 1 5 male, 2 5 female). Most mathematical and statistical procedures cannot be applied to nominal data.

nominal scales Scales that partition data into mutually exclusive and collectively exhaustive categories.

nonbalanced scales Measurement scales that are weighted toward one end or the other of the scale.

noncomparative scales Measurement scales in which judgment is made without reference to another object, concept, or person.

nonprobability sample A subset of a population in which the chances of selection for the various elements in the population are unknown.

nonprobability samples Samples in which specific elements from the population have been selected in a nonrandom manner.

nonresponse bias Error that results from a systematic difference between those who do and those who do not respond to a measurement instrument.

nonsampling error All error other than sampling error; also called *measurement error*.

normal distribution Continuous distribution that is bell-shaped and symmetric about the mean; the mean, median, and mode are equal.

null hypothesis The hypothesis of status quo, no difference, no effect.

observation research Systematic process of recording patterns of occurrences or behaviors without normally communicating with the people involved.

observation research Typically, descriptive research that monitors respondentsí actions without direct interaction.

one-group pretest–posttest design Pre-experimental design with pre- and postmeasurements but no control group.

one-shot case study design Pre-experimental design with no pretest observations, no control group, and an after measurement only.

one-way frequency table Table showing the number of respondents choosing each answer to a survey question.

one-way mirror observation Practice of watching behaviors or activities from behind a one-way mirror.

online focus groups Focus groups conducted via the Internet.

open observation Process of monitoring people who know they are being watched.

open online panel recruitment Any person with Internet access can self-select to be in a research panel.

open-ended questions Questions to which the respondent replies in her or his own words.

operational definition Statement of precisely which observable characteristics will be measured and the process for assigning a value to the concept.

opportunity identification Using marketing research to find and evaluate new opportunities.

ordinal scales Scales that maintain the labeling characteristics of nominal scales and have the ability to order data.

outsourcing Having personnel in another country perform some, or all, of the functions involved in a marketing research project.

pvalue Exact probability of getting a computed test statistic that is due to chance. The smaller the p value, the smaller the probability that the observed result occurred by chance.

paired comparison scales Measurement scales that ask the respondent to pick one of two objects in a set, based on some stated criteria.

Pearson's product–moment correlation Correlation analysis technique for use with metric data.

People Reader Machine that simultaneously records the respondent's reading material and eye reactions.

personification Drawing a comparison between a product and a person.

photo sort Projective technique in which a respondent sorts photos of different types of people, identifying those people who she or he feels would use the specified product or service.

physical control Holding constant the value or level of extraneous variables throughout the course of an experiment.

pilot studies Surveys using a limited number of respondents and often employing less rigorous sampling techniques than are employed in large, quantitative studies.

point estimate Particular estimate of a population value.

population distribution Frequency distribution of all the elements of a population.

population parameter A value that accurately portrays or typifies a factor of a complete population, such as average age or income.

population specification error Error that results from incorrectly defining the population or universe from which a sample is chosen.

population standard deviation Standard deviation of a variable for the entire population.

population Entire group of people about whom information is needed; also called universe or population of interest.

portable people meter Device worn by people that measures the radio and TV programming to which the participant was exposed during the day.

predictive function Specification of how to use descriptive and diagnostic research to predict the results of a planned marketing decision.

predictive validity Degree to which a future level of a criterion variable can be forecast by a current measurement scale.

pre-experimental designs Designs that offer little or no control over extraneous factors.

pretest Trial run of a questionnaire.

primary data New data gathered to help solve the problem under investigation.

probability sample A subset of a population where every element in the population has a known nonzero chance of being selected.

probability samples Samples in which every element of the population has a known, nonzero likelihood of selection.

processing error Error that results from the incorrect transfer of information from a survey document to a computer.

profession Organization whose membership is determined by objective standards, such as an examination.

professionalism Quality said to be possessed by a worker with a high level of expertise, the freedom to exercise judgment, and the ability to work independently.

programmatic research Research conducted to develop marketing options through market segmentation, market opportunity analyses, or consumer attitude and product usage studies.

projective test Technique for tapping respondents' deepest feelings by having them project those feelings into an unstructured situation.

prompters Short encouraging statements to rebuild respondent interest.

proportional allocation Sampling in which the number of elements selected from a stratum is directly proportional to the size of the stratum relative to the size of the population.

proportional property of the normal distribution Feature that the number of observations falling between the mean and a given number of standard deviations from the mean is the same for all normal distributions.

purchase intent scales Scales used to measure a respondent's intention to buy or not buy a product.

qualitative research Research findings that are not subject to quantification or quantitative analysis.

quantitative research Research that uses mathematical analysis.

quasi-experiments Studies in which the researcher lacks complete control over the scheduling of treatments or must assign respondents to treatments in a nonrandom manner.

questionnaire costs and profitability Factors affecting costs and profits include overestimating, overbidding, incidence rate, roadblocks to completed interviews, and premature interview terminations.

questionnaire Set of questions designed to generate the data necessary to accomplish the objectives of the research project; also called an *interview schedule* or *survey instrument*.

quota samples Nonprobability samples in which quotas, based on demographic or classification factors selected by the researcher, are established for population subgroups.

random error, or random sampling error Error that results from chance variation.

random-digit dialing Method of generating lists of telephone numbers at random.

randomization Random assignment of subjects to treatment conditions to ensure equal representation of subject characteristics.

rank-order scales Measurement scales in which the respondent compares two or more items and ranks them.

ratio scales Scales that have the characteristics of interval scales, plus a meaningful zero point so that magnitudes can be compared arithmetically.

recommendations Conclusions applied to marketing strategies or tactics that focus on a client's achievement of differential advantage.

refusal rate Percentage of persons contacted who refused to participate in a survey.

regression coefficients Estimates of the effect of individual independent variables on the dependent variable.

regression to the mean Tendency of subjects with extreme behavior to move toward the average for that behavior during the course of an experiment.

related samples Samples in which measurement of a variable in one population may influence measurement of the variable in the other.

reliability Degree to which measures are free from random error and, therefore, provide consistent data.

request for proposal (RFP) A solicitation sent to marketing research suppliers inviting them to submit a formal proposal, including a bid.

research design The plan to be followed to answer the marketing research objectives.

research management Overseeing the development of excellent communication systems, data quality, time schedules, cost controls, client profitability, and staff development

research panel A group of individuals who agree to participate in a series of research studies over time.

research proposal A document developed, usually in response to an RFP, that states the research objectives, research design, time line, and cost.

research request An internal document used by large organizations that describes a potential research project, its benefits to the organization, and estimated costs; it must be formally approved before a research project can begin.

respondent biasing Leading questions that give away the research goal or sponsor identity.

respondent's question-answering ability Factors affecting this ability include lack of required information, forgetfulness, or incomplete recall ability.

respondent's willingness to answer Embarrassing, sensitive, or threatening questions or questions divergent from respondent's self-image may cause them to refuse to answer.

response bias Error that results from the tendency of people to answer a question incorrectly through either deliberate falsification or unconscious misrepresentation.

return on quality Management objective based on the principles that (1) the quality being delivered is at a level desired by the target market and (2) that level of quality must have a positive impact on profitability.

rule Guide, method, or command that tells a researcher what to do.

sample design error Systematic error that results from an error in the sample design or sampling procedures.

sample distribution Frequency distribution of all the elements of an individual sample.

sample size The identified and selected population subset for the survey, chosen because it represents the entire group.

sample Subset of all the members of a population of interest.

sampling distribution of the mean Theoretical frequency distribution of the means of all possible samples of a given size drawn from a particular population; it is normally distributed.

sampling distribution of the proportion Relative frequency distribution of the sample proportions of many random samples of a given size drawn from a particular population; it is normally distributed.

sampling error Error that occurs because the sample selected is not perfectly representative of the population.

sampling frame List of population elements from which units to be sampled can be selected or a specified procedure for generating such a list.

sampling frame List of population elements or members from which units to be sampled are selected.

sampling Process of obtaining information from a subset of a larger group.

scale Set of symbols or numbers so constructed that the symbols or numbers can be assigned by a rule to the individuals (or their behaviors or attitudes) to whom the scale is applied.

scaled-response questions Closed-ended questions in which the response choices are designed to capture the intensity of the respondent's feeling.

scaling of coefficients A method of directly comparing the magnitudes of the regression coefficients of independent variables by scaling them in the same units or by standardizing the data.

scaling Procedures for assigning numbers (or other symbols) to properties of an object in order to impart some numerical characteristics to the properties in question.

scanning technology Form of data entry in which responses on questionnaires are read in automatically by the data entry device.

scatter diagram Graphic plot of the data with dependent variable on the Y (vertical) axis and the independent variable on the X (horizontal) axis. Shows the nature of the relationship between the two variables, linear or nonlinear.

screeners Questions used to identify appropriate respondents.

secondary data Data that have been previously gathered.

selection bias Systematic differences between the test group and the control group due to a biased selection process.

selection error Error that results from incomplete or improper sample selection procedures or not following appropriate procedures.

selective research Research used to test decision alternatives.

self-administered questionnaires Questionnaires filled out by respondents with no interviewer present.

semantic differential scales Measurement scales that examine the strengths and weaknesses of a concept by having the respondent rank it between dichotomous pairs of words or phrases that could be used to describe it; the means of the responses are then plotted as a profile or image.

sentence and story completion test Projective test in which respondents complete sentences or stories in their own words.

simple random sample Probability sample selected by assigning a number to every element of the population and then using a table of random numbers to select specific elements for inclusion in the sample.

situation analysis Studying the decision-making environment within which the marketing research will take place.

skip pattern Sequence in which later questions are asked, based on a respondent's answer to an earlier question or questions.

snowball samples Nonprobability samples in which additional respondents are selected based on referrals from initial respondents.

split-half technique Method of assessing the reliability of a scale by dividing the total set of measurement items in half and correlating the results.

spurious association A relationship between a presumed cause and a presumed effect that occurs as a result of an unexamined variable or set of variables.

stability Lack of change in results from test to retest.

standard deviation Measure of dispersion calculated by subtracting the mean of the series from each value in a series, squaring each result, summing the results, dividing the sum by the number of items minus 1, and taking the square root of this value.

standard error of the mean Standard deviation of a distribution of sample means.

standard normal distribution Normal distribution with a mean of zero and a standard deviation of one.

Stapel scales Measurement scales that require the respondent to rate, on a scale ranging from 15 to 25, how closely and in what direction a descriptor adjective fits a given concept.

statistical control Adjusting for the effects of confounded variables by statistically adjusting the value of the dependent variable for each treatment condition.

statistical power Probability of not making a type II error.

statistical significance A difference that is large enough that it is not likely to have occurred because of chance or sampling error.

storytelling Projective technique in which respondents are required to tell stories about their experiences, with a company or product, for example; also known as the *metaphor technique*.

strategic partnership An alliance formed by two or more firms with unique skills and resources to offer a new service for clients, provide strategic support for each firm, or in some other manner create mutual benefits.

stratified sample Probability sample that is forced to be more representative though simple random sampling of mutually exclusive and exhaustive subsets.

sum of squares due to regression Variation explained by the regression.

supervisor's instructions Written directions to the field service firm on how to conduct the survey.

surrogate information error Error that results from a discrepancy between the information needed to solve a problem and that sought by the researcher.

survey objectives Outline of the decision-making information sought through the questionnaire.

survey research Research in which an interviewer (except in mail and Internet surveys) interacts with respondents to obtain facts, opinions, and attitudes.

syndicated service research firms Companies that collect, package, and sell the same general market research data to many firms.

systematic error, or bias Error that results from problems or flaws in the execution of the research design; sometimes called non-sampling error.

systematic sampling Probability sampling in which the entire population is numbered and elements are selected using a skip interval.

systems orientation The creation of systems to monitor the external environment and deliver the desired marketing mix to the target market.

ttest Hypothesis test used for a single mean if the sample is too small to use the Z test.

temporal sequence An appropriate causal order of events.

test market Testing of a new product or some element of the marketing mix using an experimental or quasi-experimental design.

testing effect Effect that is a by-product of the research process itself.

test–retest reliability Ability of the same instrument to produce consistent results when used a second time under conditions as similar as possible to the original conditions.

third-person technique A projective technique in which the interviewer learns about respondents' feelings by asking them to answer for a third party, such as "your neighbor" or "most people."

traffic counters Machines used to measure vehicular flow over a particular stretch of roadway.

treatment variable Independent variable that is manipulated in an experiment.

true experimental design Research using an experimental group and a control group, to which test units are randomly assigned.

type I error (α error) Rejection of the null hypothesis when, in fact, it is true.

type II error (β error) Failure to reject the null hypothesis when, in fact, it is false.

unidimensional scales Scales designed to measure only one attribute of a concept, respondent, or object.

unrestricted Internet sample Self-selected sample group consisting of anyone who wishes to complete an Internet survey.

utilities The relative value of attribute levels determined through conjoint analysis.

validation Process of ascertaining that interviews actually were conducted as specified.

validity Degree to which what the researcher was trying to measure was actually measured.

variable A symbol or concept that can assume any one of a set of values.

web community Carefully selected group of consumers who agree to participate in an ongoing dialogue with a corporation.

word association test Projective test in which the interviewer says a word and the respondent must mention the first thing that comes to mind.

Ztest Hypothesis test used for a single mean if the sample is large enough and drawn at random.

INDEX

Note: Page numbers followed by "t" indicate the entry is in a table, those followed by an "f" indicate the entry is in a figure.